THE RIGHT TO INCLUSIVE EDUCATION IN INTERNATIONAL HUMAN RIGHTS LAW

Education is a fundamental human right that is recognised as essential for the attainment of all civil, political, economic, social and cultural rights. It was not until 2006, with the adoption of the UN Convention on the Rights of Persons with Disabilities (CRPD), that the right to inclusive education was codified. This volume fills a major gap in the literature on the right of disabled people to education. It examines the theoretical foundations and core content of the right to inclusive education in international human rights law, and explores the various ways of implementing this right through a study of legal strategies and mechanisms. With contributions by leaders in the field, this volume advances scholarship on the right to inclusive education by examining the content and practice of the right at the national, regional and international levels.

Gauthier de Beco is Reader in Human Rights at the University of Huddersfield, and previously taught at the University of Leeds, the KU Leuven and University College London. He has widely published in the field of international human rights law, including on the issue of inclusive education, and is on the editorial board of the *Revue trimestrielle des droits de l'homme*. He has worked as an expert to several governments, international organisations and NGOs.

Shivaun Quinlivan lectures in law at NUI Galway. She is a founding member of the Centre for Disability Law and Policy NUI Galway and now serves on the management committee of the CDLP. Most recently she has been appointed to the role of vice dean for equality, diversity and inclusion in the College of Business, Public Policy and Law. She has worked as a legal expert to several international organisations, as well as national and local NGOs, with a particular focus on education and equality.

Janet E. Lord is a leading authority on international human rights law and the rights of persons with disabilities. She has advised UN agencies, governments, human rights institutions and disability organisations in more than forty countries. She is currently a senior fellow at the Harvard Law School Project on Disability. A scholar as well as a practitioner, she has taught human rights law at universities in Europe, Africa, Asia and the United States.

CAMBRIDGE DISABILITY LAW AND POLICY SERIES

Edited by
Peter Blanck and Robin Paul Malloy

The Disability Law and Policy series examines these topics in interdisciplinary and comparative terms. The books in the series reflect the diversity of definitions, causes, and consequences of discrimination against persons with disabilities while illuminating fundamental themes that unite countries in their pursuit of human rights laws and policies to improve the social and economic status of persons with disabilities. The series contains historical, contemporary, and comparative scholarship crucial to identifying individual, organizational, cultural, attitudinal, and legal themes necessary for the advancement of disability law and policy.

The book topics covered in the series also are reflective of the new moral and political commitment by countries throughout the world toward equal opportunity for persons with disabilities in such areas as employment, housing, transportation, rehabilitation, and individual human rights. The series will thus play a significant role in informing policy makers, researchers, and citizens of issues central to disability rights and disability antidiscrimination policies. The series grounds the future of disability law and policy as a vehicle for ensuring that persons with disabilities participate as equal citizens of the world.

Books in the Series

Ruth Colker, *When Is Separate Unequal? A Disability Perspective*

Larry M. Logue and Peter Blanck, *Race, Ethnicity, and Disability: Veterans and Benefits in Post–Civil War America*

Lisa Vanhala, *Making Rights a Reality? Disability Rights Activists and Legal Mobilization*

Eilionóir Flynn, *From Rhetoric to Action: Implementing the UN Convention on the Rights of Persons with Disabilities*

Isabel Karpin and Kristin Savell, *Perfecting Pregnancy: Law, Disability, and the Future of Reproduction*

Alicia Ouellette, *Bioethics and Disability: Toward a Disability-Conscious Bioethics*

Arie Rimmerman, *Social Inclusion of People with Disabilities: National and International Perspectives*

Andrew Power, Janet E. Lord and Allison S. DeFranco, *Active Citizenship and Disability: Implementing the Personalisation of Support*

Lisa Schur, Douglas Kruse and Peter Blanck, *People with Disabilities: Sidelined or Mainstreamed?*

Eliza Varney, *Disability and Information Technology: A Comparative Study in Media Regulation*

Jerome E. Bickenbach, Franziska Felder and Barbara Schmitz, *Disability and the Good Human Life*

Robin Paul Malloy, *Land Use Law and Disability: Planning and Zoning for Accessible Communities*

Arie Rimmerman, *Family Policy and Disability*

Peter Blanck, *eQuality: The Struggle for Web Accessibility by Persons with Cognitive Disabilities*

Anna Arstein-Kerslake, *Restoring Voice to People with Cognitive Disabilities: Realizing the Right to Equal Recognition Before the Law*

Arie Rimmerman, *Disability and Community Living Policies*

Paul Harpur, *Discrimination, Copyright and Equality: Opening the e-Book for the Print-Disabled*

Aisling de Paor, *Genetics, Disability and the Law: Towards an EU Legal Framework*

Piers Gooding, *A New Era for Mental Health Law and Policy: Supported Decision-Making and the UN Convention on the Rights of Persons with Disabilities*

Larry M. Logue and Peter Blanck, *Heavy Laden: Union Veterans, Psychological Illness, and Suicide*

Karrie A. Shogren, Michael L. Wehmeyer, Jonathan Martinis and Peter Blanck, *Supported Decision-Making: Theory, Research, and Practice to Enhance Self-Determination and Quality of Life*

Gauthier de Beco, Shivaun Quinlivan and Janet E. Lord, *The Right to Inclusive Education in International Human Rights Law*

The Right to Inclusive Education in International Human Rights Law

Edited by

GAUTHIER DE BECO
University of Huddersfield

SHIVAUN QUINLIVAN
National University of Ireland, Galway

JANET E. LORD
Harvard Law School Project on Disability

CAMBRIDGE
UNIVERSITY PRESS

CAMBRIDGE
UNIVERSITY PRESS

University Printing House, Cambridge CB2 8BS, United Kingdom

One Liberty Plaza, 20th Floor, New York, NY 10006, USA

477 Williamstown Road, Port Melbourne, VIC 3207, Australia

314–321, 3rd Floor, Plot 3, Splendor Forum, Jasola District Centre, New Delhi – 110025, India

79 Anson Road, #06–04/06, Singapore 079906

Cambridge University Press is part of the University of Cambridge.

It furthers the University's mission by disseminating knowledge in the pursuit of education, learning, and research at the highest international levels of excellence.

www.cambridge.org
Information on this title: www.cambridge.org/9781107121188
DOI: 10.1017/9781316392881

First published 2019

A catalogue record for this publication is available from the British Library.

ISBN 978-1-107-12118-8 Hardback

Contents

Notes on Contributors

ANA LAURA AIELLO is a lawyer from Argentina. She completed a master of human rights degree in Spain and recently concluded her PhD in the United Kingdom (University of Leeds). Her thesis employs socio-legal research and empirical methods, and explores the potential of strategic litigation for addressing human rights violations suffered by people with learning disabilities who have lived in institutional residential settings. In addition to her PhD, she has rich experience in conducting research for leading human rights and disability organisations, both in the United Kingdom and internationally. She has employed research methods such as legal documentary analysis, qualitative interviews, surveys and focus groups with disabled people. She also has various publications on disability rights, covering issues such as equality and non-discrimination, accessibility and the legal interpretation of the Convention on the Rights of Persons with Disabilities by national courts.

SARAH ARDUIN is an adjunct assistant professor at the School of Law at Trinity College Dublin. She is a graduate of the University of Paris II Pantheon-Assas (Licence de Droit) and of Trinity College Dublin (TCD) (LLM). She holds a PhD from the School of Law at TCD on comparative constitutional and regulatory regimes in the context of the right to education of persons with disabilities. Her research interests sit at the intersection of regulation and human rights with an emphasis on the right to education. Her current research project looks at the emergence of gaps between educational policies as expressed by law and the level of compliance with legal norms in the lived experience of schools. She is also looking at the theory of experimentalist governance in the context of the legal architecture of the UN Convention on the Rights of Persons with Disabilities.

PETER BARNETT PETER is a litigation lawyer in ClientEarth's climate programme, using strategic litigation to fight climate change and to drive the clean energy transition. Prior to joining ClientEarth, Peter practised at specialist disputes firm Boies Schiller Flexner in London and Russell McVeagh in New Zealand. He has acted in a number of leading cases on the government non-discrimination standard in New Zealand, including appearing for the Human Rights Commission in *Spencer* v. *Attorney-General* (challenging denial of funding for disability support provided by family members) and the successful claimant in *IDEA Services Ltd* v. *Attorney-General* (challenging age discrimination in the provision of disability support services). In his previous practice, Peter also acted for companies and institutional investors in financial litigation and international commercial and investor–state arbitration. Peter is admitted as a barrister and solicitor in New Zealand (non-practising) and a solicitor in England and Wales. He holds a master of laws from Harvard Law School and a bachelor of laws (honours) and bachelor of commerce (finance) from the University of Otago.

DR THOMAS BERNHARD studied law at the Friedrich-Alexander University Erlangen-Nurnberg in Germany from 2006 to 2010, and international and comparative disability law and policy at the National University of Ireland in Galway (2012/13). From 2011 to 2015, he worked as a research fellow and was a PhD student at the University of Erlangen-Nurnberg, where he obtained his PhD in December 2015. Since October 2015, he is a legal trainee (referendar) at the district court in Regensburg. Furthermore, he is the lecturer of the module 'Rights of Persons with Disabilities' in the MA programme in human rights at the University of Erlangen-Nurnberg. His research focusses on public law, international human rights law, the rights of persons with disabilities and inclusive education.

JAPHET BIEGON is an international human rights law and policy expert. His primary area of focus is the normative and institutional structures of the African human rights system. He is currently the Africa regional advocacy coordinator at Amnesty International, where he leads its organisational engagement with the African Union. He has published widely on issues of human rights in Africa. In 2011, he pioneered academic research on disability rights in the African human rights system. A lawyer by profession and duly admitted to practise law in Kenya, Biegon sits on the advisory board of the Human Rights Law Implementation Project (HRLIP), a collaborative research initiative between four academic human rights centres (Bristol, Essex, Middlesex and Pretoria) and the Open Society Justice Initiative. He holds a doctor of laws degree (LLD) in international human rights law from the University of Pretoria, South Africa.

CARLA BONINO COVAS, born in Buenos Aires, Argentina, is a sociologist by the Complutense University of Madrid, Spain, and has a master's degree in corporate social responsibility leadership from IE Business School. Carla has wide experience as a social researcher and in leading and developing social studies in different fields such as gender issues, migrations, employment or social dialogue, with different publications as a result of her work. In 2004, she joined Fundación ONCE, based in Madrid, focussing since then on the issue of disability, with special attention given to inclusive education, thus becoming an expert in this area. Since 2010, she has led European initiatives, including the European Network on Inclusive Education and Disability (incluD-ed), promoted by Fundación ONCE between 2009 and 2015 with the co-funding of the European Social Fund. While leading this network, she has coordinated policy analyses and contributions, advocacy actions, good practice exchange, research and studies on disability and inclusive education in the context of the EU.

ANDREA BRODERICK is an assistant professor in the Department of International and European Law at the Faculty of Law, Maastricht University. She completed a Marie Curie fellowship at Maastricht University under the framework of the DREAM (Disability Rights Expanding Accessible Markets) network of researchers. Her doctoral thesis was nominated for the Max van der Stoel human rights award (2016), and has been published as a book. Andrea holds a BA international (law and French) degree, with first-class honours, and an LLB from the National University of Ireland, Galway (NUIG). Andrea Broderick also holds an LLM in international and comparative disability law and policy from NUIG (first-class honours). She is a qualified solicitor at the Law Society of Ireland, and worked in professional legal practice for many years. Andrea Broderick's current research interests lie in the areas of international and European disability law, EU equality law, inclusive education, non-state actors and the case law of the European Court of Human Rights. She has published widely in academic journals and books. She has also written and co-written thematic reports for, among others, the European Commission and the Council of Europe.

MIGUEL ÁNGEL CABRA DE LUNA holds a law degree (Granada's University, Qualified, First Class, 1977) and a PhD in law, *cum laude* (Granada's University, 1997). He is the director of social relations, international affairs and strategic planning for Fundación ONCE. He is also a member of the European Economic and Social Committee, the board of the Spanish Business Confederation of the Social Economy, the Permanent European Conference for Social Economy Europe and the Royal Board on Disability Council. He has been secretary general of the Spanish Red Cross, director of the General Secretariat Technical Bureau for Spanish Social Security and deputy director general for research and regulations of the Ministry of Labour and Social Security. Miguel Ángel Cabra de Luna is the author of several books, including *The Third Sector and Foundations in*

Spain and *Towards the New Millennium: An Economic, Sociological and Legal Study*, as well as numerous articles. He has taught courses on social services, human rights and social economy for several universities.

BO CHEN is a PhD student at the Centre for Disability Law and Policy, School of Law, National University of Ireland, Galway. His research interests include disability law, the UN Convention on the Rights of Persons with Disabilities and mental health law.

PROFESSOR MARÍA SOLEDAD CISTERNAS REYES is the Special Envoy of the Secretary General of the United Nations on Disability and Accessibility. She obtained a law degree with the highest distinction, is an attorney and a master in political science and the former chairperson of the Committee on the Rights of Persons with Disabilities (2013–2016). She is a professor of law (undergraduate and graduate) and a researcher. She has been the director of various legal and interdisciplinary projects, such as training of judges, public officials and civil society (including indigenous sectors). She has authored several publications and has been invited to national and international conferences. Her activities have been numerous at the UN: expert for the ad hoc committee that drafted the United Nations Convention on the Rights of Persons with Disabilities; participant in various activities in UNICEF, UNESCO, UNPD, WHO and ONUWOMEN; and speaker to the General Assembly High Level Meeting on Disability and Development (2013), among others. She has received different awards: the National Human Rights Award, Chile (2014–2015); the 'Chamber of Deputies Medal' (2013); '100 Women Leaders 2012–2014', *El Mercurio*; the Elena Caffarena Prize on International Women's Day (2009); a Distinction of the House of Representatives and Senate of Chile (2008–2009); 'Equality and Non-Discrimination', Mexico (2008); and the Star of Hope International, Colombia (1999).

DR GAUTHIER DE BECO (JD, University of Leuven; LLM, University of Nottingham; PhD in law, University of Louvain) is Reader in Human Rights at the University of Huddersfield, and previously taught at the University of Leeds, the KU Leuven and University College London. He has also worked as an expert for several governments, international organisations and NGOs, including the Office of the UN High Commissioner for Human Rights (OHCHR) and the European Commission. He worked at the Chambers of the International Criminal Court (ICC) and the Human Rights Unit of the Belgian Ministry of Justice. Gauthier de Beco's expertise lies in the topic of human rights and disability with a special focus on the right to inclusive education. He has widely published in the field of international human rights law, including two monographs and many articles in peer-reviewed journals, and is on the editorial board of the *Revue trimestrielle des droits de l'homme*. He is currently writing a monograph on *Disability in International Human Rights Law* for Oxford University Press. He has been involved in a number of research projects related to disability and is providing advice to many civil society organisations.

ELISABETH DE SCHAUWER is working in the field of disability studies at Ghent University. She is responsible for the course 'Diversity and Inclusion' in the master's degree in special needs education. Her research focusses on the role of difference on pedagogical relations. She works closely with children, parents and schools in the praxis of inclusive education. For her, activism, research and teaching go hand in hand.

DR DELIA FERRI is a lecturer in law at Maynooth University Department of Law, where she lectures primarily in the fields of EU law and international and European disability law. She is a member of the Maynooth University Social Sciences Institute, and of the Maynooth Centre for European and Eurasian Studies. She is an affiliated researcher at the Dirpolis Institute of Scuola Superiore Sant'Anna (Italy) within the research cluster on social rights, social inclusion and disability, and a fellow at the Burton Blatt Institute of Syracuse University (United States). In addition, Delia Ferri is a qualified lawyer (*Avvocato*) and has been a member of the Italian bar since 2008. She holds a JD in law (*Laurea Magistrale in Giurisprudenza*), and was awarded *magna cum laude* from the University of Verona School of Law (Italy), a first-class honours with distinction for her LLM from Trinity College Dublin (Ireland) and a doctorate in Italian and European constitutional law from the University of Verona.

JÁNOS FIALA-BUTORA is a research fellow at the Legal Studies Institute of the Hungarian Academy of Sciences and the director of the Central European programme of the Harvard Law School Project on Disability (HPOD). He is a graduate of the human rights programme of the Central European University LLM 2004 and of Harvard Law School LLM 2010 and SJD 2016. As a human rights lawyer, he actively consults with governments on their human rights laws and policies, has advised a number of Council of Europe and UN bodies and has brought landmark litigation before international courts on behalf of persons with disabilities. In his research, he focusses on international human rights mechanisms and the rights of persons with disabilities, ethnic minorities and refugees.

ZHIJUN FU is a legal lecturer, a PhD candidate at China Shanghai University of Finance and Economics and the director of the Shanghai Zhijun Public Interest and Law Institute. He also holds a master's degree in law in international and comparative disability law and policy from the National University of Ireland, Galway. His interest areas include international law, domestic disability law and policy, inclusive education and employment. He has published a book, *A Study on Legal Institutions of Protection of*

Rights of Persons with Disabilities (in Chinese) (2014), and several articles regarding inclusive education and disability law and policy in China.

G. ANTHONY GIANNOUMIS' research focusses on technology law and policy. He is currently researching the implementation of policies aimed at ensuring equal access to technology. His research interests include universal design, international governance, sustainable development, social regulation and standardisation. He has conducted research on assistive technology and intellectual property. He is currently an associate professor of universal design in the Department of Computer Science at Oslo and Akershus University College, and an international research fellow at the Burton Blatt Institute at Syracuse University. Anthony has previously acted as a researcher with DISCIT (making persons with disabilities full citizens) and as a legal and ethical advisor for Cloud4All (cloud platforms lead to open and universal access for people with disabilities and for all). He was awarded a Marie Curie fellowship in 2011 as part of DREAM (Disability Rights Expanding Accessible Markets), and has been a visiting researcher and guest lecturer throughout Europe, North America, Asia and Africa.

ANNA GILMER is a recent graduate of the BCL/LLB programme at McGill University's Faculty of Law. She also holds a BA from the University of Western Ontario in linguistics and First Nations studies. Throughout each degree, much of her summer and co-curricular work focussed on Indigenous issues in Canada.

YOSHIKAZU IKEHARA is a senior attorney at Tokyo Advocacy Law Office, which is one of the prominent law offices for disability rights advocacy in Japan. He established it in 1999. He is a member of the Committee on Anti-Discrimination Law for Persons with Disabilities and a member of the Committee on Rights of Aged Persons and Persons with Disabilities under the Japan Federation of Bar Associations. He is an adjunct researcher for the Project Research Institute, Comprehensive Research Organization, Waseda University. He is the chief of the researching body of the Disability Rights Tribunal in Asia and the Pacific. He was a member of the Task Force on Anti-Discrimination Law for Persons with Disability under the Cabinet Office. He has published many books on disability rights, including and especially on persons with psychosocial disabilities.

ELIZABETH KAMUNDIA is assistant director in the Research, Outreach and Advocacy Directorate at the Kenya National Commission on Human Rights. She holds an LLM in International and Comparative Disability Law and Policy from the Centre for Disability Law and Policy – National University of Ireland, Galway (NUIG). Elizabeth has worked with the Centre for Disability Law and Policy, NUIG (Legal Researcher) and the Centre for Human Rights, University of Pretoria (Disability Rights and Law Schools Project Coordinator). She has also worked at the Commission on the Implementation of the Constitution of Kenya (Consultant on Disability) and the Committee of Experts on Constitutional Review – Kenya (Legal Researcher). Elizabeth is an advocate of the High Court of Kenya. She is currently a PhD Candidate at the University of Pretoria, writing her thesis on Article 12 of the UN Convention on the Rights of Persons with Disabilities on equal recognition before the law.

PROFESSOR ARLENE KANTER lectures and writes extensively on domestic and international human rights law, disability law and inclusive education law, as well as legal capacity and personhood. In addition to her many law review articles and book chapters, she is the author of *The Development of Disability Rights under International Law: From Charity to Human Rights* (2015), and a co-editor of *Righting Educational Wrongs: Disability Studies in Law and Education* (2013) and *Cases and Materials on International Human Rights and Domestic Mental Disability Law* (2006), the first law casebook on international and comparative disability law. Arlene Kanter is the founder and editor of the first international SSRN e-journal on disability law, co-founder and co-editor of Syracuse University's Press' Critical Perspectives on Disability series, co-founder and past chair of the Disability Law Section of the American Association of Law Schools and co-founder of the Disability Studies Research Network of the Law and Society Association. She is a former commissioner of the ABA Commission on Disability Rights, has served on the editorial boards of several journals and is the recipient of numerous awards. Arlene Kanter received her JD degree from New York University School of Law and her LLM degree from Georgetown University Law Center.

ROSEMARY KAYESS is an international human rights lawyer and a leading expert on the rights of persons with disabilities. She was elected to the United Nations Committee on the Rights of Persons with Disabilities in 2018. She has devoted her career to the study and promotion of human rights and discrimination law in Australia and internationally. Currently a visiting fellow and a senior lecturer in the Faculty of Law at the University of New South Wales, she participated in all of the drafting of the CRPD and was appointed to the Australian government delegation to serve as a legal advisor during the negotiation process. Rosemary Kayess has served as a member of the AusAID Disability Reference Group. In 2010, she was appointed director of the Human Rights and Disability Project at the University of New South Wales (UNSW) and, in 2011, she was appointed senior research fellow at the Social Policy Research Centre at UNSW. From 1989 to 1995, Rosemary Kayess served as the director of Spinal Cord Injuries Australia while also serving on the ethics committee at the Benevolent Society of New South Wales and as the director of the Physical Disability Council of New South Wales. Since 1995, Rosemary Kayess has served as chairperson of the Australian Centre for Disability Law, lending her voice to the Centre's work to promote and protect the human and legal rights of people with disabilities through strategic legal advocacy. She was appointed to the Disability Council of New South Wales in 1996, serving until 2000. In 1996, Rosemary Kayess was honoured with a University of New South Wales Alumni Award. She graduated from the University of New South Wales with a bachelor of laws and a bachelor of social science (honours) degree. She also has an associate diploma of management (community organisations) and a graduate diploma of legal practice from the College of Law. She has published numerous scholarly works on the human rights of persons with disabilities.

KATE LAPHAM is the deputy director of the Education Support Program of the Open Society Foundations. Her work is focussed on overcoming barriers to education for communities facing exclusion or discrimination. Based in New York, Kate Lapham has worked with communities, civil society groups and education policy makers in the Caucasus, Central Asia, Central and Eastern Europe and Mongolia and Russia for more than fifteen years. She comes to the Open Society Education Support Program from IREX, a non-profit organisation dedicated to building quality education, independent media and strong civil society. Kate Lapham has developed initiatives to strengthen civil society, including research for evidence-based advocacy, support for organisational development among young or small NGOs, and direct work with teachers and schools. She is also a PhD candidate in comparative and international education at Lehigh University with publications that include *Learning to See Invisible Children: Inclusion of Children with Disabilities in Central Asia*. She holds an MPA from Columbia University's School of International and Public Affairs and a BS in foreign service from Georgetown University.

JANET E. LORD is an international human rights lawyer who specialises in the rights of persons with disabilities. A senior fellow at the Harvard Law School and an independent disability inclusive development consultant, she brings more than fifteen years of practice in designing, implementing, monitoring and evaluating disability rights and inclusive development programming. She served as legal counsel to Disabled Peoples International and several lead governments throughout the drafting of the Convention on the Rights of Persons with Disabilities. Most recently, she served as team leader under the Services to Improve Performance Management Enhance Learning and Evaluation (SIMPLE) mechanism for USAID/Egypt, resulting in the first-ever assessment on the accessibility of students with disabilities to Egyptian public higher education. An affiliated adjunct professor of law at the

American University, Washington College of Law and the University of Maryland Carey School of Law, Janet E. Lord has more than fifteen years of experience teaching and training on international and comparative disability rights law, international human rights law, health and human rights, humanitarian law and criminal law standards relating to trafficking in persons. She holds an LLM in international and comparative law with highest honours from the George Washington University Law School and an LLB and LLM from the University of Edinburgh in Scotland. She sits on the board of directors for Amnesty International USA.

DR SHIVAUN QUINLIVAN is a law lecturer at the Centre for Disability Law and Policy and the School of Law at NUI Galway. She teaches constitutional law and disability law and policy subjects, including a module on inclusive education law and policy. Her research interests and publications focus primarily on the rights of people with disabilities, with a particular focus on education and employment. In that capacity, she has worked with and for a range of statutory and other agencies in Ireland and Europe, including the Equality Authority, the National Council for Special Education, the Association of Higher Education Access and Disability and the Health Service Executive, as well as a number of European Commission–funded projects. She is currently working on a disability legislative project with the States of Guernsey and on an inclusive education pilot in NUI Galway. Shivaun Quinlivan was the first director of the LLM in international and comparative disability law and policy, and in that capacity she was fundamental to the development of the programme. She is a member of the management committee of the Centre for Disability Law and Policy in NUI Galway. She has recently completed an O'Brien Residential fellowship in the Centre for Human Rights and Legal Pluralism in McGill University in Canada. Most recently, Shivaun Quinlivan was appointed to the role of Vice Dean for Equality, Diversity and Inclusion in NUI Galway. Dr Quinlivan holds a BA and an LLB from NUI Galway, an LLM from King's College London, a BL (barrister at law) from The Honourable Society of King's Inns and a PhD from Trinity College Dublin.

DEEPTI S. RAJA has worked for more than a decade on the socioeconomic inclusion of persons with disabilities and mainstreaming disability in development programming. Her work has spanned research, policy analysis and capacity-building programmes. She currently works as a senior consultant to the World Bank's global disability advisor. Deepti S. Raja's work has extensively focussed on technology as an enabler of educational, economic and broader social participation. Previously, she worked as the director of international programmes and as a senior researcher at the Burton Blatt Institute at Syracuse University, a senior research analyst at the Global Initiative for Inclusive ICTs and a research coordinator for the Secretariat of the Global Partnership for Disability and Development. Her educational qualifications include a master of science degree in rehabilitation counselling from the University of Illinois at Urbana-Champaign and a master of science degree in electrical and computer engineering from the University of California, Irvine.

PROFESSOR MICHAEL SHEVLIN joined the School of Education in Trinity College Dublin in 1996, having worked as a post-primary teacher. He has developed a number of inclusive education programmes in initial teacher education and in continuing professional development for established teachers. He has participated in a number of governmental and non-governmental initiatives designed to enhance educational inclusion. Michael Shevlin chairs AHEAD, an organisation dedicated to improving access to further and higher education and employment for people with disabilities within Irish society. He is also the director of the Trinity Centre for People with Intellectual Disabilities, which has been established to provide a higher education programme for young people with intellectual disabilities and to enable these young people to access employment opportunities. He has been published widely and is currently engaged in research on transitions to post-secondary education for young people with disabilities.

PROFESSOR MICHAEL ASHLEY STEIN is the co-founder and executive director of the Harvard Law School Project on Disability; a visiting professor of law at Harvard Law School; extraordinary professor at the University of Pretoria Faculty of Law, Centre for Human Rights; and formerly professor (and Cabell Professor) at William & Mary Law School. An internationally acclaimed expert on disability law and policy, Michael Ashley Stein participated in the drafting of the United Nations Convention on the Rights of Persons with Disabilities, works with disabled persons' organisations around the world, actively consults with governments on their disability laws and policies, advises a number of United Nations bodies, has brought landmark litigation and has written extensively on disability rights. He holds a JD from Harvard Law School and a PhD from Cambridge University.

INGE VAN DE PUTTE is working in the field of disability studies at Ghent University. She has several years of experience in supporting youngsters, parents, teachers and support workers in inclusive education. At the moment she is finishing her PhD on the position of the care coordinator in dealing with diversity.

PROFESSOR GERRY WHYTE, who lectures in law at Trinity College Dublin, has published widely in the areas of public interest law and constitutional law. He is also active in a number of social justice and legal aid organisations and is a former member of the steering group of the Irish Council of People with Disabilities. The second edition of his book, *Social Inclusion and the Legal System: Public Interest Law in Ireland*, was published in 2015.

NI ZHEN works in the disability rights field. He is a consultant to various DPOs and NGOs in China. He has an LLM in human rights law from the University of Hong Kong and an MA in education from Durham University. Ni Zhen spent most of his student life in special schools. His research interests include inclusive education, disability rights and civil society participation.

Acknowledgements

The genesis of this book came from a conversation between Gauthier de Beco and Shivaun Quinlivan during a conference organised at the National University of Ireland, Galway, on 22 February 2014, entitled 'Article 24 UNCRPD: Is This a *Brown* v. *Board of Education* Moment?' From that humble beginning, we agreed on the necessity of a volume that would place the right to inclusive education within the broad context of international human rights law and we began to plot what that volume would look like. We were delighted when Janet Lord agreed to come on board as a co-editor, and this volume is the result of our combined thinking on the subject. We would in the first instance like to thank each other, as it has been a pleasure to work on this project from start to finish. This is important when you are trying to coordinate thirty authors in twenty-two different jurisdictions. We would also like to thank each and every contributor for their understanding as we brought the manuscript together.

We share in the recognition that it would have been considerably more difficult – perhaps impossible – to bring the volume together were it not for the incredible work of our sub-editor, Alice Kuzmenko. Alice was a fabulous addition to our team. Her work was efficient, accurate and detail orientated, and we share the view that this volume benefitted significantly from her sharp observations and comments. These words do not do justice to her work, but we hope she knows how much we appreciate that work.

Gauthier de Beco, Shivaun Quinlivan and Janet E. Lord

***

This project has had an important role in shaping my current research on human rights and disability. It has given me the chance not only to reflect about what the right to inclusive education actually means but also, most important, to explore many of the issues I will be dealing with over the coming years. It also helped to forge important global connections with all the people involved. This volume therefore represents more of a beginning than an end to this large-scale endeavour. I would like to thank the two employers I have been working for while coordinating it, namely the KU Leuven, Belgium, and the University of Leeds, UK. Both of them provided me with the ideal professional environment in which to carry out my work. I am grateful for both the time and the advice I received from several colleagues in order to work on the volume. I am also enormously grateful to my two co-editors, who showed their unwavering commitment and enthusiasm. Finally, I wish to thank my family, namely my wife, Aurélie, and my two children, Pierre and Victoria, who inspire me and give meaning to my work.

Gauthier de Beco, Leeds

I would like to extend my thanks to my employer, NUI Galway, for facilitating me in arranging the original conference and then later for affording me the opportunity for sabbatical which allowed me to complete my contributions to this volume. I am grateful also to the O'Brien Fellows in Residence programme that allowed me to spend four months of my sabbatical at McGill University in the McGill Centre for Human Rights and Legal Pluralism in Montreal. This time in Canada gave me the time, space and opportunity to discuss and develop my work for this volume. I am incredibly grateful to both institutions for their support. I am grateful to my co-editors for the commitment and the sense of fun they brought to this project, it has been a pleasure working with them. Finally, I would as always like to thank my parents, Jim and Mary, and my daughter, Síofra, who are always there for me.

Shivaun Quinlivan, Galway

My co-editors have greatly advanced my thinking on the subject of inclusive education and its current configuration in the international human rights system. They are a delight to work with, and our location in three countries and different time zones was a challenge we were able to overcome with ease given our strong sense of collaboration and congeniality. I am grateful to have them both as colleagues and as friends. My colleague at the Harvard Law School Project on Disability, Michael Stein, is a constant bulwark and support in all things related to academic writing and research; our chance meeting one evening during the drafting of the Convention on the Rights of Persons with Disabilities set off a collaboration and friendship that is not possible to adequately account for in a few words. I am grateful to my family for their encouragement and support. My children, Lynne and Daniel, responded to my mutterings about needing to 'finish a book chapter' with a collective groan and a directive to 'get it done, Mom!' And finally, above all, there would be no writing of any kind in this or any other work had Julie not, years ago, admonished me to stop spinning my wheels and pressed me to 'just put yourself out there'.

Janet E. Lord, Baltimore, Maryland
July 2018

Preface by Theresia Degener

The Convention on the Rights of Persons with Disabilities (CRPD) has been called an empowerment treaty, and this characterises first and foremost the right to inclusive education as enshrined in Article 24. Inclusive education as a fundamental human right empowers disabled people to flourish, to enjoy equal opportunity, to lead self-determined lives and to participate in the political, economic, social and cultural systems of society. The development of the right to education as a human right has best been described in the early 1990s by the first United Nations Special Rapporteur on the Right to Education, Katharina Tomasèvsky, who distinguished four phases of realising the human right to education for marginalised groups: exclusion, segregation, integration and inclusion. The history of disabled people reflects these development stages. First, disabled people were excluded from education; then they were segregated in special schools; thirdly, those deemed fit for the mainstream were integrated, and now is the time of inclusion. Of course, nothing of this belongs to the past. During its first decade, the Committee on the Rights of Persons with Disabilities has adopted more than seventy Concluding Observations on States Parties' reports. During the preceding dialogues with governments from all over the world, we have seen horrifying statistical and anecdotal evidence about the exclusion of a large number of disabled children from education. We have heard testimonies about educational discrimination through segregation and integration. Disabled children were prevented from developing their personality and talents because they were relegated to special schools and offered few opportunities to learn while overloaded by therapeutic interventions. We have heard about disabled children being left behind in integrated settings without accommodation relating to Braille, sign language interpretation, Easy Read or other modes and formats of communication. But with the CRPD disabled people have been vested with a normative framework that provides the right to education as a right to inclusive education. Without this normative framework the fourth stage of realising the human right to education cannot be reached. The Committee has provided some jurisprudence in this regard. In our Concluding Observations and General Comments, we have developed the human rights model of disability as the conceptual basis and given guidance on how to apply the human rights–based approach to inclusive education. We have developed the concept of inclusive equality and explained its relation to the human rights model of disability. Some scholars say we have developed the most modern international human rights law; others see it as a normative overdose. However, most of this rich normative framework has reached neither legal practice nor legal theory. This book is thus timely and greatly needed. I salute the editors and the authors for providing such a comprehensive overview of the development of the right to inclusive education, its normative content and conceptual basis and its theoretical and practical aspects. The volume closes a gap on reflection about the understanding of the right to inclusive education, especially from a legal perspective.

Geneva, August 2018
Theresia Degener

The Arthur Cox Foundation

Arthur Cox, solicitor, classical scholar and former president of the Incorporated Law Society of Ireland, was associated with the setting up of many Irish companies, not least the ESB. He was a specialist in company law and was a member of the Company Law Reform Committee which sat from 1951 and reported to the government in 1958, ultimately giving rise to the Companies Act 1963. When he decided to retire from practice as a solicitor in 1961, a number of his clients, professional colleagues and other friends, in recognition of his outstanding contribution to Ireland and his profession, thought that a fund should be established as a tribute to him which would be used to encourage the writing and publication of legal textbooks. There was a generous response to this appeal.

After his retirement, Arthur Cox studied for the priesthood and was ordained in 1963. He went to Zambia to do missionary work. He died there in 1965 as a result of a car accident.

The Foundation was established to honour Arthur Cox and was for many years administered by Mr Justice John Kenny in conjunction with the Law Society. John Kenny was the encouraging force behind the publication of a number of Irish legal textbooks. Without his quiet drive and enthusiasm there would have been no Foundation. To both Arthur Cox and John Kenny we pay tribute.

The Foundation's funds have been used to assist in the writing and publication of Irish legal textbooks and the development of electronic databases of Irish legal materials. The Foundation has recently inaugurated an annual prize for the best overall results in the business and corporate law modules of the Law Society's Professional Practice Courses.

The Law Society, as the continuing trustee of the Foundation, is pleased to have been able to assist in the publication of this book.

Patrick Dorgan
President
Law Society of Ireland
Feb. 2019

1

Introduction

Gauthier de Beco, Shivaun Quinlivan and Janet E. Lord

The title of this volume – *The Right to Inclusive Education in International Human Rights Law* – suggests an underlying normative perspective. It seeks to improve the understanding and application of the notion of inclusive education within the field of law and, in addition, to define inclusive education as a human rights issue under international human rights law.

The volume proceeds from the following three bases. First, we understand that inclusive education is rule bound since it found its way into Article 24 of the Convention on the Rights of Persons with Disabilities (CRPD). Second, we acknowledge that there is no consensus around the precise contours of inclusive education as an institutionalised norm in the international human rights system, although many of its elements are settled. Third, we can say definitively that its inclusive and participatory character as a legal standard places conditions on education. Furthermore, we can now speak of the right to inclusive education as a part of international human rights law; it is not a separate, marginal topic untethered to the larger international legal framework of human rights, as disability rights for so long tended to be in practice, if not in theory. The contributions in this volume reflect the insight that international human rights law, on the one hand, and its subfield of disability rights, on the other, are mutually constitutive, even if that project is incomplete and still emerging.

Having said this, it is worth recalling that the right to education is a fundamental human right and its realisation is essential for the exercise of all human rights, including economic, social and cultural rights, such as the right to work and the right to food, and civil and political rights, such as the right to vote and the right to free speech. Access to education is very often a vehicle for, among other things, access to information critical for the exercise of health rights, democratic participation and cultural engagement, to name a few. Education is therefore a powerful facilitator, one that can ensure that those who are marginalised in society, including but not only disabled people, can lift themselves out of poverty and participate as citizens.[1] In that sense, education is most elementally about inclusion and full participation in all facets of life.

1.1 INCLUSIVE EDUCATION AS A HUMAN RIGHTS ISSUE

As the US Supreme Court famously stated in the seminal 1954 decision of *Brown* v. *Board of Education*: 'Separate educational facilities are inherently unequal.' In the context of disability, disabled children are still segregated and separated from their peers or are excluded from education altogether. Inclusive education challenges the view that it is acceptable to segregate and to exclude some children on the basis of their disability.

Thus, the achievement of inclusive education is a vital yet unrealised goal for many disabled people. Inclusive education has gradually received recognition as a human rights issue at the international level, resulting, at the first instance, in the adoption of several non-binding international instruments. The accretion of the idea of inclusion in the area of education in these soft law documents, however, has some normative impact, as several chapters in this volume plainly disclose.

The World Declaration on Education for All: Meeting Basic Learning Needs (Jomtien Declaration), adopted in 1990, and the Standard Rules on the Equalization of Opportunities for Persons with Disabilities (Standard Rules), adopted in 1993, recommended that disabled people be able to attend regular schools and that measures be taken in order to support them within mainstream settings. In 1994, inclusive education was, for the first time, explicitly declared in the UNESCO World Conference on Special Needs Education: Access and Equality. The ensuing Salamanca Statement requested states 'to adopt as a matter of law or policy the principle of inclusive education, enrolling all children in regular schools, unless there are compelling reasons for doing otherwise'.[2] Again, the aforementioned international instruments were not legally binding and instead reflected international consensus in the form of a soft law instrument. Furthermore, even with the nominal monitoring associated with the Standard Rules, no effective

[1] Although the CRPD uses the term 'persons with disabilities', this introduction opts for the term 'disabled people'. In contrast to the former term which reflects the 'people first' language, the latter term stresses that it is society that creates barriers to their participation.

[2] World Conference on Special Needs Education: Access and Equality, Salamanca Statement and Framework for Action on Special Needs Education, Salamanca, 7–10 June 1994 http://unesdoc.unesco.org/images/0009/000984/098427eo.pdf.

monitoring was undertaken of achievements in providing an inclusive education to disabled children.

In contrast, the right to education more generally has been protected by several legally binding international instruments. Beginning with the adoption of the Universal Declaration on Human Rights (UDHR) in 1948 and continuing with the adoption of the International Covenant on Economic, Social and Cultural Rights (ICESCR) in 1966 and the Convention on the Rights of the Child (CRC) in 1989, international human rights law recognises education as a human right.[3] While neither the ICESCR nor the CRC explicitly provides for the right to inclusive education, the CRC prohibits discrimination on the basis of disability and includes a stand-alone provision on the rights of disabled children.[4] The UNESCO Convention against Discrimination in Education, enacted in 1960, also sought to prohibit discrimination in the context of education, but failed to include disability as one of the protected grounds. As a result, there was no legal basis for the goal of inclusive education under international human rights law. The seminal statement that '[s]eparate educational facilities are inherently unequal' was not applied to disabled children in international human rights law. Only in 2006 did the Committee on the Rights of the Child (CRC Committee) declare that inclusive education must be the objective for disabled children, although it allowed for exceptions to the rule and gave States Parties certain leeway in its educational policies.[5] Meanwhile, in 2001, the UN General Assembly created an Ad Hoc Committee that paved the way for a human rights treaty for disabled people.

Adopted by the UN General Assembly in 2006, the CRPD aims to protect the rights of disabled people and to eliminate the discriminatory barriers that exclude these people from society. Article 24 of the CRPD recognises, for the very first time in a human rights treaty, a right to inclusive education. It provides that disabled children have the right to participate in the general education system, that States Parties must adopt a series of measures to allow these children to be educated with their non-disabled peers, and that the failure to accommodate them in regular schools amounts to a form of discrimination.

It should be noted at the outset, though, that the drafting history of Article 24 was not an easy matter. There was significant disagreement among the

3 Articles 13 and 14, ICESCR; Articles 28 and 29, CRC.

4 Articles 2 and 23, CRC.

5 Committee on the Rights of the Child, 'General Comment No. 9: The Rights of Children with Disabilities' (2006) UN Doc. CRC/C/GC/9, para. 66.

drafters about education for disabled people and whether and how segregated education ought to be retained as a choice for parents of disabled children.[6] After considerable debate, the drafters eventually decided in favour of the goal of inclusive education. Article 24(1) of the CRPD provides that 'States Parties shall ensure an inclusive education system at all levels and lifelong learning.' The Convention thereby legally anchored the goal of inclusive education in international human rights law. While there was evidence of a growing consensus on inclusive education, the CRPD established that it is a human rights issue. The right to inclusive education has been further embedded in international human rights law with the introduction of General Comment No. 4 on the Right to Inclusive Education in 2016 by the Committee on the Rights of Persons with Disabilities (CRPD Committee) (adopted during the writing of this volume).[7] In addition to accelerating the need for inquiry in legal scholarship on this topic, this attention has made the examination of the different issues of concern relating to the right to inclusive education more compelling and urgent. This is what the volume aims to achieve by relying on the expertise of the most prominent scholars working in this new field.

1.2 MAJOR ISSUES OF CONCERN RELATING TO THE RIGHT TO INCLUSIVE EDUCATION

This volume sets out the primary conceptual and practical aspects of the right to inclusive education in international human rights law. Further, it tackles some of the primary challenges in analysing the content of this right from a legal perspective, how the law may best be used as an instrument for combatting barriers to the inclusion of disabled people in education and the complexities of translating this objective into reality. Although inclusive education was recognised prior to the adoption of the CRPD, it remains a new and unfamiliar concept in international human rights law. Inclusive education has been addressed principally by scholars in the fields of education, disability studies and, more recently, moral philosophy. The engagement of legal academics and lawyers with this topic is fairly recent, which explains why legal scholarship on the topic is still scarce, and it is also the rationale for this volume.

6 G. de Beco, 'The Right to Inclusive Education According to Article 24 of the UN Convention on the Rights of Persons with Disabilities: Background, Requirements and (Remaining) Questions' (2014) 32 (3) *Netherlands Quarterly of Human Rights* 263, 272–274.

7 Committee on the Rights of Persons with Disabilities, 'General Comment No. 4. Article 24: Right to Inclusive Education' (2016) UN Doc. CRPD/C/GC/4.

Given that the goal of inclusive education is legally anchored in Article 24 of the Convention, it follows that its analysis must be informed by the various legal standards and principles of international human rights law. The right to inclusive education must be interpreted and applied with specific reference to international human rights law and its mechanisms. The CRPD is part of that context and must be seen in the continuity of other human rights treaties. At the same time, the CRPD provides the specific context for understanding the right to inclusive education for disabled people. In so doing, it gives international human rights law a new direction with regard to the education of disabled children and, indeed, of other marginalised groups.

The right to inclusive education reflects the perils of negotiating group-specific human rights treaties, which were readily apparent to the drafters of the CRPD. On the one hand, a human rights treaty for disabled people could confer legitimacy on disability as a human rights issue, place disability rights squarely on the human rights agenda, and lend conceptual clarity to international human rights law. On the other hand, there was the risk that adopting a separate human rights treaty for disabled people could further marginalise disability rights within the international human rights system, undercut existing human rights protections as they apply to disabled people, and provide a basis for their marginal status in domestic law and policy. This would be the case especially if great care was not taken to draw out the specific context of discrimination on the basis of disability and to integrate that along with core disability rights concepts into existing human rights protection in a way that gradually developed international human rights law. Nowhere was this peril greater, perhaps, than in the negotiation of the right to inclusive education.

While it is important to study the right to inclusive education from a legal perspective, the realisation of inclusive education is an interdisciplinary project. Work across disciplines and areas of study informs the content of the legal standards. In this sense, the present volume should be considered as part of the broader, interdisciplinary endeavour to draw greater attention to the educational needs of disabled people, and, indeed, to inclusive education for all people generally. It aims to fill a gap in the literature and does so principally through the following inquiry: what norms and duties does the right to inclusive education impose upon States Parties and what can be done to ensure this right is being properly implemented and monitored in the future?

This volume seeks to resolve a number of issues. It provides an insight into the understanding and application of inclusive education as a human rights issue, offering an examination of this principle from a legal perspective in light of the development of international human rights law and in particular the CRPD. Further, it analyses the range of legal obligations for the right to inclusive education, including the duty to provide reasonable accommodation and the obligation to take steps towards the full realisation of the right in question. This volume further examines the various ways of implementing and monitoring progress in realising this right with a particular focus on the role both of the CRPD Committee and of disabled peoples' organisations (DPOs). It studies the potential avenues for the adjudication of the right to inclusive education, both before domestic and before regional courts, and looks into the practical implementation of this right in particular jurisdictions around the world, taking into account their historical development, constitutional structure, level of development and education systems.

In sum, the contributions in this volume shed light on the role of international human rights law in advancing the right to inclusive education and provide insight on how to bring about the realisation of that right in practice.

1.3 CONCEPTUALISING THE RIGHT TO INCLUSIVE EDUCATION

The volume takes due account of the fact that the CRPD has found inspiration in the social model of disability.[8] According to this model, disability connotes the social oppression of disabled people that results from the way in which society is organised and structured.[9] In contrast, the medical model of disability assumes that any reduction in the ability to participate in society is due to a medical condition intrinsic to an individual with impairment and requires medical intervention and remediation. The social model is reflected in Article 1 of the Convention, which states that disabled people include 'those who have long-term physical, mental, intellectual or sensory impairments which in interaction with various barriers may hinder their full and effective participation in society on an equal basis with others'. As a result, in the context of education, the focus should be on barriers to a child's participation in education, not on requiring all children to fit a certain standard curriculum.[10] The contributions to the present volume all emphasise the need to work on

[8] R. Kayess and P. French, 'Out of Darkness into Light? Introducing the Convention on the Rights of Persons with Disabilities' (2008) 8 *Human Rights Law Review* 1, 21; P. Bartlett, 'The United Nations Convention on the Rights of Persons with Disabilities and Mental Health Law' (2012) 75 (5) *Modern Law Review* 752, 758–761; R. Traustadóttir, 'Disability Studies, the Social Model and Legal Developments' in O. Arnardottir and G. Quinn (eds), *The UN Convention on the Rights of Persons with Disabilities: European and Scandinavian Perspectives* (London/Boston, MA: Martinus Nijhoff Publishers, 2009) 3, 16.

[9] M. Oliver, *Understanding Disability: From Theory to Practice*, 2nd edn (New York, NY: Palgrave Macmillan, 2009) 42–48.

[10] de Beco, 'The Right to Inclusive Education', 286.

the creation of enabling educational systems, rather than dwelling on the alleged shortcoming of pupils with different kinds of impairments.

This volume adopts a human rights approach to inclusive education. Participation in the general education system is a right, not a form of welfare. As such, the right to inclusive education triggers a series of legal obligations for States Parties. As inclusive education is a human rights issue, the right to inclusive education has the purpose of protecting the dignity of disabled children and of preventing their further marginalisation. Recognising that the full realisation of this right is a process and will take time in accordance with the differing capacities of States Parties, the volume draws particular attention to the duty to provide reasonable accommodation along with mandates to ensure the accessibility of education systems. At the same time, it fully acknowledges that States Parties must with alacrity use their available resources to make immediate progress towards the achievement of inclusive education. These legal obligations are to be fulfilled together if the objectives of the CRPD are to be met. In this way, the Convention bridges the divide between civil, political and economic and social and cultural rights,[11] and demonstrates that the historical dichotomy between categories of human rights does not work for disabled people (nor indeed for any group facing discrimination of any kind). In order to make the whole of education inclusive, meeting the educational needs of disabled children and remedying the failures of education systems to eliminate exclusionary practices and dismantle persistent barriers is required.

The CRPD Committee has signalled its prioritisation of the right to inclusive education, and its work serves as a barometer of where we are now – in the second decade of CRPD implementation in attaining the goal of inclusive education for disabled children. Gleaning from the concluding observations of the CRPD Committee and its General Comment No. 4, it is apparent that many barriers remain entrenched in practice and very often in law and policy.

This lack of implementation cannot be ignored. The challenges are widespread and are evident in all the regions of the world albeit in different ways. These challenges are far-reaching for education systems in developing countries, where ongoing challenges of resource limitations, underdeveloped legal and regulatory frameworks and data gaps persist. They are likewise particularly affecting displaced persons, whether those living in refugee camp settings or, increasingly, the growing population of urban refugees who have limited access to education. This does not mean that high-income countries always fare better, as despite the resources at their disposal many of them continue to

[11] T. Degener, '10 Years of Convention on the Rights of Persons with Disabilities' (2017) 35 (3) *Netherlands Quarterly of Human Rights* 152, 153–154.

deny disabled people education or to refer them to 'special' (that is, segregated) schools. The barriers are not only physical in nature as is sometimes suggested. Indeed, as the chapters in this volume bear out, the barriers are often multi-faceted and overwhelmingly the result of social attitudes. This is evident as the arrival of disabled children in mainstream schools is regarded with apprehension because it is thought to bring overall performance down or simply because of strong prejudice against disabled children. The volume acknowledges the challenges that persist in ensuring that educational programmes, facilities and services are inclusive and does so by addressing the conceptual and practical aspects of the right to inclusive education.

1.4 THE WAY FORWARD AND AN AGENDA FOR FUTURE RESEARCH

The volume provides an in-depth examination of the most relevant issues pertaining to the right to inclusive education in international human rights law, and yet it is by no means exhaustive. It aims to chart out an agenda for continued research on a dynamic area of international human rights law. The most important message conveyed, perhaps, is that this is new terrain on which more research is needed. While inclusive education has been the subject of inquiry in the fields of education and, subsequently, disability studies, it is not yet well established in legal scholarship. The volume hopes to remedy this lack of attention, while encouraging continued academic work on inclusive education as a human rights issue in the field of law. Given the many conceptual and practical questions raised by the right to inclusive education,[12] it is again important that legal academics and lawyers do so, or continue to do so, in collaboration with those of other disciplines across the board.

As is clear throughout the volume, a number of issues require further examination if the right to inclusive education is to be better understood and, eventually, practically implemented. Such issues include: inclusive education within the context of emergencies; accessible information and communication technologies (ICTs) in the general education system; support for children with different forms of impairment (including those with intensive support needs); the meaning of reasonable accommodation and progressive realisation in current political environments where shrinking budgets undercut the very aims of education; the incorporation of monitoring the

[12] G. de Beco, 'The Right to Inclusive Education: Why Is There So Much Opposition to Its Implementation?' (2018) 14(3) *International Journal of Law in Context* 396, 404–407.

implementation of the right to inclusive education into the international legal framework of human rights; and the issue of data gathering in order to facilitate the full realisation of inclusive education over time. Of particular relevance in the field of law will be the design of domestic legal frameworks that incorporate the duty to provide reasonable accommodation in education and that can offer supports for education that is available, accessible, acceptable and adaptable to disabled people.

Finally, insofar as inclusive education features as a core right of disabled people and, increasingly, as a right for all and in particular those groups so often left behind, what then are the implications of Article 24 for international human rights law? It stands to reason that the international legal framework developed by the CRPD for understanding and applying the notion of inclusive education represents an important and progressive development of international human rights law, not only for disabled people but equally for all groups that so often experience exclusion and discrimination in education, whether on the basis of gender, race, language, religion, ethnicity, indigeneity, sexual orientation and gender identity, health status, geographical location, refugee or migrant status, socioeconomic status, age, emergency and conflict, among others. Inclusive education directs attention to those students who are at high risk or on those who may be at risk of marginalisation, whatever the basis for that marginalisation; it seeks to ensure that, where necessary, proactive steps are taken to ensure and affirm their presence, participation and achievement in the education system.[13] There is therefore much to learn from the right to inclusive education beyond the issue of disability itself. It is about education and the way it can either alleviate or exacerbate various kinds of marginalisation and close, or open, the doors of opportunities for those regarded as falling outside the (imagined) educational norm.

1.5 PRESENTATION OF THE VOLUME: CHAPTER BY CHAPTER

This volume provides a comprehensive analysis of the various aspects of the right to inclusive education under international human rights law. It does so by exploring the core content of the right to inclusive education, the methods currently used to advance this right at the regional and international levels and the challenges related to its implementation at the domestic level. In addition

[13] S. Quinlivan, 'The Right to Inclusive Education for Children with Psychosocial Disability', 9th International Summer School on Disability Law and Policy, Centre for Disability Law and Policy, NUI Galway, June 2017.

to focussing on the theoretical foundation for the right to education, it examines practical and legal tools that can be used to further the right to inclusive education within the UN as well as the European, African and Inter-American human rights systems. Thereafter, it provides a number of case studies to inform how the right to inclusive education is being implemented in a diverse range of country contexts.

Following this introduction, Part I of the volume examines the background of the right to inclusive education under international human rights law. Arlene Kanter's chapter (Chapter 2) canvasses the historical and conceptual development of the right to inclusive education. She painstakingly traces the gradual convergence of human rights and disability within the context of education, following the development of international human rights law to its final proclamation in the CRPD. Gauthier de Beco's chapter (Chapter 3) subsequently offers a comprehensive legal analysis of Article 24 of the Convention in light of the recommendations of UN treaty bodies as well as the jurisprudence on the topic. He thoughtfully examines the various questions raised by a reading of the right to inclusive education, in the order of the different paragraphs, as well as any issues of contention that remain.

Part II of the volume addresses the theoretical foundations for the right to inclusive education, including conceptual and substantive issues. Starting with the conceptual issues, Michael Shevlin (Chapter 4) examines the topic from the perspective of education in order to give a good grasp of the concept of inclusive education, both looking at its origins and undertaking its evaluation. Rosemary Kayess (Chapter 5) examines the links between disability, equality and education leading to the enactment of the right to inclusive education and discusses certain ambiguities around a number of different interpretations. Sarah Arduin (Chapter 6) goes on to examine what information is conveyed by Article 24 of the CRPD, using expressivism as a methodology, and what understanding of this right emerges from the national legislations of five European states, namely England, Finland, France, Ireland and Norway. Moving to the substantive issues, Shivaun Quinlivan (Chapter 7) explores the core content of the CRPD's most significant contribution to equality under international human rights law, namely the concept of reasonable accommodation. In so doing, she contextualises reasonable accommodation within education. Gauthier de Beco (Chapter 8) follows by analysing the notion of progressive realisation with regard to Article 24 of the Convention. After examining the concept of inclusive education according to the CRPD, he provides a detailed overview of the measures to be taken with a view to realising the right to inclusive education by States Parties.

János Fiala-Butora (Chapter 9) addresses the same issue through a case study, by providing a picture of the achievement of inclusive education in Tanzania and Vietnam, thereby offering a clear illustration of the practical application of the notion of progressive realisation.

Part III of the volume deals with the implementation of the right to inclusive education, including strategies and mechanisms for its realisation. Peter Barnett and Michael Stein (Chapter 10) study the use of strategic litigation to advance inclusive education, referring to a number of important cases globally as well as their effects on the right to inclusive education. Carla Bonino Covas and Miguel Ángel Cabra de Luna (Chapter 11) examine the effectiveness of advocacy and lobbying on the basis of their experience with several programmes carried out by the European Disability Forum (EDF) in the European Union (EU). Janet E. Lord (Chapter 12) addresses the right to inclusive education within the framework of international cooperation and as a component of achieving the Sustainable Development Goals (SDGs). She further examines two elements of international cooperation and disability-inclusive development in addressing inclusive education in the context of humanitarian emergencies and in an area neglected by development donors, namely accessibility in higher education in developing countries. Deepti Raja and Anthony Giannoumis (Chapter 13) explore the adoption of a bottom-up approach in harnessing technology to advance the goals of inclusive education, consistent with the CRPD's provisions on accessible ICTs. Anna Gilmer (Chapter 14) looks to Indigenous knowledge of First Nations people as a means of achieving inclusive education. Chapters that follow address inclusive education within the work of international mechanisms. María Soledad Cisternas Reyes (Chapter 15) examines the work of the CRPD Committee through the prism of the international human rights system. This chapter is followed by an assessment of regional protections of the right to inclusive education. Andrea Broderick (Chapter 16) analyses the jurisprudence of the European Court of Human Rights, while Shivaun Quinlivan (Chapter 17) examines the jurisprudence emerging from the (Revised) European Social Charter. Japhet Biegon (Chapter 18) finally situates the right to inclusive education within an African regional framework by explicating the African disability architecture and its promise for disabled students.

Part IV of the volume focusses on putting inclusive education into practice through a number of case studies on the right to inclusive education across the different regions of the world. These case studies cover Ireland (Gerry Whyte) (Chapter 19), Belgium (Elisabeth De Schauwer, Inge Van de Putte and Gauthier de Beco) (Chapter 20), Germany (Thomas Bernhardt) (Chapter 21), Italy (Delia Ferri) (Chapter 22), China (Zhijun Fu, Bo Chen and Zhen Ni) (Chapter 23), Kenya (Elizabeth Kamundia) (Chapter 24), Japan (Yoshihara Ikehara) (Chapter 25), Tajikistan (Kate Lapham) (Chapter 26) and Argentina (Ana Laura Aiello) (Chapter 27). Taking into account the national particularities of each of the aforementioned countries, these case studies examine not only domestic legislation for the protection of the right to inclusive education but also the potential gaps and questions still to be resolved in order to improve such protection. They demonstrate what it means to be included in education in a given country's context and analyse where the law supports or undermines the right to inclusive education.

PART I

BACKGROUND

2

The Right to Inclusive Education for Students with Disabilities under International Human Rights Law

Arlene Kanter*

INTRODUCTION

In most, if not all, countries in the world today, children and adults with disabilities are denied their basic right to education.[1] Through policies and practices of outright exclusion, segregation or indirect discrimination and neglect, children and adults with disabilities are denied access to mainstream schools and classroom learning. Many potential students with disabilities are simply unable to attend school because of the inaccessibility of the schools and classrooms, and because of the unavailability of accessible transportation to and from school. Further, of those students with disabilities who do attend school, many of them are subjected to inferior education in separate schools or classrooms. They are often denied accommodations and supports, and taught by teachers who are either untrained or unwilling to include students with disabilities in their classrooms. The lack of educational opportunities for children and youth with disabilities is particularly acute in the Global South.[2] Yet without education, children and adults with disabilities will remain on the margins of society, without the tools they need to live

* Arlene S. Kanter was an autumn 2017 visiting scholar at Harvard Law School. At Syracuse University College of Law, she is a Bond, Schoeneck & King Distinguished Professor of Law, the Laura J. and L. Douglas Meredith Professor of Teaching Excellence, and the founder and director of the Disability Law and Policy Program.

[1] This chapter is based in large part on my involvement with the drafting of the Convention on the Rights of People with Disabilities at the United Nations from 2001 to 2006. The summary of the process that led to the adoption of Article 24 on inclusive education in the CRPD is based on my contemporaneous notes of those meetings and the official UN summaries. I wish to thank Jamie Glashow (SUCOL and SUSOE 2016) and Megan Brooks (SUCOL and SUSOE 2018) for their research assistance. Correspondence about this chapter may be directed to Professor Arlene Kanter at kantera@law.syr.edu.

[2] See, for example, Shaun Grech and Karen Soldatic (eds), *Disability in the Global South: The Critical Handbook* (Springer 2016) 187–216.

a meaningful life. Society too will be forced to pay the price and will be denied the valuable contributions of the significant segment of their population with disabilities.

In this chapter, I explore the history of the development of the right to education for people with disabilities under international human rights law, and the potential for realising this right since the adoption of the Convention on the Rights of People with Disabilities (CRPD) by the United Nations in 2006. The chapter begins with a discussion of the barriers to accessing quality education for children, youth and adults with disabilities. It continues, in Part II, with an overview of the development of the right to education for students with disabilities under international law generally, and the right to inclusive education in particular, prior to the adoption of the CRPD. Part III discusses the drafting of Article 24 of the CRPD. Article 24 is one of the fifty articles of the CRPD that was adopted by the United Nations after five years of negotiations. It is the first comprehensive treaty designed to 'promote, protect and ensure the full and equal enjoyment of all human rights and fundamental freedoms by all persons with disabilities, and to promote respect for their human dignity' (as stated in Article 1 of the Convention). To implement this goal, the CRPD in Article 3(c) guarantees the right of all children and adults with disabilities to '[f]ull and effective participation and inclusion in society'. These rights are enhanced with specific recommendations regarding how they will be enforced, including in Article 24, which declares the right to education and 'life long learning' in an 'inclusive education system' for all children and adults with disabilities.[3] This section of the chapter includes a detailed analysis of the drafting process of Article 24, based in part on the author's own observations of the CRPD drafting committee's negotiation on Article 24. Following this discussion of the background of the CRPD, Part IV discusses the work of the CRPD Committee, which oversees the implementation of the CRPD, including Article 24. This section includes a discussion of General Comment No. 4, the most comprehensive analysis of Article 24, which the CRPD committee published in September 2016. The chapter concludes by identifying the challenges that remain in implementing Article 24's goal of inclusive education for all children, youth and adults with disabilities throughout the world. Even after the adoption of the CRPD and its ratification by 174 countries (as of September 2017), millions of children and adults with disabilities are not realising their right to inclusive education. Yet, without inclusive education, the CRPD's goal of ensuring equality for people with

3 UNGA Convention on the Rights of Persons with Disabilities (13 December 2006) A/RES/61/106 [hereinafter CRPD].

disabilities will remain elusive in most countries in the world. Indeed, as one commentator has observed, 'it makes no sense politically or economically not to have all the world's children in quality inclusive schools'.[4]

I BARRIERS TO ACCESS TO EDUCATION FOR CHILDREN WITH DISABILITIES

UNICEF estimates that, on any given day, more than 100 million children throughout the world are out of school.[5] Most of those children are girls, despite efforts to narrow the gender gap in education. In areas of conflict, UNICEF estimates that girls 'are 2.5 times more likely to be out of school than boys'.[6] Further, of those children who are in school, millions receive inadequate education, delivered by untrained teachers in overcrowded, unhealthy and ill-equipped classrooms.[7] Even worse, however, is the lack of access to quality education for girls as well as for boys with disabilities. Millions of children with disabilities throughout the world are never even enrolled in school. These children are 'hidden at home',[8] or unable to travel to school, or prevented from attending school by their own families or the local schools.[9] Some parents of children with disabilities are so ashamed of their children's disabilities that they are reluctant to let their children leave their homes,

4 Richard Rieser, Implementing Inclusive Education: A Commonwealth Guide to Implementing Article 24 of the UN Convention on the Rights of Persons with Disabilities, 2nd edn (Commonwealth Secretariat 2012) [hereinafter *Commonwealth Guide*] 31.

5 UNICEF, The State of the World's Children 2002: Leadership (UNICEF 2002) 52 www.unicef.org/sowc/archive/ENGLISH/The%20State%20of%20the%20World's%20Children%202002.pdf, accessed 11 July 2017.

6 UNICEF, 'Education in Emergencies' (UNICEF, 12 June 2017) www.unicef.org/education/bege_70640.html, accessed 7 August 2017. The World Bank has found that the exclusion of girls from education hinders the productive potential of a country's economy, as well as its overall development. For example, it has been estimated that between US$16 billion and US$30 billion is lost annually in East Asia and the Pacific region as a result of gender gaps in education. See http://womensmediasummit.org/wp-content/uploads/2017/03/WEF_Global_Gender_Gap_Report_2016.pdf, at 27.

7 UNGA, 'A World Fit for Children' (11 October 2002) A/Res/S-27/2 [38], UNICEF (2002) (n. 5) generally; *see also* Katarina Tomaševski, *Education Denied: Costs and Remedies* (Zed Books 2003); UNICEF, World Declaration on the Survival, Protection and Development of Children (UNICEF 1990) www.unicef.org/wsc/declare.htm, accessed 11 July 2017.

8 Hisayo Katsu and others, 'Questioning Human Rights: The Case of Education for Children and Youth in Ethiopia' in Shaun Grech and Karen Soldatic (eds), *Disability in the Global South: The Critical Handbook* (Springer 2016) 189–190 (citing Lorraine Wapling, 'Exploratory Mission to Assess the Opportunity for Inclusive Education in Ethiopia' [2010] Handicap International 15, 38).

9 UNICEF, *The State of the World's Children 2006: Excluded and Invisible* (UNICEF 2006) 19, 28.

thereby 'inhibiting them from fulfilling their potential, obtaining access to education and leading independent lives'.[10]

Many other millions of children with disabilities live locked away in orphanages or other institutions, where little or no learning ever takes place.[11] 'UNICEF estimates that 2.4 million of all children of primary-school age are missing from school in ... South Eastern Europe ..., Central Europe ... and [the] Commonwealth of Independent States region.'[12] The numbers are lower in other regions of the world, including the Global South, where fewer resources are allocated for education than in European countries.[13] UNESCO estimates that fewer than 10 per cent of children with disabilities in the African region attend school, with even lower numbers in the southern region, where only 1–2 per cent of children with disabilities attend schools – this is attributed, in large part, to poverty.[14]

In Tanzania, for example, '[m]ore than one-third of Tanzanians ... live below the basic poverty line, set at approximately one US dollar per day'.[15] In an attempt to address this problem, the Tanzanian government launched the Primary Education Development Programme.[16] This policy framework 'sought to provide equitable, quality, basic education and vocational skills for all'.[17] The Programme also sought to ensure adequate teachers, management and learning environments conducive for students and teachers at all levels.[18] The Programme accomplished some of these goals.

According to the 2006 UNESCO Global Monitoring Report, in Tanzania, the 'number of out-of-school children fell by over 3 million to less than

10 Katsu and others (n. 8) 190.

11 Estimates of the number of children in institutions, as of 2014, range from 'more than 2 million' to 8 million. These figures are often reported as underestimates, due to lack of data from many countries and to the large proportion of unregistered institutions (UNICEF, Progress for Children: A Report Card on Child Protection No. 8 [UNICEF 2009] 19); see also Disability Rights International's 'Worldwide Campaign to End the Institutionalization of Children' at www.driadvocacy.org/learn-about-the-worldwide-campaign-to-end-the-institutionalization-of-children, accessed 11 July 2017.

12 UNICEF, The Right of Children with Disabilities to Education: A Rights-Based Approach to Inclusive Education: Position Paper (UNICEF 2012) 15.

13 UNESCO, Teaching and Learning: Achieving Quality for All (UNESCO 2014); see also Katsu and others (n. 8) 189.

14 UNESCO, Strong Foundations: Early Childhood Care and Education, 2nd edn (UNESCO 2006) 74, 138.

15 Filiz Polat, 'Inclusion in Education: A Step towards Social Justice' (2011) 31 *International Journal of Educational Development* 50, 52.

16 Ibid. 53.

17 Ibid. 53.

18 Ibid.

150,000' in the years between 2002 and 2006.[19] The Tanzanian government's strategy also aimed to increase the enrolment of children with disabilities from 2 per cent to 30 per cent from 2006 to 2010. However, Tanzania's lack of water, sanitation and school buildings poses additional problems to the realisation of the government's educational goals. Further, the lack of qualified teachers and teaching materials, as well as cultural barriers, such as 'lack of community awareness and negative attitudes towards disabled people and inclusive education', makes realisation of the goals of integrating students with disabilities into regular classrooms with children without disabilities more difficult.[20] It is believed that once the Tanzanian government can combat these challenges, it will be able to continue its path towards an inclusive education system.

Moreover, in many other countries, data on the number of children with disabilities who attend school are not available, and if they are, they are not reliable. One reason for the lack of data is that in some countries, children who are born with disabilities or who develop disabilities immediately after birth are not registered at birth. Accordingly, they are not included in data on the number of people with disabilities. Another reason for the lack of data on children in school is that families may choose not to identify their children with disabilities to government authorities due to the shame and stigma that attaches to the label of disability in many (if not most) countries of the world today. Without such information, ministries of education will never know about those children who are not registered at birth, who are not counted in school reports which record the number of children who do not attend or who are absent from school on any given day.[21] Moreover, children with less severe disabilities, such as learning disabilities or ADD/ADHD, may not be considered 'disabled' in many countries. If they are not considered disabled, they are not included in data on people with disabilities, nor are they provided with the services or accommodations they may need to learn in school and, later, to live their lives.

To make matters worse, many countries have no mandatory education laws, so often there are no data at all on the school attendance of children with or without disabilities. Further, in those countries that do mandate education up to a certain age, some countries exempt children with disabilities altogether or create barriers that make it impossible for school-aged children with disabilities to access education by denying them accommodations. Without accommodations, such as accessible

[19] Ibid.
[20] Ibid. 53–54.
[21] Ibid.

transportation, a child who uses a wheelchair cannot go to school; without a sign language interpreter, a deaf student cannot understand or speak with teachers or classmates; without books and assignments in braille, large-print texts or access to text-to-speech software, a student with vision impairments cannot complete assignments; and, without extra time on tests or the assistance of an aide, notetaking, tutoring or other modifications, a student with a learning or other cognitive or developmental disability is effectively denied the opportunity to receive any education at all.[22] In short, in many countries, particularly in the Global South, where resources are more limited, researchers have found that 'little is known about how children with disabilities advance and succeed in education'.[23]

Children with disabilities (as well as those without disabilities) who live in poverty face additional barriers to accessing education. The connection between disability and poverty is well documented. Disability increases the risk of poverty, while living in poverty increases the risk of developing or worsening a disabling condition.[24] Therefore, the poorer the children are, the greater is their risk of developing disabling impairments that will prevent them from attending and benefitting from school. As a study in four African countries found, 'even when children with disabilities ... access education, the poverty of their families challenges their advancement and survival'.[25]

In 2006, UNESCO estimated that 80 per cent of the world's population of children with disabilities live in developing countries, with only 10 per cent of disabled children in Africa attending primary school.[26] A more recent 2012 report by UNESCO identified additional barriers to education, including tuition costs, child labour, lack of proximity to schools and stringent entrance examinations, as well as poor teacher recruitment and teacher training programmes, especially in rural areas.[27] Lack of access to basic learning materials (e.g. books, notebooks, pencils,

[22] A report in Tanzania, for example, found that '[a]ccess without quality leaves the education system vulnerable, as this would negatively affect access and achievement as well as fail to meet the goals of equity and justice' (Polat [n. 15] 53).

[23] Katsu and others (n. 8) 191.

[24] Jill Hanass-Hancock and Sophie Mitra, 'Livelihoods and Disability: The Complexities of Work in the Global South' in Shaun Grech and Karen Soldatic (eds), *Disability in the Global South: The Critical Handbook* (Springer 2016) 138.

[25] Katsu and others (n. 8) 192.

[26] *See* UNESCO, *Strong Foundations* (n. 14) 74.

[27] UNESCO, Addressing Exclusion in Education: A Guide to Assessing Education Systems towards More Inclusive and Just Societies (UNESCO 2012) ED/BLS/BAS/2012/PI/1, 13.

drinking water and lunch) and governments' failure to provide financial resources to schools are additional, and often insurmountable, barriers, according to UNESCO.[28] Similar findings are documented in a 2007 UNICEF report which found that access to education is often hindered by 'income poverty, exposure to child labour, conflict and natural disasters, location, migration and displacement, HIV/AIDS, disability, gender, ethnicity, language of instruction, religion and caste'.[29]

Despite these many barriers to education, especially for children with disabilities who live in poverty, access to education is a critical need. Education provides the most direct route out of poverty. It also increases a person's value as a participating and contributing member of society. Research has shown too that children (with and without disabilities) who attend school exhibit marked improvement in physical, emotional and social abilities; are better able to care for themselves and to participate in family life; and are better able to secure employment as adults.[30] Indeed, education has the potential to increase a person's earnings, stimulate the economic growth of a society and break the cycle of poverty and exclusion for many people, with and without disabilities.[31] As the USAID Executive Education Strategy of 2011 highlighted, education can transform 'individuals from "subjects" to citizens – allowing them to participate meaningfully in the political life of their countries'.[32] Given these findings, the two questions we must ask is why it took so long for the right to education for children and adults with disabilities to be recognised under international human rights law and what more can be done to ensure the realisation of the important right to education for all children and adults with disabilities.

28 Ibid. 15.

29 'Social Inclusion and Respect for Diversity' (Generation 2030) www.generation2030.ru/crossroads/education/research/social_inclusion_and_respect_for, accessed 11 July 2017. Lack of access to education also has been documented as one of the effects of the recent refugee crisis resulting from the Syrian conflict. See Khawla Wakkaf and Arlene S. Kanter, 'Children with Disabilities and the Syrian Conflict' (2017) 7 *Impunity Watch Annual Review* 1.

30 James McLeskey and Nancy L. Waldron, 'School Change and Inclusive Schools: Lessons Learned from Practice' (2002) 84 *Phi Delta Kappan* 65; Rachel Morrison and Imelda Burgman, 'Friendship Experiences among Children with Disabilities Who Attend Mainstream Australian Schools' (2009) 76 *Canadian Journal of Occupational Therapy* 145.

31 UNICEF Innocenti Research Centre, Promoting the Rights of Children with Disabilities (UNICEF 2007).

32 USAID, *Education: Opportunity through Learning: USAID Education Strategy 2011–2015* (USAID 2011) 3, www.usaid.gov/sites/default/files/documents/1865/Education%20Strategy.pdf, accessed 11 July 2017.

II THE DEVELOPMENT OF THE RIGHT TO INCLUSIVE EDUCATION FOR PEOPLE WITH DISABILITIES UNDER INTERNATIONAL LAW

A *The Right to Education for People with Disabilities Under International Law Prior to the Convention on the Rights of People with Disabilities*

The Universal Declaration on Human Rights (UDHR), adopted by the United Nations in 1948, acknowledges unequivocally education as a universal human right. Article 26 of the UDHR proclaims:

> (1) Everyone has the right to education. Education shall be free, at least in the elementary and fundamental stages. Elementary education shall be compulsory. Technical and professional education shall be made generally available and higher education shall be equally accessible to all on the basis of merit.
>
> (2) Education shall be directed to the full development of the human personality and to the strengthening of respect for human rights and fundamental freedoms. It shall promote understanding, tolerance and friendship among all nations, racial or religious groups, and shall further the activities of the United Nations for the maintenance of peace.
>
> (3) Parents have a prior right to choose the kind of education that shall be given to their children.[33]

Article 26 does not exempt children with disabilities; nor does it specifically include them, either. It also does not mention the right to services, accommodations or modifications, without which many children with disabilities cannot realise their right to education on an equal basis with nondisabled children.

Following the adoption of the UDHR, subsequent treaties continued to affirm the right to education for all. The Convention on the Elimination of All Forms of Racial Discrimination of 1965, for example, prohibits discrimination in education and affirms the right to education for everyone, without distinction as to race, colour or national or ethnic origin, but not disability.[34] Similarly, Article 13 of the International Covenant on Economic, Social and Cultural Rights (ICESCR) of 1966 guarantees the right to free primary education for all. The ICESCR also specifically requires States Parties to

[33] UNGA Res. 217 (III) A 10 December 1948 Art. 26.

[34] UNGA Res. 2106 (XX) 21 December 1965 Art. 5.

'agree that education shall be directed to the full development of the human personality and the sense of its dignity, and shall strengthen the respect for human rights and fundamental freedoms'.[35] States Parties must also agree according to Article 13(1) that

> education shall enable all persons to participate effectively in a free society, promote understanding, tolerance and friendship among all nations and all racial, ethnic or religious groups, and further the activities of the United Nations for the maintenance of peace.[36]

However, the ICESCR does not specifically refer to students with disabilities and, like the UDHR, does not require the provision of services, accommodations or modifications necessary to enable students with disabilities to attend school and to participate in educational opportunities on an equal basis with nondisabled children.

In 1999, Special Rapporteur on Education Katarina Tomaševski produced a report on the right to education in General Comment No. 13 of the ICESCR.[37] Although General Comment No. 13 reaffirms the importance of education to all, it fails to acknowledge students with disabilities:

> Education is both a human right in itself and an indispensable means of realizing other human rights. As an empowerment right, education is the primary vehicle by which economically and socially marginalized adults and children can lift themselves out of poverty and obtain the means to participate fully in their communities. Education has a vital role in empowering women, safeguarding children from exploitative and hazardous labour and sexual exploitation, promoting human rights and democracy, protecting the environment, and controlling population growth. Increasingly, education is recognized as one of the best financial investments States can make. But the importance of education is not just practical: a well-educated, enlightened and active mind, able to wander freely and widely, is one of the joys and rewards of human existence.[38]

General Comment No. 13 also includes a new international conceptualisation of the right to education, commonly referred to as 'The 4 A's', which are 'availability', 'accessibility', 'acceptability' and 'adaptability' to all.[39] This

35 UNGA Res. 2200A (XXI) 16 December 1966 [hereinafter ICESCR] Art. 13(1).

36 In addition, Article 13 of the ICESCR (n. 35) places further obligations relating to the full realisation of the right in subsection 2(a)–(e).

37 Committee on Economic, Social and Cultural Rights, General Comment No. 13: The Right to Education (Article 13 of the Covenant) (8 December 1999) E/C.12/1999/10.

38 Ibid. 1.

39 Ibid. 6.

conceptualisation has been adopted by the UN and now applies to all countries that have ratified the ICESCR. In addition, the ICESCR Committee itself has recognised that education at all levels should exhibit these four 'interrelated and essential features' of which the best interests of the student must be the primary consideration.[40] However, neither the ICESCR nor General Comment No. 13 specifically mentions people with disabilities nor do they affirm the right to services, accommodations or modifications that some students with disabilities may need to exercise their right to education.

Another international initiative recognising the right to education is in the Convention on the Elimination of All Forms of Discrimination against Women (CEDAW) of 1979.[41] Article 10 of CEDAW reaffirms the right to education for girls and women. However, women and girls with disabilities are not specifically included or excluded from CEDAW, as it states that:

> States Parties shall take all appropriate measures to eliminate discrimination against women in order to ensure to them equal rights with men in the field of education and in particular to ensure, on a basis of equality of men and women[.][42]

It was not until 1989 with the adoption of the Convention on the Rights of the Child (CRC)[43] that the right to education for children with disabilities was included in a binding treaty. Prior to the CRC, the UN World Programme of Action (WPA), in 1982, proclaimed a global strategy intended to advance full participation of persons with disabilities in social life and national development, using a human rights perspective.[44] The WPA also recognised that 'whenever pedagogically possible, education should take place in the ordinary school system'.[45] However, unlike a treaty or convention, the WPA is not binding. Therefore, the right to education for children with disabilities did not become a legally binding obligation under international law until the CRC was adopted by the UN in 1989. The goal of the CRC is to prepare children to participate fully 'in a free society, in the spirit of understanding, peace, tolerance, equality . . ., and friendship'.[46] To that end, it ensures that all

40 Ibid. 4.

41 UNGA, Convention on the Elimination of All Forms of Discrimination against Women (18 December 1979) A/RES/34/180.

42 Ibid. Art. 10.

43 UNGA Res. 44/25, Convention on the Rights of the Child (20 November 1989) [hereinafter CRC].

44 UNGA Res. 37/52 (3 December 1982) UN Doc. A/RES/37/52.

45 As reprinted in Theresia Degener and Yolan Koster-Dreese (eds), *Human Rights and Disabled Persons: Essays and Relevant Human Rights Instruments* (Martinus Nijhoff 1995) 326.

46 CRC (n. 43) Art. 29(1)(d).

children have the right to receive education without discrimination for any reason. Today, the CRC is the most widely adopted treaty, with 195 ratifications.[47]

The CRC applies equally to all children 'below the age of eighteen years unless under the law applicable to the child, majority is attained earlier'.[48] The CRC Drafting Committee noted that children with disabilities must be specifically included in the CRC because '[d]iscrimination against children with disabilities is also pervasive in many formal educational systems and in a great many informal educational settings, including in the home'.[49] Article 2 of the CRC, therefore, affirms the right of *all* children to enjoy their human rights 'without discrimination of any kind, irrespective of the child's or his or her parent's or legal guardian's race, colour, sex, language, religion, political or other opinion, national, ethnic or social origin, property, *disability*, birth or other status'.[50] This provision in the CRC is the first time disability has been included in an international treaty's list of protected groups.

In addition to Article 2 of the CRC, Articles 23, 28 and 29 refer to educational rights of children with disabilities. Article 23 addresses the needs of children with disabilities to effectively access and receive an education, recognising that all children 'should enjoy a full and decent life, in conditions which ensure dignity, promote self-reliance and facilitate the child's active participation in the community'.[51] Article 23 states that education should be designed in a manner that is 'conducive to the ... fullest possible social integration and individual development', and that children with disabilities may need additional support to ensure effective exercise of their right to education, 'subject to available resources'.[52] Article 28 goes on to recognise

47 Noticeably absent from the list of countries that have ratified the CRC is the United States. The only other country that has not yet ratified the CRC is South Sudan. Somalia is the most recent country to ratify the CRC. See Omar Faruk, 'Somalia to Join Child Rights Pact: UN' Reuters (London, 20 November 2009) www.reuters.com/article/2009/11/20/ozatp-somalia-children-idAFJOE5AJ0IT20091120, accessed 11 July 2017. See also www.un.org/apps/news/story.asp?NewsID=49845#.WWoD6IjyuyI, accessed 20 July 2017.

48 CRC (n. 43) Art. 1. By definition, this age range of birth to eighteen years covers most, but not all, school-aged children since educational programming for students with disabilities may extend beyond their eighteenth year. The CRC is written to leave open this possibility. For example, a child identified with a disability in a school system in the United States is allowed three additional years to complete public schooling, thereby graduating at twenty-one years of age instead of at the age of eighteen. See the Code of Federal Regulations, in particular at 34 C.F.R. §300.101.

49 Committee on the Rights of the Child, General Comment No. 1: The Aims of Education (Article 29) (17 April 2001) CRC/GC/2001/1 [10].

50 CRC (n. 43) Art. 2 (emphasis added).

51 Ibid. Art. 23(1).

52 Ibid. Art. 23(2).

the right of all children to a free and compulsory education and imposes a duty on States Parties to provide free primary education and to do so on the basis of equality of opportunity.[53] Article 28 also requires States Parties to 'recognize the right of the child to education, and with a view to achieving this right progressively and on the basis of equal opportunity', although it also imposes a lesser duty on States Parties with respect to secondary, vocational and tertiary education.[54] When Article 28 is read in conjunction with Articles 2 and 14 of the ICESCR, it appears that States Parties also have a duty to provide free primary education to the maximum extent of their available resources under the CRC.

Article 29 is the third article of the CRC that specifically addresses the rights of children with disabilities. This article requires education to be grounded in human rights, respectful of the child's family, cultural and national identity, and focussed on the child's 'personality, talents and *mental and physical abilities*', so that all children will reach their maximum potential.[55] Article 29, together with Articles 2, 23 and 28 of the CRC, upholds the right to education of all children, including children with disabilities. However, even after the adoption of the CRC, UNICEF found that millions of children with disabilities around the world were still excluded altogether from school 'due to poor data collection and a lack of knowledge on how to include them in education planning and implementation'.[56] Thus, although the CRC may have won nearly universal ratification, its goal of education for all children has not been achieved for children with disabilities.

B *The Right to Inclusive Education under International Law Leading Up to the Convention on the Rights of People with Disabilities*

Following the adoption of the CRC in 1989, the UN began to actively promote inclusive education. In 1990, the UN adopted the World Declaration on Education for All (EFA).[57] Known as the Jomtien Declaration, this Declaration represents the first international agreement identifying the goal

[53] Ibid. Art. 28(1) and subsection (a) in particular.
[54] Ibid. subsection (1).
[55] CRC (n. 43) Art. 29(1)(a) (emphasis added).
[56] UNICEF, *Children and Young People with Disabilities: Fact Sheet* (UNICEF 2013) 20 www.unicef.org/disabilities/files/Factsheet_A5__Web_NEW.pdf, accessed 24 August 2017.
[57] UNESCO, World Conference on Education for All: Meeting Basic Learning Needs: A Vision for the 1990s: Background Document. Jomtien, Thailand, 5–9 March 1990 (Inter-Agency Commission 1990).

of inclusive education for all. This Declaration guarantees the right of every child to be educated based on his or her individual needs. It also recognises the importance of training teachers about including students with disabilities in their classrooms in order to realise the goal of inclusive education.[58] The Jomtien Declaration also recognises the value of individual differences and diversity among primary schoolchildren, and calls for overall improvement in the quality of primary education.[59] Despite the Jomtien Declaration's laudable language, as a declaration, it is not binding or enforceable as law.

Following the Jomtien Declaration, the UN adopted another non-binding international document in 1994, known as the Standard Rules on the Equalization of Opportunities for Persons with Disabilities.[60] The Standard Rules were adopted following the end of the Decade of the Disabled, and were intended to assist member states in developing national plans for people with disabilities to ensure their equal rights and to remove barriers to their inclusion in society.[61] The Standard Rules recognise the responsibility of each country to ensure equal education for all of its citizens. For example, Standard Rule 6 affirms the equal right to education of all children, youth and adults with disabilities by providing that 'States should recognize the principle of equal primary, secondary and tertiary educational opportunities for children, youth and adults with disabilities, in integrated settings'.[62] Rule 6 goes on to instruct States to 'ensure that the education of persons with disabilities is an integral part of the educational system'.[63] Thus, the two important aspects of this Rule include the expectation that educational programmes are to be provided in integrated settings and that students with disabilities are to be recognised as equal participants within the educational system. Standard Rule 6 also states that if special programming is required, it 'should reflect the same standards and ambitions as general education and should be closely linked to it [and that] students with disabilities should be afforded the same portion of educational resources as students without disabilities'.[64] In short, the Standard Rules require equal access to education in inclusive settings for all students with disabilities. The Standard Rules also include a section for monitoring progress whereby individual member states

58 Ibid.

59 Ibid.

60 UNGA, 'Standard Rules on the Equalization of Opportunities for Persons with Disabilities' (20 December 1993) A/RES/48/96.

61 Ibid.

62 Ibid. Annex II Rule 6.

63 Ibid.

64 Ibid. Annex II Rule 6(8).

are expected to evaluate the effectiveness of their programmes and to provide plans for improvements.[65]

Although the Standard Rules are not binding, they have resulted in the promulgation of reports submitted to the Commission for Social Development by the Special Rapporteur on Disability. In 1994, the first UN Special Rapporteur on the Commission for Social Development, Bengt Lindqvist, was charged with monitoring the implementation of the Standard Rules. He acknowledged the important role of education to people with and without disabilities:

> All children and young people of the world have the right to education. It is not our education systems that have a right to certain types of children. It is the school system of a country that must be adjusted to meet the needs of all children.[66]

This statement is noteworthy, even today. It clarifies the responsibility of schools to educate *all* students, by acknowledging that it is the job of teachers to learn how to educate those children; it is not the obligation of the children to change their behaviours (even if they could) to adjust to the needs of the schools.[67]

Also in 1994, UNESCO adopted the Salamanca Statement and Framework for Action on Principles, Policy, and Practice in Special Needs Education in Salamanca, Spain.[68] More than 300 participants, representing ninety-two governments and twenty-five international organisations, attended the Salamanca conference, and signed on to this statement.[69] The goal of the Salamanca conference was to further the objectives of the EFA by promoting inclusive education for all children, particularly those with 'special educational needs'.[70] The conference resulted in the Salamanca Statement, which reaffirms the need to provide equal education to all people with special educational needs throughout the world.[71] The Salamanca Statement is

[65] Ibid. Annex II Rule 20.

[66] Bengt Lindqvist, 'Summary of Thematic Presentations and Discussions: Theme 1: Policy and Legislation: Special Needs Education: Conceptual Framework, Planning and Policy Factors' in UNESCO and Ministry of Education and Science Spain (ed.), World Conference on Special Needs Education: Access and Quality: Salamanca, Spain, 7–10 June 1994 (UNESCO and Ministry of Education and Science Spain 1995) 28.

[67] Ibid.

[68] See UNESCO and Ministry of Education and Science Spain, The Salamanca Statement and Framework for Action on Special Needs Education (ED-94/WS/18, UNESCO 1994) [hereinafter Salamanca Statement].

[69] Ibid.

[70] Ibid. ix.

[71] Ibid.

unequivocal in calling upon governments to 'adopt as a matter of law or policy the principle of inclusive education, enrolling all children in regular schools, unless there are compelling reasons for doing otherwise'.[72] The Salamanca Statement makes inclusive education for students with disabilities the highest priority and also requires governments to establish ongoing systems of monitoring and evaluation for such inclusive education programmes.[73]

The Salamanca Statement also requires schools to include all children 'regardless of [their] individual differences or difficulties'.[74] The Salamanca Statement recognises that 'every child has unique characteristics, interests, abilities, and learning needs'.[75] Thus when the Salamanca Statement refers to 'special educational needs', it refers to all children who experience barriers in equal access and participation in education and declares their right to be educated together with all other children,[76] including children with 'physical, intellectual, social, emotional, linguistic or other conditions', as well as 'gifted children, street and working children, children from remote or nomadic populations, children from linguistic, ethnic or cultural minorities and children from other disadvantaged or marginalized areas or groups'.[77] Children with such 'special educational needs' require access to regular schools which should 'accommodate them within a child-centered pedagogy capable of meeting these needs'.[78]

The Salamanca Statement also includes the first definition of what the right to inclusive education actually means. Inclusion is defined as follows:

> The fundamental principle of the inclusive school is that all children should learn together, wherever possible, regardless of any difficulties or differences they may have. Inclusive schools must recognize and respond to the diverse needs of their students, accommodating both different styles and rates of learning and ensuring quality education to all through appropriate curricula, organizational arrangements, teaching strategies, resource use and partnerships with their communities. There should be a continuum of support and services to match the continuum of special needs encountered in every school.[79]

72 Ibid.
73 Ibid. iii–xii.
74 Ibid. ix.
75 Ibid. viii.
76 Ibid. 6.
77 Ibid.
78 Ibid. at viii. The Salamanca Statement also urges States Parties in seven other ways in Section 3 on pages ix–x.
79 Ibid. 11–12.

The difference between the Salamanca Statement and previous international documents is its exclusive focus on students with disabilities and its call for inclusive education. The Salamanca Statement provides detailed suggestions on how best to address the numerous levels of special education needs of students with disabilities. It also recognises the differing views on inclusive education among and within different countries of the world but affirms also the relationship between inclusive education and inclusive societies. It states that

> regular schools with this inclusive orientation are the most effective means of combatting discriminatory attitudes, creating welcoming communities, building an inclusive society and achieving education for all; moreover, they provide an effective education to the majority of children and improve efficiency and ultimately cost-effectiveness of the entire educational system.[80]

By its language, therefore, the Salamanca Statement seeks to change the view of disability in society by focussing on changing the educational system to fit the student – rather than changing the student to fit the system. In this way, the Salamanca Statement is seen as rejecting the medical model of disability, which focusses on distinctions between those with and without certain medical conditions, in favour of the social model of disability, which focusses on removing barriers that interfere with a person's ability to access society.[81] As such, the Salamanca Statement puts the responsibility on governments to remove barriers and to provide services and accommodations to students with disabilities to enable them to exercise their right to education on an equal basis with others. Although the Salamanca Statement is not binding, it reaffirms the obligation of governments to provide education in neighbourhood schools for all children, regardless of their physical, intellectual, emotional, social, linguistic or other abilities.[82] It also lays the groundwork for Article 24 of the

80 Ibid. ix.

81 For a discussion of the various models of disability, including the medical and social models mentioned here, see Arlene S. Kanter, 'The Law: What's Disability Studies Got to Do with It or an Introduction to Disability Legal Studies' (2011) 42 *Columbia Human Rights Law Review* 403, 419–432.

82 Ibid. The Salamanca Statement was updated in 2009 at the Global Conference on Inclusive Education entitled 'Confronting the Gap: Rights, Rhetoric, Reality? Return to Salamanca: Initiative 24 – Salamanca Conference Resolution' (Inclusion International Global Conference on Inclusive Education, Salamanca, 11 June 2010) http://inclusion-international.org/salamanca-conference-resolutio/, accessed 12 July 2017. The 2009 Statement reaffirms the Salamanca Statement's original commitment to fully implement Article 24's mandate to develop an inclusive education system in every country of the world (particularly paragraphs one to three).

CRPD which guarantees, in a binding treaty, the right to inclusive education, as discussed in the next section of this chapter.

The Salamanca Statement requires States Parties to develop national educational policies that require children with disabilities to attend the same neighbourhood schools that they would attend if they did not have a disability.[83] However, the Salamanca Statement also recognises the wide diversity of educational opportunities in the various countries of the world.[84] Although it recognises 'the necessity and urgency of providing education for children, youth and adults with special educational needs within the regular education system',[85] it also proclaims that '[t]he practice of "mainstreaming" children with disabilities should be an integral part of national plans for achieving education for all' and that '[n]ecessary provision should also be made for ensuring inclusion of youth and adults with special needs in secondary and higher education as well as in training programmes'.[86] As such, the Salamanca Statement is the first international document to recognise the right of every child to attend neighbourhood, inclusive schools as 'the most effective means of combatting discriminatory attitudes, creating welcoming communities, building an inclusive society and achieving education for all'.[87] For this reason, the Salamanca Statement is considered the most important international statement on inclusive education prior to the CRPD.[88]

Following the 1994 Salamanca Statement, the UN adopted the Dakar Framework for Action at the World Education Forum held in Dakar, Senegal, in 2000.[89] This Forum was attended by more than 1,100 participants from 164 countries.[90] The Dakar Framework reaffirms the goals of the 1990 EFA presented in Jomtien, Thailand, to make primary education accessible to all children by 2015 and to reduce significantly illiteracy by the year 2015.[91] At the Dakar meeting, the results of the global EFA 2000 Assessment involving more than 180 countries were presented. This study found that the numbers of

83 Salamanca Statement (n. 68) 17.
84 Ibid. 5–7.
85 Ibid. viii.
86 Ibid. 18.
87 Ibid. ix.
88 As mentioned earlier, the Salamanca Statement was subject to review in 2009 (see n. 82). The updated Statement reaffirms support for the development of an inclusive education system in every country of the world. It also specifically calls for the ratification of the CRPD throughout the world, and, 'in particular, Article 24 which gives new impetus to the Human Right of inclusive education for all people with disabilities' (1).
89 UNESCO, The Dakar Framework for Action: Education for All: Meeting Our Collective Commitments (UNESCO 2000) [hereinafter Dakar Framework] 8.
90 Edward B. Fiske, Final Report (UNESCO 2000) 7.
91 Dakar Framework (n. 89) 8.

children in school had risen dramatically, with many countries approaching full primary school enrolment for the first time in history, while the number of children out of school was more than 113 million. Even this number was considered an underestimate since the data on many excluded groups of children, including children with disabilities, are not routinely collected. Thus, although '[t]he EFA 2000 Assessment demonstrates that there has been significant progress in many countries', it also recognises that 'it [was] unacceptable in the year 2000 that more than 113 million children have no access to primary education, [and] 880 million adults are illiterate'.[92] Accordingly, the Dakar Framework calls for a new framework with different strategies and increased levels of international accountability to realise the goal of education for all.

The Dakar Framework also recognises that education is not only a basic human right but also a necessity in addressing serious global problems, such as illiteracy, poverty and even war.[93] The newest vision of the Dakar Framework, therefore, 'ensur[ed] that by 2015 all children, particularly girls, children in difficult circumstances and those belonging to ethnic minorities, have access to and complete, free and compulsory primary education of good quality'.[94] The need for inclusive education is specifically included in the Notes on the Dakar Framework for Action, which states that

> [i]n order to attract and retain children from marginalized and excluded groups, education systems should respond flexibly [and] must be inclusive, actively seeking out children who are not enrolled, and responding flexibly to the circumstances and needs of all learners.[95]

In the section on 'Challenges and Opportunities', the Dakar Framework calls for more inclusive approaches to education that must address

> the needs of the poor and the most disadvantaged, including working children, remote rural dwellers and nomads, and ethnic and linguistic minorities, children, young people and adults affected by conflict, HIV/AIDS, hunger and poor health; and those with special learning needs.[96]

Another major goal of the Dakar Framework was to 'create safe, healthy, inclusive and equitably resourced educational environments conducive to

92 Ibid.
93 Ibid. 15.
94 Ibid. 8.
95 Ibid. 16.
96 Ibid. 14. See also UNESCO, Education for All and Japanese Funds-in-Trust, *Towards Inclusive Education for Children with Disabilities: A Guideline* (UNESCO Bangkok 2009) 2.

excellence in learning, with clearly defined levels of achievement for all'.[97] The Dakar Framework also anticipates obstacles to national government and funding policies while crediting civil society organisations for their increasing involvement in demanding a more inclusive view of education that addresses the needs of all, rather than the needs of a few.[98]

During the same year that the Dakar Framework was developed, the UN adopted the Declaration on Education for All.[99] This Declaration highlights as one of its main goals the integration of all children with disabilities into mainstream schools.[100] It provided the background for the 2001 Flagship on Education for All and the Right to Education for Persons with Disabilities: Towards Inclusion, which was developed to connect the Declaration on Education for All with the Salamanca Framework for Action, and the need to include disabled and other marginalised children in all educational programmes.[101] The Flagship on Education for All seeks to enforce the goals of the Dakar Framework for all children and adults with disabilities, by recognising the universal right to education and uniting all EFA partners in their efforts to provide access to education and to promote the completion of quality education for every child, youth and adult with a disability.[102] The Flagship was led by UNESCO and included the World Bank, UNICEF, the International Disability Alliance and other NGOs, international development agencies, intergovernmental agencies and experts in the fields of special and inclusive education from the Global North and South.[103]

Also in 2000, when the Dakar Framework and the EFA were adopted, representatives of 147 countries met in New York to develop the Millennium Development Goals (MDG) for 2015, including goals relating to education.[104] The MDG were developed by the UN, in conjunction with the Organisation for Economic Co-operation and Development (OECD), the World Bank and

97 Dakar Framework (n. 89) 20.

98 Ibid. 14.

99 See UNESCO, 'The Flagship on Education for All and the Right to Education for Persons with Disabilities: Towards Inclusion' (UNESCO) www.unesco.org/education/efa/know_sharing/flagship_initiatives/disability_last_version.shtml, accessed 5 February 2016 [hereinafter Flagship].

100 Dakar Framework (n. 89) 70.

101 Flagship (n. 99).

102 Ibid.

103 The Flagship intends to reach its goals in various ways, which can be found on its website (n. 99) under the title of 'Flagship Actions and Activities'.

104 United Nations, *The Millennium Development Goals Report: 2010* (United Nations Department of Economic and Social Affairs 2010) 3; 'UN Millennium Summit' (United Nations Systems) www.unsystem.org/content/united-nations-millennium-summit-6-8-september-2000, accessed 21 July 2017.

the International Monetary Fund. Among the eight goals of this document are achieving universal primary education and cutting poverty in half by 2015.[105] The MDG also affirm (among other things) the right of every individual to dignity, freedom, equality, a basic standard of living that includes freedom from hunger and violence, and encourage tolerance and solidarity.[106]

Following the development of the MDG, the World Bank launched the Education for All Fast-Track Initiative (FTI) in 2002.[107] The FTI is a global partnership to help low-income countries meet the goal of education for all children completing primary education by 2015.[108] On 21 September 2011, the Fast Track Initiative was renamed the Global Partnership for Education, and was launched at the UN General Assembly.[109] In 2015, the UN issued its report on the implementation of the MDG and concluded that despite some progress, disability remains a 'major impediment to accessing education'.[110] Taken together, the Standard Rules, the Salamanca Statement, the Dakar Framework and the other international initiatives discussed earlier in this chapter provided the foundation for the legally binding right to inclusive education that is now included in the Convention on the Rights of People with Disabilities.

III THE DRAFTING OF ARTICLE 24 OF THE CONVENTION ON THE RIGHTS OF PEOPLE WITH DISABILITIES

Based on this history leading up to the formation of the UN Ad Hoc Committee on a Comprehensive and Integral International Convention on the Protection and Promotion of the Rights and Dignity of Persons with Disabilities (as it was called), the right of children with disabilities to education, generally, and their right to inclusive education had gained momentum throughout the world.[111] Therefore it was no surprise that this Committee,

105 United Nations (n. 104) 6–19.

106 Ibid. 3.

107 World Bank, *Guyana: Education for All – Fast Track Initiative (EFA – FTI) Program: Amerindian Peoples' Strategy* (IPP95, World Bank 2004) www-wds.worldbank.org/external/default/WDSContentServer/WDSP/IB/2015/06/05/090224b0828a5df4/1_0/Rendered/PDF/Guyana000Educa0iative00FTI00Program.pdf, accessed 12 July 2017; Government of Guyana, 'Education for All-Fast Track Initiative – Overview' (Ministry of Education, Guyana 17 April 2014) www.education.gov.gy/web/index.php/projects/education-for-all-fast-track-initiative/item/498-efa-fti-overview, accessed 12 July 2017.

108 Ibid.

109 'Global Partnership for Education' (*Wikipedia* 23 May 2016) https://en.wikipedia.org/wiki/Global_Partnership_for_Education, accessed 21 July 2017.

110 United Nations, *The Millennium Development Goals Report: 2015* (United Nations 2015) 26.

111 Roger Slee, 'Social Justice and the Changing Directions in Educational Research: The Case of Inclusive Education' (2001) 5 *International Journal of Inclusive Education* 167.

which was charged with negotiating the CRPD, included an article requiring States Parties to provide inclusive education for children and adults with disabilities. Article 24 requires States Parties to 'recognize the right of persons with disabilities to education ... without discrimination and on the basis of equal opportunity'.[112] It also requires States Parties to 'ensure an inclusive education system at all levels and lifelong learning'.[113] This language is consistent with the prior (non-binding) international documents. Therefore, the UN Ad Hoc Committee saw its job as 'simply' to extend existing human rights to people with disabilities.[114] Yet, as we see from the following discussion, Article 24 not only built on prior international documents but also expanded their influence by establishing, for the first time as a matter of international law, the right to inclusive education for all children and adults with disabilities. As we also see, Article 24 was one of the most debated articles in the entire CRPD.

Article 24 has been hailed as the most comprehensive statement in international law guaranteeing the right to inclusive education for children and adults with disabilities.[115] It prohibits the exclusion of children and adults with disabilities from educational opportunities based on their disability.[116] It also requires that education for children with disabilities and lifelong learning for adults with disabilities be provided in an 'inclusive education system'. Although many hours of the Ad Hoc Committee meetings focussed on Article 24, including nearly the entire Sixth Ad Hoc Committee meeting, it was not until the final and Eighth Ad Hoc Committee meeting in December 2006 when Article 24 was finally approved. The most controversial aspect of Article 24 related to the scope and mandate of each State Parties' obligation to ensure an 'inclusive education system at all levels and lifelong learning', as provided in the first paragraph of the final version.[117]

The first area of dispute about the article on education was whether it should include the right to 'choose' education or a right to education itself.

112 CRPD (n. 3) Art. 24(1).

113 Ibid.

114 See Arlene S. Kanter, *The Development of Disability Rights under International Law: From Charity to Human Rights* (Routledge 2016) 5, 52.

115 CRPD (n. 3) Art. 24 is formed of five subsections, each in detail exemplifying the various obligations relating to the right of persons with disabilities to education.

See also UNGA, 'Comprehensive and Integral International Convention to Promote and Protect the Rights and Dignity of Persons with Disabilities' (19 December 2001) A/Res/56/168.

116 CRPD (n. 3) Art. 24(2)(a).

117 Ibid. Art. 24(1). Until the final version of the CRPD, Article 24 was referred to as Article 17. As Article 17, it went through several drafts, and was the subject of nearly the entire Sixth Ad Hoc Committee meeting.

Some members of the drafting committee expressed the view that the right to education must be specifically included in the article; others suggested that the right to choose education was sufficient. In the end, the right to education prevailed based on the view that, like other human rights, education should not be something governments can choose to provide or not.

The second area of dispute regarding the proposed article on education was whether States Parties should be required to provide education that is in the 'best interest' of the child. Those who opposed including this standard viewed the right to education as a basic human right, not an optional service that may or may not be provided, depending on someone's judgement about whether education is in the student's best interests. Those States Parties who viewed the right to education as a basic human right prevailed on this point too, since, as written, the Article declares education a human right, not a service provided according to a best interest standard.[118]

The third area of controversy during the drafting process of Article 24 related to its scope and coverage. Early drafts of Article 24 referred to a 'child with a disability'. But as opposition mounted regarding limiting the article to children, the draft was changed to read a 'person with a disability'. This change reflected an agreement among the drafters that the right to education in the CRPD should apply not only to children, but also to adults with disabilities who are engaged in 'lifelong learning'. As written, therefore, Article 24 protects the right to primary and secondary education as well as to post-secondary education, vocational education, informal adult education and all other 'lifelong learning'.

In addition to the drafting committee's discussion about who should be covered under Article 24, another disagreement arose regarding the timing of the obligations on States Parties of the implementation of Article 24. It is a well-established principle of international human rights law that civil and political rights must be realised immediately, whereas social, economic and cultural rights, including the right to education, are subject to progressive realisation under Article 2 of the ICESCR.[119] Article 2 reads as follows:

> Each State Party to the present Covenant undertakes to take steps, individually and through international assistance and co-operation, especially economic and technical, to the maximum of its available resources, with a view to achieving progressively the full realization of the rights recognized in the present Covenant by all appropriate means, including particularly the adoption of legislative measures.[120]

118 Ibid. Art. 24.
119 ICESCR (n. 35) Art. 2(1).
120 Ibid.

The phrase 'to the maximum of its available resources, with a view to achieving progressively the full realization of the rights' was included in the Covenant to recognise differences among countries in the nature and extent of economic, social and cultural policies, programmes and services.[121]

The right to education is subject to progressive realisation because it is included in the ICESCR and not the International Covenant on Civil and Political Rights (ICCPR). Article 13 of the ICESCR provides in part:

> The States Parties to the present Covenant recognize the right of everyone to education. They agree that education shall be directed to the full development of the human personality and the sense of its dignity, and shall strengthen the respect for human rights and fundamental freedoms.[122]

Based on this provision, therefore, some members of the drafting committee proposed a specific statement calling for the progressive realisation of the right to education, particularly the right to inclusive education. Other participants observed that even if the right to education is subject to progressive realisation, States Parties still must immediately examine their current laws, practices and procedures to ensure that they do not conflict with the obligations under the CRPD.

While acknowledging that the right to education, like all other social, economic and cultural rights, is subject to the principle of progressive realisation, the CRPD drafting committee insisted that progressive realisation does not mean that States Parties may ignore their obligations to provide education in an 'inclusive education system'. To the contrary, the principle of progressive realisation means what it says: it requires States Parties to realise the provisions of the article by 'tak[ing] deliberate steps immediately and in the future towards the full realization' of the right to education under Article 24.[123] Therefore, even if the right to education under Article 24 is not intended to be effectuated immediately, as are civil and political rights, States Parties are prohibited from taking any regressive steps that would deprive people with disabilities from enjoying their rights under Article 24.[124] In other words, States Parties are still required, even under the principle of progressive realisation, to refrain immediately from any actions, such as decreasing or reallocating funding, which would have the effect of interfering with Article 24's goal of ensuring the right to inclusive education for all students with disabilities.

121 Ibid.
122 Ibid. Art. 13(1).
123 'Progressive Realisation and Non-Regression' (ESCR-Net, 3 August 2012) www.escr-net.org/docs/i/401627, accessed 12 July 2017; see also ICESCR (n. 35) Art. 2(1).
124 'Progressive Realisation and Non-Regression (n. 123).

Although most parties may have agreed on the impact of the doctrine of progressive realisation on the right to education under Article 24, they did not agree on the application of the right to inclusive education. Despite the international mandate for inclusive education contained in prior international instruments, as discussed earlier in this chapter, the drafting committee was deeply divided regarding whether the CRPD should contain an explicit right to inclusive education for all students with disabilities. Some delegates argued for a right to inclusive education whereas others argued that parents should retain their right to choose where to send their children to school, including the right to decide to send their children to an inclusive or segregated school. In fact, of all of the issues discussed at the Ad Hoc Meetings during the five-year drafting process of the CRPD, this issue of inclusive education was one of the most hotly contested; it resulted in the most lobbying within the Ad Hoc Committee meetings at the UN, with more pamphlets and information sheets distributed by NGOs representing both sides of this issue than most, if not all, other issues considered by the Ad Hoc Committee.[125]

The discussion about inclusive education reflected deep divisions regarding the right to education, generally, and the right of children with disabilities to education, in particular. On the one hand, some delegates and organisations rejected the 'separate but equal' principle,[126] expressing the view that separating students into certain schools and classrooms on the basis of their disability is inherently unequal. According to this view, students with disabilities can realise their right to equal education only when they are included in the general education system and receive whatever supports, accommodations or modifications they may need to remain there.[127] On the other hand, equally committed advocates for students with disabilities argued that, for children and adults with certain disabilities, inclusion in general classrooms is not always the path towards equality. To them, children who are blind or deaf or who have other learning or cognitive disabilities should be able to attend schools with their peers who have the same disability in order to avoid the

125 I attended these meetings and witnessed the intense lobbying and dissemination of piles of position papers, flyers and announcements. Only Article 12 and (at the last meeting) the challenged footnote in the preamble provoked greater controversy.

126 The US Supreme Court rejected this principle in *Brown* v. *Board of Education of Topeka* 347 US 483 (1954) 495. In *Brown*, the US Supreme Court overturned a prior decision that had permitted segregation by race and upheld the right of all children to attend integrated schools.

127 For a discussion of inclusive education under international law, see Arlene S. Kanter, Michelle L. Damiani and Beth A. Ferri, 'The Right to Inclusive Education under International Law: Following Italy's Lead' (2014) 17 *Journal of International Special Needs Education* 21, 22ff.

isolation that may occur if they are placed in a classroom with students who do not have any or the same disabilities as they do.[128]

As this disagreement unfolded during the drafting process, some participants advocated for the right to education of children with disabilities in the general education system to be the rule, and the provision of special education to be the exception, requiring schools to consider first whether a student should be included in a regular classroom before ever considering the placement of a student in a self-contained or separate classroom.[129] Other members of the committee argued that special education should be provided where the general education system was inadequate in meeting a child's needs, but that there should be no presumption that one approach was more desirable than the other.[130] Still, other participants focussed on the need for deaf and blind children to be educated with each other and not in general education because of their unique communication and linguistic needs.[131] But even this group supported an explicit obligation on all States Parties to ensure the accessibility of the general education system, so that all children would be able to choose to attend classes in the general education system or in special education.[132]

Some members of the Ad Hoc Committee's Working Group preferred to limit Article 24's application to children without sensory disabilities, so deaf children could be taught sign language separately from non-deaf students.[133] Other members questioned whether Article 24 should be broadened to include all children who might need alternative communication systems.[134] But in both cases, wherever sign language, braille or alternative communication systems would be taught, most of the group believed that such systems should be taught in addition to, and not instead of, national languages.[135]

The European Union, for example, proposed that Article 24 should ensure the right to education without discrimination for all persons with disabilities. The EU also proposed that States Parties commit themselves to the goal of

128 For a discussion of the benefits of separate education, see Naomi P. Zigmond and Amanda Kloo, 'General and Special Education Are (and Should Be) Different' in James M. Kauffman and Daniel P. Hallahan (eds), *Handbook of Special Education* (Routledge 2011).

129 Rehabilitation International, 'Daily Summary of Discussion at the Sixth Session 4 August 2005' (United Nations Enable 4 August 2005) Word document downloaded from www.un.org/esa/socdev/enable/rights/ahc6sum4aug.htm, accessed 12 July 2017 [hereinafter Ad Hoc Committee Daily Summaries, 6th Sess.].

130 Ibid.

131 Ibid. 3.

132 Ibid. 4.

133 Ibid. 1–2.

134 Ibid. 6.

135 Ibid. 2.

inclusiveness of their general education systems, and if the general education systems do not adequately meet the needs of persons with disabilities, States Parties shall take appropriate measures to ensure effective alternative forms of education, bearing in mind the goal of full inclusion.[136] To the extent that the EU proposal was seen as providing a right to inclusive education only in some cases, this position was opposed by several countries, including Panama, as well as several NGOs.[137] Other participants suggested that indeed, most NGOS – as well as most countries who spoke at the 4 August meeting – affirmed their position that Article 24 should specifically state that general or mainstream education is not only preferred but also a right. Other countries continued to suggest that special education may be permissible and, at times, a desirable alternative to inclusion.[138]

At the Sixth Meeting of the Ad Hoc Committee, a disability rights organisation from Israel, Bizchut, argued that in order for Article 24 to result in the right to education for people with disabilities on the basis of equal opportunity, States Parties must 'ensure that persons with disabilities can choose inclusive education and will [receive] the required support' necessary to participate in such education.[139] This suggestion was based on the concern that if schools could offer 'special and alternative forms of learning' (i.e. special education) as a choice for children whose needs were not being met in the general education system, States Parties would be absolved from their responsibility of making inclusive education a realistic choice for all children.[140] In such cases, the State would only appear to but not actually 'meet its responsibility by offering an unrealistic choice, between the mainstream system without the assistance necessary to enable inclusion, and the special education system'.[141]

In response to this discussion, Mexico suggested the following proposed language: 'States Parties shall ensure that where the general education system does not adequately meet the needs of persons with disabilities special and

[136] 'Contribution by Governments: European Union: European Union Proposal for Article 15' (United Nations Enable) www.un.org/esa/socdev/enable/rights/ahc6eu.htm, accessed 7 August 2017.

[137] Ad Hoc Committee Daily Summaries, 6th Sess. (n. 129).

[138] Ibid. 2–4.

[139] Bizchut, 'Comments, Proposals and Amendments Submitted Electronically: Article 24 – Education, 3rd Session' (United Nations Enable 2004) www.un.org/esa/socdev/enable/rights/ahcstata24tscomments.htm#bizchut, accessed 12 July 2017.

[140] Japan Disability Forum, 'Comments, Proposals and Amendments Submitted Electronically: Article 24 – Education, 3rd Session' (United Nations Enable 2004) www.un.org/esa/socdev/enable/rights/ahcstata24tscomments.htm#jdf, accessed 12 July 2017.

[141] Bizchut (n. 139).

alternative forms of learning should be made available.'[142] To further this goal, Mexico added that

> [a]ny such special and alternative forms of [teaching] should:
> (a) reflect the same standards and objectives provided in the general education system; (b) be provided in such a manner to allow children with disabilities to participate in the general education system to the maximum extent possible; (c) allow a free and informed choice between general and special systems; (d) in no way limit the duty of States Parties to continue to strive to meet the needs of students with disabilities in the general education system.[143]

The Ontario Human Rights Commission also suggested that '[i]n keeping with the notion that integration should be the norm of general application', the term 'appropriately' should be substituted for the word 'adequately', so that the article on education would read: 'States Parties shall ensure that where the general education system does not adequately meet the needs of persons with disabilities special and alternative forms of learning should be made available.'[144] The intent of this change, according to the Commission, was to provide the right of States Parties to choose inclusive and accessible education, without creating an obligation on students with disabilities to attend general schools where their needs may not be adequately met.[145]

The Commission and other participants who supported this language argued that the individualised needs of all persons with intellectual disabilities could not be met in the general education system. Therefore, Article 24 should include a provision authorising the acceptability of separate education for persons with intellectual disabilities. This proposal was met with strong opposition, however, including from Mental Disability Rights International (now known as Disability Rights International) (DRI). DRI argued that if Article 24 included an exception from the requirement of inclusive education for children with certain disabilities, then separate education would become the rule and not the exception. In short, States Parties would feel justified in maintaining a separate education system for

142 Mexico, 'Comments, Proposals and Amendments Submitted Electronically: Article 24 – Education, 3rd Session' (United Nations Enable 2004) www.un.org/esa/socdev/enable/rights/ahcstata24tscomments.htm#mexico, accessed 12 July 2017.

143 Ibid.

144 Ontario Human Rights Commission, 'Comments, Proposals and Amendments Submitted Electronically: Article 24 – Education, 3rd Session' (United Nations Enable 2004) www.un.org/esa/socdev/enable/rights/ahcstata24tscomments.htm#ohrc, accessed 12 July 2017.

145 Ibid.

students with certain impairments.[146] In response, DRI insisted that the right to inclusive education 'should not be one of exceptions . . . but rather one of strong principles and commitments to work toward systematically on a targeted and tireless basis'.[147] In the end, the provision was bitterly disputed, with China serving as the holdout until the final, Eighth Session.

Representatives from Australian NGOs also helped to move along the contentious debate that erupted about inclusive education. Their intervention suggested that even specialised learning, such as learning in braille or sign language, should take place in mainstream educational settings. The Australian NGOs reasoned as follows:

> It is important that people with disability have the opportunity to interact with other students and teachers without disability for at least three reasons: (a) people with disability, during and once we have completed our education, will be interacting with the wider community where broad life experience and skills are essential for continuing participation in society; (b) interaction between students with disability and students and teachers who do not have disability promotes a general understanding and awareness of disability which in itself promotes a more inclusive society; and (c) people with disability form life-long networks during their education. It is important that they have the opportunity to develop these networks with non-disabled as well as disabled people.[148]

The Ad Hoc Committee was eventually persuaded. It concluded that research supported the view that '[i]t is not acceptable to separate disabled students from their peers into separate settings on a permanent basis in order for them to receive the supports and accommodations that they need and which are necessary for their learning'.[149] Notwithstanding this research, the European Disability Forum (EDF) observed that '[t]he decision between special and mainstream education is an issue for which the level of economic development of countries needs to be taken into account'.[150] According to EDF, the existence of special schools would be difficult to justify in

146 Tara J. Melish, 'An Eye toward Effective Enforcement: A Technical-Comparative Approach to the Drafting Negotiations' in Maya Sabatello and Marianne Schulze (eds), *Human Rights and Disability Advocacy* (University of Pennsylvania Press 2014) 70.

147 Ibid. 90.

148 Australian NGOs, 'Comments, Proposals and Amendments Submitted Electronically: Article 24 – Education, 3rd Session' (United Nations Enable 2004) www.un.org/esa/socdev/enable/rights/ahcstata24tscomments.htm#ango, accessed 12 July 2017.

149 Ad Hoc Committee Daily Summaries, 6th Sess. (n. 129) 3.

150 See EDF, 'Comments on the Draft Text: Draft Article 17: Education, 3rd Session' (United Nations Enable 2004) www.un.org/esa/socdev/enable/rights/wgdca17.htm#edf, accessed 12 July 2017.

economically challenged countries, except by organisations for the deaf, who defend special schools as the preferred option for teaching sign language as a first language.[151] All other groups, EDF acknowledged, consider mainstream education the preferred option.[152] The Forum continued, however, by stating that:

> inclusion in mainstream schools can only be the best option if the adequate support is provided to the disabled child. As long as this support is not provided, special schools need to continue to exist to ensure the right for a quality education. However, the general objective to be promoted is the integration in mainstream education.[153]

The International Save the Children Organization also supported a mandate for inclusive education during the negotiations on Article 24. Citing the Salamanca Statement, the Dakar Framework for Action and the Standard Rules, which (as discussed earlier in this chapter) emphasise the importance of equal access to education and the right of all children to achieve their full potential, Save the Children reiterated the importance of transforming special education towards the preparation for and support of persons with disabilities in inclusive settings and supporting the education system to become inclusive for all children and adults with disabilities.[154] However, the organisation did not go as far as others in calling for a prohibition on special education, as Save the Children proposed that

> States Parties recognise the right of all children and adults with disabilities to inclusive education. The education and training of students with disabilities shall be directed to: … building a society that is inclusive to all …

151 Ibid. In reference to the right of deaf children to receive education in their own language, the World Federation of the Deaf clarified that sign language is not only a means of communication but also a spoken, written and signed language, with its own grammar and structure. Sign language therefore differs from braille, which is not a language but a method of communication. Accordingly, at the Third Session of the Ad Hoc Committee, the World Federation of the Deaf proposed that:

> Deaf children have the right to receive education in their own groups and to become bilingual in sign language and their national spoken and written language. They also have the right to learn additional foreign languages, both signed and spoken/written. Each state Party shall take legislative, administrative, political and other measures needed to provide quality education using sign language, by ensuring the employment of Deaf teachers and also hearing teachers who are fluent in sign language.

www.un.org/esa/socdev/enable/rights/ahc3wfd.htm, accessed 12 July 2017.

152 EDF (n. 150).

153 Ibid.

154 Save the Children, 'NGO Comments on the Draft Text: Draft Article 17 – Education' (United Nations Enable 2003) www.un.org/esa/socdev/enable/rights/ahc3ngoa17.htm, accessed 12 July 2017.

> In realising this right, States Parties shall endeavour to ensure:
> (a) that all persons with disabilities can participate in inclusive and accessible education in their own community (including access to early childhood and pre-school education)
> (b) the provision of adequate support for change of the education system, positive attitudes of stakeholders; appropriate training and mentoring of teachers and educational support staff, student centred curriculum, flexible teaching methods, appropriate teaching aids and equipment, alternative and augmentative communication modes, an inclusive physical and learning environment, parent and community involvement, to ensure the full participation of students with disabilities
> (c) that no person with a disability shall be required to undergo any medical treatment or intervention, to correct, improve or alleviate any actual or perceived disability as a condition to inclusive and full education.[155]

Interestingly, the proposal of Save the Children was one of the only proposals to include the term 'communication disabilities'. This phrase referred not only to people who are blind and/or deaf but also to people who have challenges expressing themselves or handling information for any reason, including students diagnosed with autism, spasticity and learning or intellectual impairments. The proposal by Save the Children, therefore, included a recommendation to ensure that students with communication disabilities would have the right to education in 'alternative language and or with alternative communication systems, to become bi-lingual and to learn the communication, learning and mobility skills for inclusive education and full participation within the class or school environment'.[156] The proposal by Save the Children also required States Parties to 'take appropriate legislative, administrative and other measures for full inclusive education of all students with disabilities by ensuring appropriately skilled teachers and basic additional resources'.[157] Accordingly, Save the Children proposed that:

> States Parties shall ensure that persons with disabilities shall access secondary and tertiary education, vocational training, adult education and lifelong learning on an equal basis with others. To that end, States Parties shall render appropriate assistance to persons with disabilities.[158]

155 Ibid. at 17.1–2.
156 Ibid. at 17.4.
157 Ibid.
158 Ibid. at 17.5.

Finally, Save the Children reminded the group that inclusive education is about changing schools to accommodate all students with their individual learning needs, not about fitting students into existing schools, as prior international instruments had recognised.[159] Save the Children found support for its position among most members of the Ad Hoc Working Group, as did the Landmine Survivors Network, which also prompted the group 'that if specialist educational settings are offered, they should not be of a lower standard than the general or mainstream settings'.[160]

A disabled persons' organisation (DPO), Disabled Peoples' International (DPI), was equally active in the negotiations about Article 24. DPI went on record stating that '[a]ccess and quality of education is particularly important, not just architecture or universal design of schools. It's how information is conveyed through new teaching materials, new technologies, that will make it possible for [people with disabilities].' DPI also stated that '[e]ffective education means teaching [people with disabilities] to use everything they have towards their social environment' in order to bring people with disabilities 'out of segregation and marginalization and away from an assisted life'.[161]

Among the strongest supporters for inclusive education was the British Council of Disabled People, on behalf of the International Disability Caucus (IDC).[162] The IDC was a network of global, regional and national organisations of persons with disabilities and allied non-governmental organisations that was a key player in the negotiation of the CRPD. According to the IDC, '[t]he problem with inclusive education is that a lot of states think they've already done it. In most cases, this is not true. Placing children in the mainstream is not inclusive education: it is integration.'[163]

The IDC stated that '[t]he "mixed economy" of inclusive education around the world is "mainly segregation with some integration and tiny islands of inclusion"'.[164] Such policies, according to the IDC, have 'led to some 40 million disabled children left out of the education system in poorer parts

159 Save the Children, 'Schools for All: Including Disabled Children in Education' (Save the Children, 2002) www.savethechildren.org.uk/resources/online-library/schools-for-all-including-disabled-children-in-education, accessed 12 July 2017.

160 Landmine Survivors Network, 'Comments on the Draft Text: Draft Article 17: Education, 3rd Session' (United Nations Enable 2004) www.un.org/esa/socdev/enable/rights/wgdca17.htm#lsn, accessed 12 July 2017. See also 'Standard Rules on the Equalization of Opportunities for Persons with Disabilities' (n. 60) Annex II Rule 6(8); UNESCO, Convention against Discrimination in Education (14 December 1960, entry into force 22 May 1962) Art. 5(1)(c).

161 Ad Hoc Committee Daily Summaries, 6th Sess. (n. 129) 3–4.

162 Ibid. 1–2.

163 Ibid. 1.

164 Ibid.

of the world' and '[i]n Europe, . . . over half of disabled children of primary age are still [attending] segregated schools', despite Europe's commitment to inclusion.[165] For example, 33 per cent of disabled children in the United Kingdom are in special schools.[166] Moreover, the achievement of students in special schools is seven times worse than that of disabled children in mainstream schools.[167] Accordingly, the IDC observed that

> [t]his lack of inclusive education has led to massive underachievement and disempowerment of disabled children, leading to a lack of employment opportunities, lack of independent living, and lack of relationships . . . Inclusion is not one size fits all. In an inclusive system, all barriers are removed, of organization, attitudes, curriculum, and environment. This would be done progressively for those countries with limited resources.[168]

The IDC also stated that the needs of students with sensory impairments can be met in mainstream schools, as it acknowledged that

> [f]or Deaf children this means qualified teachers of the deaf and sign language interpreters. For blind children this means teachers qualified in these methods of communication but with a curriculum organized by mainstream teachers. This amounts to massive teacher training projects around the world. There is much concern among teachers' organizations, not about the principle of inclusion, which they support, but for lack of training and support by governments.[169]

Finally, the IDC called for inclusive education to be the 'overriding principle'.[170] The IDC representative stated that:

> [T]here is a need to work for inclusion, for all learners, those with sensory impairments, as well as the much larger groups – those with speech and language, physical, behavioral and psychiatric impairments. This will require a flexible approach and resources. Inclusive education has to also mean including persons with disabilities in the curriculum. If disabled people growing up do not see themselves in books, pictures, the curriculum, and the talk, they will be invisible, including in the human rights curriculum as Israel suggested. Therefore there is much work to be done on this article to achieve the IDC vision of inclusive education.[171]

165 Ibid.
166 Ibid. 1.
167 Ibid.
168 Ibid.
169 Ibid.
170 Ibid. 1–2.
171 Ibid.

Following this lengthy discussion, the chair of the Ad Hoc Working Group noted the exemplary plan of action by the Indian government towards the objective of inclusive education by 2020. The following is an excerpt of this plan of action:

> In a country like India where only 2% of disabled people get some education, and there are only 3000 NGOs, inclusive education is the only way out. Education is a means to a life of independence, self reliance, a livelihood, employment, a place in mainstream society. Words like 'Shall endeavor to' and 'to the possible extent' defeat the purpose ... 'To the possible extent' would only lead states either to deny education, a fundamental right, or to an instrument towards more segregated environments. India is in the process of drafting a policy on education and the request by the Indian delegate for 'to the possible extent' is a retrograde step that defeats the purpose of its own policy. Choice is made by the state or parents, not the child. Therefore inclusive education should become compulsory.[172]

Even after this lengthy discussion, no consensus was reached by the end of the Sixth Ad Hoc Meeting. Moreover, when no consensus could be reached in floor debate during the Seventh Ad Hoc Meeting, or even by the Eighth and final meeting of the Ad Hoc Committee, the chair sent the draft text of Article 24 to be negotiated privately in state-to-state consultations and informal small group settings. As a result of these negotiations, the Ad Hoc Committee eventually approved a right to 'an inclusive education' within Article 24.

The final language of Article 24 represents a clear compromise between those who wanted the CRPD to guarantee inclusive education for all students and those who wanted it only as an option. As written, Article 24 guarantees the right to education for all children and adults with all types of disabilities, as well as the 'right to an inclusive education system'. Beginning in Paragraph 2 of Article 24, the right to education for students with disabilities is affirmed. It states that States Parties shall ensure that:

> a) Persons with disabilities are not excluded from the general education system on the basis of disability, and that children with disabilities are not excluded from free and compulsory primary education, or from secondary education, on the basis of disability;
> b) Persons with disabilities can access an inclusive, quality and free primary education and secondary education on an equal basis with others in the communities in which they live;

[172] Ibid. 3.

c) Reasonable accommodation of the individual's requirements is provided;
d) Persons with disabilities receive the support required, within the general education system, to facilitate their effective education; and
e) Effective individualized support measures are provided in environments that maximize academic and social development, consistent with the goal of full inclusion.

Yet nowhere does Article 24 state that children, youth and adults with disabilities must be educated only in mainstream or neighbourhood 'regular' schools and inclusive classrooms. By requiring States Parties to ensure an 'inclusive education system', rather than inclusive classrooms for all students with types of disabilities, at all levels of education, Article 24 appears to concede that for some children and adults with disabilities, some of the time, separate educational programmes may be permitted. As Article 24(3)(c) provides, education must be 'delivered in the most appropriate languages and modes and means of communication for the individual, and in environments which maximize academic and social development'.[173]

In summary, Article 24 was one of the most debated articles of the CRPD. The drafting committee discussed it at several of its meetings, including as the sole focus of the Ad Hoc Committee's Sixth meeting. The primary disagreement about Article 24 stemmed from the inability of the Ad Hoc Committee members, state delegations, NGOs, and DPOs to reach a consensus about the meaning of inclusive education and whether it should be required in all cases. In the end, Article 24 affirms the right to inclusive education for all children, youths and adults with disabilities. But it also fails to prohibit segregated settings. In this way, Article 24 leaves open the possibility that States Parties may believe they are free to continue to support separate schools and classrooms. Thus in some countries, some children with disabilities will remain in segregated schools or classrooms, yet children with the same disabilities will be required to attend inclusive classrooms in other countries.

[173] CRPD (n. 3) Art. 24(3)(c). In fact, this is the position that the Spanish Constitutional Court took in a 2014 case which cited both Spanish law and Article 24 of the CRPD. The Court held that an autistic child had no right to attend an inclusive classroom and that his school district could send him to a special school for autistic children. The court reasoned that given the student's need for an individual tutor, his need for the adaptation of the courses to his learning skills, his need to limit his class to a maximum of four students, and the seriousness of his disability, the decision of the school to register the child in a special education school was not 'unreasonable or discriminatory'. Constitutional Court Judgment 10/2014 of 27 January 2014 (BOE [*Official State Gazette*] no. 48 of 25 February 2014).

Following the discussion of the final version of Article 24, the chair of the Ad Hoc Committee took note of '[t]he unusually high number of interventions and the wide range of views' about this article.[174] The chair then added a personal observation that, in his view, '[i]f the committee gets this article right, it will get a lot of the convention right and will add a huge amount of value to existing law. If not, then it will be extremely unfortunate.'[175] For those who fought for the right to inclusive education, the Committee got it 'almost' right. Inclusive education is now enshrined in international law. However, to ensure this mandate for every student with any type of disability in every country throughout the world, additional action is required by the CRPD Committee and according to changes in domestic laws, as discussed in the following section of this chapter.

IV ENFORCEMENT OF ARTICLE 24 BY THE COMMITTEE ON THE RIGHTS OF PERSONS WITH DISABILITIES

A *The CRPD Committee's Concluding Observations on Country Reports*

The CRPD was adopted by the United Nations General Assembly on 13 December 2006, and opened for signature on 30 March 2007. Following ratification by the twentieth State Party, the CRPD came into force on 3 May 2008. As of July 2017, 174 countries have ratified the CRPD.[176] Of those, 92 countries have also ratified the Optional Protocol.[177] Once a country ratifies the CRPD, it is required to submit a report to the Committee on the Rights of Persons with Disabilities (CRPD Committee) within two years and, thereafter, every four years. Article 34 of the CRPD establishes the CRPD Committee as an independent body of eighteen experts that monitors the implementation of the CRPD. The CRPD Committee reviews and responds to each country report, offering recommendations to the country on how to better enforce and implement the provisions of the CRPD, in a document known as Concluding Observations. The CRPD Committee also reviews shadow reports prepared by civil society organisations in response to country reports.

174 Ad Hoc Committee Daily Summaries, 6th Sess. (n. 129) 7.

175 Ibid.

176 Division for Social Policy Development: Disability, 'Convention on the Rights of Persons with Disabilities' (UN) www.un.org/development/desa/disabilities/convention-on-the-rights-of-persons-with-disabilities.html, accessed 30 July 2017.

177 Ibid.

To date, 102 countries and the European Union have filed country reports. Of those, fifty-three country reports and the report of the European Union discuss Article 24.[178] Of those fifty-three countries, all but six and the European Union already have received Concluding Observations from the CRPD Committee. In the Concluding Observations, the CRPD Committee summarises its assessment of the progress and deficits in the implementation of Article 24 by a particular country; it also provides recommendations on how each country can improve its implementation of the CRPD and ensure compliance with Article 24 and the rest of the CRPD. Of the Concluding Observations that the CRPD issued as of February 2017, all of them highlight the need for greater inclusive educational opportunities for students with disabilities.[179]

The CRPD Committee has made clear in its Concluding Observations that Article 24 requires States Parties to do nothing less than to promote and to provide inclusive education to all students with all types of disabilities, despite the controversy over Article 24 during the negotiation process. In fact, in most (if not all) of the Concluding Observations, the Committee recommends that the country should work to promote greater inclusion as well as training for

178 These countries are Spain, Tunisia, Peru, China, Argentina, Hungary, Paraguay, Austria, Australia, El Salvador, Sweden, Azerbaijan, Costa Rica, Mexico, Republic of Korea, Belgium, Denmark, Ecuador, Germany, Croatia, Czech Republic, United Kingdom, Dominican Republic, Turkmenistan, Mongolia, Cook Islands, New Zealand, Kenya, Ukraine, Brazil, Qatar, Serbia, Slovakia, Portugal, Chile, Lithuania, Thailand, Ethiopia, Moldova, Armenia, Italy, Uganda, United Arab Emirates, Bosnia and Herzegovina, Uruguay, Colombia, Cyprus, Gabon, Guatemala, Honduras, Iran, Mauritius and Turkey, as well as the European Union.

179 The countries that submitted reports with a discussion of Article 24 are: Spain, Tunisia, Peru, China, Argentina, Hungary, Paraguay, Austria, El Salvador, Sweden, Azerbaijan, Costa Rica, Mexico, Republic of Korea, Belgium, Denmark, Ecuador, Germany, Croatia, Czech Republic, United Kingdom, Dominican Republic, Turkmenistan, Mongolia, Cook Islands, New Zealand, Kenya, Ukraine, Brazil, Serbia, Slovakia, Portugal, Lithuania, Jordan, Thailand, Ethiopia, Moldova, Armenia, Italy, Uganda, United Arab Emirates, Bosnia and Herzegovina, Uruguay, Colombia, Cyprus, Gabon, Guatemala, Honduras, Iran, Mauritius and Turkey.

Of those, the forty countries that have received Concluding Observations from the CRPD Committee in response to their country reports on Article 24 are: Argentina, Austria, Australia, Azerbaijan, Belgium, Brazil, Chile, China, Cook Islands, Costa Rica, Croatia, Czech Republic, Denmark, Dominican Republic, Ecuador, El Salvador, Gabon, Germany, Hungary, Kenya, Lithuania, Mauritius, Mexico, Mongolia, New Zealand, Paraguay, Peru, Portugal, Qatar, Republic of Korea, Serbia, Slovakia, Spain, Sweden, Thailand, Turkmenistan, Tunisia, Uganda, Ukraine and the European Union. See Concluding Observations by the Committee on the Rights of Persons with Disabilities at http://tbinternet.ohchr.org/_layouts/treatybodyexternal/TBSearch.aspx?Lang=en&TreatyID=4&DocTypeID=5, accessed 21 July 2017.

teachers about including students with disabilities in their schools and classrooms.[180]

The observations of the CRPD Committee in response to these country reports demonstrate a wide variation in country practice, with respect to separate schools, treatment of students with physical and sensory disabilities and accessibility. Even those countries that were praised for the development of inclusion in the past (such as Italy and Spain) were also criticised by the Committee for lacking a continuing momentum towards the goal of full implementation of inclusive education. As a result, the CRPD Committee has urged most if not all countries that have ratified the CRPD to do more to ensure inclusive education for every child with a disability (as well as lifelong inclusive education), in order to fulfil their obligations under Article 24. Moreover, what we see from these reports and the CRPD Committee's responses is that no region or nationality stands out as 'the best' or 'the worst' in terms of compliance with Article 24. In fact, it appears that the development of inclusive education is proceeding along parallel courses throughout the world, with varying degrees of success. Most countries share concerns about lack of funding, albeit at different levels, and all countries seem to call for adequate teacher training, and national plans and strategies for ensuring full compliance with Article 24.[181]

180 Ibid.

181 Ninety-nine countries and the EU (as of 30 January 2017) filed reports relating to the CRPD. Each report can be found at http://tbinternet.ohchr.org/_layouts/treatybodyexternal/TBSearch.aspx?Lang=en&TreatyID=4&DocTypeID=29, accessed 21 July 2017. The countries that discuss Article 24 are Spain, Tunisia, Peru, China, Argentina, Hungary, Paraguay, Austria, Australia, El Salvador, Sweden, Azerbaijan, Costa Rica, Mexico, Republic of Korea, Belgium, Denmark, Ecuador, Germany, Croatia, Czech Republic, United Kingdom, Dominican Republic, Turkmenistan, Mongolia, Cook Islands, New Zealand, Kenya, Ukraine, Brazil, Qatar, Serbia, Slovakia, Portugal, Chile, Lithuania, Thailand, Ethiopia, Moldova, Armenia, Italy, Uganda, United Arab Emirates, Bosnia and Herzegovina, Uruguay, Colombia, Cyprus, Gabon, Guatemala, Honduras, Iran, Mauritius and Turkey, as well as the European Union.

The countries that submitted reports with a discussion of Article 24 are: Spain, Tunisia, Peru, China, Argentina, Hungary, Paraguay, Austria, El Salvador, Sweden, Azerbaijan, Costa Rica, Mexico, Republic of Korea, Belgium, Denmark, Ecuador, Germany, Croatia, Czech Republic, United Kingdom, Dominican Republic, Turkmenistan, Mongolia, Cook Islands, New Zealand, Kenya, Ukraine, Brazil, Serbia, Slovakia, Portugal, Lithuania, Jordan, Thailand, Ethiopia, Moldova, Armenia, Italy, Uganda, United Arab Emirates, Bosnia and Herzegovina, Uruguay, Colombia, Cyprus, Gabon, Guatemala, Honduras, Iran, Mauritius and Turkey.

Of those, the forty countries that have received Concluding Observations from the CRPD Committee in response to their country reports on Article 24 are: Argentina, Austria, Australia, Azerbaijan, Belgium, Brazil, Chile, China, Cook Islands, Costa Rica, Croatia, Czech Republic, Denmark, Dominican Republic, Ecuador, El Salvador, Gabon, Germany, Hungary, Kenya, Lithuania, Mauritius, Mexico, Mongolia, New Zealand, Paraguay, Peru,

B *The CRPD Committee's General Comment No. 4*

One of the reasons for the lack of progress or even consistency regarding the implementation of Article 24 among the various countries that have filed country reports to date may be the confusion that remains (even after the adoption of Article 24) regarding the meaning and scope of inclusive education. This confusion (and disagreement) was evident during the negotiation process, as discussed earlier in this chapter, and it continues today.

Efforts are under way, however, to clarify the meaning and scope of Article 24 throughout the international human rights community. For example, in March 2014, the Human Rights Council passed a resolution urging domestic implementation of the right to inclusive education.[182] To fully achieve the goal of inclusive education, the resolution recommends that States 'ensur[e] that all children have equal opportunity for access to an inclusive education system of good quality' and 'strengthen further the process of developing inclusive education systems'.[183] To achieve this goal, the resolution recognises the necessity of training teachers and allocating the necessary resources for suitable teaching facilities and materials.[184] The resolution further recognises the importance of raising awareness to combat prejudice and stereotypes, including sources of discrimination in schools.[185]

On 2 September 2016, further clarification about the importance and meaning of inclusive education was provided by the CRPD Committee itself in its

Portugal, Qatar, Republic of Korea, Serbia, Slovakia, Spain, Sweden, Thailand, Turkmenistan, Tunisia, Uganda and Ukraine, along with the European Union.

182 UN Human Rights Council, The Right to Education of Persons with Disabilities (25 March 2014) Res. A/HRC/25/L.30. The resolution '[c]alls upon States [P]arties to the CRPD to adopt and implement appropriate measures, including legislative measures, to ensure that persons with disabilities enjoy the right to education without discrimination and on the basis of equal opportunity by ensuring an inclusive education system at all levels and life-long learning, in accordance with the [CRPD]' (8). See the preamble and paragraphs 19–20 for further information relating to the development of inclusive education systems, the appointment of the Secretary General Special Envoy on Disability, the expiry of the mandate of the Special Rapporteur on Disability of the Commission on Social Development, Resolution 7/9 of 27 March 2008, and its next annual interactive debate on the rights of persons with disabilities. In March 2014, the High Commissioner for Human Rights, Navi Pillay, presented to the Council of Human Rights a study on the rights to education for persons with disabilities, which can be viewed here: http://bice.org/en/bice-defends-the-right-to-inclusive-education-of-children-with-disabilities-at-the-un-human-rights-council/, accessed 12 July 2017; See also 'HRC Meeting on Persons with Disabilities Focuses on Inclusive Education' at www.unmultimedia.org/photo/detail.jsp?id=583/583248&key=264&query=%22Human%20Rights%20Council%22&lang=&sf=date, accessed 12 July 2017.

183 Ibid. preamble.

184 Ibid. 9.

185 Ibid. preamble.

General Comment No. 4. This General Comment seeks to resolve such doubts and to fill in any information considered missing from the language of Article 24.[186] The General Comment clarifies the Committee's view that Article 24 (like the UDHR, the ICESCR, the CRC and other international documents before it) includes a right to education which is necessary to the 'full development of the human potential and sense of dignity and self-worth, strengthening of respect for human rights and human diversity'.[187] The General Comment recognises further that for people with disabilities, accommodations may be necessary in order to fulfil the goal of education that is accessible, adaptable, available and inclusive. The Comment also highlights the importance of Article 24 given the fact that even today, after the ratification of the CRPD by most countries in the world, millions of children and adults with disabilities are denied a right to education.

In short, General Comment No. 4 is the most comprehensive statement on the meaning and scope of the right to inclusive education for people with disabilities. Also, unlike Article 24 itself, it begins with a definition of inclusive education, which is to be understood as:

a) A fundamental right of all learners. Notably, education is the right of the individual learner, and not, in the case of children, the right of a parent or caregiver. Parental responsibilities in this regard are subordinate to the rights of the child.
b) A principle that values the well-being of all students, respects their inherent dignity and autonomy, acknowledges individual requirements and ability to effectively be included in and contribute to society.
c) A means of realizing other human rights. It is the primary means by which persons with disabilities can lift themselves out of poverty, obtain the means to participate fully in their communities, and be safeguarded from exploitation.[188] It is also the primary means through which to achieve inclusive societies.
d) The result of a process of continuing and pro-active commitment to eliminate barriers impeding the right to education, together with changes to culture, policy and practice of regular schools to accommodate and effectively include all students.[189]

186 Committee on the Rights of Persons with Disabilities, General Comment No. 4 (2016) Article 24: The Right to Inclusive Education (2 September 2016) CRPD/C/GC/4.
187 Ibid. 15.
188 Committee on Economic, Social and Cultural Rights, General Comment No. 13: The Right to Education (Article 13 of the Covenant) (8 December 1999) E/C.12/1999/10.
189 General Comment No. 4 (n. 186) 10.

General Comment No. 4 also includes a definition of inclusive education that differentiates it from exclusion, segregation and integration. As the General Comment makes clear, inclusive education is

> a process of systemic reform embodying changes and modifications in content, teaching methods, approaches, structures and strategies in education to overcome barriers with a vision serving to provide all students of the relevant age range with an equitable and participatory learning experience and environment that best corresponds to their requirements and preferences. Placing students with disabilities within mainstream classes without accompanying structural changes to, for example, organisation, curriculum and teaching and learning strategies, does not constitute inclusion. Furthermore, integration does not automatically guarantee the transition from segregation to inclusion.[190]

In General Comment No. 4, the CRPD Committee also refers to the Thematic Study on the Rights of Persons with Disabilities to Education, which declares 'that only inclusive education can provide both quality education and social development for persons with disabilities, and a guarantee of universality and non-discrimination in the right to education'.[191] The General Comment also references the UNESCO Convention against Discrimination in Education, which affirms that the right to education must be assured without discrimination and on the basis of equality of opportunity.[192] Overall, these are only highlights of the content of General Comment No. 4, which actually contains seventy-four detailed paragraphs on how to include all students in inclusive education, as well as a detailed discussion of the nature of schooling and accessibility, communication access, and the need for teacher training that must be in place in order to ensure education for all students with all types of disabilities.

CONCLUSION

Article 24 of the CRPD includes a new international human right to inclusive education. All of the 174 countries that have ratified the CRPD to date are now obligated to enforce the mandate of Article 24, which ensures to all its citizens

> an inclusive education system at all levels and life long learning directed to . . . [t]he full development of human potential and sense of dignity and self-

190 Ibid. 11.

191 Ibid. 2, quoting the OHCHR 'Thematic Study on the Right of Persons with Disabilities to Education' (18 December 2013) A/HRC/25/29 [3].

192 General Comment No. 4 (n. 186) 13.

worth, and the strengthening of respect for human rights, fundamental freedoms and human diversity.[193]

The promise of Article 24 will only be realised, however, with coordination and collaboration among many levels of governments and with leadership by people with disabilities themselves. Article 32 specifically recognises the importance of international cooperation and its promotion, in support of national efforts for the realisation of the purposes and objectives of the CRPD, including Article 24.[194]

New domestic laws that comply with Article 24 as well as enforce existing national regulations, policies and practices are necessary to ensure the right of all children, youth and adults with disabilities to be included within general education programmes. In addition, and perhaps even more important, local implementation of Article 24 is critical. Local implementation of Article 24 is hard work; it involves working with teachers, providing them with sufficient resources and training, building new buildings or retrofitting existing buildings and adapting course materials and methods of teaching. It also involves supporting families and the students with disabilities themselves. Moreover, in order for inclusive education to be successful, attitudes about people with disabilities, generally, must change. For children with disabilities in particular, education systems will not serve their needs until each child, with or without a disability, is viewed and valued as competent. In order to fully implement Article 24 and its goal of inclusive education, we all (States Parties, members of the public, teachers and families of people with disabilities, as well as people with disabilities themselves) must be willing to presume the competence of people with disabilities.[195] When all aspects of society can embrace a presumption of competence of people with disabilities, educational systems will necessarily shift their focus away from what a student cannot do towards what a student can do and what supports are necessary for the student

193 CRPD (n. 3) Art. 24(1) and (1)(a).

194 Ibid. Art. 32(1).

195 A presumption of competence, first described by my Syracuse University colleagues Douglas Biklen and Jamie Burke in 'Presuming Competence' (2006) 39 *Equity & Excellence in Education* 166. A presumption of competence requires educators, parents and professionals to start from a place that assumes individuals are competent and capable. For educators to presume competence, it is critical for them to accept their students as they are, and to assist these students in reaching their individual potential through knowing the students, their strengths and their individual needs. For a discussion of the presumption of competence as applied to Article 12 of the CRPD and guardianship, see Carrie E. Rood, Arlene S. Kanter and Julie Causton, 'Presumption of Incompetence: The Systematic Assignment of Guardianship within the Transition Process' (2015) 39 *Research and Practice for Persons with Severe Disabilities* 319.

to realise his or her goals. Through this process, educators, together with families and students with disabilities, will end the stigma about disability that inhibits opportunities for students with disabilities in so many countries today. Such efforts, together with domestic laws based on international mandates that promote inclusion, expectations of students with disabilities will increase and segregated schools and settings based on narrow visions of their future potential should disappear.

Changing the attitudes and educational systems that for decades have prevented children and adults with disabilities from being included in schools (as well as in society) will require major shifts in the thinking of governments as well as of school personnel, parents, students with disabilities and their peers. Moreover, providing the accommodations, adaptations and modifications that some students with disabilities may require to learn and participate in the classroom will also be challenging. Such accommodations must include full and equal access to services, materials, information, activities and classroom learning as well as access to buildings, programmes and transportation to and from school. As one commentator has written, the evidence from around the world is clear:

> When disabled people are included in education, they can escape the inequalities and prejudices which for so long have confined them to poverty and denial of their human rights. Moreover, the changes in education systems that this will require will mean that all learners benefit, leading to more humane, educated and equal societies.[196]

Finally, the voices of people with disabilities, families and teachers in the Global South must especially be heeded, given that millions of children with disabilities in that region never attend any sort of school. Particularly in sub-Saharan Africa, where resources are more limited, a human rights argument for inclusive education may not be persuasive. There, for example, support for implementation of Article 24 may be particularly daunting as many believe that the solution to educational problems faced by under-resourced countries in the Global South is not the application of international human rights norms.[197] As some scholars have claimed, 'the growth of "inclusive education" in the developing world . . . in part reflects the export of first-world thinking to

196 *Commonwealth Guide* (n. 4) 297.

197 Nidhi Singal and Nithi Muthukrishna, 'Reflexive Re-storying of Inclusive Education: Evidence from India and South Africa' in Shaun Grech and Karen Soldatic (eds), *Disability in the Global South: The Critical Handbook* (Springer 2016) 212, citing Ann Cheryl Armstrong, Derrick Armstrong and Ilektra Spandagou, *Inclusive Education: International Policy & Practice* (Sage 2009) 12.

countries which reinforces dependency'.[198] Such concerns are important and require thoughtful and comprehensive responses. Hopefully, as more local people with disabilities and teachers are directly involved in the development of their own inclusive educational systems, schools will be based on their local communities' own 'situated needs and priorities'.[199] When that happens, there can be a more nuanced understanding of inclusive education so that the 'monolithic understanding of inclusive education [is] contested because of the diversity and complexity of local contexts in which international and national policies are enacted'.[200] Because of the importance of education to all children, youth and adults with disabilities, in whatever country they reside, such challenges must be addressed – and soon.

198 Ibid. 202.
199 Ibid. 212.
200 Ibid.

3

Comprehensive Legal Analysis of Article 24 of the Convention on the Rights of Persons with Disabilities

Gauthier de Beco

INTRODUCTION

Article 24 of the CRPD proclaims the right to inclusive education. Although it has started to receive wider attention around the world, it remains largely unexplored. No human rights treaty protected the right in question prior to the CRPD. While the Universal Declaration of Human Rights (UDHR), the International Covenant on Economic, Social and Cultural Rights (ICESCR) and the Convention on the Rights of the Child (CRC) do protect the right to education,[1] they do not provide for a right to inclusive education. Although the goal of inclusive education has gradually been recognised at the international level, only with the adoption of the CRPD has it been firmly instantiated in international human rights law. The right to inclusive education moreover sparked heated debate among the drafters of the Convention, especially with regard to the continued existence of special education. Only towards the end of the negotiation of this Convention was the goal of inclusive education agreed upon, and that goal is still contested by some scholars today. As a human rights treaty, the Convention therefore raises new questions that need to be addressed if the right to inclusive education is to be fulfilled.

Indeed, Article 24 of the CRPD is far from being implemented in reality. Although the CRPD establishes the right to inclusive education, disabled children are largely excluded from the general education system. In many parts of the world, these children simply cannot go to school because of their disability. The issue has recently been elevated through the adoption of Sustainable Development Goal (SDG) 4, which refers explicitly to disabled

[1] International Covenant on Economic, Social and Cultural Rights (adopted 16 December 1966, entered into force 23 March 1976) 993 UNTS 3 (ICESCR); Convention on the Rights of the Child (adopted 20 November 1989, entered into force 2 September 1990) 1577 UNTS 3 (CRC).

people among its targets.[2] If disabled children are included in education at all, they are often enrolled in so-called special schools, particularly in more developed countries.[3] This includes the region of Western Europe, where strongly segregated education systems have been built since the 1970s. These special schools often provide a lower standard of education and decrease their pupils' future chances in life. This was originally done in order to better address issues related to disability, but also due to teachers' inability to deal with these issues. As a result, despite the CRPD's high level of ratification, as well as a resolution supporting the goal of inclusive education by the Human Rights Council,[4] evidence indicates that disabled children remain largely absent in regular schools.[5]

This chapter explores the various questions that currently emerge from a close reading of the right to inclusive education. It does so by offering a comprehensive legal analysis of Article 24 of the CRPD in the sequence of its paragraph.

Article 24(1) of the Convention starts with requiring that States Parties set up an 'inclusive education system at all levels and life long learning'. It then defines the aims of developing such an 'inclusive education system'. According to Article 24(1), these aims are:

a) [t]he full development of human potential and sense of dignity and self-worth, and the strengthening of respect for human rights, fundamental freedoms and human diversity;
b) [t]he development by persons with disabilities of their personality, talents and creativity, as well as their mental and physical abilities, to their fullest potential;
c) [e]nabling persons with disabilities to participate effectively in a free society.

2 SDG Target 4.5 sets out the aim to 'eliminate gender disparities in education and ensure equal access to all levels of education and vocational training for the vulnerable, including *persons with disabilities*, indigenous peoples and children in vulnerable situations' by 2030 (emphasis added).

3 UNICEF Innocenti Research Centre, *Promoting the Rights of Children with Disabilities* (UNICEF 2007) 17, www.un.org/esa/socdev/unyin/documents/children_disability_rights.pdf, accessed 1 July 2018.

4 Human Rights Council (HRC), The Right to Education of Persons with Disabilities (24 March 2014) A/HRC/25/L.30.

5 Inclusion International, *Better Education for All: When We're Included Too: A Global Report: People with an Intellectual Disability and Their Families Speak Out on Education for All, Disability and Inclusive Education* (INICO 2009) 65–6, http://ii.gmalik.com/pdfs/Better_Education_for_All_Global_Report_October_2009.pdf, accessed 1 July 2018.

Article 24(2) of the Convention, then, outlines the measures to be taken in order to realise the right to inclusive education. Article 24(2)(a) provides that States Parties must ensure that '[p]ersons with disabilities are not excluded from the general education system on the basis of disability, and that children with disabilities are not excluded from free and compulsory primary education, or from secondary education, on the basis of disability'. Article 24(2)(b) goes on, stipulating that '[p]ersons with disabilities can access an inclusive, quality and free primary education and secondary education on an equal basis with others in the communities in which they live'. According to Article 24(2)(c), States Parties must also guarantee that '[r]easonable accommodation of the individual's requirements is provided'. Furthermore, Article 24(2)(d) provides that disabled children must 'receive the support required within the general education system, to facilitate their effective education'. Article 24(2)(e) also provides that '[e]ffective individualized support measures are provided in environments that maximize academic and social development, consistent with the goal of full inclusion'. In this way, States Parties should make inclusive education a reality for disabled people.

Article 24 of the CRPD continues by addressing a number of specific aspects of the education process. Article 24(3) deals with those who are blind, deaf or deaf-blind. It provides that 'persons with disabilities to learn life and social development skills to facilitate their full and equal participation in education and as members of the community'. It further enumerates a number of measures in order to achieve this:

a) [f]acilitating the learning of Braille, alternative script, augmentative and alternative modes, means and formats of communication and orientation and mobility skills, and facilitating peer support and mentoring;
b) [f]acilitating the learning of sign language and the promotion of the linguistic identity of the deaf community;
c) [e]nsuring that the education of persons, and in particular children, who are blind, deaf or deafblind, is delivered in the most appropriate languages and modes and means of communication for the individual, and in environments which maximize academic and social development.

Article 24(4) concerns the important question of teacher education, stipulating that States Parties must 'take appropriate measures to employ teachers, including teachers with disabilities, who are qualified in sign language and/or Braille, and to train professionals and staff who work at all levels of education'. Finally, Article 24(5) provides that 'persons with disabilities are able to access general tertiary education, vocational training, adult education and lifelong learning without discrimination and on an equal basis with others'. It thereby completes the full circle of the education of disabled people.

This chapter opens with an outline of the relevant international legal instruments that relate to inclusive education before the adoption of the CRPD and a brief review of the drafting history of Article 24 of the Convention. Thereafter, it provides a legal analysis of Article 24 examining the meaning of its various provisions, their relationship to previous human rights treaties and the issues of contention that remain. It does so in light of existing scholarship on the topic as well as the jurisprudence of the Committee on the Rights of Persons with Disabilities (CRPD Committee), including its general comment on the right to inclusive education,[6] and the work of other UN treaty bodies, including the Committee on Economic, Social and Cultural Rights (CESCR Committee) and the Committee on the Rights of the Child (CRC Committee). It also refers to the jurisprudence of national and regional courts that have clarified or confirmed a number of issues relating to this right and that have upheld that right for disabled people.

I BACKGROUND

A *CRPD Antecedents*

The right to education is protected by several international legal instruments. Article 26(1) of the UDHR provides that '[e]veryone has the right to education' and that '[e]ducation shall be free, at least in the elementary and fundamental stages', and that '[e]lementary education shall be compulsory'. Article 13(1) of the ICESCR also recognises 'the right of everyone to education'. Article 13 of the Covenant further outlines obligations relating to primary, secondary and tertiary education. It covers both the content of education (i.e. the social aspect of the right to education) and the right of parents to choose the education of their children according to their religious and moral convictions along with the right to establish private schools (i.e. the freedom aspect of the right to education).[7] Article 14 of the ICESCR establishes the obligation to set up a plan of action in case the right to free and compulsory education is not achieved within two years after the ratification of the Covenant. The CESCR

6 CRPD Committee, General Comment No. 4. Article 24: Right to Inclusive Education (2 September 2016) CRPD/C/GC/4.

7 The latter aspect is provided for both by Article 13(3) of the ICESCR and by Article 18(4) of the International Covenant on Civil and Political Rights (ICCPR).

Committee moreover issued two general comments pertaining to the topic, one on the right to education in general and another on plans of action for primary education.[8]

The CRC also includes detailed provisions on the right to education that have a broad reach, as it is the most widely ratified human rights treaty.[9] Article 28 of the CRC repeats most of the standards enunciated in Article 13 of the ICESCR. It goes on to add new standards to the right to education,[10] and Article 29 of the CRC is more expansive with regard to the aims of education (discussed later in this chapter). Furthermore, the CRC is the first human rights treaty to pay particular attention to disability. Article 2 of the Convention mentions it in the list of prohibited discrimination grounds, and Article 23(3) states that disabled children must have access to education 'in a manner conducive to the child achieving the fullest possible social integration and individual development'.[11] The CRC Committee itself has contributed to the progressive development of the right to inclusive education in its issuance of two general comments, one on the aims of education and another on the rights of disabled children.[12] The latter general comment particularly advanced this right both by providing that inclusive education 'should be the goal of educating children with disabilities' and by explicitly endorsing the CRPD's drafters' approach to the issue of education.[13]

Although neither the ICESCR nor the CRC provides for a right to inclusive education, both recognise the right to education. A close reading of the CRC, however, reveals that some of the standards set forth in this Convention offer weaker protection than those set forth in the ICESCR.[14] To circumvent this problem, the CRC has a savings clause, which stipulates that if other human

[8] CESCR Committee, General Comment No. 13: The Right to Education (Art. 13) (8 December 1999) E/C.12/1999/10; CESCR Committee, General Comment No. 11: Plans of Action for Primary Education (Art. 14) (10 May 1999) E/C.12/1999/4.

[9] The CRC has been ratified by all States except the United States.

[10] These include the obligation to '[m]ake educational and vocational information and guidance available and accessible to all children' and to 'take all appropriate measures to ensure that school discipline is administered in a manner consistent with the child's human dignity' (Articles 28(1)(d) and 28(2), CRC).

[11] The UNESCO Convention against Discrimination also prohibits discrimination in education on the basis of various grounds, but not disability (Convention against Discrimination in Education [14 December 1960, entry into force 22 May 1962] 429 UNTS 93).

[12] CRC Committee, General Comment No. 1: The Aims of Education (Art. 29(1) [17 April 2001] CRC/GC/2001/1); CRC Committee, General Comment No. 9: The Rights of Children with Disabilities (27 February 2007) CRC/C/GC/9.

[13] General Comment No. 9 (n. 12) para. 66.

[14] While Article 13(2)(b) of the ICESCR stipulates that '[s]econdary education in its different forms ... shall be made generally available and accessible to all by every appropriate means, and in particular by the progressive introduction of free education', Article 28(1)(b) of the CRC

rights treaties contain higher standards, the latter are applicable.[15] As such, to the extent that the CRC weakens the right to education of disabled people, the ICESCR governs the scope of protection.

While the CRPD is the first international legally binding instrument to proclaim the right to inclusive education, the idea was already expressed in previously adopted documents. Following the World Conference on Education in 1990, the World Declaration on Education for All: Meeting Basic Learning Needs (Jomtien Declaration) declared that '[s]teps need to be taken to provide equal access to education to every category of disabled persons as an integral part of the education system'.[16] The Standard Rules on the Equalization of Opportunities for Persons with Disabilities (Standard Rules) adopted in 1993 subsequently provided that '[e]ducation for persons with disabilities should form an integral part of national educational planning, curriculum development and school organisation', and that '[e]ducation in mainstream schools presupposes the provision of interpreter and other appropriate support services ... [a]dequate accessibility and support services, designed to meet the needs of persons with different disabilities'.[17]

The next significant step was the UNESCO World Conference on Special Needs Education: Access and Equality which took place in 1994. For the first time, specific attention was paid to inclusive education. The resulting Salamanca Statement[18] provided that 'those with special educational needs must have access to regular schools which should accommodate them within a child-centred pedagogy capable of meeting these needs', and that 'regular schools with this inclusive orientation are the most effective means of combating discriminatory attitudes, creating welcoming communities, building an inclusive society and achieving education for all'.[19] This was the first international instrument to affirm the goal of inclusive education. States committed 'to adopt as a matter of law or policy the principle of inclusive education, enrolling all children in regular schools, unless there are compelling reasons for doing otherwise'.[20]

provides that States Parties shall '[e]ncourage the development of different forms of secondary education ... make them available and accessible to every child, and take appropriate measures such as the introduction of free education and offering financial assistance in case of need'.

15 Article 41, CRC.

16 Article 3(5), Jomtien Declaration.

17 Rules 6(1) and 6(2), Standard Rules.

18 World Conference on Special Needs Education: Access and Equality, Salamanca Statement and Framework for Action on Special Needs Education (7–10 June 1994) http://unesdoc.unesco.org/images/0009/000984/098427eo.pdf, accessed 1 July 2018.

19 Para. 2, Salamanca Statement.

20 Para. 3, Salamanca Statement.

B Travaux préparatoires

Despite the adoption of the aforementioned documents, the drafters of the CRPD did not achieve an easy consensus on the content of Article 24. In fact, the text was not settled until the final phase of the drafting process. The task to work on the right to education of disabled people was entrusted to a Working Group, which started to meet during the third session of the Ad Hoc Committee. A core point of contention concerned whether States Parties should be required to make special education available.[21] These discussions were the focus of debate at the sixth session of the Ad Hoc Committee. A key question, then, was whether parents had to be given the right to choose the form of education for their children. There was no consensus on the matter of separate versus regular schooling, although there was general agreement on the principles that should animate such education.

The Ad Hoc Committee initially opted for language that affirmed the right to choose between inclusive and special education. Proposed by Mexico at the third session,[22] draft Article 17(3) of the (future) Convention provided that 'where the general education system does not adequately meet the needs of persons with disabilities special and alternative forms of learning should be made available'.[23] Any such forms should:

a) reflect the same standards and objectives provided in the general education system;
b) be provided in such a manner to allow children with disabilities to participate in the general education system to the maximum extent possible;
c) allow a free and informed choice between general and special systems;
d) in no way limit the duty of States Parties to continue to strive to meet the needs of students with disabilities in the general education system.[24]

This provision reflected differing perspectives among governments and stakeholders regarding the right to education of disabled people. While some considered that special education should still be made available, others thought that inclusive education should constitute the norm.[25] The former

[21] Bronagh Byrne, 'Hidden Contradictions and Conditionality: Conceptualisations of Inclusive Education in International Human Rights Law' (2013) 28 *Disability & Society* 239.

[22] Mexico, 'Draft Article 17 Education' https://static.un.org/esa/socdev/enable/rights/ahcstata24tscomments.htm#mexico, accessed 1 July 2018.

[23] Report of the Working Group to the Ad Hoc Committee (27 January 2004) A/AC.265/2004/WG/1.

[24] Ibid.

[25] Byrne (n. 21) 239.

indeed questioned whether the goal of inclusive education was the preferable option in all circumstances for disabled children. In this regard, the Standard Rules recognised that '[i]n situations where the general school system does not *yet* adequately meet the needs of all disabled people, special education may be considered', although it 'should be aimed at preparing students for education in the general school system'.[26] The term 'yet' suggested that the provision of inclusive education was not necessarily the ultimate objective. The contingent phrasing was used early on in the drafting, but was omitted in later drafts.[27] This helped to achieve the purpose of those who favoured an unqualified embrace of inclusive education in the text of Article 24.

At the sixth session of the Ad Hoc Committee, while the matter was not definitively settled, consensus emerged that inclusiveness was the key issue to be addressed with regard to the education of disabled children.[28] This was to be a primary aim, yet allowing for the provision of special education in certain, narrowly defined circumstances. Following proposals by Australia and the European Union,[29] a new draft Article 17(1) stipulated that States Parties committed themselves to 'the goal of inclusiveness of their general education systems'.[30] It still made room for 'alternative forms of education', but only '[w]here exceptionally the general education system does not adequately meet the needs of persons with disabilities'.[31] While disabled people's organisations (DPOs) had stressed at length the importance of inclusive education and highlighted the measures to be adopted for its achievement, the goal of inclusive education was not fully recognised by the negotiators.

Following the subsequent adoption of the CRPD in 2006, the CRC Committee adopted a general comment on the rights of disabled children. It had actually elaborated this general comment during the very course of Ad Hoc Committee discussions on the content of Article 24. While the CRC Committee affirmed that inclusive education 'should be the goal of educating children with disabilities', it recognised that 'the measure in which the inclusion occurs, may vary' and that '[a] continuum of services and programme

26 Rule 6(8), Standard Rules (emphasis added).

27 Rosemary Kayess and Jennifer Green, 'Today's Lesson Is on Diversity: A Reflection on Inclusive Education' in Peter Blanck and Eilionóir Flynn (eds), *Routledge Handbook of Disability Law and Human Rights* (Routledge 2016) 62.

28 Report of the Working Group to the Ad Hoc Committee (17 August 2005) A/60/266.

29 Oddný Mjöll Arnardóttir, 'The Right to Inclusive Education for Children with Disabilities: Innovations in the CRPD' in Asbjørn Eide, Jakob Möller, Ineta Ziemele and Gudmundur Alfredsson (eds), *Making Peoples Heard: Essays on Human Rights in Honour of Gudmundur Alfredsson* (Martinus Nijhoff Publishers 2011) 213.

30 Report of the Working Group to the Ad Hoc Committee (17 August 2005) A/60/266.

31 Ibid.

options must be maintained in circumstances where fully inclusive education is not feasible to achieve in the immediate future'.[32] It thereby aligned its position with the emerging consensus of the drafters of the (coming) CRPD.

On the basis of a final version circulated by the facilitator,[33] it was eventually decided that inclusive education had to feature as an explicit guarantee for all disabled people in the Convention. The Ad Hoc Committee accordingly put to one side the reservations reflected in the Standard Rules and in the ongoing work of the CRC Committee. Noting that 'considerable improvement' had been made by the Working Group, the chair of the Ad Hoc Committee declared that substantive issues had been resolved.[34] The only remaining question was how to square the goal of inclusive education with specific regard to the education of deaf, blind or deaf-blind people. Representative organisations, including the World Blind Union (WBU), the World Federation of the Deaf (WFD) and Deafblind International (DbI), expressed strong resistance in this regard during the negotiation of the CRPD and urged that the element of choice in school environment be kept for their constituents.[35]

The CRPD now lays down the goal of inclusive education. In order to satisfy the differing sides of the debate on Article 24, the final text reflects a compromise and is a clear example of negotiated ambiguity. While it was agreed that inclusiveness had to be a primary aim, left unclear is the scope of inclusion or where, exactly, inclusive education must take place. Accordingly, Article 24 does not explicitly prevent States Parties from establishing special schools.[36] Nor does it compel them to do so. It embraces a strong preference for inclusive education, but seems to leave open the possibility of maintaining a segregated education system.

II ESTABLISHMENT OF AN INCLUSIVE EDUCATION SYSTEM

Article 24(1) of the CRPD provides that States Parties must 'ensure an inclusive education system at all levels and life long learning'. This is the objective

[32] General Comment No. 9 (n. 12) para. 66.

[33] Report of the Working Group to the Ad Hoc Committee (17 August 2005) A/60/266.

[34] Letter dated 7 October 2005 from the chairman to all members of the Committee (14 October 2005) A/AC.265/2006/1, para. 92.

[35] Seventh Session, 'Comments, Proposals and Amendments Submitted Electronically', https://static.un.org/esa/socdev/enable/rights/ahcstata24sevscomments.htm, accessed 1 July 2018.

[36] A proposal made by the Centre for Studies on Inclusive Education (CSIE) to prohibit providing special education for disabled children was rejected by the Convention's drafters (Belinda Shaw, 'Inclusion or Choice? Securing the Right to Inclusive Education for All' in Maya Sabatello and Marianne Schulze [eds], *Human Rights & Disability Advocacy* [University of Pennsylvania Press 2013] 63).

towards which they must strive by committing a sufficient level of resources and adopting a series of measures that will enable them to attain that objective. Through their efforts, they must gradually establish an 'inclusive education system' throughout.

The precise meaning of 'inclusive education' in Article 24 of the CRPD is not easy to establish, especially as it is not defined in the Convention. Emerging jurisprudence does not shed light on its meaning. As discussed later in this volume, the concept of inclusive education can be seen as a requirement of changing the different practices of education so as to increase the abilities and skills of all children and, thereby, fostering an inclusive school environment conducive to the learning of all children.

Article 24(1) of the Convention outlines the aims of the establishment of an 'inclusive education system'. The drafters draw inspiration from the ICESCR in spelling out these aims, the wording of which is to a large extent similar to that of this Covenant. Article 13(1) of the ICESCR provides that 'education shall be directed to the full development of the human personality and the sense of its dignity, and shall strengthen the respect for human rights and fundamental freedoms'. It also states that States Parties 'agree that education shall enable all persons to participate effectively in a free society, promote understanding, tolerance and friendship among all nations and all racial, ethnic or religious groups, and further the activities of the United Nations for the maintenance of peace'. Article 29(1) of the CRC echoes this view, but it also contains a number of aims not listed in Article 13(1) of the ICESCR.[37] Moreover, the CRC Committee has been much more expansive about such aims than the CESCR Committee, and even produced its first general comment ever on the issue.[38] It is worth inquiring into the extent to which Article 24(1) of the CRPD diverges from Articles 13(1) of the ICESCR and 29(1) of the CRC, by adding or deleting certain terms, thereby shifting the focus with regard to disabled children. It is also useful to examine how those terms that are similar have already been understood by the corresponding treaty bodies.

[37] These aims are: '[t]he development of respect for the child's parents, his or her own cultural identity, language and values, for the national values of the country in which the child is living, and for civilizations different from his or her own'; '[t]he preparation of the child for responsible life in a free society, in the spirit of understanding, peace, tolerance, equality of sexes, and friendship among all peoples, ethnic, national and religious groups and persons of indigenous origin'; and '[t]he development of respect for the natural environment' (Article 29(1)(c), (d) and (e), CRC).

[38] General Comment No. 1 (n. 12). Nonetheless, the CESCR Committee recommended that States Parties to the Covenant ensure that those aims be 'interpreted in the light of [the Jomtien Declaration]' and that they include 'gender equality and respect for the environment' (General Comment No. 13 [n. 8] para. 5).

The creation of an 'inclusive education system' should have a threefold purpose outlined in the three paragraphs of Article 24(1) of the CRPD.

Article 24(1)(a) provides that the 'inclusive education system' should 'be directed' to '[t]he full development of human potential and sense of dignity and self-worth, and the strengthening of respect for human rights, fundamental freedoms and human diversity'. This is almost a verbatim iteration of Article 13(1) of the ICESCR. However, the term 'personality' (which found its way into Article 24(1)(b) of the CRPD) has been replaced by 'potential', and two others have been added, namely 'self-worth' and 'human diversity'.[39] The term 'self-worth' is quite relevant given that disabled children have for a long time been regarded as inferior in comparison to non-disabled children. The term 'human diversity' also makes sense in the context of disability, since a key principle of the Convention is precisely to advance consideration of disabled people as a reflection of 'human diversity'.[40] The term 'dignity' furthermore is very much linked to the notion of human rights, and is related to the sense of 'self-worth' mentioned previously. Not only is the promotion of respect for 'dignity' part of the aims of the Convention,[41] but it can also be used as a benchmark for making the achievement of inclusive education ethically acceptable for disabled children.[42] As noted by the CRPD Committee, inclusive education should have the purpose of 'promoting mutual respect and value for all persons and at building educational environments in which the approach to learning, the culture of the educational institution, and the curriculum itself, reflect the value of diversity'.[43]

Education should furthermore integrate the values of human rights, including those that underpin the CRPD, and cultivate an attitude of tolerance and respect for others. This can be achieved by the provision of human rights education, which has received considerable attention in recent decades. The CRC Committee indicates by way of example that '[e]mphasis must be placed upon the importance of teaching about racism as it has been practised historically, and particularly as it manifests or has manifested itself within particular communities'.[44] Similarly, an 'inclusive education system' should

[39] The latter were inserted during the third session of the Ad Hoc Committee, albeit without any discussion (Report of the Working Group to the Ad Hoc Committee [9 June 2004] A/AC.265/2004/5).

[40] Article 3(d), CRPD.

[41] Article 1, CRPD.

[42] Gauthier de Beco, 'The Right to Inclusive Education: Why Is There So Much Opposition to Its Implementation?' (2018) 14 *International Journal of Law in Context* 405–406.

[43] General Comment No. 4 (n. 6) para. 15.

[44] General Comment No. 1 (n. 12) para. 11.

be aimed at combating historical prejudices against disabled people and promoting a positive image of these throughout the school curriculum.[45]

Article 24(1)(b) of the CRPD further stipulates that the 'inclusive education system' should 'be directed' to '[t]he development by persons with disabilities of their personality, talents and creativity, as well as their mental and physical abilities, to their fullest potential'. While the term 'personality' is used in Article 13(1) of the ICESCR (which refers to 'the full development of the human personality and the sense of its dignity'), its appearance in Article 24(1)(b) of the CRPD links more directly to Article 29(1)(a) of the CRC (which refers to '[t]he development of the child's personality, talents and mental and physical abilities to their fullest potential'). This aim should be understood in a broad sense. According to the CRC Committee, education 'goes far beyond formal schooling to embrace the broad range of life experiences and learning processes which enable children, individually and collectively, to develop their personalities, talents and abilities and to live a full and satisfying life within society'.[46] This confirms that inclusive education should allow the determination of how all children's skills and abilities can effectively be developed through the provision of education.[47] The CRC Committee also mentions that 'teaching methods should be tailored to the different needs of different children',[48] which is particularly relevant for those who are disabled and emphasises that education should cater for human differences. According to the CRPD Committee, the aim should be to 'support the creation of opportunities to build on the unique strengths and talents of each [disabled person]'.[49] The CRPD Committee also noted that '[t]he education of persons with disabilities too often focuses on a deficit approach, on their actual or perceived impairment and limiting opportunities to pre-defined and negative assumptions of their potential'.[50] While disability may sometimes lead to diminished capacity, this does not

45 This is also reflected in the general principles of the CRPD, which include '[r]espect for difference and acceptance of persons with disabilities as part of human diversity and humanity' (Article 3(d), CRPD).

46 General Comment No. 1 (n. 12) para. 2.

47 Serge Ebersold, 'Accessibilité, politiques inclusives et droit à l'éducation: considérations conceptuelles et méthodologiques' (2015) 9 *ALTER European Journal of Disability Research* 27; Michele Moore and Roger Slee, 'Disability Studies, Inclusive Education and Exclusion' in Nick Watson, Alan Roulstone and Carol Thomas (eds), *Routledge Handbook of Disability Studies* (Routledge 2012) 235.

48 General Comment No. 1 (n. 12) para. 9.

49 General Comment No. 4 (n. 6) para. 16.

50 Ibid. para. 16.

mean that the 'mental and physical abilities' referred to in Article 24(1)(b) are necessarily affected nor, indeed, that they cannot be further enhanced.

Article 24(1)(c) of the CRPD finally provides that the 'inclusive education system' should 'be directed' to '[e]nabling persons with disabilities to participate effectively in a free society'. This aim is reflected in in Article 13(1) of the ICESCR. The CRPD, by contextualising such participation, clarifies what that aim ought to encompass. 'Full and effective participation and inclusion in society' is one of the general principles of the Convention,[51] and embodies the core objective of this Convention. While Article 24(1)(c) of the CRPD provides that society should be 'free' (as Article 13(1) of the ICESCR), it clearly echoes the general principle of '[f]ull and effective participation and inclusion in society'. This general principle highlights the long-term purpose of inclusive education. Education that is inclusive must not only put an end to the exclusion of disabled children, but also be a vehicle for the improvement of social attitudes and creation of open societies. The impact of inclusive education therefore goes beyond the mere inclusion of disabled children. In the words of Global Campaign for Education and Handicap International, it can 'help to shape more equal societies [and] offers a chance to challenge widely-held and discriminatory attitudes and behaviours, to celebrate and embrace the rich tapestry of diversity in our societies, and to promote social values that combat discrimination'.[52] Education can foster the participation of disabled children in society by equipping them to face adult life challenges and facilitating relationships with their non-disabled peers. It can likewise accustom non-disabled children to live with disabled people once they have become adults.

III OBLIGATIONS FOR THE RIGHT TO INCLUSIVE EDUCATION

A *Non-Exclusion of Disabled People*

Article 24(2)(a) of the CRPD provides that States Parties must ensure that '[p]ersons with disabilities are not excluded from the general education system on the basis of disability, and that children with disabilities are not excluded from free and compulsory primary education, or from secondary education, on the basis of disability'. It thereby provides for the non-exclusion of disabled people

[51] Article 3(c), CRPD.

[52] Global Campaign for Education and Handicap International, *Equal Right, Equal Opportunity: Inclusive Education for Children with Disabilities*, 16, http://campaignforeducation.org/docs/reports/Equal%20Right,%20Equal%20Opportunity_WEB.pdf, accessed 1 July 2018.

because of their disability. Despite the important function of this principle in achieving inclusive education, very little has actually been written about this requirement.

Article 24(2)(a) of the CRPD consists of two parts. The first one affirms non-exclusion in general. The second one specifies that education should be 'free and compulsory' for any child in line with both the ICESCR and the CRC. This differs somewhat, however, from the ICESCR, which provides that '[p]rimary education shall be compulsory and available free to all' and that '[s]econdary education in its different forms . . . shall be made generally available and accessible to all by every appropriate means, and in particular by the progressive introduction of free education'.[53] There is therefore a hierarchy between the different levels of education within the Covenant. Article 24(2) of the CRPD does not differentiate to such an extent between primary and secondary education. It limits itself to providing that disabled children shall not be excluded from 'secondary education' without the caveat stipulated by the ICESCR (although it refers in contrast to 'free and compulsory primary education'). It must also be read in light of Article 24(1) of the CRPD, which provides that education systems must be inclusive 'at all levels and life long learning'. Whatever the level of provision of inclusive education in a given State Party, disability may not be a motive to hinder the enrolment of a disabled child.

The result is that disabled children must be able to attend regular schools. Refusal to admit these children due to their disability by such schools is a form of discrimination prohibited by the CRPD.[54] Such refusal can be precluded by the so-called non-rejection clause, which sanctions the refusal to enrol a child under the motive of disability and which can be provided for by domestic legislation.[55] This kind of rejection has been condemned in different jurisdictions where a number of children have been denied education for the reason of being 'uneducable'. In the United States, two landmark (district court) cases[56] led to other similar cases and, subsequently, the adoption of the

53 Articles 13(2)(a) and 13(2)(b), ICESCR. Articles 28(1)(a) and 28(1)(b) of the CRC provide similarly that States Parties must '[m]ake primary education compulsory and available free to all' and '[e]ncourage the development of different forms of secondary education . . . and take appropriate measures such as the introduction of free education and offering financial assistance in case of need'. As mentioned earlier, this wording is weaker than that of the ICESCR. See n. 14.

54 Article 5(2), CRPD.

55 OHCHR, Thematic Study on the Right of Persons with Disabilities to Education (18 December 2013) A/HRC/25/29, para. 26.

56 *Pennsylvania Association for Retarded Children (PARC)* v. *Pennsylvania* 343 F Supp. 279 (ED Pa 1972); *Mills* v. *Board of Education* 348 F Supp. 866 (DDC 1972).

Education for All Handicapped Children Act of 1975 (EAHCA) later replaced by the Individuals with Disabilities Education Act of 1990 (IDEA).[57] In Ireland, the High Court, citing the aforementioned developments in the United States as well as both the UDHR and the CRC, ruled that even children with profound learning difficulties should be entitled to free and compulsory primary education in the *O'Donoghue* v. *Minister for Health* case.[58] By enacting the non-exclusion of disabled people, Article 24(1) of the CRPD has taken stock of this case law and confirmed that disabled children may not be denied education altogether.

The prohibition of discrimination includes the duty to provide reasonable accommodation.[59] As is further discussed in what follows, this is not only a general obligation underlying all the rights protected by the CRPD but it is also repeated – twice – in relation to the right to inclusive education (in Articles 24(2)(c) and 24(5)). The duty to provide reasonable accommodation, as an element of ensuring non-discrimination in education for disabled people, thus is further underscored by Article 24(2)(a) of the Convention.

Children may not be discriminated against because of disability either directly or indirectly. First, States Parties to the CRPD may not invoke the existence of an impairment in order to refuse to educate a child, although this direct form of discrimination has become rather infrequent. Second, they are forbidden to impose a requirement that effectively leads to the same result, which is the usual way by which disabled children are 'excluded from the general education system on the basis of disability' as per Article 24(2)(a) of the CRPD. Indirect forms of discrimination are covered by the CRPD, as can be seen from an implicit reading of the Convention.[60] This can happen in different ways that indirectly target disabled children. According to the CRPD Committee, for instance, conditions that focus on the potential of children through 'a common test as a condition for school entry without reasonable accommodations and support' create a situation of '[n]on-direct exclusion'.[61] If evidence demonstrates that such a 'common test' de facto results in most disabled children being rejected from regular schools, this will result in a violation of Article 24(2)(a) of the Convention.

57 For a more detailed discussion on the issue, see the chapter on 'Strategic Litigation and Inclusive Education' by Peter Barnett and Michael Ashley Stein in the present volume (Chapter 10).
58 *O'Donoghue* v. *Minister for Health* [1993] IEHC 2, [1996] 2 IR 20.
59 Article 5(3), CRPD.
60 Andrea Broderick, *The United Nations Convention on the Rights of Persons with Disabilities* (Intersentia 2015) 95–96.
61 General Comment No. 4 (n. 6) para. 18.

B Access to Inclusive Education for Disabled Children

Article 24(2)(b) of the CRPD provides that States Parties must ensure that '[p]ersons with disabilities can access an inclusive, quality and free primary education and secondary education on an equal basis with others in the communities in which they live'. Like Article 24(2)(a), Article 24(2)(b) has not been the subject of much attention. However, guaranteeing access to disabled children is fundamental in order to put into effect the right to inclusive education. Avoiding the exclusion of disabled children from the general education system will not be achieved in practice if the barriers that prevent them from attending regular schools remain.

Like Article 24(2)(a), Article 24(2)(b) seems to make a distinction between primary and secondary education, although it is less clear here whether the terms 'inclusive, quality and free' only apply to 'primary education'. The fact that it stipulates 'primary education and secondary education' (instead of 'primary and secondary education') reveals, at first sight, that only 'primary education' should be 'inclusive, quality and free'. However, it would be discriminatory if secondary education would be free and compulsory for non-disabled children but not for disabled children, as was stressed during the negotiation of the CRPD.[62] This pleads in favour of making secondary education 'inclusive, quality and free' as well. Even if a contrary interpretation would be more consistent with Article 24(2)(a) of the CRPD and other human rights treaties, it could therefore be argued that both primary and secondary education should be 'inclusive, quality and free'. At a minimum, the same regime must be applied to all children, disabled or not. The question remains, though, why the term 'quality' has been inserted between 'inclusive' and 'free' in Article 24(2)(b) and not in Article 24(2)(a) (which stipulates that primary education should be just 'free and compulsory').

The key term of Article 24(2)(b) of the Convention is arguably the 'access' to inclusive education. Accessibility is an issue especially related to disability, which is emphasised here with regard to inclusive education. The CRPD provides that States Parties must take measures to ensure access to '[b]uildings, roads, transportation and other indoor and outdoor facilities, including schools' for disabled people.[63] It also enumerates accessibility among its general principles[64] and refers in this regard explicitly to 'schools'.[65] With regard to education, it is not just about

62 Report of the Working Group to the Ad Hoc Committee (17 August 2005) A/60/266. Note also that the original draft provided for 'free and compulsory primary *or* secondary education' and did not include the term 'quality' in contrast to the final version (emphasis added).

63 Article 9(1)(a), CRPD.

64 Article 3(f), CRPD.

65 Article 9(1)(a), CRPD.

the physical world but also affects teaching and assessment methods. According to the CRPD Committee, 'it is the entire process of inclusive education that must be accessible, not just buildings, but all information and communication' and the '[m]odes and means of teaching'.[66] Furthermore, accessibility concerns 'buildings, information and communication, comprising ambient or frequency modulation assistive systems, curriculum, education materials, teaching methods, assessment and language and support services'.[67] It also applies to information and communication through the use of 'sign language, Braille, alternative script, and augmentative and alternative modes, means and formats of communication and orientation'.[68] Accessibility concerns wider school life as well, including 'school transport, which should be inclusive, accessible and safe; water and sanitation facilities, including hygiene and toilet facilities; school cafeterias; and recreational spaces'.[69] Therefore, infrastructure, including classrooms and toilets, as well as transport to school must be made fully accessible to disabled children.[70] Article 24(2)(b) of the CRPD furthermore stipulates that inclusive education should be made accessible to disabled people 'in the communities in which they live'. In order to do so, the CRPD Committee recommends that regular schools 'must be within safe physical reach for persons with disabilities, including safe and secure transport, or accessible via information communication technology'.[71] The Italian Constitutional Court, for instance, held that the provision of transportation for disabled children is an essential element of the right to inclusive education.[72]

The requirement of accessibility has been confirmed within the Council of Europe. In two cases against France (which was referring some of its pupils to special schools in neighbouring Belgium), the European Committee of Social Rights considered that the lack of access to regular schools by autistic children was a violation of the (Revised) European Social Charter.[73] Laying down a presumption in favour of inclusive education,[74] the Committee noted that

66 CRPD Committee, General Comment No. 2. Article 9: Accessibility (22 May 2014) CRPD/C/GC/2, para. 39.
67 General Comment No. 4 (n. 6) para. 21.
68 General Comment No. 2 (n. 66) para. 39.
69 General Comment No. 4 (n. 6) para. 21.
70 UNICEF Innocenti Research Centre (n. 3) 16–17; Inclusion International (n. 5) 82.
71 Ibid. para. 26.
72 Italian Constitutional Court, Decision No 275/2016.
73 *European Action of the Disabled (AEH)* v. *France* Complaint No. 81/2012 (11 September 2013); *International Association Autism Europe* v. *France* Complaint No. 13/2002 (4 November 2003).
74 See on this point the chapter on 'Emerging Jurisprudence on Inclusive Education under the European Social Charter (Revised)' by Shivaun Quinlivan in the present volume (Chapter 17).

the said Charter does not 'leave [S]tates [P]arties a wide margin of appreciation when it comes to choosing the type of school in which they will promote the independence, integration and participation of persons with disabilities, as this must clearly be a mainstream school'.[75] While the Committee had previously condemned Bulgaria for the absence of measures to ensure access to inclusive education by children with profound learning difficulties,[76] these cases demonstrate the willingness of supranational (quasi-)jurisdictional bodies to challenge the existence of barriers that prevent disabled children from attending regular schools.

Article 24(2)(b) should also be read in light of the right to education, as interpreted through the prism of the '4-A framework' adopted by Katarina Tomaševski, the former UN Special Rapporteur on the right to education,[77] and subsequently endorsed by the CESCR.[78] Under that '4-A framework', education must be 'Available', 'Accessible', 'Acceptable' and 'Adaptable'. This '4-A framework' emphasises both the quantitative and qualitative aspects of the right to education, by focussing not only on the right to education as such but also on respect *for* human rights in education and enhancing human rights *through* education. This means that States Parties to the CRPD must ensure that inclusive education is available for disabled children, that all of its aspects are accessible to them, that the education provided is of good quality and that teaching is adapted to their particular needs throughout.[79]

Although efforts have been made to guarantee access to inclusive education, regular schools often remain inaccessible to most disabled people.[80] The CRPD Committee has expressed its concern about inaccessibility to several States Parties.[81] The problem is that much of the infrastructure has

75 *European Action of the Disabled (AEH)* v. *France* Complaint No. 81/2012 (11 September 2013) para. 78.

76 *Mental Disability Advocacy Center (MDAC)* v. *Bulgaria* Complaint No. 41/2007 (3 June 2008).

77 Katarina Tomaševski, *Annual Report of the Special Rapporteur on the Right to Education* (7 January 2002) E/CN.4/2002/60, paras 12–13; Katarina Tomaševski, *Preliminary Report of the Special Rapporteur on the Right to Education* (13 January 1999) E/CN.4/14999/49, paras 15–25.

78 General Comment No. 13 (n. 8) para. 6.

79 General Comment No. 4 (n. 6) paras 19–25.

80 Inclusion International (n. 5) 82.

81 CRPD Committee, Concluding Observations on the Initial Report of Belgium (28 October 2014) CRPD/C/BEL/CO/1, para. 36; CRPD Committee, Concluding Observations on the Initial Report of Brazil (29 September 2015) CRPD/C/BRA/CO/1, para. 44; CRPD Committee, Concluding Observations on the Initial Report of Lithuania (11 May 2016) CRPD/C/LTU/CO/1, para. 45(e); CRPD Committee, Concluding Observations on the Initial Report of Colombia (30 September 2016) RPD/C/COL/CO/1, para. 54; CRPD Committee, Concluding Observations on the Initial Report of Italy (6 October 2016) CRPD/C/ITA/CO/1, para. 59.

been established without disabled children in mind. Complying with CRPD requirements will inevitably be harder for existing schools built without taking into account accessibility. Barrier removal plans therefore should be adopted and mechanisms put into place to ensure that new schools are made accessible from the very beginning. The CRPD Committee indeed recommends that States Parties 'prohibit and sanction the building of any future education infrastructures that are inaccessible'.[82]

C Provision of Reasonable Accommodation to Disabled People

Article 24(2)(c) of the CRPD provides that States Parties shall ensure that '[r] easonable accommodation of the individual's requirements is provided'. The Convention defines the concept of 'reasonable accommodation' as follows: 'necessary and appropriate modifications and adjustments not imposing a disproportionate or undue burden, where needed in a particular case, to ensure to persons with disabilities the enjoyment or exercise on an equal basis with others of all human rights and fundamental freedoms'.[83] While the duty to provide reasonable accommodation is guaranteed by Article 5(3),[84] it is repeated in Article 24(2)(c) and also referenced again in Article 24(5) (which is examined later in this chapter). This demonstrates its importance for the implementation of the right to inclusive education. As a result, special attention should be given to ensure that the duty to provide reasonable accommodation is reflected in domestic legislation in the area of education and that measures are taken to enable regular schools to provide such accommodation to disabled children.

The CRPD makes explicit that 'denial of reasonable accommodation' is a form of discrimination.[85] It is therefore an obligation that has to be fulfilled immediately by States Parties. This has been confirmed by the European Court of Human Rights. The Court addressed the exclusion of Roma children from the general education system on the basis of (alleged) disability in the *DH and others* v. *Czech Republic* and a number of other cases.[86] It has even recognised the duty to provide reasonable accommodation to disabled people

82 General Comment No. 4 (n. 6) para. 21.

83 Article 2, CRPD.

84 For a more detailed discussion on the issue, see the chapter on 'Reasonable Accommodation' by Shivaun Quinlivan in the present volume (Chapter 7).

85 Article 2, CRPD.

86 *DH and others* v. *Czech Republic* App No. 57325/00 (13 November 2007). See also *Sampanis and others* v. *Greece* App No. 32526/05 (5 June 2008); *Oršuš and others* v. *Croatia* App No. 15766/03 (16 March 2010); *Horváth and Kiss* v. *Hungary* App No. 15766/03 (29 January 2013).

in the context of education in the more recent *Çam* v. *Turkey* case. Referring explicitly to the CRPD (to which Turkey is a State Party), the Court has ruled that failure to comply with this duty results in a violation of the European Convention of Human Rights.[87]

Reasonable accommodation aims to ensure that disabled people can participate on the same level as other students in all aspects of the education process. The duty to provide reasonable accommodation is an individualised obligation, as stressed by the term 'individual's requirements' in Article 24(2)(c) of the Convention. As such, the provision of reasonable accommodation should be flexible. It must meet the individual needs of a disabled child in a particular context and may have to be amended over time. In contrast to accessibility, which is an '*ex ante* duty' applicable to disabled people as a whole, reasonable accommodation is an '*ex post* duty' that must be discharged on an individual basis.[88] States Parties must make adjustments upon the request of the disabled child provided the requested accommodation can be considered 'reasonable'.[89] While the reasonableness of any accommodation will be evaluated against the totality of the available resources of the State Party under examination, examples include 'changing the location of a class, providing different forms of in-class communication, enlarging print, materials and/or subjects in sign, or providing all handouts in an alternative format, providing students with a note-taker, or a language interpreter or allowing students to use assistive technology in learning and assessment situations'.[90] Also involved are the '[p]rovision of non-material accommodations, such as allowing a student more time, reducing levels of background noise, sensitivity to sensory overload, alternative evaluation methods or replacing an element of curriculum by an alternative element'.[91]

A question that often arises is when a requested accommodation may be considered 'reasonable'. This is indeed a delicate question, which will never be subject to a definitive answer and which must be considered on a case-by-case basis.[92] It can be answered through a two-stage process. First, there should be an assessment of whether the requested accommodation is effective to reach the objective sought. Second, there should be an evaluation of the reasonableness of this accommodation. The question, then, is whether the

87 *Çam* v. *Turkey* App No. 51500/08 (23 May 2016) paras 64 and 69.
88 General Comment No. 2 (n. 66) paras 25–26.
89 General Comment No. 4 (n. 6) para. 23.
90 Ibid. 29.
91 Ibid.
92 Nicholas Bamforth, Maleiha Malik and Colm O'Cinneide, *Discrimination Law: Theory and Context* (Sweet and Maxwell 2008) 1077–1078.

accommodation in question does not create disproportionate or undue burden.[93] There may well be a burden, which means that efforts will be required, but this burden may not be disproportionate or undue, which ultimately means that the potential impact of the requested accommodation will have to be weighed against its advantages. This entails a comparison between potential costs, which should be calculated taking into account any compensations that can be obtained, and potential advantages, which should include those for parties other than those for whom the measures are taken.[94] If a ramp is useful for disabled children, for instance, it can likewise be beneficial to pregnant mothers, small children and older people. There will also be a difference between a small organisation and a bigger one that might be funded publicly.

Reasonable accommodation should not entail any cost for the child concerned.[95] According to the CRPD Committee, States Parties must 'ensure that the parents of children with disabilities are not obliged to pay . . . for the measures of reasonable accommodation in mainstream schools'.[96] The CRPD Committee requires that education 'be free of charge at all compulsory levels of education'.[97] Furthermore, reasonable accommodation should be provided by both public and private actors. While private actors are allowed to offer education, States Parties must guarantee that such actors do not discriminate, because they may not discharge themselves from their legal obligations under the international human rights law.

Even though the reasonable character of an accommodation for the purpose of inclusive education can be difficult to determine, several sources point out that pertinent cost is usually overestimated and that most of the time that cost remains relatively low. The *Handbook for Parliamentarians on the Convention on the Rights of Persons with Disabilities and Its Optional Protocol* considers that this should be possible for approximately 80 to 90 per cent of disabled children, including those who have intellectual disabilities.[98] According to the UNICEF Innocenti Research Centre, '[i]

93 Article 2, CRPD. For an example outside of the context of education, see CRPD Committee, *HM* v. *Sweden* (21 May 2012) CRPD/C/7/D/3/2011, para. 85.

94 Letícia de Campos Velho Martel, 'Reasonable Accommodation: The New Concept from an Inclusive Constitutional Perspective' (2011) 8 *International Journal on Human Rights* 104.

95 General Comment No. 4 (n. 6) para. 23.

96 CRPD Committee, Concluding Observations on the Initial report of Spain (19 October 2001) CRPD/C/ESP/CO/1, para. 44.

97 General Comment No. 4 (n. 6) para. 17. See also CRPD Committee, Concluding Observations on the Initial Report of Spain (19 October 2011) CRPD/C/ESP/CO/1, para. 44.

98 OHCHR, *From Exclusion to Equality: Realizing the Rights of Persons with Disabilities: Handbook for Parliamentarians on the Convention on the Rights of Persons with Disabilities*

nclusive policies and practices required to promote the enjoyment of the rights of children with disabilities are both feasible and practical'.[99] As a result, most of the barriers to inclusive education can be removed.

Finally, the way in which the reasonable accommodations are determined should be decided in consultation with all involved parties. Whatever the outcome, the decision must be the result of an objective and fair procedure creating a dialogue in which they can debate on all available options. The procedure must therefore meet certain formal guarantees, including publicity and transparency. The process is as, if not more, important than the outcome. It is possible for a certain accommodation to be deemed unreasonable, as long as all parties have had the chance to put forward their arguments and decisions are made taking those arguments into account.

D Provision of Support for Purpose of Education

Article 24(2)(d) of the CRPD stipulates that States Parties must ensure that '[p]ersons with disabilities receive the support required within the general education system, to facilitate their effective education'. To start with, it is worth clarifying that the provision of support must be embedded in the overall educational policies of States Parties and not be foreseen in a way that leads to the establishment of a segregated education system. Such interpretation is consistent with the phrase 'within the general education system'. Furthermore, as indicated by Article 24(2)(d), the purpose is to make education 'effective' for disabled children. This refers to the elements of 'Acceptability' and 'Adaptability', as per the '4-A framework', and aims to ensure that education is beneficial to these children.[100] The underlying idea is that disabled children should not just be 'placed' in regular schools, but should be provided with the necessary support to develop their skills and talents or, in other words, be enabled to progress in their learning in an inclusive school environment.

Support includes not only appropriate equipment and materials, such as Braille and sign language, but also personal assistance. The latter can be 'a qualified learning support assistant, either shared or on a one-to-one basis, depending on the requirements of the student'.[101] It includes 'the provision of sufficient trained and supported teaching staff, school counsellors, psychologists,

and Its Optional Protocol (UN 2007) 85 www.un.org/disabilities/documents/toolaction/ipuhb.pdf, accessed 1 July 2018.

99 UNICEF Innocenti Research Centre (n. 3) 1.

100 Broderick (n. 60) 294.

101 General Comment No. 4 (n. 6) para. 32.

and other relevant health and social service professionals, as well as access to scholarships and financial resources'.[102] According to Special Rapporteur on the Right to Education Vernor Munoz, support also involves 'the provision of supplementary classes, alternative/additional forms of communication, special tutors or support staff, and nutritious meals'.[103] States Parties must ensure that such support is provided to disabled children by regular schools, which can be achieved through an individual action plan that identifies the different kinds of support required.[104] This individual action plan must be tailored to children's particular needs and be modified according to the circumstances.

The CRPD Committee has expressed its concern that support is either missing or inadequate to a number of States Parties.[105] If the support provided does not actually meet their needs, disabled children will be unable to participate in the general education system. These children might, then, prefer special schools where they are better accommodated. States Parties therefore must offer disabled children different kinds of support in the general education system. The fact that many of them still allocate resources to special schools, however, does not help to increase the availability of that support. This is the case in several Western European states, which have made massive investments in establishing such schools. It is contended that governments ought to transfer resources from the special schools to regular schools in order to realise the right to inclusive education.[106] In Italy, for instance, where special schools were abolished in the 1970s, the provision of support had to be secured by the enactment of domestic legislation.[107] Yet this support has often been inadequate, and the Italian courts have had to remind the different regions of the State Party's duty to make more support teacher hours available to disabled children. Following a decision of the Italian Constitutional Court

[102] Ibid. para. 31.

[103] Vernor Munoz, *The Right to Education of Persons with Disabilities: Report of the Special Rapporteur on the Right to Education* (19 February 2007) A/HRC/4/29, para. 14.

[104] OHCHR (n. 55) 47.

[105] CRPD Committee, Concluding Observations on the Initial Report of Austria (30 September 2013) CRPD/C/AUT/CO/1, para. 40; CRPD Committee, Concluding Observations on the Initial Report of Sweden (12 May 2014) CRPD/C/SWE/CO/1, para. 47; CRPD Committee, Concluding Observations on the Initial Report of Portugal (18 April 2016) CRPD/C/PRT/CO/1, para. 44; CRPD Committee, Concluding Observations on the Initial Report of Denmark (30 October 2014) CRPD/C/DNK/CO/1, para. 52; CRPD Committee, Concluding Observations on the Initial Report of Mexico (27 October 2014) CRPD/C/MEX/CO/1, para. 47(c).

[106] Gauthier de Beco, 'The Right to Inclusive Education According to Article 24 of the UN Convention on the Rights of Persons with Disabilities: Background, Requirements and (Remaining) Questions' (2014) 32 *Netherlands Quarterly of Human Rights* 277.

[107] For further details, see the chapter on Italy by Delia Ferri in the present volume (Chapter 22).

in which it stated that resource availability should not be an obstacle while citing the CRPD on its own motion,[108] a number of regional administrative courts have taken up the issue by annulling individual education plans that included only a limited number of such support teacher hours.[109]

Support supplements reasonable accommodation. Its provision must also be at the expense of the State, which is responsible for the realisation of the right to inclusive education. Since children should not have to pay for their primary education, there is no reason why it should be any different for those who are disabled. Should secondary education entail any cost, disabled children should not be in a position where they have to pay additional costs (such as transport or special educational materials) due to their disability, as often happens in practice. The opposite would be against the prohibition of discrimination provided for in Article 5(2) of the CRPD. It is, however, worth recalling that the provision of support is subject to the notion of progressive realisation (contrary to the duty to provide reasonable accommodation). Consequently, States Parties are not obliged to provide all of this support straightaway, provided that their available resources are used for the purpose of implementing Article 24 of the Convention.

E Individualised Support with the Goal of Full Inclusion

Article 24(2)(e) of the CRPD stipulates that States Parties must ensure that '[e]ffective individualized support measures are provided in environments that maximize academic and social development, consistent with the goal of full inclusion'. At first sight, this provision seems to prescribe the same as Article 24(2)(d), although the wording varies in different ways. What they have in common is the provision of support and the issue of effectiveness. Article 24(2)(e) nonetheless uses a number of different terms that bring another dimension to the support to be provided. In order to understand this dimension, it is worth going back to its drafting history.

In its original proposal, Articles 24(2)(d) and 24(2)(e) of the Convention were a single provision, namely Article 17(3). This provision included a second sentence which indicated that '[i]n exceptional circumstances where the general school system cannot adequately meet the needs of all persons with

108 Italian Constitutional Court, Decision No. 80/2010. See also Italian Constitutional Court, Decision No. 25011/2014.

109 See inter alia Tribunale Amministrativo Regionale (TAR) del Lazio Sezione 3B, Decision No. 2796/2017; TAR per la Sicilia Sezione Terza, Decision No. 557/2017 (cited in the chapter on Italy by Delia Ferri in the present volume, Chapter 22).

disabilities, States Parties shall ensure that effective alternative support measures are provided, consistent with the goal of full inclusion'.[110] The drafters could not agree at that time on whether inclusive education had to be the norm for disabled children. '[E]ffective alternative support measures' were indeed to be understood as special education or a mixed form of education.[111] The obligation to 'ensure that effective alternative support measures are provided' was subsequently replaced by the obligation to 'ensure that effective *individualized* support measures are provided in environments that maximize academic and social development' (emphasis added). The possibility that 'the general school system cannot adequately meet the needs of all persons with disabilities' was removed in the process. In the end, the whole sentence was moved out in order to become what is now Article 24(2)(e) of the CRPD.

As a result, Articles 24(2)(d) and 24(2)(e) of the Convention underline different aspects of support provision. A first noticeable difference is the term 'individualised'. Article 24(2)(d) refers only to 'support', whereas Article 24(2)(e) mentions 'individualised support'. The latter echoes the importance of taking into account the actual circumstances of any given child. Disability does not refer to a homogenous group of people, but includes people with varied kinds of impairments. As with reasonable accommodation, support does not make sense if it is not adapted to their particular needs. While the provision of support is fundamental for all children, the measures taken towards this end must take into consideration the different situations in which disabled children might find themselves.

The fact that the Convention stipulates that the support must be 'individualised' has been criticised, though, because it escalates 'the difficulties children themselves have with legitimised practices of teaching and learning'.[112] It is true that too much individualisation may lead to further marginalisation. It is therefore important that 'individualised support' does not lead to the stigmatisation of disabled children by unnecessarily singling them out and categorising them as less capable than other children, but that it is integrated into overall educational strategies in order to be equitable and to preserve esteem.

Another difference is the phrase 'environments that maximize academic and social development', which is even more difficult to interpret. This phrase was added when 'effective alternative support measures' was replaced by

110 Report of the Working Group to the Ad Hoc Committee (13 February 2006) A/AC.265/2006/2, Annex II Article 24(4), www.un.org/esa/socdev/enable/rights/ahc7docs/ahc7report-e.pdf, accessed 1 July 2018.

111 Arnardóttir (n. 29) 217.

112 Byrne (n. 21), 241.

'effective individualized support measures' in (former) Article 17(3) of the CRPD. It is moreover found in Article 24(3)(c) of the Convention, which, as discussed in what follows, concerns the education of blind, deaf or deaf-blind people. While a degree of ambiguity remains, it can, however, be argued that Article 24(2)(e) should be read more narrowly than Article 24(3)(c). Article 24(2)(e) provides that 'individualised support' has to be given 'consistent with the goal of full inclusion', which some have interpreted as a requirement of educating all disabled children in regular schools.[113] In addition, Article 24(2)(e) was originally in the drafting process as part of Article 24(2)(d), which does not aim to provide a special regime for a particular group of disabled people.

In view of this, Article 24(2)(e) of the CRPD may point to the requirement of further adaptation in order to meet the needs of disabled children. While the drafters of the Convention initially thought of making an exception to the support that must be provided to these children by regular schools, this exception was eventually removed, although the emphasis on its individualisation was retained. The phrase 'environments that maximize academic and social development', therefore, could mean that this support may be 'individualised' even more and less integrated into the States Parties' overall educational policies. Such support, then, could more so take the form of reasonable accommodation. It can also be seen as an obligation to equip regular schools with specific forms of support with a view to facilitating the transition to inclusive education systems.[114] However, the result should not be a segregated education system, as confirmed by the phrase 'consistent with the goal of full inclusion', which remains the objective of education for disabled children.

IV DEAF, BLIND OR DEAF-BLIND PEOPLE

Article 24(3) of the CRPD provides that States Parties must enable 'persons with disabilities to learn life and social development skills to facilitate their full and equal participation in education and as members of the community'. It focusses, in fact, on the education of people who are deaf, blind or deaf-blind. The phrase 'learn life and social development skills' must be read with

113 Gary Hornby, 'Inclusive Special Education: Development of a New Theory for the Education of Children with Special Educational Needs and Disabilities' (2015) 42 *British Journal of Special Education* 239–240; James Kauffman, Dimitris Anastasiou, Jeanmarie Badar, Jason Travers and Andrew Wiley, 'Inclusive Education Moving Forward' (2016) 32 *Advances in Special Education* 169–171.

114 Gauthier de Beco, 'Transition to Inclusive Education Systems According to the Convention on the Rights of Persons with Disabilities' (2016) 34 *Nordic Journal of Human Rights* 43.

this subgroup of disabled people in mind. Article 24(3) of the Convention therefore deals principally, though not exclusively, with different forms of communication.

Article 24(3) is probably the most difficult to interpret and reflects again the controversy surrounding the education of disabled people during the drafting process of the Convention. Before inquiring further into this negotiation, it is worth mentioning some singular characteristics of the group concerned. Although the CRPD mentions 'sensory impairments' in its scope of application,[115] persons who are deaf do not necessarily regard themselves as disabled. Rather, deaf people may self-identify as members of a cultural and/or linguistic community and, in equal manner, view sign language as much more than a tool of communication.[116] As such, they lay claim to a shared and distinct identity associated to 'Deaf culture'.

During the Convention's negotiation, organisations representing people who are deaf, blind or deaf-blind emphasised their often negative experience of inclusive education (pointing to the failures of purportedly inclusive education systems to accommodate these people effectively), and also feared that the objective was to assimilate them and, thereby, ignore their singular characteristics. As indicated by the WBU, WFD and DbI, 'inclusion as a simple placement in a regular school without meaningful interaction with classmates and professionals at all times is tantamount to exclusion'.[117] These representative organisations defended therefore the position that deaf, blind or deaf-blind children must have the possibility of attending special schools.[118] They advanced the argument that special education was often the best way of educating such children, while stressing the need to give them the opportunity to maintain and to develop relationships with those who have a similar kind of impairment.[119] Achieving this in every single regular school would actually be impossible for many of them, especially in countries with a lower amount of resources. The problem means that uncertainty remains as to how to provide inclusive education to those who are deaf, blind or deaf-blind.

The question, then, was whether and how Article 24 of the CRPD would provide an exception to the goal of inclusive education. While the text makes

115 Article 1, CRPD.

116 Sarah Batterbury, 'Language Justice for Sign Language Peoples: The UN Convention on the Rights of Persons with Disabilities' (2012) 11 *Language Policy* 256–258.

117 WBU, WFD and DbI, 'Article 17 Statement on Inclusive Education for Persons Who Are Deaf, Blind and Deafblind: The Rationale for Choice in Education' https://static.un.org/esa/socdev/enable/rights/ahcstata24sevscomments.htm#multi, accessed 1 July 2018.

118 Seventh Session, 'Comments, Proposals and Amendments Submitted Electronically' https://static.un.org/esa/socdev/enable/rights/ahcstata24sevscomments.htm, accessed 1 July 2018.

119 Kayess and Green (n. 27) 66.

no explicit exception for deaf, blind or deaf-blind people, Article 24(3)(c) has sometimes been interpreted in this way. It was, however, well understood by the drafters that such a position would undermine the general principles and, arguably, the very purpose of the Convention. It would also oblige States Parties to uphold both an inclusive and a segregated education system. Article 24(3) must be understood in light of this dilemma. As with several other questions, the ambiguity of Article 24 is an indication that the drafters left the matter open to interpretation, which means that the debate around what this provision entails is still unsettled.

Article 24(3)(a) of the CRPD requires that States Parties must facilitate the 'learning of Braille, alternative script, augmentative and alternative modes, means and formats of communication and orientation and mobility skills, and facilitating peer support and mentoring'. This provision reflects the aforementioned discussion on the education of deaf, blind or deaf-blind children. While the greatest attention goes to the different forms of communication, other aspects are highlighted, including 'peer support and mentoring'. These aspects as well as 'orientation and mobility skills' concern not only those who are deaf, blind or deaf-blind but also people with other kinds of impairment[120] and, perhaps, some who are not considered disabled at all. Thus, the CRPD Committee recommends that States Parties 'invest in developing expertise, technology and services in order to promote access to appropriate technology and alternative communication systems to facilitate learning' and 'provide the required support, including by way of resources, assisted technology, and provision of orientation and mobility skills'.[121] Article 24(3)(a) of the Convention nonetheless is silent about the environment where the measures outlined must be implemented. Given the general aim of Article 24 and the object of Article 24(3)(a), it can be argued that these measures are relevant for any regular schools.

Article 24(3)(b) of the CRPD provides that States Parties must also facilitate 'the learning of sign language and the promotion of the linguistic identity of the deaf community', and links to the recognition of 'linguistic identity' in Article 30(4) of the Convention.[122] Despite the crucial function and, indeed,

[120] Arnardóttir (n. 29) 220. The CRPD Committee has also referred to 'persons on the autism spectrum' in its discussions on Article 24(3) of the Convention (General Comment No. 4 [n. 6] para. 33).

[121] General Comment No. 4 (n. 6) para. 34.

[122] Article 30(4) stipulates that disabled people must 'be entitled, on an equal basis with others, to recognition and support of their specific cultural and linguistic identity, including sign languages and deaf culture' (note the term 'deaf' without capital letter, though). It thereby specifies further what is meant by 'linguistic identity'.

victory, of this provision for the 'deaf community', it has unfortunately not been given much attention to date, except by that community, albeit only recently. Article 24(3)(b) goes clearly beyond the different forms of communication and takes account of the singular characteristics of deaf people. The term 'linguistic identity' is the result of the understanding of the Convention's drafters that these people again see themselves as a cultural and/or linguistic minority. How 'the promotion of the linguistic identity of the deaf community' should be achieved by States Parties to the Convention remains an unanswered question, however. The CRPD Committee simply advises that deaf people 'must be provided with the opportunity to learn sign language, and measures taken to recognise and promote the linguistic identity of the deaf community'.[123] More guidance will be required if this objective is to be reached.

Finally, Article 24(3)(c) of the CRPD provides that States Parties must ensure that 'the education of persons, and in particular children, who are blind, deaf or deafblind, is delivered in the most appropriate languages and modes and means of communication for the individual, and in environments which maximize academic and social development'. This is probably the most delicate provision in Article 24. While it has been argued that this provision is a 'masterpiece' and the credit should go to its facilitator, Rosemary Kayess,[124] it is at the same time a 'ticking bomb'. To be sure, it was the best compromise that could have been found to resolve the issue.

Article 24(3)(c) is the only paragraph that explicitly mentions 'blind, deaf or deafblind' people (besides the 'deaf community' in Article 24(3)(b)), and none of these terms are used elsewhere in Article 24, or indeed in the rest of the CRPD.[125] The Convention, moreover, does not focus more on any other particular group of disabled people as much as it does with these people. It is therefore clear for whom Article 24(3)(c) is intended. The phrase 'in environments which maximize academic and social development' has attracted particular attention and is generally regarded as code for the term 'special education'.[126] It is therefore understood as an authorisation to educate blind, deaf or deaf-blind children in special schools. Such children would have the option to attend these schools, although they should not be prevented from participating in the general education system.

[123] General Comment No. 4 (n. 6) para. 34.

[124] Theresia Degener, 'A Human Rights Model of Disability' in Blanck and Flynn (n. 27) 39–40.

[125] Article 30(4) of the CRPD also refers to 'deaf culture'. See also n. 122.

[126] Arnardóttir (n. 29) 219–220.

The interpretation of this provision continues to evolve, even among those organisations who advocated strongly for the preservation of parental choice for special schools. While the WBU, WFD and DbI have started to inquire as to whether and how the goal of inclusive education can be adequately attained with regard to blind, deaf or deaf-blind children, they continue to advocate for offering them the possibility of attending such schools.[127] At the same time, upholding a segregated education system would be in clear contradiction with the prohibition of discrimination, and would resuscitate the principle of 'separate but equal' for a particular group of disabled people.[128] There is no indication that the CRPD Committee sees things differently.

A remaining issue is that the phrase 'in environments that maximize academic and social development' is used not only in Article 24(3)(c) of the CRPD. This phrase is also to be found in Article 24(2)(d) of the Convention, yet in that case it is accompanied by the qualification that such environments be 'consistent with the goal of full inclusion'.[129] The result is as follows. On the one hand, Article 24(2)(d) includes terminology that is elsewhere applicable to the education of blind, deaf or deaf-blind people, and consistent with the position of those who still view inclusive education with apprehension. On the other hand, Article 24(3)(c) omits the phrase 'consistent with the goal of full inclusion', which raises the question whether the phrase 'environments which maximize academic and social development' refers to an 'inclusive education system'.[130] While the former seems (Article 24(2)(d)) to at one and the same time embrace segregated and inclusive education, pushing in opposite directions, the latter (Article 24(3)(c)) is not altogether clear. Taken in combination, these provisions create confusion and internal inconsistency.

127 Joseph Murray, Maartje De Meulder and Delphine le Maire, 'An Education in Sign Language as a Human Right? The Sensory Exception in the Legislative History and Ongoing Interpretation of Article 24 of the UN Convention on the Rights of Persons with Disabilities' (2018) 40 (1) *Human Rights Quarterly* 59–60.

128 Kayess and Green (n. 27), 67.

129 Articles 24(2)(d) and 24(3)(c) of the Convention use exactly the same expression with the minor exception that the term 'that' in Article 24(2)(d) has been replaced by 'which' in Article 24(3)(c).

130 The CRPD Committee, however, recommended that 'for such *inclusive* environments to occur, States Parties should provide the required support, including by way of resources, assisted technology, and provision of orientation and mobility skills' (General Comment No. 4 [n. 6] para. 34) (emphasis added). The term 'environments' would thus refer to an 'inclusive education system' in the eyes of the Committee even though it did not state this explicitly.

V TEACHERS

Article 24(4) of the CRPD provides that States Parties must take measures to 'employ teachers, including teachers with disabilities, who are qualified in sign language and/or Braille, and to train professionals and staff who work at all levels of education'. Article 24(4) deals with an important precondition for the provision of inclusive education. Although it highlights 'sign language and/or Braille' – thereby focussing again on the education of blind, deaf or deaf-blind people – it is relevant for all disabled children. Perhaps it is even the starting point for the development of an 'inclusive education system', especially since training students takes a certain period of time and affects the competences of the next generation of teachers.

Article 24(4) provides that States Parties must 'take appropriate measures . . . to train professionals and staff who work at all levels of education'. As indicated by the CRPD Committee, States Parties must 'ensure that all teachers are trained in inclusive education'.[131] The scope of the training must be broad so that teachers are able to accommodate disabled children on the whole. Article 24(4) further specifies that '[s]uch training shall incorporate disability awareness and the use of appropriate augmentative and alternative modes, means and formats of communication, educational techniques and materials to support persons with disabilities'. This has been requested, for instance, by the Western Cape High Court in South Africa.[132] Teachers should, therefore, not only master different tools of communication but also be able to adapt their teaching methods to the particular needs of disabled children. This includes training in techniques such as 'the provision of individualized instruction; teaching the same content using varied teaching methods to respond to the learning styles and unique abilities of each person; the development and use of individual educational plans to support specific learning requirements; and the introduction of a pedagogy centred around students' educational objectives'.[133]

Thus, teachers should be enabled to change their educational methods and to utilise new forms of target assessments. In order to do so, they should receive adequate support by regular schools.[134] It is also important that teachers

[131] General Comment No. 4 (n. 6) para. 35.

[132] *Western Cape Forum for Intellectual Disability* v. *Government of the Republic of South Africa and another* [2010] ZAWCHC 544, 2011 (5) SA 87.

[133] Ibid. para. 69.

[134] Ibid. para. 25. See also CRPD Committee, Concluding Observations on the Initial Report of Gabon (2 October 2015) CRPD/C/GAB/CO/1, para. 53; CRPD Committee, Concluding Observations on the Initial Report of Qatar (2 October 2015) CRPD/C/QAT/CO/1, para. 44;

continue to be supported during their teaching career. It is necessary to train them on how to deal with issues related to disability, not only through their core training but also through their continuing education.[135]

Furthermore, Article 24(4) of the CRPD emphasises an important element of realising the right to inclusive education. It points out – albeit indirectly – that the corpus of teachers should encompass people who are disabled themselves, as can be seen from the phrase 'including teachers with disabilities'. As with any other right protected by the Convention, the right to inclusive education requires the involvement of disabled people for its implementation. This is an issue that deserves more attention, as the employment of disabled people in regular schools can be a stepping stone towards greater understanding of the ways of achieving inclusive education. In the words of the CRPD Committee, the inclusion of teachers with disabilities 'will serve to promote equal rights for persons with disabilities to enter the teaching profession, bring unique expertise and skills into learning environments, contribute to breaking down barriers and serve as important role models'.[136] For this to be achieved, it is necessary to facilitate their inclusion in teacher programmes and to encourage more disabled people to become teachers.

Despite its essential function for realising the right to inclusive education, teachers by and large lack the knowledge and skills for the effective accommodation of disabled children (which was one of the reasons why special schools were established in the first place). The CRPD Committee has noted that teacher education is woefully inadequate to implement Article 24 in many States Parties to the Convention.[137] From the teachers' perspective, it should, however, be noted that staff members frequently have to work in isolation with pressure from school administrators to meet educational targets and without help to find adequate solutions.[138] As a result, they are afraid that they will not be able to cope with disabled children and that inclusive education will in fact increase their workload. Another problem is that disability as a rule remains an optional course in university curricula or a topic taught in order to subsequently find employment in special schools. The CRPD Committee has

CRPD Committee, Concluding Observations on the Initial Report of Colombia (30 September 2016) CRPD/C/COL/CO/1, para. 55.

135 Global Campaign for Education and Handicap International (n. 52) 24.

136 General Comment No. 4 (n. 6) para. 36.

137 CRPD Committee, Concluding Observations on the Initial Report of the United Arab Emirates (3 October 2016) CRPD/C/ARE/CO/1, para. 44(c); CRPD Committee, Concluding Observations on the Initial Report of El Salvador (8 October 2013) CRPD/C/SLV/CO/1, para. 22.

138 UNICEF, *The State of the World's Children 2013: Children with Disabilities* (UNICEF 2013) 33.

expressed its regret that the training of staff members remains within the framework of special education.[139] Training on inclusive education should not be included only in specialisation courses but also in any teacher programmes which must pay attention to the existence of human diversity.

VI HIGHER EDUCATION

Article 24(5) of the CRPD – the last paragraph of Article 24 – stipulates that States Parties must guarantee that 'persons with disabilities are able to access general tertiary education, vocational training, adult education and lifelong learning without discrimination and on an equal basis with others', and also to ensure 'that reasonable accommodation is provided to persons with disabilities'. This provision addresses post-secondary education. Article 24(5) signals the interest of the drafters of the Convention to ensure coverage of education throughout the life course.[140] It was necessary since Article 24(2)(b) does not mention higher levels of education. Although Article 24(5) does not say so explicitly, there is no doubt that its purpose here is likewise to provide access to inclusive education. Article 24(1) moreover provides that States Parties must 'ensure an inclusive education system at all levels and life long learning' and, thereby, covers the higher levels of education.

The CRPD strengthens the protection of disabled people in higher education by going beyond the standards of the ICESCR.[141] Article 13(2)(c) of the ICESCR provides that '[h]igher education shall be made equally accessible to all, on the basis of capacity, by every appropriate means, and in particular by the progressive introduction of free education'. This provision uses the phrase 'on the basis of capacity', which can be prejudicial to disabled people, because it may automatically rule out access for these people (in particular in the case of intellectual disabilities). While it is true that some of them will have no such access in practice, others might be able to pursue higher education if the necessary adaptations are made to meet their needs. Moreover, Article 13(2)(c) of the ICESCR recalls the issue of progressiveness in contrast to Article 24(5) of the CRPD. While Article 24 of the Convention does not align the higher levels

[139] CRPD Committee, Concluding Observations on the Initial Report of Costa Rica (12 May 2014) CRPD/C/CRI/CO/1, para. 45.

[140] It is regrettable in this regard that the Convention does not deal with early education, including preschool, considering its importance to achieve inclusive education at further levels of education.

[141] The CRC does not address post-secondary education, as its scope of application is limited to children.

of education with secondary education, it limits itself to require 'access . . . on an equal basis with others'. This stronger protection is reflected in the CRPD Committee's recommendation that '[a]ttitudinal, physical, linguistic, communication, financial, legal and other barriers to education at these levels must be identified and removed in order to ensure equal access'.[142]

Higher education is an important pathway to employment opportunities for disabled people. Article 24(5) of the Convention, therefore, is strongly related to the right to work, especially since it also refers to 'education and lifelong learning'. As with inclusive education in general, Universal Design for Learning (UDL) has been promoted in the context of higher education in order to improve access to course materials and communication with teachers.[143] Another issue is 'vocational training', which is listed in Article 24(5) but has received little attention despite the fact that many disabled people are oriented to vocational training in practice. SDG 4 focusses on this issue both in general terms and in relation to disabled people.[144]

Finally, Article 24(5) of the CRPD stipulates that States Parties must ensure that 'reasonable accommodation is provided to' disabled people. This provision is a repetition of the duty to provide such accommodation guaranteed by Article 24(2)(c) of the Convention, which applies to all levels of education. What has been said in relation to Article 24(2)(c), therefore, is applicable here. States Parties must ensure that reasonable accommodation is made so that disabled people can have access to 'general tertiary education, vocational training, adult education and lifelong learning'. The explicit reference to the duty to provide reasonable accommodation probably aims to avoid higher education falling through the net, and to stress that inclusive education does not stop after traditional schooling. Some States have emerging good practice in making higher education more accessible to disabled students, such as the United States (which is not a State Party to the CRPD), where universities have tried to make reasonable accommodation more available to such students pursuant to the Americans with Disability Act (ADA) as well as the Rehabilitation Act.[145] That being said, much more work is needed to open up

142 General Comment No. 4 (n. 6) para. 37.

143 Tracy Hall and Skip Stahl, 'Using Universal Design for Learning to Expand Access to Higher Education' in Mike Adams and Sally Brown (eds), *Towards Inclusive Learning in Higher Education: Developing Curricula for Disabled Students* (Routledge 2006) 72–73.

144 SDG Target 4.4 also commits states to 'substantially increase the number of youth and adults who have relevant skills, including technical and vocational skills, for employment, decent jobs and entrepreneurship'. See also n. 3.

145 Laura Rothstein, 'Forty Years of Disability Policy in Legal Education and the Legal Profession: What Has Changed and What Are the New Issues?' (2014) 22 *American*

higher education to disabled students.[146] In addition, more attention is required to ensure accessibility to non-university programmes, especially in 'vocational training, adult education and lifelong learning', as disabled people remain disproportionally underemployed in modern societies.

CONCLUSION

This chapter provided a comprehensive legal analysis of Article 24 of the CRPD. The purpose was both to analyse its core content and to assess existing issues of contention in its interpretation. Many of these provisions and issues are also discussed further throughout the present volume.

The CRPD proclaims the right to inclusive education. Although this right started to take shape prior to the CRPD, the Convention is the first human rights treaty to do so explicitly. Article 24(1) exhorts States Parties to set up 'an inclusive education system', while declaring what the aims of developing such an 'inclusive education system' are. Article 24(2) goes on to identify a series of measures for the realisation of the right to inclusive education. Article 24(3) focusses on the education of deaf, blind or deaf-blind people, and Article 24(4) underscores the vital role of training in inclusive education. Article 24(5) finally deals with post-secondary education. In this way, Article 24 of the CRPD provides comprehensive coverage of the right to inclusive education, as can be seen from its length. It not only establishes the objectives of the Convention in this regard but also outlines the steps to be taken in order to attain these objectives.

However, the examination of Article 24 of the Convention is still in its infancy. Despite the importance of the education of disabled people, it remains largely underexplored. While clarifying a number of points, the present chapter sought to answer some of the essential questions surrounding the right to inclusive education, making use of the most up-to-date available jurisprudence and scholarship on the topic. Article 24 will of course continue to spur debate, and this chapter is by no means the last word. It will yet hopefully set a benchmark for all stakeholders, and offer some clarification to the numerous misunderstandings about its content.

University Journal of Gender Social Policy and Law 519; Kevin Smith, 'Disabilities, Law Schools, and Law Students: A Proactive and Holistic Approach' (1999) 32 *Akron Law Review* 1.

146 For a more detailed discussion on the issue, see the chapter on 'Advancing the Right to Inclusive Education in Development Cooperation' by Janet Lord in the present volume.

PART II

THEORETICAL FOUNDATIONS

A

CONCEPTUAL ISSUES

4

Moving towards Schools for All

Examining the Concept of Educational Inclusion for Disabled Children and Young People

Michael Shevlin

The concept of societal inclusion has achieved international prominence in the past couple of decades and is referenced in the policies adopted by international bodies and appears regularly in policy documents produced by national governments. However, despite this prominence, societal inclusion remains an elusive concept, and an agreed definition of its meaning has not emerged. This is understandable given the variety of influences and ideologies that have blended to produce the concept of an inclusive society. This chapter focusses on the emergence and development of educational inclusion within the context of the shift towards a more inclusive society. An historical overview examines how segregated educational provision became an established feature of educational provision for disabled children and young people. The origins of change are examined within the context of greater recognition of the exclusion marginalised groups experience within society. The move towards more integrated provision is addressed along with the inherent shortcomings that made these developments increasingly obsolete as inclusive perspectives gained prominence. The influence of supranational bodies who advocated for a more socially inclusive society on international developments is examined. The increasing prominence of educational inclusion within the education system is analysed, and the implications for educational provision are explored.

HISTORICAL OVERVIEW

In order to understand how the concept of educational inclusion has evolved, an understanding of the historical perspectives informing the development of special education is essential. Disabled people had occupied a marginal position within society over the centuries, and attitudes were heavily influenced by belief systems that attributed many disabling conditions to supernatural or demonological causes.[1] Poverty and disability remained closely related and in certain periods, begging by disabled people attracted contrasting responses. On the one hand, disabled people were viewed as a social menace, while from a religious perspective, the presence of disabled people was seen as an opportunity to give alms and to please God through this charitable action. Disability was a serious impediment to social and economic participation, and disabled people tended to be regarded as inferior with few rights or privileges.[2] Education for disabled people was not seen as a priority and only emerged in the middle of the eighteenth century, prompted by the philosophy and principles of the European Enlightenment.[3] Innovative pedagogies were developed to support those who were deaf, blind, and intellectually disabled, and these initiatives emerged initially in France and later in continental Europe, Britain and North America. Educational interventions, despite national variations, tended to follow a common pattern, with those who were deaf as the initial recipients, followed by those who were blind and, finally, those who had an intellectual disability. The European Enlightenment movement was characterised by a humanitarian philosophy informed by beliefs about the equality of all people and the human responsibility to care for others within society. As a result, reform movements were established to address the inequalities experienced by marginalised groups within society, including disabled people, poor people, slaves and those deemed insane. Pioneering educators devised a variety of strategies to address the educational needs of disabled people, including sign language for the deaf, a raised print method for the blind and an appropriate pedagogy for those who were intellectually disabled. In the early nineteenth century, institutional provision was established and tended to be informed and supported by a humanitarian philosophy and evangelical beliefs. Three major principles of child rescue – protection, separation and dependence – informed institutional developments. It was envisaged that these institutions would protect the most vulnerable (disabled/disenfranchised); however, the very existence of these institutions limited opportunities within wider society for disabled children and young people.[4] A sociological analysis of this type of provision would maintain that these institutions served as a form of social control by separating those who were disabled and often deemed to have

1 David L. Braddock and Susan L. Parish, 'An Institutional History of Disability' in Gary L. Albrecht, Katherine D. Seelman and Michael Bury (eds), *Handbook of Disability Studies* (Sage 2001) 11–68.

2 Margret A. Winzer, 'Confronting Difference: An Excursion through the History of Special Education' in Lani Florian (ed.), *The Sage Handbook of Special Education* (Sage 2007) 23.

3 Ibid. 21.

4 Sally Tomlinson, *A Sociology of Special Education* (Routledge and Kegan Paul 1982).

extraordinary needs from their peers, who could continue with their schooling without any interference from disabled children and young people.[5] These institutions developed as public charities whose inmates were designated as different and deficient.

In the early twentieth century, as general schooling became more organised and came under the remit of the state, special classes within regular schools emerged to accommodate those deemed intellectually deficient or capable of undesirable behaviour. Compulsory attendance laws forced the state to make provision for disabled children and young people, generally through institutions and emergent segregated classes. Parallel systems of regular and special education became established with different locations, specialised training for teachers in special education settings and the development of specialist provision, including therapeutic disciplines.[6] Many interlinked factors had a considerable influence on developments within special education, including the testing movement, developments in the disciplines of psychology and psychiatry, the mental hygiene movement and persistent complaints about the efficacy of public residential institutions.[7] The educational segregation of disabled people was considerably strengthened by the nascent science of psychometrics and an emerging eugenics movement. In Britain and the United States, the idea that intelligence was a fixed entity assumed prominence, and psychometric testing was used to establish categories of disabilities applied to disabled children who were then to be accommodated within segregated settings. The psychometric tests were often subject to cultural bias, which resulted in disproportionate numbers of African Americans, members of immigrant communities and families experiencing poverty being classified as learning disabled and assigned to segregated settings. The eugenics movement was supported by many eminent psychiatrists, doctors, scientists, politicians and political commentators. Supporters of the eugenics movement argued that people with intellectual disabilities constituted a social menace associated with increased criminality and immoral behaviour.[8] As a result, a number of countries pursued a sterilisation policy over many decades designed to protect the general population from this

5 Sally Tomlinson, 'The Expansion of Special Education' (1985) 11 *Oxford Review of Education* 157, 158.

6 Sally Beveridge, *Special Educational Needs in Schools* (2nd edn) (Routledge 1999) 4.

7 Gary Thomas, David Walker and Julie Webb, *The Making of the Inclusive School* (Routledge 1997) 3.

8 Adrienne Asch, 'Disability, Bioethics and Human Rights' in Gary L. Albrecht, Katherine D. Seelman and Michael Bury (eds), *Handbook of Disability Studies* (Sage 2001) 298.

imminent social menace.[9] Segregated educational provision became the norm.

TRACING THE ORIGINS OF CHANGE

Segregated educational provision remained largely unchallenged until the 1960s, when the civil rights movement in the United States and the normalisation movement in Scandinavia challenged the societal attitudes and approaches to disenfranchised and marginalised groups.[10] Minority ethnic groups challenged the barriers preventing their full participation in society, and this provided a powerful stimulus to profound changes in policy and practice. Other marginalised groups, including those with a disability, copied this example. This resulted in a serious questioning of the role of educational bodies and professionals in the conceptualisation and delivery of special educational provision. This marked the beginning of an authentic movement towards dismantling institutional segregated provision and establishing more integrated special educational provision. The normalisation movement originating in Scandinavian countries provided another powerful rationale for significant change in overall provision for disabled people, and this had an impact on how special educational provision was conceptualised and delivered. The specialisation of services developed for disabled people (medical, educational, social) inevitably resulted in separate provisions supported by highly trained professionals. According to normalisation principles, disabled people should be enabled to participate in the mainstream of community life and live their lives as close to the cultural norm as possible.[11] Education, health and social services needed to be reoriented towards an integration framework designed to ensure that disabled people could participate to the greatest extent possible in their communities. The practice of segregated educational provision was challenged as it appeared to violate these normalisation principles.

Existing special educational provision began to be critiqued in parallel with the civil rights movement and the development of normalisation principles. Goffman, for example, challenged the rationale for separate provision and concluded that this type of provision enabled mainstream provision to avoid the challenges involved in responding appropriately to diversity of needs.[12]

9 Ibid.

10 Doug Biklen, 'Achieving the Complete School' in Gary Thomas and Mark Vaughan (eds), *Inclusive Education: Readings and Reflections* (Oxford University Press 2004) 74.

11 Ibid. 78.

12 Erving Goffman, *Asylums: Essays on the Social Situation of Mental Patients and Other Inmates* (Pelican Books 1968).

Dunn reinforced this perspective through his analysis of the inadequacies of special educational provision.[13] He asserted that poverty and social deprivation were major contributory factors to the learning difficulties experienced by children labelled as 'mildly mentally retarded' rather than inherent within-child factors. Furthermore, he pointed out that the special programmes had not resulted in a significant increase in the learning outcomes for children and young people receiving special educational provision. Dunn was particularly concerned about the negative impact of the special needs label on children's self-esteem and how their life opportunities were often shaped by their experience of special educational provision.

The United States enacted legislation to respond to the serious issues raised by the civil rights movement and the critique of existing special educational provision. Public Law 94–142 (1975) marked a significant breakthrough in the shift away from segregated provision towards more integrated settings where disabled children and young people could be enabled to learn alongside their peers. This federal law required states to provide free appropriate public education for disabled children and young people aged three to twenty-one years. The legislation also introduced the concept of the 'least restrictive environment', which meant that these children and young people should be placed in the 'least restrictive environment' where their educational needs could be appropriately met.

A parallel process had also emerged in the United Kingdom and culminated in the Warnock Report, which provided a national review of special educational provision.[14] The Report challenged the traditional practice of identifying the child according to a category of disability and assigning the child to a special disability-specific school. The Report concluded that this approach to education for disabled children and young people was inappropriate. Identifying children according to disability categories often stigmatised them and provided limited relevant information about their actual educational needs. In fact, children with the same disability label were treated as a homogeneous group with broadly similar educational needs, yet in practice, these needs often varied widely. The Report decided to replace the existing multiple categories of disability with the generic term 'special educational need'. This term applied to any pupil who required additional educational support (either short or long term) focussed on specific aspects of learning/

[13] Lloyd M. Dunn, 'Special Education for the Mildly Retarded: Is Much of It Justifiable?' (1968) 35 *Exceptional Children* 5, 10.

[14] Department of Education and Science, *Report of the Committee of Enquiry into the Education of Handicapped Children and Young People* (Cmnd 7212, 1978).

subjects or more generally across the majority of subjects. The Warnock Report marked a significant shift away from the traditional conceptualisation of educational needs according to assigned disability category and represented:

> an explicit attempt to break with traditional notions of educational difficulty as being primarily rooted and fixed within the individual child. It did not deny that within-child factors can have a significant impact on learning, but the concept of special educational need which was put forward was far more concerned with the interaction between the child and the learning contexts which the child experiences.[15]

INTEGRATION

Advocates of integration cogently argued that the integration of disabled pupils involved a fundamental moral choice for society.[16] Enabling disabled pupils to participate fully in the educational system became a question of how committed governments were to developing more equitable systems of educational provision that valued diversity. More equitable provision should reduce the marginalisation and stigmatisation experienced by disabled pupils and their families. As a result, addressing the issue of equity for disabled pupils and their families would contribute to the development of more tolerant societies capable of responding appropriately to diversity. Advocates of integration anticipated that integrated education would be of benefit to disabled pupils and their same-age peers. However, despite agreement about the fundamental thrust of the integration movement, no generally accepted definition of integration emerged. This was probably due to the wide variation in special educational provision across and within countries, which rendered it difficult to make judgements about levels of integration in place in each jurisdiction.[17]

It is clear that the Warnock Report (United Kingdom) and enabling legislation (United States) marked significant turning points in the thinking around disability/special educational needs and the organisation and delivery of special educational provisions.[18] Immediate improvements were evident as

[15] Beveridge (n. 6) 4.

[16] Thomas Hehir, *New Directions in Special Education: Eliminating Ableism in Policy and Practice* (Harvard Education Press 2005) 65.

[17] Sip Jan Pijl, Cor J. W. Meijer and Seamus Hegarty, *Inclusive Education: A Global Agenda* (Routledge 1997) 3.

[18] Seamus Hegarty, 'Reviewing the Literature on Integration' (1993) 8 *European Journal of Special Needs Education* 194, 195.

increased funding was made available, enabling legislation was enacted and parents became more active participants in the decision-making processes around the education of their children. Developing integrated educational provision involved all participants and stakeholders in education and had moved significantly from its traditional marginalised position.

The Warnock Committee identified three main types of integration:[19] locational, social and functional. Locational integration was characterised by the placement of disabled pupils within a mainstream setting, though often in a special unit/class with little interaction between disabled pupils and their same-age peers. Social integration focussed on enabling disabled pupils to interact socially with their same-age peers, though not necessarily in shared classrooms. Functional integration was epitomised by the participation of disabled pupils in mainstream classrooms alongside their same-age peers.

Policy options regarding integration varied across countries, and three broad policy options in integration practices can be identified.[20] In countries such as Italy and Sweden, a 'one-track' integration policy operated where disabled children were educated in mainstream schools alongside their same-age peers to the greatest possible extent. 'Two-track' integration policies were evident in the Netherlands, Belgium and Germany, where the two parallel school systems existed and worked independently of each other. The third group of countries, including Denmark, England and Wales and the United States, followed 'multi-track' policies where a flexible system of educational provision was devised, and a continuum of services was made available to disabled pupils. It was clear that how the concept of need was conceptualised often determined the type of educational provision available. The belief that learning difficulties arose from individual pupil deficits resulted in an emphasis on separate educational provision, whereas flexible and responsive systems of provision tended to be associated with the belief that learning difficulties are caused by a combination of individual and environmental factors.

Provision in the United Kingdom spanned a continuum from greater levels to lesser forms of integration where the disabled child[21] (a) was fully included in class and an active participant in curricular activities; (b) received specialist support within class; (c) was withdrawn from mainstream class for specialist work; (d) was part time in special class and part time in ordinary class; (e) was full time in special class in mainstream school; (f) was part time in special

19 Department of Education and Science (Cmnd 7212, 1978) (n. 14) 100–101.

20 Sip J. Pijl and Cor J. W. Meijer, 'Does Integration Count for Much? An Analysis of the Practices of Integration in Eight Countries' (1991) 6 *European Journal of Special Needs Education* 100, 101.

21 Hegarty (n. 18) 197.

school and part time in mainstream school. The first level of integration requires all teachers (not just specialist teachers) to be competent in teaching disabled children and represents a considerable challenge to many schools. The special class option could be regarded as little more than locational integration. This representation of the continuum of integration arrangements enables us to understand a very complex reality. The process of integration did not consist of a smooth progression from more segregated to more integrated provisions. This type of transition requires an alignment between the national special education policy, how resources are distributed and the development of the capacity of schools to deliver integrated provisions.

The research literature on integration identified three broad strands:[22] (i) investigations of the effectiveness of segregated and/or integrated provision; (ii) features of successful integration programmes; (iii) the centrality of attitudinal factors. Analysing the effectiveness of segregated and integrated provisions proved very difficult due to the immense variety of variables involved in each type of provision. The results of studies of social and academic outcomes for disabled children and young people from each type of provision proved inconclusive. Advocates of integration maintained that unless segregated provision is demonstrably superior to integrated provision, it is difficult to justify its existence. Proponents of separate and integrated provision engaged in highly politicised debates where the location rather than the quality of provision became the dominant feature. Hegarty concluded that '[t]here has to be a presumption in favour of integration and, in the absence of decisive countervailing evidence, it must be regarded as a central principle governing provision'.[23]

However, by the 1990s, it was becoming increasingly evident that progress towards integration was inconsistent. Despite the enabling legislation and ground-breaking national and international reports, enormous divisions remained between proponents of separate and integrated provision. There appeared to be a number of reasons why progress towards integration was intermittent. Long-established patterns of separate provision proved resistant to change and support for integration within mainstream schools was limited. Integrated provision tended to be conceptualised in placement terms rather than considering the support infrastructure required to deliver effective educational provision for disabled children and young people: 'Placement in

22 Thomas M. Skrtic, *Behind Special Education: A Critical Analysis of Professional Culture and School Organisations* (Love Publishing Company 1991).

23 Hegarty (n. 18) 198.

a mainstream school is a necessary, but not a sufficient, condition for realising the goals of integration.'[24]

It became increasingly evident that the arguments about choosing between separate and integrated provision were becoming sterile and unproductive. A new paradigm was needed to address how disabled children and young people can be fully included within mainstream provision. This would require a fundamental overhaul of existing mainstream provision and a re-orientation of teaching, curricula and accreditation to address the learning needs of all children. There was evidence that some groups of disabled children (physical/sensory) were making more progress in mainstream provision than others (emotional/behavioural difficulties, mild/moderate intellectual disability). This appeared to support the emerging contention that there were limits to the types of children that can be successfully integrated in mainstream schools. There has been a gradual acceptance that '[i]ntegration is in the end a matter of school reform. It entails creating schools that respond to students' individual differences within a common framework'.[25]

INTERNATIONAL PERSPECTIVES

The rights of persons with disabilities have been the focus of sustained attention in the United Nations and other international organisations over a prolonged period of time. Over the past forty years, international conventions and agreements have had a significant impact in the promotion of the inclusion of people with disabilities within mainstream society.[26] In 1975, for example, the UN Declaration on the Rights of Disabled Persons called on states to encourage the integration of people with disabilities into all aspects of the economic and social life of mainstream society.[27] The World Programme of Action,[28] initiated by the UN in 1982 and building on earlier UN initiatives, had a strong focus on education and promoted the equalisation of opportunities for people with disabilities and their full participation in society. The World Programme of Action Concerning Disabled Persons emerged from the designated International Year of Disabled Persons, 1981 (adopted by the UN General Assembly in 1982). The International Year and the World Programme of Action provided a strong momentum for significant progress in

24 Ann Lewis, *Children's Understanding of Disability* (Routledge 1995) 4.

25 Hegarty (n. 18) 199.

26 Sonali Shah and Mark Priestley, *Disability and Social Change: Private Lives and Public Policies* (Policy Press 2011).

27 United Nations General Assembly Res. 3447 (XXX) 9 December 1975.

28 United Nations General Assembly Res. 37/52 (3 December 1982) UN Doc A/RES/37/52.

promoting the rights of people with disabilities to the same opportunities as other citizens to equitable access to education and employment. For the first time, this World Programme recognised that people with disabilities were often rendered disabled by a disabling society which failed to address their need to participate on an equal basis with other citizens within society.

The World Declaration on Education for All (1990) expanded on earlier UN initiatives by focussing specifically on the urgent need to develop international and national structures to meet the basic learning needs of all children, including those with disabilities.[29] It was pointed out that the assertion in the Universal Declaration of Human Rights that 'everyone has a right to education' was not the current reality for many children throughout the world. It was acknowledged that the world faced many difficult and intractable problems such as mounting debt burdens, widening economic disparities and high levels of infant mortality which severely limited attempts to guarantee that basic learning needs are addressed. It is recognised that meeting basic learning needs:

> empowers individuals in any society and confers upon them a responsibility to respect and build upon their collective cultural, linguistic and spiritual heritage, to promote the education of others, to further the cause of social justice, to achieve environmental protection, to be tolerant towards social, political and religious systems which differ from their own, ensuring that commonly accepted humanistic values and human rights are upheld, and to work for international peace and solidarity in an interdependent world.[30]

An expanded vision of education for all has been formulated with five key components; universalising access and promoting equity; focussing on learning; broadening the means and scope of basic education; enhancing the environment for learning; strengthening partnerships. Ensuring access and promoting equity will involve a sustained effort to remove educational inequalities and it is acknowledged that:

> The learning needs of the disabled demand special attention. Steps need to be taken to provide equal access to education to every category of disabled persons as an integral part of the education system.[31]

29 UNESCO, World Conference on Education for All: Meeting Basic Learning Needs: A Vision for the 1990s: Background Document: Jomtien, Thailand, 5–9 March 1990 (The Inter-Agency Commission 1990).

30 Ibid. 11.

31 Ibid. 34.

The authors of the Declaration are aware that achieving the aims of the Education for All initiative will require the establishment of supportive policy contexts encompassing economic, health, employment and trade policies. These policies need to be designed to create a suitable infrastructure to support an education system capable of meeting the basic learning needs of all children and young people.

The Standard Rules on the Equalization of Opportunities for Persons with Disabilities were based on the knowledge and experience gained during the United Nations Decade of Disabled Persons (1983–1992).[32] While these Rules are not compulsory, they affirm a strong moral commitment by states to develop policy and legislation designed to enable people with disabilities to exercise the same rights and obligations as other citizens in society. There was an explicit recognition that substantial obstacles existed within societies, preventing people with disabilities exercising the same rights and obligations as other citizens. Under these Rules it is expected that:

> States should recognize the principle of equal primary, secondary and tertiary educational opportunities for children, youth and adults with disabilities, in integrated settings. They should ensure that the education of persons with disabilities is an integral part of the educational system.[33]

The Salamanca Statement and Framework for Action on Special Needs Education[34] represented a milestone in international initiatives designed to enable disabled children and young people and those with special educational needs to access an equitable education within an inclusive learning environment. Representatives from ninety-two governments and twenty-five international organisations met to advance the principles contained within the Education for All initiative adopted at Jomtien, Thailand, in 1990. For the first time, the Education for All initiative focussed specifically on addressing the learning needs of children and young people with disabilities and/or special educational needs within an inclusive education framework. The Salamanca Statement reaffirmed the fundamental right of every child to education and the educational needs of children and young people were conceptualised through a strengths-based rather than the more traditional deficits-based approach. Critically, the emphasis shifted from the individual child who has difficulties in learning towards assigning responsibility to education systems to design and to deliver educational programmes that

32 United Nations General Assembly Res. 48/96 (20 December 1993) UN Doc A/RES/48/96.

33 Ibid. annex rule 6.

34 UNESCO and Ministry of Education and Science Spain, The Salamanca Statement and Framework for Action on Special Needs Education (ED-94/WS/18, UNESCO 1994).

take into account the wide diversity of educational needs presented by children. In particular, children and young people with special educational needs require access to mainstream schools capable of responding appropriately to the diversity of educational needs within these schools.

The Salamanca Statement articulated a paradigm shift in our understanding of special needs education within the wider context of inclusive learning environments:

> The guiding principle that informs this Framework is that schools should accommodate *all children* regardless of their physical, intellectual, social, emotional, linguistic or other conditions. This should include disabled and gifted children, street and working children, children from remote or nomadic populations, children from linguistic, ethnic or cultural minorities and children from other disadvantaged or marginalized areas or groups.[35]

Mainstream schools with a focus on inclusion are:

> the most effective means of combating discriminatory attitudes, creating welcoming communities, building an inclusive society and achieving education for all; moreover, they provide an effective education to the majority of children and improve the efficiency and ultimately the cost-effectiveness of the entire education system.[36]

Mainstream schools face the challenge of creating a child-centred pedagogy capable of effectively educating all children, including those who experience substantial disadvantages, disabilities and/or special educational needs. Developing more inclusive learning environments confronts traditional discriminatory attitudes towards disabled people within society and facilitates a fundamental shift in social perspectives. Special needs education adopts an inclusive perspective which:

> assumes that human differences are normal and that learning must accordingly be adapted to the needs of the child rather than the child fitted to preordained assumptions regarding the pace and nature of the learning process.[37]

The Dakar Framework for Action reviewed progress towards the goals outlined in the Education for All strategy introduced in 1990 and followed by the Salamanca Statement in 1994.[38] Progress towards achieving these goals was

35 Ibid. 6. Emphasis added.

36 Ibid. ix.

37 Ibid. 7.

38 UNESCO, The Dakar Framework for Action: Education for All: Meeting Our Collective Commitments (UNESCO 2000).

noted; however, there was a discernible dissatisfaction with the slow rate of progress as it was noted that more than 113 million children worldwide had no access to primary education, 880 million adults were illiterate, gender discrimination was rife, and significant numbers of disabled people continued to be excluded from education, gainful employment and full participation in their societies. Specific targets for increased literacy levels were established for 2015 along with greater participation by girls from disadvantaged groups and ensuring that disabled people achieved equitable access to appropriate learning and life-skills programmes. States will be expected to develop specific Education for All programmes within the wider context of a poverty reduction framework. Strong political commitment and partnerships within civil society have achieved some notable outcomes in the past decade, including increased primary school enrolments (82 million) with more than 80 per cent enrolment rates within developing countries. It can be concluded that there is a substantial correlation between low enrolment, poor retention and inadequate learning outcomes and high incidence of poverty. In addition, it is evident that measuring and comparing performance and achievements is extremely difficult across the multiple and diverse contexts. The Framework for Action identified the need to 'ensure that the broad vision of Education for All as an inclusive concept is reflected in national government and funding agency policies'.[39] Six key goals were identified and articulated as follows: (1) expanding and improving comprehensive early childhood care and education, especially for the most vulnerable and disadvantaged children; (2) ensuring that by 2015 all children, particularly girls, children in difficult circumstances and those belonging to ethnic minorities, have access to complete free and compulsory primary education of good quality; (3) ensuring that the learning needs of all young people and adults are met through equitable access to appropriate learning and life-skills programmes; (4) achieving a 50 per cent improvement in levels of adult literacy by 2015, especially for women, and equitable access to basic and continuing education for all adults; (5) eliminating gender disparities in primary and secondary education by 2005, and achieving gender equality in education by 2015, with a focus on ensuring girls' full and equal access to and achievement in basic education of good quality; (6) improving every aspect of the quality of education, and ensuring their excellence so that recognised and measurable learning outcomes are achieved by all, especially in literacy, numeracy and essential life skills. The strategies designed to achieve these goals focus on developing national action plans cognisant of the centrality of poverty

[39] Ibid. 14.

elimination, and the need to enhance the professionalism of teachers combined with harnessing new information and communication technologies.

The United Nations Convention on the Rights of Persons with Disabilities (UNCRPD) represents the culmination of a dedicated commitment by the UN over many decades to transform societal attitudes towards disabled people.[40] The Convention marks a significant shift from a deficit perspective which views disabled people as 'objects' of charity who are dependent towards a perspective that views disabled people as 'subjects' capable of being full participants within society. The Convention is designed as a human rights instrument which emphasises that disabled people must be enabled to exercise their fundamental human rights as citizens. The principles underpinning the Convention are articulated in Article 3: (a) Respect for inherent dignity, individual autonomy, including the freedom to make one's own choices, and independence of persons; (b) Non-discrimination; (c) Full and effective participation and inclusion in society; (d) Respect for difference and acceptance of persons with disabilities as part of human diversity and humanity; (e) Equality of opportunity; (f) Accessibility; (g) Equality between men and women; (h) Respect for the evolving capacities of children with disabilities and respect for the right of children with disabilities to preserve their identities. Article 24(1) explicitly recognises the right of disabled people to education and recommends that an inclusive education system needs to be established at all levels of education, including opportunities for lifelong learning to:

> ensure an inclusive education system at all levels and life long learning directed to:
> (a) The full development of human potential and sense of dignity and self-worth, and the strengthening of respect for human rights, fundamental freedoms and human diversity;
> (b) The development by persons with disabilities of their personality, talents and creativity, as well as their mental and physical abilities, to their fullest potential;
> (c) Enabling persons with disabilities to participate effectively in a free society.

The UNESCO Strategy for Education (2014–2021) provides an overview of achievements in advancing the Education for All agenda.[41] Significant progress has been made in achieving universal access to and completion of primary education. However, significant challenges remain in relation to expanding early childhood provision, ensuring quality and relevance of education

40 13 December 2006 UN Doc A/RES/61/106.
41 UNESCO, 37 C/4 2014–2021 Medium-Term Strategy (UNESCO 2014).

available and offering opportunities for young people who have received little or no education. The limited progress towards achievement of Education for All goals disproportionately affects those who are poor and/or disabled.

The European Union (EU) and the Council of Europe have also been proactive in recent decades in developing strategies to address the educational inequalities experienced by disabled people. From the 1970s onwards, the EU disability agenda was dominated by a focus on employment and rehabilitation goals. The 1990s marked a significant shift in EU policy that began to recognise how structural societal barriers can marginalise disabled people and, for example, limit their access to education. A series of initiatives and actions followed, including the European Community Disability Strategy[42] (1996), the European Disability Action Plan[43] (2006) and the European Disability Strategy[44] (2010–2020). The European Community Disability Strategy (1996) focussed on the need to identify and to remove all barriers to equal opportunities and to achieve full societal participation for disabled people. The European Disability Action Plan (2006) aims to promote equality of opportunity for disabled people through the mainstreaming of disability issues in relevant Community policies and processes. The European Disability Strategy 2010–2020: A Renewed Commitment to a Barrier-Free Europe recommends the elimination of barriers to full societal participation for disabled people and promotes the implementation of the UNCRPD across the EU. As a result of these EU initiatives, the European Agency for Development in Special Needs Education (EADSNE) has been established and has been prominent in leading discussions among member states about how to develop inclusive learning environments. For example, EADSNE (2009) has published a set of indicators for inclusive education in Europe focussing on enabling legislation and policies linked to developing knowledgeable professionals and schools capable of responding appropriately to the diversity of learning needs.[45]

42 [42] European Commission, 'Communication of the Commission of 30 July 1996 on Equality of Opportunity for People with Disabilities: A New Community Disability Strategy' COM(96) 406 Final.

43 Council of Europe, Rec(2006)5 of the Committee Ministers on the Council of Europe Action Plan to Promote the Rights and Full Participation of People with Disabilities in Society: Improving the Quality of Life of People with Disabilities in Europe 2006–2015 (adopted 5 April 2006).

44 European Commission, European Disability Strategy 2010–2020: A Renewed Commitment to a Barrier-Free Europe (Communication from the Commission to the European Parliament, the Council, the European Economic and Social Committee and the Committee of the Regions, 2010).

45 Mary Kyriazopoulou and Harald Weber (eds), *Development of a Set of Indicators for Inclusive Education in Europe* (European Agency for Development in Special Needs Education 2009).

As is evident from this review of international developments, international human rights initiatives have played a significant role in conceptualising the right to education for disabled people within the framework of inclusion within a mainstream learning environment. The international instruments promoted by the UN have established that inclusion within a mainstream educational environment represents a fundamental right. However, it is apparent that the standards outlined in the international initiatives have not been incorporated into the legal systems of many EU countries.[46] Furthermore, the right to participation in inclusive learning environments has often been narrowly interpreted to mean access to existing facilities rather than the development of a learning environment designed to support the learning and social needs of disabled children/young people. As a result, few European states have explicitly included reasonable accommodation clauses to guarantee equitable access to learning environments.

KEY PERSPECTIVES

Key perspectives emerge in reviewing how special educational provision has evolved. These key perspectives consist of: the psycho-medical legacy, the sociological response, curricular approaches, school improvement strategies and disability studies critique.[47] It is important to note that '[t]hese perspectives are never wholly exclusive of each other, nor are they strictly chronologically sequential'.[48] There is always the risk that complex historical developments can be reduced to simplistic overviews that view these developments as purely linear. The psycho-medical legacy, for example, has retained a powerful influence in the development of special educational provision through the systems of identification and assessment of disabled children and young people and subsequent distribution of resources.

Until relatively recently, the psycho-medical perspective has occupied a dominant position in policy and practice in special educational provision.[49] From the beginning of organised special educational provision, the medical profession has been centrally involved. Many physicians were at

[46] Fiona Smyth, Michael Shevlin, Tobias Buchner, Gottfried Biewer, Paula Flynn, Camille Latimier, Jan Siska, Mario Toboso-Martin, Susana Rodriguez Diaz and Miguel A. V. Ferreira, 'Inclusive Education in Europe: Policy Evolution in Four European Countries' (2014) 29 *European Journal of Special Needs Education* 433, 434.

[47] Peter Clough and Jenny Corbett, *Theories of Inclusive Education: A Student's Guide* (Sage 2000).

[48] Ibid. 8.

[49] Gary Thomas and Andrew Loxley, *Deconstructing Special Education and Constructing Inclusion* (2nd edn) (Open University Press 2007).

the forefront of establishing educational provision for disabled children and young people. Within this perspective there was an emphasis on 'within-child' deficits that required remediation. Identifying individual deficits within the child became the focus of the assessment process and usually children were assigned to disability-specific schools for their education. This became the foundation for separate schooling systems with little if any connection to mainstream schooling.

The rationale for separate education and the professional disciplines involved in the delivery of special educational provision was subjected to a sustained sociological critique. It was asserted that '[i]f the psychomedical perspective saw special educational need as arising from children's own characteristics, by contrast the sociological response sees them as the outcome of social processes'.[50] Sociologists pointed out that separate educational provision needed to be reviewed within a broader critique of societal inequality and by considering how disadvantage can be reproduced through special educational provision. The presumed benign nature of special schooling informed by concerned and committed professionals was questioned. It was recognised that power relationships within special education systems were heavily skewed in favour of medical and support professions in maintaining their pre-eminent position within the decision-making mechanisms.[51] Sociological analysis also revealed a strong link between familial poverty and the higher incidence of children with learning difficulties from this background.[52] Also, it was argued that the existence of separate provision provided an 'escape route' for mainstream schools that did not wish to include disabled children and young people.

While the sociological analysis tackled the broader issues of inequality and disadvantage at the societal level, educators began to develop appropriate curricula for disabled children and young people. Accepting that the interaction of within-child and environmental factors contributed significantly to learning difficulties prompted mainstream schools to re-evaluate their provision. Disabled children had generally been expected to adapt to mainstream curricula, and their failure to achieve was attributed to within-child factors. Gradually educators began to focus on developing curricula and opportunities for accreditation that took into account the difficulties experienced by disabled children and young people.

50 Clough and Corbett (n. 47) 15.
51 Sally Tomlinson, *A Sociology of Special Education* (Routledge 2012) 82.
52 Ibid. 108.

There was a gradual recognition that enhancing the capacity of schools to respond appropriately to diversity had to become a central feature of establishing inclusive learning environments.[53] Existing inflexible school structures combined with inappropriate teaching methodologies was a significant factor in accounting for learning failure. School improvement strategies focussed on schools, examining school policies and classroom practices in depth.[54]

The final perspective (social model of disability) consisted of an analysis of existing provision by an alliance of disabled people's advocacy movements and academics based on the thinking which informed the social model of disability. This perspective was apprised by serious concerns about the impact of exclusion and segregation on the lives of disabled people. Oliver, for example, argued passionately for the deconstruction of the whole special education system as it has, in his view, patently failed to deliver equitable educational opportunities for disabled children and young people.[55] He, among others, located the inclusive education discussion within the broader framework of societal inclusion for people from marginalised groups.[56]

CONCEPTS OF INCLUSION

By the late 1980s and early 1990s, a consensus was emerging that the movement towards integration had stalled and failed to achieve the overall aim of dismantling segregated educational provision. There was growing dissatisfaction with what was perceived as limited progress in realising the goals of the integration movement. It was cogently argued that integration, in many cases, more closely represented assimilation as the disabled children and young people were expected to 'fit in' to existing arrangements and the anticipated transformation of mainstream schooling had not occurred.[57] In effect, this model of assimilation failed to challenge mainstream provision, which often remained relatively unaltered. There was a gradual realisation that mainstream schools could not guarantee equitable access for disabled children and young people. A new paradigm was required.

[53] Mel Ainscow (ed.), *Effective Schools for All* (David Fulton Publishers 1991).

[54] Mel Ainscow, Tony Booth and Alan Dyson, *Improving Schools, Developing Inclusion* (Routledge 2006).

[55] Michael Oliver, *Understanding Disability: From Theory to Practice* (Palgrave Macmillan 1996).

[56] For further discussion, see Colin Barnes, Geof Mercer and Tom Shakespeare, *Exploring Disability: A Sociological Introduction* (Polity 1999); Dan Goodley, *Disability Studies: An Interdisciplinary Introduction* (Sage 2011); Shah and Priestley (n. 26).

[57] Seán Griffin and Michael Shevlin, *Responding to Special Educational Needs: An Irish Perspective* (2nd edn) (Gill and MacMillan 2011).

The inclusion movement originated in Canada and the United States in the mid-to-late 1980s as there was a concerted effort to develop programmes to include all disabled children and young people in mainstream classrooms. Since then, the inclusion movement has gained considerable momentum. The convergence between international policy and legislation has not produced a clear, uncontested definition of inclusive education.[58] There is a general consensus that an inclusive education system needs to be established which prioritises the embedding of the values of tolerance, diversity and equity. However, the failure to develop a generally acceptable definition of inclusion demonstrates the complexity and inherent tensions involved in establishing inclusive learning environments. Many definitions of inclusive educational provision have emerged, each with a slightly different emphasis.

The Centre for Studies of Inclusive Education, for example, focussed very clearly on the rights of disabled children and young people to participate in mainstream education alongside their peers:

- All children have the right to learn and play together;
- Children should not be devalued or discriminated against by being excluded or sent away because of their disability or learning difficulty;
- There are no legitimate reasons to separate children for the duration of their schooling. They belong together rather than need to be protected from one another.[59]

A minimalist interpretation of inclusive educational provision focussing on adjusting organisational arrangements is evident in the following definition from the Department of Education and Skills (United Kingdom):

> Inclusion is about engendering a sense of community and belonging, encouraging mainstream and special schools and others to come together to support each other and pupils with special educational needs.[60]

A more expansive version of inclusive educational provision is apparent in the British Psychological Society's definition which signals a significant shift towards assigning responsibility for developing inclusive practice to schools and education authorities rather than disabled children and their families adjusting to existing realities:

58 Roger Slee, 'Inclusion in Practice: Does Practice make Perfect?' (2001) 53 *Educational Review* 113.

59 Centre for Studies on Inclusive Education, 'Ten Reasons for Inclusion' www.csie.org.uk/resources/ten-reasons-02.pdf, accessed 11 March 2017.

60 Department for Education and Skills, Inclusive Schooling: Children with Special Educational Needs (DfES 2001) [8].

- Rejecting segregation or exclusion of learners for whatever reason – ability, gender, language, care status, family income, disability, sexuality, colour, religion or ethnic origin;
- Maximising the participation of all learners in the community schools of their choice;
- Making learning more meaningful and relevant for all, particularly those learners most vulnerable to exclusionary pressures;
- Rethinking and restructuring policies, curricula, culture and practices in schools and learning environments so that diverse learning needs can be met, whatever the origin or nature of those needs.[61]

Definitions of inclusive education have expanded to include all learners within the school settings and not just disabled children and young people as originally envisaged in the integration movement as summarised by Ainscow and his colleagues:

> Inclusive practice requires significant changes to be made to the content, delivery and organisation of mainstream programmes and is a whole school endeavour which aims to accommodate the learning needs of all students. The discourse on inclusion has moved beyond simply focusing on the response to individuals to explore 'how settings, policies, cultures and structures can recognise and value diversity'.[62]

The Committee on the Rights of Persons with Disabilities, in its review of the UNCRPD, succinctly articulates what the right to inclusive education involves in practice:

> Ensuring the right to inclusive education entails a transformation in culture, policy and practice in all formal and informal educational environments to accommodate the differing requirements and identities of individual students, together with a commitment to remove the barriers that impede that possibility. It involves strengthening the capacity of the education system to reach out to all learners. It focuses on the full and effective participation, accessibility, attendance and achievement of all students, especially those who, for different reasons, are excluded or at risk of being marginalized.[63]

The UNCRPD established inclusive education as a device to ensure the right to education for people with disabilities. The commitment to inclusive education enshrined in Article 24 became a legal obligation that becomes legally

61 The British Psychological Society, 'Inclusive Education Position Paper' www.bps.org.uk/system/files/images/final_inclusion_statement_july_2005.doc, accessed 22 April 2015, 2.
62 Ainscow and others (2006) (n. 54) 2.
63 Committee on the Rights of Persons with Disabilities, General Comment No. 4 (2016) Article 24: Right to Inclusive Education (2 September 2016) CRPD/C/GC/4 [9].

enforceable upon a country's ratification of the UNCRPD.[64] States have the responsibility to ensure that disabled children and young people are supported through a series of measures including reasonable accommodations, individualised education programmes and giving them a sense of ambition for their educational career. In addition, disabled people should be enabled to access tertiary education, vocational training and adult education as appropriate on an equal basis to their peers.

Though the concept of educational inclusion appears to be informed by similar principles emphasising human rights, rights to participate and zero exclusion policies, it has been difficult to arrive at a commonly accepted definition of educational inclusion. Some commentators suggest that this is due to educational inclusion being heavily context dependent, while others have argued that educational inclusion is in essence part of a wider political struggle to achieve equality for those from marginalised groups within society. A typology of educational inclusion has been developed which spans a conceptual range from quite limited to very expansive notions of what constitutes educational inclusion.[65]

Establishing inclusive educational inclusion involves a radical shift from the traditional categorical approaches and conceptualising educational inclusion as involving the presence, participation and achievement of all pupils in local mainstream schools, and not focussing specifically on members of marginalised groups within the school community.[66] Essentially, the move to establish inclusive schools is based on a human rights agenda designed to identify barriers to participation for all marginalised groups and to ensure that these schools can respond appropriately to a diversity of needs within the context of establishing a more inclusive society:

> [T]he history of inclusion is the history of these struggles for an educational system which served the interests of communities, and which does not exclude anyone within those communities. It needs to trace its roots within community and comprehensive education as well as within the struggles for rights of women, black people, gay people and disabled people and other groups who's participation is made conditional and vulnerable. The history of inclusion doesn't take you back to special education.[67]

64 Jo Walker, *Equal Right, Equal Opportunity: Inclusive Education for Children with Disabilities* (Global Campaign for Education and Handicap International 2013) 14.

65 Mel Ainscow, Andy Howes, Peter Farrell and Jo Frankham, 'Making Sense of the Development of Inclusive Practices' (2003) 18 *European Journal of Special Needs Education* 227.

66 Tony Booth and Mel Ainscow, *Index for Inclusion: Developing Learning and Participation in Schools* (Centre for Studies on Inclusive Education 2002).

67 Tony Booth, 'Reflection' in Peter Clough and Jenny Corbett (eds), *Theories of Inclusive Education: A Student's Guide* (Paul Chapman Publishing 2000) 64.

The concept of educational inclusion is generally accepted as a fundamental principle underpinning policy and enabling legislation and practice within the education system. It is generally understood that inclusion is a process concerned with: the identification and removal of barriers in mainstream schooling; the presence, participation and achievement of all pupils within mainstream schools; those groups within society particularly prone to exclusion and marginalisation. Over the past few decades, educational inclusion has evolved from being merely an idea and has become the dominant ideology informing contemporary education for disabled pupils and young people. Few would disagree with this rights-based philosophy; however, difficulties have arisen in attempting to translate the principles underpinning educational inclusion into practice within the 'lived worlds of teachers and the hard realities of general classrooms'.[68]

A number of major challenges to the development of inclusive education systems have been identified:

- Despite adopted policies on inclusive education, all countries struggle with the management and implementation of an education system that truly caters for diversity;
- Funding mechanisms seem to be the key predictor to the set-up for the provision targeted to address the diversity of learning needs;
- Curricula should be flexible enough to accommodate the diversity of learning styles and pace;
- As inclusive education systems require new skills and knowledge from teachers, teacher education should be revisited and designed to support inclusion;
- The importance of community and parental involvement in education is recognised, although a lot needs to be done in order to make their participation real;
- Structures or procedures to facilitate multi-sectoral collaboration need to be developed;
- Attitudes are the greatest barrier, or the greatest asset, to the development of inclusion in education;
- Education for All means 'ALL, not all, BUT'[69]

At a systemic level, support for disabled pupils and young people is often based on an individually based assessment of need and this is often mandated in enabling legislation. As a result, while policy is framed within an inclusive

[68] Winzer (n. 2) 31.

[69] Sai Vayrynen, *Inclusive Education: A Challenge, a Process* (ISEC: Including the Excluded, University of Manchester, 24–28 July 2000) 4.

perspective, the allocation of resources is clearly based on traditional categories of disability:

> On the one hand, we are encouraged to work towards 'inclusion'; on the other, the language of SEN, rooted in the medical model of disability, legitimizes the idea that some children are 'normal' while others are 'special'. As a consequence, groups and individual children are assigned specific labels, often leading to special or segregated provision.[70]

Categorisation processes and the consequent provision represent a substantial barrier to developing inclusive learning environments:

> If disabled children are to be genuinely included in the mainstream of education, this cannot involve special education thought and practice. Categorising and naming children as 'special' identifies them as different from others, and different in ways that are not valued in present mainstream schools and society.[71]

Critics of inclusion have challenged the view that educational inclusion represents an indisputable moral imperative for all disabled children and young people and argue that 'the rights of the child to have maximum access to mainstream education need to be balanced by their right to an effective education, appropriate to their needs'.[72]

Over the past two decades, establishing inclusive learning environments at the local level has involved:

- Understanding and acknowledging inclusion as a continuous evolving process;
- Creating learning environments that respond to the needs of all learners;
- Developing educational settings that identify and reduce barriers to learning;
- Enabling the participation of pupils, teachers, parents and members of the community in the work of the school;
- Reorganising school culture, policies and practices to respond to the diversity of pupils in the local community;
- Developing appropriate supports for pupils, staff and other professionals;

70 Caroline A. Jones, *Supporting Inclusion in the Early Years* (Open University Press 2004) 11.

71 Keith Ballard, 'Children and Disability: Special or Included?' in the University of Waikato (ed.), *Waikato Journal of Education*, vol. 10 (University of Waikato School of Education 2004) 318.

72 Norah Frederickson and Tony Cline, *Special Educational Needs, Inclusion and Diversity: A Textbook* (Open University Press 2002) 73.

- Providing accessible information on inclusive policies and practices within the school to the whole school community and anyone involved in the education of pupils.[73]

Systematic programmes designed to establish and to review inclusive educational provision at the school level have been developed, including the Index for Inclusion. The Index 'is concerned with improving educational attainments through inclusive practice'.[74] The concept of 'special educational need' is not used in the Index and is replaced by the designation 'barriers to learning and participation', which emphasises how barriers to learning and participation can occur at all levels of education and affect many children rather than just those traditionally identified as having 'special educational needs'. The Index enabled schools to evaluate the strengths and shortcomings in their inclusive practice and to address aspects of 'gender, disability, class, ethnicity and sexual orientation'.[75] Critical factors include: participation of the whole school community in developing shared vision and practice; collaborative teamwork and planned time for teachers to work together; effective child/parental/family involvement and adaptation of existing curricula and instructional practice. Putting inclusion into practice in schools involves a commitment to valuing pupils and their teachers equally; substantial restructuring of school cultures, policies and practices to address diversity within the community; reducing barriers to learning and encouraging participation of all in the school community; fostering mutually sustaining relationships between schools and communities; realising that educational inclusion is a vital aspect of wider societal inclusion.

CONCLUDING COMMENTS

The concept of educational inclusion has been firmly established within policy and legislation in many countries throughout the world. However, it is equally evident that there are many contrasting and, in some cases, conflicting interpretations of how educational inclusion should be implemented in practice. We should not underestimate the enduring strength and influence of traditional conceptualisations of special education that continue to exert a hold over current procedures through the emphasis on defining educational needs according to traditional categories of disability and allocating resources on this basis. This emphasis on developing increasingly sophisticated systems

73 Booth and Ainscow (n. 66).
74 Ibid. 7.
75 Ibid.

of categorisation designed to determine eligibility for resources deflects attention away from wider systemic factors that preserve existing power inequalities and social disadvantage.[76] In addition, the increasing marketisation of education with accompanying competition between schools for status and resources can produce a hostile environment quite unsympathetic to the inclusion agenda. We also need to facilitate access to curricula and accreditation, to support teachers and school personnel in developing appropriate responses to any child experiencing difficulties in school, to encourage pupil participation in decision-making processes within schools and to challenge exclusionary procedures within schools and the education system. A human rights approach to educational inclusion demands that exclusionary practices at all levels within the education system are challenged to become socially just and equitable.[77] Achieving educational inclusion is a process that challenges societies at a fundamental level to demonstrate who is really valued within our communities and how the human rights of all children and young people can be realised within our education systems.

76 Roger Slee, *The Irregular School: Exclusion, Schooling and Inclusive Education* (Routledge 2011).

77 Anastasia Liasidou, *Inclusive Education, Politics and Policymaking: Contemporary Issues in Education Studies* (Continuum 2012).

5

Drafting Article 24 of the Convention on the Rights of Persons with Disabilities

Rosemary Kayess

1 INTRODUCTION

Equality for all members of the human family is a central pillar of human rights law. If societies are to achieve equality, their systems and structures must recognise human diversity in all its forms and their policies must reflect that diversity. Until twenty years ago, international human rights standards were focussed on equality and non-discrimination based on race and gender, giving little attention to or guidance for states on disability. Increasing awareness of the failure of existing instruments to improve the situation of many of the world's persons with disabilities led to calls for a thematic convention on these rights.[1] Although the various developments in 'soft law' had not stimulated reform and social change, they did provide a significant framework of principles for the task.[2]

The 2006 adoption of the Convention on the Rights of Persons with Disabilities (CRPD) signalled a move away from reliance on general human rights norms and non-binding soft law standards on disability to explicit, formally binding legal obligations for those states that become party to the Convention, a significant legal and policy advance. The aim of the Convention was to stand on existing human rights norms and to apply them expressly within a disability context. This was to ensure equality by persons with disabilities in the exercise and enjoyment of all human rights and fundamental freedoms. Although some of the rights in the Convention are

[1] T. Degener and G. Quinn, 'The Moral Authority for Change: Human Rights Values and the Worldwide Process of Disability Reform' in G. Quinn and T. Degener (eds), *Human Rights and Disability: The Current Use and Future Potential of United Nations Human Rights Instruments in the Context of Disability* (United Nations, 2002) 13–28.

[2] R. Kayess and T. French, 'Out of Darkness into Light? Introducing the Convention on the Rights of Persons with Disabilities' (2008) 8(1) *Human Rights Law Review* 1.

simply transposed from other human rights treaties (e.g. the right to life), the majority have been reformulated for their specific context, providing clearer and more detailed guidance for States Parties seeking to comply with their obligations to respect, protect and fulfil the rights of persons with disabilities. The CRPD is an international charter of rights, but one which is specific to persons with disabilities. Importantly, the Convention provides both a framework for policy analysis, design and implementation and a binding source of law for advocacy by disabled persons' organisations regarding the rights of persons with disabilities.

Based on a conceptualisation of disability as a part of human diversity and a substantive equality approach, the call for inclusive education presented a significant challenge for the CRPD negotiations. Enshrining and defining the principle of inclusive education was a highly contentious issue for both state and civil society delegations. The most contentious issue was whether inclusive education incorporated a right to choose a segregated education setting. This chapter briefly explores the paradigm shift that framed the drafting of Article 24 and how the drafters negotiated these complex and contentious issues.

Part 2 of this chapter analyses the way disability has been conceptualised in the context of education. The right to education is one of the core group of economic, social and cultural rights enshrined in the International Bill of Human Rights,[3] with the 1948 Universal Declaration of Human Rights (UDHR) stating the right of everyone to education. Article 26 of the UDHR provides that education shall be free and compulsory, at least in the elementary and fundamental stages, that technical and professional education shall be generally available and that higher education shall be equally accessible to all. It defines the aim of education as being 'directed to the full development of the human personality and to the strengthening of respect for human rights and fundamental freedoms'. When the International Covenant on Economic, Social and Cultural Rights (ICESCR) came into force in 1976, the right to education took its place as a norm of binding international law. This chapter also explains that, in practice, persons with disabilities are still consistently denied equal access to education and to the opportunity for lifelong learning. In all regions of the world, including in the industrialised societies, persons with disability are typically excluded from this fundamental human right.

3 The International Bill of Human Rights incorporates the three instruments of general application: the Universal Declaration of Human Rights (1948), the International Covenant on Civil and Political Rights (1966) and the International Covenant on Economic, Social and Cultural Rights (1966).

They experience greatly inferior education compared to their non-disabled peers, often as a result of inadequate levels of support to accommodate their disabilities, with poor-quality curricula and instructional methods greatly diminishing their academic development. Moreover, children and young persons with disabilities are commonly channelled into segregated education,[4] and the education opportunities provided to them in these segregated environments, away from their non-disabled peers, greatly diminish their social development.

Although there is a scarcity of reliable global data on the educational circumstances of people with disabilities, in 2011, the World Health Organization (WHO) partnered with the World Bank to gather 'the best available scientific evidence' on disability, including data relating to disability and education.[5] Drawing on multiple surveys of the educational experience of persons with disabilities undertaken in all regions of the world, the WHO presents a global portrait of exclusion and obstructed capability. Across fifty-one countries participating in the World Health Survey, people with disabilities experienced significantly lower rates of primary school completion and fewer years of education than those without.[6] The rates of young people with disabilities who are not attending school are particularly high in developing countries, but even in more prosperous regions, such as Eastern Europe, large numbers do not attend school.[7] The WHO report notes a range of systemwide factors which contribute to this global outcome, including divided ministerial responsibility, lack of legislation, policy, targets and plans and inadequate resources.[8] A number of school-based barriers were also identified by the WHO through surveys: curricula and teaching methods which are not sufficiently flexible to meet the needs of all learners, inadequate training and resourcing of teachers, physical barriers in school buildings and school transport, the consequential effects of labelling of children, negative societal or community attitudes towards disability generally and bullying or violence.[9]

4 The Warnock Report (1978) Special Educational Needs Report of the Committee of Enquiry into the Education of Handicapped Children and Young People, available at www.educationengland.org.uk/documents/warnock/warnock1978.html (last accessed 24 August 2016) p. 28.

5 World Health Organization, *World Report on Disability*, Chapter 7, 'Education'.

6 Ibid., page 206 and table 7.1. See also World Health Organization, *World Health Survey* (Geneva, 2002–2004), available at www.who.int/healthinfo/survey/en (last accessed 24 November 2018).

7 Ibid., pages 207–208 and tables 7.1 and 7.2.

8 Ibid., pages 212–215.

9 Ibid., pages 215–216.

A similar portrait emerges from a survey of the Concluding Observations of the UN Committee on the Rights of Persons with Disabilities between 2011 and 2017.[10] The overwhelming placement of people with disabilities in segregated schools and the lack of access to inclusive education are almost universal, even in countries which are very highly developed, such as Australia, Germany, Austria and Portugal. As the Committee observed in relation to Cyprus, '[s]egregated education remains rooted in the education system [and] is reflected in the attitude of teachers and other professionals'.[11] And while most states are taking steps towards greater inclusion, not nearly enough is being done. Where data are available, countries report lower levels of enrolment and lower educational achievements by people with disabilities. The Committee repeatedly observes that resources allocated to the education of people with disabilities, and especially to their inclusive education, are too low. This is closely related to inadequate teacher training and resourcing, and to the lack of accessible teaching and learning materials. Other barriers present for people with disabilities in many of the countries surveyed are negative social attitudes in schools, refusal of enrolment in mainstream schools, lack of support when placed in inclusive education, lack of planning (including physical accessibility and transport) and an emphasis on vocational and craft skills rather than on academic skills.

The Convention was negotiated with groundbreaking civil society participation, particularly by disabled persons' organisations. With regard to education, the negotiations brought together people from all parts of the world who had had quite different experiences, which made the development of CRPD Article 24 highly contentious. For example, there were people from a generation which had been educated in segregated schools with full augmentative communication and access to alternative scripts. Their advocacy organisations were aware of students with similar disability in mainstream schools who had received inadequate support, and this had had a significant adverse impact on their education and life opportunities. There were members of a younger generation who had experienced mainstream education with adequate support and who valued the experience of attending the local neighbourhood school.[12]

10 OHCHR Committee on the Rights of Persons with Disabilities, Concluding Observations, available at www.ohchr.org/EN/HRBodies/CRPD/Pages/CRPDIndex.aspx (last accessed 24 November 2018).

11 Ibid., page 5.

12 R. Kayess and J. Green, 'Today's Lesson Is on Diversity' in P. Blanck and E. Flynn (eds), *Routledge Handbook of Disability Law and Human Rights* (Taylor & Francis Group, 2017) chapter 4.

Part 3 of this chapter looks at the development of Article 24 in the CRPD and explains the reasoning behind one of its most contentious aspects, the right to an inclusive education. Article 24 guarantees the right to education for persons with disabilities without discrimination, based on the principle of inclusive education, and requires reasonable accommodation of individual requirements. The provision recognises the great importance of access to adequate education for persons with disabilities, particularly its importance to their prospects of gaining employment and of achieving economic independence, including the pathways it offers to escape poverty and disadvantage. Education is also self-empowering, providing persons with disabilities with the means to acquire the knowledge and the skills necessary for participation, advocacy and effecting social change. Education is also recognised as a crucial mechanism for social inclusion, playing a central role in social development and interaction, as well as offering opportunities to form support networks and lifelong friendships.

Article 24 obliges States Parties to take 'effective measures to support persons with disabilities in the general education system at all levels' and requires that all support measures are provided in environments that maximise the academic and social development of persons with disabilities.[13] The emphasis is on establishing 'an inclusive education system', and the provision sets clear goals for States Parties regarding education for persons with disabilities. These include 'the full development of human potential and sense of dignity and self-worth', as well as 'the strengthening of respect for . . . human diversity'; the development by persons with disabilities 'of their personality, talents and creativity, as well as their mental and physical abilities, to their fullest potential'; and 'enabling persons with disabilities to participate effectively in a free society'.[14]

During the Convention negotiations, Article 24 arose as an acutely contentious one and was extensively and intensively debated throughout the negotiations, including over three days at the Sixth Session, with more than 110 interventions from Member States and NGO delegations. The tensions in these debates highlighted underlying differences in the ways disability was being conceptualised, and centred on three points: the principle of inclusive education, the right to choose and ensuring equality of education for all

[13] United Nations (2006), Convention on the Rights of Persons with Disabilities (CRPD), United Nations Treaty Series, vol. 2515, 3 Article 24 (2(b) (c)(e)).

[14] United Nations (2006), Convention on the Rights of Persons with Disabilities (CRPD), United Nations Treaty Series, vol. 2515, 3 Article 24(1) (a) (b) (c)).

persons with disabilities through reasonable accommodation and individualised support.

2 CONCEPTUALISING DISABILITY

The education experience of people with disabilities has been and continues to be framed by a conceptualisation in public discourse and policy of disability as 'deficit'. This conceptualisation focusses on the individual, rather than on the society, and 'locates the causes of social inequality and disadvantage in the body or mind of individuals with impairments'.[15] People with disability are perceived as not meeting a normative standard, and their impairments are viewed as an individualised problem, in which individuals have 'special needs' and require care, treatment and protection within a social welfare regime. This social conceptualisation of disability has been a powerful and enduring one throughout modern history.[16] Framed as a medical model of disability, 'it has guided and dominated clinical practice with the resulting assumption that both problems and solutions lie within people with disabilities rather than within society'.[17]

Under this conceptualisation, disability is perceived as a 'problem' which derives directly from the individual impairment, giving little or no recognition to the role of the social environment in *disabling* persons with impairments. This approach, which sees disability as a deficiency of the individual, has reinforced ideas of disability as 'different' or 'other'. The typical public policy response has been to establish separate, parallel institutions and services, isolating those for persons with disabilities from the mainstream systems, including in residential care, education, employment and justice diversion measures.[18] Hence, the overall experience for people with disability remains one of separation and segregation, excluding them from key social institutions and isolating them – and disability issues – from mainstream public policy. In the context of education, segregation has resulted in historically low levels of academic achievement and prevented people with disabilities from expressing their capabilities, including in key professions and public administration,[19] with the consequence that they have not been

15 A. Lawson and M. Priestly, 'The Social Model of Disability: Questions for Law and Legal Scholarship?' in P. Blanck and E. Flynn (eds), *Routledge Handbook of Disability Law and Human Rights* (Taylor & Francis Group, 2017) 6.

16 Kayess and French, note 2, at 5.

17 S. French, 'What Is Disability?' in S. French(ed.), *On Equal Terms: Working with Disabled People* (Butterworth-Heinemann, 1994) 3–16.

18 R. Kayess and B. Smith, 'Charters and Disability' in Matthew Groves and Colin Campbell (eds), *Australian Charters of Rights a Decade On* (Federation Press, 2017) 151–168.

19 S. Linton, *Claiming Disability: Knowledge and Identity* (New York University Press, 1998) chapter 3, p. 4.

represented in public policy decision-making processes. Linton notes that disability has not been a topic of academic concern in the areas of law, policy, public administration, planning and architecture, and argues that this has led to limited understanding of the issues it raises.[20]

As a result, people with disability are perceived as a vulnerable 'special interest' group.[21] When perceived as such, people with disabilities are seen as an exception to the norm. Similar to norms of sexism and racism, the pervasive and enduring norm of 'ableism' idealises ablebodiedness.[22] As Goodley elaborates, the 'valued citizen' of the twenty-first century is 'cognitively, socially, and emotionally able and competent; biologically and psychologically stable; genetically and hormonally sound, and ontologically responsible; hearing, mobile, seeing, walking'; and 'normal: sane, autonomous, self-sufficient, self-governing, reasonable, law abiding and economically viable'.[23] Being a norm, ableism has been observed to be generally internalised,[24] often unstated and appearing natural, neutral[25] and benign.

The argument that people with disability are perceived as only partial citizens is substantiated by the existence of economically based reservations about disability equality claims, reservations that would be unthinkable if the accommodations involved were gender or race related.[26] As Kayess and Smith argue, 'employers are not permitted to reject female job applicants simply because the woman might get pregnant and need maternity leave, and thereby cost the employer more. In contrast, it is still considered acceptable for employers to reject a person with disability if hiring them could impose some costs'.[27] They conclude that 'apart from care, protection and welfare, disability is apparently irrelevant – that it only needs to be considered in respect of

20 Ibid. chapter 4; see also C. Barnes, G. Mercer and T. Shakespeare, *Exploring Disability: A Sociological Introduction* (Polity Press, 1999).

21 Kayess and Smith, note 18, at 5.

22 Ibid. 5.

23 D. Goodley, *Dis/Ability Studies: Theorising Disablism and Ableism* (Routledge, 2014) 88–89.

24 F. Campbell, 'Exploring Internalised Ableism Using Critical Race Theory' (2008) 23(2) *Disability and Society* 151.

25 M. Minow, *Making All the Difference: Inclusion, Exclusion, and American Law* (Cornell University Press, 1990), chapter 2.

26 F. Campbell, 'Problematizing Vulnerability: Engaging Studies in Ableism and Disability Jurisprudence' (Draft). Keynote Legal Intersections Research Centre, Disability at the Margins: Vulnerability, Empowerment and the Criminal Law, University of Wollongong, Wednesday, 27 November 2013. See A. Lawson, 'UN Convention on the Rights of Persons with Disabilities and European Disability Law: A Catalyst for Cohesion?' in O. Arnardottir and G. Quinn (eds), The United Nations Convention on the Rights of Persons with Disabilities: European and Scandinavian Perspectives (Brill, 2009) 320.

27 Kayess and Smith, note 18, at 5.

special needs, but can be otherwise ignored'.[28] As summarised by Campbell, 'disability remains largely invisible on the policy and equity agendas of governments and is viewed largely as a state of exception'.[29]

These approaches contrast sharply with a more contemporary approach to conceptualising disability, which is to view it as part of human diversity. Instead of impairments being exceptional or abnormal, they are understood as 'an infinitely various but universal feature of the human condition'.[30] As Bickenbach explains, 'no human has a complete repertoire of abilities, suitable for all permutations of the physical and social environment'.[31] This approach acknowledges that each of us is relatively limited in some way, at some time, and that it is how we characterise and treat the multiplicity of permutations that determines whether someone is a 'person with disability'. What makes certain traits 'matter' is how they are perceived and labelled. Even traits which would be irrelevant were social arrangements different may 'matter' where those traits do not sit comfortably within dominant social arrangements.[32] An example is deafness which, being different, is used to characterise and establish hearing as the norm. For Minow, the law not only operates without requiring that the norm be stated, it also responds as though the chosen differences and the norm were premised on objective fact, rather than being a subjective ordering of priorities and expectations.[33]

This conceptualisation draws strongly on two contemporary approaches to disability – the social model and ableism. The social model of disability locates the experience of disability in the social environment, rather than in the impairment, and locates the need to change or to accommodate in the society, not in the person with the impairment. For example, for a wheelchair user, it is the stairs which are the disabling factor, not the physical impairment; similarly, a conformist behavioural code for a classroom may be disabling for a child with autism, because it does not accommodate different modes of learning and expression. The theory of ableism offers a way of understanding the current conceptualisation, a way which illuminates the unstated characteristics of the 'normative citizen' and then challenges the assumptions that underpin law and public policy based on this conceptualisation.

28 Ibid. 5

29 Campbell, note 26, at 13.

30 J. E. Bickenbach, 'Minority Rights or Universal Participation: The Politics of Disablement' in M. Jones and L. Basser Marks (eds), *Disability, Divers-Ability and Legal Change* (Martinus Nijhoff Publishers, 1999) 101–115, at 111.

31 Ibid.

32 Minow, note 25, at 55.

33 Ibid. 52.

The fundamental tenet of conceptualising disability as part of human diversity is universalism. It requires modification of the dominant and pervasive ableist social norm to reflect, instead, human diversity.[34] Approaching disability as part of human diversity challenges the essentialism of the ableist foundations of modern society.[35] The human diversity conceptualisation resonates with Fineman's 'vulnerable subject' thesis, where she argues that:

> the 'vulnerable subject' must replace the autonomous and independent subject asserted in the liberal tradition. Far more representative of actual lived experience and the human condition, the vulnerable subject should be at the center of our political and theoretical endeavors.[36]

She contends that 'understanding the significance, universality, and constancy of vulnerability mandates that politics, ethics, and law be fashioned around a complete, comprehensive vision of the human experience if they are to meet the needs of real-life subjects'.[37] She identifies vulnerability as the universal axiom, and concludes that the 'vulnerable subject approach does what the one-dimensional liberal subject approach cannot: it embodies the fact that human reality encompasses a wide range of differing and interdependent abilities over the span of a lifetime'.[38]

This conceptualisation of disability also exhibits a deep and applied understanding of substantive equality. Adopting a policy approach based on formal equality merely involves the consistent, or facially neutral, application of law and policy, and is aimed at eliminating stereotyping and overtly prejudicial treatment of identity groups. Effectively assuming that the existing social norm is benign, formal equality does not challenge or seek to change the fundamental structure of that norm. A policy approach based on substantive equality, by contrast, acknowledges the different impacts of even facially neutral laws and policies in social contexts, and recognises that existing patterns of disadvantage and differentiation result in disparate outcomes. A substantive equality approach seeks to achieve the outcome of full participation in society by all persons equally, whatever their personal characteristics or their membership in a particular identity group. Drawing on Fredman's four main purposes or dimensions of substantive equality and applying them to the disability context, this would extend to: redistribution to address economic and social disadvantage of people with disability; recognition

34 Kayess and French, note 2, at 10.

35 Kayess and Smith, note 18, at 6.

36 M. Fineman, 'The Vulnerable Subject: Anchoring Equality in the Human Condition' (2008) 20(1) *Yale Journal of Law and Feminism* 2.

37 Ibid. 10.

38 Ibid. 12.

that addresses 'stigma, stereotyping, humiliation and violence'; participation that requires the genuine inclusion of the views and experiences of all disadvantaged people in political and other decision-making; and transformation supporting normative reform.[39]

The CRPD negotiations were framed by these paradigm shifts, with Article 24 ultimately incorporating both the conceptualisation of disability as part of human diversity and a substantive equality approach to the development of disability law and policy.

3 THE DRAFTING OF CRPD ARTICLE 24

The CRPD was developed under a UN General Assembly mandate based on the premise that the new Convention would apply existing human rights to the particular circumstances of persons with disabilities, applying existing norms and standards rather than establishing any new human rights, and not derogating from or lowering the standards set out in existing norms. The General Assembly established the Ad Hoc Committee on a Comprehensive and Integral International Convention on the Protection and Promotion of the Rights and Dignity of Persons with Disabilities (Ad Hoc Committee), and it was within this Committee that the desirability of a new convention was discussed, and negotiations and drafting of the new convention's provisions took place. The Ad Hoc Committee established a Working Group (WG) at its second session, in June 2003, to develop the proposed convention's draft text.

The text which the WG produced included an education provision which was premised on an approach to education for persons with disabilities which was and remains common among governments: to provide a few opportunities for integration of persons with disabilities in mainstream education but to rely, for the main, on segregated education systems, often under the policy and administrative direction of departments of welfare or health.[40]

Disability advocates and education scholars had been pushing for many years for inclusive education.[41] Based on the assumption that first and foremost every

39 S. Fredman, 'Substantive Equality Revisited', University of Oxford Legal Research Paper Series, Paper No. 70/2014, page 21.

40 Kayess and Green, note 12, at 61.

41 A. J. Artiles and E. B. Kozleski, 'Inclusive Education's Promises and Trajectories: Critical Notes about Future Research on a Venerable Idea' (2016) 24 *Analysis Archives/Archivos Analíticos de Políticas Educativas*, Arizona State University, available at www.redalyc.org/articulo.oa?id=275043450022 (last accessed 24 November 2018); see also D. Konza, 'Inclusion of Students with Disabilities in New Times: Responding to the Challenge' in P. Kell, W. Vialle, D. Konza and G. Vogl (eds), *Learning and the Learner: Exploring Learning for New Times* (University of Wollongong, 2008) 39–64.

child can be accommodated in their neighbourhood school, inclusive education was seen as central to the paradigm shift sought in the CRPD: an education system to meet the needs of all students irrespective of the level of support required. It was noted in the Ad Hoc Committee negotiations that the WG text fell short of this notion of inclusive education as well as existing standards set out in human rights treaties on education for persons with disabilities. First, delegates said, the WG draft of what was to become CRPD Article 24 did not enshrine the principle of inclusive education, even though that principle had previously been accepted under the UN Standard Rules on the Equalization of Opportunities for Persons with Disabilities.[42] The Standard Rules provided that:

> General educational authorities are responsible for the education of persons with disabilities in integrated settings. Education for persons with disabilities should form an integral part of national educational planning, curriculum development and school organization.[43]

Second, delegates pointed out that the Salamanca Statement had expressly called on governments to 'adopt as a matter of law or policy the principle of inclusive education'.[44] Third, the 1989 UN Convention on the Rights of the Child (CRC) jurisprudence endorsed the principle of inclusive education. Delegates drew attention to the fact that the focus of the Committee on the Rights of the Child had turned increasingly to the inclusion of children in mainstream education, moving away from the segregated education approach. In fact, that Committee had earlier concluded that segregating children with disabilities 'for care, treatment or education' constituted a breach of the CRC.[45]

These factors supported a compelling argument – which enjoyed significant support – that the CRPD article should be based on the principle of inclusive education. That principle was incorporated into the first Facilitator's Text, developed at the Sixth Session of the Ad Hoc Committee in August 2005,[46] and, ultimately, into the final wording of CRPD Article 24(1).

42 UN Standard Rules on the Equalization of Opportunities for Persons with Disabilities, United Nations, 1993 ('Standard Rules').

43 Ibid. Rule 6 'Education'.

44 UNESCO Salamanca Statement and Framework for Action on Special Needs Education (1994) 3(b).

45 Committee on the Rights of the Child, Day of General Discussion: Children with Disabilities 1997 Document ref CRC/C/66, Annex V, para. 338(d). Available at www.ohchr.org/EN/HRBodies/CRC/Pages/DiscussionDays.aspx (last accessed 7 August 2015).

46 UNGA Ad Hoc Committee on a Comprehensive and Integral International Convention on the Protection and Promotion of the Rights and Dignity of Persons with Disabilities (UNGA Ad Hoc Committee) (2005c), 'Facilitator's Text – Draft Article 17 – Education', 'Revisions and

Two (related) contentious issues arose from this change. The issue of legislative and departmental responsibility in relation to inclusive education was raised on several occasions by delegates and civil society.[47] Adopting the principle of inclusive education in the CRPD should mean that education for persons with disability would henceforth be governed by the same legislation and departmental responsibility as education for the rest of the community. The inclusive education approach in Article 24 has the potential to reverse the historical emphasis (by community or human service/welfare departments) on therapeutic and avocational endeavours over academic outcomes, an approach which experience shows has continually left students with an academic and vocational disadvantage. Including all education within the one legislative and departmental area of responsibility is consistent with the international law principle of equality and the guarantee of non-discrimination. Moreover, there are compelling operational arguments for the single portfolio approach, including the instrumental impetus it generates towards meeting the objectives of the Salamanca Statement. Through giving policy and budgetary priority to improving the education system overall, as well as to establishing mechanisms for planning, monitoring and evaluating educational provision, the approach promotes the development of an inclusive education system.[48]

While the point is not overtly referred to within the final text of Article 24, the single portfolio approach is the concept behind the language of 'general education system' and it is within this context that it should be interpreted. However, one point that is expressly referred to, a point which achieved universal agreement during the negotiations and which is directly related to the operational benefits of a single portfolio approach, is the importance of support to successful inclusion. Article 24(4) requires States Parties to train and employ teachers, including teachers with disabilities, who are qualified in augmentative and alternative modes, means and formats of communication, educational techniques and materials to support persons with disabilities.

The second contentious issue arising was that, even though the principle of inclusive education had been incorporated, the WG draft text still presented

Amendments at the Sixth Session of the Ad Hoc Committee, Facilitator', available at www.un.org/esa/socdev/enable/rights/ahc6facilitator.htm (last accessed 24 November 2018).

47 In particular Canada, Centre for Studies on Inclusive Education and Canadian Community Living Association. See UNGA Ad Hoc Committee, Daily Summaries of Discussions. Available at www.un.org/esa/socdev/enable/rights (last accessed 14 May 2015).

48 UNESCO, note 44.

segregated education as a valid exception to inclusive education.[49] Several text variants were proposed to address this. The European Union (EU) proposed a variation that allowed for 'effective alternative forms of education' in cases 'where exceptionally the general education system does not adequately meet the needs of persons with disabilities', but 'bearing in mind the goal of full inclusion'.[50] The weakness of this variation was that it potentially established a broad exception, without sufficiently emphasising the obligation to progressively realise inclusive education. Both Australia and Canada proposed variations that emphasised the standard of non-discrimination, each arguing that it was not necessary to build in exceptions. Rather, they said, 'what was needed is a clear statement that persons with disabilities receive the support required to facilitate their education within the general education system and the communities in which they live'.[51] This approach was broadly supported by governments and strongly supported by civil society, and it ultimately formed the basis for CRPD Article 24.[52]

These debates were linked by some to the guarantee set out in UDHR Article 26, by which 'parents have a prior right to choose the kind of education that shall be given to their children'. ICESCR Article 13(3) requires States Parties to 'have respect for the liberty of parents . . . to choose for their children schools, other than those established by the public authorities', where those parents wish 'to ensure the religious and moral education of their children in conformity with their own convictions'. The right is subject to the condition that such schools 'conform to such minimum educational standards as may be laid down or approved by the State'. This provision allows the development of 'private' schools catering to particular religious beliefs, for the specific purpose of accommodating religious plurality, and envisages an educational system which offers state-provided education to all but in which private, religious (or affiliated linguistic) alternative schools also operate.

The concept of parents' right to choose a private, religious education for their children was carried over from the ICESCR into the disability convention negotiations, where it was presented as a right to choose a particular, state-

49 United Nations 2004: Draft art. 17(2).

50 UNGA Ad Hoc Committee – Sixth Session – Contributions by Governments (August 2005) EU Proposal Draft Article 17 Education. Available at: www.un.org/esa/socdev/enable/rights/ahc6eu.htm (last accessed 14 May 2017).

51 UNGA Ad Hoc Committee on a Comprehensive and Integral International Convention on the Protection and Promotion of the Rights and Dignity of Persons with Disabilities (UNGA Ad Hoc Committee) (2006b), Daily Summaries of Discussions, 24 January 2006, available at www.un.org/esa/socdev/enable/rights/ahc7sum24jan.htm (last accessed 14 May 2015).

52 Ibid.

established education setting based on disability. However, this claim was not supported by either international human rights law or its related jurisprudence. ICESCR Article 13(3) is perfectly specific in recognising a limited right of parents to choose alternative schools, where those schools are private and where the objective of the parents is to enable education to be provided in conformity with their religious and moral convictions. The analogous claim in the CRPD negotiations was misguided, for two reasons. First, the right in ICESCR Article 13(3) is essentially one of non-interference by the state, as distinct from one entitling parents to demand state-funded, separate education for their children. As is explained in The Hague Recommendations Regarding the Education Rights of National Minorities, 'persons belonging to national minorities ... have the right to establish and manage their own *private* educational institutions' (emphasis added).[53] Secondly, there is no comparable parental right in relation to disability, nor would such a right (if it existed) be consistent with the international human rights law standards of equality and non-discrimination, directed as Article 13(3) is towards the preservation of difference.

Domestically, many Member States had adopted policies based on a 'right to choose' and had established special education systems for people with disabilities.[54] As previously mentioned, although the WG text had been altered in relation to inclusive and accessible education within communities, it still included provisions requiring that, 'where the general education system does not adequately meet the needs of persons with disabilities special ... alternative forms of learning should be made available' and that these should 'allow a free and informed choice between general and special systems'.[55]

The lack of consensus on this issue is recorded in the footnotes to the WG text. Delegates in favour of inclusive education without state-established segregation raised the arguments mentioned earlier in this chapter, regarding the Standard Rules, the Salamanca Statement and the developing jurisprudence in relation to the CRC, which had increasingly emphasised the obligation to include all children in mainstream education, rather than in segregated education.[56] It was

53 The Hague Recommendations Regarding the Education Rights of National Minorities & Explanatory Note, October 1996, Paragraph 8.

54 Though see Germany's comment in relation to this issue, stating that the similar right under the German Constitution extends to the right of parents to choose specialised schools for children with disability (Germany 2016).

55 Ibid. Draft Art. 17(3).

56 Centre for Inclusive Education. As mentioned earlier, the Committee on the Rights of the Child, following a day of General Discussion in 1997 on the rights of children with disabilities, concluded that the segregation of children with disabilities 'for care, treatment or education' represented a breach of the Convention: Document ref. CRC/C/66, Annex V, para. 338(d),

clear to the negotiators that, under the UN Standard Rules, the provision of separate, 'special' education is only acceptable as a temporary measure, where mainstream education has not yet developed sufficiently to accommodate all children.[57] Rule 7(8) of the Standard Rules provides:

> In situations where the general school system does not *yet* adequately meet the needs of all persons with disabilities, special education may be considered ... States should aim for the gradual integration of special education services into mainstream education. It is acknowledged that in some instances special education *may currently* be considered to be the most appropriate form of education for some students with disabilities. (emphasis added)

Rule 7(8) clearly refers in its construction to states' obligations generally under the ICESCR, with segregated education considered as a stage in the progressive realisation of the goal of inclusive education within the general education system. It should not be interpreted as an endorsement of segregated education systems where states have neglected to take steps to ensure that the general education system has inclusive practises and supports.

At this stage in the negotiations, the WG text had imported the Standard Rules wording from Rule 7(8) but, critically, it had omitted the word 'yet' appearing in the first line of that Rule, which dramatically altered the nature of the text provision. Hence, instead of requiring that segregated education should only be maintained where steps were being taken to progressively realise inclusive education, the WG text provision purported to create an exception to the norm of inclusive education. The consequence of this formulation was that a choice was offered between two state-established options, legitimising a system of parallel, segregated education for persons with disabilities. This outcome was in direct contravention of UN treaty body jurisprudence.[58] The fundamentally flawed nature of this approach had been made clear fifty years earlier in the United States, where a policy of 'separate but equal' had been advanced to justify public schools being segregated on the basis of race. The US Supreme Court had held that separate educational facilities were inherently unequal and discriminatory.[59] Yet the WG text provision would have applied a similar 'separate but equal' policy

available at www.unhchr.ch/html/menu2/6/crc/doc/days/disabled.pdf (last accessed 24 November 2018).

57 Standard Rules on the Equalization of Opportunities for Persons with Disabilities A/RES48/96 of 20 December 1993 www.unhchr.ch/huridocda/huridoca.nsf/(Symbol)/A.RES.48.96.En?Opendocument (last accessed 24 November 2018).

58 ICESCR General Comment No. 13.

59 In *Brown* v. *Board of Education of Topeka*, 347 U.S. 483 (1954) the US Supreme Court declared that laws establishing separate education for black children were unconstitutional, finding that 'separate educational facilities are inherently unequal'. Overturning earlier rulings going back to

and permitted the segregation of persons with disabilities from the general public education system.

What emerged during these debates in the negotiations was that generating the desired 'paradigm shift' through the CRPD broadly would require building inclusion deeply in to provisions like Rule 7(8). It needed to be unequivocal that public education systems should accommodate people with disabilities, instead of people with disabilities accommodating the education systems. States should provide the necessary infrastructure and supports to ensure equality of education in a system that aims to meet the needs of the full diversity of students in schools' local areas. This approach has particularly important consequences for resources and funding. The ICESCR enables States Parties to meet their educational human rights obligations progressively, but it also obliges them to apply the maximum of available resources to their endeavours and to eradicate existing discrimination. While it is true that shortage of resources is cited as the most common reason for states' failure to fully implement inclusive education,[60] it is also true that permitting temporary segregation pending adequate resources enables existing state resources to be diverted away from inclusive services. During the negotiations, civil society delegations argued that:

> While resources (human and financial) are used to develop inclusive education *and* to support exclusion and segregation, most obviously by maintaining a dual system of 'ordinary' and 'special' education, inclusive education will not be developed to maximum effect. Economically, it is far more efficient to target resources towards a single inclusive education system from the outset than to develop a dual system of separate education for disabled and non-disabled persons and then have to work towards bringing about inclusive education.[61]

A contrary view was presented by deaf, deaf-blind and blind representatives, who pressed for choice and argued that segregated education was essential to ensure equality in language and literacy instruction.[62] Their perspective was

Plessy v. *Ferguson* in 1896 which endorsed the policy of 'separate but equal'. For an example, see Towong State, 'School Bilingual and Bicultural, English and Auslan, Hearing and Deaf', https://toowongss.eq.edu.au/Supportandresources/Studentservicesandsupportprograms/Pages/Bilingual-Bicultural.aspx.

60 UNESCO Economic and Social Council, 'Inclusive Dimensions of the Right to Education: Normative Bases. A Concept Paper'. Eighth and Ninth Meetings of the Joint Expert Group UNESCO (CR) ECOSOC (ICESCR) on the Monitoring of the Right to Education (2008).

61 Centre for Studies in Inclusive Education, Ad Hoc Committee 2005, 6. Available at www.un.org/esa/socdev/enable/rights/ahc6contngos.htm (last accessed 7 August 2015) 5.

62 UNGA Ad Hoc Committee, Daily Summaries of Discussions, 2005. Available at www.un.org/esa/socdev/enable/rights (last accessed 14 May 2015).

that deaf, deaf-blind and blind persons need to develop particular, essential skills, such as Braille, sign language and orientation and mobility skills, and that those skills would be more effectively acquired in segregated environments than in inclusive settings. It was, however, noted that those skills are fundamental and may be acquired at a later stage of life and more broadly, not just in the context of education. Access to such fundamental skills should be available broadly both pre- and post-education. They could be integrated into and facilitated by the education system, but delegates questioned whether it should be the basis for segregated education.[63] Representative organisations for blind, deaf and deaf-blind persons also suggested that the choice of special education settings is important for establishing a peer group, which typically provides support throughout a person's life. Also emphasised was the cultural dimension of segregated education environments for deaf persons, as the deaf community identifies as a discrete cultural and linguistic group, the members of which share a language (sign) and a common heritage of beliefs, attitudes, history, norms and values that are maintained through engagement with deaf peers.[64]

No clear consensus emerged when the issue was referred to and discussed at the Ad Hoc Committee, although it was evident that, even among persons with sensory disability, there was a diversity of views on the issue of a deaf, blind and deaf-blind person's right to choose a special public educational environment. Ultimately, however, the arguments in favour of inclusion prevailed. There was no evidence that effective sign language and Braille instruction could not be provided in inclusive settings. The importance of children and young people with sensory disability establishing relationships with a broad range of peers was acknowledged, relationships which would assist them to function effectively within the general community as adults. Without undervaluing the importance of the peer support of others with sensory disability, such support could be facilitated through extracurricular activities. In countries where resources will probably never be available to establish special schools in all communities, inclusive education would allow children and young people with sensory disability to not have to travel extensive distances or to live away from home in order to attend school. Bilingual schools[65] would allow children and young people with sensory disability to attend school with their siblings and non-disabled peers. Such

63 Ibid. See Australia. Available at www.un.org/esa/socdev/enable/rights/ahc6sum2aug.htm (last accessed 14 May 2015).

64 World Federation of the Deaf.

65 UNGA Ad Hoc Committee 2005, Informal Facilitator Discussions – Draft Article 17 Education. For an example, see Towong State, note 59.

schools would facilitate social development in a more diverse environment and would be a catalyst to promote the use and broader awareness of sign language.

Importantly too, there would be economies of scale in such arrangements. To have taken the path of choice would have created an obligation on states to maintain parallel education systems, with the likely budgetary consequence that neither system would be adequately resourced. Even though the WG text provided for 'free and informed' choice between general and segregated education, it is unlikely that the general education system would have sufficient resources to duplicate the services offered by the special, separate schools. As a result, it is not likely that people with disabilities would choose the general education option, which would further direct resources into segregated education. As delegates noted, 'this is in fact a false choice enforced by a lack of resources and access to support'.[66]

Finally, and perhaps most fundamentally, to have enshrined choice would have been to work against the standard of non-discrimination, which is set out in Article 5 of CRPD and is one of the core pillars of international human rights law more broadly. CRPD Article 24 in its final form does not include a right to choose between the general education system and segregated education system. Instead, States Parties are obliged to ensure an inclusive public education system. However, that system must be non-discriminatory, meaning that states must ensure that persons with disabilities are not disadvantaged in their access to inclusive education. States must also give attention to the specific educational requirements of persons who are Deaf, Blind or Deaf/Blind, but this does not justify states maintaining segregated education, since the overall obligation is to establish an inclusive education system, not a parallel 'separate but equal' segregated education system.

4 CONCLUSION

The negotiations were an opportunity to embed the much sought-after paradigm shift. The resulting Article has achieved the enshrining of inclusive education as an outcome for people with disabilities, recognising that disability is merely one aspect of the human condition and that people with disability should participate fully in community life. This means that children are educated together, share common development experiences and have the opportunity to form lifelong relationships and connections, and that the

66 See, for example, New Zealand (UNGA Ad Hoc Committee 2005b); Blanck and Flynn, eds, note 12, page 67.

experience of children without disability is enriched. Article 24 is the first step and, as the Concluding Observations demonstrate, there is a long way to go. What we now have is a clear foundation for addressing disability and a binding instrument to guide states in ensuring an inclusive education system.

6

The Expressive Dimension of the Right to Inclusive Education

Sarah Arduin

1 INTRODUCTION

Article 24 of the UN Convention on the Rights of Persons with Disabilities (CRPD)[1] consolidates the pedigree of the right to inclusive education in international law.[2] Its status as a landmark legal principle is further strengthened by policies within the European Union[3] and at national levels.[4] Compliance with, and enforcement of, the right remains, however, a challenge in practice.[5] This difficulty may be, in part, attributed to the level of ambiguity linked to the social meaning of inclusive education, its underlying value(s) and the purpose of its regulation.[6]

The aim of this chapter is not so much to focus on the meaning per se of the concept of inclusive education, although its social meaning is important.

1 United Nations General Assembly, Convention on the Rights of Persons with Disabilities (13 December 2006) A/RES/61/106 (hereinafter the Convention or CRPD).

2 For further analysis on the recognition of the right in international law, see Kanter, Chapter 2, this volume.

3 In 2011, the European Union ratified the UN CRPD (Council Decision 2010/48/EC); see also the EU Disability Strategy 2010–2020 (COM(2010) 636), which refers to inclusive education.

4 As is further discussed in Section 2 of this chapter, several European countries have undertaken legal reforms subsequent to the ratification, or signature, of the CRPD.

5 In General Comment No. 4 (2016) Article 24: Right to Inclusive Education, the UN Committee on the Rights of Persons with Disabilities has provided a list of the remaining barriers faced by persons with disabilities in accessing inclusive education (2 September 2016) CRPD/C/GC/4 [4].

6 For further analysis on the different definitions of inclusive education adopted in some European countries, see Sarah Arduin, 'A Review of the Values That Underpin the Structure of an Education System and Its Approach to Disability and Inclusion' (2015) 41 *Oxford Review of Education* 105; see also Cor Meijer and Amanda Watkins, 'Changing Conceptions of Inclusion Underpinning Education Policy' in Amanda Watkins and Cor Meijer (eds), *Implementing Inclusive Education: Issues in Bridging the Policy–Practice Gap* (Emerald 2016) vol. 8.

Rather, this chapter is concerned with the information expressed in Article 24 of the CRPD and how it affects national legal frameworks. In this sense, the chapter seeks to analyse the extent to which a gap exists between, on the one hand, the audience meaning of the right to inclusive education and, on the other hand, the information expressed in Article 24 of the Convention.

From a European perspective, expressive theory is a relatively novel field.[7] Expressivism is a methodology that looks at the ability of a law to affect the meaning of social norms and to influence individual behaviours.[8] Richard McAdams points out that there are three approaches to understanding the meaning of a statement for the purposes of expressive theories.[9] The first approach looks at the intention of the speaker – that is, what the speaker seeks to express; the second perspective focusses on the audience – that is, how a law is understood by the audience, regardless of the intention of the speaker; the third approach zeroes in on the conventional meaning of a statement.[10] By pinpointing the information that a law expresses, one is using the second perspective – that is, through the lens of the audience. From this perspective, what matters when we look at the information conveyed by a law is not what the speaker intends to mean, nor what the convention's meaning is; it is how the information is perceived and understood by the audience. In this

7 Since the 1990s, scholarship on expressive theories has been abundant in the United States. The situation is slightly different in Europe, where expressivism has not attracted the same level of attention yet. Khaitan has started to refer to expressivism as a mechanism for distinguishing the concept of dignity from other values, such as equality and autonomy. For further analysis, see Tarunabh Khaitan, 'Dignity As an Expressive Norm: Neither Vacuous nor a Panacea' (2012) 32 *Oxford Journal of Legal Studies* 1.

8 This chapter draws from the expressive law scholarship as developed in the late 1990s and early 2000s by American scholars. In *The Expressive Powers of Law: Theories and Limits* (Harvard University Press 2015), Richard H. McAdams provides an excellent analysis of the four theories of expressive law developed in recent years. See also Elizabeth S. Anderson and Richard H. Pildes, 'Expressive Theories of Law: A General Restatement' (2000) 148 *University of Pennsylvania Law Review* 1503; Alex C. Geisinger and Michael Ashley Stein, 'Expressive Law and the American with Disabilities Act' (2016) *Michigan Law Review* 1061; Alex C. Geisinger and Michael Ashley Stein, 'A Theory of Expressive International Law' (2007) 60 *Vanderbilt Law Review* 77; Deborah Hellman, 'The Expressive Dimension of Equal Protection' (2000) 85 *Minnesota Law Review* 1; Lawrence Lessig, 'The Regulation of Social Meaning' (1995) 62 *University of Chicago Law Review* 943; Cass R. Sunstein, 'On the Expressive Function of Law' (1996) 144 *University of Pennsylvania Law Review* 2021; Michael Ashley Stein, 'Under the Empirical Radar: An Initial Expressive Law Analysis of the Americans with Disabilities Act' (2004) 90 *Virginia Law Review* 1151.

9 McAdams (n. 8) 19.

10 Ibid.; see also Matthew D. Alder, 'Expressive Theories of Law: A Skeptical Overview' (2000) 148 *University of Pennsylvania Law Review* 1363.

sense, whether some scholars support or disagree with a statement made by law depends on how the law has been interpreted.[11]

Methodologically, this chapter combines an empirical analysis with a normative study of the right to inclusive education as enshrined in Article 24. From an empirical perspective, the chapter identifies how the right to inclusive education has been understood by the audience, which is composed, in our case, of legislators in European countries. From a normative perspective, the chapter examines the extent to which the European legal norm(s) correlate(s) with the information expressed in Article 24 of the CRPD.

Accordingly, the chapter is divided into three parts. It begins by providing an overview of how the right to inclusive education has been interpreted in five European legal frameworks, namely England, Finland, France, Ireland and Norway. It then benchmarks the empirical findings against the information expressed in Article 24. Finally, it concludes by highlighting the salience of bridging normative expressivism and consequentialism in order to monitor the effectiveness of Article 24.

2 OVERVIEW

Since the Salamanca Statement, differing interpretative approaches have been adopted within the European Union.[12] As the European Agency for Development of Special Needs Education has pointed out, when policy and practice relating to inclusive education are discussed, European legal frameworks may not talk about the same concept or principle.[13]

Two interpretative approaches to the right to inclusive education have been suggested. One interpretation is primarily concerned with the placement of a child with disability into a mainstream setting; a second interpretation zeroes in on the individual learning capacities of the students, providing a wide range of educational supports in different settings.[14] As Norwich has pointed out,

11 See Sunstein (n. 8) 2022.

12 UNESCO and Ministry of Education and Science Spain, The Salamanca Statement and Framework for Action on Special Needs Education (ED-94/WS/18, UNESCO 1994).

13 This absence of a common understanding of the concept is exacerbated by the realities of using different national languages. For further analysis on this latter observation, see European Agency for Development in Special Needs Education, *Organisation of Provision to Support Inclusive Education: Literature Review* (European Agency for Special Needs and Inclusive Education 2013); see also Meijer and Watkins (n. 6) 3.

14 When these two interpretations are summarised in terms of rights, it seems that the first interpretation gives priority to the right *to* education, whereas the second emphasises rights *within* education. See Michael Oliver and Colin Barnes, *The New Politics of Disablement* (Palgrave Macmillan 2012); see also Arduin (n. 6); Simona D'Alessio and Amanda Watkins,

these two interpretations relate to two different responses to students' differences in learning.[15] On the one hand, the differentiation stance gives priority to the individual needs of the students, justifying at times alternative educational settings. On the other hand, the commonality stance focusses on the communal aspect of education with a view to establishing a common curriculum for all within a mainstream educational setting.[16]

In most European education systems, special settings are still part of the educational landscape for children with disabilities, although the overall number of special schools has been decreasing over the past few years.[17] What differentiates some countries from others is the perceived role of

'International Comparisons of Inclusive Policy and Practice: Are We Talking about the Same Thing?' (2009) 4 *Research in Comparative and International Education* 233; UNESCO, *Education for All: The Quality Imperative* (UNESCO 2004); UNESCO, *Policy Guidelines on Inclusion in Education* (UNESCO 2009) ED-2009/WS/31; World Health Organization and World Bank, *World Report on Disability* (World Health Organization 2011). For a more exhaustive analysis of the two approaches to inclusive education as implemented in Europe, see European Agency for Development in Special Needs Education (n. 13) 11; Garry Hornby, 'Inclusive Special Education: Development of a New Theory for the Education of Children with Special Educational Needs and Disabilities' (2015) 42 *British Journal of Special Education* 234; Brahm Norwich, 'Changing Policy and Legislation and Its Effects on Inclusive and Special Education: A Perspective from England' (2014) 41 *British Journal of Special Education* 403; Lorella Terzi, 'Reframing Inclusive Education: Educational Equality As Capability Equality' (2014) 44 *Cambridge Journal of Education* 479; Mary Warnock and Brahm Norwich, *Special Educational Needs: A New Look* (Lorella Terzi, ed. Continuum 2010).

15 Brahm Norwich, 'Perspectives and Purposes of Disability Classification Systems: Implications for Teachers and Curriculum and Pedagogy' in Lani Florian and Margaret J. McLaughlin (eds), *Disability Classification in Education: Issues and Perspectives* (Corwin 2008); Brahm Norwich, 'What Future for Special Schools and Inclusion? Conceptual and Professional Perspectives' (2008) 35 *British Journal of Special Education* 136; Brahm Norwich, 'Can We Envisage the End of Special Educational Needs? Has Special Educational Needs Outlived Its Usefulness?' (2010) 34 *Psychology of Education Review* 13; Brahm Norwich, *Dressing Tensions and Dilemmas in Inclusive Education: Living with Uncertainty* (Routledge 2013).

16 This tension is also addressed by Martha Minow in *Making All the Difference: Inclusion, Exclusion and American Law* (Cornell University Press 1990) and in *In* Brown's *Wake: Legacies of America's Educational Landmark* (Oxford University Press 2010). In the latter, Minow provides a thorough analysis of the mixed legacy of *Brown* v. *Board of Education* in bringing about educational reforms in the treatment of children with diverse needs. Minow points out that the decision in *Brown* has a 'protean quality ... as a symbol of equality and justice'; this multifaceted approach to the decision may be also linked to the 'irreducible tension between the goal of equality understood as access to mainstream success regardless of personal identity and the goal of pluralism understood as latitude for adults as individuals and groups to pass on the traditions and identities that matter to them ... *Brown*'s ideals can be mobilized both against forced assimilation and for expanding intergroup contact' (at 187).

17 Note that this section only provides an overview of how the right to inclusive education has been interpreted in some European countries. For a more in-depth analysis of the approach

alternative educational settings and their relevance – or not – in the legal framework on inclusive environment.

a England

England signed the CRPD in 2007 and ratified it in 2009. In 2014, the English legal framework was reformed by the Children and Families Act. Among other things,[18] the new Act reaffirms the general presumption in law of mainstream education in relation to decisions about educational placement of students with special educational needs (SEN).[19] This presumption, which was previously set in the Education Act 1996,[20] provides that students with special educational needs 'must' be educated in mainstream schools,[21] 'unless that is incompatible ... with the wishes of the child's parent or the young person, or ... the provision of efficient education for others'.[22]

At first sight, it seems that this presumption enshrined in Sections 33 and 34 of the 2014 Act does not refer to the individual needs of the student nor to his/her best interest when a decision on his/her educational placement is made – principles that are respectively enshrined in Article 24(2)(d) and (e) and Article 7 of the CRPD. According to Section 33(2) of the Act, there are two reasons for justifying the placement of a student with SEN in a setting other than a mainstream school: (1) when the parents or student decide(s) so, or (2) when the mainstream placement prevents the provision of effective education

adopted by each European country, see the European Agency for Special Needs and Inclusive Education, *Organisation of Provision to Support Inclusive Education: Summary Report* (European Agency for Special Needs and Inclusive Education 2013); European Agency for Special Needs and Inclusive Education, *Agency Position on Inclusive Education Systems* (European Agency for Special Needs and Inclusive Education 2015); and Meijer and Watkins (n. 6).

18 For an analysis of the changes brought under the new framework, see Brahm Norwich and Andrew Eaton, 'The New Special Educational Needs (SEN) Legislation in England and Implications for Services for Children and Young People with Social, Emotional and Behavioural Difficulties' (2015) 20 *Emotional and Behavioural Difficulties* 117; Norwich (2014) (n. 14); Peter Gray and Brahm Norwich, 'The Coalition Government's Policy on SEND: Aspirations and Challenges' (2014) 14 *Journal of Research in Special Educational Needs* 122, 120–138.

19 See Sections 33 and 34 of the Children and Families Act 2014. See also *Special Educational Needs and Disability Code of Practice: 0 to 25 Years: Statutory Guidance for Organisations Which Work With and Support Children and Young People Who Have Special Educational Needs or Disabilities* (Department for Education 2015) ('Code of Practice') [1.26].

20 Education Act 1996 S316.

21 The Act distinguishes between children with special educational needs who also have Education, Health and Care (EHC) plans (S33) and children with special educational needs without EHC plans (S34).

22 Children and Families Act 2014 S33(2).

for other students.[23] Yet Sections 33 and 34 should be read in conjunction with Section 19, which sets out the general principles that govern Part 3 of the 2014 Act.[24] Among these principles are 'the views, wishes and feelings of the child' and 'the need to support the child and his or her parent, or the young person, in order to facilitate the development of the child or young person and to help him or her achieve the best possible educational and other outcomes'.[25] Although these principles are somewhat ambiguous, it seems that they refer to the best interests of the student and to the right to effective educational support in light of the evolving individual learning capacities. In this sense, through Section 19, the 2014 Act implements, to some extent, the principles of the best interests of the child[26] and effective individualised support[27] – principles that are essential for realising effectively the right to education for students with disabilities. Perhaps one noticeable difference is that the CRPD does not emphasise the salience of educational outcomes to the same extent as the English Act.[28]

In addition, the provisions of the 2014 Act should be read in conjunction with the Equality Act 2010, which prohibits schools from discriminating against students with disabilities in respect of admissions and treatment for a reason related to their disability.[29]

Finally, and perhaps most interestingly, the 2015 Code of Practice specifies that:

> Children and young people with SEN have different needs and can be educated effectively in a range of mainstream or special settings. Alongside the general presumption of mainstream education, parents of children with

[23] See, in particular, Article 7 of the CRPD, which refers to the best interests of the child, and Article 24(2)(d) and (e), which refer to effective individual support in realising the right to education of persons with disabilities.

[24] Section 19 of the Act provides that local authorities must have regard to the general principles when implementing their statutory duties.

[25] Children and Families Act 2014 S19(a) and (d).

[26] CRPD Article 7.

[27] CRPD Article 24(2)(d) and (e).

[28] For further analysis on the novel emphasis of the Act on educational outcomes of students with special educational needs, see Norwich (2014) (n. 14) and Gray and Norwich (n. 18).

[29] Section 91(3) of the Equality Act 2010. Nevertheless, note that the English Ofsted inspection framework, which evaluates students' academic progression in education and identifies schools that do not reach the academic level as set out by the government, is silent when it comes to evaluating schools' admission and exclusion policy relating to students with special educational needs. This raises the question as to what extent Section 91(3) of the Equality Act is being monitored and effectively enforced in practice. See Norwich (2014) (n. 14) 416; Ofsted, *The Framework for Inspecting Schools in England under Section 5 of the Education Act 2005 (As Amended)* (Ofsted 2013).

an EHC [Education, Health and Care] plan and young people with such a plan have the right to seek a place at a special school.[30]

It seems that this latter approach expressed in the Code may be in conflict with the provisions of the 2014 Act. The provisions of the 2014 Act, read in conjunction with the Equality Act 2010, emphasise primarily the placement of the child with SEN into a mainstream school. In contrast, the 2015 Code of Practice seems to primarily emphasise the different learning 'needs' of children with SEN ahead of their educational placement.

Accordingly, it is not entirely clear how the English legal framework has interpreted Article 24 of the CRPD. Whilst the 2014 reform occurred after the ratification of the CRPD, one will note that the Children and Family Act does not make any reference to the concept of inclusive education or to the right to education in an inclusive environment.

b Ireland

The Irish legal framework provides, to some extent, a clearer approach to its interpretation of the right to inclusive education than the one provided in the English framework. Ireland signed the CRPD in 2007; however, it has not yet ratified the Convention.[31]

The legal framework is regulated by, inter alia, the Education Act 1998,[32] the Education for Persons with Special Educational Needs (EPSEN) Act 2004[33] and the Equal Status Act 2000.[34]

Section 7(1)(a) of the Education Act requires the state to ensure that a level and quality education appropriate to meet the needs and abilities of each person residing in the state, including persons with disabilities, is available.[35]

30 Code of Practice (n. 19) 28.

31 As of January 2017, Ireland is the only European Union member state which has not ratified the CRPD. Finland and the Netherlands were the latest two countries to ratify the Convention (in 2016). Related information is available at <http://fra.europa.eu/en/theme/people-disabilities/ratified-crpd> (accessed January 2017).

32 No. 51 of 1998.

33 No. 30 of 2004. Note that, at the time of writing (early 2017), parts of the EPSEN Act have still not been implemented.

34 No. 8 of 2000. For further analysis on the Irish legal framework, see Whyte, 'Litigating the Right to Inclusive Education under Irish Law' in the present volume (Chapter 19).

35 Section 7(1)(a) states that the minister is required 'to ensure, subject to the provisions of this Act, that there is made available to each person resident in the State, including a person with a disability or who has other special educational needs, support services and a level and quality of education appropriate to meeting the needs and abilities of that person'.

In addition, like the English framework, Section 2 of the EPSEN Act establishes a general presumption in law in favour of mainstream education, although this section has not yet commenced.[36] Unlike the English framework, the Irish EPSEN Act does expressly refer to the concept of inclusive education. What is striking is that Section 2 of the EPSEN Act links the principle of inclusive education with decisions relating to the place where the child 'shall' be taught, bearing in mind that the general presumption could be reversed when the mainstream placement is inconsistent with the best interests of the student or with the effective education of other students.[37]

Finally, Section 7(2) of the Equal Status Act prohibits an educational establishment from discriminating on the basis of, inter alia, disability, in relation to, inter alia, the admission of the student to the establishment and access of the student to any course provided by the establishment.[38] This prohibition is, however, not absolute; it should not apply 'to the extent that compliance with any of its provisions in relation to a student with a disability would, by virtue of the disability, make impossible, or have a seriously detrimental effect on, the provision by an educational establishment of its services to other students'.[39] Note that the onus is on the school to prove that the provision of educational services to a student with disability may be detrimental to his/her education and the education of others.[40]

When these provisions are analysed together, it appears that the right to inclusive education has been interpreted in the Irish framework as a right to education in a mainstream school, prioritising the educational placement of a student with a disability ahead of his/her specific individual learning needs.

36 Section 2 provides that 'A child with special educational needs shall be educated in an inclusive environment with children who do not have such needs unless the nature or degree of those needs of the child is such that to do so would be inconsistent with (a) the best interests of the child as determined in accordance with any assessment carried out under this Act, or (b) the effective provision of education for children with whom the child is to be educated'. As it stands, the Irish government has indefinitely delayed its implementation. For further analysis, see Roisin Webb, *ANED Country Report on Equality of Educational and Training Opportunities for Young Disabled People* (ANED 2010) VT/2007/005.

37 For further analysis on the Irish legal framework, see Sarah Arduin, 'Implementing Disability Rights in Education in Ireland: An Impossible Task?' (2013) 36 *Dublin University Law Journal* 93.

38 Section 7(2) provides that 'An educational establishment shall not discriminate in relation to – (a) the admission or the terms or conditions of admission of a person as a student to the establishment, (b) the access of a student to any course, facility or benefit provided by the establishment, (c) any other term or condition of participation in the establishment by a student, or (d) the expulsion of a student from the establishment or any other sanction against the student'.

39 Section 7(4)(b) of the Act.

40 For a detailed analysis of the case law that arose under this section, see Whyte (n. 34).

Perhaps, in reaction to – or in light of – this legislative approach to the right, some schools have adopted narrow enrolment policies that are far from inclusive. As has been observed, some schools have been reported as having caveats suggesting that students with special educational needs will be enrolled only if resources are in place or if their behaviour does not adversely affect other students.[41] Others have suggested that 'soft' barriers are being placed hindering the enrolment of children with individual educational needs by advising their parents that a different school may be more suitable for them.[42]

c *France*

With respect to the French legal framework, the Code of Education introduced the concept of inclusive education in 2013,[43] subsequent to the ratification of the CRPD in 2010. Prior to 2013, the Code was silent with respect to the principle of inclusion in education; it provided that students with disabilities should be enrolled in the school closest to their home, be it a mainstream school or a special school.[44]

This principle of neighbourhood schools has been consolidated by the 2013 Act. As it stands, Article L111-1 of the Code provides that inclusive education is ensured to all students, without any distinction.[45] Note that this provision represents an interesting departure from the English and Irish frameworks. The concept of inclusive education, as expressed in the French legal framework, does not seem to be exclusively linked to disability or special educational needs. Instead, the concept seems to be understood in universal terms, applying to every child.

Similarly, through the principle of neighbourhood schools established in Article L112-1 of the Code, the French legal framework seems to differentiate

41 See National Council for Special Education (NCSE), *Supporting Students with Special Educational Needs in Schools* (National Council for Special Education 2013) Policy Advice Paper No. 4; see also Arduin (2015) (n. 6).

42 NCSE (n. 41). Note that the Education (Admission to Schools) Bill 2016 (No. 58 of 2016) seeks to remedy the exclusionary practice observed in many schools. In particular, the Bill prohibits schools from discriminating against a student in their admission policies based on certain characteristics, such as the student's disability or special educational needs, among others (Section 61).

43 Law n° 2013–595 of 8 July 2013 for the Refoundation of the School of the French Republic (Loi pour la Refondation de l'École de la République).

44 Article L112-1 of the Code of Education, modified by Law no. 2005–102 of 11 February 2005 (Loi du 11 février 2005 pour l'égalité des droits et des chances, la participation et la citoyenneté des personnes handicapées).

45 According to paragraph 1 of Article L111-1, 'L'éducation est la première priorité nationale. Le service public de l'éducation est conçu et organisé en fonction des élèves et des étudiants . . . Il veille à l'inclusion scolaire de tous les enfants, sans aucune distinction.'

itself from the common law framework, which prioritises a general presumption in favour of mainstream education.[46] When the French Commission for the Rights and Autonomy of Persons with Disabilities decides the appropriate educational setting in light of the information provided by the multidisciplinary team and the wishes of the student concerned, or his/her legal representative,[47] close attention is paid to the individual needs of the student.[48] Whilst the Code of Education does express a preference for the provision of education in a mainstream school for children with a personalised schooling project,[49] the legal priority is centred on the individual learning needs and wishes of the student concerned.[50] In other words, the general presumption in law in favour of mainstream education, which has been observed in the English and Irish legal frameworks, is absent in the French legal interpretation.

To some extent, this latter perspective appears similar to the one adopted in the Norwegian legal framework.

d Norway

In the Norwegian framework, the legal principle for determining the educational placement of any child is that of neighbourhood schools. As seen earlier with the French Code of Education, the principle guarantees the right of every child to attend the school that is closest to where he or she lives. This principle is affirmed in Section 8(1) of the Norwegian Act of 17 July 1998 (no. 61) relating to Primary and Secondary Education and Training (the Education Act) as amended in June 2010.[51] In addition, in 2008, Section 1(3) was added to the Education Act

[46] This principle was first established in Nordic countries, as is observed later in this chapter. It is also referred to in Article 24(2)(b) of the CRPD.

[47] Article L146-9 of the Code de l'action sociale et des familles.

[48] This is particularly manifested when the personalised schooling project of the child is designed. See Article L112-2 of the Code of Education.

[49] Article L112-2.

[50] See Articles L111-1 and L112-1 of the French Code of Education. See also Circulaire n° 2015–129 du 21.8.2015 sur la scolarisation des élèves en situation de handicap: Unités localisées pour l'inclusion scolaire (Ulis), dispositifs pour la scolarisation des élèves en situation de handicap dans le premier et le second degrés (Regulation Relating to the Schooling of Students with Disabilities in Primary and Secondary Education: Inclusive Education Classes). This Regulation relates to the establishment, organisation and functions of special classes in mainstream schools for students with a personalised schooling project.

[51] The Norwegian government provides a translation of the Education Act 1998 at www.regjeringen.no/contentassets/b3b9e92cce6742c39581b661a019e504/education-act-norway-with-amendments-entered-2014–2.pdf (accessed January 2017). According to Section 8(1), '[p]rimary and lower secondary school pupils have the right to attend the school that is closest to where they live or the school designated for the catchment area where they live'. For further analysis on the Norwegian and Finnish legal frameworks, see Arduin (2015) (n. 6).

1998 to the effect that '[e]ducation shall be adapted to the abilities and aptitudes of the individual pupil'.[52]

Three observations are noteworthy. First, aside from the neighbourhood schooling principle, no general presumption in law or preference towards mainstream education is mentioned in the Norwegian Act. Second, the Act does not expressly refer to students with disabilities. Whilst Section 5(1)of the Act is entitled 'The right to special education', this section applies to 'pupils who either do not or are unable to benefit satisfactorily from ordinary teaching',[53] hence emphasising the learning needs of students as opposed to their personal characteristic. This legal priority on the individual needs of the student is also expressed in Section 5(1) paragraph 2 of the Act, which places strong emphasis on the 'pupil's developmental prospects' when assessing the content of the education to be provided to the student falling under the scope of Section 5.[54] Third, the absence of any explicit reference to the concept of inclusive education should be noted, bearing in mind that the concept of 'adapted education' was introduced in 2008, and that Norway signed the CRPD in 2007 and ratified the Convention in 2013.[55]

Accordingly, as far as the Norwegian legal framework is concerned, it seems that adapted education is the prevalent legal norm, the nature of which is universal, in the sense that it applies to every student. Whilst many special schools have been closed since the 1990s, they have not totally disappeared from the educational landscape; instead, they have been reorganised into resource centres, which, along with the local municipal support system – in particular, the Educational Psychology Service – are available to schools to ensure that expert assessments are prepared and that special support is suited and appropriate to the educational needs of students.[56]

52 Section 1(3) was added by the Act of 20 June 2008 no. 48 of 2008, pursuant to the Decree of 20 June 2008 no. 621 of 2008.

53 Education Act 1998 S5(1) [1].

54 As per paragraph 2 of Section 5.1 of the Act, '[i]n assessing what kind of instruction shall be provided, particular emphasis shall be placed on the pupil's developmental prospects. The content of the courses offered shall be such that the pupil receives adequate benefit from the instruction as a whole in relation to other pupils and in relation to educational objectives that are realistic for the pupil. Pupils who receive special education shall have the same total number of teaching hours as other pupils.'

55 Information available at https://treaties.un.org/Pages/ViewDetails.aspx?src=TREATY&mtdsg_no=IV-15&chapter=4&clang=_en (accessed January 2017) ('UN CRPD Depositary').

56 Rolf B. Fasting, 'Adapted Education: The Norwegian Pathway to Inclusive and Efficient Education' (2013) 17 *International Journal of Inclusive Education* 263; see also European Agency for Special Needs and Inclusive Education (n. 13) 49.

e Finland

These Norwegian features are also prevalent in the Finnish legal framework.[57] Aside from the legal provision established in the Finnish Basic Education Act 1998 to the effect that a pupil's school is determined by the principle of neighbourhood schools, the diversity of learners' needs is also given priority in the legislation.[58] For instance, Sections 16 and 16A of the Act, which were introduced in 2010, provide for remedial teaching, part-time special needs education and enhanced support. Both sections emphasise the learning difficulties of the students, regardless of their personal characteristic. In addition, the Finnish National Core Curriculum is formulated on the basis of a situational approach to learning, that is, 'as an individual and communal process of building knowledge and skills'.[59]

Like the system in Norway, the Finnish system guarantees a continuum of provisions and placements options aimed at responding to the individual learning needs of Finnish pupils in their local school.[60] Similarly, the

57 For further analysis on the Finnish education system, see Henri Pesonen, Irmeli Halinen, Pirjo Koivula, Matti Kyrö, Hanna-Mari Sarlin and Kristiina Volmari, 'The Implementation of New Special Education Legislation in Finland' (2015) 29 *Educational Policy* 162; Marjatta Takala and Astrid Ahl, 'Special Education in Swedish and Finnish Schools: Seeing the Forest or the Trees?' (2014) 41 *British Journal of Special Education* 59; Tiina Itkonen and Maekku Jahnukainen, 'An Analysis of Accountability Policies in Finland and the United States' (2007) 54 *International Journal of Disability, Development and Education* 5; Irmeli Halinen and others, *The Development of Education: National Report of Finland* (Finnish National Board of Education 2008).

58 Section 6(1) of the Finnish Basic Education Act 628/1998, as amended in 2010 by 1136/2010.

59 Finnish National Board of Education, *Regional Preparatory Workshop on Inclusive Education: Eastern and South Eastern Europe* (UNESCO and International Bureau of Education 2007) www.ibe.unesco.org/fileadmin/user_upload/Inclusive_Education/Reports/sinaia_07/finland_inclusion_07.pdf (accessed January 2017) 4.

60 The reform adopted in 2010 introduced one additional educational support, known as intensified support, on top of the already established general educational support and special support. According to Section 16(a)(1) of the Basic Education Act:

> A pupil who needs regular support in learning or schoolgoing shall be provided enhanced support in accordance with a learning plan devised for him or her. The learning plan must be prepared, unless there is an apparent reason not to do so, in collaboration with the pupil, the parent, carer or, where necessary, some other legal representative of the pupil. The enhanced support shall comprise forms of pupil support, especially those referred to in Sections 16, 31 and 31a, and the required pedagogical arrangements. The salient content of the enhanced support and the learning plan shall be laid down in the core curriculum.

In other words, pupils in need of regular support for their learning or schooling or in need of several forms of support at the same time must be provided with *intensified support* that is based on a pedagogical assessment in accordance with a learning plan prepared for them. Intensified support is provided when general support is not sufficient (S4.1 of the

Finnish legal framework does not explicitly refer to the concept of inclusive education, despite the reform adopted in 2010 and the signature of the CRPD in 2007.[61]

In autumn 2015, 8.4 per cent of Finns received intensified support[62] and 7.3 per cent received special support in comprehensive schools.[63] In other words, around 16 per cent of comprehensive school students received some form of additional support in Finland, whilst only 8 per cent of students received additional support in Norway during the same period.[64] Perhaps one of the main reasons behind this difference in proportion stems from the fact that additional support in Norway requires the provision of an Individual Education Plan (IEP), whilst in Finland such a plan is established only for students benefiting from support in the form of full-time special education.[65]

f The Information Inferred by the Audience in Relation to Article 24 of the CRPD

In light of these differing interpretations of the right to inclusive education in national legal frameworks, of the reservations made by the United Kingdom on Article 24 of the Convention with respect to the maintenance of special

Amendments and Additions to the National Core Curriculum for Basic Education, Finish National Board of Education 2010).

61 Finland ratified the Convention on 11 May 2016. This information was retrieved from the UN CRPD Depositary (n. 55). It has been argued that the principle of inclusive education constitutes a fundamental value of the Finnish education system. See Halinen and others (n. 57) 20; see also Essi Kesälahti and Sai Väyrynen, *Learning from Our Neighbours: Inclusive Education in the Making* (University of Lapland Printing Centre 2013).

62 Official Statistics of Finland, 'Special Education' (*Statistics Finland*, 13 June 2016) www.stat.fi/til/erop/index_en.html (accessed January 2017).

63 Ibid. As pointed out by the Amendments to the National Core Curriculum, every pupil has a right to high-quality education as well as an opportunity to receive guidance and support for learning and schooling on all school days. General support is the first type of support available. It may take the form of remedial teaching or any alternative teachings required to meet the students' needs. See Halinen and others (n. 57).

64 Division for Education Statistics, 'Pupils in Primary and Lower Secondary School, 1 October 2016' (*Statistics Norway*, 14 December 2016) www.ssb.no/en/utdanning/statistikker/utgrs (accessed 12 June 2017).

65 Finnish National Board of Education, *National Core Curriculum for Basic Education 2004* (Finnish National Board of Education 2004) www.oph.fi/download/47671_core_curricula_basic_education_1.pdf (accessed 14 June 2017) [5.4]; Norwegian Directorate for Education and Training, 'National Curriculum for Knowledge Promotion in Primary and Secondary Education and Training: The Quality Framework' (*Utdanningsdirektoratet*) www.udir.no/globalassets/upload/larerplaner/fastsatte_lareplaner_for_kunnskapsloeftet/prinsipper_lko6_eng.pdf (accessed 14 June 2017); Takala and Ahl (n. 57); and Arduin (n. 6).

schools,[66] of the approach adopted by the Committee on Social and Economic rights in *Autism* v. *France*[67] and in *Action Européenne des Handicapés* v. *France*,[68] which seems to reject any notion of 'separate but equal', and of the recent General Comment on Article 24,[69] the task of clarifying the information expressed in Article 24 of the CRPD, whilst challenging, is salient.

As observed in France, the right to inclusive education is understood as the right to education for all in an inclusive environment. In contrast, the Irish legal framework understands the right to inclusive education as the right to education in a mainstream school. In England, there is no reference to a legal right to inclusive education; the prevailing norm is that of mainstream education for students with SEN, although this norm is not absolute. Finally, the Norwegian and Finnish legal frameworks do not refer to the right to inclusive education either. They refer, instead, to the universal right to education, which should be adapted to the learning needs of pupils. Accordingly, out of five national legal frameworks reviewed, two refer expressly to the right to inclusive education and, out of the two, one – i.e. Ireland – has yet to ratify the Convention and to implement Section 2 of the EPSEN Act, which establishes the right to inclusive education.

To the extent that only France and Ireland refer exclusively to the right to inclusive education in their legislation, the following syllogism is specifically designed for their legal interpretation, although it could be argued that it also applies to the English approach:

[66] The United Kingdom made a reservation to Article 24 to enable it to educate children with disabilities 'outside their local community where more appropriate education provision is available elsewhere'. Note the following declaration from the United Kingdom: 'The General Education System in the United Kingdom includes mainstream, and special schools, which the UK Government understands is allowed under the Convention.' Mauritius made a similar reservation with regard to Article 24(2)(b) to the effect that a special education system would be maintained along with an inclusive education system. Information retrieved from UN CRPD Depositary (n. 55) under 'Declarations and Reservations'.

[67] *International Association Autism-Europe* v. *France* Complaint no. 13/2002 (European Committee on Social Rights, 4 November 2003).

[68] Complaint no. 81/2012 (European Committee on Social Rights, 11 September 2013).

[69] Although the Comment distinguishes between segregation, exclusion, integration and inclusion, the Committee remains silent as to whether, based on the learning capacity of the student, alternative forms of education should be provided as a tool to promote the well-being of the student and his or her participation in society.

1. Students with disabilities are traditionally seen as not being able to benefit from the same educational standard than others, which is why they have been traditionally educated in separate settings.
2. A law is passed to the effect that everyone should be educated in mainstream school. Accordingly, persons with disabilities are entitled to this right to learn in a mainstream school and the onus is on schools to provide reasonable accommodation to the students so that they can learn along with their peers.
3. By imposing a duty on schools to educate everyone in the same mainstream environment, the intervention of the law may actually reinforce the existing stigma associated with disability and difference. In other words, inclusive education, understood according to a universalist approach or to a forced presumption, may be another form of affirmative action measures, the implication of which may be to reinforce the prevailing stereotype of students with disabilities.[70]

The next section benchmarks the aforementioned legal interpretations against the information expressed in Article 24. Accordingly, the following sections provide a normative framework for analysing the expressive dimension of Article 24(1) and (2).

3 THE INFORMATION EXPRESSED IN ARTICLE 24(1) OF THE CRPD

Article 24(1) provides that, in order to realise the right to education for persons with disabilities 'without discrimination and on the basis of equal opportunity', States Parties shall guarantee an 'inclusive educational system' aimed at the full development of persons with disabilities and their effective participation in society.[71] Two types of information may be inferred from this first provision. First, it is argued that the right to inclusive education is a non-discriminatory right; second, its purpose is to promote the well-being of persons with disabilities.

[70] Tarunabh Khaitan provides an excellent analysis of the importance of the design of affirmative action measures. In *A Theory of Discrimination Law* (Oxford University Press 2015), Khaitan observes that the design of these measures may convey two contrary expressive implications for the disadvantaged group. On the one hand, they 'may send a message' that the state has acknowledged the relative disadvantage and injustice faced by the group historically; on the other hand, they may be interpreted as 'fortify[ing] a negative stereotype that members of the group are lazy or unintelligent' (at 222).

[71] Similarly, this association may be observed, although to a lesser extent, in Article 3 of the CRPD, which pinpoints the general principles that govern the Convention.

a Inclusive Education as a Non-Discriminatory Right

With respect to its nature, the right to inclusive education enshrined in Article 24(1) fulfils the four characteristics of a non-discriminatory right.[72] The first characteristic emphasises the connection between what is prohibited and certain attributes or personal grounds that a person has, such as disability.[73] It is well acknowledged that inclusive education emerged from the field of special education and is linked to the concept of disability.[74] The fulfilment of this condition is not contentious.

The second characteristic of a non-discriminatory right relates to its cognate group – that is, the protected personal ground, disability, classifies persons into groups – such as persons with disabilities versus persons without disabilities.[75] This condition is essential, for it suggests that a right that is universal and not sensitive to grounds is not a discriminatory right.[76] Accordingly, the right to inclusive education for all observed in the French Code of Education is not a discriminatory right; it is a universal right.

The third characteristic emphasises the substantial disadvantages that the members of one group experience relative to the members of the other cognate group.[77] Again, it is well acknowledged that students with disabilities are more likely to suffer disadvantages in our societies than non-disabled students. This observation is not contentious; it is affirmed in paragraphs k (acknowledging the persistence of barriers faced by persons with disabilities and violation of their human rights) and p (acknowledging multiple and aggravated forms of discrimination) of the Preamble of the Convention, Articles 6 and 7 of the

72 These characteristics have been summarised by Khaitan (n. 70); in particular, see chapter 2.

73 Ibid. 29.

74 See, for instance, the Salamanca Statement (n. 12), which was exclusively concerned with disability and special education. For further analysis, see also Gary Thomas, 'A Review of Thinking and Research about Inclusive Education Policy, with Suggestions of a New Kind of Inclusive Thinking' (2013) 39 *British Educational Research Journal* 473.

75 Khaitan (n. 70) 30. Note that the term 'group' is defined loosely as referring to the universal order ground, such as disability. It does not require the existence of a group identity, which would be contentious in the context of disability. On disability identity, see the scholarship of Samuel R. Bagenstos, *Law and the Contradictions of the Disability Rights Movement* (Yale University Press 2009).

76 Surprisingly, the Committee on the Rights of Persons with Disabilities has recently affirmed in its fourth General Comment that '[i]nclusive education is central to achieving high quality education for all learners, including those with disabilities' (n. 5) [2]. This perspective suggests that, although the CRPD was designed exclusively for persons with disabilities, as expressed in Article 1, the scope of the right to inclusive education would extend beyond disability and special educational needs. In other words, the Committee interprets the right to inclusive education as a universal right. This interpretation seems at odds with the nature of the right expressed in Article 24(1) of the CRPD.

77 Khaitan (n. 70) 31.

Convention, which cover respectively the groups of women with disabilities and children with disabilities,[78] and the recent General Comment of the Committee on the Rights of Persons with Disabilities.[79]

Finally, the fourth condition of a non-discriminatory right relates to its design. Whilst a norm of discrimination law seeks to distribute the substantial benefits in question to some members of the intended beneficiary group, it does not intend to distribute the benefits to all of them.[80] It has been argued that even positive norms of discrimination law are not designed to benefit every member of the group.[81] The eccentric characteristic of the norm of inclusive education is particularly manifest when one looks closely at the language used in Article 24. At no point does the Article refer to *every* or *all* person(s) with disabilities. When the Convention seeks to refer to all persons with disabilities, the text mentions it explicitly. For instance, Article 4(1) reaffirms the general obligations that States Parties undertake to implement 'the full realization of all human rights . . . for *all* persons with disabilities'.[82] Similarly, Article 5(1) of the CRPD emphasises that 'all persons are equal before and under the law and are entitled without any discrimination to the equal protection and equal benefit of the law'. Accordingly, when one reads Article 24(1) in light of Article 24(2)(a) of the CRPD, which imposes a duty on States Parties to ensure that '[p]ersons with disabilities are not excluded from the general education system on the basis of disability', this duty should not be read as ensuring that every person with disability is educated in the general schooling system.[83] In other words, if Article 24(2)(a) is a typical discriminatory

78 For an analysis of the intersectionality of the CRPD, see Oddný Mjöll Arnardóttir, 'A Future of Multidimensional Disadvantage Equality?' in Oddný Mjöll Arnardóttir and Gerard Quinn (eds) *The UN Convention on the Rights of Persons with Disabilities: European and Scandinavian Perspectives* (Martinus Nijhoff Publishers 2009) 41–66; see also Gerard Quinn and Eilionóir Flynn, 'Transatlantic Borrowings: The Past and Future of EU Non-Discrimination Law and Policy on the Ground of Disability' (2012) 60 *The American Journal of Comparative Law* 23, 46.

79 (n. 5) [4].

80 Khaitan (n. 70) 39.

81 Ibid.

82 Emphasis added. The full text of Article 4(1) reads as follows: 'States Parties undertake to ensure and promote the full realization of all human rights and fundamental freedoms for all persons with disabilities without discrimination of any kind on the basis of disability.' Note that this chapter does not reject the view that education is a universal right, although to what extent the right to inclusive education is a human right remains unclear. For instance, see John-Stewart Gordon, 'Is Inclusive Education a Human Right?' (2013) 41 *Journal of Law, Medicine and Ethics* 754.

83 Kanter makes an interesting point in relation to the design of Article 24(1). She observes that Article 24 refers to an 'inclusive education system' as opposed to 'inclusive classrooms or schools for all students with types of disabilities, at all levels of education'. Accordingly, she

prohibition that applies to every person with disability and is, a fortiori, universal,[84] Article 24(2)(b) applies, however, to some members of the group, as opposed to the entire group of persons with disabilities. It provides that persons with disabilities 'can' access educational provision in the local schooling system. The use of the verb 'can' suggests, first, that persons with disabilities have the opportunity to access an inclusive local school;[85] it imposes, therefore, a duty on States Parties to remove barriers that prevent a student with disability from accessing and participating in their local school.[86] Second, it suggests that persons with disabilities may choose to attend their local school or not.[87] Interestingly, UNESCO pointed out, during the seventh session, that this principle of choice is embedded within the goal of inclusion in education.[88]

From this normative analysis it follows that the right expressed in Article 24 is a non-discriminatory right as opposed to a universal right. It is not designed, nor does it seek, to secure a place in mainstream school for *every* child with a disability. Its purpose is twofold: first, to protect all students from discrimination based on their disability, and, second, to guarantee opportunities for students with disabilities to access and participate in their local school. Once again, this latter objective does not express the ideal according to

concludes that, through this design, Article 24 may permit the education of some students with disabilities in separate educational settings (n. 2, at 33).

84 The universal scope of the anti-discriminatory prohibition on the basis of disability is explicitly affirmed at Article 5(2) of the CRPD: 'States Parties shall prohibit *all* discrimination on the basis of disability and guarantee to persons with disabilities equal and effective legal protection against discrimination on all grounds' (emphasis added).

85 Note the interpretation provided by the Committee in its General Comment No. 4 (n. 5) [33] on the purpose of support measures required under paragraph 2(e) of Article 24: 'they must be designed to *strengthen opportunities* for students with disabilities to participate in the classroom and in out-of-school activities alongside their peers' (emphasis added).

86 It could also be argued that, due to the emphasis on the principle of 'access to' an inclusive education, Article 24(2)(b) is in fact complementary of Article 24(2)(a), which ensures that persons with disabilities are not excluded from education on the basis of disability.

87 This observation should not be interpreted as suggesting that one has a right to choose to be educated or not. The right to education is a universal human right, which cannot be derogated from. See Article 13(1) of the UN International Covenant on Economic, Social and Cultural Rights, which provides that '[t]he States Parties to the present Covenant recognize the right of everyone to education' (United Nations General Assembly Res. 2200A (XXI) 16 December 1966).

88 See UNESCO observations at www.un.org/esa/socdev/enable/rights/ahcstata24sevscomments .htm (accessed December 2016). For a detailed analysis of the different approaches suggested during the drafting process of the CRPD, in particular as to whether the CRPD should contain an explicit right to inclusive education for all students with disabilities, see Kanter (n. 2) 23–25.

which all educational services for all students with disabilities should be provided in the general schooling system.

Accordingly, the universal interpretation of the right to inclusive education as adopted in France is at odds with the nature of the right as it finds expression in Article 24(1) of the Convention.

b The Purpose of the Right Expressed in Article 24(1)

As mentioned briefly, Article 24 seeks to regulate conduct that is discriminatory and that prevents students with disabilities from accessing and participating in primary and secondary education in their local school. In other words, this part argues that the normative basis on which the second objective is based relates to the well-being of persons with disabilities. From this perspective, it follows that Article 24 seeks to promote, protect and fulfil the individual well-being of students with disabilities. Whilst the concept of well-being is not expressly referred to in Article 24(1), it may be inferred from the 'full development of human potential and sense of dignity and self-worth' of persons with disabilities, expressed in Article 24(1)(a), and from the development 'of their personality, talents and creativity, as well as their mental and physical abilities, to their fullest potential', expressed in Article 24(1)(b). In addition, this purposive dimension has been stated by the Committee on the Rights of Persons with Disabilities in its General Comment on Article 24.[89] As per the Committee, the right to inclusive education seeks not only to 'combat discrimination, including harmful stereotypes' based on disability but also to promote participation of persons with disabilities by adopting proactive measures that focus on their well-being.[90]

To the extent that this perspective is intertwined with the notion of well-being, some form of definition is required for clarity's sake. As per Sen, the concept of well-being refers to the 'wellness' of the person's state.[91] Sen

89 General Comment No. 4 (n. 5) [9].

90 Ibid. [10]: 'Inclusive education is to be understood as [a] principle that values the well-being of all students, respects their inherent dignity and autonomy, [and] acknowledges individual requirements and ability to effectively be included in and contribute to society.'

91 As per Sen, 'functionings are seen as central to the *nature* of well-being, even though the *sources* of well-being could easily be external to the person . . . The claim is that the functionings make up a person's being, and the evaluation of a person's wellbeing has to take the form of an assessment of these constituent elements.' See Martha Nussbaum and Amartya Sen, *The Quality of Life* (Oxford University Press 1993) 36–37. See also Amartya Sen, 'Well-Being, Agency and Freedom: The Dewey Lectures 1984' (1985) 82 *Journal of Philosophy* 169; and Amartya Sen, *Inequality Reexamined* (Clarendon Press 1992).

suggests that the wellness of a person is linked to the guarantee of essential functionings – such as being educated – and to the promotion of more complex and 'refined' functionings – such as the nurture of individual talents.[92] In this sense, it has been suggested that the concept of well-being is both objective and subjective.[93] On the one hand, it is objective as it identifies a set of functionings that are essential for the achievement of individual well-being; on the other hand, it is subjective, for it is relative to the individual's set of functionings.[94] When someone is excluded from access to essential functionings or to more refined functionings, this person's well-being is not secured. In turn, this lack of well-being achievement may lead to individual disadvantages, which may further impair the person's well-being. In this context, the purpose of a norm of discrimination law, such as a norm of inclusive education, is to protect individuals from disadvantages based on personal characteristics so as to promote and secure their individual well-being.

In light of this normative analysis on Article 24(1), the information expressed in Article 24(2) becomes clearer.

4 THE INFORMATION EXPRESSED IN ARTICLE 24(2) OF THE CRPD

In order to achieve the regulated purpose of the right to inclusive education, two instruments are provided in Article 24(2): (1) 'reasonable accommodation',[95] and (2) 'individualized support measures' in 'environments that maximize academic and social development, consistent with the goal of full inclusion'.[96]

92 Sen notes that, in day-to-day parlance, we may refer to functionings in a 'refined way', which 'relates to the relevance of choice in our life'. Nussbaum and Sen (n. 91) 40. See also Hugh Collins, 'Discrimination, Equality and Social Inclusion' (2003) 66 *Modern Law Review* 16, 32; Michael Ashley Stein, 'Disability Human Rights' (2007) 95 *California Law Review* 75; Michael Ashley Stein and Penelope J. S. Stein, 'Beyond Disability Civil Rights' (2007) 58 *Hastings Law Journal* 1203.

93 Collins (n. 92) 23–24.

94 Instead of referring to 'functionings' and 'capabilities', Collins refers to the distinction between access to material goods – such as food and shelter – and access to non-material goods – such as education, employment and participation in politics. He points out that to achieve a state of well-being, an individual should have access to and benefit from both goods (ibid.).

95 Article 24(2)(c).

96 Article 24(2)(e).

The provision of reasonable accommodation is a well-established international and regional principle,[97] the denial of which is a form of discrimination.[98] Reasonable accommodation refers to 'necessary and appropriate modification and adjustments not imposing a disproportionate or undue burden, where needed in a particular case, to ensure to persons with disabilities the enjoyment or exercise on an equal basis with others of all human rights and fundamental freedoms'.[99] In other words, reasonable accommodation is an individualised obligation, relative to the needs of the student concerned.[100] It is commonly accepted that the duty to make reasonable accommodation is not absolute; its limitation relates to the 'disproportionate' or 'undue burden' that would result from making the accommodation, wherever that line is drawn.[101] When the implementation of this duty is not proportionate in the context of education, Article 24(2) suggests that a second anti-discriminatory instrument may be supplemented in order to achieve the goal of inclusion – that is, the achievement of individual well-being in a 'learning-friendly' and 'safe' environment.[102] Note that the promotion of opportunities for students with disabilities to access and participate in their local school is only a component of well-being achievement.

97 For further analysis on the provision of reasonable accommodation in the context of disability, see Michael Ashley Stein, 'Same Struggle, Different Difference: ADA Accommodations as Antidiscrimination' (2004) 153 *University of Pennsylvania Law Review* 579; Michael Ashley Stein, Anita Silvers, Bradley A. Areheart, Leslie Pickering Francis, 'Accommodating Every Body' (2014) 81 *University of Chicago Law Review* 689; Lisa Waddington and Mark Bell, 'Exploring the Boundaries of Positive Action under EU Law: A Search for Conceptual Clarity' (2011) 48 *Common Market Law Review* 1503; Lisa Waddington and Aart Hendriks, 'The Expanding Concept of Employment Discrimination in Europe: From Direct and Indirect Discrimination to Reasonable Accommodation Discrimination' (2002) 18 *International Journal of Comparative Labour Law and Industrial Relations* 403; Lisa Waddington, 'Reassessing the Employment of People with Disabilities in Europe: From Quotas to Anti-Discrimination Laws' (1996) 18 *Comparative Labor Law and Policy Journal* 62; Grainne de Búrca, 'The EU in the Negotiation of the UN Disability Convention' (2010) 35 *European Law Review* 174.

98 CRPD Art 2.

99 Ibid.

100 See Lisa Waddington and Anna Lawson, *Disability and Non-Discrimination Law in the European Union: An Analysis of Disability Discrimination Law within and beyond the Employment Field* (Publications Office of the European Union 2009) 52. For an excellent summary of the duty to accommodate as interpreted by member states, see Lisa Waddington and Andrea Broderick, *Disability Law and Reasonable Accommodation beyond Employment: A Legal Analysis of the Situation in EU Member States* (Publications Office of the European Union 2016).

101 This is reflected in Article 2 of the CRPD, which refers to the 'disproportionate or undue burden' as a limitation of the duty to provide reasonable accommodation.

102 General Comment No. 4 (n. 5) [12(f)].

This second instrument is referred to as 'individualized support' in 'environments that maximize academic and social development'.[103] During the drafting process, the initial provision was referring to 'alternative educational settings'.[104] In day-to-day parlance, these settings are most commonly referred to as special classes or special schools and, at times, are interpreted as being the antonym of inclusive education. Two comments are noteworthy.

First, a literal interpretation of the text of the Convention does not support the assumption according to which alternative settings are contrary to the goal of inclusive education. Recall that the goal of the right is to prevent discriminatory behaviour based on disability and to promote individual well-being achievement in educational settings. Similarly, the design of Article 24 has been left intentionally general so as to allow flexible interpretation of the principles embedded in the Convention.[105] What is manifest is that the introduction of the provision in paragraph (e), which is distinct from reasonable accommodation (paragraph c) and from support in the general education system (paragraph d), suggests that individual support may be also provided in settings that are different from settings provided in the general education system.[106] This interpretation seems consonant with the approach adopted by the Committee on the Rights of Persons with Disabilities in its concluding observations to Spain[107] and the Committee on the Rights of the

103 Article 24(2)(e).

104 United Nations General Assembly, 'Report of the Ad Hoc Committee on a Comprehensive and Integral International Convention on the Protection and Promotion of the Rights and Dignity of Persons with Disabilities' 3rd Session (2004) UN Doc A/AC.265/2004/5.

105 See, for instance, Canada's statement on 3 August 2005 during the sixth session: 'Canada also believes that it is important to avoid overly prescriptive detail in the convention. As we have noted several times, it is important that the convention serve as a principled document that is capable of interpretation over time.' Available at www.un.org/esa/socdev/enable/rights/ahcstata24sevscomments.htm (accessed 25 October 2018)

106 This interpretation further bolsters Kanter's analysis, which provides that 'nowhere does Article 24 state that children, youth and adults with disabilities must be educated only in mainstream or "regular" schools and classrooms' and concludes that 'Article 24 leaves open the possibility that State Parties may be free to continue to support separate schools and classrooms' (n. 2) 33.

107 Committee on the Rights of Persons with Disabilities, Concluding Observations on the Initial Report of Spain (19 October 2011) CRPD/C/ESP/CO/1 [44(b) and (d)]. The Committee did not express the view according to which Article 24(2) prohibits children with disabilities from being placed in separate schools or special classes; instead, the Committee recommended that these decisions to place children with disabilities in a separate school or special classes be 'taken in consultation with the parents' and be capable of being 'appealed swiftly and effectively'. This approach has also been expressed by the Committee on the Rights of the Child, to the extent that inclusion may 'includ[e] a certain portion of special education' (Committee on the Rights of the Child, General Comment

Child, which stated that inclusion may 'includ[e] a certain portion of special education'.[108]

Second, the CRPD *travaux préparatoires* discloses a number of views among states, non-governmental organisations (NGOs), intergovernmental organisations (IGOs) and national human rights institutions (NHRIs) towards a flexible approach in providing education in alternative settings. For instance, during the third session of the Ad Hoc Committee, the draft of the then Article 17 of the Convention provided that '[w]here the general education system does not adequately meet the needs of persons with disabilities special and alternative forms of learning education should be made available'.[109] In subsequent sessions, several states[110] and UNESCO supported the EU proposal, which expressly referred to appropriate 'effective alternative forms of education' in meeting educational needs and in the interest of promoting full inclusion. The final draft of the Convention replaced the expression of appropriate 'effective alternative forms of education' with the more general expression of 'environments that maximise academic and social developments' of the student concerned. This generality should be interpreted in a flexible manner – that is, in a manner reflecting the individual needs of the students. It should allow for different forms of education that are adaptable to the capabilities of the students and acceptable for them, with the caveat that decisions solely based on personal characteristics will be rejected. In this context, alternative educational provisions become complementary instruments, designed to promote students' well-being in educational settings.

From this normative analysis, it follows that the information expressed in Article 24(1) and (2) may be summarised in the following syllogism:

1. The law seeks to promote the well-being of students with disabilities in learner-friendly environments. Evidence demonstrates that, historically, persons with disabilities have suffered substantive barriers to access

No. 9 [2006]: The Rights of Children with Disabilities [27 February 2007] CRC/C/GC/9 [67]).

108 Committee on the Rights of the Child, General Comment No. 9 (2006): The Rights of Children with Disabilities (27 February 2007) CRC/C/GC/9 [67].

109 UN Doc A/AC.265/2004/5 (n. 104) 40.

110 See for instance the observations made by Canada, the European Union, Japan, Kenya, Philippines, Sudan and Thailand during the sixth session of the Ad Hoc Committee in the following daily summaries by Rehabilitation International: Daily Summary 2 August 2005 www.un.org/esa/socdev/enable/rights/ahc6sum2aug.htm (accessed 14 June 2017); Daily Summary 3 August 2005 www.un.org/esa/socdev/enable/rights/ahc6sum3aug.htm (accessed 14 June 2017); Daily Summary 4 August 2005 www.un.org/esa/socdev/enable/rights/ahc6sum4aug.htm (accessed 14 June 2017).

a number of goods and services on the ground of their personal characteristics. In this context of persistent discrimination, the law prohibits schools from discriminating on the basis of disability.

2. Within the general education system, schools have a duty to provide reasonable accommodation, adapted according to the individual needs of the student. The purpose of this instrument is to further promote the well-being of the student concerned.
3. When this accommodation may not prove effective for reasons outside financial constraints, alternative forms of education should be provided to the individual student *on a temporary basis* and with regular reviews of his/her situation.
4. Accordingly, the law on inclusive education is prima facie concerned with the best interests of the student and the ideal of individual well-being achievement.[111]

5 CONCLUSION

This chapter has sought to demonstrate that the statement made by Article 24 may be different from the statement heard by the audience. When one looks at the legal interpretation of the right to inclusive education adopted in some European frameworks and the information expressed in Article 24(1) and (2) of the Convention, it seems that the two do not always converge. The legal presumption observed in the English and Irish legal frameworks to place children with disabilities into mainstream school does not seem to be required by a close reading of Article 24. Similarly, the expansion of the right to inclusive education to all children observed in the French legal framework is at odds with the non-discriminatory nature of the right as it finds expression in Article 24 of the Convention. Had the French legal framework adopted the same interpretation as the Norwegian and Finnish frameworks, which refer to the universal right to education adapted to the individual needs of the students, there would not be any such contradiction. Once again, the main difference is that the Norwegian Education Act and the Finnish Act are both silent with respect to the concept of inclusive education. Accordingly, their legal norm is different from the legal norm as it finds expression in Article 24 of the CRPD.

111 Recall that Article 7(2) of the CRPD provides that '[i]n all actions concerning children with disabilities, the best interests of the child shall be a primary consideration'.

From a normative perspective, this chapter suggests that the right to inclusive education as it finds expression in Article 24 is a non-discriminatory right, not a universal right. Through expressivism, it has sought to clarify the nature of the right, its purpose and its regulatory instruments. The purpose of this exercise is to monitor the audience interpretation to further refine the language used in future legislative frameworks and to ensure their effectiveness. Further research is needed in order to understand why a gap has emerged between the information expressed in Article 24 of the CRPD and the audience meaning.

Ultimately, the question as to how Article 24 should be interpreted is epistemological; it requires empirical evidence of testable assumptions on which the legal principle of inclusive education is premised. As it stands, there is a dearth of empirical evidence. Accordingly, the debate on the interpretation of Article 24 remains semantic. As Sunstein has observed, support for a law should be rooted not only in the intrinsic value of the statement but also in its consequences on norms.[112]

112 Sunstein (n. 8) 2045.

B

SUBSTANTIVE ISSUES

7

Reasonable Accommodation

An Integral Part of the Right to Education for Persons with Disabilities

Shivaun Quinlivan

1 INTRODUCTION

The United Nations Convention on the Rights of Persons with Disabilities (CRPD) is the first international human rights convention to explicitly hold that the failure to provide reasonable accommodation amounts to an act of discrimination.[1] This follows from a prior interpretation, by the United Nations Committee on Economic, Social and Cultural Rights (CESCR), which defined discrimination as including the denial of reasonable accommodation.[2] The express incorporation within the CRPD 'highlights the centrality of reasonable accommodation in the quest for equal rights for people with disabilities'.[3] Arguably, the inclusion of the duty to accommodate is one of the more important features of the CRPD, as it provides a legal tool to assist in the enforcement of equality provisions in both the public and private spheres. Moreover, the duty to accommodate is situated within the CRPD articles of general application, thus ensuring that the duty to accommodate is explicitly linked 'to the realization of *all* human rights – civil, political,

[1] United Nations General Assembly, Convention on the Rights of Persons with Disabilities (adopted 13 December 2006, opened for signature 30 March 2007, entered into force 3 May 2008) A/RES/61/06 [hereinafter CRPD] Art. 5. The European Court of Human Rights in *Glor* v. *Switzerland* App. No. 13444/04 (ECtHR, 30 April 2009) interpreted Article 14 of the European Convention on Human Rights and Fundamental Freedoms as including a duty to accommodate. Moreover, the UN Committee on Economic, Social and Cultural Rights (CESCR), in General Comment No. 5: Persons with Disabilities (9 December 1994) E/1995/22, defined discrimination as including the denial of reasonable accommodation [15].

[2] CESCR, General Comment No. 5 (n. 1) [15].

[3] Piers Gooding and Shivaun Quinlivan, 'Reasonable Accommodation: A Tool for Disability Justice in the 21st Century' in Annika Pabsch and Petra Söderqvist (eds), *UNCRPD Implementation in Europe – a Deaf Perspective: Article 27: Work and Employment* (European Union of the Deaf 2015) 2.

economic, social, cultural',[4] therefore including the right to education. Additionally, the right to education contains two additional references to reasonable accommodation and the duty to accommodate learners with disabilities, suggesting it is particularly important in the education context.

The right to education has been variously described as an 'empowerment'[5] or 'multiplier'[6] right, and, for many, it is a prerequisite to accessing and availing of other human rights. The Committee on the Rights of the Child (CRC) highlights that denying educational opportunities impacts people with disabilities 'by denying them job opportunities in the future'.[7] In effect, the denial of equal access to the right to education has the potential to impact negatively a person's life opportunities. Therefore it seems self-evident that if a society improves a person's educational opportunities, this might in turn improve that person's employment prospects, access to health care and political participation, as well as help to ensure the 'full and equal enjoyment of all human rights'.[8] It is equally clear that people with disabilities are not provided the same educational opportunities as people without disabilities.[9]

It is against this backdrop that the implementation of effective non-discrimination duties, including the duty to provide reasonable accommodation, might be expected to improve the educational opportunities for people with disabilities. Commentators have described the inclusion of the duty to accommodate as 'novel',[10] 'transformative',[11] 'innovative'[12]

4 Janet E. Lord and Rebecca Brown, 'The Role of Reasonable Accommodation in Securing Substantive Equality for Persons with Disabilities: The UN Convention on the Rights of Persons with Disabilities' (SSRN Scholarly Paper 2010) 1 https://ssrn.com/abstract=1618903 (accessed 31 July 2017).

5 Fons Coomans, 'Clarifying the Core Elements of the Right to Education' in Fons Coomans and Fried Van Hoof (eds), *The Right to Complain about Economic, Social and Cultural Rights*, vol. 18 (SIM Special, Netherlands Institute of Human Rights 1995) 11.

6 Katarina Tomaševski, *Human Rights Obligations in Education: The 4-A Scheme* (Wolf Legal Publishers 2006) 7.

7 UN Committee on the Rights of the Child (CRC), General Comment No. 9 (2006): The Rights of Children with Disabilities (27 February 2007) CRC/C/GC/9 [8].

8 CRPD (n. 1) Article 1.

9 For examples of the educational disadvantage experienced by children with disabilities, see the following two reports: Vernor Muñoz, 'The Right to Education of Persons with Disabilities' (A/HRC/4/29, UNGA 19 February 2007); World Health Organization and World Bank, *World Report on Disability* (World Health Organization 2011).

10 Frédéric Mégret and Dianah Msipa, 'Global Reasonable Accommodation: How the Convention on the Rights of Persons with Disabilities Changes the Way We Think about Equality' (2014) 30 *South African Journal on Human Rights* 252, 254.

11 Kelley Ann Loper, 'Equality Law and Inclusion in Education: Recommendations for Legal Reform' (SSRN Scholarly Paper 2010) [2] https://ssrn.com/abstract=1712710 (accessed 31 July 2017).

12 Office of the United Nations High Commissioner for Human Rights, 'Equality and Non-Discrimination under Article 5 of the Convention on the Rights of Persons with Disabilities:

and 'the most fundamental instrumental element of the convention'.[13] While arguably all of these statements are accurate, it is also fair to suggest that the duty to provide reasonable accommodation is a widely misunderstood concept, confused at times with affirmative action or with progressively realisable rights such as accessibility.[14] The lack of clarity surrounding this duty coupled with the fact that this is an unfamiliar concept in many legal systems may negatively impact the ability of States Parties to effectively legislate and implement the duty to provide reasonable accommodation. It is therefore important to set out the parameters or contours of the duty to accommodate as enshrined within the CRPD.

This chapter is broken down into two parts. Part 2 addresses the specific references to reasonable accommodation contained in Article 24 of the CRPD, and then sets out the contours of the duty to provide reasonable accommodation. Part 3 assesses the cross-cutting nature of the anti-discrimination measures in the CRPD and the immediate nature of this legal duty.

2 REASONABLE ACCOMMODATION

2.1 *Article 24 and Reasonable Accommodation*

It may be inferred, from the specific inclusion of the duty to provide reasonable accommodation within Article 24, that the duty to provide reasonable accommodation is particularly pertinent in the context of education. Article 24 seeks to give expression to the international human right to education as it applies to people with disabilities. Article 24 was a particularly disputed

Report of the Office of the United Nations High Commissioner for Human Rights' (A/HRC/34/26, UNGA 9 December 2016) [76].

13 Rosemary Kayess and Phillip French, 'Out of Darkness into Light? Introducing the Convention on the Rights of Persons with Disabilities' (2008) 8 *Human Rights Law Review* 1, 27.

14 See generally Anna Lawson, 'Reasonable Accommodation in the UN Convention on the Rights of Persons with Disabilities and Non-Discrimination in Employment: Rising to the Challenges?' in Charles O'Mahony and Gerard Quinn (eds), *Disability Law and Policy: An Analysis of the UN Convention* (Clarus Press 2017); Lisa Waddington, 'When It Is Reasonable for Europeans to Be Confused: Understanding When a Disability Accommodation Is "Reasonable" from a Comparative Perspective' (2008) 29 *Comparative Labor Law and Policy Journal* 317; Gerard Quinn and Shivaun Quinlivan, 'Disability Discrimination: The Need to Amend the Employment Equality Act 1998 in Light of the EU Framework Directive on Employment' in Cathryn Costello and Eilis Barry (eds), *Equality in Diversity: The New Equality Directives*, vol. 29 (Irish Centre for European Law 2003).

provision and 'it was not adopted without controversy'.[15] A significant strength of the final provision is that it contains the first explicit treaty reference to inclusive education. The resulting Article 24(1) provides:

1. States Parties recognize the right of persons with disabilities to education. With a view to realizing this right without discrimination and on the basis of equal opportunity, States Parties shall ensure an inclusive education system at all levels and life long learning directed to:

a) The full development of human potential and sense of dignity and self-worth, and the strengthening of respect for human rights, fundamental freedoms and human diversity;
b) The development by persons with disabilities of their personality, talents and creativity, as well as their mental and physical abilities, to their fullest potential;
c) Enabling persons with disabilities to participate effectively in a free society.

It is noteworthy that the addressees of the right to education are 'persons' with disabilities as opposed to children with disabilities. By implication, the right to education conceivably does not cease at the attainment of majority. Interestingly, the CRPD is entirely silent on the role of parents or the rights of parents in respect of their children's education. This may be more to do with the fact that the addressees of this article are not just children with disabilities but persons with disabilities. Further, the right to education is a right to an inclusive education system. The term 'inclusive education' is not defined within the CRPD, but Committee on the Rights of Persons with Disabilities (the Committee) has provided further guidance on the full meaning of this provision in General Comment No. 4 on the Right to Inclusive Education.[16] What we can establish is that an inclusive education system is directed to the 'full development of human potential', and that it should also enable persons with disabilities to 'participate effectively in a free society'.

Article 24 makes two specific references to the duty to provide reasonable accommodation: Article 24(2) and 24(5). The first reference in Article 24(2) provides States Parties with clear guidance on how to realise the right to

[15] See Arlene S. Kanter in this volume (Chapter 2) for a full discussion of the various controversies and the debates that led to the introduction of Article 24. See also Kayess and French (n. 13); Richard Rieser, *Implementing Inclusive Education: A Commonwealth Guide to Implementing Article 24 of the UN Convention on the Rights of People with Disabilities* (2nd edn) (Commonwealth Secretariat 2012).

[16] UN Committee on the Rights of Persons with Disabilities, General Comment No. 4 (2016): Article 24: Right to inclusive Education (2 September 2016) CRPD/C/GC/4; Kanter (n. 15).

inclusive education. Article 24(2) includes a general prohibition on excluding people on the 'basis of disability' from an inclusive education system, both primary and secondary. Access should be achieved on an equal basis with other members of the community, and there is a requirement to provide effective individualised support measures, as well as to ensure that persons with disabilities receive the necessary support to 'facilitate their effective education'. In addition to these actions, Article 24(2)(c) provides that States Parties must ensure that '[r]easonable accommodation of the individual's requirements is provided'.

Accordingly, a student with a disability has a right to education, and the onus is on States Parties to ensure that the education provided is an inclusive setting. Moreover, the tools deemed necessary to assist in accessing that right include the provision of reasonable accommodation. The Committee supports this point, stating that 'reasonable accommodation must be adopted at national, local and education institution levels and at all levels of education'.[17] A notable element of the imposition of a duty to provide reasonable accommodation within the CRPD is that private actors, in this case education institutions, are in fact engaged in the enforcement of the Convention. Traditionally, human rights treaties are addressed to States Parties and require those States Parties to undertake certain actions to enforce or to enhance the human rights of a particular group. Mégret and Msipa note that '[i]t is almost as if the CRPD, through state's accession, spoke directly past the sovereign to the various non-state actors that in practice will have to do much of the work of reasonable accommodation'.[18] These non-state actors include education providers, and Article 24(5) specifies the necessity for the provision of reasonable accommodation in 'general tertiary education, vocational training, adult education and lifelong learning'. There is therefore a duty on all education providers to deliver reasonable accommodation for learners with disabilities; it seems clear that for this to work in practice, it should have a legislative basis. Article 5 of the CRPD introduces a clear onus on States Parties to introduce anti-discrimination legislation and to ensure that the duty to provide reasonable accommodation is enshrined in those measures.[19] Those measures should ensure that there is a legal duty to provide reasonable accommodation in education.

17 General Comment No. 4 (n. 16) [27].
18 Mégret and Msipa (n. 10) 270.
19 CRPD (n. 1) Article 5(3).

2.2 *Reasonable Accommodation*

Article 5 provides that States Parties ensure that there is 'effective legal protection against discrimination'.[20] This has been further clarified by the Committee, which notes that the CRPD imposes extensive obligations on States Parties including a duty to legislate 'to ensure that reasonable accommodation provisions are enshrined in law as an immediately enforceable right in all areas of law and policy'.[21] Such laws should ensure that the definition of reasonable accommodation is recognised 'and punishable as a form of discrimination'.[22] Moreover, the Office of the United Nations High Commissioner of Human Rights (OHCHR) states that the CRPD enforces a legal 'obligation to provide reasonable accommodation in all sectors, at every level of government'.[23] From the foregoing we can deduce that States Parties to the CRPD are under a duty to introduce non-discrimination legislation, and that that legislation should define the failure to provide reasonable accommodation as discrimination. Furthermore, all rights addressed within the CRPD, including the right to education, should be covered by such anti-discrimination provision. Additionally, it is important at this junction to clarify one point regarding the duty to accommodate, which is often confused with positive or affirmative action. Article 5(4) is permissive of actions that 'are necessary to accelerate or achieve *de facto* equality of persons with disabilities' (emphasis added), thus clarifying that reasonable accommodation and affirmative or positive action are two distinct and separate concepts.[24] Affirmative action or positive discrimination is permitted by the CRPD, but it is not required. This is in contrast to the duty to accommodate, which is required as is evident from the definition of discrimination contained in Article 2. That article defines 'discrimination on the basis of disability' to mean:

> any distinction, exclusion or restriction on the basis of disability which has the purpose or effect of impairing or nullifying the recognition, enjoyment or exercise, on an equal basis with others, of all human rights and fundamental freedoms in the political, economic, social, cultural, civil or any other field. *It includes all forms of discrimination, including denial of reasonable accommodation*[.][25]

20 Ibid. Article 5(2).
21 Committee on the Rights of Persons with Disabilities, Concluding Observations on the Initial Report of Germany (13 May 2015) CRPD/C/DEU/CO/1 [14(b)].
22 Ibid.
23 Office of the United Nations High Commissioner for Human Rights (n. 12) [64].
24 For a more detailed discussion on some of the confusion and misunderstandings of this concept, see Lawson (2017) (n. 14).
25 CRPD (n. 1) Article 2, emphasis added.

Reasonable accommodation is defined within the CRPD as:

> necessary and appropriate modification and adjustments not imposing a disproportionate or undue burden, where needed in a particular case, to ensure to persons with disabilities the enjoyment or exercise on an equal basis with others of all human rights and fundamental freedoms[.][26]

From this we can extrapolate that the duty to provide reasonable accommodation can be broken down into two constituent parts. In the first instance there is a duty to provide a 'modification' or an 'adjustment' that is 'necessary and appropriate' where it is required 'in a particular case' to ensure that a person with a disability is able to enjoy or to exercise her or his rights, including the right to education on an 'equal basis with others'. Lawson contends that this provision 'imposes positive obligations to identify barriers in the way of a disabled person's enjoyment of their human rights and to take appropriate steps to remove them'.[27]

The second part of this duty provides that any required accommodations should not impose a 'disproportionate or undue burden' on the duty-bearer. A number of factors need to be considered in order to determine what amounts to a 'disproportionate or undue burden', including the cost, disruption and potential benefit of any proposed accommodation. If the analysis of a proposed accommodation determines that such an accommodation does impose a disproportionate or undue burden on a duty-bearer, then it is contended that they are no longer bound by the duty to provide reasonable accommodation. Commentators have noted some confusion around the parameters and impact of this duty,[28] a confusion that is evident in some court decisions.[29] It is therefore proposed to address the elements of the duty to accommodate in detail.

26 Ibid.

27 Anna Lawson, 'The UN Convention on the Rights of Persons with Disabilities and European Disability Law: A Catalyst for Cohesion?' in Oddný Mjöll Arnardóttir and Gerard Quinn (eds), *The UN Convention on the Rights of Persons with Disabilities: European and Scandinavian Perspectives* (International Studies in Human Rights, Martinus Nijhoff 2009) 103.

28 Shelagh Day and Gwen Brodsky, 'The Duty to Accommodate: Who Will Benefit?' (1996) 75 *Canadian Bar Review* 433. In this article the authors contend that reasonable accommodation lacks the capacity to address inequality and to foster inclusive institutions, in effect arguing it is a flawed concept. For an alternative perspective, see Lawson (2017) (n. 14). See generally Mégret and Msipa (n. 10); Waddington (n. 14).

29 For example, in *In Re Article 26 and the Employment Equality Bill 1996* [1997] 2 IR 321.

2.2.1 Individualised Duty

The duty to provide reasonable accommodation is, in the main, an individualised reactive duty in that it must respond to the specific circumstances of the individual disabled persons as well as to the needs of the duty-bearer concerned.[30] This point is reinforced within Article 24(2)(c), which requires reasonable accommodation of the 'individual's requirements'. As this duty is both individualised and reactive, the Committee has held that '[t]here is no "one size fits all" formula to reasonable accommodation, and different students with the same impairment may require different accommodations'.[31] For example, two students with visual impairments may have different accommodation needs, assuming that the barrier to equal participation is a difficulty or an inability to access the reading materials for the course. It is now necessary for the educational institution to identify the necessary modification or adjustment to allow both students to participate on an equal basis. It does not follow that because both students have a visual impairment and face the same barrier that the necessary modification or adjustment will be the same. The nature of the visual impairments may vary and it may be that one of the students could be accommodated by the use of large print while the other student may require braille text. The accommodation or adjustment necessary must be what is required for that individual in a 'particular case'.

People with disabilities do not form a homogenous group; consequently any adjustment or modification will depend entirely on the individual needs of the person in question. Impairments vary greatly both in range and extent, and can be physical, mental or sensory as well as permanent and intermittent in nature. Different impairments in interaction with society may give rise to the need for a variety of different accommodations. Moreover, the context in which the accommodation is sought will also influence the nature of any accommodations to be made. It is the sensitive and particularised nature of the duty to accommodate that ensures it can respond in a nuanced way to an individual's need in a particular circumstance. It is arguably this incredibly individualised nature of the duty in addressing barriers to participation that 'makes reasonable accommodation effective'.[32]

This is not an unbounded obligation, and it is limited by the need to avoid imposing a 'disproportionate and undue burden' on the duty-bearer. The limit

[30] See Office of the United Nations High Commissioner for Human Rights (n. 12) [40], where it is suggested that 'entities offer accommodation without waiting for a request; this should be regarded as good practice'.

[31] General Comment No. 4 (n. 16) [29].

[32] Mégret and Msipa (n. 10) 263.

to the duty to provide reasonable accommodation is also a reactive limit, as it responds to the needs and resources of the duty-bearer. What would be considered a disproportionate and undue burden for a small private preschool may differ considerably from what would be considered an undue and disproportionate burden on a publicly funded education system. Thus, determining whether an accommodation gives rise to an undue or disproportionate burden on a particular duty-bearer requires analysis on a case-by-case basis.

2.2.2 Process of Dialogue

The duty to accommodate is deemed 'triggered'[33] or 'enforceable'[34] from the moment an individual with an impairment needs the accommodation in a particular situation. Due to the greatly individualised nature of this duty, it seems self-evident that for an accommodation to be appropriate, some level of dialogue should happen between the duty-bearer and the person with a disability.[35] This position is supported by the OHCHR, who note that once the duty has been triggered, '[b]oth the requesting and the obligated parties should then engage in a dialogue'.[36] In the context of education, the duty-bearer may be a school, an educational institution or the relevant government department. In the provision of reasonable accommodation, the requesting party would normally be the person requiring a reasonable accommodation; however, it may also be that due to the age of the student concerned, the parents or guardians request an educational accommodation on behalf of their child: such accommodations may also be requested in expert reports, such as a report from an educational psychologist or a medical report. What is important in this context is that regardless of how the request for an accommodation is made, it is the request that initiates the process.

Once an accommodation has been requested, the duty-bearer should engage in a process of dialogue with the individual to determine the extent of the barrier and the most appropriate response to that barrier. The nature of any dialogue will depend to a large extent on the nature of the relationship between the duty-bearer and the individual. Short-term or transitory relationships should not necessitate any ongoing dialogue. For example, where a student with a mobility impairment wishes to attend a university open day, a brief conversation notifying the university of his or her intention to attend

33 Office of the United Nations High Commissioner for Human Rights (n. 12) [40].
34 UN Committee on the Rights of Persons with Disabilities, General Comment No. 2 (2014) Article 9: Accessibility (22 May 2014) CRPD/C/GC/2 [26].
35 Lawson (2017) (n. 14); Mégret and Msipa (n. 10).
36 Office of the United Nations High Commissioner for Human Rights (n. 12) [40].

should suffice. The university may hold the open day in an accessible venue or provide a removable ramp to ensure that the venue is accessible on the day. In contrast, where a relationship is ongoing or long term, such as the relationship between a student and a school, the dialogue may be 'formal and extensive'.[37] As education is a process, and the accommodation needs for a student with disability are not necessarily stationary or fixed (as they may vary or change over time), the accommodation provided could 'be ended, modified, expanded or replaced, as needed', which gives rise to the necessity for ongoing dialogue.[38] Such a process does not need to be overly burdensome on both parties, and can just involve ongoing discussions about the needs of the child in particular situations. Some situations may require more formal interventions such as state examinations. Others could involve a brief chat with the parents and/or student about participation in a school event such as a school tour and how that would work best for all involved. Ideally, such dialogue would be uncontentious and facilitative of the individual student's right to participate on an equal basis with others.

2.2.3 Limits to the Duty

As is clear from the foregoing discussion, accommodations are entirely determined by the requirement of the individual and the ability of the duty-bearer to respond to that requirement. As with the duty to provide reasonable accommodation, the requirements of a duty-bearer require an assessment of the proposed 'burden' on a particular duty-bearer. Any such assessment must be sensitive to the unique needs of the particular duty-bearer. The 'burden' on a duty-bearer is not limitless, and any required accommodation should not give rise to a 'disproportionate and undue burden'.[39] In addition, some jurisdictions have interpreted the word 'reasonable' (as used in the phrase 'reasonable accommodation') as an independent modifier of the duty to accommodate. It is a matter of debate whether this is the correct interpretation of this phrase, and this is discussed in more detail in what follows.[40]

2.2.3.1 DISPROPORTIONATE OR UNDUE BURDEN A duty-bearer is under an obligation to provide an accommodation as long as such accommodations do not amount to a 'disproportionate or undue burden'. It has been asserted that

37 Ibid. [45].
38 Ibid. [41].
39 CRPD (n. 1) Article 2.
40 For further discussions on the meaning of the word 'reasonable' in the phrase 'reasonable accommodation', see Mégret and Msipa (n. 10) and Waddington (n. 14).

the term 'disproportionate or undue burden' should be considered a single concept, and that the words '"[d]isproportionate" and "undue" should be considered synonyms'.[41] Consequently, this chapter refers to both as one concept.

In order to assess whether an accommodation imposes a disproportionate or undue burden, it is necessary to be sensitive to the particularities of the duty-bearer. Such analysis involves more than a mere cost analysis of any proposed accommodation; burdens can be financial, structural or organisational in nature. Determining what could be an undue or disproportionate burden necessitates an assessment of the impact of a particular accommodation on a particular duty-bearer. Accommodations can vary in cost, duration, frequency, benefit and disruption, but equally duty-bearers vary in their ability to withstand such impacts. Each assessment must be made on a case-by-case basis. An accommodation may in one instance give rise to an undue or disproportionate burden, but with a different duty-bearer it may not impose such a burden.

It is undoubted that the issue of the proposed or feared burden of reasonable accommodations has given rise to confusion, as evidenced by the Irish Supreme Court decision in *In Re Article 26 and the Employment Equality Bill 1996*.[42] In that action, the Irish Supreme Court held that a legislative provision, which attempted to impose a duty to provide reasonable accommodation on private actors, was unconstitutional.[43] The proposed reasonable accommodation provision required the imposition of the duty to deliver reasonable accommodation subject to the defence of 'undue hardship'. In order to determine what could give rise to an undue hardship, consideration could be given to: the cost and the number of beneficiaries, the financial situation of the employer, the disruption involved, the nature of any other benefits or detriments and the nature of the treatment or facilities. The Irish Supreme Court held that requiring an employer to bear the costs of reasonable accommodation unless the cost gave rise to an 'undue hardship' was a violation of the employer's property rights. In this action, the Irish Supreme Court recognised the 'laudable aim of making provision for such of our fellow citizens as are disabled', but contended that the cost of this could not be placed on employers, because of their right to private property.[44] The impact of this decision was that property rights, in this instance the right to earn a profit, outweighed the

41 Office of the United Nations High Commissioner for Human Rights (n. 12) [31].

42 *In Re Article 26 and the Employment Equality Bill 1996* (n. 29).

43 Ibid. For a detailed discussion on why it was unconstitutional, see Quinn and Quinlivan (n. 14) and Lawson (2017) (n. 14).

44 *In Re Article 26 and the Employment Equality Bill 1996* (n. 29) 367.

right to equality of a person with a disability. What is evident from the discussion on reasonable accommodation is that the Supreme Court assumed that all reasonable accommodations entail some level of cost and that those costs would be considerable. It is respectfully suggested that this highlights a misunderstanding by the Irish Supreme Court of the duty and the actual costs of reasonable accommodations.[45] For example, the Job Accommodation Network undertook research on the cost of accommodations required by employees under the Americans with Disabilities Act. That research surveyed employers and the majority of the respondents (59 per cent) stated that the accommodations required by the employees cost absolutely nothing; 36 per cent experienced a one-time cost; 4 per cent noted an ongoing annual cost, with just 1 per cent requiring a combination of a one-time and annual cost. The typical one-time expenditure was in the region of $500.[46] The OHCHR reaffirms this, stating that most accommodations have 'either a low cost or none at all'.[47] It is equally clear 'that the cost to the individual who is not accommodated is excessive'.[48]

A 'burden' is not confined to a financial assessment of a duty-bearer and might for example include what are described earlier in this chapter as structural or organisational burdens. Many accommodations entail little or no financial cost, but require a change in practice: for example a student with dyslexia may experience issues with reading, and so a resulting accommodation could be additional time in an exam situation. Such an accommodation has no or minimal cost implications for an education provider, but does involve some reorganisation of the academic institution's practices. Another consideration in determining a disproportionate or undue burden could be the potential disruptiveness or disadvantage for the education provider by the provision of a particular accommodation. The focus is on the impact on a particular duty-bearer and whether any such disruption gives rise to a disproportionate or undue burden – some disruption is arguably acceptable. Equally it would be important as part of that assessment to address any possible advantages by the introduction of an accommodation. The oft-cited example is the provision of a ramp for a wheelchair user as an accommodation. Initially

45 The Italian courts have taken a very different approach to the Irish Supreme Court; for this discussion, see Delia Ferri, 'The Past, Present and Future of the Right to Inclusive Education in Italy' in this volume (Chapter 22).

46 Beth Loy, *Workplace Accommodations: Low Cost, High Impact: Annually Updated Research Findings Address the Costs and Benefits of Job Accommodations* (Office of Disability Employment Policy, 9 January 2016) https://askjan.org/media/LowCostHighImpact.html#findings (accessed 24 July 2017).

47 Office of the United Nations High Commissioner for Human Rights (n. 12) [38].

48 Quinn and Quinlivan (n. 14) 225.

this accommodation could be both costly and disruptive, but the introduction of a ramp could benefit a much broader cohort of people than that one individual; for example, other potential beneficiaries include parents of small children who may need to use buggies, people using crutches, elderly people and other disabled and non-disabled individuals. Therefore an assessment of a 'burden' should also assess the extent of any benefit. For example, a possible accommodation for a child with autism would be the ability to access a sensory or calm room throughout the school day. Depending on the school, the investment required for such a room could potentially give rise to an undue or disproportionate burden. However, it is suggested that any assessment of that burden should consider 'reasonably predictable indirect benefits'[49] to that school such as the ability of other children to benefit from that accommodation, and those benefits could impact any assessment of what amounts to an undue or disproportionate burden.

The primary issue in assessing whether an accommodation could give rise to a disproportionate or undue burden is the ability of the duty-bearer to withstand that accommodation. It seems evident, for example, that the analysis of a burden would be different for a large, publicly funded university to that imposed on a small, private preschool. The assessment of a financial or other burden requires an assessment of the budget of the education provider in question. Where the cost of an accommodation gives rise to a cost that accounts for a fraction of the overall budget of the organisation, arguably it does not represent an undue or disproportionate burden on that body. That analysis necessarily suggests that the same accommodation may amount to a burden on a small and less financially robust education provider. Moreover, it supports the position that different standards should exist for public or state bodies over private entities. The OHCHR states that 'stricter standards exist for states when justifying a denial of reasonable accommodation'.[50]

Importantly, in the education context, an education provider needs to identify in consultation with the student the barriers that that student may face. Valid considerations for an education provider include identifying the barrier, the measures to address that barrier and whether such measures give rise to an undue or disproportionate burden. Issues of perceived unfairness (by, for example, other students) to the provision of accommodations do not amount to valid considerations for an education provider, as they do not relate to the core aspect of the right concerned.[51] Ideally, an education provider

49 Office of the United Nations High Commissioner for Human Rights (n. 12) [56].
50 Ibid. [61].
51 For a general discussion on the issue of valid versus invalid criteria, see ibid. paras 47–50.

should, in consultation with the student, identify the necessary modification or adjustment that would allow that student to exercise the right to education on an equal basis with other students.

2.2.3.2 REASONABLE There is some confusion surrounding the impact of the word 'reasonable' as it relates to the legal duty to accommodate.[52] Prior to the introduction of the CRPD, a number of jurisdictions had incorporated a duty to provide reasonable accommodation; consequently there is a body of pre-existing interpretations of this duty. However, there is little agreement about the impact of the word 'reasonable'. Specifically, does it act as an independent modifier or a qualifier of the duty to accommodate, or is it a term of art that refers to the actual accommodation concerned? Mégret and Msipa contend that the more common understanding of the term 'reasonable' 'is that it modifies the *duty* to make reasonable accommodation'.[53] This position is implicitly accepted by Lawson when she states that:

> It is remarkable that a duty, which is explicitly limited by concepts of 'reasonableness', 'undue hardship' or 'disproportionate burden' should have been met with such alarm.[54]

Moreover, Waddington has assessed various European jurisdictions' interpretation of the term 'reasonable accommodation' and identified a number of distinct approaches to the use of the word 'reasonable'.[55] In contrast, Broderick suggests that the drafting history of the reasonable accommodation duty contained in the CRPD shows 'that the term "reasonable accommodation" is a single concept'.[56] Therefore she contends that it was not intended under the CRPD that the word 'reasonable' should act as a qualifier or modifier to that duty. This position receives support from the Committee in its General Comment on the right to inclusive education, which provided that:

> 'Reasonableness' is understood as the result of a contextual test that involves an analysis of the relevance and the effectiveness of the accommodation, and the expected goal of countering discrimination. The availability of resources

52 Andrea Broderick, *The Long and Winding Road to Equality and Inclusion for Persons with Disabilities: The United Nations Convention on the Rights of Persons with Disabilities* (School of Human Rights Research Series, Intersentia 2015) vol. 74; Lawson (2017) (n. 14); Mégret and Msipa (n. 10); Waddington (n. 14).

53 Mégret and Msipa (n. 10) 266.

54 Lawson (2017) (n. 14) 368.

55 Waddington (n. 14); see also *US Airways Inc.* v. *Barnett* 535 US 391 (US Supreme Court 2002); *Vande Zande* v. *Wisconsin Dep't of Admin* 44 F3d 538 (US Seventh Circuit 1995).

56 Broderick (n. 52) 159.

> and the financial implications is recognized when assessing disproportionate burden.[57]

The Committee suggests here that the term 'reasonable' refers to the effectiveness of the accommodation concerned, and, more fundamentally, it does not refer to an assessment of what amounts to a burden.[58]

This position further reinforces the earlier, more tentative enunciation of this position set out by the CRPD Committee in the individual complaint of *HM* v. *Sweden*.[59] In this action, the complainant had a condition known as Ehlers-Danlos Syndrome (EDS) – a connective tissue disorder. As a result of this condition, she could no longer stand or walk, and had difficulty sitting or lying down. She had been confined to her bed for almost two years, and she was unable to take medication for her condition due to hypersensitivity to medication. At the point of the complaint, due to the high risk of injury involved in transporting her to hospital or therapy, she no longer left her home. The only feasible therapy for the complainant was to avail of hydrotherapy in her home. She had applied for planning permission to build a hydrotherapy pool on her own property; this application involved an extension to her house, a large part of which would be on land where building was not permitted under the Planning and Building Acts.[60] Because of the building restriction, she was denied planning permission. She appealed this decision to various bodies, but was not successful in any of the national fora, so she lodged an individual petition under the CRPD.[61] On the issue of reasonable accommodation, the Committee noted that the complainant's health was now critical and as a consequence:

> access to a hydrotherapy pool at home is essential and an effective – in this case the only effective – means to meet her health needs. Appropriate modification and adjustments would thus require a departure from the development plan, in order to allow the building of a hydrotherapy pool. The Committee notes that the State party has not indicated that this departure would impose a 'disproportionate or undue burden'.[62]

57 General Comment No. 4 (n. 16) [27].

58 This position contrasts directly with the position adopted in *US Airways Inc.* v. *Barnett* (n. 55).

59 UN Committee on the Rights of Persons with Disabilities, 'Communication No. 3/2011' CRPD/C/7/D/3/2011 [hereinafter *HM* v. *Sweden*]; for a discussion of this case, see Ilze Grobbelaar-Du Plessis and Annelize Nienaber, 'Disability and Reasonable Accommodation: HM v Sweden Communication 3/2011 (Committee on the Rights of Persons with Disabilities)' (2014) 30 *South African Journal on Human Rights* 366.

60 *HM* v. *Sweden* (n. 59) [2.3].

61 She raised arguments relating to articles 1, 5, 9, 10, 14, 19, 20, 25, 26 and 28.

62 Ibid. [8.5].

The Committee in this action adopted a two-stage process in determining whether there was a failure to accommodate the applicant. The first step was to assess what would be a reasonable accommodation – this would require the identification of the barrier to participation and then the identification of the accommodation necessary in a particular case. The Committee held that for an accommodation to be reasonable, the primary concern is that it is effective. The test of effectiveness requires the accommodation to address the relevant barrier. The second stage addressed what amounted to a disproportionate burden and this did not look at or assess the reasonableness or otherwise of the complainant's case. In the case of *HM* v. *Sweden*, the accommodation necessary was a departure from the development plan. The Committee did not consider that such a departure would impose a 'disproportionate or undue burden' on the State Party, as the Planning and Building Acts already permitted some departures from the Acts where necessary. The departure from the planning acts necessary in the complainant's case in order for her to access her human rights on an equal basis with others did not amount to a disproportionate or undue burden.[63] Two different tests are, therefore, employed in the assessment of the duty to accommodate; in the first instance, there is an assessment of the effectiveness or the reasonableness of the accommodation suggested, and the second stage assesses whether that accommodation gives rise to a disproportionate or undue burden on the relevant duty-bearer.

Practice to date (albeit under a variety of different legal provisions, many of which predate the CRPD) suggests that the word 'reasonable' has been interpreted as an additional qualifier to the duty to accommodate. This appears to contradict the position adopted by the Committee in its General Comments and more tentatively in the case of *HM* v. *Sweden*.[64] Moreover, the OHCHR, in a recent report on 'Equality and Non-Discrimination under Article 5 of the Convention on the Rights of Persons with Disabilities', assessed the duty to accommodate. In this report there is no reference to 'reasonable' as a modifier or qualifier to the duty of accommodation. However, the Committee stated that 'reasonable accommodation should not be confused with procedural accommodations in the context of access to justice'.

63 Ibid. The Committee found a violation of articles 5(1), 5(3), 25, 26, 3(b), (d) and (e) and 4(1)(d). It further noted that the failure to provide her with the necessary accommodation may in time violate her right to independent living in the future guaranteed under Article 19(b).

64 General Comment No. 2 (n. 34); UN Committee on the Rights of Persons with Disabilities, General Comment No. 3 (2016): Article 6: Women and Girls with Disabilities (2 September 2016) CRPD/C/GC/3; General Comment No. 4 (n. 16); *HM* v. *Sweden* (n. 59).

> During the negotiations on the Convention, the term 'reasonable' was intentionally left aside in the framing of article 13. Article 13 requires 'procedural accommodations', which are not limited by the concept of 'disproportionate or undue burden'. This differentiation is fundamental, because the right of access to justice acts as the guarantor for the effective enjoyment and exercise of all rights.[65]

This does appear to suggest that the word 'reasonable' within 'reasonable accommodation' serves a purpose more than being part of a term of art. The Committee is currently considering a General Comment on Article 5, so it is therefore respectfully suggested that a definitive comment on the impact of the word 'reasonable' and on the duty to accommodate generally by the CRPD Committee would be welcome to clarify the full extent of this duty.[66]

3 EQUALITY AND NON-DISCRIMINATION IN THE CRPD

It is evident from reading the CRPD that it is imbued with the concept of equality. 'Equality is complemented by the principle of non-discrimination.'[67] Both concepts underlie all human rights treaties, and the CRPD is no exception.[68] There are multiple references to both equality and non-discrimination throughout the preambular paragraphs and the cross-cutting articles, as well as the substantive articles of the CRPD. The very purpose of this Convention is 'to promote, protect and ensure the full and equal enjoyment of all human rights . . . by all persons with disabilities'.[69] The CRPD is for all intents and purposes an equality convention focussing on how to achieve the 'full and equal enjoyment of all human rights' for persons with disabilities.

Equality is the goal to be achieved; non-discrimination is one of the tools employed to help achieve that goal. When considering equality and non-discrimination on other grounds (race for example), it is often, though not exclusively, the case that an educator, employer or service provider is required to ignore irrelevant factors such as race when making their services available to

65 Office of the United Nations High Commissioner for Human Rights (n. 12) [35].
66 'Day of General Discussion (DGD) on the Right of Persons with Disabilities to Equality and Non-Discrimination, on 25 August 2017 (Conference Room XVII, Palais des Nations, Geneva)' (Committee on the Rights of Persons with Disabilities) www.ohchr.org/EN/HRBodies/CRPD/Pages/EqualityAndNon-discrimination.aspx (accessed 27 July 2017).
67 Office of the United Nations High Commissioner for Human Rights (n. 12) [3].
68 Ibid.
69 CRPD (n. 1) Article 1.

an individual. In the disability context, it may be that the service provider is required to see past disability to facilitate participation for people with disabilities by focussing on the individual's ability. To that end, a non-discrimination provision must be robust enough to help overcome historical barriers that isolated, segregated, institutionalised and marginalised people with disabilities. The OHCHR notes that the CRPD enshrines a 'strengthened vision of substantive equality',[70] one that is innovative 'by including denial of reasonable accommodation as a form of discrimination'.[71] This lends support to the proposition that the duty to provide reasonable accommodation is one of the more important inclusions within the CRPD and, indeed, human rights law more generally.

The OHCHR described the CRPD as innovative in respect of its vision of equality; perhaps as important is the structure of the CRPD, which adopts articles that are of general application to all other articles within the Convention.[72] These articles of general application or cross-cutting articles serve as guiding norms that apply to the remainder of the Convention and consequently underpin all other articles within the Convention, including the right to education.[73] The right to equality and non-discrimination in Article 5 is clearly situated among the cross-cutting articles. These cross-cutting articles articulate the underlying principles upon which the CRPD is based and include the right to equality, non-discrimination, accessibility and awareness raising.[74] Thus any assessment of the right to education contained in Article 24 also requires an assessment of that right through the prism of the principles espoused within the articles of general application – including that of equality and non-discrimination.

The expressed goal of the CRPD is to achieve the 'equal enjoyment of all human rights' by people with disabilities, and in order to achieve that goal, a number of different tools and strategies are employed.[75] The CRPD is

70 Office of the High Commissioner for Human Rights (n. 12) [3].

71 Ibid [23].

72 CRPD (n. 1) Articles 3–9.

73 Shivaun Quinlivan, 'The United Nations Convention on the Rights of Persons with Disabilities: An Introduction' (2012) 13 *ERA Forum* 71. Article 4 of the Convention sets out the General Obligations, which include an obligation to adopt legislation and other appropriate measures to implement the Convention, to modify or to repeal existing laws or practices that discriminate and to take all appropriate measures to eliminate disability discrimination, among other requirements. Article 6 addresses issues that apply to women with disabilities, Article 7 children with disabilities, Article 8 awareness raising and Article 9 accessibility.

74 References to the principle of equality and/or non-discrimination are also made in articles 3, 4, 6, 7, 8 and 9 of the CRPD (n. 1).

75 For a discussion of the innovative enforcement mechanisms employed within the CRPD, see Frédéric Mégret, 'The Disabilities Convention: Towards a Holistic Concept of Rights' (2008) 12 *International Journal of Human Rights* 261.

primarily addressed to States Parties, and to that end a number of obligations are imposed on States Parties in order to achieve the overarching goal of equality for people with disabilities. The nature of state obligations may vary: some are immediate in nature while others are to be progressively realised.[76] The principle of non-discrimination is considered a civil and political right, and one that is capable of immediate enforcement. It is noteworthy that the application of the non-discrimination duty 'has not been subject to any condition for other constituencies'[77] in denominated human rights treaties such as the Convention on the Rights of the Child (CRC) or the Convention on the Elimination of All Forms of Discrimination against Women (CEDAW). Because historically non-discrimination duties are immediately enforceable in all other UN treaties, it is fair to extrapolate that the non-discrimination duty enshrined within the CRPD should also be one that is not subject to any conditionality and is therefore a legal duty capable of immediate enforcement. The immediacy of the duty of non-discrimination coupled with the inclusion of the duty to provide reasonable accommodation injects the necessary robustness into non-discrimination norms of the CRPD.

The duty to provide reasonable accommodation applies to all rights within the Convention, including socioeconomic rights. Lawson describes reasonable accommodation as playing a 'peculiar bridging role'[78] in the context of human rights. Traditionally, socioeconomic rights have been considered programmatic in nature. The inclusion of the duty to provide reasonable accommodation within the non-discrimination norm injects some immediacy to the enforcement of socioeconomic rights, therefore linking the immediacy of civil and political rights to the traditionally programmatic socioeconomic rights. It is suggested here that this duty to provide reasonable accommodation arguably highlights the artificial dichotomy between both sets of rights.[79]

76 For a full discussion of progressive realisation, see Gauthier de Beco, 'Progressive Realisation and the Right to Inclusive Education' in the current volume (Chapter 8).

77 Office of the United Nations High Commissioner for Human Rights (n. 12) [5].

78 Lawson (2009) (n. 27) 104.

79 Brynhildur Flóvenz, 'The Implementation of the UN Convention and the Development of Economical and Social Rights as Human Rights' in Oddný Mjöll Arnardóttir and Gerard Quinn (eds), *The UN Convention on the Rights of Persons with Disabilities: European and Scandinavian Perspectives* (Martinus Nijhoff 2009); Sandra Fredman, *Human Rights Transformed: Positive Rights and Positive Duties* (Oxford University Press 2008); Ida Elisabeth Koch, 'From Invisibility to Indivisibility: The International Convention on the Rights of Persons with Disabilities' in Oddný Mjöll Arnardóttir and Gerard Quinn (eds), *The UN Convention on the Rights of Persons with Disabilities: European and Scandinavian Perspectives* (Martinus Nijhoff 2009); Scott Leckie, 'Another Step towards Indivisibility: Identifying the Key Features of Violations of Economic, Social and Cultural Rights' (1998) 20 *Human Rights Quarterly* 81; María Magdalena Sepúlveda

According to this author, defining the duty to accommodate as a form of discrimination is one of the most important inclusions within the CRPD. The positive legal obligation imposed by the duty to accommodate has the effect or potential to act as 'a Trojan horse for the enforceability of more and more slices of social and economic rights'.[80] It provides a legal tool to ensure that certain elements or aspects of socioeconomic rights, including the right to education, can be immediately enforced.

4 CONCLUSION

People with disabilities experience pervasive educational disadvantage or discrimination. Moreover, 'it is doubtful that any child may reasonably be expected to succeed in life if he is denied the opportunity of an education'.[81] The CRPD enunciates that people with disabilities are entitled to a right to education and that that education should be provided within an inclusive education system. In order to combat a history of educational exclusion, marginalisation and segregation, the CRPD needed to adopt robust enforcement mechanisms. It is suggested in this chapter that providing that the failure to give reasonable accommodation amounts to an act of discrimination goes some way towards addressing educational disadvantage experienced by people with disabilities. It is also important that the duty to provide reasonable accommodation is reiterated in the article on the right to education as this suggests that it is particularly important in this context.

The failure to provide reasonable accommodation is an act of discrimination. Non-discrimination within the CRPD is situated among the cross-cutting rights and therefore applies to all substantive rights within the Convention, including the right to education, and the non-discrimination duty is immediately applicable. States Parties are required to introduce anti-discrimination legislation; such legislation should define the failure to provide reasonable accommodation as an act of discrimination and address all rights contained within the CRPD, including the right to education. The impact of such legislation ensures that non-state actors such as educational institutions must provide reasonable accommodation.

The duty to accommodate is an individualised reactive duty that can be broken down into two constituent parts. The first part of the duty requires the

Carmona, *The Nature of the Obligations under the International Covenant on Economic, Social and Cultural Rights* (Intersentia 2003).

80 Gerard Quinn, 'A Short Guide to the United Nations Convention on the Rights of Persons with Disabilities' (2009) 1 *European Yearbook of Disability Law* 89, 100.

81 *Brown* v. *Board of Education of Topeka* (1954) 347 US 483, 493.

identification and removal of a discriminatory barrier – arguably the identification of the appropriate accommodation should arise after a process of dialogue between the individual and the duty-bearer. In addition, accommodations are not static: they may change, be expanded or be ended as necessary. The second part of the duty assesses whether the provision of a particular accommodation would amount to a disproportionate or undue burden on the duty-bearer. In order to assess whether an accommodation imposes a disproportionate or undue burden, it is necessary to be sensitive to the particularities of the duty-bearer. Such analysis involves more than a mere cost analysis of any proposed accommodation; burdens can be financial, structural or organisational in nature, but do not include invalid considerations such as the perceptions of the accommodation by other students. The assessment of both the impact on the duty-bearer and what would be a 'necessary and appropriate' accommodation must be analysed on a case-by-case basis. There is some confusion surrounding the duty to accommodate as is evident from the Irish Supreme Court case of *Re Employment Equality Bill 1996* and the obvious differences in interpretation of the impact of the word 'reasonable'. It is undoubted that the interpretations provided by the Committee of the duty to accommodate in the case law like that of *HM* v. *Sweden*, the concluding observations and the General Comments go a considerable distance to clarify the full extent of this duty. Arguably, however, there is still a need for a definitive interpretation of the duty to accommodate to overcome some of the confusions that surround this important provision.

8

Progressive Realisation and the Right to Inclusive Education

Gauthier de Beco

INTRODUCTION

The Convention on the Rights of Persons with Disabilities (CRPD) obliges States Parties to the Convention to realise economic, social and cultural rights. Article 4(2) of the CRPD provides that 'each State Party undertakes to take measures to the maximum of its available resources ... with a view to achieving progressively the full realization of these rights'. Since the right to education traditionally belongs to economic, social and cultural rights, progressive realisation applies likewise to the right to inclusive education. An in-depth examination of this obligation is necessary, given the numerous misunderstandings around progressive realisation and its important function for the implementation of the right in question. While it is known that economic, social and cultural rights require states to take steps towards their full realisation, it is not always clear what the criteria exactly are for evaluating compliance with human rights treaties.

An analysis of the concept of progressive realisation requires an understanding of the obligation in light of the International Covenant on Economic, Social and Cultural Rights (ICESCR),[1] as well as an investigation of the meaning of 'inclusive education' according to Article 24 of the CRPD. While acknowledging that the goal of inclusive education relates to broader questions beyond those related to disabled people, the focus here is on disability because of its endorsement by the Convention. Since achieving inclusive education is an ambitious objective, it is also important to look at the whole range of measures to be adopted for the progressive realisation of the right to inclusive education. The Committee on the Rights of Persons with Disabilities (CRPD Committee) has already provided guidance on these

[1] International Covenant on Economic, Social and Cultural Rights (adopted 16 December 1966, entered into force 23 March 1976) 993 UNTS 3 (ICESCR).

measures and noticed their adoption (or lack thereof) by States Parties to the Convention. Likewise, the CRPD Committee has made recommendations as to the measures required to make further progress towards the full realisation of the right to inclusive education. Accordingly, this chapter examines not only what is expected from States Parties to the CRPD but also what strategy they must adopt in order to fulfil this obligation. In addition to academic scholarship on the right to inclusive education, this chapter relies on both the Concluding Observations and General Comment No. 4 on the Right to Inclusive Education of the CRPD Committee.[2]

This chapter is divided into four parts. Part 1 discusses the international legal framework of progressive realisation, taking into account the well-established jurisprudence of the Committee on Economic, Social and Cultural Rights (CESCR Committee). In Part 2, the meaning of 'inclusive education' under the CRPD is examined, along with the remaining ambiguities of this concept. The third part outlines the type of measures that States Parties to the Convention must adopt in order to realise the right to inclusive education and discusses the related findings of the CRPD Committee. The chapter concludes in Part 4 with an analysis of the strategy for achieving inclusive education by considering the necessity of planning, budgeting and monitoring progress towards the full realisation of the right to inclusive education.

A LEGAL FRAMEWORK

The right to education falls within the category of economic, social and cultural rights.[3] This right is recognised in articles 13 and 14 of the ICESCR as well as articles 28 and 29 of the Convention on the Rights of the Child (CRC).[4] Neither the ICESCR nor the CRC, however, provide for a right to inclusive education.

As far as economic, social and cultural rights are concerned, Article 2(1) of the ICESCR provides that a State Party must 'take steps . . . to the maximum of its available resources, with a view to achieving progressively the full realization of the rights recognized in the present Covenant'. This provision is found again, with more or less the same wording, in the CRPD. Article 4(2) of the

[2] Committee on the Rights of Persons with Disabilities, General Comment No. 4 (2016) Article 24: Right to Inclusive Education (2 September 2016) CRPD/C/GC/4.

[3] Manisuli Ssenyonjo, *Economic, Social and Cultural Rights in International Law* (Hart Publishing 2009) 357.

[4] Convention on the Rights of the Child (adopted 20 November 1989, entered into force 2 September 1990) 1577 UNTS 3 (CRC).

CRPD stipulates that '[w]ith regard to economic, social and cultural rights, each State Party undertakes to take measures to the maximum of its available resources . . . with a view to achieving progressively the full realization of these rights'.[5]

As stated by the CESCR Committee, progressive realisation recognises that the 'full realization of all economic, social and cultural rights will generally not be able to be achieved in a short period of time'.[6] Therefore, States Parties to the ICESCR may delay fulfilling some of their obligations for implementing economic, social and cultural rights. Progressive realisation is chiefly a procedural obligation, which requires the adoption of various measures to make a right effective for its beneficiaries.[7] It does not mean that states can make no effort whatsoever or that they may postpone such efforts indefinitely. According to the CESCR Committee, States Parties to the ICESCR must 'move as expeditiously and effectively as possible towards' the full realisation of economic, social and cultural rights.[8] They must thus use their resources in a way that is compliant with the Covenant.[9] This means that they have to put in place a framework for budget allocation and to take steps in order to reach the objective, even if this objective must not be reached straightaway.

As mentioned earlier, Article 4(2) of the CRPD includes a provision similar to Article 2(1) of the ICESCR. What applies to economic, social and cultural rights in the ICESCR, therefore, similarly applies to economic, social and cultural rights in the CRPD. Consequently, the right to inclusive education is subject to progressive realisation. It must be clear, however, that the intended outcome is the achievement of the full realisation of the right to inclusive education within a reasonable period of time. The CRPD requires that States Parties to the Convention adopt a series of measures towards this end shortly after this Convention's ratification. While their education systems must not be made inclusive overnight, the States Parties are required without delay to do their utmost to incrementally transform these education systems with a view to

5 The CRC also includes such a provision. Article 4 of the CRC provides that '[w]ith regard to economic, social and cultural rights, States Parties shall undertake such measures to the maximum extent of their available resources' 'for the implementation of the rights recognized in the present Convention'.

6 Committee on Economic, Social and Cultural Rights, General Comment No. 3: The Nature of State Parties Obligations (Art. 2, para. 1 of the Covenant) (14 December 1990) E/1991/23 [9].

7 Olivier De Schutter, *International Human Rights Law: Cases, Materials, Commentary* (2nd edn) (Cambridge University Press 2014) 530.

8 General Comment No. 3 (n. 6) [9].

9 Maria Magdalena Sepúlveda, *The Nature of the Obligations under the International Covenant on Economic, Social and Cultural Rights* (Intersentia 2003) 315.

implementing the Convention. As a result, they are obliged to put in place their available resources in such a way as to realise the right to inclusive education and to immediately take steps to this end.

This said, immediate obligations also result from the attendant economic, social and cultural rights. The CESCR Committee has recommended that States Parties to the ICESCR fulfil 'a minimum core obligation to ensure the satisfaction of, at the very least, minimum essential levels of each of the rights' in the Covenant.[10] A State Party 'in which any significant number of individuals is deprived of . . . the most basic forms of education is, *prima facie*, failing to discharge its obligations under the Covenant'.[11] For the purpose of the right to education, the Committee considers that the 'minimum core obligation' includes ensuring 'the right of access to public educational institutions and programmes on a non-discriminatory basis [and] that education conforms to the objectives set out in article 13(1)' of the Covenant.[12] Failure to do so constitutes a violation of the ICESCR, unless the state in question is able to demonstrate the actual unavailability of the resources.[13]

Therefore, States Parties to the CRPD must at all times fulfil 'a minimum core obligation' to provide the 'most basic forms of education' to disabled children. This concerns not only primary education but also other levels of education, because of the great importance of education for the life opportunities of disabled people. It can still be argued that this 'minimum core obligation' should be more stringent with regard to the lower levels of education. States Parties to the CRPD must take minimal steps to ensure that disabled children from an early age are included in mainstream schools. These steps include facilitating access to buildings, giving minimal assistance, using available tools and coaching teachers, which again must be done instantly upon the Convention's ratification. Granting disabled children access to a segregated education arguably does not apply, because they must be able to 'access an inclusive, quality and free primary education and secondary education on an equal basis with others in the communities in which they live'.[14] In contrast to progressive realisation, the 'minimum core

[10] General Comment No. 3 [10].

[11] Ibid.

[12] CESCR Committee, General Comment No. 13: The Right to Education (Art. 13 of the Covenant) (8 December 1999) E/C.12/1999/10 [57].

[13] Ben Saul, David Kinley and Jacqueline Mowbray, *The International Covenant on Economic, Social and Cultural Rights: Commentary, Cases, and Materials* (Oxford University Press 2014) 147.

[14] Article 24(2)(b) of the CRPD.

obligation' requires that States Parties to the Convention achieve a certain outcome. It provides a 'bottom line' under which the progressive realisation of the right to inclusive education does not apply.

The prohibition of discrimination is likewise an obligation of immediate application.[15] This prohibition includes the duty to provide 'reasonable accommodation',[16] an obligation that attaches to the right to inclusive education and that is reiterated (twice) in Article 24,[17] which confirms its important function for this right.[18] The failure to satisfy that duty, therefore, constitutes discrimination on the basis of disability and a violation of the Convention.[19] When accommodation can be considered 'reasonable' is a delicate question which will never have a definite answer and which must be considered on a case-by-case basis.[20] As far as this question involves a cost-benefit comparison, several sources point out that the cost is often overestimated and that most of the time reasonable accommodation is in fact available.[21]

As a result, States Parties to the CRPD must behave in a certain manner to realise the right to inclusive education. Whether a given State Party has correctly done so will depend not only on the outcome but, above all, on the steps it has taken in order to do so. However, States Parties to the Convention must also ensure that disabled people can access inclusive education in its 'most basic forms' in addition to providing reasonable accommodation. What matters in relation to this is not how they are fulfilling the obligation, but whether this is actually done to the extent required. Having fulfilled the 'minimum core obligation', States Parties to the CRPD of course cannot be complacent about the result and must pursue their efforts in realising the right to inclusive education. While this 'minimum core

[15] 'Maastricht Guidelines on Violations of Economic, Social and Cultural Rights' (1998) 20 *Human Rights Quarterly* 691 [11].

[16] Article 5(3) of the CRPD.

[17] Articles 24(2)(c) and 24(5) of the CRPD.

[18] For a more detailed discussion on the issue, see the chapter on 'Reasonable Accommodation' by Shivaun Quinlivan in the present volume (Chapter 7).

[19] Article 2 of the CRPD.

[20] Nicholas Bamforth, Maleiha Malik and Colm O'Cinneide, *Discrimination Law: Theory and Context: Text and Materials* (Sweet and Maxwell 2008) 1077–1078.

[21] Office of the UN High Commissioner for Human Rights (OHCHR), From Exclusion to Equality: Realizing the Rights of Persons with Disabilities: Handbook for Parliamentarians on the Convention on the Rights of Persons with Disabilities and Its Optional Protocol (United Nations, Office of the UN High Commissioner for Human Rights and Inter-Parliamentary Union 2007) 84–85 www.ohchr.org/Documents/Publications/training14en.pdf (accessed 18 June 2017); United Nations International Children's Emergency Fund (UNICEF) Innocenti Research Centre, Promoting the Rights of Children with Disabilities (United Nations International Children's Emergency Fund 2007) 1 www.un.org/esa/socdev/unyin/documents/children_disability_rights.pdf (accessed 18 June 2017).

obligation' is a 'bottom line', they must go further than that and guarantee that disabled people will be able to fully enjoy their right to inclusive education in the not too distant future.

The question remains, therefore: what does progressive realisation actually imply for the right to inclusive education? This question has not been thoroughly examined to date, although doing so is necessary to determine what is expected from States Parties to the CRPD with regard to the right in question. While the CRPD Committee has not provided much guidance in this regard, it has made clear that progressive realisation 'is not compatible with sustaining two systems of education: mainstream and special/segregated education systems'.[22] It has thus clearly ruled out the provision of special education for disabled people as a means of realising economic, social and cultural rights. As provided for by Article 24(1) of the Convention, the right to inclusive education requires the establishment of 'an inclusive education system at all levels and lifelong learning'. This is the objective towards which States Parties must strive by committing a sufficient level of resources and by adopting a series of measures that will enable them to achieve that objective over time. Through the elaboration of an appropriate strategy for the implementation of the right to inclusive education, they must gradually build an 'inclusive education system'. What is meant by 'inclusive education' in this context is explored in the next part of this chapter.

B INCLUSIVE EDUCATION

In order to understand the progressive realisation of the right to inclusive education, one must first inquire into the meaning of 'inclusive education' according to the CRPD. Unlike other concepts, such as reasonable accommodation,[23] inclusive education is not defined in the Convention. There are nonetheless some clear indications as to its content. First, inclusive education cannot amount to education in special schools for children according to the different kinds of impairment.[24] This would result in the segregation of disabled children and thereby contradict the very aims of the Convention, which includes the general principle of inclusion reflected in its Article 3. Second, inclusive education is not the same as integration, which gives disabled children access to mainstream schools without altering the way in

[22] General Comment No. 4 (n. 2) [39].
[23] Article 2 of the CRPD.
[24] General Comment No. 4 (n. 2) [11].

which schools work.[25] Education systems that are not adapted to the particular needs of disabled children and that fail to guarantee true participation in classes cannot be considered inclusive.

What 'inclusive education' exactly means in the sense of Article 24 of the CRPD, however, is not easy to establish. Given the novelty of the concept of inclusive education and given the absence of research about the issue of social inclusion in international human rights law, the task is both delicate and perilous. The risk lies especially in setting the threshold: if it is too high, it is impossible to reach, and, if it is too low, it may hinder efforts.

In the context of disability, the concept of inclusive education has emerged as a reaction to the traditional paradigm for educating disabled children, namely special education.[26] From this viewpoint, inclusive education means having as many disabled children as possible in mainstream schools. This is wrong and a simplistic approach to the issue. More often than not, such practice is referred to as inclusive education, although it ultimately amounts to integration. As stated by the CRPD Committee, '[p]lacing students with disabilities within mainstream classes without accompanying structural changes to, for example, organisation, curriculum and teaching and learning strategies, does not constitute inclusion'.[27] When the purpose remains to make disabled children reach the 'norm' and to separate them from others in order to achieve this, the result will be some form of segregated education but not inclusive education according to Article 24 of the CRPD.

The lack of adaptation of education systems to the individual needs of disabled people explains why disabled children may find the experience of attending mainstream schools poor despite the substantial advantages it holds for them in terms of participation in society.[28] These children often feel they are not accepted in such schools. They are sometimes even victims of

[25] Gary Thomas, 'Inclusive Schools for an Inclusive Society' (1997) 24 *British Journal of Special Education* 103; Anastasia Liasidou, *Inclusive Education, Politics and Policymaking* (Continuum 2012) 8–9.

[26] Gary Thomas, 'A Review of Thinking and Research about Inclusive Education Policy, with Suggestions for a New Kind of Inclusive Thinking' (2013) 39 *British Educational Research Journal* 473, 475.

[27] General Comment No. 4 (n. 2) [11]. See also Committee on the Rights of the Child, General Comment No. 9: The Rights of Children with Disabilities (27 February 2007) CRC/C/GC/9 [67]. This interpretation was confirmed by the CRPD Committee, which noted 'that there exists some confusion between inclusive education and integrated education' (CRPD Committee, Concluding Observations on the Initial Report of Austria [30 September 2013] CRPD/C/AUT/CO/1 [40]).

[28] Sonali Shah and Mark Priestley, *Disability and Social Change: Private Lives and Public Policies* (Policy Press 2011) 107.

violence, including harassment and bullying.[29] Because disabled children are subject to mistreatment and stigmatisation, their families may dislike inclusive education and prefer special education for them.[30] Disabled people, therefore, use negative social attitudes to explain their refusal to participate in the general education system. The schools also fear that disabled children will drag down the level of education.[31] This fear is fuelled by the fact that the standard tests which are used to determine this level of education are generally inappropriate for inclusive education.[32] Forcing children to be educated in mainstream schools might thus do more harm than good, and, as Rioux and Pinto argue, end up being 'a charade of inclusion'.[33]

Indeed, inclusive education is not about 'placing' disabled children in mainstream schools. Rather, it concerns ensuring that education systems are accommodating disabled children. As the CRPD Committee has indicated, the general 'education system must provide a personalized educational response, rather than expecting the student to fit the system'.[34] The full realisation of the right to inclusive education, therefore, involves a more far-reaching adaptation of the general education system. The purpose should not be to identify the 'problems' of disabled children to help them fill the 'gap', but to determine how all children's abilities and skills can be effectively strengthened through the provision of education.[35]

The question remains of what could be the true meaning of 'inclusive education' in Article 24 of the CRPD. The CRPD Committee considers that inclusive education

> involves a process of systemic reform embodying changes and modifications in content, teaching methods, approaches, structures and strategies in

29 Marcia H. Rioux and Paula C. Pinto, 'A Time for the Universal Right to Education: Back to Basics' (2010) 31 *British Journal of Sociology of Education* 621, 630–631.

30 Global Campaign for Education and Handicap International, Equal Right, Equal Opportunity: Inclusive Education for Children with Disabilities, 26 http://campaignforeducation.org/docs/reports/Equal%20Right,%20Equal%20Opportunity_WEB.pdf (accessed 23 June 2017).

31 UNICEF Innocenti Research Centre (n. 21) 17.

32 Anastasia Liasidou, 'Inclusive Education and Critical Pedagogy at the Intersections of Disability, Race, Gender and Class' (2012) 10 *Journal for Critical Education Policy Studies* 168, 175.

33 Rioux and Pinto (n. 31) 622.

34 General Comment No. 4 (n. 2) [12(c)].

35 Serge Ebersold, 'Accessibilité, politiques inclusives et droit à l'éducation: considérations conceptuelles et méthodologiques' (2015) 9 *ALTER European Journal of Disability Research* 22, 27; Michele Moore and Roger Slee, 'Disability Studies, Inclusive Education and Exclusion' in Nick Watson, Alan Roulstone and Carol Thomas (eds), *Routledge Handbook of Disability Studies* (Routledge 2012) 235.

education to overcome barriers with a vision serving to provide all students of the relevant age range with an equitable and participatory learning experience and environment that best corresponds to their requirements and preferences.[36]

This definition of the concept of inclusive education implies that States Parties to the Convention make constant and ongoing efforts through taking steps to recognise the abilities and skills of all children and to change and to adapt the various practices of education to meet this objective. It requires revisiting the different facets of education so that disabled children can acquire the same level of educational opportunities as other children.

In view of this, States Parties to the Convention should aim to apply a 'universal design' to education, a concept that was originally developed in architecture and subsequently applied to technology and other areas, including education. This means that States Parties must ensure that from the very beginning, 'goods, services, equipment and facilities' can be used by everybody.[37] 'Universal design' means looking not only at how schools address the individual needs of disabled people but also at how to establish education systems that make room for the variety of children from inception.[38] As stated by the CRPD Committee, '[c]urricula must be conceived, designed and applied to meet and adjust to the requirements of every student' while 'providing teachers and other staff members with a structure to create adaptable learning environments and develop instruction to meet the diverse needs of all learners'.[39]

C MEASURES

The next question is how to reach the objective: what needs to be done in order to realise the right to inclusive education? The CRPD sets out the steps to be taken in order to bring about an 'inclusive education system'. Although it does not define the concept of inclusive education, it obliges States Parties to adopt a number of measures for the progressive realisation of the right to inclusive education. On the basis of the CRPD, these measures can generally be divided into four main categories: accessibility, support provision, teacher education and raising awareness. This typology corresponds to that reflected in

36 General Comment No. 4 (n. 2) 11.
37 Article 4(f) of the CRPD.
38 Martha Minow, 'Universal Design in Education: Remaking All the Difference' in Arlene S. Kanter and Beth A. Ferri (eds), *Righting Education Wrongs* (Syracuse University Press 2013) 56.
39 General Comment No. 4 (n. 2) 25.

the work of UN agencies and disabled people's organisations and that interpreted by the CRPD Committee in its Concluding Observations to States Parties to the CRPD on the bases of their reports on the implementation of the Convention as well as its General Comment on the Right to Inclusive Education. The discussion that follows addresses these four categories in succession.

First, disabled children must have full access to mainstream schools. Access to education for different groups of people has mainly been viewed through the issue of non-discrimination with a special focus on physical and economic obstacles.[40] The CRPD, in turn, has not only made it a general obligation for the implementation of the entire Convention's rights but also broadened it to include issues that go beyond physical and economic accessibility. Article 9 of the CRPD provides that States Parties to the Convention must take measures to ensure access to '[b]uildings, roads, transportation and other indoor and outdoor facilities, including schools' for disabled people.[41] In addition, they must make accessible '[i]nformation, communications and other services, including electronic services and emergency services'.[42] Such accessibility can again be achieved through ensuring 'universal design'. As far as education is concerned, '[t]he entire education system must be accessible, including buildings, information and communication, comprising ambient or frequency modulation assistive systems, curriculum, education materials, teaching methods, assessment and language and support services'.[43] This also applies to information and communication through the use of 'sign language, Braille, alternative script, and augmentative and alternative modes, means and formats of communication and orientation'.[44] Accessibility concerns wider school life as well, including 'school transport, which should be inclusive, accessible and safe; water and sanitation facilities, including hygiene and toilet facilities; school cafeterias; and recreational spaces'.[45] Therefore, buildings, including classrooms and toilets, as well as transport to school must be made fully accessible to disabled children.[46] Although efforts have been made in this regard, educational environments remain inaccessible to most disabled

40 General Comment No. 13 (n. 12) [6].
41 Article 9(1)(a) of the CRPD.
42 Article 9(1)(b) of the CRPD.
43 General Comment No. 4 (n. 2) [21].
44 CRPD Committee, General Comment No. 2 (2014) Article 9: Accessibility (22 May 2014) CRPD/C/ GC/2 [39].
45 General Comment No. 4 (n. 2) [21].
46 UNICEF Innocenti Research Centre (n. 21) 16–17; Inclusion International, Better Education for All: When We're Included Too: A Global Report: People with an Intellectual Disability and Their Families Speak Out on Education for All, Disability and Inclusive Education

people.[47] Much of the infrastructure has been established without disabled children in mind, not only in Western countries that are equipped with special schools but also in developing countries which have received funding to build new schools that are still very often inaccessible. Complying with CRPD requirements, however, will inevitably be harder for existing schools built without taking into account accessibility. Barrier removal plans should be adopted and mechanisms put into place to ensure that new schools are made accessible from the very beginning. Thus, the CRPD Committee recommends that States Parties to the CRPD 'prohibit and sanction the building of any future education infrastructures that are inaccessible'.[48] Accessibility is an area in which they must progress promptly if disabled people are ever to enjoy their right to inclusive education.

The practice of the CRPD Committee indicates numerous aspects of inaccessibility in education. For instance, the Committee was 'concerned about poor accessibility in schools' in Belgium and 'a lack of . . . accessible school environments in the mainstream education system' in Brazil.[49] In its review of Lithuania, the Committee regretted that '[t]he number of accessible means of transport is insufficient to accommodate the needs of students with disabilities and to allow them to participate fully in the education system' in Lithuania.[50] The Committee noticed 'the lack of teaching and reading materials in accessible formats and modes of communication' in Colombia and 'the lack of availability of accessible learning materials and the lack of assistive technology' in Italy.[51]

Second, disabled people must be provided with the supports they require in order to be included in education. Article 24(2)(d) of the CRPD stipulates that '[p]ersons with disabilities receive the support required within the general education system, to facilitate their effective education'. Such support includes not only equipment and materials, such as Braille and sign language, but also personal assistance. The latter can be 'a qualified learning support

(Instituto Universitario de Integración en la Communidad 2009) 82 http://ii.gmalik.com/pdfs/Better_Education_for_All_Global_Report_October_2009.pdf (accessed 23 June 2017).

47 Inclusion International (n. 46) 82.

48 General Comment No. 4 (n. 2) [21].

49 CRPD Committee, Concluding Observations on the Initial Report of Belgium (28 October 2014) CRPD/C/BEL/CO/1 [36]; CRPD Committee, Concluding Observations on the Initial Report of Brazil (29 September 2015) CRPD/C/BRA/CO/1 [44].

50 CRPD Committee, Concluding Observations on the Initial Report of Lithuania (11 May 2016) CRPD/C/LTU/CO/1 [45(e)].

51 CRPD Committee, Concluding Observations on the Initial Report of Colombia (30 September 2016) RPD/C/COL/CO/1 [54]; CRPD Committee, Concluding Observations on the Initial Report of Italy (6 October 2016) CRPD/C/ITA/CO/1 [59].

assistant, either shared or on a one-to-one basis, depending on the requirements of the student'.[52] Support also includes 'the provision of sufficient trained and supported teaching staff, school counsellors, psychologists, and other relevant health and social service professionals, as well as access to scholarships and financial resources'.[53] However, it appears that support is frequently either missing or inadequate in reality.[54] This is a serious obstacle that prevents many disabled children from receiving meaningful and quality education. If the support provided does not meet their individual needs, these children will be unable to participate in the general education system. Disabled people might then prefer special education where their impairments are better taken into account. States Parties to the CRPD must ensure that support is provided to disabled children within mainstream schools. Still, the fact that States allocate resources to special schools does not help to increase the availability of the support. Therefore, it is contended here that governments ought to transfer resources from the special schools to mainstream schools in order to build an 'inclusive education system'.

The CRPD Committee has expressed its concern regarding the matter to a number of States Parties to the Convention through the reporting process. To Austria, it indicated 'that insufficient effort has been made to support the inclusive education of children with disabilities'.[55] To Sweden, it noted that there were 'reports indicating that some children who need extensive support cannot attend school due to a lack of such support' and, to Portugal, that 'although the great majority of students with disabilities attend regular schools in the State party, there is a lack of support'.[56] It also regretted 'the lack of clarity regarding the extent to which pupils with disabilities can receive adequate support' in Denmark and '[t]he lack of accessible schools and didactic materials, including textbooks in Braille and sign-language interpreters' in Mexico.[57]

Third, a crucial aspect of inclusive education is the training of staff members. Article 24(4) of the CRPD provides that teachers must be trained in 'the use of appropriate augmentative and alternative modes, means and formats of

52 General Comment No. 4 (n. 2) [32].

53 Ibid. [31].

54 Inclusion International (n. 46) 65–66.

55 CRPD/C/AUT/CO/1 (n. 26) [40].

56 CRPD Committee, Concluding Observations on the Initial Report of Sweden (12 May 2014) CRPD/C/SWE/CO/1 [47]; CRPD Committee, Concluding Observations on the Initial Report of Portugal (18 April 2016) CRPD/C/PRT/CO/1 [44].

57 CRPD Committee, Concluding Observations on the Initial Report of Denmark (30 October 2014) CRPD/C/DNK/CO/1 [52]; CRPD Committee, Concluding Observations on the Initial Report of Mexico (27 October 2014) CRPD/C/MEX/CO/1 [47c].

communication, educational techniques and materials to support persons with disabilities'. Such training will allow them to address the issues arising and to change their teaching methods for disabled children. In fact, staff members often have to work in isolation with pressure from the top to meet educational targets and do not get help to find solutions.[58] They are also afraid that they will not be able to cope with disabled children and that inclusive education will further increase their workload. It is therefore important that the training is done for 'all teachers at pre-school, primary, secondary, tertiary and vocational education levels'.[59] This includes training in the following techniques:

> the provision of individualized instruction; teaching the same content using varied teaching methods to respond to the learning styles and unique abilities of each person; the development and use of individual educational plans to support specific learning requirements; and the introduction of a pedagogy centred around students' educational objectives.[60]

The problem is that disability usually remains an optional course in teacher education and a topic taught in order to work subsequently in special schools. For instance, the CRPD Committee regretted 'the continuing existence of the special education model … and that training for teachers and other professional staff continues to be provided within this specialized framework' in Costa Rica.[61] In order to enable teachers to educate disabled children in mainstream schools, it is necessary to teach all of them how to deal with disabilities both by teacher core training and by continuing education.[62]

The CRPD Committee further noted that teacher education left a lot to be desired in many States Parties to the Convention. It recommended, to the United Arab Emirates, 'that training on inclusive education and teaching children with disabilities [be] compulsory and an integral part of core teacher training curricula in universities' and, to El Salvador, 'promoting disability education as a cross-cutting theme in university courses'.[63] In order to help

58 United Nations International Children's Emergency Fund (UNICEF), The State of the World's Children 2013: Children with Disabilities (United Nations International Children's Emergency Fund 2013) 33.
59 General Comment No. 4 (n. 2) [69].
60 Ibid.
61 CRPD Committee, Concluding Observations on the Initial Report of Costa Rica (12 May 2014) CRPD/C/CRI/CO/1 [45].
62 Global Campaign for Education and Handicap International (n. 30) 24.
63 CRPD Committee, Concluding Observations on the Initial Report of the United Arab Emirates (3 October 2016) CRPD/C/ARE/CO/1 [44(c)]; CRPD Committee, Concluding Observations on the Initial Report of El Salvador (8 October 2013) CRPD/C/SLV/CO/1 [22].

teachers adapt their education methods and to utilise new forms of target assessments, they should likewise receive adequate support within mainstream schools.[64] The CRPD Committee recommended that Gabon ensure 'mandatory pre- and in-service training for all teachers and other education personnel on inclusive quality education', that Qatar give 'mandatory in-service training of all teachers and all staff in education facilities on quality, inclusive education' and that Colombia make 'inclusive education and the rights of persons with disabilities key components of teacher training . . . before and during the exercise of their functions'.[65]

Fourth, disabled children must feel welcome in mainstream schools. Article 8(2)(b) of the CRPD provides for measures fostering 'at all levels of the education system, including in all children from an early age, an attitude of respect for the rights of persons with disabilities'. The creation of welcoming school environments is a fundamental step towards the full realisation of the right to inclusive education. Without the changing of social attitudes, other measures to realise the right to inclusive education are doomed to failure. As explained in the previous section, disabled children continue to suffer stigmatisation in mainstream schools. In order to improve social attitudes, States Parties to the CRPD should

> adopt measures to build a culture of diversity, participation and involvement into community life and to highlight inclusive education as a means to achieve a quality education for all students, with and without disabilities, parents, teachers and school administrations, as well as the community and society.[66]

Therefore, they should allocate their resources to provide 'awareness raising initiatives to address stigma and discrimination, particularly bullying in educational settings'.[67] States Parties to the Convention must work on making disabled children accepted by raising awareness of the Convention and promoting a positive image of disabled people in mainstream schools. This is perhaps the most difficult to achieve, especially since it requires working on underlying stereotypes and prejudices that surround disabled people, which is reflected in the belief that disabled children are generally ill-fitted to the general education system.

64 General Comment No. 4 (n. 2) [25].
65 CRPD Committee, Concluding Observations on the Initial Report of Gabon (2 October 2015) CRPD/C/GAB/CO/1 [53]; CRPD Committee, Concluding Observations on the Initial Report of Qatar (2 October 2015) CRPD/C/QAT/CO/1 [44]; CRPD/C/COL/CO/1 (n. 53) [55].
66 General Comment No. 4 (n. 2) [46].
67 Ibid. [67].

While the CRPD Committee has not paid a lot of attention to social attitudes, it has addressed the issue to a few States Parties to the CRPD. To New Zealand, it expressed its concern 'at reports indicating that children with disabilities experience bullying in schools', while it asked Chile to have 'a plan for transitioning towards inclusive education . . . which provides for . . . the roll-out of comprehensive awareness-raising campaigns and the promotion of a culture of diversity'.[68] It also encouraged States Parties to the Convention to 'ensure that mechanisms are in place to foster, at all levels of the education system, and among parents and the wider public, an attitude of respect for the rights of persons with disabilities'.[69] It also asked them repeatedly to overcome stereotypes and prejudices by promoting a 'positive image of persons with disabilities' in accordance to Article 8 of the CRPD.[70] While these recommendations are useful, it would have been well-considered to place a greater emphasis on sensitisation in the context of education. The acceptance of disabled children in mainstream schools is an essential prerequisite for the establishment of an 'inclusive education system'.

A final point to be made is the legal nature of the measures to be adopted for the progressive realisation of the right to inclusive education and the provision of reasonable accommodation to disabled people. On the one hand, progressive realisation applies to the achievement of inclusive education with respect to the general education system as a whole. It is a legal obligation which for its fulfilment largely depends on available resources. It moreover requires that States Parties to the CRPD acquire a high level of expertise in achieving inclusive education that most of them are still lacking. On the other hand, reasonable accommodation is a duty that must be satisfied instantaneously as part of the non-discrimination obligation. If asked for by an individual, measures such as holding classes on a ground level, waiving certain entry requirements (including medical exams) and flexing assessment regulations must be adopted upon request of that individual.

Despite their different approach and application scope, progressive realisation and reasonable accommodation are to be considered together. This can

68 CRPD Committee, Concluding Observations on the Initial Report of New Zealand (31 October 2014) CRPD/C/NZL/CO/1 [49]; CRPD Committee, Concluding Observations on the Initial Report of the Republic of Chile (13 April 2016) CRPD/C/CHL/CO/1 [50(a)].

69 General Comment No. 4 (n. 2) [46].

70 See, among others, CRPD Committee, Concluding Observations on the Initial Report of Croatia (15 May 2015) CRPD/C/HRV/CO/1 [14]; CRPD Committee, CRPD/C/DNK/CO/1 (n. 59) [23]; CRPD/C/GAB/CO/1 (n. 67) [21]; CRPD Committee, Concluding Observations on the Initial Report of the Republic of Kenya (30 September 2015) CRPD/C/KEN/CO/1 [16]; CRPD Committee, Concluding Observations on the Initial Report of Paraguay (15 May 2013) CRPD/C/PRY/CO/1 [22].

be seen in the CRPD Committee's emphasising 'the necessity for the provision of individualised education plans, which can identify the reasonable accommodations and specific support required for an individual student'.[71] It immediately adds, though, that any measures 'must be designed to strengthen opportunities for students with disabilities to participate in the classroom and in out-of-school activities alongside their peers, rather than marginalise them'.[72] Therefore, the goal must remain to create an 'inclusive education system'.

D STRATEGY

In order to realise economic, social and cultural rights, States Parties to the CRPD need a strategy that is effective, realistic and well-funded. Starting with the last point, it is worth recalling that the progressive realisation of the right to inclusive education requires the use of a State Party's maximum available resources. The CRPD Committee considers in this regard that States Parties to the Convention 'must commit sufficient financial and human resources . . . to support the implementation of inclusive education, *consistent with progressive realisation*'.[73] They must therefore make inclusive education a priority by utilising the means at their disposal to develop an 'inclusive education system'. Resources in this context need to be understood broadly and should be evaluated in terms of both expenditure and revenues.[74] These resources include natural, human, technological and informational resources as well as potentially available national resources, such as land reform and wealth taxes, and international resources.[75] States Parties to the Convention must in such a way allocate a budget with a view to achieving the full realisation of the right to inclusive education.

States often put forward that inclusive education is too costly and that they do not have the necessary resources. This is contradicted by a number of international organisations. Both the United Nations Children's Fund (UNICEF) and the Organisation for Economic Co-operation and Development (OECD), for instance, have held that inclusive education systems are less expensive than segregated education systems.[76] This is also

71 General Comment No. 4 (n. 2) [32].

72 Ibid. [33].

73 Ibid. [67] (emphasis added).

74 Saul, Kinley and Mowbray (n. 13) 143–144.

75 Robert E. Robertson, 'Measuring State Compliance with the Obligation to Devote the "Maximum Available Resources" to Realizing Economic, Social, and Cultural Rights' (1994) 16 *Human Rights Quarterly* 693, 695–700.

76 United Nations International Children's Emergency Fund (UNICEF), The Right of Children with Disabilities to Education: A Rights-Based Approach to Inclusive Education

stated in the Salamanca Statement, which declares that inclusive education 'would improve the efficiency and ultimately the cost-effectiveness of the entire education system'.[77] Money could arguably be saved not only on school buildings but also on administration, materials and transport. To be sure, inclusive education could bring additional costs in the short term and only become profitable in the long term. The achievement of inclusive education can be compared to the construction of a 'passive house', which is cheaper in the long run compared to the heavy reconstruction costs subsequently carried out on a badly insulated house. Inclusive education is economically feasible and will eventually be more beneficial. However, it should be seen not just as the more economical route but also as a more efficient way for providing education to all children.[78]

This being said, resources remain an important obstacle to inclusive education. While most States Parties to the CRPD have adopted national legislation allowing disabled children to enrol in mainstream schools, there are as a rule no or limited resources for that purpose. The lack of resources to realise the right to inclusive education has been pointed out on numerous occasions by the CRPD Committee. While reacting positively to legal frameworks, the CRPD Committee has expressed its concern about the lack of practical implementation by many States Parties to the Convention.[79] The failure to apply the maximum available resources for establishing an 'inclusive

(Position paper) (United Nations International Children's Emergency Fund, 2012) 38–39 www.unicef.org/ceecis/UNICEF_Right_Children_Disabilities_En_Web.pdf; Organisation for Economic Co-operation and Development (OECD), Inclusive Education at Work: Students with Disabilities in Mainstream Schools (Organisation for Economic Co-operation and Development, 1999) 21 www.oecd-ilibrary.org/education/inclusive-education-at-work_9789264180383-en. See also OHCHR (21) [84]; Inclusion International (n. 46) [41].

77 Para. 2, Salamanca Statement.

78 Global Campaign for Education and Handicap International (n. 30) [21].

79 To Spain, the Committee requested 'allocating sufficient financial and human resources to implement the right to inclusive education' (CRPD Committee, Concluding Observations on the Initial Report of Spain [19 October 2011] CRPD/C/ESP/CO/1 [44(a)]). To Peru, it recommended that the state 'allocate sufficient budget resources to achieve advances in the progress for an inclusive education system for children and adolescents with disabilities' (CRPD Committee, Concluding Observations on the Initial Report of Peru [16 May 2012] CRPD/C/PER/CO/1 [37]) and, to Argentina, that the state 'allocates sufficient budgetary resources to ensure progress towards the establishment of an education system that includes students with disabilities' (CRPD Committee, Concluding Observations on the Initial Report of Argentina [8 October 2012] CRPD/C/ARG/CO/1 [38]). To Hungary, it called upon the state 'to allocate sufficient resources for the development of an inclusive education system for children with disabilities' (CRPD Committee, Concluding Observations on the Initial Report of Hungary [22 October 2012] CRPD/C/HUN/CO/1 [41]), to the Czech Republic, 'to allocate sufficient financial and human resources for reasonable accommodations that will enable boys and girls with disabilities, including intellectual disabilities and autism, and deaf-blind

education system' is not in conformity with the CRPD. While the CRPD Committee has been succinct about this failure and did not clarify its precise legal impact, the consequence of not allocating these resources to realise the right to inclusive education obviously results in a violation of the Convention.

The progressive realisation of the right to inclusive education also involves the redefinition of budgetary allocations, which includes transferring budgets for special education to build an 'inclusive education system'. A lot of states allocate significant resources to special schools. The resources therefore are available but not committed in the way that they should be according to international human rights law. In order to realise the right to inclusive education, the CRPD Committee has requested States Parties to the CRPD 'to achieve a transfer of resources from segregated to inclusive environments'.[80] For instance, it recommended, to China, to 'reallocate resources from the special education system to promote the inclusive education in mainstream schools' and, to Qatar and the United Arab Emirates, to '[r]eorient resources from segregated educational settings towards quality inclusive education'.[81] Consequently, States Parties to the Convention that continue to fund extensively special schools without endeavouring to redirect the resources for mainstream schools so as to make their education system inclusive fail to implement the right to inclusive education. This might mean an investment at first instance, as it is possible that they do not recover these resources straightaway, because the budget might be used for those disabled children who are already enrolled in mainstream schools. Inclusive education therefore could bring additional costs in the short term and only become profitable in the long term for States Parties to the CRPD. It involves a process that will enable the general education system to gradually meet the various needs of all disabled children.

Moreover, progressive realisation involves a planning exercise.[82] An essential tool to ensure sound planning for the achievement of inclusive

children, to receive inclusive quality education' (CRPD Committee, Concluding Observations on the Initial Report of Czech Republic [15 April 2015] CRPD/C/CZE/CO/1 [48]) and, to Ukraine, to 'allocate sufficient financial and human resources to train all teachers and ensure the accessibility of school environments and educational facilities, material and curricula' (CRPD Committee, Concluding Observations on the Initial Report of Ukraine [2 October 2015] CRPD/C/UKR/CO/1 [45]).

80 General Comment No. 4 (n. 2) [68].

81 CRPD Committee, Concluding Observations on the Initial Report of China (15 October 2012) CRPD/C/CHN/CO/1 [36]; CRPD/C/QAT/CO/1 (n. 67) [44]; CRPD/C/ARE/CO/1 (n. 65) [44(b)].

82 Saul, Kinley and Mowbray (n. 13) 166–167.

education, therefore, is the elaboration of national action plans.[83] While such plans are not mentioned in the CRPD, they are provided for by Article 14 of the ICESCR and have been highlighted by the CRPD Committee. The latter recommended that a 'comprehensive and co-ordinated legislative and policy framework for inclusive education must be introduced, together with a clear and adequate time frame for implementation' by States Parties to the CRPD.[84] Such a 'legislative and policy framework' should include measures to improve accessibility, to expand support provision, to review teacher education and to foster raising awareness. Given the importance to consider disability throughout the general education system, it is moreover preferable to integrate any national action plan for inclusive education into the overall strategy for the education of all children.

The CRPD Committee has confirmed that planning is indispensable to realise the right to inclusive education to States Parties to the CRPD. To Italy, it recommended that it should 'implement an action plan – with sufficient resources, timelines and specific goals – . . . to improve the quality of inclusive education in classrooms, support provisions and teacher training across all levels', to Germany, that it '[i]mmediately develop a strategy, action plan, timeline and targets to provide access to a high-quality, inclusive education system across all Länder' and, to Colombia, that it '[a]dopt a national plan to transform the system into one that provides inclusive and quality education for all persons with disabilities'.[85] The planning exercise will thus vary according to the particularities of a given State Party (which may have a federal constitutional structure like Germany's). It may also involve a transition from segregated to inclusive education systems in those States Parties to the Convention that have been relying more than others on special education. To Kenya, the CRPD Committee requested that it should '[e]stablish a time frame for the transition process from segregated to inclusive quality education and ensure that budgetary, technical and personal resources are available to complete the process' and, to Chile, that it should '[i]mplement a plan for transitioning towards inclusive education at all levels up to higher education'.[86]

A final aspect is the importance of assessing progress towards the full realisation of the right to inclusive education. Because inclusive education is

83 Gauthier de Beco, 'Transition to Inclusive Education Systems According to the Convention on the Rights of Persons with Disabilities' (2016) 34 *Nordic Journal of Human Rights* 40, 55–56.

84 General Comment No. 4 (n. 2) [61].

85 CRPD/C/ITA/CO/1 (n. 53) [56]; CRPD Committee, Concluding Observations on the Initial Report of Germany (13 May 2015) CRPD/C/DEU/CO/1 [46(a)]; CRPD/C/COL/CO/1 (n. 53) [55(a)].

86 CRPD/C/KEN/CO/1 (n. 72) [44(a)]; CRPD/C/CHL/CO/1 (n. 70) [50(a)].

a process rather than a goal, and because it involves ongoing efforts, monitoring is of particular importance to keep abreast of this progress over a period of time. This can be done through the development of indicators relating to the right to inclusive education, as advocated by several international organisations[87] and advanced by scholarship on the potential use of human rights indicators.[88] These indicators could be divided into structural, process and outcome indicators, thereby following the methodology of the Office of the UN High Commissioner for Human Rights (OHCHR) which drafted a guide outlining this methodology and provided lists of illustrative indicators relating to several human rights (including the right to education).[89] These indicators can address the essential aspects of human rights implementation, that is, intention, effort and result.[90] As far as the right to inclusive education is concerned, the structural indicators could focus on legislation, planning, budget and monitoring bodies, the process indicators on accessibility, support measures, flexible curricula, teacher education and promotion campaigns, and the outcome indicators on attendance, completion and drop-out (by education level) as well as social attitudes and recreational activities in mainstream schools.[91]

Article 31(1) of the CRPD also requires that States Parties to the Convention 'collect appropriate information, including statistical and research data, to enable them to formulate and implement policies to give effect to 'the present Convention'. They should gather such data so that their achievements can be measured regularly through the aforementioned indicators, and submit this data in their reports for the attention of the CRPD Committee so that it can make recommendations to them. In order to detect instances of discrimination, the data must furthermore be 'disaggregated, as appropriate', as provided by Article 31(2) of the Convention, that is, not only by disability but also age, gender and so on. The CRPD Committee has confirmed that 'States Parties to the Convention should gather disaggregated data and evidence on the barriers that prevent persons with disabilities from having access to, remaining in, and

87 UNICEF (2013) 27–28; Global Campaign for Education and Handicap International (n. 32) 22.

88 Gauthier de Beco, 'Human Rights Indicators: From Theoretical Debate to Practical Application' (2013) 5 *Journal of Human Rights Practice* 380.

89 Office of the UN High Commissioner for Human Rights (OHCHR), *Human Rights Indicators: A Guide to Measurement and Implementation* (Office of the UN High Commissioner for Human Rights 2012) www.ohchr.org/Documents/Publications/Human_rights_indicators_en.pdf (accessed 23 June 2017).

90 Gauthier de Beco, 'Human Rights Indicators: From Theoretical Debate to Practical Application' (2013) 5 *Journal of Human Rights Practice* 380, 381–382.

91 de Beco (2016) (n. 82) 56–58.

making progress in inclusive quality education'.[92] Of course, this will demand a further allocation of resources for the implementation of the right to inclusive education, but developing indicators and gathering data are preconditions for sound policy making and, therefore, a necessary tool to ensure that States Parties to the CRPD are actually realising economic, social and cultural rights.

The CRPD Committee has noted the role of data collection in evaluating the extent to which the right to inclusive education has been realised to States Parties to the CRPD. It has successively expressed its concern about the importance of data collection. For instance, to Italy, the Committee noted 'the absence of data and indicators to monitor the quality of education and inclusion of students with disabilities in mainstream schools and classes' and, to the United Arab Emirates, it referred to 'the lack of disaggregated statistical data on children with disabilities in inclusive education and of teachers trained on inclusive education and teaching children with disabilities'.[93] It also asked Kenya to 'collect disaggregated data on the advancement of the inclusive education system' and Lithuania to '[s]et clear timelines, targets, baselines and indicators to secure time-bound and measurable progress'.[94] The indicators can help to track the pace at which the creation of an 'inclusive education system' is taking place and what steps are still needed in order to make further progress towards the full realisation of the right to inclusive education. Such indicators also could benefit from the data collected for the purpose of indicators measuring progress towards the achievement of the Sustainable Development Goals (SDGs), several of which address disability in the context of education.[95]

CONCLUSION

The right to inclusive education is subject to progressive realisation. The latter has an important function for the implementation of this right. Developing an 'inclusive education system' presents significant challenges for States Parties to the CRPD, and can indeed not be achieved adequately in a hurry. The concept of progressive realisation indeed acknowledges that the target

92 General Comment No. 4 (n. 2) [66].
93 CRPD/C/ITA/CO/1 (n. 53) [55]; CRPD/C/ARE/CO/1 (n. 65) [43(f)].
94 CRPD/C/KEN/CO/1 (n. 72) [44(a)]; CRPD/C/LTU/CO/1 (n. 52) [45].
95 See https://sustainabledevelopment.un.org/sdg4 (accessed 23 June 2017). For a more detailed discussion on the issue, see the chapter on 'Advancing the Right to Inclusive Education in Development Cooperation' by Janet Lord in the present volume (Chapter 12).

cannot be reached overnight. This is especially so with the right to inclusive education. Inclusive education must not aim just to enable mainstream schools to educate disabled children but also to open up education systems for the benefit of all children alike, including not only these children but also those from ethnic minorities and poorer backgrounds.

The discussion should not stop there. It is worth recalling that the purpose of the obligation is to achieve the *full* realisation of the right to inclusive education over a reasonable period of time. This purpose should be kept in mind, especially since it appears that changes are not happening on the ground despite the Convention's high ratification level and since only minor adaptations have been done to transform education systems up until now. This is why it is necessary to signal the requirements of achieving inclusive education to States Parties to the CRPD beyond the fulfilment of the 'minimum core obligation' and the provision of reasonable accommodation and to stress the imperative of adopting measures for the progressive realisation of the right to inclusive education.

The main lesson to be learned from this analysis, perhaps, is that careful attention should not only go to the outcome – the achievement of inclusive education – but also to the process – the transformation of education systems. The measures to realise the right to inclusive education should be further scrutinised through a thorough evaluation of the policies adopted as well as the budget allocated for inclusive education. Looking at legislation is not enough, since without such policies the right in question will never become a reality. This leads to the importance of monitoring progress in realising the right to inclusive education. States Parties to the CRPD need much more guidance on how to bring about an 'inclusive education system'. In addition to the reviews of state reports by the CRPD Committee, it would be advisable to activate a large range of other mechanisms that could indicate to them how to reach this objective. These mechanisms include not only the communications and inquiry procedures before this Committee but also the Conference of States Parties to the CRPD and the UN Department of Economic and Social Affairs.

Finally, the full realisation of the right to inclusive education cannot be achieved without the involvement of disabled people themselves. These people must be associated in the elaboration of the strategy and participate in the choice of the approach to allow disabled children to be educated in mainstream schools. In order to realise the right to inclusive education, these children must feel much more welcome in such schools and have their particular needs addressed. Both disabled people's organisations and families of disabled children, therefore, must be invited to express their concerns about the real-life experience of disabled children, who should likewise be able to express their views on the matter. What is true for the CRPD in general is true for the right to inclusive education. Inclusive education should be a viable option for disabled people, the failure of which would mean that the right to inclusive education will never be fully realised.

9

Financing Inclusive Education

Lessons from Developing Countries

János Fiala-Butora

I INTRODUCTION

The right to inclusive education applies to all countries ratifying the Convention on the Rights of Persons with Disabilities (CRPD), including developing countries, where the vast majority of persons with disabilities live. While developing inclusive education might require significant investments, lack of funds is not an excuse for fulfilling the right, as according to Article 24 of the CRPD, all States Parties must ensure an inclusive education system.[1]

The right to education is a socioeconomic right subject to progressive realisation under Article 4(2) of the CRPD. Accordingly, the full realisation of the right must be achieved progressively. This, however, does not mean that fulfilling the right could be postponed until economic conditions improve. As Gauthier de Beco explains in this volume (Chapter 8), all States Parties must take the necessary measures to the maximum of their available resources to fully realise the right. Article 24 of the CRPD provides a list of such measures, which include teacher training, awareness raising, accessibility, individualised support and facilitation of communication.[2] While some of these measures can require significant investments, all States Parties 'must commit sufficient financial and human resources' to develop inclusive education, as the Committee on the Rights of Persons with Disabilities (CRPD Committee) underlined in its General Comment No. 4 on the right to inclusive education.[3]

[1] United Nations General Assembly, Convention on the Rights of Persons with Disabilities (13 December 2006) A/RES/61/106 (CRPD) Article 24(1).

[2] CRPD Article 24(2)–(4).

[3] Committee on the Rights of Persons with Disabilities, General Comment No. 4 (2016) Article 24: Right to Inclusive Education (2 September 2016) CRPD/C/GC/4 [67].

This chapter looks into the example of two developing countries, Tanzania and Vietnam, to analyse how they proceeded in committing their resources to fulfil the right to inclusive education. Both countries have ratified the CRPD,[4] but neither has submitted its first state report yet. However, they have submitted state reports in the past under the Convention on the Rights of the Child (CRC) and the International Covenant on Economic, Social and Cultural Rights (ICESCR), which provide useful information about the state of their education systems and the situation of children with disabilities in them. The countries' progress is assessed in this chapter in light of their reports to their respective UN treaty bodies, and two analyses of their budgetary processes, which provide detailed information about how they allocate funds to educational goals.[5]

II TANZANIA

Tanzania is one of the world's least developed countries, with an estimated gross domestic product (GDP) per capita of 1,032 USD.[6] Its economy relies heavily on agriculture, which makes up 45 per cent of its GDP and 75–80 per cent of exports.[7]

1 *Tanzania's Education System*

Tanzania's oldest school, the Uhuru Mchanganyiko primary school in Dar es Salaam, was established in 1921.[8] After its independence in 1961, the country started building a comprehensive national education system.[9] Since 1978,

4 Tanzania in 2009, Vietnam in 2015.

5 For analysis concerning Tanzania, see Comprehensive Community Based Rehabilitation in Tanzania (CCBRT), 'Budget Analysis with Disability Perspective' (December 2013) www.ccbrt.or.tz/fileadmin/downloads/Government_of_Tanzania_Budget_Analysis_with_Disability_Perspective.pdf (accessed 25 March 2017); for analysis concerning Vietnam, see Nguyen Thi Van Anh, Ngo Huy Duc, Le Ngoc Hung and Luu Van Quang, *Child-Focused Budget Study: Assessing the Rights to Education of Children with Disabilities in Vietnam* (Hanoi 2000).

6 Committee on Economic, Social and Cultural Rights, 'Combined Initial, Second and Third Periodic Reports Submitted by States Parties under Articles 16 and 17 of [the] International Covenant on Economic, Social and Cultural Rights: United Republic of Tanzania' (28 March 2011) E/C.12/TZA/1–3 [8]; International Monetary Fund, 'Report for Selected Countries and Subjects – Tanzania' www.imf.org/external/pubs/ft/weo/2017/01/weodata/weorept.aspx?pr.x=56&pr.y=3&sy=2017&ey=2021&scsm=1&ssd=1&sort=country&ds=.&br=1&c=738&s=NGDPD%2CNGDPDPC%2CPPPGDP%2CPPPPC&grp=0&a=#download (accessed 25 April 2017).

7 Committee on Economic, Social and Cultural Rights (n. 6) [8]

8 Committee on the Rights of the Child, 'Initial Reports of States Parties Due in 1993: United Republic of Tanzania' (25 September 2000) CRC/C/8/Add.14/Rev.1 [274].

9 'Combined Initial, Second and Third Periodic Reports Submitted by States Parties under Articles 16 and 17 of [the] International Covenant on Economic, Social and Cultural Rights: United Republic of Tanzania' (n. 6) [136].

with the adoption of the National Education Act,[10] enrolment in and attendance of primary schools has become compulsory for children aged seven to thirteen.[11]

The obligation to attend school was implemented with difficulty in practice due to the lack of schools and trained teachers. The distance from schools prevented children from participating in education, especially in rural areas.[12] Nevertheless, the country has achieved significant successes in developing its education system. According to the government's claim, in the 1970s, the gross enrolment ratio of children in basic education reached 98 per cent, and girls achieved parity with boys.[13] Adult literacy has also surpassed 90 per cent.[14]

In the 1980s and the 1990s, Tanzania underwent an economic crisis, which negatively affected the public funds available for education.[15] Together with the high rate of population growth, this meant a significant decrease of per capita spending in the education sector.[16] Lack of public funds for schools in turn transferred into higher school fees and other out-of-pocket costs for education for schoolchildren and their families.[17] As a result, the gross enrolment ratio declined to about 75 per cent in 1996.[18] In 1990, the gross enrolment rate was 77.6 per cent, while the net enrolment rate (reflecting the percentage of schoolchildren in the given age group)[19] was 58.8 per cent.[20] Adult illiteracy also increased from 10 per cent to 16 per cent in the period from 1981 to 1996, and continued to grow with an estimated rate of 2 per cent per year.[21] Children

10 National Education Act 1978.

11 United Nations Economic and Social Council, 'Reports Submitted in Accordance with Council Resolution 1988 (LX) by States Parties to the Covenant Concerning Rights Covered by Articles 10 to 12: United Republic of Tanzania' (21 December 1979) E/1980/6/Add.2, 2.

12 'Initial Reports of States Parties Due in 1993: United Republic of Tanzania' (n. 8) [273].

13 Ibid. [313].

14 Ibid.

15 Ibid. [314].

16 Ibid.

17 Ibid. [315].

18 Ibid.

19 The gross enrolment rate (GER) reflects the ratio of pupils enrolled in schools to the total number of children in a particular age group. The net enrolment ratio (NER) reflects the ratio of pupils of a particular age group enrolled in schools out of the total number of children in that particular age group. If there are eight children in second grade, out of them five of second grade age and three older children, and a total of ten children of second grade age, the GER is 80 per cent (because there are eight pupils in second grade), while the NER is 50 per cent (because only five children of second grade age are in school). The GER can rise above 100 per cent if a large number of older children (who are statistically not part of the relevant age group) are enrolled with younger children in grades for younger children.

20 Committee on the Rights of the Child, 'Second Periodic Reports of States Parties Due in 2004: United Republic of Tanzania' (24 August 2005) CRC/C/70/Add.26 [210].

21 'Initial Reports of States Parties Due in 1993: United Republic of Tanzania' (n. 8) [315].

from low-income social groups were especially affected negatively by the collapse of the school system's public funding.[22]

The Tanzanian government addressed the deplorable state of affairs in the education sector by adopting the Primary Education Development Plan 2000–2005,[23] which aimed to provide compulsory primary as well as secondary education to every child by 2015.[24] The government committed to allocate 20 per cent of its budget to finance the plan and to maintain the 20 per cent ratio from then on.[25]

As a response to the recommendations of the Committee on the Rights of the Child (CRC Committee), school fees and other contributions were formally abolished in 2002,[26] although they continue to be demanded by individual schools on an informal basis.[27] The government also invested in teacher training and rebuilding the school infrastructure. Two thousand eight hundred and twenty-seven schools opened between 2001 and 2006.[28] Two hundred and two satellite schools were also built in rural communities,[29] reducing the furthest walking distance to schools to three kilometres according to the government,[30] although this seems to be an overly optimistic view of the situation.[31] The government addressed the difficulties of retaining girls in schools by constructing more sanitary facilities for girls.[32] The government also organised enrolment campaigns and recruited additional teachers.[33]

22 Ibid.

23 Committee on the Rights of the Child, 'Consideration of Reports Submitted by States Parties under Article 44 of the Convention: Concluding Observations: United Republic of Tanzania (Second Report)' (21 June 2006) CRC/C/TZA/CO/2 [55].

24 'Combined Initial, Second and Third Periodic Reports Submitted by States Parties under Articles 16 and 17 of International Covenant on Economic, Social and Cultural Rights: United Republic of Tanzania' (n. 6) [137].

25 Ibid. [152].

26 'Second Periodic Reports of States Parties Due in 2004: United Republic of Tanzania' (n. 20) [210].

27 Committee on the Rights of the Child, Concluding Observations on the Combined Third to Fifth Periodic Reports of the United Republic of Tanzania (3 March 2015) CRC/C/TZA/CO/3–5 [60].

28 'Combined Initial, Second and Third Periodic Reports Submitted by States Parties under Articles 16 and 17 of International Covenant on Economic, Social and Cultural Rights: United Republic of Tanzania' (n. 6) [138].

29 'Second Periodic Reports of States Parties Due in 2004: United Republic of Tanzania' (n. 20) [216].

30 Ibid. [222].

31 Concluding Observations on the Combined Third to Fifth Periodic Reports of the United Republic of Tanzania (n. 27) [60].

32 'Second Periodic Reports of States Parties Due in 2004: United Republic of Tanzania' (n. 20) [216].

33 Ibid. [210].

As a result of these efforts, the gross enrolment rate reached 105.3 per cent[34] in 2003[35] and 112.7 per cent in 2006,[36] while the net enrolment rate rose to 88.5 per cent in 2003[37] and 96.1 per cent in 2006.[38] The education system was, however, still suffering from several shortcomings. The number of schools was still insufficient, and they provided a poor physical environment.[39] The drop-out rate was very high, especially among girls due to pregnancy and early marriage.[40] The quality of learning and teaching was also low due to the lack of qualified teachers.[41] Children from low-income families continued to face disproportionate difficulties in accessing schools due to the ongoing practice of unofficial financial contributions and the absence of school meal programmes.[42]

2 *The Right to Education of Children with Disabilities in Tanzania*

The lack of attention to the education of children with disabilities can be characterised as a pervasive historical problem in Tanzania. Although the Uhuru Mchanganyiko primary school in Dar es Salaam started integrating visually impaired children already in 1961, and by 1993 10.6 per cent of its student body was reported to have a disability, integration was far from becoming the norm.[43] The government in its initial report to the UN Economic and Social Council admitted that children with disabilities were mainly educated in special schools,[44] but the number of these schools was far from satisfactory.[45]

34 The GER can rise above 100 per cent if a large number of older children (who are statistically not part of the relevant age group) are enrolled with younger children in grades for younger children. See note 19 for definitions.

35 'Second Periodic Reports of States Parties Due in 2004: United Republic of Tanzania' (n. 20) [210].

36 'Combined Initial, Second and Third Periodic Reports Submitted by States Parties under Articles 16 and 17 of International Covenant on Economic, Social and Cultural Rights: United Republic of Tanzania' (n. 6) [138].

37 'Second Periodic Reports of States Parties Due in 2004: United Republic of Tanzania' (n. 20) [210].

38 'Combined Initial, Second and Third Periodic Reports Submitted by States Parties under Articles 16 and 17 of International Covenant on Economic, Social and Cultural Rights: United Republic of Tanzania' (n. 6) [138].

39 Concluding Observations on the Combined Third to Fifth Periodic Reports of the United Republic of Tanzania (n. 27) [60].

40 'Concluding Observations: United Republic of Tanzania (Second Report)' (n. 23) [55].

41 Ibid.

42 Concluding Observations on the Combined Third to Fifth Periodic Reports of the United Republic of Tanzania (n. 27) [60].

43 'Initial Reports of States Parties Due in 1993: United Republic of Tanzania' (n. 8) [274].

44 'Reports Submitted in Accordance with Council Resolution 1988 (LX) by States Parties to the Covenant Concerning Rights Covered by Articles 10 to 12: United Republic of Tanzania' (n. 11) 2.

45 'Initial Reports of States Parties Due in 1993: United Republic of Tanzania' (n. 8) [129].

In the twentieth century, disability was mainly considered an issue of health care, rehabilitation and social protection, but not an educational priority. The Tanzanian government considered rehabilitation centres as its main measure fulfilling the rights of children with disabilities (there were thirty-four in the country in 2000, with a capacity of more than 700 children).[46] In 1982, Tanzania passed laws on the employment[47] and care and maintenance[48] of persons with disabilities, but not on their education. In the same year, the National Advisory Council was established with regional and district committees to look after the interests of persons with disabilities,[49] but it only had competence to monitor the aforementioned rehabilitation centres, not educational institutions.[50]

In the absence of focussed attention, the education of children with disabilities was sporadic at best, and left to the families' initiative. In 2000, the government reported 138 special schools for children with disabilities in the country. However, it was unaware of how many children attended them, how many attended mainstream schools and how many did not go to school at all.[51] By 2005, due to specific questions by UN treaty bodies, the government's research revealed that 39,139 children with disabilities (47.2 per cent of the relevant age group) attended primary school.[52] This number seems to be an overestimation, a result of the fact that the government was unaware of how many children with disabilities there actually were in the country.[53] For example, in 2000, the government reported to know about only 1,245 'mentally retarded' children for the whole country.[54] It seems that a large number of children with disabilities are not recognised by the education authorities and do not appear in the education statistics.

46 Ibid. [277].
47 Disabled Persons (Employment) Act 1982.
48 Disabled Persons (Care and Maintenance) Act 1982.
49 'Initial Reports of States Parties Due in 1993: United Republic of Tanzania (n. 8) [273].
50 Committee on the Rights of the Child, 'Concluding Observations of the Committee on the Rights of the Child: United Republic of Tanzania (First Report)' (9 July 2001) CRC/C/15/Add.156 [52].
51 'Initial Reports of States Parties Due in 1993: United Republic of Tanzania' (n. 8) [278].
52 Committee on the Rights of the Child, 'Written Replies by the Government of the United Republic of Tanzania Concerning the List of Issues (CRC/C/TZA/Q/2) Received by the Committee on the Rights of the Child Relating to the Consideration of the Second Periodic Report of Tanzania' (CRC/C/70/Add.26) (20 April 2006) CRC/C/TZA/Q/2/Add.1 [4]; the government reports the figure of 53.85 per cent for mainland Tanzania. From its tables, however, it can be deduced that the overall number of school-age children with disabilities was 82 975; hence the ratio is 47.2 per cent for the whole of Tanzania.
53 Ibid.
54 'Initial Reports of States Parties Due in 1993: United Republic of Tanzania' (n. 8) [278].

In 2006, Tanzania adopted the comprehensive Persons with Disabilities (Rights and Privileges) Act (2006) recognising, among others, the right to education of persons with disabilities.[55] In 2012, it adopted the 2012 Strategic Plan of Inclusive Education.[56] The government claims that by 2013, the number of inclusive schools in Zanzibar alone increased to eighty-six, and the number of children with disabilities enrolled in them had risen from 450 in 2005 to 3,883 in 2011.[57] Thousands of teachers were reported to be trained on sign language and Braille.[58] The government, however, still did not have data of sufficient quality on children with disabilities across the whole territory of the country, contrary to its obligations under Article 31(2) of the CRPD.[59] The primary school enrolment of children with disabilities was also still very low, not meeting the requirements of Article 24(2) of the CRPD.[60] The government planned to have at least one teacher in each primary school trained in inclusive education, which, even if fulfilled, was insufficient to meet children's needs and the government's obligations under Article 24(4) of the CRPD.[61]

Among the obstacles of inclusive education, the government mentioned the reluctance of parents of children with disabilities to send them into regular schools,[62] and the lack of available schools, learning materials, teachers trained in inclusive education,[63] accessible facilities,[64] including water and sanitation,[65] and the all-important lack of funds to remedy all these problems.[66] Children with disabilities were also disproportionately affected

55 Committee on the Rights of the Child, 'Consideration of Reports Submitted by States Parties under Article 44 of the Convention: Third to Fifth Periodic Reports of States Parties Due in 2012: United Republic of Tanzania' (4 November 2013) CRC/C/TZA/3–5 [9].

56 Committee on Economic, Social and Cultural Rights, Concluding Observations on the Initial to Third Reports of the United Republic of Tanzania (13 December 2012) E/C.12/TZA/CO/1–3 [28].

57 'Third to Fifth Periodic Reports of States Parties Due in 2012: United Republic of Tanzania' (n. 55) [43].

58 Ibid.

59 'Concluding Observations on the Combined Third to Fifth Periodic Reports of the United Republic of Tanzania' (n. 27) [16].

60 Ibid. [52].

61 'Combined Initial, Second and Third Periodic Reports Submitted by States Parties under Articles 16 and 17 of International Covenant on Economic, Social and Cultural Rights: United Republic of Tanzania' (n. 6) [145].

62 'Initial Reports of States Parties Due in 1993: United Republic of Tanzania' (n. 8) [129].

63 Ibid. [273].

64 'Concluding Observations: United Republic of Tanzania (Second Report)' (n. 23) [43].

65 Concluding Observations on the Initial to Third Reports of the United Republic of Tanzania (n. 56) [26].

66 'Initial Reports of States Parties Due in 1993: United Republic of Tanzania' (n. 8) [275].

by the continued demand for out-of-pocket payments in primary education, such as for textbooks, uniforms and school lunches.[67] These obstacles are not specific to Tanzania; they are all identified in Article 24 of the CRPD as common barriers to inclusive education. By recognising them, the government made the first important steps; the next one, required by Article 24(2), is to 'take appropriate measures' to overcome them, and to commit the 'maximum of its available resources' to these measures according to Article 4(2) of the CRPD.[68]

3 *Budgeting as a Means of Meeting Human Rights Obligations*

Lack of funds is a major obstacle to fulfilling the right to education for children with disabilities in Tanzania. The following part therefore analyses whether the government uses its resources efficiently in allocating funds for the needs of children with disabilities. The analysis relies on figures from the report of the Comprehensive Community-Based Rehabilitation in Tanzania (CCBRT) on government spending during five fiscal years, from 2009/10 to 2013/14.[69]

In the examined period, Tanzania was implementing the National Strategy for Growth and Reduction of Poverty (MKUKUTA), which was divided to sector strategic plans.[70] All expenditures can therefore be divided into recurrent expenditures, mostly covering services provided on a regular long-term basis, and development expenditures, related to the implementation of the National Strategy.[71] Total spending was rising constantly in both categories in the examined period, more than doubling by 2014. Tanzania's GDP also doubled during this period, suggesting a correlation with the expansion of public spending.[72]

It is difficult to establish how much money was allocated to advance the inclusive education of children with disabilities, because the public budgets are rarely specific enough about this type of expenditure. The Strategic Plan on development does not contain education as its main priority. Some subprogrammes are investing in human capital, mainly in employment and social services. Even in these programmes, persons with disabilities are not listed as

67 Concluding Observations on the Initial to Third Reports of the United Republic of Tanzania (n. 56) [26].
68 CRPD Articles 24(4) and 4(2).
69 CCBRT (n. 5) 6.
70 Ibid.
71 Ibid. 9.
72 Ibid. 8; although obviously this does not necessarily mean causation.

a specific budget category. They are included in the category of 'vulnerable groups', together with other children such as orphans, pastoralist communities, girls, persons living with HIV and others.[73] Overall, development expenditures in the examined period were mostly allocated to building infrastructure, without any ascertainable figure allocated to inclusive education.[74]

Recurrent expenditures comprised 70 per cent of all government spending in the examined period.[75] A very small proportion of these expenditures could be identified as allocated specifically to disability-related programmes. Strategic plans of ministries and local governments list a number of programmes that can be related to furthering the rights of persons with disabilities, such as health and rehabilitation services, labour market programmes, vocational education and training and others.[76] However, in the absence of disaggregated data it is impossible to estimate whether any funds were allocated specifically to persons with disabilities.

The programmes specifically addressing disability were very small. They received funds in the magnitude of only 0.2 per cent of the state budget, or 0.1 per cent of the GDP.[77] This is highly insufficient compared to the average of countries in the Organisation for Economic Co-operation and Development that spend 1.2 per cent of their GDP on similar programmes,[78] or even to neighbouring Kenya, which allocated ten times more money on disability-related programmes than Tanzania, despite having only a 50 per cent higher GDP.[79]

Tanzania's very poor performance on financing disability programmes stems partly from methodological problems related to a lack of disaggregated data on the level of planning, budget allocation and actual spending. The unavailability of disability-specific data not only undermines the success of education policies, but also violates Article 31(2) of the CRPD, which obliges States Parties to collect such data. The insufficient information masks funding streams that most likely indirectly benefit persons with disabilities as well. For example, in line with the government's promises, 20 per cent of the overall budget was spent on education, the vast majority of which was spent on teachers' salaries.[80] Children with disabilities studying in primary

73 Ibid. 5.
74 Ibid. 9.
75 Ibid.
76 Ibid. 12.
77 Ibid. 11.
78 Ibid. 12.
79 Ibid.
80 'Combined Initial, Second and Third Periodic Reports Submitted by States Parties under Articles 16 and 17 of International Covenant on Economic, Social and Cultural Rights: United Republic of Tanzania' (n. 6) [152].

schools were consuming services maintained from this budget, even if it was not specifically for disability-related programmes.

Such unidentifiable funds for disability education should not be considered to meet the government's obligations to fulfil the rights of children with disabilities. As stated earlier in this chapter, under Article 24 of the CRPD, the government needs to take specific measures to overcome the obstacles to inclusive education, and under Article 4(2) of the CRPD, it must commit resources to these measures. A lack of available funds might justify a gradual expansion of the measures to the whole population. However, not taking any specific steps at all, and not committing any funds to specific steps intended to overcome the correctly identified obstacles, falls beyond the requirements of Article 24 of the CRPD read in conjunction with Article 4(2).

If Tanzania's schools were all providing inclusive education, the lack of disability-specific funding would be less concerning. However, the foregoing analysis showed that Tanzania has a long history of excluding children with disabilities from mainstream education. The significant shortages in the education system began to be remedied at the time when children with disabilities were segregated in special schools or not attending school at all. Transforming mainstream schools to inclusive ones was not a priority in those years. Significant funds are required to achieve these goals on top of schools' regular expenditures. This means not only refitting the inadequate infrastructure but also equipping schools with learning materials accessible to children with disabilities, and training teachers in inclusive education. These are objectives recognised by the Ministry of Education and Vocational Training,[81] but if they are not followed up with specific budget allocations, it is hard to meet them. It is also very difficult to establish the effectiveness of any programmes aimed at promoting inclusive education if budgets are not transparently allocated to such programmes.

The lack of disaggregated data is also preventing the authorities from coordinating funding from various sources. There are private and church donors providing inclusive education in Tanzania,[82] and international aid is also available.[83] By using these donors strategically, the government could multiply the effects of its own programmes aimed at promoting inclusive education. It is hard to achieve that if the government does not design any programmes for this specific task and does not allocate a budget for them.

81 CCBRT (n. 5) 9.
82 'Initial Reports of States Parties Due in 1993: United Republic of Tanzania' (n. 8) [276].
83 CCBRT (n. 5) 5.

It can be concluded that despite the recent surge in the amount of recurrent spending, the state budget is financing services in which persons with disabilities have not been mainstreamed, and therefore cannot access them, contrary to the requirements of Article 24(2) of the CRPD. Transformation of the services to make them adaptable to the needs of children with disabilities is not an identified priority in either recurrent spending or development spending.[84]

Tanzania is among the world's least developed countries; therefore, the lack of resources constitutes an important obstacle in fulfilling the right to education of children with disabilities. It is thus especially important that the government uses its funds effectively. Tanzania allocated a significant proportion of its budget to develop education services which were not adapted to the needs of children with disabilities. Currently it fails to design specific programmes and to allocate funds to transform existing services and to develop inclusive services, while continuing to spend a significant proportion of its budget on an education system which children with disabilities could access only accidentally. Confronting this issue explicitly is not only a question of budget; it is also a question of recognising the problem and having the political will to resolve it.

III VIETNAM

Vietnam is a developing country, with an estimated GDP per capita of 2,321 USD. It is one of the remaining socialist states of the world, although it has undergone significant transformation to introduce market capitalism, and is currently one of the fastest growing economies.

1 *Vietnam's Education Sector*

Vietnam's recent history was marked by wars. The liberation war after World War II against the French colonisers ended in 1954. The country was then divided into a communist North Vietnam and a Western-oriented South Vietnam. North Vietnam defeated South Vietnam and its allies by 1975 and unified the country.

The long period of wars devastated the country's economy and infrastructure. This seriously affected the education sector as well. In 1992, Vietnam was still suffering from a shortage of teachers and schools.[85] There was no

84 Ibid. 9.

85 Committee on the Rights of the Child, 'Consideration of Reports Submitted by States Parties under Article 44 of the Convention: Initial Reports of States Parties Due in 1992: Viet Nam' (22 October 1992) CRC/C/3/Add.4 [202].

guaranteed free primary education.[86] Teachers were badly trained and paid, while pupils' parents had to complement their salaries to keep them teaching.[87] Parents also had to pay for schoolbooks and for the maintenance of school buildings,[88] practices still prevalent today.[89]

As a result of the deplorable state of the education infrastructure, many children were not going to school at all.[90] A growing number of children worked on farms in rural areas and in urban centres, involved in illegal activities such as prostitution and drug trafficking.[91]

The government's priority at that time was to increase the education budget to raise enrolment rates and the quality of education.[92] Nonetheless, the education of children with disabilities did not appear among the government's or the CRC Committee's concerns.[93]

To meet its education goals, the government increased its spending on education from 12.7 per cent of the state budget in 1995 to almost 15 per cent in 1998,[94] which further increased to 20 per cent by the beginning of the new century.[95] The government also encouraged private individuals and organisations to invest in education.[96] As a result, several private schools were established, attracting a significant proportion of pupils. By 2001, 34 per cent of pupils of secondary schools were attending private institutions, which children from poorer families could hardly afford.[97] In the state sector, despite the constitution guaranteeing

86 Committee on Economic, Social and Cultural Rights, 'Consideration of Reports Submitted by States Parties under Articles 16 and 17 of the Covenant: Concluding Observations of the Committee on Economic, Social and Cultural Rights: Viet Nam' (9 June 1993) E/C.12/1993/8 [10].

87 'Initial Reports of States Parties Due in 1992: Viet Nam' (n. 85) [202].

88 Ibid. [203].

89 Committee on the Rights of the Child, 'Consideration of Reports Submitted by States Parties under Article 44 of the Convention: Concluding Observations: Viet Nam (Third and Fourth Reports)' (22 August 2012) CRC/C/VNM/CO/3–4 [67].

90 'Initial Reports of States Parties Due in 1992: Viet Nam' (n. 85) [201].

91 'Concluding Observations of the Committee on Economic, Social and Cultural Rights: Viet Nam' (n. 86) [10].

92 'Initial Reports of States Parties Due in 1992: Viet Nam' (n. 85) [204].

93 'Concluding Observations of the Committee on Economic, Social and Cultural Rights: Viet Nam' (n. 86) [10].

94 Committee on the Rights of the Child, 'Consideration of Reports Submitted by States Parties under Article 44 of the Convention: Periodic Reports of States Parties Due in 1997: Viet Nam (Second Report)' (5 July 2002) CRC/C/65/Add.20 [207].

95 Committee on Economic, Social and Cultural Rights, 'Consideration of the Combined Second to Fourth Periodic Reports of States Parties Due in 2005 under Articles 16 and 17 of the Covenant: Vietnam' (14 March 2013) E/C.12/VNM/2–4 [526].

96 'Periodic Reports of States Parties Due in 1997: Viet Nam (Second Report)' (n. 94) [202].

97 'Consideration of the Combined Second to Fourth Periodic Reports of States Parties Due in 2005 under Articles 16 and 17 of the Covenant: Vietnam' (n. 95) [507].

free primary education, out-of-pocket payments relating to education continued to be imposed in practice, preventing the enrolment of some children.[98] Overall, the government achieved significant results in increasing the enrolment rate. However, the cost of education in both the private and the public sectors has had a disproportionate impact on some vulnerable categories of children, mainly children from ethnic minority and immigrant communities,[99] children living in remote areas such as mountains and the Mekong Delta and children with disabilities.[100]

2 *The Education of Children with Disabilities in Vietnam*

The lack of attention towards the education of children with disabilities can be seen from the statistics gathered by the government. The authorities are unaware of the real number of children with disabilities who do not attend schools.[101] In 1992, the government reported that it estimates that there are about 1 million children with disabilities in the country.[102] Special education was provided only to deaf, mute and blind children, and even so it was in a very limited way. In one third of the country's provinces, no education was provided to children with disabilities at all.[103]

By 2002, the government reported that only 200,000 children with disabilities lived in Vietnam.[104] Presumably this decline in reported numbers was caused by many children being invisible for the education authorities and not appearing in the statistics. The government admitted that it has no comprehensive system of data collection on children with disabilities,[105] and was therefore unaware of the needs of most of those not attending schools.[106] From the reported 200,000 of whom the government was aware, only 42,000 attended integrated schools in forty-two provinces of the country (out of fifty-eight).[107] An additional 4,000 children attended a network of eighty special schools.[108]

98 'Concluding Observations: Viet Nam (Third and Fourth Reports)' (n. 89) [67].
99 Ibid.
100 Ibid. [17].
101 Committee on the Rights of the Child, 'Consideration of Reports Submitted by States Parties under Article 44 of the Convention: Concluding Observations: Viet Nam (Second Report)' (18 March 2003) CRC/C/15/Add.200 [16].
102 'Initial Reports of States Parties Due in 1992: Viet Nam' (n. 85) [174].
103 Ibid. [175].
104 'Periodic Reports of States Parties Due in 1997: Viet Nam (Second Report)' (n. 94) [168].
105 'Concluding Observations: Viet Nam (Second Report)' (n. 101) [16].
106 Ibid. [44].
107 'Periodic Reports of States Parties Due in 1997: Viet Nam (Second Report)' (n. 94) [170].
108 Ibid.

Even according to the government's statistics, approximately 54 per cent of school-age children with disabilities did not attend school.[109] However, comparing the reported attendance to the estimated number of 1 million of children with disabilities gives us the astounding figure of 90 per cent of school-age children with disabilities not enrolled in schools.[110] Many lived outside of the authorities' attention, not having access to rehabilitation services besides being unable to attend school.[111]

The government was heavily criticised for this dire state of affairs by the Committee on Economic, Social and Cultural Rights (CESCR Committee), and took steps in the following years to remedy it.[112] By 2011, it claimed to have established and developed an education system for children with disabilities nationwide.[113] At that time, persons with disabilities constituted 6.63 per cent of Vietnam's population. Among them were 1,150,000 children with six main disabilities.[114] Integrated education has been expanded to sixty-three provinces, where more than 7,000 children attended nearly 100 special schools. The number of children integrated into mainstream schools rose to 70,000 by 2003, and to 230,000 by 2006.[115] According to the government, nearly half of all school-age children with disabilities were enrolled in some kind of educational programme.[116]

The accessibility of mainstream schools was still limited,[117] and so was the quality of education. The government took a number of steps to enrol and keep children with disabilities in schools, such as exempting them from tuition fees and other contributions.[118] Education management officers were appointed to schools, and teachers were trained in inclusive

109 This figure rests on a rough estimate of children of primary school age (six to fourteen years old) comprising approximately half of all children.

110 Similarly, the number of primary school-age children with disabilities was estimated to comprise 50 per cent of the estimated 1 million children with disabilities.

111 'Concluding Observations: Viet Nam (Second Report)' (n. 101) [43].

112 Ibid. [44].

113 Committee on the Rights of the Child, 'Consideration of Reports Submitted by States Parties under Article 44 of the Convention: Third and Fourth Periodic Reports on the Implementation of the Convention in the Period 2002–2007: Viet Nam' (25 November 2011) CRC/C/VNM/3–4 [85].

114 Ibid. [191].

115 Ibid. [220].

116 Committee on the Rights of the Child, 'List of Issues Concerning Additional and Updated Information Related to the Consideration of the Third and Fourth Combined Periodic Reports of Viet Nam (CRC/C/VNM/3–4): Written Replies of Viet Nam' (24 May 2012) CRC/C/VNM/Q/3–4/Add.1 [32].

117 'Third and Fourth Periodic Reports on the Implementation of the Convention in the Period 2002–2007: Viet Nam' (n. 113) [195].

118 Ibid. [220].

education.[119] The effectiveness of these steps, however, is dubious.[120] Teachers, for example, reported that they felt unprepared to teach children with disabilities, as the training was so short and simple that it did not provide them with enough skills.[121] There has been a lack of equipment, tools and materials for teaching children with disabilities.[122] As the policy initiatives were not supported by an adequate budget, their implementation relied on the voluntary efforts of teachers and school staff, putting their sustainability in doubt.[123]

Despite the authorities' attempts to enrol children with disabilities in schools, it seems that unfounded perceptions of disability were undermining the efforts at integration.[124] In the past, families of children with disabilities did not consider it necessary or even useful to enrol their children in schools.[125] These attitudes were changing very slowly despite public awareness campaigns.[126]

Public policies often strengthened rather than undermined the widespread stigma[127] against children with disabilities.[128] Despite official statements to the contrary, public policies were underlined by an outdated medical model of disability, which considers that barriers to inclusion stem from persons' impairments rather than from social and economic structures surrounding them.[129] Discrimination against children with disabilities was not prohibited, despite laws emphasising their needs.[130] For example, the 1998 Education Law stressed that the state should create favourable conditions for the enrolment of children with disabilities in school, but did not make education an enforceable right for children with disabilities.[131] Nor did the 2005 Law on Education.[132]

119 'List of Issues Concerning Additional and Updated Information Related to the Consideration of the Third and Fourth Combined Periodic Reports of Viet Nam (CRC/C/VNM/3–4): Written Replies of Viet Nam' (n. 116) [109].

120 'Concluding Observations: Viet Nam (Third and Fourth Reports)' (n. 89) [56].

121 Van Anh and others (n. 5) 55.

122 'Concluding Observations: Viet Nam (Third and Fourth Reports)' (n. 89) [55].

123 Van Anh and others (n. 5) 55.

124 'Concluding Observations: Viet Nam (Third and Fourth Reports)' (n. 89) [56].

125 Van Anh (n. 5) 45.

126 Ibid. 55.

127 'Concluding Observations: Viet Nam (Third and Fourth Reports)' (n. 89) [56].

128 János Fiala-Butora and Michael Ashley Stein, 'The Law as a Source of Stigma and Empowerment: Legal Capacity and Persons with Intellectual Disabilities' in Katrina Scior and Shirli Werner (eds), *Intellectual Disability and Stigma: Stepping Out from the Margins* (Palgrave Macmillan 2016) 196.

129 'Concluding Observations: Viet Nam (Third and Fourth Reports)' (n. 89) [55].

130 'Concluding Observations: Viet Nam (Second Report)' (n. 101) [22].

131 'Consideration of the Combined Second to Fourth Periodic Reports of States Parties Due in 2005 under Articles 16 and 17 of the Covenant: Vietnam' (n. 95) [490].

132 Ibid. [493].

Besides sending the wrong messages, state policies also had undesired consequences. The 2010 Law on Persons with Disabilities, for example, was ineffective in combating discrimination and in fact promoted segregated education and employment.[133] The CRC Committee recommended that Vietnam ratify the Convention on the Rights of Persons with Disabilities and that the country revise its policies to develop a rights-based approach towards the education of children with disabilities.[134] Vietnam signed the CRPD in 2007,[135] and ratified it in 2015, but did not create an effective legislative framework for enforcing non-discrimination provisions of international treaties.[136]

3 *Budgeting as an Obstacle to Policy Implementation*

As the foregoing historical excurse shows, Vietnam has to overcome several obstacles in fulfilling the right to education. The country experienced a very low attendance rate of children generally in the 1970s due to an insufficient school network. As a response to low attendance, the government made primary education formally free and compulsory, and took steps to make it available to most children. To implement the policy of free education, the government gradually increased the proportion of its budget spent on education from 8 per cent in 1990 to 15 per cent in 2000,[137] and to 20 per cent by 2008,[138] which constituted 5.6 per cent of the GDP.[139] The funds were used to build schools and to train teachers, and were generally successful in increasing the enrolment rates.

The government was less successful in enrolling children from more remote communities, and children who required a modification of the universal school curriculum, such as children from minority communities and children with disabilities. This reflects an underlying short-term cost-benefit analysis: it was cheaper to concentrate on children whose education needs required less investment. This approach perhaps had its benefits, but it is not necessarily the most effective in the long run, if the goal is to enrol all children into the mainstream educational system.

133 Committee on Economic, Social and Cultural Rights, Concluding Observations on the Second to Fourth Periodic Reports of Viet Nam (15 December 2014) E/C.12/VNM/CO/2–4 [15].

134 'Concluding Observations: Viet Nam (Third and Fourth Reports)' (n. 89) [56].

135 'Consideration of the Combined Second to Fourth Periodic Reports of States Parties Due in 2005 under Articles 16 and 17 of the Covenant: Vietnam' (n. 95) [90].

136 Concluding Observations on the Second to Fourth Periodic Reports of Viet Nam (n. 133) [13].

137 'Consideration of the Combined Second to Fourth Periodic Reports of States Parties Due in 2005 under Articles 16 and 17 of the Covenant: Vietnam' (n. 95) [526].

138 Ibid. [527].

139 Ibid. [526].

Children with disabilities were not at the forefront of education reform until the 1990s. When the government's attention turned to them, extra funds were allocated to increase the enrolment of children with disabilities. So far, the effects have been limited for several reasons.

Funds allocated to the education of children with disabilities fall into two main categories. Children with disabilities were exempt from tuition and other out-of-pocket expenses,[140] including contributions to building and renovating school buildings. The amount spent on reduction of school fees made up the largest part of the expenses relating to disability, reaching VND 120 billion in 2013 (more than 5 million USD).[141] Although the government claims the exemption was full,[142] this depended on local policies. The government allocates approximately 25,000 to 30,000 VND (CCA 1.10 to 1.30 USD) yearly for every child with a moderate disability, which covers around half of the school fees. Children with severe disabilities receive twice this amount, exempting them fully from paying the school fees.[143]

The other significant expense, around VND 100 billion in 2013 (CCA 4.4 million USD), was used to subsidise books and other learning materials for children with disabilities.[144] About 20,000 to 30,000 VND (CCA 0.9 to 1.30 USD) was allocated for children with severe disabilities, and around half of this sum for children with moderate disabilities.[145]

It can be argued that the government took the wrong approach by addressing the exclusion of children with disabilities from schools as a question of social deprivation. However, in Vietnam, access to education in fact has been, at least in part, a question of social deprivation. Persons with disabilities were disproportionately rural and poor: 87.2 per cent lived in rural areas, and one third of their households were classified as poor by the government.[146] Case studies found an even higher rate; in the district of Vinh Tuong, 38 per cent of children with disabilities lived in poor families compared to the provincial average of 2.7 per cent.[147] Given that the high cost of education was a nationwide problem,[148]

140 Ibid. [492].
141 Ibid. [228].
142 'Third and Fourth Periodic Reports on the Implementation of the Convention in the Period 2002–2007: Viet Nam' (n. 113) [220].
143 Van Anh and others (n. 5) 53.
144 'Consideration of the Combined Second to Fourth Periodic Reports of States Parties Due in 2005 under Articles 16 and 17 of the Covenant: Vietnam' (n. 95) [228].
145 Van Anh and others (n. 5) 54.
146 'Consideration of the Combined Second to Fourth Periodic Reports of States Parties Due in 2005 under Articles 16 and 17 of the Covenant: Vietnam' (n. 95) [220].
147 Van Anh and others (n. 5) 32.
148 'Concluding Observations: Viet Nam (Third and Fourth Reports)' (n. 89) [67].

it is not surprising that many families could not afford to send their children with disabilities to school. Or, rather, based on the widespread disbelief about the usefulness of education for children with disabilities, families did not consider it worthwhile to invest in their children's education.[149]

In these circumstances it seems defensible for the government to alleviate the costs of education for children with disabilities. Indeed, that was one of the recommendations of the CRC Committee.[150] The problem, rather, is that very little funds were allocated to meet other expenses, such as training teachers in inclusive education and making schools accessible. The reasons only partly have to do with the lack of funds.

Vietnam adopted a policy to allocate a per capita expenditure norm 63 per cent higher for the education of children with disabilities compared to children in general: 800,000 VND/pupil with disabilities (CCA 35 USD) compared to the general norm of 490,000 VND (CCA 21.5 USD).[151] However, very few children in fact benefit from this higher amount; in 2000, only 3,900 did.[152] In fact, the budget per child in schools is much lower than the official amount at around 242,000 VND per child (CCA 10.5 USD), and is not dependent on the number of children with disabilities enrolled.[153] This can be explained by the fact that the extra amount is utilised only in the case of children who are accommodated in the educational process. For the vast majority of children with disabilities, the goal is not accommodation, but simply enrolment, which is achieved through the aforementioned subsidies on school fees and learning materials. This, of course, is helping only those children with disabilities who can participate in the education without accommodations. Those who would require modifications to the teaching process are left behind, despite official public policy to the contrary.

This state of affairs goes contrary to the requirements of Article 24 of the CRPD. Vietnam is required to identify the obstacles to inclusive education, to take measures to overcome the obstacles under Article 24(4) of the CRPD and to commit resources to these measures under Article 4(2) of the CRPD. While the state adopted national-level policies to foster inclusion, these only have a declaratory effect in practice and are insufficient to meet the state's obligations under the CRPD. Measures ensuring effective integration on the school and individual levels are lacking in Vietnam. Children with disabilities who need accommodation to enrol in schools are not benefitting from specific

149 Ibid. [56].
150 'Concluding Observations: Viet Nam (Second Report)' (n. 101) [44].
151 Van Anh and others (n. 5) 27.
152 Ibid.
153 Ibid. 49.

measures taken by the government to overcome the obstacles they are facing, as Article 24(2)–(4) requires, nor are sufficient resources allocated to policies aimed at helping them.

The poor implementation of state policies can be explained by the complexity of the budget-planning process. Vietnam's state education budget is divided among the provinces, which transfer funds to districts, and these fund individual communities where schools are located. The budget is balanced at the province level,[154] and lower levels play a minor role in planning.[155] The planning process mostly takes place at the provincial level, using numbers supplied by local authorities based on previous years. The main budget items such as salaries and social insurance are clearly defined. The district authorities report to the provincial level the schools' approved manpower items, upon which a budget is prepared on the provincial level.[156] Schools have very little opportunity to influence this process. They are only given a budget to implement, without knowing how it was prepared.[157]

This difficult and complex process results in very rigid budgets, which mostly reflects existing activities rather than future policies.[158] As a result, the budget is not sufficiently adequate to meet new education priorities, such as accommodating pupils with disabilities in schools.[159] Any expansion of planned activities can only be incremental, which means quite a degree of lag between planned activities and budget allocation.[160]

The budget's rigidity is underlined by the fact that very few provinces can increase it from their own resources. Rich cities like Hanoi, Ho Chi Minh City or Vung Tau spend 22 per cent, 20 per cent and 19 per cent of their budget on education. The national average, however, is 26 per cent, and it is above 30 per cent in some poorer provinces.[161] This does not reflect a strong commitment to education in poorer provinces. Quite the contrary, it shows that even fulfilling the central government's mandate on the number of schools and teachers is straining their budget, and provides little scope for flexibility and additional funds from the provinces themselves.

The resulting budgets for schools are spent on two major expenses. The vast majority, around 95 per cent, is spent on teachers' salaries, including

154 Ibid. 39.
155 Ibid. 57.
156 Ibid. 48.
157 Ibid.
158 Ibid. 57.
159 Ibid. 5.
160 Ibid. 42.
161 Ibid. 40.

mandatory social security contributions.[162] The remaining 5 per cent is mostly spent on books and other teaching materials.[163] Renovation and other costs are covered by local communities', mostly parents', contributions. Parents also pay subsidies towards teachers' salaries to keep them at work.

The way budgets are allocated means that schools have little possibility to cover additional expenses to accommodate pupils with disabilities. Children with disabilities are not even taken into account during the planning process if they do not yet attend schools.[164] If they do attend school, in terms of expenditures they are taken into account as regular pupils, not considering the cost of any accommodations they might have received.

There is one major expense reported by schools that keeps schools from enrolling more children with disabilities; teachers require subsidies for teaching children with disabilities due to the increased workload.[165] Reportedly, two groups of children especially require extra effort from teachers, for which they require extra pay – children with paralysis and epilepsy, who make up about 20 per cent of pupils with disabilities.[166] Schools are meeting these demands by contributions from the community, or by increasing the teacher-to-student ratio. One local-level analysis revealed that from the twenty teachers whose salary was allocated to Binh Duong I school, only fifteen were in fact teaching.[167] The salaries of the remaining five teachers were presumably used as contributions to the salaries of those teaching.

According to the calculations of Van Anh and colleagues, the education budget would have to be increased by less than 1 per cent for schools to have enough funds to supplement teachers for the extra workload related to teaching pupils with disability.[168] This does not seem to be an extravagant amount; in fact, Vietnam's education budget has been growing steadily, therefore an increase of 1 per cent does not seem hard to accommodate.[169] Of course, this would require a change in the education planning process, so that the amount indeed gets allocated for this specific purpose on the school level.

Increasing teachers' subsidies might be a necessary precondition for the enrolment of children with disabilities, but it does not in itself result in inclusive education. Indeed, many teachers report that they feel unable to

162 Ibid. 49.
163 Ibid. 42.
164 Ibid. 41.
165 Ibid. 49.
166 Ibid. 53.
167 Ibid. 47.
168 Ibid. 53.
169 'Consideration of the Combined Second to Fourth Periodic Reports of States Parties Due in 2005 under Articles 16 and 17 of the Covenant: Vietnam' (n. 95) [527].

teach pupils with disabilities, as the little training they received did not equip them with the necessary skills.[170] This goes contrary to the requirements of Article 24(4) of the CRPD, which mandates the training of teachers at all levels of education. Schools also do not have the funds to make their buildings and the teaching process itself accessible, as CRPD Article 24(2) requires. Some are able to provide teaching materials to children with different types of sensory impairments from community contributions; others are not. This falls short of Article 24(2) of the CRPD, which makes it the States Parties' obligation to support children with disabilities in the education process to facilitate their effective education.

Building inclusive education would require the transformation of the educational process, where teacher training and educational materials would be the starting point. This could be achieved if schools were able to play a more active role in estimating the costs necessary to accommodate pupils with disabilities, and to report on expected expenditures.[171] State budget might or might not be able to cover all the costs from the very beginning, but the current situation (where the inflexibility of the budget process ignores these expenses in the planning phase) is inadequate to meet international obligations. A more effective approach would recognise the rights of children with disabilities to accommodation and support in the education process. National policies should include specific steps implementing support measures overcoming obstacles to inclusion on the local school level with budgets allocated to specific measures. In the absence of local implementation, national policies themselves cannot be considered to constitute appropriate measures to ensure the realisation of the right to education in the meaning of CRPD Article 24(4). In the absence of these measures, Vietnam is also not allocating sufficient funds to fulfil the right to education under Article 4(2) of the CRPD.

IV CONCLUSION

The foregoing analysis showed that both Tanzania and Vietnam allocate very little of their available resources to finance inclusive education. While both countries have made progress in expanding their educational sector to raise enrolment rates of children in general, the needs of children with disabilities were not at the forefront of their education reforms. As a result, new schools were built and teachers were trained without considering how the education

170 Van Anh (n. 5) 55.
171 Ibid. 53.

process can be accessible to children with disabilities – contrary to the requirements of Article 24(2) of the CRPD.

Currently, both countries recognise the importance of inclusive education, and have adopted laws and other public policy documents to promote it. However, inclusive education must be introduced now into an already established school system. This means refitting buildings, retraining teachers and redesigning teaching materials at a substantially higher cost than it would cost to build, train and design these initially in an inclusive way. Both countries' experience seems to underline that short term cost-benefit analyses are insufficient to fulfil the right to education. While ignoring accessibility requirements possibly might have allowed expanding infrastructure faster and cheaper at early stages of development, making education accessible to all will come at a higher cost at later stages. Investing in inclusive education from the beginning might not be only the option required by human rights treaties, such as Article 24 of the CRPD, but also the more cost-effective one in the long run.

For this reason it is regrettable that UN human rights bodies at early stages of reporting paid little attention to the situation of children with disabilities in their concluding observations. There is some indication that Vietnam and Tanzania started taking steps to improve the situation of children with disabilities once the CRC Committee and the CESCR Committee reminded them of their obligations. At least there is a strong overlap between the committees' observations to that effect and the countries' resulting steps as evidenced in subsequent reports. Unfortunately both committees ignored the issue of inclusive education when reviewing early reports, at times when it could matter the most – when the countries were developing their education systems. This underlines the need for the adoption of the Convention on the Rights of Persons with Disabilities, since as Stein notes, without the CRPD persons with disabilities had 'implied but not actual human rights protection'.[172] Fortunately, in later stages of reporting, both the CRC Committee and the CESCR Committee endorsed inclusive education and prompted Tanzania and Vietnam to take action. Hopefully these committees will also endorse the CRPD Committee's approach to inclusive education as expressed in its General Comment No. 4.

Another shortcoming in promoting inclusive education in both Tanzania and Vietnam stems from a lack of dedicated budget lines to implement otherwise progressive policies. This falls short of the CRPD Committee's General Comment No. 4, which recommends transferring budgets to develop

[172] Michael Ashley Stein, 'Disability Human Rights' (2007) 95 *California Law Review* 75, 82.

inclusive education.[173] Children in both countries face obstacles that are identified in Article 24(4) of the CRPD as typical barriers to inclusive education. States Parties are required to adopt specific steps to overcome these barriers, and to allocate sufficient resources to these specific measures under Article 4(2) of the CRPD. However, both Tanzania and Vietnam commit a very small proportion of their state budgets to measures specifically dedicated to fulfil the right to inclusive education. Education materials adapted to the needs of children with disabilities are either non-existing or not fully covered by the state; teachers are poorly, if at all, trained to teach children with disabilities. These shortcomings violate the states' obligations under Article 24 of the CRPD, and the guidelines provided by the CRPD Committee in General Comment No. 4.

In Tanzania, it is hard to analyse the issue because the authorities are not disaggregating data on disability, contrary to the requirements of Article 31(2) of the CRPD, therefore it is hard to assess the effectiveness of budget use. In general, however, there is a shortage of funds allocated to promote inclusive education, so steps can only be taken by schools from their own resources. While it is commendable that the authorities are in favour of mainstreaming on all levels, this should not mean losing control over the specific situation of persons with disabilities. Mainstreaming can only work if the government knows precisely how children with disabilities are doing in the education sector, what interventions are needed to help them and how effective these turn out.

In Vietnam, the problem stems not from the lack of funds as such, but the very rigid budgetary process which hinders the implementation of official policies. The needs of children with disabilities do not reach the specific administrative levels most important for determining future budgets of specific schools where these children will study. In this situation, it is up to the schools to meet children's needs on their own initiative and from their own resources, which are scarce. It is not a surprise that in both countries a significant number of children with disabilities do not attend school. Enrolment is open mostly to those who do not need a major adaptation of the education process, which leaves children with more severe disabilities behind. The education sector thus falls short of several criteria of the right to education identified by the CESCR Committee and endorsed by the CRPD Committee in General Comment No. 4: it is not accessible to persons with disabilities, it is not acceptable as it does not

[173] General Comment No. 4 (n. 3) [39].

provide a good-quality education to pupils with disabilities and it is not adapted to the needs of children with disabilities.[174]

Both countries can hardly be seen as utilising their existing resources effectively to promote inclusive education. They are not committing sufficient financial resources as required by General Comment No. 4.[175] Hopefully, their experience will be informative for other developing countries to commit to long-term economic analysis to include children with disabilities from the beginning of education reform, and to include disability as a factor on all levels of policy and budget planning.

174 Ibid. [19].
175 Ibid. [67].

PART III

IMPLEMENTATION

A

STRATEGIES

10

Strategic Litigation and Inclusive Education

Peter Barnett and Michael Ashley Stein

INTRODUCTION

Strategic litigation has played a visible and occasionally instrumental role in implementing the right to education of children with disabilities (CWD). Historically, these lawsuits challenged the exclusion or segregation of CWD in educational systems. More recent efforts have sought court-driven structural reforms to better incorporate and accommodate the needs of CWD within mainstream schools. Collectively, the reported decisions speak to the benefits and limitations of lawsuits as a mechanism for advancing this human rights agenda. Strategic litigation has played and can continue to play a meaningful role, particularly as courts, scholars and policy makers increase our social and legal understandings of the theoretical content and practical implications of inclusive education. Ultimately, however, the efficacy of these lawsuits depends heavily on their relationship with broader disability rights advocacy and mobilisation strategies.

Article 24 of the Convention on the Rights of Persons with Disabilities (CRPD)[1] marks an important milestone in recognising a specific and actionable legal right to inclusive education, building on a more general provision contained in the Convention on the Rights of the Child[2] as well as several soft law instruments.[3] The fundamental importance of quality education for children generally, and of inclusive education for CWD in particular, was

[1] Convention on the Rights of Persons with Disabilities (adopted 13 December 2006, entered into force 3 May 2008) 2515 UNTS 3.

[2] Convention on the Rights of the Child (adopted 20 November 1989, entered into force 2 September 1990) 1577 UNTS 3 Art. 23.

[3] Most significantly, United Nations General Assembly (UNGA), 'Standard Rules on the Equalization of Opportunities for Persons with Disabilities' (20 December 1993) UN Doc. A/RES/48/96, and United Nations Educational, Scientific and Cultural Organization (UNESCO), The Salamanca Statement and Framework for Action on Special Needs Education (ED-94/WS/18, UNESCO 1994).

strongly reaffirmed by Article 24's inclusion in the Sustainable Development Goals.[4] Yet transforming an acknowledged human right or global programming initiative via strategic litigation into cognisable changes for CWD poses two key challenges. The first is defining the content of the right to inclusive education in order to obtain a judicial remedy for its violation. The second is that remedies for transformative and lasting change are often institutional and structural in nature, hence traditionally the preserves of democratic governments rather than courts.

The right to education has been established as a justiciable right in international and national fora.[5] Nevertheless, an immediate obstacle to implementing this justiciably recognised right is that 'there is no consensus on the definition of the concept of "inclusive education"'.[6] Article 24 outlines certain legal obligations and provides guidance on what sorts of features a state should include or avoid to achieve inclusive education, but does not explicitly define the term. Hence, its contours are subject to debate regarding the availability of effective remedies via domestic or international law. Some scholars have made valuable contributions in elucidating the content of the right to inclusive education,[7] and the Special Rapporteur on the right to education has underlined the importance of adjudication in its effective realisation.[8] Most recently, the Committee on the Rights of Persons with Disabilities provided additional definition on the content of the right to inclusive education in its General Comment No. 4,[9] and continues to do so through state-specific concluding observations.[10] Soft law

[4] UNGA, 'Transforming Our World: The 2030 Agenda for Sustainable Development' (21 October 2015) UN Doc. A/RES/70/1, Goal 4.

[5] Justiciability is defined as 'the ability to claim a remedy before an independent and impartial body when a violation of a right has occurred or is likely to occur'. International Commission of Jurists, *Courts and the Legal Enforcement of Economic, Social and Cultural Rights: Comparative Experiences of Justiciability* (International Commission of Jurists 2008) 6.

[6] Gauthier de Beco, 'The Right to Inclusive Education According to Article 24 of the UN Convention on the Rights of Persons with Disabilities: Background, Requirements and (Remaining) Questions' (2014) 32 *Netherlands Quarterly of Human Rights* 263, 275.

[7] Ibid.; Oddný Mjöll Arnardóttir, 'The Right to Inclusive Education for Children with Disabilities: Innovations in the CRPD' in Asbjørn Eide, Jakob Th. Möller and Ineta Ziemele (eds), *Making Peoples Heard: Essays on Human Rights in Honour of Gudmundur Alfredsson* (Martinus Nijhoff 2011).

[8] United Nations Human Rights Council (UNHRC), 'Report of the Special Rapporteur on the Right to Education, Kishore Singh: Justiciability of the Right to Education' (10 May 2013) UN Doc. A/HRC/23/35 [3].

[9] United Nations Committee on the Rights of Persons with Disabilities (UNCRPD), General Comment No. 4 (2016) Article 24: Right to Inclusive Education (2 September 2016) CRPD/C/GC/4.

[10] See International Commission of Jurists (n. 5) 17–18 on the role of international treaty bodies in defining the content of economic, social and cultural rights. See also United Nations

instruments are likewise significant.[11] But in the end, effective judicial enforcement of inclusive education depends as a baseline matter on tribunals' ability to clearly ascertain the content and scope of that right.[12]

The transition from segregated special education to mainstreamed inclusive education poses a complex, long-term challenge requiring deep-seated structural change in the face of institutional resistance and additional political and social barriers.[13] Despite inclusive education being more efficient and cost-effective than segregated education in the long run, the transition to meaningfully inclusive education can incur significant costs in the short term, with fiscal constraints constantly flagged as an obstacle.[14] Careful planning, an effective legislative and policy framework and adequate and sustainable resource allocations will be important, as will genuine political resolve.[15]

The right to inclusive education contained in CRPD Article 24 – with the exception of the obligation to provide reasonable accommodation, the denial of which is recognised as discrimination – is also subject to progressive realisation. Each state is required, according to Article 4(2), 'to take measures to the maximum of its available resources' to progressively achieve a full national-level realisation of the right to inclusive education. Implementing inclusive education thus requires states, even the wealthier ones, to engage in decisions regarding policy trade-offs and resource allocation. As we observe further in Part III.B, this is a function traditionally reserved to democratically elected officials rather than the judiciary.

The role of courts in implementing inclusive education is thus somewhat vexed, and might take various forms depending on the competencies, cultures and predilections of national legal schemes and their respective actors. Certainly, as underscored by recent reports of the Special Rapporteur on the right to education and the Office of the UN High Commissioner on Human Rights, there is an acknowledged role for the courts in monitoring and enforcing CWD's right to education.[16] Courts can therefore play an important

Convention on the Rights of the Child (UNCRC), General Comment No. 9 (2006): The Rights of Children with Disabilities (27 February 2007) CRC/C/GC/9 and United Nations Committee on Economic, Social and Cultural Rights (UNCESCR), General Comment No. 5: Persons with Disabilities (9 December 1994) E/1995/22.

11 See n. 3.

12 See International Commission of Jurists (n. 5) 15.

13 See, for example, UNHRC, 'The Right to Education of Persons with Disabilities: Report of the Special Rapporteur on the Right to Education, Vernor Muñoz' (19 February 2007) A/HRC/4/29 [12] and [50]; de Beco (n. 6) 277–278.

14 de Beco (n. 6) 276–277.

15 See, for example, Muñoz (n. 13) [26]–[34], [51].

16 See, for example, ibid. [43] (role of courts '[o]f particular relevance . . . in providing remedies for breaches of the right to education'); UNICEF, *The State of the World's Children 2013: Children with Disabilities* (UNICEF 2013) 75 (making good on the promises of the CRPD will

function in driving necessary systemic changes. More controversially, strategic litigation might directly shape systemic change as it has done, with varying degrees of success, in the United States. Conversely, in some states or cultural circumstances, courts may well be deemed inapposite or inappropriate to the social engineering exercise implicated by wide-ranging educational reform. Courts may also prove inaccessible to CWD and their champions, or may not be conducive to effecting justice beyond the needs of the immediately aggrieved individuals. In all locales, intelligently and sensitively devised strategies need to be applied by the stakeholders involved, their cause lawyers and other allies in order for long-term changes to take hold.

This chapter proceeds as follows. Part I sets forth prior strategic litigation successes for the rights of CWD to education. Next, Part II examines the future role courts could play in implementing Article 24 of the CRPD. Then, drawing on the extensive literature regarding the efficacy of cause lawyers in the United States (which has a long history both of strategic litigation and of inclusive education), Part III offers some caveats on the prospects of strategic litigation for effectuating progressive transformations on behalf of CWD. We conclude that potential strategic litigants should consider their court-based options as one tool that can be utilised within the broader legal mobilisation possibilities of community-based advocacy.

I STRATEGIC LITIGATION SUCCESSES

A considerable body of international case law considers the right of CWD to education. This Part delineates three categories of such cases. Part I.A reviews challenges to the outright exclusion from schools of CWD. Part I.B details contestations to the segregation of CWD within educational settings. Part I.C explores cases adjudicating on or engaging in structural reform of school systems. These cases introduce themes and features explored within the chapter: the use of international and foreign law in domestic courts, the respective roles of courts and legislatures in matters of social policy and

require not only diligent enforcement but also rigorous monitoring and an unflagging commitment by all to accountability and adaptation); Office of the High Commissioner of Human Rights (OHCHR), 'Thematic Study on the Right of Persons with Disabilities to Education' (18 December 2013) A/HRC/25/29 [63] ('Remedies and reparation in cases of violations are important components of the national implementation process'). See also Maritza Formisano Prada, *Empowering the Poor through Human Rights Litigation* (UNESCO 2011) 27 (the role of justiciability more generally) and 29 (role for judges in assisting with achieving the transformative potential of economic, social and cultural rights).

the appropriate place for strategic litigation in conjunction with broader community-based disability rights advocacy.

A *Securing Access to Education*

The first strategic litigation category concerns basic access to education, meaning legal challenges to the barring of CWD from education. CWD historically have faced outright exclusion from public education systems, often with legislative underpinning or judicial blessing. The English Education Act 1944, for instance, empowered education authorities to classify children as 'uneducable' and to segregate them into congregate settings until as late as 1970.[17] The Ohio Court of Appeals upheld a similar remit in 1934, finding that the state education department was empowered to exclude pupils with IQs below 50. 'As a matter of common sense', the Court stated, 'it is apparent that a moron of very low type, or an idiot or imbecile who is incapable of absorbing knowledge or making progress in the schools, ought to be excluded'.[18] Litigation as a means of advancing the educational outcomes of CWD began, in a number of countries, with challenges to similar modes of exclusion.

i United States

Litigation has been unquestionably influential in securing educational opportunities for CWD in the United States.[19] Two 1972 cases in particular directly paved the way for reform of the American education system. In *Pennsylvania Association for Retarded Children* v. *Pennsylvania* (PARC),[20] the plaintiffs

17 Education Act 1944 S57. See Dympna Glendenning, *Education and the Law* (2nd edn) (Bloomsbury Professional 2012) [5.21].

18 *Board of Education of Cleveland Heights* v. *State ex rel Goldman* 191 NE 914, 916 (Ohio CA 1934).

19 See, for example, Michael Ashley Stein, Charlotte McClain-Nhlapo and Janet E. Lord, 'Education and HIV/AIDS: Disability Rights and Inclusive Development' in Malcolm Langford, Andy Sumner and Alicia Ely Yamin (eds), *The Millennium Development Goals and Human Rights: Past, Present and Future* (Cambridge University Press 2013) 281 (efforts to use the courts to force states to provide an equal educational opportunity for students with disabilities 'were very successful and eventually led to the passage of federal legislation'); Mitchell L. Yell, David Rogers and Elisabeth Lodge Rodgers, 'The Legal History of Special Education: What a Long, Strange Trip It's Been!' (1998) 19 *Remedial and Special Education* 219; R. Shep Melnick, *Between the Lines: Interpreting Welfare Rights* (Brookings Institution 1994) 135–137.

20 *Pennsylvania Association for Retarded Children (PARC)* v. *Pennsylvania* 343 F Supp. 279 (ED Pa 1972).

challenged a state law permitting the exclusion of children certified as 'uneducable and untrainable'[21] under both the Fourteenth Amendment to the US Constitution guaranteeing equal protection and *inter alia* the right to education. The parties agreed to settle the equal protection claim after a single day of expert testimony – described as 'an intelligent response' on the defendants' part 'to overwhelming evidence against their position'.[22] The ensuing consent decree required the defendants to provide every individual with intellectual disabilities between the ages of six and twenty-one 'access to a free public program of education and training appropriate to his learning capacities'.[23] *Mills* v. *Board of Education*[24] raised a similar challenge and reached a comparable result, with the district court ordering the District of Columbia to 'provide to each child of school age a free and suitable publicly-supported education regardless of the degree of the child's mental, physical or emotional disability or impairment' and forbidding the exclusion of any child on the basis of a claim of insufficient resources.[25] *PARC* and *Mills* initiated a flood of similar litigation – some forty-six cases filed in twenty-eight states by 1975.[26] This spate of litigation directly paved the way for the Education for All Handicapped Children Act of 1975 (EAHCA) (later re-enacted as the Individuals with Disabilities Education Act of 1990),[27] requiring a 'free appropriate public education' for CWD and providing the current framework for education for CWD in the United States.[28]

ii Ireland

Litigation has also been influential in securing access to education in Ireland. The High Court's 1993 decision in *O'Donoghue* v. *Minister for Health*[29] has been described as a 'landmark catalyst' in the state's

21 Ibid. 282.
22 Ibid. 291.
23 Ibid. 314.
24 *Mills* v. *Board of Education* 348 F Supp. 866 (DDC 1972).
25 Ibid. 878.
26 Thomas Hehir and Sue Gamm, 'Special Education: From Legalism to Collaboration' in Jay Philip Heubert (ed.), *Law and School Reform: Six Strategies for Promoting Educational Equity* (Yale University Press 1999) 212.
27 Education for All Handicapped Children Act, Pub. L No. 94-142 (1975), later replaced by the Individuals with Disabilities Education Act, Pub. L No. 101-476, 104 Stat 1142 (1990). See, for example, Melnick (n. 19) 141 (participants and academic commentators agree that *PARC* and *Mills* were central to the development of the EAHCA).
28 See Benjamin Michael Superfine, *Equality in Education Law and Policy, 1954–2010* (Cambridge University Press 2013) 82.
29 *O'Donoghue* v. *Minister for Health* [1993] IEHC 2, [1996] 2 IR 20.

developing entitlements to and provisions for CWD.[30] *O'Donoghue* concerned a challenge to Ireland's refusal to educate certain CWD. The applicant challenged the government's position that her child, 'by reason of being profoundly mentally and physically disabled, is ineducable' in consequence of which 'all that can be done for him to make his life more tolerable is to attempt to train him in the basics of bodily function and movement'.[31] The Court found that CWD were constitutionally entitled to a free primary education and granted declaratory relief 'appropriate to vindicate' those rights.[32] Citing developments in the United Kingdom and the United States (including *PARC*, *Mills* and the EAHCA), as well as the right to education expressed in the Universal Declaration of Human Rights (UDHR) and the CRC, and international declarations, it concluded that Ireland had a duty to enable CWD 'to make the best possible use of his [or her] inherent and potential capacities'.[33] Commentators credit *O'Donoghue* as having 'far-reaching implications' for establishing a 'clear legal obligation to provide *appropriate* education for all children' via a legislative mandate.[34]

iii Significance of the Access Cases

In both the United States and Ireland, litigation significantly increased access to education for CWD, with two necessary qualifications. First, the impact of the cases themselves was limited. The two US cases had little bearing within their respective state jurisdictions.[35] In Ireland, 'administrative foot dragging continued for' at least five years after *O'Donoghue*.[36] Instead, the cases served as important catalysts for legislative reforms that were more influential in changing educational outcomes than the litigation itself. Second, judicial and legislative focus on access to education – rather than the substance of education – came to represent a limitation. As an illustration of this, the US Supreme Court in *Board of Education* v. *Rowley*[37] noted that neither *PARC* nor *Mills* purported to require any particular substantive level of education, and that the EAHCA itself was silent regarding the substantive

30 See Sarah Meegan and Ann MacPhail, 'Inclusive Education: Ireland's Education Provision for Children with Special Educational Needs' (2006) 25 *Irish Educational Studies* 53, 60.

31 *O'Donoghue* (n. 29) 25.

32 Ibid. 71.

33 Ibid. 62.

34 Ibid. 58–60 (citing Education Act 1998).

35 Melnick (n. 19) 149.

36 *Sinnott* v. *Minister for Education* [2001] 2 IR 545, 575.

37 *Board of Education* v. *Rowley* 458 US 176 (1982).

standard for its required 'free appropriate public education'.[38] As a result, courts began to turn to the substantive content of the right to education (Part I.B) and how it might best be secured through structural reforms (Part I.C).

B Substantive Content of the Right to Education: Challenging Segregation

The second category of cases concerns challenges to the segregation of CWD into 'special education'. The courts here engaged in giving substantive content to legislative, constitutional and international law prescriptions.

i Least Restrictive Environment: United States

The US Supreme Court's 1954 decision in *Brown* v. *Board of Education*[39] marked a turning point in judicial attitudes around segregation, and its effect was clearly felt in special education litigation.[40] The Utah District Court's 1969 decision in *Wolf* v. *Legislature of Utah*[41] is a case in point. The Court paraphrased *Brown* in ordering that two CWD, previously excluded from school, be admitted to the public school system:

> Today it is doubtful that any child may reasonably be expected to succeed in life if he is denied the right and opportunity of an education . . . Segregation, even though perhaps well intentioned, under the apparent sanction of law and state authority, has a tendency to retard the educational, emotional and mental development of the children.[42]

The EAHCA, passed in 1975 as described earlier in this chapter, reflected a similar approach by providing for access to a free appropriate public education for CWD within 'the least restrictive environment'. It fell to the courts to

[38] Ibid. 189 (citing the Education of the Handicapped Act), 194. The US Supreme Court recently returned to the substantive standard required of a 'free appropriate public education' in *Endrew F* v. *Douglas County School District* 580 US ___ (2017), finding that to meet its substantive obligation a school must offer an individualised education programme (IEP) 'reasonably calculated to enable a child to make progress appropriate in light of the child's circumstances' (at 11 of the slip opinion). In doing so, it rejected the holding of the appellate court that a child's IEP was adequate so long as it was calculated to confer an educational benefit that was 'merely . . . more than *de minimus*' (at 8 of the slip opinion).

[39] *Brown* v. *Board of Education of Topeka* 347 US 483 (1954).

[40] See, for example, Hehir and Gamm (n. 26) 211 (*Brown* 'foreshadowed a fundamental change in judicial attitudes toward children with disabilities').

[41] *Wolf* v. *Legislature of Utah* No. 182 646 (3rd Jud. Dist. Utah, 8 January 1969), as cited in ibid. 210–211.

[42] Ibid.

give content to that later legislative prescription.[43] In 1989, the Fifth Circuit Court of Appeals in *Daniel RR* v. *State Board of Education* found for 'a strong preference in favor of mainstreaming'.[44] The Court articulated a two-part test for determining compliance with the mainstreaming requirement: asking whether education in a regular classroom could be satisfactorily achieved with supplementary aids and services, and, if not, whether the school had mainstreamed the child to the maximum extent possible, meaning participation with non-disabled peers in academic, non-academic and extracurricular activities to the maximum extent appropriate.[45]

The Third Circuit Court of Appeals returned to the mainstreaming preference in *Oberti* v. *Board of Education* in 1993, focussing on the use of 'supplementary aids and services' to enable schools to educate CWD for at least a majority of the time within a regular classroom.[46] The trial court had found a violation of the mainstreaming requirement, emphasising that '[i] nclusion is a right, not a privilege for a select few'.[47] The appellate panel agreed, citing experts' suggestions of a modified curriculum, parallel instruction within the classroom, special instruction in a separate resource room, a behaviour management plan and special education training for the regular teacher as among the supplementary aids and services that might have been considered in order for the school district to meet the mainstreaming presumption.[48]

ii Inclusive Education: Israel

The importance of inclusion in education was also recognised in the Israeli case of *Yated* v. *Ministry of Education* – an important decision and an illustration of the increasing cross-fertilisation of ideas between jurisdictions.[49] Israel's law provided for both regular and special schools. The question in *Yated* was whether the state was required to provide free special education not only to children at special schools (as specifically provided for by statute) but also to those who, while having special educational needs, had been found suitable for integration into regular schools (on which

43 See n. 38 as to the standard required of a 'free appropriate public education'.

44 *Daniel RR* v. *State Board of Education* 874 F 2nd 1036 (5th Cir. 1989) 1048–1050.

45 Ibid. 1044.

46 *Oberti* v. *Board of Education of Clementon School District and Others* 995 F 2nd 1204 (3rd Cir. 1993) 1214.

47 *Oberti* v. *Board of Education of the Borough of Clementon School District and Others* 801 F Supp. 1392 (DNJ 1992) 1404.

48 See *Oberti* (3rd Cir.) (n. 46) 1220–1223.

49 *Yated* v. *Ministry of Education* HCJ 2599/00 [2002] IsrLR 57.

the statute was silent). Israel did not dispute the advantages of integration – nor indeed that its policy was to encourage such integration – but it denied an obligation to pay for special education within regular schools. Yated claimed that the state's refusal to extend free special education to children integrated into regular schools violated the rights to education and equality. The Court agreed, interpreting the relevant statute in accordance with the basic values of the legal system, the right to education in the UDHR, the CRC, foreign constitutions, Judaic sources and Israeli law, and the derivative right to special education recognised in the CRC, US law (including *Daniel RR* and *Oberti*) and Israeli law. It held that these collective principles mandated 'that the funding duty of the State also applies to the assistance required for a child with special needs integrated into a regular educational institution'.[50] Accordingly, the Court ordered the state to quickly adopt the measures necessary for it to come into compliance with the statutory requirements no later than the preparatory stages for the coming fiscal year's budget.[51]

iii Twin Tracking: Canada

Other decisions have attracted criticism for reinforcing a two-track regular and special educational system, including the Supreme Court of Canada's 1997 decision in *Eaton* v. *Brant County Board of Education*.[52] Emily Eaton, a twelve-year-old girl with cerebral palsy, had been placed in a special education class contrary to the wishes of her parents. The Court upheld the decision of the tribunal of first instance, leaving Emily placed in special education. In doing so, the Court declined to recognise a presumption in favour of integration and, indeed, cast special education as part of a positive duty of reasonable accommodation. The Court observed that:

> In some cases, special education is a necessary adaptation of the mainstream world which enables some disabled pupils access to the learning environment they need in order to have an equal opportunity in education. While integration should be recognized as the norm of general application because of the benefits it generally provides, a presumption in favour of integrated schooling would work to the disadvantage of pupils who require special education in order to achieve equality ... Integration can be either a benefit or a burden depending on whether the individual can profit from the advantages that integration provides.[53]

[50] Ibid. 71.
[51] Ibid.
[52] *Eaton* v. *Brant County Board of Education* [1997] 1 SCR 241.
[53] Ibid. [69].

Malhotra and Hansen describe the decision as 'enormously disappointing to many in the disability rights community and effectively setting a clear precedent that separate education constitutes equality'.[54] Pothier describes the case as evocative of *Plessy* v. *Ferguson*'s 'doctrine of "separate but equal"' and marginalising for CWD.[55] Significantly, Malhotra and Hansen argue that *Eaton*, and a number of other Canadian decisions, 'are wrong when regarded through the prism of the values contained in the *CRPD*'.[56] The *Eaton* decision is returned to later in this chapter when considering the impact that CRPD Article 24 might have on future cause lawyering for inclusive education.

C *Substantive Content of the Right to Education: Court-Led Structural Reform*

The third category of cases directly concerns the extensive structural reform needed to realise the right to education for CWD. Such restructuring is normally regarded as falling outside the institutional competence of courts. The following cases illustrate the tension between observing the separate functions of the legislature, executive and judiciary and ensuring that courts discharge their ultimate responsibility for warranting effective substantive protection of fundamental rights.

i United States

The most controversial example of structural reform litigation is the *Jose P.* v. *Ambach* class action.[57] The case was initiated as a straightforward challenge to the New York City school system's failure to promptly evaluate and place students with disabilities, and Jose P. was quickly placed in an appropriate school. But the district judge declined to declare the lawsuit moot,

54 Ravi Malhotra and Robin F. Hansen, 'The United Nations Convention on the Rights of Persons with Disabilities and Its Implications for the Equality Rights of Canadians with Disabilities: The Case of Education' (2011) 29 *Windsor Yearbook of Access to Justice* 73, 94.

55 Dianne Pothier, 'Eaton v Brant County Board of Education' (2006) 18 *Canadian Journal of Women and the Law* 121.

56 Malhotra and Hansen (n. 54) 102.

57 *Jose P.* v. *Ambach* 669 F 2nd 865 (2nd Cir. 1982). The following discussion is drawn from Ross Sandler and David Schoenbrod, *Democracy by Decree: What Happens When Courts Run Government* (Yale University Press 2003) 46–97; Samuel R. Bagenstos, 'The Judiciary's Now-Limited Role in Special Education' in Joshua M. Dunn and Martin R. West (eds), *From Schoolhouse to Courthouse: The Judiciary's Role in American Education* (Brookings Institution 2009) 130–136; and Superfine (n. 28) 84–86.

certifying some 14,000 students then awaiting evaluation or placement as a class, and subsequently consolidating that case with another, much broader challenge seeking structural relief to address issues including a lack of individualised placement procedures, inadequate preparation of individual education programmes and an unavailability of mainstreaming opportunities. Despite an order in 1979 of fundamental structural reforms, the case remains under the supervision of the court, with a number of highly detailed supplemental orders and stipulations issued since.[58]

The litigation has its supporters and its critics. Supporters (prominent among them the plaintiffs' counsel) cite increased priority and resources for CWD as successful outcomes of the litigation.[59] Critics argue that political pressure would have delivered enhanced special education programmes irrespective of the court's role;[60] the litigation undermined general education by prioritising resource allocation to special education;[61] the administrative and financial burden is crushing;[62] and judicial intervention significantly removed the New York City school system's flexibility to adapt to evolving, evidence-based, professional understanding of what structures work best in promoting good outcomes.[63] The latter point is of heightened salience considered against the evolving understanding of the right to inclusive education itself over the past thirty-five years.

The equivocal record of the *Jose P.* case should raise serious questions about the utility and propriety of structural reform litigation where courts are expected to play a close and continuing role. In this respect, Bagenstos contrasts *Jose P.* with the more narrowly focussed *Ray M.* v. *Board of Education* class action.[64] *Ray M.* began in 1994, challenging New York City's failure to provide special education to preschool students in the least restrictive environment. The parties entered into a consent decree in 1999 that terminated in 2002. Hence, the *Ray M.* litigation can be viewed as 'remarkably

58 See Advocates for Children of New York, 'Jose P. v. Mills', www.advocatesforchildren.org/litigation/class_actions/jose_p_vs_mills, accessed 29 January 2017.

59 Sandler and Schoenbrod (n. 57) 90–91; Bagenstos (n. 57) 133–134; Superfine (n. 28) 85.

60 Sandler and Schoenbrod (n. 57) 94. See Bagenstos (n. 57) 133.

61 See Bagenstos (n. 57) 133–134 (suggesting that criticism is misplaced and, to the extent valid, compelled by the legislation rather than the litigation).

62 Sam Dillon, 'Special Education Absorbs School Resources', *New York Times* (New York, 7 April 1994), www.nytimes.com/1994/04/07/us/special-education-absorbs-school-resources.html?pagewanted=all, accessed 17 June 2017 (reporting that New York spent hundreds of thousands of dollars annually on legal costs and was forced to maintain ten full-time employees).

63 Bagenstos (n. 57) 134–135.

64 Ibid. 135–136, from which the following discussion is drawn.

successful' owing to the proportion of preschoolers with disabilities served in integrated settings rising from 20 per cent to 50 per cent between the initial challenge in 1994 and the 2005–2006 school year.[65]

ii Europe (France, Bulgaria)

In other cases, litigants have called on judicial and quasi-judicial bodies to find state-level structural reform efforts insufficient, but without attendant structural relief. The decisions of the European Committee of Social Rights in *Autism Europe* v. *France* and *Mental Disability Advocacy Center* v. *Bulgaria (MDAC)* are illustrative.[66] In the first case, Autism Europe alleged that France had made insufficient provision for the education of children and adults with autism due to quantitative and qualitative shortfalls in both mainstream and specialised schools.[67] The Committee agreed, finding a breach of the rights to education to non-discrimination under the European Social Charter and concluding that France's reform efforts had 'failed to achieve sufficient progress in advancing the provision of education for persons with autism'.[68] The complainant in *MDAC* similarly alleged that Bulgaria was in breach of the rights to education and non-discrimination under the Charter in respect of children with moderate, severe or profound disabilities living in institutions. In response, Bulgaria invited the Committee to recognise its efforts to secure equal access to education, and the legal and practical steps it had taken to overcome problems of access to education. The Committee found that Bulgaria's financial constraints did not justify its 'patently insufficient' progress and that the children in question were denied an effective right to education and were discriminated against.[69] Notably, the Committee is limited to conclusions as to the satisfactory application of rights under the European Social Charter. While it can serve a significant role in monitoring structural reform, it cannot itself engage in that reform. But even in the case of a national court with broad remedial jurisdiction, it will often be appropriate to entrust the crafting of the proper remedial response to the executive as in the case examined in what follows.

65 Ibid.

66 *International Association Autism Europe* v. *France* Complaint no. 13/2002 (ECSR, 4 November 2003) and *Mental Disability Advocacy Center (MDAC)* v. *Bulgaria* Complaint no. 41/2007 (ECSR, 3 June 2008). These cases and others under the European Social Charter are considered in detail in Chapter 4 of this volume.

67 *Autism Europe* (n. 66) [16].

68 Ibid. [54]. See also *European Action of the Disabled (AEH)* v. *France* Complaint no. 81/2012 (ESCR, 11 September 2013).

69 *MDAC* (n. 65) [47], [48], [54].

iii Canada

The Supreme Court of Canada considered an appeal from a finding that a school district's denial of necessary intensive remedial instruction to a child with a severe learning disability constituted unjustified discrimination in *Moore* v. *British Columbia (Education)*.[70] The tribunal below had granted both individual and systemic remedies, and remained seized of jurisdiction to oversee their implementation. The Supreme Court upheld the tribunal's finding of discrimination and the individual remedies granted. It acknowledged that this remedy had 'clear broad remedial repercussions for how other students with severe learning disabilities are educated',[71] but it declined to uphold the specific systemic remedies granted, finding them outside the scope of the individual claim and in excess of the tribunal's role as an adjudicator of the particular claim before it. The question of the institutional competence of the courts in shaping remedies for breaches of fundamental rights is returned to in Part III.B.

iv South Africa (Western Cape)

The 2010 decision of the Western Cape High Court in *Western Cape Forum for Intellectual Disability* v. *South Africa*[72] provides a recent example of a court closely involving itself both in adjudication of the discrete constitutional question before it and also the structural reform necessary to give effect to the rights in question. South Africa had established 'special schools' catering to children with moderate to mild intellectual disabilities. Children with severe or profound disabilities, however, were regarded as uneducable and excluded from both special and mainstream schools.[73] The applicant challenged that exclusion. The respondents argued that they had limited resources and had to make difficult policy choices as to the distribution of such resources in the face of competing demands, and were not, accordingly, able to further contribute to the education of the affected children. The Court considered the constitutional right to education and the right expressed in the CRC, the African Charter on the Rights and Welfare of the Child, the European Social Charter (including the decision in *Autism Europe*), the CRPD and *O'Donoghue*. It held that the affected children's rights to education, equality

70 *Moore* v. *British Columbia (Education)* 2012 SCC 61, [2012] 3 SCR 360.

71 Ibid. [63].

72 *Western Cape Forum for Intellectual Disability* v. *Government of the Republic of South Africa and Another* [2010] ZAWCHC 544, 2011 (5) SA 87.

73 Ibid. [17].

and dignity were unjustifiably infringed.[74] Significantly, the Court granted a detailed structural interdict directing reasonable measures (including interim measures) to give effect to the rights in question, including ensuring affordable access to adequate education, funding, transport and staff training. The respondents were ordered to report on implementation within twelve months.

The *Western Cape* decision followed thirteen years' lobbying and is a landmark decision in securing education for children with severe or profound disabilities in South Africa. However, the implementation of the judgment has relied in large part on the continuing and considerable efforts of the Western Cape Forum in ongoing policy and budgetary measures.[75] The experience underscores that a courtroom victory represents a step along the path towards inclusive education (an often important, sometimes pivotal one) rather than a destination.

v The Spectrum of Remedial Responses

Simply because a lawsuit alleges or implicates structural failures does not mean that the court must involve itself in the structural reform to which the lawsuit is directed. The traditional starting point, reflected in *O'Donoghue*, is that the court will grant general 'declaratory relief in the expectation that the institutions of the State would respond by taking whatever action was appropriate'.[76] This judicial restraint acknowledges that there will often be a number of options open to the government to bring itself into compliance, particularly in an area of social policy such as inclusive education. The Supreme Court of Canada's decision in *Eldridge* v. *British Columbia (Attorney General)* is illustrative.[77] In considering the appropriate remedy for a discriminatory failure to provide sign language interpretation in hospitals, the Court observed that:

> A declaration, as opposed to some kind of injunctive relief, is the appropriate remedy in this case because there are myriad options available to the government that may rectify the unconstitutionality of the current system. It is not this Court's role to dictate how this is to be accomplished.[78]

74 Ibid. [45]–[46].
75 See Western Cape Forum, 'Advocacy', www.wcfid.co.za/page26.html, accessed 17 June 2017.
76 *O'Donoghue* (n. 29) 71.
77 *Eldridge* v. *British Columbia (Attorney General)* [1997] 3 SCR 624. See generally Kent Roach, 'Remedial Consensus and Dialogue under the Charter: General Declarations and Delayed Declarations of Invalidity' (2002) 35 *University of British Columbia Law Review* 211.
78 *Eldridge* ibid. [96].

The cases considered earlier in this chapter reflect a spectrum of remedial responses. At one end, the decisions of the European Committee of Social Rights reflect the boundaries of its jurisdiction, under which it is limited to conclusions on the application of the rights in question. There is then the traditional position in *O'Donoghue*, in which courts prefer general declaratory relief as a matter of remedial discretion. This gives the executive (the more institutionally competent and closely accountable body) maximum flexibility in crafting a remedial response. But such an approach is highly dependent on good faith and political will to ensure substantive protection of the relevant right. Towards the other end of the spectrum are the structural interdicts ordered in the South African case of *Western Cape* and (at the most extreme end) the US case of *Jose P*. The question of the proper remedial role of the courts is returned to in Part III.B.

II FUTURE ROLE FOR STRATEGIC LITIGATION

The future role that strategic litigation might play in implementing Article 24 of the CRPD will be informed, in part, by the past successes and limitations considered earlier in this chapter. This Part considers three areas in which the courts might play a productive role: securing specific outcomes, interpreting the right to inclusive education and shifting priorities.

A *Securing Specific Outcomes*

One clear role for the courts is in applying specific minimum standards under Article 24 of the CRPD and domestic implementing legislation, in order to secure specific outcomes. While the precise content and scope of the right to inclusive education will continue to evolve (and the courts will play an important role in that),[79] Article 24 does provide for certain detailed legal obligations, to be transposed into and supplemented by domestic law.

The Office of the High Commissioner of Human Rights (OHCHR) recommended in 2013, for example, that states adopt inclusive education laws with a clear definition of inclusive education, a 'no-rejection clause' and provision for reasonable accommodation and effective remedies.[80] The Special Rapporteur on the right to education similarly emphasised

[79] See Part III.B.
[80] OHCHR, 'Thematic Study on the Right of Persons with Disabilities to Education' (n. 16) [26], [56], [63].

the importance of an adequate, focussed and effective legislative framework, including recognising inclusive education as an inherent component of the right to education, identifying minimum standards and providing for effective remedies.[81]

As in the cases concerning access to education considered in Part I.A, the courts may be successful in enforcing specific outcomes (such as a 'no-rejection clause' preventing the denial of admission into mainstream schools). The clearer the content and scope of the right to inclusive education in domestic legislation, the more straightforward and predictable the courts' adjudicative role under this head will be.

B *Interpreting the Right to Inclusive Education*

The second, and more broadly applicable, role for the courts is in drawing on Article 24 in interpreting and applying domestic constitutional and legislative rights to education, equality and non-discrimination. The cross-fertilisation of ideas between jurisdictions (and between treaty bodies and national courts) in cases such as *O'Donoghue*, *Yated* and *Western Cape* illustrates the important role the courts might play in incorporating and enforcing the substantive protections of Article 24 at the national level.

The status of international law (and international treaties in particular) in domestic law varies across jurisdictions. Generally, in dualist systems, implementing legislation is required to give a treaty domestic legal effect. But even in the absence of implementing legislation, domestic courts will often look to international law in interpreting and applying constitutional and legislative rights.

The South African Constitution, for example, provides that in interpreting the Bill of Rights a court *must* consider international law and may consider foreign law (though it is not bound to follow either).[82] In most other countries, it remains a matter of judicial discretion. In the United States, Hathaway and others write, '[c]ourts often look to treaties when interpreting statutes and, more controversially, constitutional provisions'.[83] Outside of the United States, courts look more readily to international law as an aid to interpreting and applying both domestic law and

81 Muñoz (n. 13) [26]–[28], [33].
82 South African Constitution S39. See S. v. *Makwanyane and Another* [1995] ZACC 3, 1995 (3) SA 391, [39].
83 Oona A. Hathaway, Sabria McElroy and Sara Aronchick Solow, 'International Law at Home: Enforcing Treaties in U.S. Courts' (2012) 37 *Yale Journal of International Law* 51, 87.

constitutional rights – as is the case in Canada,[84] New Zealand,[85] Israel[86] and Botswana.[87]

The importance of this 'interpretive enforcement'[88] of international human rights law in domestic legal systems is reflected in the experience to date. The courts considered international law in interpreting the right to education in Ireland, the rights to education and equality in South Africa, the rights to special education and equality in Israel and the rights to education, equality and non-discrimination in Colombia.[89] It is also relevant to note that the European Court of Human Rights considered obligations under the CRPD in interpreting and applying rights under the European Convention on Human Rights (ECHR) in *Kiss* v. *Hungary*[90] (a voting rights case) – suggesting that Article 24 of the CRPD will prove relevant if the Court were to consider the non-discrimination standard in the ECHR as it relates to education for CWD. Interpretive enforcement would, finally, provide a mechanism to revisit decisions such as the Canadian case of *Eaton* in light of the CRPD.[91]

Interpretive enforcement of Article 24 thus might play a valuable role in incorporating its substantive protections into the rights to education, non-discrimination and equality expressed in most domestic legal systems.

84 *Baker* v. *Canada (Minister of Citizenship and Immigration)* [1999] 2 SCR 817 [70] ('international human rights law as an aid in interpreting domestic law' and 'a critical influence on the interpretation of the scope of [*Charter*] rights'). See generally Malhotra and Hansen (n. 54) 84–90.

85 See generally Andrew S. Butler and Petra Butler, 'The Judicial Use of International Human Rights Law in New Zealand' (1999) 29 *Victoria University of Wellington Law Review* 173.

86 See, for example, *Yated* (n. 49) 70.

87 See, for example, Obonye Jonas, 'The Right to Inclusive Education in Botswana: Present Challenges and Future Prospects' (2014) 2 *African Disability Rights Yearbook* 3, 11.

88 Hathaway, McElroy and Solow (n. 83) 88.

89 *O'Donoghue* (n. 29); *Western Cape Forum for Intellectual Disability* (n. 72) [20]–[26] and see generally Sue Philpott, 'Too Little, Too Late? The CRPD as a Standard to Evaluate South African Legislation and Policies for Early Childhood Development' (2014) 2 *African Disability Rights Yearbook* 51, 73; *Yated* (n. 49) 64–70 (considering the right to education in the UDHR, the ICESCR, the CRC and foreign constitutions, as well as the right to special education in the CRC and foreign law); Corte Constitucional, Sala Séptima de Revisión de Tutelas noviembre 30, 2010, MP Jorge Ignacio Pretelt Chaljub, Sentencia T-974/10 (Colombia) (considering the ICESCR and the CRPD), and see 'Decision T-974/10' (*ESCR-Net*), www.escr-net.org/docs/i/1600445, accessed 29 January 2017.

90 *Alajos Kiss* v. *Hungary* App. no. 38832/06 (ECtHR, 20 May 2010).

91 See Malhotra and Hansen (n. 54) 75.

C Shifting Priorities

Successfully implementing Article 24 of the CRPD will ultimately require considerable political will, deep-seated structural change and complex social and fiscal policy decisions. Here the potential role for the courts is arguably more vexed.

i To What Extent Has Strategic Litigation Succeeded in Shifting Priorities to Date?

There has been remarkable progress in education for CWD over the past decades – both in the normative evolution of the right to inclusive education and in improved educational opportunities and outcomes for CWD. What has driven that progress, and what has been the impact and effectiveness of litigation within it?

In the authors' view, the change is attributable, in the most part, to UN-led programming, progress marked by such policy milestones as the Jomtien World Declaration on Education for All, the Salamanca Statement on Principles, Policy and Practice in Special Needs Education and Article 24 of the CRPD itself. Litigation has played a comparatively modest role.

That said, the cases considered in this chapter demonstrate that litigation has resulted in a number of successes – contributing to improved outcomes as well as an important 'transnational judicial dialogue'[92] around the right to education for CWD. It has been an important catalyst for legislative change in the United States (which contributed in turn to international legal and policy developments) and Ireland. It is credited with a significant impact on school practices in the United States and South Africa. It has added to pressure for a more rapid pace of change in France and Bulgaria. This suggests that significant potential remains for court-led change in implementing Article 24, albeit situated within a broader strategic frame.

ii Specific Priorities

Before turning to a critical appraisal of the role for inclusive education litigation, it is worthwhile considering where it might sit within specific priorities in implementing Article 24 of the CRPD. There are at least three notable gaps in implementation.

92 Malhotra and Hansen (n. 54) 102.

The first is a generic failure of implementation: a persisting gap between the rhetoric and reality of implementation. Botswana (as analysed by Jonas) provides a good example.[93] Despite having expressed a policy commitment to inclusive education (albeit not having ratified the CRPD), as Jonas describes, little has been done to implement it in practice, with an inadequate legislative framework, no comprehensive special education curriculum in mainstream schools, a structurally exclusive education system, inadequate infrastructure and resources to implement inclusive education and, as a result, CWD remaining excluded from education.[94]

The second concerns governments' focusing attention and resources on achieving universal primary education (Millennium Development Goal 2),[95] but failing to focus on CWD. Stein et al. state that many countries' 'lagging challenge remains reaching the last 15 per cent of out-of-school children, of whom children with disabilities are disproportionally represented'.[96] The authors refer to the need for specific interventions to reach marginalised children, including 'the explicit targeting of children with disabilities in national education sector plans' and the development of inclusive educational policies consistent with Article 24 of the CRPD.[97]

The third notable implementation gap concerns governments' focussing attention and resources on CWD, but focussing it on *special* rather than inclusive education. China is a case in point.[98] China has ratified the CRPD and championed the rights of CWD internationally and domestically, including pledging increased funding for education of CWD.[99] But Human Rights Watch describes China as 'continu[ing] to devote too few resources to the education of students with disabilities in mainstream schools while at the same time actively developing a parallel system of segregated special education schools'.[100] It reports a nearly fourfold increase in funding for special education schools in the past decade, with little growth in funding for education of students with disabilities in mainstream schools.[101]

The role litigation might play in addressing some of these high-priority implementation gaps seems likely a peripheral one. The principal drivers of

93 Jonas (n. 87).
94 Ibid. 22, 20, 28, 23, 26, 27.
95 UNGA Res. 55/2 (18 September 2000) UN Doc. A/RES/55/22 [19].
96 Stein, McClain-Nhlapo and Lord (n. 19) 284 (citations omitted).
97 Ibid. 285.
98 See Human Rights Watch, *"As Long as They Let Us Stay in Class": Barriers to Education for Persons with Disabilities in China* (Human Rights Watch 2013).
99 Ibid. 2.
100 Ibid. 1–2.
101 Ibid. 20.

change are more likely to remain UN and disabled people's organisation–led programming – assisted, hopefully, by the international cooperation measures anticipated in Article 32 of the CRPD.

But that is not to foreclose a strategic role for litigation. The European Committee of Social Rights' decisions in *Autism Europe* and *MDAC* show the value of litigation in focussing a government's attention on gaps between rhetoric and reality in implementing educational policy. The US cases, *O'Donoghue*, *Western Cape* and *MDAC* demonstrate that litigation can be used to highlight exclusion of certain marginalised groups. *Yated* illustrates a successful challenge to the misallocation of funding in favour of special rather than inclusive education. More generally, litigation drawing on statistical information (structural, process and outcome indicators) might play an important role in monitoring and evaluating state-by-state implementation of inclusive education.[102]

iii How Far Should the Courts Be Willing to Go?

The cases considered earlier in this chapter illustrate the tension that can arise between the traditionally (and sensibly) limited role of the courts in determining questions of social policy, and the need for the courts to act as effective guardians of substantive rights. Given the deep-seated structural change required in realising inclusive education and the institutional resistance it might face,[103] it seems likely that the courts will be faced with difficult questions as to the proper extent of their role.

The proper preference is that the courts act to ensure substantive protection of the right to inclusive education without recourse to intrusive judicial supervision or injunctive relief. But the broader experience suggests that institutional resistance may require bolder judicial intervention in the appropriate case. Both litigants and courts should direct efforts at ensuring a robust, participatory executive response to violations of the right to inclusive education, backed up by a more active judicial role if necessary. It seems fair to add that improved social outcomes will ultimately rest more on litigants' broader advocacy and mobilisation strategies than on the particular form of relief granted in an individual case.

102 See Singh (n. 8) [72]–[73].

103 Muñoz (n. 13) [12] and [50].

III CAUTIONS AND QUALIFICATIONS

This Part raises critiques that might be applied to the types of strategic litigation strategies and their consequences as described earlier in this chapter. In doing so, it considers three specific objections, putting them forward in their strongest terms. First, that a court-centred strategy places naïve faith in litigation's ability to directly advance social change. Second, that courts lack institutional competence to adjudicate questions of social policy such as inclusive education. Third, that limited access to lawyers and courts by those affected by exclusion, as well as the potential for their individual concerns to override systemically transformative goals, renders the prospects of strategic litigation nugatory. We add a caveat that these critiques draw on the heavily American literature on cause lawyering. Accordingly, despite guidance that can be taken from this extensive research, individual stakeholders need to evaluate the prospects of going to court as a means of implementing the right to inclusive education within their respective national, cultural, legal, economic and other circumstances.[104]

A Court-Centred

The first critique of strategic litigation notes that by definition it is inherently court-centred, and thus places naïve faith in litigation's ability to directly advance social change.[105] This reliance on the courts is said to lack historical perspective given that social change has primarily been the result of political rather than judicial processes,[106] overlooks that courts are ill equipped to perform the monitoring and follow-up role necessary to effect meaningful change,[107] and arise from a glamorisation of strategic litigation and an over-representation of the ability of cause lawyers to affect social reform.[108]

[104] This is true when considering applying any human rights model as a precedent. See Michael Ashley Stein and Janet E. Lord, 'Forging Effective International Agreements: Lessons from the UN Convention on the Rights of Persons with Disabilities' in Jody Heymann and Adèle Cassola (eds), *Making Equal Rights Real: Taking Effective Action to Overcome Global Challenges* (Cambridge University Press 2012).

[105] Michael E. Waterstone, Michael Ashley Stein and David B. Wilkins, 'Disability Cause Lawyers' (2012) 53 *William and Mary Law Review* 1287, 1336–1347. A classic critique of faith in the power of courts is Gerald N. Rosenberg, *The Hollow Hope: Can Courts Bring About Social Change?* (University of Chicago Press 1991).

[106] Sandler and Schoenbrod (n. 57) 30–34.

[107] Waterstone, Stein and Wilkins (n. 105) 1337.

[108] Sandler and Schoenbrod (n. 57) 32.

Litigation is also claimed to misallocate time, energy and financial resources from more productive, community-led advocacy and mobilisation efforts.[109]

Inclusive education litigation successes will not automatically or necessarily lead to real change. Where litigation has led to significant institutional reform, the underlying drivers are more plausibly regarded as changes in social attitudes than the initiative of the courts. Thus, Sandler and Schoenbrod's reflection on *Brown* v. *Board of Education* – that 'the courts rode the wave of history rather than set it in motion'[110] – may be appropriately applied to each of the successful strategic litigation cases considered in Part I. Further, the court decisions themselves often played a lesser role in causing real change than did subsequent developments – either legislative (as in *PARC*, *Mills* and *O'Donoghue*) or ongoing, collaborative implementation between the parties (as in *Western Cape*).[111]

Strategic litigation was, however, instrumental in bringing about developments that led to change, illustrating the potential value of litigation as a political tool – with courtroom victories used 'as leverage in other political forums'[112] – and thus an effective catalyst for change.[113] Inclusive education litigation can therefore be used pragmatically and strategically, as part of broader community-led advocacy and mobilisation efforts by cause lawyers.[114] This more nuanced and favourable assessment of the potential role for strategic litigation aligns with research into its use by disability rights lawyers in the United States.[115] *Western Cape* provides a good international example of such an approach in practice.

B *Institutional Limits of the Courts*

The second critique of strategic litigation focusses on the institutional limits of the courts in adjudicating questions of social policy and then implementing the transformative changes they deem necessary. This account follows from

109 Waterstone, Stein and Wilkins (n. 105) 1343. See also Jay P. Heubert, 'Six Law-Driven School Reforms: Developments, Lessons, and Prospects' in Heubert (ed.) (n. 26) 8.

110 Sandler and Schoenbrod (n. 57) 33.

111 For several models of this dynamic, see Stuart A. Scheingold, *The Politics of Rights: Lawyers, Public Policy, and Political Change* (2nd edn) (University of Michigan Press 2004).

112 Melnick (n. 19) 139.

113 This is a pattern that has been taken up by cause lawyers for the LGBT community in the United States. See, for example, Scott L. Cummings and Douglas NeJaime, 'Lawyering for Marriage Equality' (2010) 57 *UCLA Law Review* 1235, 1241.

114 See Waterstone, Stein and Wilkins (n. 105) 1337–1342.

115 See ibid. 1337.

the discussion of the justiciability of the right to inclusive education and the remedial role of the courts discussed in Part I.C.

Sandler and Schoenbrod describe the courts as drifting, in cases like *Jose P.*, from enforcing negative rights (i.e. prohibiting discrimination) to making policy in pursuit of 'soft rights',[116] by which they mean the realm of social rights.[117] Moreover, these soft rights – which clearly include the right to an inclusive education[118] – are only enforced to the extent a court, or those negotiating a consent decree, think it proper to balance that right against a government's competing social priorities.[119] This is a function traditionally reserved to democratically elected officials, especially in those jurisdictions such as the United States that eschew recognition of social rights.[120]

The institutional limits of courts is therefore a valid point to consider, and particularly in relation to outlier cases such as *Jose P.* Overall, though, the decisions described in Part I.C suggest that courts can play a useful role in monitoring and enforcing the right to education of CWD without overstepping institutional bounds. Further, the adjudicative role of the courts will become more straightforward as the right to inclusive education is given increased content by the Committee on the Rights of Persons with Disabilities, decisions of regional and national courts and academic scholarship.[121] Sandler and Schoenbrod are correct to require an ultimate balancing of rights and state interests, but courts are frequently called on to undertake such balancing tests, and do so in an analytically rigorous manner.[122]

116 Sandler and Schoenbrod (n. 57) 102–103.

117 See Michael Ashley Stein and Malcolm Langford, *Disability Social Rights* (Cambridge University Press, forthcoming).

118 Cf. Sandler and Schoenbrod (n. 57) 104 (characterising the statutory right to special education in the EAHCA as an aspiration or soft right). The New Zealand Court of Appeal described the CRPD in similar terms (as 'largely aspirational') in *Smith* v. *Air New Zealand Ltd* [2011] NZCA 20, [2011] 2 NZLR 171 (18 February 2011) [22]. One notable exception from this categorisation are instances where the right of children to education is deemed an immediately remedial (read: civil and political) right such as in South Africa, where the right to education is enumerated in the Constitution.

119 Sandler and Schoenbrod (n. 57) 7, 103.

120 Cass R. Sunstein, 'Why Does the American Constitution Lack Social and Economic Guarantees?' (2003) University of Chicago Public Law and Legal Theory Working Paper No. 36, 5, http://ssrn.com/abstract_id=375622, accessed 26 February 2017.

121 See, for example, Paul Harpur and Michael Ashley Stein, 'Children with Disabilities, Human Rights, and Sustainable Development' in Claire Fenton-Glynn (ed.), *Children's Rights and Sustainable Development: Implementing the UNCRC for Future Generations* (Cambridge University Press, forthcoming).

122 See, for example, *R.* v. *Oakes* [1986] 1 SCR 103 and *Paul Rodney Hansen* v. *R* [2007] NZSC 7, [2007] 3 NZLR 1 [92] for the tests applied under the Canadian Charter and the New Zealand Bill of Rights Act 1990, respectively.

The more pertinent question is the proper approach to remedies, and in particular the role of courts in granting supervisory and injunctive relief. There the issue of relative institutional competence becomes acute. On this question, the Canadian Supreme Court's decision in *Doucet-Boudreau* v. *Nova Scotia (Minister of Education)* provides useful general principles.[123] There, Francophone parents sought publicly funded French-language educational facilities, as guaranteed by constitutional minority language rights, for their CWD. The trial judge, in the face of a long history of non-compliance and an 'urgent context of ongoing cultural erosion',[124] ordered the government to make its best efforts to provide schools and services by specific dates, and retained jurisdiction to hear reports on compliance.

The Supreme Court, by a bare majority, upheld the trial judge's order and set out a number of principles bearing on the appropriateness and justice of remedies under the Canadian Charter. The majority emphasised that an appropriate remedy must meaningfully vindicate the right, must be relevant to the claimant's experience 'and must address the circumstances in which the right was infringed'.[125] A remedy must respect the separate functions of the legislature, the executive and the judiciary, and while it might touch on functions that are principally assigned to the executive it must not depart unduly from courts' adjudicative role.[126] Likewise, it must ensure that the claimant's right is fully vindicated, while also being fair to the party against whom it is made.[127] Finally, the majority stressed that the constitutional scheme is ultimately directed at the vindication of fundamental rights, and therefore remedies should be allowed to evolve to meet the challenges and circumstances of the individual case.[128]

The Canadian Supreme Court's approach stands in direct contrast to the Irish Supreme Court's earlier decision in *TD* v. *Minister for Education*.[129] In *TD*, the court below had granted a mandatory injunction requiring the Minister for Education to adhere to plans the government had put forward for secure, high-support residential units for children with very high support needs, within the deadlines specified in those plans. The judge had acknowledged that the relief granted touched on the separation of powers and that

[123] *Doucet-Boudreau* v. *Nova Scotia (Minister of Education)* 2003 SCC 62, [2003] SCR 3.

[124] Ibid. [40].

[125] Ibid. [55].

[126] Ibid. [56]. Ibid. [57]: 'It will not be appropriate for a court to leap into the kinds of decisions and functions for which its design and expertise are manifestly unsuited.'

[127] Ibid. [58].

[128] Ibid. [59].

[129] *TD (a Minor Suing by His Mother and Next Friend MD) and Others* v. *The Minister for Education and Others* [2001] 4 IR 259.

judicial intervention would 'occur only in limited circumstances and where it was absolutely necessary for the court to carry out its duties under the Constitution in securing, vindicating and enforcing constitutional rights'.[130] However, given the long history of the defendants' culpable delays in addressing 'the quite scandalous situation' which had obtained for some years,[131] the judge granted the order sought.

The Supreme Court (with the now chief justice dissenting) overturned the judge's decision. It found the mandatory injunction had breached the separation of powers and that such intervention was only permitted if there was a 'clear disregard' of the executive's constitutional obligations, which Murray J would have limited to 'a conscious and deliberate decision' to act in breach of such obligations, 'accompanied by bad faith or recklessness'.[132] The unfortunate consequence of the Supreme Court's decision is effectively to foreclose injunctive relief even in the face of state inaction of the degree present in *TM*, leaving litigants with little or no effective remedy.

Doucet-Boudreau establishes a preferable set of general principles that, applied in the context of inclusive education, would seek to meet concerns around the institutional competence and legitimacy of courts adjudicating the right to inclusive education, while ultimately ensuring that that right is meaningfully protected. The long history of discrimination, exclusion and marginalisation of CWD, coupled with likely institutional resistance to change, argues strongly in favour of a flexible and responsive approach to remedies in cases where a violation of the right to inclusive education can be upheld.

C Access to Lawyers and Courts

The third critique of strategic litigation raises concerns regarding effective access to justice.[133] Aggrieved parties – in this case, the parents, guardians or supporters of CWD – have limited access to lawyers and thence courts, rendering as academic (or at least severely circumscribing) the prospects of strategic litigation.[134] As an initial and general matter, this is because legal

[130] Ibid. 273.

[131] Ibid. 327.

[132] Ibid. 336–337.

[133] See generally Yash Ghai and Jill Cottrell (eds), *Marginalized Communities and Access to Justice* (Routledge 2010) (global context); Deborah L. Rhode, *Access to Justice* (Oxford University Press 2004) (American context).

[134] See Mark C. Weber, 'Litigation under the Individuals with Disabilities Education Act after *Buckhannon Board & Care Home, Inc. v. West Virginia Department of Health & Human Resources*' (2004) 65 *Ohio State Law Journal* 357.

representation itself can be prohibitively expensive.[135] Additionally, when remedies exist for violations of the right to inclusive education at the national level, they may be limited to declaratory or (as in the United States) injunctive relief, and may not provide successful claimants with legal fees or damages.[136] There thus can be little economic incentive for cause lawyers to take on strategic litigation cases involving inclusive education claims.[137]

Moreover, contracting for legal assistance often requires a fairly high level of educational and/or socioeconomic power. Those individual clients who do obtain legal assistance are then placed in tension with broader institutional reform aspirations – seeking remedies for their children rather than for the class of similarly situated CWD – and in doing so strip away the greater transformative potential of these lawsuits.[138] And although some of the cases reviewed in this chapter, notably *Jose P.*, were converted from single person–single remedy lawsuits into broader-based institutional reform cases, this dynamic is a notable exception and dependant on the individuals adjudicating the claims. In addition, the history of disability-based rights claims, at least in the United States, indicates that more frequently than not these suits are not conceived of and empowered by disability rights attorneys but rather by other types of lawyers;[139] the point being that the issues may not be framed with the same care, and with equal concern for systemic change, as if by the hand of a knowledgeable disability rights cause lawyer.

CONCLUSION

Strategic litigation can play an important role in advancing the right to inclusive education, with the qualification that such a role should be carefully situated within broader, community-led advocacy and mobilisation strategies.

135 Ibid.; Samuel R. Bagenstos, 'The Perversity of Limited Civil Rights Remedies: The Case of "Abusive" ADA Litigation' (2006) 54 *UCLA Law Review* 1 (noting the shift in incentives for litigants after the stripping of statutory legal and other fees).

136 See Mark C. Weber, Ralph Mawdsley and Sarah Redfield, *Special Education Law: Cases and Materials* (3rd edn) (LexisNexis 2010).

137 The same is true for American disability rights cause lawyers in the context of employment discrimination claims, which lose at federal court at a 95 per cent rate and do not have fees attached. These lawyers have adjusted their dockets instead towards public accommodation and other claims more likely to see victory and with available state-level fees. See Waterstone, Stein and Wilkins (n. 105) 1348–1353; Michael Ashley Stein, Michael E. Waterstone and David B. Wilkins, 'Cause Lawyering for People with Disabilities' (2010) 123 *Harvard Law Review* 1658, 1682–1686.

138 See Michael Ashley Stein and Michael E Waterstone, 'Disability, Disparate Impact, and Class Actions' (2006) 56 *Duke Law Journal* 861.

139 Stein, Waterstone and Wilkins (n. 137) 1670–1678.

Article 24 of the CRPD brings increased justiciable content to the right to inclusive education – the express and binding recognition of the right itself, the 'no-rejection' clause and the clear and immediate requirement for reasonable accommodation. The content of the right to inclusive education will be further elucidated by the Committee on the Rights of Persons with Disabilities, academic scholarship and judicial decisions. Article 24 of the CRPD can also be expected to play a significant role in directing and aligning judicial approaches to the rights to education and non-discrimination expressed in domestic law. If approached carefully, litigation can provide a useful tool in monitoring and enforcing national implementation – in particular, countering political or institutional resistance to change. It is, however, a limited means of social change. The international experience suggests that the effectiveness of litigation will depend in large part on who brings suit, the manner in which such claims are brought, the nature of the relief sought and – most importantly – how it is integrated into a broader 'legal mobilization framework' that looks beyond the date of the judgment.[140]

[140] Ibid. 1691.

11

Advocacy for Inclusive Education

A European Approach

Carla Bonino Covas and Miguel Ángel Cabra de Luna

INTRODUCTION

This chapter examines the different means through which advocacy can help improve legislation and policies related to inclusive education, taking a European approach. Although, as explained in Section 1.2, in the European Union the competence on education remains at the Member State level, relevant policy developments and related advocacy experiences on inclusive education deserve our attention due to the role they play in promoting a real European society inclusive for all.[1]

The purpose of strengthening the European social model defined the criteria for building the content of this chapter. The authors believe that the idea that 'Europe' materialised in the 'European Union' (EU) is a live and dynamic reality, based on legislation and policies but also, and not less importantly, on concrete experiences coming from civil society aiming at consolidating a 'European citizenship'.

In this sense, the authors have identified and selected pioneering advocacy experiences that, inspired in the United Nations Convention on the Rights of Persons with Disabilities (CRPD), seek to foster inclusive education with

Fundación ONCE for the Cooperation and Social Inclusion of People with Disabilities (Fundación ONCE) has the main goal of promoting the quality of life of people with disabilities and their families, particularly focussed on the areas of training, employment and universal accessibility of environments, products and services. Based in Spain, it was founded in 1988 by the National Organization of Spanish Blind (ONCE) as an instrument of cooperation and solidarity from the Spanish blind towards other people with disabilities. Within Fundación ONCE, Carla Bonino co-ordinates various European initiatives, one of them being the European Network on Inclusive Education and Disability (incluD-ed), examined in this text as one of the advocacy practices.

[1] Despite education being a competence that remains at the Member State level, the European Union has increasingly paid attention to this issue through policies as well as through relevant programmes such as Erasmus+.

a European scope. All of these experiences share this factor and are led by different actors and showcase different advocacy instruments. Together, we believe they reflect how the rights of people with disabilities, in the field of education, can be fostered in a variety of ways and thanks to the actions of various stakeholders. Moreover, all of them have Europe as a common aim.

With this perspective, this chapter begins by analysing relevant European policies and instruments that set the background for advocacy on inclusive education (Section 1). These are the European Disability Strategy 2010–2020; the EU 2020 Strategy for Smart, Sustainable and Inclusive Growth; and the Strategic Framework for European Cooperation in Education and Training.

Afterwards, the chapter addresses four selected advocacy experiences from a pan-European perspective coming from different sectors such as the European disability movement, EU and governmental authorities acting in a European framework, the social economy and the students themselves (Section 2).

Lastly, the authors make final reflections about advocacy on inclusive education in Europe, including remarks that they believe should not be left aside, taking into consideration current demands on skills for the job market that bring new challenges for people with disabilities and advocacy (Section 3).

1 THE PLACE OF INCLUSIVE EDUCATION IN RELEVANT EUROPEAN POLICIES: SETTING THE SCENE FOR ADVOCACY

1.1 The European Disability Strategy 2010–2020 and the EU 2020 Strategy for Smart, Sustainable and Inclusive Growth

Closely linked with demands by the disability movement at the European level and with the conclusion of the United Nations Convention on the Rights of Persons with Disabilities (UNCRPD), the European Commission adopted in 2010 the European Disability Strategy 2010–2020: A Renewed Commitment to a Barrier-Free Europe.[2] The declared overall aim of this Strategy was to empower people with disabilities so that they can enjoy their full rights, and benefit entirely from participating in society and in the European economy, notably through the European single market, promoting effective

[2] European Commission, 'European Disability Strategy 2010–2020: A Renewed Commitment to a Barrier-Free Europe' (Communication) COM(2010) 636 Final.

implementation of the UNCRPD across the EU. For this purpose, the European Disability Strategy identifies eight main areas for action: accessibility, participation, equality, employment, education and training, social protection, health and external action.

Under the area of education and training, the Strategy sets the objective of promoting inclusive education and lifelong learning for pupils and students with disabilities (in the context that it is the Member States' responsibility to define the content of teaching and to organise their education systems). In this document, the Commission declares its support for the goal of inclusive, quality education and training, and sets different objectives in this field: to remove legal and organisational barriers for people with disabilities to general education and lifelong learning systems; to provide timely support for inclusive education and personalised learning as well as early identification of special needs; to give adequate training and support for professionals working at all levels of education; and to report on participation rates and outcomes.

Other areas of the European Disability Strategy 2010–2020 are specifically related to inclusive education, such as the ones referring to employment and accessibility. In regard to employment, the Strategy points out the issue of developing adequate skills for employment and highlights the importance of the process of transition from education to the job market. Additionally, in the accessibility area, the Strategy refers to the incorporation of accessibility and design for all in academic curricula.

Throughout its approach, the European Disability Strategy connects its objectives with the EU's Europe 2020 Strategy for Smart, Sustainable and Inclusive Growth, with the recognition that building a society that includes everyone also brings market opportunities and fosters innovation.[3]

The EU 2020 Strategy is structured around three focussed areas that define the concept of future growth in Europe: smart growth, referred to as developing an economy based on knowledge and innovation; sustainable growth, aimed at promoting a more resource-efficient, greener and more competitive economy; and, lastly, inclusive growth, oriented to fostering a high-employment economy delivering social and territorial cohesion.

With this framework, the EU 2020 Strategy sets a series of headline targets to be achieved by 2020. The following are highlighted for the purpose of the discussion in this chapter: 75 per cent of the population aged twenty to sixty-four should be employed; the share of early school leavers should be under

[3] European Commission, 'Europe 2020: A Strategy for Smart, Sustainable and Inclusive Growth' COM(2010) 2020 Final.

10 per cent; at least 40 per cent of the younger generation should have a tertiary degree; and 20 million fewer people should be at risk of poverty.

The UNCRPD, which became a legally binding instrument for the EU on 22 January 2011, impacted the way in which disability policy, as part of the EU 2020 Strategy, needed to be devised. The Convention, which is the first human rights treaty ratified by a regional organisation like the EU, includes substantive provisions regarding accessibility (Article 9), education (Article 24) and work and employment (Article 27), all of which are of crucial importance for the EU 2020 Strategy. Since the Convention, States Parties are bound to take into account the protection and promotion of the human rights of persons with disabilities in all policies and programmes. It is thus justified that the UNCRPD explicitly serves as a frame of reference for both targeted disability policy and disability mainstreaming across the various fields of action under the EU 2020 Strategy.

Concerning EU 2020 education targets, the reality reflects a strong disadvantage for people with disabilities, as stated in a European Commission (EC) Staff Working Document from 2014, reporting on the implementation of the UNCRPD by the European Union. The report highlights that around 19 per cent of young disabled people (aged eighteen to twenty-four) are early school leavers, as compared with 11 per cent of non-disabled young persons. These high rates of early school leavers among young disabled people may indicate problems relating to accessibility and a lack of adapted programmes, says the report. Also, it mentions that only around 27 per cent of people with disabilities in the thirty-to-thirty-four age group have successfully completed tertiary-level education, as compared with 37 per cent of non-disabled people.[4]

The EC working document also refers to an earlier report in 2012, compiled for the Commission by the Network of Experts in Social Science of Education and Training (NESSE).[5] This 2012 Report, specifically focussed on education and students with disabilities, stressed that despite Member States' stated commitment to promote inclusive education, too many learners with special needs were still placed in segregated institutions or in mainstream settings with inadequate support. The Report therefore called on Member States to work harder to develop inclusive education systems and to remove the barriers

4 European Commission, 'Report on the Implementation of the UN Convention on the Rights of Persons with Disabilities (CRPD) by the European Union' (Staff Working Document) SWD (2014) 182 Final 61.

5 Network of Experts in Social Science of Education and Training (NESSE), *Education and Disability/Special Needs: Policies and Practices in Education, Training and Employment for Students with Disabilities and Special Educational Needs in the EU* (European Commission 2012).

faced by vulnerable groups when it comes to participation and success in education, training and employment. It also underlined a wide variation between Member States as to how children with special needs are identified, and whether, after identification, they are placed in mainstream or special schools. The report emphasised as well the need to harmonise definitions in this field across the EU and to improve data gathering to enable Member States to compare their approaches more effectively and to learn from each other's experience. The European Agency for Special Needs and Inclusive Education, which is one of the advocacy experiences reviewed in this text (Section 2.2), has made a significant effort in this field.

Lastly, when reviewing the implementation of the right to education and how some of the quantitative targets seen earlier apply to people with disabilities, the occurrence of the economic crisis cannot be forgotten. The 2012 study *Assessing the Impact of European Governments' Austerity Plans on the Rights of Persons with Disabilities*, conducted by the European Consortium of Foundations on Human Rights and Disability, gathered crisis-specific data affirming that restricting resources for inclusive education is likely to result in higher school dropout rates by pupils with disabilities and to diminish the proportion of students going on to tertiary education.[6] Many of the measures taken in the times of crisis and identified by the study have the potential to seriously inhibit progress towards the EU 2020 Strategy objectives relating to employment, education, poverty and social exclusion.

1.2 *Strategic Framework for European Cooperation in Education and Training (ET2020)*

In the European Union, legislation on education relies on EU Member States. Therefore, EU institutions have limited power for regulation in this field, which they primarily implement through the so-called Open Method of Coordination (OMC), created in the framework of the Luxembourg process[7] and defined as an instrument of the Lisbon Strategy.[8] The OMC takes place in areas that fall within the competence of the Member States, education being one of them.

6 European Foundation Centre, *Assessing the Impact of European Governments' Austerity Plans on the Rights of Persons with Disabilities* (European Foundation Centre 2012).

7 It is the process evolved from the Luxembourg Jobs Summit in November 1997, with the result of the creation of the European Employment Strategy.

8 The Lisbon Strategy for Growth and Jobs was launched in 2000 as a response to globalisation, aimed at generating growth and more and better jobs by investing in people's skills, the greening of the economy and innovation.

In consequence, under this scheme of competences, Member States are responsible for the organisation of their education and training systems and for the content of teaching programmes, in accordance with the Treaty on the Functioning of the European Union (TFEU).[9] Its Article 165 establishes that the Union's role is to contribute to the development of quality education by encouraging cooperation between Member States and, if necessary, by supporting and supplementing their action.

This is where the OMC comes into play, acting as an intergovernmental process based on actions such as the following (which apply in the field of education): jointly identifying and defining objectives; establishing measuring instruments like statistics, indicators and guidelines; benchmarking the Member States' performance; or exchanging best practices. In this context, the European Commission's role is limited to surveillance and recommendations, including for example the revision of the National Reform Programmes to be established by the EU Member States.[10]

A key instrument of policy cooperation among Member States and the EU institutions pertaining to education is the Strategic Framework for European Cooperation in Education and Training (ET2020).[11] Through ET2020, Member States have identified four common objectives, which are: first, making lifelong learning and mobility a reality; second, improving the quality and efficiency of education and training; third, promoting equity, social cohesion and active citizenship; and fourth, enhancing creativity and innovation, including entrepreneurship, at all levels of education and training. The Education and Training Monitor[12] supports the implementation of ET2020 by strengthening the evidence-base and by linking it more closely to the broader Europe 2020 Strategy.

The third objective in ET2020 on promoting equity, social cohesion and active citizenship deserves special attention regarding inclusive education. Under this objective, it is stated that educational disadvantage should be addressed by providing high-quality early childhood education and targeted support, and by promoting inclusive education. Furthermore, it underlines that

9 Consolidated Version of the Treaty on the Functioning of the European Union [2012] OJ C326/47.

10 National Reform Programmes are documents which annually present the different EU Member States' policies and measures to sustain growth and jobs, and to reach the Europe 2020 targets.

11 Council Conclusions of 12 May 2009 on a Strategic Framework for European Cooperation in Education and Training (ET 2020) [2009] OJ C119/2.

12 The Education and Training Monitor can be accessed at http://ec.europa.eu/education/tools/et-monitor_en.htm.

education and training systems should aim to ensure that all learners – including those from disadvantaged backgrounds, those with special needs and migrants – complete their education, including, where appropriate, second chance education and the provision of more personalised learning. Education should promote intercultural competences, democratic values and respect for fundamental rights and the environment, as well as combat all forms of discrimination, and provide all young people with the right tools to interact positively with their peers from diverse backgrounds. Various needs for action are pointed out, such as to develop cooperation on the issue of learners with special needs, to promote inclusive education and personalised learning through timely support, to identify special needs early, to count with well-coordinated services the integration of services within mainstream schooling and to ensure pathways to further education and training.

The 2012 report on implementing ET2020[13] re-validates the references to inclusive education, stressing the need for EU Member States to reinforce mutual learning on effective ways to raise educational achievement in an increasingly diverse society, in particular by implementing inclusive educational approaches which allow all learners to achieve their full potential. This 2012 report also mentions that the situation of learners with special needs regarding mobility (seen as a factor to strengthen Europe's knowledge-based growth and as connected to the advocacy experience dealt with in Section 2.4) is insufficiently addressed, with specific reference to people with disabilities.

Finally in this context, the 2012 Communication on Rethinking Education: Investing in Skills for Better Socio-Economic Outcomes[14] is worth mentioning to highlight the support teachers need in relation to, among others, abilities on how to cater for diversity and inclusion and to meet the needs of disadvantaged learners, such as children with disabilities.

To conclude, although it cannot be said that the ET2020 leaves aside inclusive education (in fact, references to it have been increasing), the analysis indicates that there is not a comprehensive approach and many concerns affecting people with disabilities remain unsolved. In other words, the implications of the UNCRPD do not seem to be fully integrated into cooperation

13 Council and European Commission, '2012 Joint Report of the Council and the Commission on the Implementation of the Strategic Framework for European Cooperation in Education and Training (ET 2020): Education and Training in a Smart, Sustainable and Inclusive Europe' [2012] OJ C70/9.

14 European Commission, 'Rethinking Education: Investing in Skills for Better Socio-Economic Outcomes' COM(2012) 669 Final.

education policies to actually promote education for all. This certainly leaves a big area for advocacy on inclusive education. As we see in the following pages, this space has been strongly taken up by the disability movement and other organisations concerned with education for which inclusive education has become a solid demand.

2 ADVOCATING FOR INCLUSIVE EDUCATION: PAN-EUROPEAN EXPERIENCES

2.1 *The European Disability Movement and Inclusive Education: The Demands by the European Disability Forum*

It can be said that identifying education as a key issue in the agenda is a common trend in the sector of organisations representing people with disabilities and their families, whether or not the specific mission activities of these organisations are particularly focussed on education. The reflection carried out in the previous part of this chapter certainly confirms that a strong improvement is needed to effectively implement the right to education for people with disabilities and to build inclusive education systems on the field.

Following family background, education is the second pillar of socialisation and sets the frame for the development of an individual's potential for social inclusion and for later participation in the labour market – which is the main source for independent life. Therefore, non-discrimination of people with disabilities demands that the right to education must be a right for all, and inclusive education helps guarantee its implementation. This is, in short, the approach of many disability organisations and indeed the approach of the European disability movement represented by the European Disability Forum.

The European Disability Forum (EDF) is an independent organisation formed by various organisations around Europe that represent people with disabilities and their families among EU Member States and throughout Europe, and that deals with different types of disabilities. The EDF is the disability EU umbrella organisation, and it plays the role of a self-advocate, campaigning for the right of persons with disabilities to be fully involved in European policy-making processes.

The work of the EDF is premised on the idea that there are 80 million Europeans who have a role to play in society and refuse to be forgotten. 'Nothing about us, without us' and 'visibility of disability everywhere' are the slogans that define the EDF's advocacy activity. The EDF actively participated in the negotiations of the UNCRPD, including its Article 24. Moreover, the content and implementation of the UNCRPD structures all of the EDF's action.

Assuming the importance of the role of education for social inclusion and equal opportunities, and despite the limited competences of the European Union in this field (which relies on national governments as we have seen before), the EDF believes that the right to education should be considered and protected by the EU as part of its fundamental values and principles and a universal human right. Therefore the EDF works with the EU institutions and the Member States to make sure that quality education and freedom of choice become a reality for all people with disabilities in Europe.

In this context, special attention needs to be paid to an advocacy instrument that concentrates the key messages, concerns and demands of the disability movement at the European level: the 2009 EDF statement 'Inclusive Education: Moving from Words to Deeds'.[15] Some of the EDF's ideas within this statement were incorporated into the European Disability Strategy 2010–2020.

The statement was elaborated on the basis of Article 24 of the UNCRPD, following its different parts and structuring the discussion around the following central topics: moving towards inclusive education, accessing education in practice, learning life and social development skills, training teachers and going beyond basic education. The statement identifies Article 24 at the core of the UNCRPD and points out how it illustrates the paradigm shift from persons with disabilities being defined by their impairments and denied access to mainstream life, to persons with disabilities as rights holders empowered to fully participate in all aspects of life, where the barriers that prevent their equal participation are addressed.

Through this statement, intended particularly to contribute to the implementation of Article 24, the EDF emphasises that education must be recognised as a fundamental right, implying that persons with disabilities have the right to receive education of the same quality as any other person, in an environment that takes their needs into account. In order to achieve this, policies and legislation must address access, not only to schools and universities, but also to all other education opportunities in a lifelong learning perspective.[16]

15 European Disability Forum, 'Inclusive Education: Moving from Words to Deeds: Statement' (2009), http://cms.horus.be/files/99909/MediaArchive/library/EDF-Statement-Inclusive-Education.doc, accessed 5 February 2015.

16 María Antonia Casanova Rodríguez, *Educación Inclusiva: un Modelo de Futuro* (Wolters Kluwer Educacion España 2011); María Antonia Casanova Rodríguez and Miguel

In this document, the EDF also deals with a relevant debate that still needs to be kept in mind, since the UNCRPD does not explicitly define what 'inclusive education' is. This debate deals with the difference between integration and inclusion. The statement highlights that integration is understood as a matter of location or the placing of students with disabilities in mainstream schools, where they have to adapt to the existing teaching and learning systems and the schools' organisation. However, inclusion requires adapting the system to meet the needs of students with disabilities. The environment, teaching and learning and schools' organisation and education system must systematically be changed in order to remove barriers so that students with disabilities can maximise their academic and social achievements. In other words, the integration concept implies that the individual must adapt, whereas inclusion involves changes to the environment, pedagogy and organisation, that is, of the whole educational system, so that education effectively becomes a right for all. In this sense, the EDF clearly advocates that an inclusive approach is beneficial to all students and not only for those with disabilities or learning difficulties.

It is largely due to the advocacy activity of the EDF that education became part of the European Disability Strategy 2010–2020 as one of the eight areas for action, thus reflecting a key priority for the European disability movement. This Strategy is currently undergoing a revision process in which the EDF is highly involved.

In 2012, the EU set up a mechanism, the EU Monitoring Framework, to monitor the implementation of the UNCRPD. The EDF is a full member and chair of the Framework, together with the European Ombudsman, the European Agency of Fundamental Rights, the European Parliament and the European Commission. Moreover, the EDF takes part in the UNCRPD monitoring process at the UN level.[17] In fact, in March 2015, the EDF issued its Alternative Report on the implementation of the UNCRPD in Europe.[18]

With respect to education and UNCRPD Article 24, the EDF Alternative Report stresses that pupils and students with disabilities, especially those in

Ángel Cabra de Luna (eds), *Educación y Personas con Discapacidad: Presente y Futuro* (Fundación ONCE 2009); Organisation for Economic Co-operation and Development (OECD), *Inclusion of Students with Disabilities in Tertiary Education and Employment: Education and Training Policy* (OECD Publishing 2011).

17 Whilst the UNCRPD States Parties prepare their report for the UN Committee on the Rights of Persons with Disabilities (the body of independent experts which monitors implementation of the UNCRPD), organisations of people with disabilities can prepare an alternative report.

18 European Disability Forum, 'Alternative Report to the UN on the Rights of Persons with Disabilities' (2014), www.edf-feph.org/Page_Generale.asp?DocID=13854%26thebloc=34244, accessed 10 February 2015.

need of high-level support, are often excluded or do not have adequate access to education services. The EDF also argues that under the Employment Equality Directive,[19] persons with disabilities are protected against discrimination in education only in regard to vocational training. However, equal opportunities can only be achieved if the right to inclusive education is granted at all levels through the adoption of relevant legislation which prohibits any discrimination on the basis of disability in all fields – not only employment. Limitations are found nevertheless in the EU since, as explained previously in Section 1.2, education competences remain at the Member State level.

In addition, and very importantly, the Alternative Report draws attention to the lack of indicators to specifically measure the share of people with disabilities within EU2020 targets.

Therefore the EDF calls on the European Commission to support EU countries in developing inclusive education systems by promoting the use of European funding instruments to fund both the training of staff and accessibility, including research on accessible pedagogical material, and reasonable accommodation in education, whilst paying special attention to children in need of high-level support. According to the EDF, the Commission should also promote participation of persons with disabilities in EU exchange programmes, collect data and best practices at the national level to monitor the access to education of pupils with disabilities, support Member States in producing adequate reports based on comparable data and statistics and include disability-specific indicators in the Europe 2020 Strategy when pursuing the target on education.

A final comment must be made in regards to another EDF campaign priority: the observatory on the impact of the economic crisis on the rights of persons with disabilities. The EDF claims that the crisis in the EU is having devastating effects on the economic, political and social structures that have been built into European societies over the past few decades. It denounces that, despite the fact that the European Union's Europe 2020 Strategy has made social inclusion one of

The purpose of the EDF's Alternative Report is to inform the UN Committee about how the UNCRPD has been implemented by the EU and its institutions, agencies and bodies. The Report based its analysis on the gaps in the EU Report on the Implementation of the UNCRPD that the EU submitted to the UN Committee on 5 June 2014 (commented on in Section 1 of this chapter) and seeks to complement it where relevant with information received by EDF members and other stakeholders.

Lastly, it is worth mentioning that a connection between the UN Committee on the Rights of Persons with Disabilities and the EDF exists as one of the eighteen experts is also a member of the EDF Executive Committee.

19 Council Directive 2000/78/EC of 27 November 2000, Establishing a General Framework for Equal Treatment in Employment and Occupation [2000] OJ L303/16.

the three pillars to bring Europe out of the crisis, the economic, social and political policies adopted by Member States and the EU may increase the number of people experiencing social exclusion in Europe. The observatory was consequently created, acting as a monitoring tool of the measures taken by EU Member States, EU institutions and international financial institutions, based on the collection of examples provided by EDF members.

Since 2008, a position paper and three resolutions have been issued by the observatory. The last resolution, of 2012, recognised that the situation of people with disabilities in education and employment was disadvantaged even before the economic crisis, but that the crisis particularly exacerbated these issues.[20] The resolution calls on EU institutions, national governments, the International Monetary Fund and the World Bank to, among other actions, boost employment through the development of sustainable services promoting independent and community living for all persons with disabilities, and also through support for education, including accessible infrastructure. Similarly, the EDF 2015 Alternative Report on the implementation of the UNCRPD stated that it has been demonstrated that the financial crisis has negatively influenced efforts towards inclusive education.

We have seen the EDF's participation in the UNCRPD EU Monitoring Framework, but other interesting examples of stable collaborations include the close cooperation between the EDF and the European Parliament (particularly through the Disability Intergroup, with decades of history and renewed for the period 2014–2019) and the strong links of the EDF and EDF personalities with the European Economic and Social Committee (EESC), the most important EU consultative body; in all aforementioned scenarios, the issue of inclusive education has been on the agenda, encouraged by the EDF.[21] Worth mentioning also are the various EESC Opinions having the EDF's president as their rapporteur. These Opinions have dealt with topics such as the UNCRPD itself,[22] the structural funds,[23] the European Disability

20 European Disability Forum, 'Resolution on a Human Rights Way out of the Crisis' (2012), www.edf-feph.org/Page_Generale.asp?DocID=13854%26thebloc=13856, accessed 5 February 2015.

21 Through the EDF president, Mr Yannis Vardakastanis, member of the EESC since 2010, the European disability movement contributed to the reinforcement of the issue of disability on the European agenda.

22 European Economic and Social Committee (EESC), 'The Implementation and Monitoring of the UN Convention on the Rights of Persons with Disabilities by the EU Institutions and the Role of the EESC', Opinion SOC/464 EESC-2012-1468 [2013] OJ C44/28.

23 EESC, 'Proposal for a Regulation of the European Parliament and of the Council Laying Down Common Provisions on the European Regional Development Fund, the European Social Fund, the Cohesion Fund, the European Agricultural Fund for Rural Development

Strategy,[24] young persons with disabilities[25] and accessibility as a human right.[26] Many of these collaborations included strong demands for inclusive education.

The EDF's experience can be seen as a successful story of self-advocacy by people with disabilities and their representative organisations at the European level having unified in a single European voice the concerns and demands of people with different types of disabilities and from various national contexts. The EDF has spread important messages for the implementation of the rights of people with disabilities, both in the field of education and otherwise, and ensured that people with disabilities are on the European agenda, having been inspired by the UNCRPD. In this process, although with some difficulties, the organisation has consolidated its role as a central partner for the EU institutions regarding disability matters, including inclusive education.

2.2 *Institutional Advocacy: Intergovernmental Action by the European Agency for Special Needs and Inclusive Education*

As we have seen in Section 1.2, in the European Union, education is a competence that relies on the EU Member States. The aforementioned Open Method of Coordination allows for cooperation in, among others, the field of education, an example of which is the previously mentioned Strategic Framework for European Cooperation in Education and Training (ET2020).

Within this context, a relevant example of collaboration by governments specifically in the field of inclusive education exists in the EU – the European Agency for Special Needs and Inclusive Education. It is the second pan-European advocacy experience examined in this chapter and reflects how cooperation among national public authorities can help to progress inclusive education, despite and beyond differences between countries' approaches to education and education systems.

and the European Maritime and Fisheries Fund Covered by the Common Strategic Framework and Laying Down General Provisions on the European Regional Development Fund, the European Social Fund and the Cohesion Fund and Repealing Regulation (EC) No 1083/2006', Opinion ECO/314 EESC-2012-1040 [2012] OJ C191/30.

24 EESC, 'Communication from the Commission to the European Parliament, the Council, the European Economic and Social Committee and the Committee of the Regions – European Disability Strategy 2010-2020: A Renewed Commitment to a Barrier-Free Europe', COM (2010) 636 Final Opinion SOC/403 EESC-2011-1382 [2011] OJ C376/81.

25 EESC, 'Young Persons with Disabilities: Employment, Inclusion and Participation in Society', Opinion SOC/439 EESC-2012-826 [2012] OJ C181/2.

26 EESC, 'Accessibility as a Human Right', (Opinion) TEN/515 EESC-2013.

Established in 1996, the European Agency for Special Needs and Inclusive Education is an independent, self-governing European organisation that brings together the ministries of education of its member countries (the European Union, Iceland, Norway and Switzerland), acting as a platform for cooperation. Born ten years prior to the approval of the UNCRPD, the Agency evolved from increasing collaboration among various European countries and the implementation of specific programmes to a more permanent and systematic structure for pan-European collaboration.

Funded by the national members and the European Commission, the Agency's aim is to improve educational policy and practice for learners with special educational needs, taking into account issues such as equal opportunities, accessibility, inclusive education and the promotion of quality education. Recognising that there are differences in countries' policies, practices and educational contexts, the Agency's work has a series of strategic objectives: to promote quality in the field of special needs education through the maintenance of a long-term framework for extended European collaboration; to provide a reliable reflection of the reality of special needs education across Europe with up-to-date information that can be related to individual countries' national contexts; to identify key factors that hinder or support positive experiences; and to facilitate effective exchange of knowledge, experience and relevant information among, as well as within, member countries.[27]

As an institutional advocacy experience, it is worth noting, the Agency's declared target groups are the policy makers and the experts and professionals who influence policy and practice in special needs education. Therefore it works as an interesting example of public authorities being simultaneously subject and object of the aim of promoting the implementation of the right to education for all, with inclusive education as a central issue.[28]

The work of the Agency was at first inspired by various relevant international documents, statements and policy instruments such as the UN Standard Rules on the Equalization of Opportunities for Persons with Disabilities (1993),[29] the Salamanca Statement (1994)[30] and the Charter

[27] European Agency for Special Needs and Inclusive Education, 'What We Do', www.european-agency.org/about-us/what-we-do, accessed 13 February 2015.

[28] European Agency for Special Needs and Inclusive Education, 'Articles of Association' (2010), www.european-agency.org/sites/default/files/about-us/articles/Articles-of-Association-2016w.pdf, accessed 13 February 2015.

[29] United Nations General Assembly, 'Standard Rules on the Equalization of Opportunities for Persons with Disabilities' (20 December 1993) A/RES/48/96.

[30] United Nations Educational, Scientific and Cultural Organization (UNESCO) and Ministry of Education and Science Spain, The Salamanca Statement and Framework for Action on Special Needs Education (ED-94/WS/18, UNESCO 1994).

of Luxembourg (1996).[31] Their work later aligned with the United Nations Educational, Scientific and Cultural Organization (UNESCO) Dakar Framework for Action Education for All: Meeting Our Collective Commitments (2000)[32] and the Madrid Declaration (2002),[33] and since 2006, the UNCRPD has been the central inspiration, along with the UNESCO Policy Guidelines on Inclusion in Education (2008).[34]

Two other milestones have importantly contributed to the basis of the Agency's later work: 'The Conference on Inclusive Education: A Way to Promote Social Cohesion', held in Madrid on 11–12 March 2010 under the EU Spanish presidency,[35] and the Conclusions from the council meeting of the Ministers of Education on the Social Dimension of Education and Training of May 2010.[36]

Considering the contributions and suggestions made by country members of priority themes, the Agency has developed several projects regarding topics relating to special educational needs and inclusive education. Some of them are: information and communication technologies (ICT) and accessibility, including accessible information provision for lifelong learning; raising the achievement for all learners in inclusive education; the organisation of provision to support inclusive education; vocational educational training and special needs; teacher education for inclusion; promoting quality in inclusive education; early childhood intervention; multicultural diversity and special needs education; and assessment in inclusive settings and indicators for inclusive education.

The Agency has produced several valuable reports that build a remarkable corpus of knowledge on inclusive education in Europe and that deal with all of

31 European Agency for Special Needs and Inclusive Education, 'Charter of Luxembourg November 1996' (1996), www.european-agency.org/sites/default/files/CHARTER-of-LUXEMBOURG-November-1996.pdf, accessed 13 February 2015.

32 UNESCO, The Dakar Framework for Action: Education for All: Meeting Our Collective Commitments (UNESCO 2000).

33 The Madrid Declaration was adopted in March 2002 at a large European disability congress held in Madrid, and can be consulted at www.disabilityworld.org/09-10_02/news/madrid.shtml.

34 UNESCO, Policy Guidelines on Inclusion in Education (UNESCO 2009) ED-2009/WS/31.

35 Ministerio de Educación de España, 'La Educación Inclusiva: vía Para Davorecer la Cohesión Social' (European Agency for Special Needs and Inclusive Education 2010), www.european-agency.org/sites/default/files/Conclusions-Madrid-conference.pdf, accessed 13 February 2015.

36 Council of the European Union, 'Council Conclusions on the Social Dimension of Education and Training' (European Agency for Special Needs and Inclusive Education 2010), www.european-agency.org/sites/default/files/Council-Conclusions-May-2010-Social-Dimension.pdf, accessed 13 February 2015.

the aforementioned topics. This material evolves from different collaborative projects involving the national partners.

Worth noting for this chapter is the work carried out on the organisation of provision to support inclusive education, which examined how systems of provision are organised to meet the needs of learners with disabilities under the terms of the UNCRPD.[37] The project included research and recommendations for policy makers, addressing several relevant issues to improve systems of support for all learners, in particular for those with disabilities in mainstream schools. The main idea was that countries needed to clarify their view of inclusion and focus on building the capability of all schools to cater for learner diversity rather than distributing additional resources to meet the needs of identified groups.[38]

The recommendations refer first to child rights and participation, calling policy makers to review national legislation and education policy to ensure that they are consistent with and actively support the principles of both the United Nations Convention on the Rights of the Child and the UNCRPD, and uphold the right of all learners to full participation in school with their own local peer group, including in particular the right to education and inclusion, non-discrimination on the grounds of disability, the right of the child to express his or her view and access to assistance.

Further recommendations point out the need to clarify the concept of inclusion across and between levels of the educational system, connecting it with quality and equity for all learners, as well as to address underachievement by all vulnerable groups, including children with disabilities. Policy makers are also encouraged to consider and to enhance collaboration and partnerships among different national and local stakeholders, including public authorities, local education and school leaders, teachers, other professionals, students, parents and local services, thus contributing to build the 'inclusive capability' of the education system as a whole. Incentives for schools to include all students should be provided in addition to methods of assessment, inspections and other accountability measures to support inclusive practice.

The Agency's recommendations finally encourage policy makers to develop a 'continuum of support' for inclusive education aimed at teachers, support staff and school leaders on the basis of research and networking. Moreover, the role of special schools and specialist knowledge should be developed as

37 The Organisation of Provision to Support the Inclusive Education Project, conducted by the Agency, was carried out from 2011 to 2013.

38 European Agency for Special Needs and Inclusive Education, 'Organization of Provision to Support Inclusive Education: Policy Brief' (2013), www.european-agency.org/sites/default/files/OoP_Policy_Brief_EN.pdf, accessed 11 February 2015.

a resource to increase the capability of mainstream schools and to improve support for learners. Furthermore, more accessible curriculum and assessment frameworks should be developed, and greater flexibility in pedagogy, school organisation and resource allocation should be provided, so that schools can work innovatively to implement a continuum of support for learners, rather than fit them into an existing system.

Besides the several collaborative projects, thematic studies and publications, the Agency is a reference for providing information on inclusive education at the national level, and is supported by the contributions of its country members. The Agency's relevant advocating role is also consolidated on the basis of its ties and stable collaborations with other relevant organisations and bodies such as Eurydice[39] and Eurostat, UNESCO,[40] the Organisation for Economic Co-operation and Development (OECD) and the European Centre for the Development of Vocational Training (CEDEFOP).

A final remark must be made on the actions carried out by the Agency to give a voice to the students themselves. The Agency has been the first to use 'hearings' in the field of inclusive education; these have been held in relevant institutions such as the European Parliament. In 2003, in the context of the European Year of People with Disabilities, a first hearing on 'young views on special needs education' was celebrated with the participation of several students with disabilities from around Europe. The outcome was the drafting of a document reflecting the main discussion, concerns and testimonials, translated into the different EU languages.[41] A similar hearing was held later in 2011, and a new document on the results was produced.[42]

This advocacy instrument was also implemented under the EU Portuguese presidency in 2007 through the hearing at the Assembleia da República which resulted in the widely known 'Lisbon Declaration',[43] and a more recent

39 The Eurydice Network provides information on and analyses of European education systems and policies.

40 The Agency has developed the Inclusive Education in Action (IEA) Project in collaboration with UNESCO, which is aimed at identifying and disseminating policies, practices, stories and different materials that exemplify the suggested actions in the UNESCO Policy Guidelines on Inclusion in Education.

41 European Agency for Special Needs and Inclusive Education, *Young Views on Special Needs Education: Results of the Hearing in the European Parliament* (European Agency for Special Needs and Inclusive Education 2005).

42 European Agency for Special Needs and Inclusive Education, Young Views on Inclusive Education: European Parliament Hearing: Brussels, November 2011 (European Agency for Special Needs and Inclusive Education 2012), www.european-agency.org/sites/default/files/young-views-on-inclusive-education_YoungViews-2012EN.pdf, accessed 11 February 2015.

43 European Agency for Special Needs and Inclusive Education, 'Lisbon Declaration: Young People's Views on Inclusive Education' (2007), www.european-agency.org/sites/default/files/lis

hearing held in October 2015 under the EU presidency of Luxembourg which led to the 'Luxemburg Recommendations'. The recommendations have been grouped around five key messages expressed by young people during their discussions and presentation of results. These messages refer to the following: 'Everything about us, with us' – young people should be directly involved in all decision-making that concerns them; 'Barrier-free schools' – all physical and technical barriers must be eliminated; 'Breaking down stereotypes' – what lies behind the concept of 'normality', because if we accept that everybody is different, who then is 'normal'? People should behave with mutual respect and tolerance; 'Diversity is the mix, inclusion is what makes the mix work' – everyone should focus on what can be done, not on what cannot be done; 'Becoming full citizens' – inclusive education in mainstream schools is a crucial aspect to lead to full inclusion in society.[44]

The Luxembourg Recommendations were presented to the Council of Ministers during the 'Education, Youth, Culture and Sports' meeting on 23 November 2015, and to the Education Committee on 2–3 December 2015, for their consideration.

Finally, an instrument that reflects the role of the Agency to advance and coordinate efforts on an issue that, in the end, remains a national domain is the 2016 Position on Inclusive Education Systems. This paper presents the Agency member countries' vision for inclusive education systems, and is focussed on ensuring that all learners of any age are provided with meaningful, high-quality educational opportunities in their local community, alongside their friends and peers. It underlines that all European countries are committed to working towards more inclusive education systems, but they do so in different ways, depending on their past and current contexts and histories.[45]

The example of the Agency as an advocacy experience showcases how even with strong differences in context, reality and resources, EU Members are willing to improve themselves in regards to inclusive education by exchanging experiences, learning from each other and setting relevant coordination mechanisms for information gathering and analysis. It could be seen as a 'circular' experience where Member States evolve from being 'subjects' of

bon-declaration-young-people2019s-views-on-inclusive-education_declaration_en.pdf, accessed 11 February 2015.

[44] European Agency for Special Needs and Inclusive Education, 'European Hearing: Luxembourg Recommendations' (2015), www.european-agency.org/sites/default/files/European_Hearing_Luxembourg_Recommendations.pdf, accessed 1 March 2016.

[45] European Agency for Special Needs and Inclusive Education, *Agency Position on Inclusive Education Systems* (European Agency for Special Needs and Inclusive Education 2015).

advocacy to 'objects' of advocacy, seeking to influence their own policy-making processes.

2.3 *The European Network for Inclusive Education and Disability: A Multi-Stakeholder and Multi-Instrument Advocacy Experience*

For the purpose of this chapter, we have selected a third advocacy experience resulting from civil society, disability and social economy organisations, with strong participation of the various actors that take part in what can be understood broadly as the 'educational community'.

The European Network on Inclusive Education and Disability (incluD-ed), is a network of organisations working on disability and inclusive education in Europe. The network is a pioneering initiative, initiated in 2009, which is co-financed by the European Social Fund (the main funding instrument of the European Employment Strategy) through the Spanish Operational Programme 'Fight against Discrimination 2007–2013', which ran until 2015.[46]

The main purpose of incluD-ed is to promote equal opportunities in the educational context for people with disabilities around Europe, and to actively contribute to the elimination of barriers in this field. The network is based on collaborative work among different social players involved in the educational process and advocates for inclusive education as a key element for an inclusive society, not only for people with disability but for all. As we see in the following pages, this network concentrates a variety of advocacy instruments used for achieving its mission and has developed a wide range of messages on specific topics dealing with inclusive education. The network involves several actors from a multi-stakeholder approach, and develops its work from a pan-European perspective.[47]

The work of incluD-ed has been inspired and developed in close connection with many policies and instruments which have already been mentioned: the UNCRPD, particularly Article 24 on education and Article 27 on work and employment; the European Strategy Europe 2020 for Smart, Sustainable and Inclusive Growth, specifically its objectives on education; the European Disability Strategy 2010–2020, especially its area focussed on promoting inclusive education and lifelong learning; the Strategic Framework for European Cooperation in Education and Training (ET2020), regarding its strategic

[46] At the time of revising this chapter, incluD-ed had formally ended since the project finished on 31 December 2015.

[47] For incluD-ed objectives, see 'About the Network', www.includ-ed.eu/about-network, accessed 3 March 2015.

objective of promoting equity, social cohesion and active citizenship; and lastly the broad concern by the EU institutions and all EU Member States on tackling youth unemployment.

Indeed, incluD-ed was conceived as an advocacy instrument and as a form of contribution to the implementation of all these policies that affect people with disabilities and the overall objective of effectively developing the right to education for all in Europe.

Led by a reference organisation from the social economy and the third sector, Fundación ONCE (for which the authors work), incluD-ed partners each contributed with their own resources to the network's activities and objectives under the so-called transnational cooperation activities foreseen by the European Social Fund.[48] incluD-ed founding partners came from four different countries with diverse situations regarding inclusive education, but all shared the same interest on the matter, which they viewed as an approach to guarantee equal opportunities for all, with special attention to people with disabilities.

The network founding partners included Fundación ONCE, based in Spain[49] (already mentioned as the leading organisation), the Association des Paralysés de France (APF),[50] the Finnish organisation Kynnys[51] and the Rytmus association[52] from the Czech Republic. As previously stated, these partners came from very different national contexts representing the western, northern and eastern regions of the EU, with their backgrounds regarding inclusive education being diverse. Thus, the network had Spain, a country

48 Transnational Cooperation was regulated in Article 10 of Regulation (EU) No. 1304/2013 of the European Parliament and of the Council of 17 December 2013 on the European Social Fund and Repealing Council Regulation (EC) No. 1081/2006 [2013] OJ L 347/470.

49 As stated at the beginning of this chapter, Fundación ONCE's mission is to promote the quality of life of people with disabilities and their families, with a special focus on the areas of training, employment and universal accessibility of environments, goods and services. Founded by the National Organization of the Blind in Spain (ONCE), Fundación ONCE gathers in its board of trustees the main Spanish organisations representing people with disabilities and their families, including the Spanish Committee of Representatives of Persons with Disabilities (CERMI). Fundación ONCE is also an associate member of the EDF.

50 The APF is a national movement representing people with physical or loco-motor disabilities, as well as their families. The APF's role is to advocate for people with disabilities in all dimensions of life, seeking for the implementation of rights and active citizenship.

51 Kynnys (with head offices in Helsinki and branches in the cities of Tampere, Kuopio, Jyvaskyla, Oulu and Turku) advocates for the rights of people with disabilities in different areas and their independent living. One of their central themes to focus on is the participation of people with disabilities in the educational system (which is not always as inclusive as could be expected in such an environment).

52 Rytmus has its main operations in Prague and in the Karlovy Vary region, but it also has extended activity throughout the Czech Republic with the mission to advocate and facilitate the participation of people with disabilities in society, with a special dedication to employment and education, implementing a set of programmes and services for this purpose.

with an inclusive approach to education but suffering strong impacts from the economic crisis; France, a complex environment regarding diversity with an evolving reality towards inclusion in education; Finland, a country widely known for its quality education system and holding top positions in rankings such as PISA;[53] and the Czech Republic, a country still very much dealing with the role of special education schools, segregation and the transition to a more inclusive model.

incluD-ed also relied on other partner organisations acting as associate members, whose role is to further spread the work done and the key messages from the network and the founding partners in the EU. The associated members represented organisations (including universities and research institutions) from other countries such as Austria, Iceland, Ireland, Romania and the United Kingdom, all of which have diverse backgrounds and approaches regarding inclusive education and people with disabilities.[54]

In addition, incluD-ed acted as a network of networks, based on the figure of the Local Promoting Groups, which enhances the multi-stakeholder and collaborative nature of this European initiative, complementing it with a necessary local approach. The Local Promoting Groups are an instrument designed for deepening the work on inclusive education using local contexts, bringing together various actors in the field that are involved in the educational system and educational community.[55]

incluD-ed understood that equal opportunities and inclusive education are key factors for employability, work and social inclusion. In this sense, and in accordance with the scope of the European Social Fund, the network focussed on four main areas, which are considered key for connecting education to

53 The Programme for International Student Assessment (PISA), run by the OECD, assesses the knowledge and skills of fifteen-year-old students on reading, mathematics, science and problem-solving. The last PISA report was issued in 2012.

54 The associated member organisations were 'Quearum. Cultural and Social Research' (a private research organisation from Austria); the University of Akureyri in Iceland; the Inclusion Ireland organisation; Association Reninco from Romania; the Centre for Studies on Inclusive Education (CSIE) from the United Kingdom; and, again from France, like the founding partner APF, the International Foundation of Applied Disability Research (FIRAH).

55 The Local Promoting Groups were led by the four network founding partners in their countries and cities of origin and gathered national, regional or local authorities; schools; organisations representing teachers, parents, people with disabilities, universities and research institutions; individual experts; companies; and corporate foundations working on the issue of education or the media, among others. Each Local Promoting Group has set its own work plan and activities according to its priorities to better advocate for the right to education for all in their local contexts.

employability and later participation in the labour market: secondary education, working to overcome specific barriers and address the challenges in this level; transition to higher levels of education (university and vocational training); transition to adult life and the labour market, including social and communicative skills and lifelong learning; and new technologies to narrow the digital divide and make them a real instrument to increase participation of people with disabilities in education and employment.

As one advocacy instrument, incluD-ed dedicated a great part of its efforts to identifying, exchanging and spreading good practices that foster inclusive education for people with disabilities across Europe. It was understood that good practices on inclusive education have an important role in showcasing that challenges can be met and that concrete organisations and people are working and using their resources for this purpose.[56] The network sought to inspire others and to advocate for the right to education by sharing specific examples of good practices in inclusive education.

The contribution of incluD-ed to the field of good practice exchange was also based on the elaboration of good practice criteria. Developed with the collaboration of experts, these criteria sought to better define what makes a good initiative, project or activity that fosters inclusive education. The criteria refer to different variables such as impact, innovation, transferability, sustainability, participation of people with disabilities, broad-based participation of different stakeholders and evaluation. incluD-ed also determined the importance of identifying individual experts and organisations that work on inclusive education around Europe. All of these individuals and entities established the 'incluD-ed virtual community', a common space from which inclusive education was promoted, with several and diverse contributors from the EU.[57]

incluD-ed founding partners, associate members, the Local Promoting Groups and their participants and the experts and organisations of the virtual community together created an outstanding network-based force of voices, seeking jointly to achieve a more inclusive Europe based on the right to education for all.

[56] incluD-ed compiled several examples of projects and initiatives focussed on inclusive education and disability led by different entities around Europe. Good practices collected in incluD-ed have been disseminated in a specific section of the initiative's website, www.includ-ed.eu/good-practices, accessed 3 March 2015.

[57] For this purpose, a database was elaborated which includes the profiles and contact details of those experts and organisations willing to have their work and expertise shared, and to connect with others with similar concerns.

incluD-ed also implemented other methods of advocacy, directly aimed at policies and policy makers. One of its undertakings worth highlighting was the Conference on Inclusive Education and Disability held at the European Parliament in Brussels on 9 April 2014, co-organised by Members of the European Parliament (MEPs) and the incluD-ed Network. Member of the European Parliament Rosa Estaràs Ferragut hosted this pioneering event at the European Parliament with the support of MEP Ádám Kósa (vice-president and co-president of the European Parliament's Disability Intergroup, respectively). With attendees representing all EU institutions, national governments and key stakeholders, the Conference offered an overview of inclusive education systems being implemented and the main actions carried out at the European level, as well as the most important future challenges. Ultimately, the Conference furthered a new momentum in the political debate on inclusive education in the EU.

For this event, the incluD-ed network elaborated and shared a statement, building on the position of the EDF.[58] The statement pointed out the key aspects to focus on regarding inclusive education and disability, and the aspects which should be considered in the legislative period 2014–2019. The statement, called 'Promoting Inclusive Education Systems in Europe', was handed formally to the MEPs, and concentrated key messages were addressed to the EU institutions. Based on the UNCRPD, particularly Article 24, and the European Charter of Fundamental Rights (articles 21 and 26 on persons with disabilities), the statement stresses that in order to take the vision of the Europe 2020 Strategy and to achieve a smart, sustainable and inclusive economy in coming years, inclusive education systems need to be promoted, developed and established throughout the EU. High levels of employment, productivity and social cohesion – priorities of EU2020 – cannot be achieved without establishing inclusive education systems.

Furthermore, the text highlights that EU Member States have already experienced positive results after implementing inclusive education for students with special educational needs, that inclusive education benefits all learners and strengthens social cohesion and that access to and permanence in the education system ensures equal opportunities for all and is a main source of labour and social inclusion.

Finally, in this statement, incluD-ed articulated key demands to the EU institutions to foster the development of inclusive education systems by

[58] incluD-ed, 'Statement on Promoting Inclusive Education Systems in Europe' (2014), www.includ-ed.eu/resource/statement-promoting-inclusive-education-systems-europe, accessed 3 March 2015.

Member States at all levels which: enable early special educational needs detection mechanisms for qualified early and personalised support; establish mechanisms that facilitate transitions between the different stages of education and from education to employment; set a framework of services that supports inclusive education, particularly for students that require high-level support; promote the participation of students with special educational needs in post-compulsory education and university; enhance universally accessible curricula for lifelong learning and accessibility of ICT in an educational context; reinforce teacher training to ensure quality inclusive education; and monitor progress, collect reliable data and promote best practices.

In September 2015, the main content of the incluD-ed statement was transformed in the Written Declaration by the European Parliament,[59] and this was circulated for signature among all MEPs under the leadership of MEP Rosa Estaràs, with the support of numerous co-authors from various countries and political groups. Open for three months, as stipulated for this kind of initiative, the Written Declaration gathered the signatures of 263 MEPs. Although this significant number did not reach the minimum necessary for a European Parliament majority (half of the seats plus one additional seat) in order for it to be formally adopted, these data are a strong indicator that inclusive education in Europe is becoming increasingly important, largely thanks to advocacy actions. A huge effort in raising awareness among and disseminating this Written Declaration to all the MEPs was made in collaboration with the incluD-ed network as well as with the EDF.[60]

59 European Parliament Written Declaration 0029/2015 of 7 September 2015 on Promoting Inclusive Education Systems, www.europarl.europa.eu/sides/getDoc.do?pubRef=-%2F%2FEP%2F%2FNONSGML%2BWDECL%2BP8-DCL-2015-0029%2B0%2BDOC%2BPDF%2BV0%2F%2FEN, accessed 7 June 2016.

60 Other advocacy actions carried out by incluD-ed and directly addressed to policy makers included the production and dissemination among key stakeholders at the European level of position papers on different topics such as the European Commissions' funding programme, 'Erasmus for all'; the U-Multirank, a university ranking system set up with European funding, publicly launched under the Irish EU presidency in Dublin in January 2013; the Commission's Proposal for a Directive on the Accessibility of Public Sector Bodies' Websites; the OECD Programmes for International Student Assessment (PISA) and for the International Assessment of Adult Competencies (PIAAC); the European Public Consultation on the Europe 2020 Strategy; the education objectives under the EU Disability, and the European Mobility Card. In this context, incluD-ed also collaborated in the preparation of European Parliament questions on inclusive education addressed to Commissioners who work in this field. References to these position papers are: incluD-ed, 'Views of the European Network on Inclusive Education and Disability on the Proposal "Erasmus for all"' (2012), www.includ-ed.eu/resource/views-european-network-inclusive-education-disability-proposal-%E2%80%9Cerasmus-all%E2%80%9D, accessed 3 March 2015; incluD-ed, 'Views of the European Network on Inclusive Education and Disability IncluD-

There are two other initiatives that drove incluD-ed's final advocacy action in 2015 which are worth noting. The first one deals with research and analysis, and the second one with generating international debate.

The first action is a pilot study called *Quality Factors of Inclusive Education in Europe. An Exploration*,[61] aimed at exploring the quality of inclusive processes in various schools in several European countries, taking into account elements for quality inclusive education relating to culture, policies and practices, as well as elements relating to available human and material resources. The study concludes that inclusive education, with its overall objective to meet the common and special needs of students, is a demanding process in which these different elements combine. The study was conducted in the four European countries of incluD-ed's founding partners (Spain, France, Finland and the Czech Republic) as well as in Austria, the United Kingdom, Ireland and Iceland (incluD-ed's associated member organisations[62]).

ed on U-Multirank' (2013), www.includ-ed.eu/resource/views-european-network-inclusive-education-disability-includ-ed-u-multirank, accessed 3 March 2015; incluD-ed, 'Views of incluD-ed on the Commission's Proposal for a Directive on the Accessibility of Public Sector Bodies' Websites' (2013), www.includ-ed.eu/resource/views-includ-ed-commission%E2%80%99s-proposal-directive-accessibility-public-sector-bodies%E2%80%99-website, accessed 3 March 2015; incluD-ed, 'Views of the incluD-ed Network on the OECD Programme for International Student Assessment (PISA)' (2013), www.includ-ed.eu/resource/views-includ-ed-network-oecd-programme-international-student-assessment-pisa, accessed 3 March 2015; incluD-ed, 'Views of the European Network on Inclusive Education and Disability on the OECD Programme for the International Assessment of Adult Competencies (PIAAC)' (2014), www.includ-ed.eu/resource/views-european-network-inclusive-education-disability-oecd-programme-international-assessme, accessed 3 March 2015; incluD-ed, 'Contribution by the European Network on Inclusive Education and Disability, incluD-ed to the European Public Consultation on the Europe 2020 Strategy' (2014), www.includ-ed.eu/resource/contribution-european-network-inclusive-education-disability-includ-ed-european-public-cons, accessed 3 March 2015; incluD-ed, 'Views of incluD-ed on the EU Disability Strategy and Education Objectives' (2015), www.includ-ed.eu/resource/views-includ-ed-eu-disability-strategy-education-objectives, accessed 3 March 2015; incluD-ed, 'Views of the European Network on Inclusive Education & Disability, incluD-ed, on EDF's proposal of a European Mobility Card' (2015), www.includ-ed.eu/resource/views-european-network-inclusive-education-disability-includ-ed-edf%E2%80%99s-proposal-european-mob, accessed 7 June 2016.

61 Jorge Calero and Ximena Pérez Benasco, *Quality Factors of Inclusive Education in Europe: An Exploration* (incluD-ed 2015), www.includ-ed.eu/sites/default/files/documents/quality_factors_of_inclusive_education_final_en.pdf, accessed 8 June 2016.

The Study has been coordinated by Carla Bonino and Maria Tussy (Fundación ONCE); the authors are Jorge Calero and Ximena Pérez Benasco (University of Barcelona), with the technical support of the incluD-ed Technical Secretariat, operated by PAU Education.

62 One of the bases of the study is the application of a questionnaire that also serves as a self-assessment tool for schools concerning the complexity of factors that can lead to inclusive education.

The second action, study visits, were derived from a figure developed within incluD-ed since 2014. Particularly, as a result of a study visit of incluD-ed founding partners to UNESCO, both platforms organised an international online debate on vocational education and training from an inclusive perspective: *Inclusive Technical Vocational Education and Training (TVET) in the Context of Lifelong Learning: Empowering People with Disabilities with Skills for Work and Life*. During the course of three weeks between October and November 2015, this debate gathered contributions from experts around the globe, and ended up with a document of conclusions and recommendations[63] in line with the UNCRPD as well as with the UN Sustainable Development Goals, in which education and employment are to be fostered in a framework of inclusiveness.[64]

In conclusion, incluD-ed represented a relevant advocacy experience that distinctively combined the participation of several different stakeholders coming from a variety of contexts that deal with inclusive education. The network operated from a global and local perspective, and took a collaborative approach, using a wide range of advocacy instruments, all aimed at promoting a more inclusive Europe, by means of inclusive education. This combined approach (involving actors, having a scope of action and variety of advocacy instruments), on top of the blend of public and private funding, made incluD-ed an outstanding story of partnership for advocating inclusive education that does not only consider its results, but also its own nature.

2.4 *Fostering Mobility in Europe, by Students for Students: ExchangeAbility*

After examining European advocacy experiences that broadly deal with the issue of inclusive education, the authors have selected a final example that focusses on a particular aspect of education and the participation of people with disabilities, which shows its increasing importance in our current societies and in the EU: educational mobility. In addition, this advocacy example has a distinctive feature that makes it worthy of special attention: it is promoted by the students themselves.

63 incluD-ed and UNESCO, 'UNESCO and incluD-ed Collaborate for a More Inclusive Society Launching an e-Discussion on Inclusive Technical Vocational Education and Training' (2015), www.includ-ed.eu/es/newsandevents/unesco-includ-ed-collaborate-more-inclusive-society-launching-e-discussion-inclusive-0, accessed 10 June 2016.

64 Other advocacy tools developed by the European Network for Inclusive Education and Disability involve communication actions (such as videos, newsletters and the website).

As noted in this chapter's Section 1, it is widely recognised that participation in higher education and mobility is one of the pillars for employability and integration in the labour market as it leads to a higher guarantee of quality employment. A study released in 2014 (by the European Commission) on the impact of the European Union's Erasmus student exchange programme found that young people who study or train abroad not only gain knowledge in specific disciplines, but also strengthen key transversal skills which employers highly value. The study shows that graduates with international experience are half as likely to experience long-term unemployment (compared with those who have not studied or trained abroad) and that five years after graduation, their unemployment rate is 23 per cent lower.[65]

According to the European Commission Staff Working Document from 2014, which reports on the implementation of the UNCRPD by the European Union, people with disabilities have a lower participation than non-disabled people in tertiary education.[66] Furthermore, students with disabilities represent a very small proportion in mobility programmes – not even 1 per cent. Students with special needs represented only 0.13 per cent of the total number of Erasmus students in 2011–2012,[67] a figure that mirrors the fact that participation of students with special needs in higher education is limited generally.

The advocacy experience selected is a network run by students for students: the International Exchange Erasmus Student Network, and its project ExchangeAbility.

The International Exchange Erasmus Student Network (ESN) was born in 1990, and works to create a more mobile and flexible education environment by supporting and developing the student exchange. The network is present in more than 430 higher education institutions from thirty-seven countries, with more than 13,500 active members, offering its services to around 180,000 international students every year.

The ESN developed a specific project called 'ExchangeAbility',[68] which is aimed at increasing the participation of students with disabilities in mobility

[65] European Commission, *Effects of Mobility on the Skills and Employability of Students and the Internationalisation of Higher Education Institutions* (European Union 2014). The study, compiled by independent experts, is the largest of its kind and received feedback from nearly 80,000 respondents, including students and businesses.

[66] European Commission Staff Working Document (n. 4) 61. According to this report, of people with disabilities in the thirty-to-thirty-four age group, only around 27 per cent have successfully completed tertiary-level education, as compared with 37 per cent of non-disabled people.

[67] European Commission, 'On the Way to ERASMUS+: A Statistical Overview of the ERASMUS Programme in 2011-12' (2013), http://ec.europa.eu/education/library/reports/erasmus1112_en.pdf, accessed 2 March 2015.

[68] The project can be accessed at http://exchangeability.esn.org/.

programmes, and at the same time making the ESN an accessible organisation itself. The ExchangeAbility project started in order to acknowledge the data reflecting the low proportion of students with special needs among Erasmus students, and to seek to improve the situation.

For this purpose, ExchangeAbility involves various partners representing disability organisations at the European level, such as the EDF, Autism Europe or the European Network for Independent Living; the sector of service providers represented by the European Association of Service Providers for Persons with Disabilities (EASPD); EU institutions including the European Commission and the European Economic and Social Committee; and specific higher education networks such as the Association for Higher Education Access and Disability (AHEAD) or the Network of Universities from Capitals of Europe (UNICA).

A key action of the ExchangeAbility project is 'MapAbility', which was funded by the Council of Europe through the European Youth Foundation funding programmes.[69] MapAbility has the objective of mapping European higher education institutions' accessibility and services for students with disabilities, in order to provide practical information, and to encourage their participation in mobility programmes.

The result of MapAbility is an online map devised using research arising out of submissions from a detailed questionnaire on the accessibility level of higher education facilities and the services offered to students with disabilities throughout Europe. This questionnaire was created by a committed team of students and submitted by disability coordinators in the different countries with the help of ESN volunteers.

Besides the practical objectives of the project, MapAbility also has a mission to promote common understanding of the different forms of disability, and the diverse range of accessibility needs in Europe.

The need for people with disabilities to participate in higher education and mobility programmes has been outlined by the disability movement at the European level, which takes us back to the first advocacy experience, thus closing the circle. According to the EDF Alternative Report on the implementation of the UNCRPD in Europe to the UN Committee on the Rights of Persons with Disabilities (stated in Section 2.1),[70] EU regulation and student exchange programmes have been improved in recent years by including financial support for the mobility of students with disabilities. However, in practice, disabled students face numerous barriers when trying to access the

69 The project can be accessed at https://exchangeability.eu/mapability.
70 European Disability Forum, 'Alternative Report' (n. 18).

national educational services of the country of destination (attitudinal, architectural, communication and information barriers and a lack of flexibility of curricula).

Therefore, states the Report, the European Commission should promote participation of persons with disabilities in EU exchange programmes (e.g. Erasmus+ including lifelong learning programmes) and should provide more accessible information on accessibility and reasonable accommodation, including information about who is responsible for the costs (which are borne by the local authorities, the university of the country of origin and the host country). The Commission should also promote the sharing of best practices about access to exchange programmes for students and teachers with disabilities.

As a result, the ESN, ExchangeAbility and MapAbility have shown how the people who are most directly involved, the students, can make a significant contribution to the change needed. Students themselves have provoked a movement in the direction of inclusion, identified a particular situation (sub-representation in mobility programmes), engaged different stakeholders relevant in the field (public and private), obtained funding and developed specific tools which were applied in a collaborative way to gather information on inclusiveness and accessibility and promoted improvement. Furthermore, this experience represents an example of solidarity, where students with and without disabilities work together under the belief that inclusive education, in this case inclusive mobility, benefits all.

3 MAIN CONCLUSIONS AND FINAL REMARKS ON ADVOCACY FOR INCLUSIVE EDUCATION IN EUROPE

In this chapter on advocacy for inclusive education from a European perspective, the authors have purposely selected four different advocacy experiences which are representative of, among others, the following aspects: the type of leading actors involved, the advocacy mechanisms used or the kind of results achieved and the mention of some of the factors considered.

The first advocacy experience was the European Disability Forum (EDF), which can be considered a successful story of self-advocacy by people with disabilities and their representative organisations at the European level, which unifies concerns and demands in a single European voice.[71] Becoming a central partner for the EU institutions on disability matters, the EDF has been able to spread relevant messages for the implementation of the rights of people with disabilities, including education, to ensure their place in the

[71] Experience analysed in Section 2.1.

European agenda, and was always inspired by the UNCRPD. In this context, inclusive education has been greatly promoted by the EDF with an important stance on this matter, has influenced European policies such as the European Disability Strategy 2010–2020 and has inspired and enriched other advocacy experiences such as the ones assessed here.

The second experience was a case of institutional advocacy with the intergovernmental action of the European Agency for Special Needs and Inclusive Education.[72] The example of the Agency showcases how EU Member States are capable of coordinating themselves and searching for improvement on inclusive education, despite their strong differences in context, reality and resources. Robust data collection and analysis, exchanging experiences and mutual learning, wide collaboration with international institutions and experts, project development, recommendations and positioning and high-level events, as well awareness-raising campaigns (involving students themselves, for example) have been some of the advocacy instruments implemented. It is interesting to see the nature and work of the Agency as a 'circular' experience where Member States evolve from being 'subjects' of advocacy to 'objects' of advocacy, seeking to influence their own policy-making processes.

The third advocacy example was incluD-ed,[73] which distinctively combined the participation of several different stakeholders that take part in the processes that can shape inclusive education,[74] building a sense and a reality of 'community' for inclusive education where contributions can come from many different sources. Furthermore, incluD-ed worked both from a global and a local perspective, developing a collaborative environment and using a wide range of advocacy instruments, all aimed at promoting a more inclusive Europe by means of inclusive education. This mixed approach as regards the actors involved, scope of action, variety of advocacy instruments and the blend of public and private funding makes incluD-ed an outstanding example of multi-stakeholder partnership for advocating for inclusive education at the EU level.

Finally, the work promoted by the International Exchange Erasmus Student Network focussed on improving the participation of students with disabilities in mobility programmes.[75] It shows that inclusive education is a complex reality that involves approaching different specific situations (such as mobility), and that inclusive education is understood as one of the

[72] Experience analysed in Section 2.2.

[73] Experience analysed in Section 2.3.

[74] Under the lead of a civil society organisation (Fundación ONCE), relying on the support of the European Social Fund.

[75] With the initiatives ExchangeAbility and MapAbility, dealt with in Section 2.4.

means to improving employability in our current globalised world. This topic-oriented advocacy experience also illustrates how students themselves can play an active role in fostering inclusive education, as advocates, identifying a particular situation (sub-representation of students with disabilities in mobility programmes). Moreover, it shows how to coordinate actions at the EU level, to develop specific initiatives and tools and to engage key stakeholders. Therefore, this experience represents an example of solidarity, where students with and without disabilities work together under the belief that inclusive education (in this case inclusive mobility) benefits all.

Despite their unique nature, what is common to all of these advocacy experiences is that they act on a European level where inclusive education, if the EU 2020 Strategy for Smart, Sustainable and Inclusive Growth targets are actually to be met, must be improved in line with the UNCRPD.[76] What is also a shared characteristic of these advocacy practices is that they work to move inclusive education forward at the European level among EU states where the competence on education remains at the Member State level, thus leaving limited power to the EU institutions. Although European policies and programmes that include the promotion of inclusive education have been very important and extremely necessary, relevant decisions on how education systems work (and the role of inclusiveness within these systems) depend on the particular countries.

This fact – linked with the matter that overall European policies on education still do not consider inclusive education in depth, and leave plenty of room for improvement – is one of the main features that, in the authors' opinion, shape the scope and nature of advocacy on inclusive education at the European level.[77] Action might be extensive, but it may face significant difficulties to become intensive and to produce real short-term (or even mid-term) changes on the field. However, European advocacy for inclusive education (supported by the incomparable instrument of the UNCRPD) is a crucial and influential path that we need to get onto, as it reinforces all the advocacy processes at the national (or even the regional[78]) level.

Through the analysis of the selected advocacy experiences, and having led incluD-ed), the authors identify some key factors the presence or absence of which do not determine, but do condition, the level of success or failure of

76 EU2020 has been dealt with in Section 1.1 as an overall European policy.

77 As discussed in Section 1.2 regarding the Strategic Framework for European Cooperation in Education and Training (ET2020).

78 For instance, in countries such as Spain, where the authors come from, the competence on education has been transferred to the regional authorities.

advocacy actions on inclusive education, particularly at the European level since it has been the focus of our text.

The elements that we specially highlight in this sense are the following: firstly, the level of interconnection of the advocacy action with authorities responsible for education, but also with other stakeholders relevant in the education environment such as representative organisations or platforms of teachers (even within the trade unions), of educational centres (schools, universities, including the different levels), of students and, of course, of people with disabilities and their families.

Another aspect to consider is how close the action is to the disability movement, particularly to families of children with disabilities, as regards perceiving integration in mainstream schools as a better option than special schooling. This is often linked with the actual available (or lack of) resources for inclusive education in mainstream schools – which vary in different countries – which can lead families to feel that their children are better taken care of in special education environments. At the same time, the more supportive the disability movement is of inclusive settings, the more pressure it can put on responsible authorities to change, with time, the situation.

A third aspect to consider is how the increasing number of analysis, studies and recommendations on inclusive education, mostly generated by experts in the educational field, are made available not only for EU institutions, governments or public authorities responsible for education but also for involved professionals and stakeholders that can put them into practice and who build education reality day by day. These analyses and studies do represent an important advocacy input, by setting efficient communication channels for education on the field, and involving the educational community while the work is being developed contributes to progress.

The aforementioned is related to another aspect: the need to extend efforts to establish robust indicators and mechanisms to follow up the evolution of inclusive education and to compare its situation in different regions and countries throughout the EU. Nowadays, indicator productions for follow-ups very much remain in the hands of national authorities, which are the ones that transfer the data available to the EU institutions. In our perspective, it would be helpful if advocacy on inclusive education in Europe reinforced the view of the importance of data collection as a relevant tool to assess reality, to make decisions and to evaluate change.

In relation to this, it is worth mentioning one of the remarks by the Committee on the Rights of Persons with Disabilities included in the concluding observations on the initial report of the implementation of the UNCRPD by the European Union. Pertaining to Article 24 of the UNCRPD on Education, the Committee shows its concern that in different EU Member States, many boys and girls and adults with disabilities cannot access inclusive, quality education in line with the UNCRPD. Consequently, the Committee recommends that the EU evaluates the situation and takes measures to improve it, including disability-specific indicators in the Europe 2020 Strategy when pursuing the education target.[79]

There is no doubt that the recession Europe has suffered recently (especially in certain countries) has damaged key social achievements, and inclusive education is not an exception. This crisis will probably affect the Member States' ability to consolidate policies and programmes, as well as data collection on inclusive education in the short- and mid-term future. However, the direction for progression must not be forgotten and, concerning indicators, we believe that the disability-related Sustainable Development Goals (SDGs), in particular Goal 4 on ensuring inclusive, equitable quality education, will contribute to the implementation of more solid data collection systems on inclusive education, which in the end will strengthen (with the proper transference channels as stated earlier) advocacy action.[80]

The authors wish to end this chapter with a short but important reflection on a factor that, from our point of view, should not be left aside in the framework of advocacy for inclusive education, as it plays an important role in the current global economy and in the participation and success in the labour market as it is shaped today. We find this is an increasingly important matter that needs to be considered in order to progress inclusive education from an extensive perspective: the so-called STEM skills (skills in science, technology, engineering and maths) and the role of people with disabilities in them.

The STEM skills are becoming a progressively substantial part of basic literacy in today's knowledge economy, since they serve as the foundation of innovation and global competitiveness. According to the European Commission, the number of researchers in Europe as a share of the population is well below that of the United States, Japan and other countries, and the

79 Committee on the Rights of Persons with Disabilities, Concluding Observations on the Initial Report of the European Union (2 October 2015) CRPD/C/EU/CO/1.

80 United Nations General Assembly, 'Transforming Our World: The 2030 Agenda for Sustainable Development' (21 October 2015) A/RES/70/1.

EU will need at least 1 million new research jobs by 2020 to adequately perform in a knowledge- and digital-based economy.[81] These new research positions are greatly linked with STEM.

Employability and quality youth employment will therefore be increasingly conditioned by the acquisition of STEM skills. However, if STEM education and training is not developed under an inclusive focus, it could become a new strong factor of inequality and lack of opportunities. This is why the authors draw attention to the importance of the participation of people with disabilities in STEM, as this will place them at the core of a moving economy. Therefore, we point out the need to consider this reality in the context of advocacy for inclusive education. The question of STEM and people with disabilities may sound too specific at first, but it is actually a key aspect that will condition people's participation in the labour market, particularly in terms of quality employment opportunities.

According to the Committee on Equal Opportunities in Science and Engineering of the National Science Foundation in the United States,[82] students with disabilities make one of the largest untapped pools of potential scientists, engineers, technologists, mathematicians and technicians. Innovative products often derive from a problem or challenge that requires a unique solution, making it imperative that all students, including those with disabilities, have access to a rigorous STEM curriculum.

Sharing experiences and examples of people with disabilities performing STEM studies or careers is a way to raise awareness and to advocate on the issue, encouraging others to follow. The STEM Disability Committee in the United Kingdom,[83] or the nomination of the so-called champions of change under the STEM Equality for Americans with Disabilities programme of the US White House,[84] are remarkable cases.[85]

81 European Commission, 'Europe 2020 Flagship Initiative: Innovation Union' COM(2010) 546 Final.

82 National Center for Technology Innovation and Center for Implementing Technology in Education (CITEd), 'Technology Supported Science, Technology, Engineering, and Math (STEM) Instruction for Students with Disabilities' (LD Online, 2009), www.ldonline.org/article/technology_supported_science,_technology,_engineering,_and_math_%28stem%29_instruction_for_students_with_disabilities?theme=print, accessed 11 March 2015.

83 The STEM Disability Committee's website is www.stemdisability.org.uk/default.aspx.

84 Individual champions can be consulted at www.whitehouse.gov/champions/STEM-equality-for-Americans-with-disabilities.

85 Recognising that STEM skills have and will remain essential for the United States to retain a leading position in the global economy, this White House initiative seeks to spread the message that when the playing field is levelled, people with disabilities can excel in STEM,

The authors conclude that it is therefore vital that educational policies on STEM connect with inclusive education policies, and that this relationship is taken into account in advocacy action. We urge the disability movement and other advocates for inclusive education in Europe to highlight STEM participation of young people with disabilities in the advocacy agenda.

develop new products, create scientific inventions, open successful businesses and contribute equally to the economic and educational future of our society.

12

Advancing the Right to Inclusive Education in Development Cooperation

Janet E. Lord*

INTRODUCTION

The right to inclusive education for persons with disabilities as set forth in the Convention on the Rights of Persons with Disabilities (CRPD)[1] should be the basis for development cooperation interventions at all levels of education. This is especially so given the interrelationship between poverty, disability and access to education in developing countries.[2] Further, access to education connects to health, for instance, through health information disseminated by educational systems and early identification and intervention as part of school screening programmes.[3] Inclusive education at all levels in developing countries is hinged to higher education. This is where the appropriate training of a wide array of specialists who can facilitate access to education at all levels needs to occur: training of educators who can master flexible pedagogy and accommodations in the classroom for all learners; engineers and architects who understand universal design; information and communication technology specialists who can design for accessibility; health and rehabilitation specialists who provide access to quality care so that persons with disabilities can attend school; sign language interpreters for deaf and deaf-blind students;

* This chapter is based in part on the author's work in the disability-inclusive development sector, and specifically in designing and implementing international cooperation programmes in higher education.

1 Convention on the Rights of Persons with Disabilities, G.A. Res. 61/106, U.N. Doc. A/61/49 (Dec. 13, 2006).

2 World Bank and World Health Organization (WHO), World Report on Disability (2011), available at: www.make-development-inclusive.org/docsen/howtonotedfid.pdf, accessed 24 November 2018; Department for International Development (DFID), How to Note: Working on Disability in Country Programmes (2007), available at: www.dfid.gov.uk/pubs/files/disability.pdf, accessed 24 November 2018; DFID, Disability, Poverty and Development (2000), available at: http://unipd-centrodirittiumani.it/public/docs/28893_poverty.pdf, accessed 24 November 2018.

3 CRPD (n.1) arts. 7, 25.

lawyers who are apprised of human rights and disability law and policy, among countless other examples.

Disability-inclusive development, defined herein as development that includes persons with disabilities as beneficiaries and participants, has the potential to make significant headway in advancing inclusive education for children and adults with disabilities in developing countries.[4] The strong inclusive development mandate set out in Article 32 of the CRPD,[5] together with the adoption of other global frameworks supporting equality and non-discrimination in the achievement of inclusive development goals, provides a basis upon which to advance inclusive education through donor-supported initiatives.

This chapter explores whether and how the right to inclusive education is being pursued through international development cooperation, consistent with the CRPD. It does so by situating the right to inclusive education within international development policy and programming and through identifying the barriers to inclusive education for learners with disabilities in developing countries, with a focus on access to higher education. Part 1 provides the overall context for addressing inclusive education in developing countries where persons with disabilities are likely to live among the poorest of the poor and where international development assistance is often a critical factor in poverty reduction. In Part 2, the international law and policy framework for inclusive education is addressed as it applies specifically to the context of international development. In so doing, it examines the progressive evolution of that framework, including through the post-2015 Sustainable Development Goals (SDGs) and in the light of the obligations set forth in the CRPD. Part 3 advances an approach for strengthening inclusive education through development cooperation. While applicable to any level of education, it draws on fieldwork undertaken regarding the barriers to accessing higher education for persons with disabilities in developing countries. This area has largely been neglected in international development programming, namely, higher education. While organisations such as the United Nations International Children's Emergency Fund (UNICEF) and international non-governmental organisations have implemented inclusive education programmes in primary and secondary education, inclusive higher education has not been the focus of education initiatives funded by international cooperation. The chapter concludes

4 AusAID, Development for All: Towards a Disability-Inclusive Australian Aid Program 2009–2014 (AusAID 2008) [hereinafter AusAID Disability Strategy], available in a range of formats at: www.ausaid.gov.au/keyaid/disability.cfm, accessed 24 November 2018; European Commission (EC), 'Guidance Note on Disability and Development, European Commission', July 2004, available at: http://ec.europa.eu/development/body/publications/docs/Disability_en.pdf, accessed 24 November 2018.

5 CRPD (n.1) art 32.

with some observations as to key strategies for advancing inclusive education in higher education through international development cooperation in the years ahead.

1 CONTEXT FOR ADDRESSING INCLUSIVE EDUCATION IN DEVELOPMENT COOPERATION

Disability stigma fuels discrimination, isolation and segregation and thereby exacerbates deprivation and human rights violations against persons with disabilities.[6] Outright exclusion from education, segregation in special school settings or placement in schools without providing necessary supports and accommodations creates lifelong barriers to economic opportunity and undermines socialisation processes required for learners to thrive as full members of society.[7] This, of course, is true for developed and developing countries alike. It poses more complex problems for developing countries reliant on multiple sources of development assistance, who often face significant challenges in responding to the needs of persons with disabilities in law, policy and institutions and in contexts where civil society is often disempowered or weak.[8]

In developing countries experiencing or emerging from conflict, risk of exclusion is intensified for all persons with disabilities, and especially children. Human Rights Watch reports that Syrian refugee children with disabilities in Jordan and Lebanon have been largely excluded from international assistance programmes providing access to education. According to its reporting, in Lebanon, thirteen humanitarian and disabilities organisations indicated that little or nothing had been done to ensure that children with disabilities can enrol in schools.[9] Research undertaken in Sierra Leone and Sudan emphasises the enhanced risk to children with disabilities who are out of school and the limited attention by donors to emergency education generally.[10] The inclusion of children with disabilities in education in crisis-

[6] World Bank and WHO (n. 2).

[7] UN Committee on the Rights of Persons with Disabilities (CRPD), General Comment No. 4 (2016), Article 24: Right to Inclusive Education, 2 September 2016, CRPD/C/GC/4.

[8] Michael Ashley Stein and Penelope J. S. Stein, 'Disability, Development, and Human Rights: A Mandate and Framework for International Financial Institutions', (2014) 47 *University of California Davis Law Review* 1231.

[9] Human Rights Watch, *'Growing Up without an Education': Barriers to Education for Refugee Children in Lebanon* (2016), www.hrw.org/report/2016/07/19/growing-without-education/barriers-education-syrian-refugee-children-lebanon, accessed 24 November 2018.

[10] Jean-Francois Trani et al., 'Disability, Vulnerability and Citizenship: To What Extent Is Education a Protective Mechanism for Children with Disabilities in Countries Affected by Conflict?' Washington University in St. Louis, Washington University Open Scholarship,

affected environments is understood by humanitarian organisations to be important for the acquisition of basic education skills such as literacy and numeracy, and skills associated with well-being and survival such as mine awareness and HIV and AIDS education.[11]

According to the International Labour Organization (ILO), persons with disabilities face greater degrees of poverty and unemployment relative to the rest of the population.[12] The cost of this labour market exclusion is high – an estimated US$338.55 billion up to US$480.21 billion for middle-income countries and, for low-income countries, between US$135.36 billion and US $192.00 billion.[13] Further, while data are incomplete, limited and unreliable, studies suggest that persons with disabilities have difficulty accessing education, with only 10 per cent of children with disabilities in school, and indicate that their global literacy rate is as low as 3 per cent, and for women with disabilities, it is as low as 1 per cent.[14] Meaningful and non-exploitative work is difficult to access for persons with disabilities, particularly those living in developing countries. When employed, they tend to earn less and too often their work is not freely chosen, as is frequently the case for persons with disabilities in segregated sheltered workshops.[15] Isolation in separate schools or congregate living serves as another

27 June 2011, http://openscholarship.wustl.edu/cgi/viewcontent.cgi?article=1035&context=brown_facpubs, accessed 24 November 2018.

11 Inter-Agency Network for Education in Emergencies (INEE), *Handbook: Minimum Standards for Education in Emergencies, Chronic Crises and Early Reconstruction* (2004), http://ineesite.org/page.asp?pid=1240, accessed 24 November 2018; Inter-Agency Network for Education in Emergencies (INEE), *INEE Pocket Guide to Supporting Learners with Disabilities* (INEE 2010); Inter-Agency Network for Education in Emergencies (INEE), *Education in Emergencies: Including Everyone* (INEE 2009).

12 International Labour Organization (ILO), 'ILO and Disability Inclusion', September 2015, www.ilo.org/wcmsp5/groups/public/–ed_emp/–ifp_skills/documents/publication/wcms_407645.pdf, accessed 24 November 2018.

13 United Nations Department of Social and Economic Affairs, 'World Population Ageing 2013', 2013, accessed 9 March 2015, www.un.org/en/development/desa/population/publications/pdf/ageing/WorldPopulationAgeing2013.pdf, accessed 24 November 2018.

14 United Nations Educational, Scientific and Cultural Organization (UNESCO), *EFA Global Monitoring Report: EFA. Strong Foundations: Early Childhood Care and Education* (2007); United Nations International Children's Emergency Fund (UNICEF), 'Children and Young Persons with Disabilities Fact Sheet' (May 2013), p. 20, www.unicef.org/disabilities/files/Factsheet_A5__Web_NEW.pdf, accessed 24 November 2018. See also Leonard Cheshire, *Disability and UNGEI, Still Left Behind: Pathways to Inclusive Education for Girls with Disabilities* (June 2017), www.ungei.org/Still_Left_Behind_Full_Report.PDF, accessed 24 November 2018.

15 Katherine Guernsey, Marco Nicoli and Alberto Ninio, *Making Inclusion Operational: Legal and Institutional Resources for World Bank Staff on the Inclusion of Disability Issues in Investment Projects* (World Bank Legal Vice Presidency, 2006).

barrier to quality education for persons with disabilities and, in turn, impacts secure livelihoods. These factors work in combination to enhance the risk of persons with disabilities to human trafficking for sexual exploitation and forced labour in often dangerous lines of work, among other abuses.[16]

Greater attention is being directed by international governmental and non-governmental organisations working in developing countries to the problems posed by segregated living arrangements for children with disabilities in social care homes, orphanages or special schools. Evidence demonstrates that such conditions reinforce isolation and diminish opportunities to obtain quality education.[17] The lack of community supports for persons with disabilities and their families who live at home creates additional barriers. Inaccessible transport or school buildings may lead parents or family members to forgo economic opportunity in order for their disabled child to obtain an education. Parents or grandparents may take responsibility for getting the child to school and remain with them to assist during the day. In other instances in developing countries, families may have to send their disabled child to reside in segregated schools away from home or to attend a mainstream school far away in a capital city.[18] This, in turn, enhances the risk they face from violence, exploitation and abuse, as is well documented by Disability Rights International and other human rights organisations.[19] Work on the part of UNICEF as well as non-governmental organisations in the education sector of international development to advance inclusive education for children with disabilities is beginning to take root.[20] The challenge, however, is to bring to

16 The link between human trafficking and disability is increasingly appreciated. See, for example, US Department of State, Trafficking in Persons Report 39 (2012) ('Persons with disabilities remain one of the groups most at risk of being trafficked'); Human Trafficking Legal Center, Trafficking of Persons with Disabilities (April 2016), www.htlegalcenter.org/wp-content/uploads/2016/04/Trafficking-of-Persons-With-Disabilities-in-the-United-States-04.12.2016, accessed 24 November 2018.

17 See LUMOS, *Funding Haitian Orphanages at the Cost of Children's Lives*, 20 November 2017; www.driadvocacy.org/media-gallery/our-reports-publications, accessed 24 November 2018.

18 See Camilla Parker, *Forgotten Europeans, Forgotten Right: The Human Rights of Persons Placed in Institutions* (Office of the High Commissioner for Human Rights, Regional Office Europe, 2010).

19 Disability Rights International (formerly Mental Disability Rights International) has documented egregious human rights violations against persons with disabilities in institutional settings, including purported schools as well as orphanages, social care homes and psychiatric hospitals. These are available at: www.driadvocacy.org/media-gallery/our-reports-publications, accessed 24 November 2018.

20 See, for example, Helen Pinnock and Marian Hodgkin, 'Education Access for All', 35 *Forced Migration Review* (July 2010). Special Issue: Disability and Displacement. Oxford: Refugee Studies Centre, University of Oxford; Save the Children, *Schools for All.*

scale the ubiquitous small-scale pilot project targeting children with disabilities and to integrate disability into large-scale development projects.

Women and girls with disabilities, who experience intersecting discrimination on account of disability, gender and often other marginal status, may be uniquely vulnerable in the educational context.[21] Research confirms that girls and young women with disabilities face heightened risk of physical and sexual abuse at or on the way to school and over-protection by family as a result of security concerns.[22] A study in Kenya revealed that women with disabilities studying in universities cited sexual violence as a major concern and risk factor that impacted their security and well-being.[23] Economic insecurity may make it difficult for some to negotiate safe sex or to avoid exploitative sex in exchange for food and other necessities.[24] Research also indicates that in some contexts, disabled boys may receive priority over disabled girls in allocation of resources for education.[25] This will impact the number of girls entering education. Yet in other contexts, however, perceptions of masculine ideals can reinforce and compound discriminatory attitudes towards disability for boys even more so than for girls.[26]

Poverty impacts educational opportunities in other ways. For example, the lack of access to clean water and sanitation at schools and higher education

Including Disabled Children in Education (Save the Children, 2002), www.eenet.org.uk/resources/docs/schools_for_all.pdfaccessed 24 November 2018.

21 Bonnie G. Smith and Beth Hutchison (eds), *Gendering Disability* (New Brunswick, NJ: Rutgers University Press, 2004).

22 See, e.g., Cheshire, (n. 14); Janet E. Lord, 'Child Rights Trending: Accommodating Children with Disabilities in the Global Human Rights Framework and US Foreign Policy,' 16 *Whittier Journal of Child and Family Advocacy* (2017).

23 Bathseba Opini, 'Barriers to Participation of Women Students with Disabilities in University Education in Kenya' (2012) 25(1) *Journal of Postsecondary Education and Disability* 65 at 72–73. See also N. N. Wane and Bathseba O. Opini, 'An Exploration of Gendered Violence in Kenyan Schools', (2006) 6(2) *Eastern African Journal of Humanities and Sciences* 44; Anne Wagner and Jamie Lynn Magnusson, 'Neglected Realities: Exploring the Impact of Women's Experiences of Violence on Learning in Sites of Higher Education' (2005) 17(4) *Gender and Education* 449.

24 Nora E. Groce, *HIV and Disability: Capturing Hidden Voices* (2004), at 3, available at: http://globalsurvey.med.yale.edu/capturing_hidden_voices_english.pdf, accessed 24 November 2018. Further, examples of such exploitation were discovered by the author during fieldwork in Zambia, where two school principals reported such exploitation in three cases where deaf female students were found to be pregnant following exploitative encounters with other students.

25 Save the Children (n. 20).

26 Ibid 34.

institutions in many developing countries presents additional barriers to school inclusion, especially for girls with disabilities and all children with mobility impairments.[27] Girls may be particularly impacted on account of privacy and personal safety concerns, for instance where disabled girls or young women need assistance using the toilet or changing clothes. Lack of access to health and rehabilitation services, such as to obtain needed assistive devices or for mobility orientation, are additional environmental factors that can inhibit access to education.[28]

Traditional solutions funded through development assistance very often reinforce disability discrimination in education.[29] Within mainstream development cooperation, this is perhaps most evident in the establishment of separate education systems and the building of segregated institutions and facilities for persons with disabilities.[30] Wrongheaded development interventions pursued without regard for disability rights principles clearly undermine the very development objectives they intend to address. Examples abound: support for segregated education for children with disabilities funded by development donors is an obvious example. Another is faith-based initiatives supported by private funding and therefore not subject to the rigours of donor monitoring schemes. These all too often perpetuate poor quality and unsustainable education programmes, living arrangements and segregated

27 World Bank Group, 'Including Persons with Disabilities in Water Sector Operations: A Guidance Note' (World Bank 2017); Hazel E. Jones & Robert A. Reed, (2005) 'Water and Sanitation for Disabled People and Other Vulnerable Groups: Designing services to improve accessibility' (WEDC, 2005) <http://wedc.lboro.ac.uk/publications/details.php?book=1%208 4380%20079%209> accessed 29 January 2019; WELL, 'Briefing Note 12: Why Should the Water and Sanitation Sector Consider Disabled People?' 1 (2005), www.wsscc.org/sites/default/files/publications/well_why should_the_watsan_sector_consider_disabled_people_bn12_2005.pdf, accessed 24 November 2018.

28 WHO, *Closing the Gap in a Generation: Health Equity through Action on the Social Determinants of Health. Final Report of the Commission on Social Determinants of Health* (Geneva: World Health Organization, 2008). Further, research discloses that only 3 per cent of individuals with disabilities needing rehabilitation services are able to access them, adding barriers for children with disabilities who could otherwise attend school but have not benefitted from rehabilitation services. Shanthi Ameratunga, Alana Officer, Bliss Temple and Sandar Tin Tin, *Rehabilitation of the Injured Child*, 87 Bulletin of the World Health Organization 327 (2009).

29 Michael Ashley Stein and Penelope Stein, 'Disability, Development, and Human Rights: A Mandate and Framework for International Financial Institutions', (2014) 47 *UC Davis Law Review*, 1231–1278.

30 Michael Stein, Janet E. Lord and Charlotte McClain-Nhlapo, 'Education and HIV/AIDS: Disability Rights and Inclusive Development', in Malcolm Langford, Andy Sumner and Alicia Ely Yamin (eds), *Millennium Development Goals and Human Rights: Past, Present and Future* (Cambridge University Press, 2013) 274–294.

('sheltered') workshops producing goods of poor quality where there is no local market, and worse, exploiting children and youth with disabilities, which results in exploitative labour conditions.[31] Such retrogressive approaches are apparent in other sectors of development where programmes are designed without attention to disability inclusion, impacting access to education.[32] These include, for instance, infrastructure projects that build inaccessible schools or inaccessible transport systems, school renovation projects that design inaccessible water and sanitation facilities, e-governance initiatives for online learning that develop inaccessible websites or civic education and human rights education activities that are inaccessible to persons with disabilities.[33] All of the foregoing undermine efforts to advance the CRPD and its vision of inclusive education as one among many elements of inclusive development.

2 INTERNATIONAL LAW AND POLICY FRAMEWORK FOR DISABILITY-INCLUSIVE DEVELOPMENT IN THE EDUCATION SECTOR

A challenge when addressing education through development interventions is the common lack of attention to law and policy frameworks and yet there has been, at the international level, a progressive development of standards supporting disability-inclusive international cooperation. Some initial action in support of disability-inclusive development occurred during the 1980s, which saw the launch of the first International Year of Disabled Persons[34] (1981) and the designation of the United Nations Decade of Disabled Persons[35] (1983–1992). These efforts highlighted the role that social and environmental barriers play in human rights enjoyment by persons with disabilities. During this period, in 1982, the World Programme of Action for Disabled Persons was

31 LUMOS (n. 17).

32 See World Bank Group, 'Understanding the Inclusivity of Inclusive Education', Disability-Inclusive Knowledge-Silo Breaker Knowledge Brief (World Bank Group, n.d.).

33 For a discussion of barriers in some of these development contexts, Michael Ashley Stein, Charlotte McClain-Nhlapo and Janet E. Lord, 'Education and HIV/AIDS: Disability Rights and Inclusive Development' in Malcolm Langford, Andy Sumner and Alicia Ely Yamin (eds), *The Millennium Development Goals and Human Rights: Past, Present and* Press 2013); Amy T. Wilson, 'The Effectiveness of International Development Assistance American Organizations to Deaf Communities in Jamaica,' 150(3) *American Annals of the Deaf* 292 (2005).

34 International Year of Disabled Persons, G.A. Res. 36/77, at 176, U.N. GAOR, 36th Sess., Supp. No. 77, U.N. Doc. A/RES/36/77 (1981).

35 Decade of Disabled Persons, G.A. Res. 48/96, U.N. Doc. A/RES/48/96 (4 March 1993), which annexed thereto (resolution 48/96 annex, 20 December 1993), available at: www1.umn.edu/humanrts/instree/disabilitystandards.html, accessed 24 November 2018.

adopted, providing a global strategy and blueprint for countries to achieve the full and equal participation of persons with disabilities.[36] Notably, its emphasis on social development and the importance of including persons with disabilities in policies and programming also formed part of an evolving international dialogue on education for individuals with disabilities and, in turn, secured livelihoods.

During the 1990s, efforts to advance disability rights proceeded, with some attention to accounting for persons with disabilities in development cooperation, especially in the Standard Rules on the Equalization of Opportunities for Persons with Disabilities (Standard Rules).[37] The Standard Rules address disability inclusion in technical and economic cooperation, reaffirming the principle of inclusive policies, plans and activities and specifying that '[t]he needs and concerns of persons with disabilities should be incorporated into general development plans and not be treated separately'.[38] Rule 21 of the Standard Rules addresses the responsibility of states in the realm of technical and economic cooperation, and Rule 22 specifies the need for states to participate actively in international cooperation concerning policies for the equalisation of opportunities for persons with disabilities.[39] The Standard Rules served to inform state policies and practices and, in some instances, helped frame bilateral donor policies on disability. Their adoption, together with the work of the Special Rapporteur on Disability, helped to situate disability as a development issue and to highlight global human rights conditions for persons with disabilities.[40] In some instances, the Standard Rules did serve as an impetus for disability-inclusion policy making in international development, as the specific reference to the Standards Rules in the Italian Cooperation illustrates.[41]

[36] World Programme of Action Concerning Disabled Persons, G.A. Res. 37/52, at 185, U.N. GAOR, 37th Sess., Supp. No. 51, U.N. Doc. A/RES/37/52 (3 December 1982).

[37] Standard Rules on the Equalization of Opportunities for Persons with Disabilities, G.A. Res. 48/96, at 202, U.N. GAOR, 48th Sess., Supp. No. 49, U.N. Doc. A/RES/48/96 (20 December 1993). For more on the role of the Standard Rules in advancing inclusive education, see Arlene Kanter's chapter in this volume (Chapter 2).

[38] Ibid, Rule 14(2).

[39] Ibid, Rule 22.

[40] See Leandro Despouy, Special Rapporteur of the Sub-Commission on Prevention of Discrimination and Protection of Minorities, *Human Rights and Disabled Persons* (1988).

[41] Janet E. Lord et al., *Disability Inclusive Development: A Review of Existing Policies and Practices* (World Bank, September 2009).

Mandating Disability-Inclusive Development in the CRPD

The negotiation of the CRPD provided further impetus for the articulation of inclusive education as part of the right to education and to advancing it within international development activities.[42] This agenda was taken up with enthusiasm by disabled people's organisations (DPOs), developing countries and a broad coalition of stakeholders who advanced the development of a legally binding treaty that was consistent with a social model, rights-based understanding of disability and responsive to the development agenda.[43] The CRPD is the first core human rights convention negotiated under the auspices of the United Nations to include a detailed, specific provision on inclusion in international development, set out in Article 32.[44] It creates a mandate for disability-inclusive development and accompanying measures to advance the full participation of persons with disabilities in rights-based development. This, together with provisions aimed to ensure access to education for persons with disabilities at all levels in Article 24, triggers an obligation that development cooperation supporting education must ensure that persons with disabilities benefit from such investments.

The CRPD, in expressly recognising the role of international cooperation in supporting national efforts to effectively implement States Parties' obligations,[45] provides that States Parties are to cooperate internationally through partnerships with other states, and/or with relevant international and regional organisations and civil society in support of national measures to give effect to the CRPD.[46] This triggers obligations on the part of donors to

[42] See Rosemary Kayess, Jenny Green and Andrew Byrnes, 'The Right to Inclusive Education', in Michael Ashley Stein and Malcolm Langford (eds), *Disability Social Rights* (Cambridge University Press, 2018).

[43] Early attention to the importance of international cooperation in development during the drafting of the CRPD is evident in the language developed by Mexico in the General Assembly resolution creating the Ad Hoc Committee. Comprehensive and Integral International Convention to Promote and Respect the Rights and Dignity of Persons with Disabilities, 19 December 2001, Res. A/RES/56/168, para. 1.

[44] CRPD, (n. 1) 32; For more on the negotiation of Article 32, see Janet E. Lord and Michael Stein, 'Article 32', in Ilias Bantekas and Michael Stein (eds), *Convention on the Rights of Persons with Disabilities: A Commentary* (Oxford: Oxford University Press, 2018).

[45] CRPD at art. 32(1). ('States Parties recognize the importance of international cooperation and its promotion, in support of national efforts for the realization of the purpose and objectives of the present Convention, and will undertake appropriate and effective measures in this regard, between and among States and, as appropriate, in partnership with relevant international and regional organizations and civil society, in particular organizations of persons with disabilities.')

[46] CRPD (n.1), art. 32(1).

ensure that their bilateral assistance is inclusive of persons with disabilities, as well as their participation in multilateral assistance schemes. Likewise, it presents obligations on the part of beneficiary governments to ensure that the design and implementation of foreign-funded programming is disability inclusive.

Article 32 identifies a range of measures that states can take within the framework of international cooperation which include the following: (1) 'capacity building, including through the exchange and sharing of information, experiences, training programs and best-practices';[47] (2) research programmes and the facilitation of access to scientific knowledge;[48] and (3) technical and economic assistance, including the facilitation of access to accessible and assistive technologies.[49] Article 32 thus makes clear that all international cooperation efforts should be accessible to and fully inclusive of persons with disabilities, from design through implementation. For education, the implications are clear – scholarships for higher education, student and faculty exchanges and collaborative research, among other programming, should be disability inclusive.

A reading of Article 32, and disability-inclusive development in particular, must take place within and across the CRPD text. In other words, it must be read in relation to the treaty's general principles, general obligations and its specific, substantive rights.[50] Understanding disability-inclusive development in the context of education projects funded by international cooperation compels a consideration of Article 24 on education, and other provisions that give meaning to and facilitate the realisation of inclusive education.[51]

The CRPD recognises education as a right and as an integral component of realising other human rights. Article 24 expressly prohibits discrimination in education on the basis of disability and applies that prohibition to all levels of

[47] Ibid., art. 32(1)(b). ('Such measures could include, inter alia: … Facilitating and supporting capacity-building, including through the exchange and sharing of information, experiences, training programmes and best practices.')

[48] Ibid., art. 32(1)(c). ('Such measures could include, inter alia: … Facilitating cooperation in research and access to scientific and technical knowledge.')

[49] Ibid., art. 32(1)(d). ('Such measures could include, inter alia: … Providing, as appropriate, technical and economic assistance, including by facilitating access to and sharing of accessible and assistive technologies, and through the transfer of technologies.')

[50] Michael Ashley Stein and Janet E. Lord, 'The United Nations Convention on the Rights of Persons with Disabilities: Process, Substance, and Prospects', in Felipe Gomez Isa and Koen De Feyter (eds), *International Protection of Human Rights: Achievements and Challenges* (Universidad de Deusto, 2009) 495.

[51] Janet E. Lord and Michael Ashley Stein, 'The Domestic Incorporation of Human Rights Law and the United Nations Convention on the Rights of Persons with Disabilities' (2008) 83 *University of Washington Law Review* 449.

education.[52] The disability discrimination includes the duty to provide reasonable accommodation. Further, human rights law requires educational services to be available, accessible, acceptable and adaptable, including through setting minimum standards, and to improve the quality of those services.[53] General Comment No. 2 on accessibility, adopted by the CRPD Committee, specifically addresses education and affirms that 'it is the entire process of inclusive education that must be accessible, not just buildings, but all information and communication, including ambient or FM assistive systems, support services and reasonable accommodation in schools'.[54] Further, accessibility as it is understood in Article 9 of the CRPD reflects the notion that persons with different disabilities and different personal circumstances may require (or desire) different strategies and supports to achieve the same goals of equal opportunity and equal enjoyment of the services offered by higher education institutions.

The CRPD recognises that people with disabilities are active agents and holders of rights, thus adopting the social model perspective of disability 'as an evolving concept . . . that . . . results from the interaction between persons with impairments and attitudinal and environmental barriers that hinders their full and effective participation in society on an equal basis with others' and not as an inherent limitation, which includes participation in education at all levels.[55] To break down these barriers, the Convention introduces into the human rights framework the concept of universal design. This is defined as 'the design of products, environments, programmes and services to be usable by all people, to the greatest extent possible, without the need for adaptation or specialized design'.[56] The Convention sets forth general principles that inform its overall approach and that apply across the treaty: (1) dignity, individual autonomy, including the freedom to make one's own choices, and independence of persons; (2) non-discrimination, participation and inclusion in society; (3) respect for difference; (4) equality of opportunity; (5) accessibility; (6) equality between men and women; and (7) respect for the evolving capacities of children with disabilities. And, notably for considering

52 CRPD (n. 1) art. 24.

53 See generally Gauthier de Beco, 'Transition to Inclusive Education Systems According to the Convention on the Rights of Persons with Disabilities', (2016) 34(1) *Nordic Journal of Human Rights* 40; Gauthier de Beco, 'The Right to Inclusive Education According to Article 24 of the UN Convention on the Rights of Persons with Disabilities: Background, Requirements and (Remaining) Questions', (2014) 32(3) *Netherlands Quarterly of Human Rights* 263.

54 CRPD Committee, General Comment No. 2, Accessibility.

55 CRPD (n.1) Preamble (e).

56 Ibid. art. 2.

the role that poverty plays as a barrier to quality education at all levels, the Convention recognises that many people with disabilities live in poverty and thus underscores 'the critical need to address the negative impact of poverty on persons with disabilities'.

Other CRPD articles provide additional direction on the inclusive education roadmap funded within the context of international cooperation programmes. Thus, the specific substantive obligations of the treaty must be harnessed to support and inform international cooperation programmes directed at poverty alleviation and inclusive development, whatever the sector of cooperation at issue. Article 27 on employment, for instance, connects to education in supporting pathways into employment and transitions from school into jobs. Implementation provisions are also germane to inclusive education. Article 31 is of particular interest as it mandates disability data collection to aid implementation of all CRPD rights and assumes tremendous importance in advancing inclusive education. Indicators developed for monitoring, evaluating and assessing development programmes in education must capture data disaggregated on the basis of disability. In programmes funding capacity building for education ministries, this obligation must be emphasised. It is for this reason, and understanding the challenge of disability data collection, that development donors such as UNICEF and USAID have worked to develop indicators on disability in various contexts.[57]

In the light of the foregoing, Article 32, together with the articles of general application and the specific CRPD provisions in the areas of education, employment and living in the community, among others, have important implications, not only for States Parties and their donor agencies, but for implementing partners as well. These developments served as the impetus for international policy advancing disability inclusion in international cooperation and in humanitarian action for education in emergency settings in both multilateral and bilateral donor initiatives.

Disability Inclusion in the Post-2015 Development Agenda

Prior to the adoption of the CRPD, mainstream development policies and frameworks did little, if anything, to account for persons with disabilities as beneficiaries or participants in development. For instance, the Millennium Development Goals (MDGs) disregarded persons with disabilities, as in MDG Goal 2, on universal primary education. Target 2A – aimed to ensure

[57] For efforts in this direction, see UNICEF, *Guidance: Including Children with Disabilities in Humanitarian Action* (2017), 13–15.

that, by 2015, children everywhere, boys and girls alike, would complete a full course of primary schooling – failed to reference children with disabilities notwithstanding their nearly complete exclusion from education in developing countries.[58] The MDGs, like so many of the early international policy frameworks, assembled persons with disabilities in and among the category of 'vulnerable groups'. As such, little account was taken for addressing their specific needs in development planning, implementation and monitoring.

Not surprisingly, failing to account for persons with disabilities in development had various consequences. It served in some instances to reinforce isolation and disadvantage (e.g. the building of inaccessible schools, failures to accommodate deaf persons in health education campaigns and developing information and communication technology without attention to the needs of blind persons or persons with low vision). The purpose of such inclusion is clear: disability-specific targets help to incorporate disability in education sector interventions (among others) funded through international cooperation directed at reducing poverty and sustainable development.

Since the adoption of the CRPD, significant progress has been made to better account for persons with disabilities in development, especially at the policy level. These include, for instance, the post-2015 development agenda, the incorporation of non-discrimination into the World Bank's Environmental and Social Framework and disability policies and guidance adopted by numerous bilateral development agency policies and strategies.[59] In addition, the adoption of the CRPD and its strong embrace of inclusive education in Article 24 is taking root. The UN Human Rights Council, for instance, adopted a resolution, The Right to Education of Persons with Disabilities, in 2014, according to which States Parties to the CRPD are directed to 'adopt and implement appropriate measures, including legislative measures, to ensure that persons with disabilities enjoy the right to education without discrimination and on the basis of equal opportunity by ensuring an inclusive education system at all levels and life-long learning, in accordance with the [CRPD]'.[60]

In contrast to the MDGs, the Sustainable Development Goals (SDGs) account for exclusion of persons with disabilities in multiple domains. In Transforming Our World: The 2030 Agenda for Sustainable Development, states committed to 'providing inclusive and equitable quality education at all

58 Stein, McClain-Nhlapo and Lord (n.33).

59 World Bank, *Environmental and Social Framework* (2016).

60 UN Human Rights Council, The Right to Education of Persons with Disabilities (25 March 2014) Res. A/HRC/25/L.30.

levels – early childhood, primary, secondary, tertiary, technical and vocational training' and, further, that all persons 'irrespective of sex, age, race or ethnicity, and persons with disabilities, migrants, indigenous peoples, children and youth . . . should have access to life-long learning opportunities'.[61]

The SDGs contain seven targets that address with specificity persons with disabilities in terms of education, accessible schools, employment, accessible public spaces and transport, empowerment and inclusion and data disaggregation. Six SDG targets refer to persons in vulnerable situations, which are understood to include persons with disabilities. Furthermore, universal targets are inclusive of all persons and therefore must also be achieved for persons with disabilities. In addition, two other targets address discrimination, a major cause of inequality and unequal access to opportunities and services for persons with disabilities.[62] SDG 4 (Ensure inclusive and equitable quality education and promote lifelong learning opportunities) requires the design of education facilities to be responsive to the needs of students with disabilities and, further, SDG 10 (Reduce inequality within and among countries) requires the social, economic and political inclusion of all, including persons with disabilities.[63] Of particular note are the following indicators:

- Parity indices (female/male, rural/urban, bottom/top wealth quintile and others such as disability status, indigenous peoples and conflict affected, as data become available) for all education indicators . . . that can be disaggregated.

Proportion of schools with access to: (a) electricity; (b) the Internet for pedagogical purposes; (c) computers for pedagogical purposes; (d) adapted infrastructure and materials for students with disabilities; (e) basic drinking water; (f) single sex basic sanitation facilities; and (g) basic handwashing facilities (as per the WASH indicator definitions).

[61] UN General Assembly, *Transforming Our World: The 2030 Agenda for Sustainable Development*, 21 October 2015, A/RES/70/1., para. 25.

[62] The International Disability Alliance (IDA) and the International Disability and Development Consortium (IDDC) have published guides on the SDGs and disability. *See especially* IDA and IDDC, *The 2030 Agenda: The Inclusion of Persons with Disabilities Comprehensive Guide*, www.internationaldisabilityalliance.org/sites/default/files/documents/2030_agenda_comprehensive_guide_for_persons_with_disabilities_comp.pdf, accessed 24 November 2018.

[63] In addition, the New Urban Agenda commits to equal access for persons with disabilities to spaces, facilities and services open to the public in rural and urban areas. The Agenda encourages the 'elimination of legal, institutional, socioeconomic and physical barriers' to promote equitable and affordable access to safe drinking water and sanitation for persons with disabilities. See UN General Assembly, New Urban Agenda, UN Doc. A/RES/71/256 (2017), http://habitat3.org/wp-content/uploads/NUA-English.pdf (accessed 24 November 2018).

Other indicators clearly intersect with disability inclusion in education. Capturing that data, appropriately disaggregated on the basis of disability, is an important message for development donors and implementers working in the education sector in developing countries. Further, providing assistance in data capture is likewise important in terms of advancing implementing of inclusive education for all learners with disabilities. The following indicators link to inclusive education and deepen understanding around barriers experienced by persons with disabilities:

- Average hourly earnings of female and male employees, by occupation, age and persons with disabilities.
- Unemployment rate, by sex, age and persons with disabilities.
- Proportion of people living below 50% of median income, by age, sex and persons with disabilities.
- Proportion of population that has convenient access to public transport, by sex, age and persons with disabilities.
- Average share of the built-up area of cities that is open space for public use for all, by sex, age and persons with disabilities.
- Proportion of persons that are victims of physical or sexual harassment, by sex, age, disability status and place of occurrence, in the previous 12 months.
- Proportions of positions (by sex, age, persons with disabilities and population groups) in public institutions (national and local legislatures, public service and judiciary) compared to national distributions.[64]

It is now widely understood that including children with disabilities in the general education system – with appropriate supports – is an important strategy for reaching universal primary education.[65] The achievement of universal inclusive education, including its reflection in education policies and practice, necessitates profound modifications in education systems. Central to this approach is the notion that schools have the duty to accommodate the diverse and unique needs of all learners while providing high-quality education to all. This requires governments to step up their efforts to reach marginalised children by designing specific interventions. This might include the explicit targeting of children with disabilities in national education sector plans, the development of inclusive educational

64 UN General Assembly, *Transforming Our World* (n. 61), para. 25.

65 CRPD Committee, General Comment No. 4 (n. 7) UNESCO, *Addressing Exclusion in Education: A Guide to Assessing Education Systems Towards More Inclusive and Just Societies* (UNESCO 2012) ED/BLS/BAS/2012/PI/1, 13; UNICEF, *The Right of Children with Disabilities to Education: A Rights-Based Approach to Inclusive Education*: Position Paper (UNICEF 2012) 15.

policies for teacher training in inclusive practices and the development of appropriate learning materials and programmes on early identification and assessment for childhood disabilities (Article 24 CRPD). These interventions, all contemplated by the CRPD, should be core to the approach taken to inclusion in development programming.

Too often, however, small-scale projects or pilot initiatives are funded without follow-up.[66] Research discloses that the inclusion of children with disabilities in the education system requires a multifaceted strategy. This includes first a coherent legislative and policy framework embracing inclusive education undergirded not only by teacher and administrative backing but also by strong community and family involvement.[67] Inclusive education policies must be financially supported to allow for accessible school infrastructure, teacher training in inclusive education and interventions that support social protection, for example, school feeding schemes, HIV and AIDS and other health education and parent training.[68] The foregoing discussion traced the gradual emergence of disability inclusion in international development policy that resulted ultimately in the specific inclusion of targets on disability in the education goals for the SDGs, among other disability-inclusive elements of the SDGs. An additional dimension of international cooperation, emergency education in humanitarian situations, is to some extent also addressing disability-inclusive approaches as the following section reviews.

International Cooperation and Disability Inclusion in Emergency Education

The role of education in humanitarian action – interventions to support populations impacted by armed conflict, natural disaster or other crises – has traditionally received little attention. The Committee on the Rights of the Child, in its General Comment No. 9, stated that States Parties must ensure access to adequate health and social services, including psychosocial recovery and social reintegration, to children with disabilities affected by an armed conflict.[69] It also recommended that, in a post-conflict context,

66 Michael Ashley Stein and Janet E. Lord, 'Forging Effective International Agreements: Lessons from the UN Convention on the Rights of Persons with Disabilities', in Jody Heymann and Adele Cassola (eds), *Making Equal Rights Real: Taking Effective Action to Overcome Global Challenges* (Cambridge University Press, 2012) 27.

67 Roeher Institute, *Inclusive Policy and Practice in Education: Best Practices for Students with Disabilities* (Roeher Institute, 2004).

68 Ibid.

69 Committee on the Rights of the Child, General Comment No. 9, CRC/C/GC/9, para. 55.

resources for education be increased to build and to reconstruct adequate school facilities and that inclusive educational systems be created, including for children with disabilities.[70]

Increasingly humanitarian actors are drawing attention to the fact that wars and natural disasters seriously impact the knowledge and opportunities that an education can provide for affected populations.[71] While education is a human right that applies in times of crisis as in times of peace, it can also contribute to physical, psychosocial and cognitive protection that can sustain and save lives. Humanitarian actors focussed on education, such as the International Network of Education in Emergencies (INEE), stress that:

> Education in emergencies ensures dignity and sustains life by offering safe spaces for learning, where children and youth who need other assistance can be identified and supported. Education mitigates the psychosocial impact of conflict and disasters by giving a sense of routine, stability, structure and hope for the future. It can save lives by protecting against exploitation and harm, including forced early marriage, recruitment into armed forces and armed groups or organised crime. Lastly, education provides the critical survival skills and coping mechanisms through the dissemination of lifesaving information about landmine safety, HIV/AIDS prevention, conflict resolution and peace-building.[72]

The dramatic increase in numbers of displaced children put out of school during emergency crises has led in recent years to a focussed effort to address emergency education. Humanitarian actors within the INEE worked to develop a coherent approach to achieve a minimum level of educational access and quality in emergencies through to recovery as well as to ensure the accountability of the workers who provide these services.[73] The first set of Minimum Standards was adopted in 2003–2004 and was followed in 2009–2010 by an updating process resulting in the adoption of the INEE Minimum Standards for Education: Preparedness, Response, Recovery in June 2010.[74] The revised Standards are designed for use in emergency

70 Committee on the Rights of the Child, Concluding Observations on the Report of Afghanistan, CRC/C/AFG/CO/1, para. 61 (a).

71 For discussion of disability inclusion in humanitarian action, see Janet E. Lord, 'International Humanitarian Law and Disability: Paternalism, Protection or Rights?', in Michael Gill and Cathy Schlund-Vials (eds), *Disability, Human Rights and the Limits of Humanitarianism* (Ashgate, 2014) 155–178. See also Janet E. Lord and Michael Stein, 'Peacebuilding and Reintegrating Combatants with Disabilities', (2015) 19 *International Journal of Human Rights* 277.

72 INEE Minimum Standards for Education: Preparedness, Response, Recovery (June 2010).

73 Ibid.

74 Ibid.

preparedness, response and recovery and in humanitarian advocacy and are applicable in a wide range of situations, including natural disasters and armed conflicts. They give guidance on how to prepare for and respond to acute emergencies in ways that reduce risk, improve future preparedness and lay a foundation for quality education. They provide flexibility in responding to needs at the most important level – the community – while providing a harmonised framework to coordinate the educational activities of national governments, other authorities, funding agencies, and national and international agencies.

The INEE Standards provide guidance for the implementation of Article 24 in the context of emergencies, as contemplated in Article 11, Situations of Risk, in the CRPD. These INEE Standards define 'inclusive education' as education that ensures the presence, participation and achievement of all individuals in learning opportunities; that guarantees that education policies, practices and facilities respond to the diversity of all individuals in the context; and that understands that exclusion from education can result from discrimination, lack of support to remove barriers or use of languages, content or teaching methods that do not benefit all learners.[75] Further, the INEE Standards specifically recognise that persons with disabilities are often the most excluded from education and that some individuals who were previously able (pre-emergency) to access education may be excluded because of circumstantial, social, cultural, physical or infrastructural factors. Inclusive education means ensuring that these barriers to participation and learning are removed and that teaching methodologies and curricula are accessible and appropriate for students with disabilities. All individuals are welcomed and supported to make progress, and their individual requirements are addressed.

The foregoing discussion traced the emergence of disability-inclusive development and its gradual impact on international cooperation in the education sector, as international actors increasingly take on the challenge of implementing inclusive education in emergency situations, a relatedly new focus of humanitarian action. The discussion that follows in Part 3 addresses an issue that is still largely ignored in development cooperation activities focussed on disability inclusion, namely the inclusion of students with disabilities in higher education.

[75] Ibid.

3 STILL NEGLECTED: ADVANCING INCLUSIVE EDUCATION IN EDUCATION PROJECT ASSESSMENTS FUNDED BY INTERNATIONAL COOPERATION

Assessments funded by international cooperation to guide education programme design in developing countries should align with the principles of inclusive education. Likewise, in undertaking social impact assessments in advance of large-scale development, whether financed through public, private or combined means, the assessment methodology should be guided by a rights-based, inclusive education approach. International human rights law as set forth in the CRPD, together with international inclusive development policy reflected in the SDGs and other instruments, combine to form the strongest basis yet for advancing the human right to inclusive education for learners with disabilities. There is a growing literature on efforts to introduce inclusive education models into development programming, with leadership in this context provided by UNICEF and other development implementers focussed on primary and secondary education.[76] Conspicuously little attention has been directed at research or development initiatives focussing on inclusive education at the level of higher education as a part of inclusive development interventions.[77] Louise Morley describes the barriers to higher education for students with disabilities in sub-Saharan Africa as 'exacerbated in higher levels of education' where 'access for disabled students to higher education or particular programmes can be formally blocked, or informally advised against' and, further, that 'exclusion from, or access only to segregated, non-academic basic education means that traditionally there has been a small pool of disabled students qualified to enter higher education'.[78]

[76] *See e.g.*, Richard Reiser, *Implementing Inclusive Education: A Commonwealth Guide to Implementing Article 24 of the UN Convention on the Rights of Persons with Disabilities* (2nd edn) (Commonwealth Secretariat 2012) [hereinafter Commonwealth Guide] 31; UNESCO, *Addressing Exclusion in Education* (2012); UNICEF, The Right of Children with Disabilities to Education (2012), 15.

[77] Many of the technical tools to facilitate CRPD implementation in the context of education for use in developing countries focus on primary and secondary education, to the exclusion of higher education. See, for example, Janet E. Lord, Allison de Franco, Joelle Balfe, Katherine Guernsey and Valerie Karr, *Human Rights. YES! Action and Advocacy on the Rights of Persons with Disabilities* (2nd edn) (2012); Betty Dion, Victor Pineda and Soren Ginnerup, Toolkit: Key Indicators of Accessibility: Reporting on the UN CRPD (Global Alliance for Accessible Technologies and Environments 2015); Reiser (n. 76) 31.

[78] Louise Morley, 'Disabled Students in Higher Education in Ghana and Tanzania: Towards Equity and Participation' University of Dar es Salaam, Tanzania, Report for the World Bank Global Review of Tertiary Education (October 2010), 14–15.

Indeed, the practice of the CRPD Committee thus far has focussed on Article 24's implementation in the context of primary and secondary school, not higher education, and the Committee's concluding observations on state reporting bear this out. In the light of this neglect, Part 2 directs attention to the implications of the CRPD and the SDGs for advancing inclusive education for persons with disabilities in higher education.

The section that follows provides a conceptual framework for assessing disability inclusion in higher education development interventions. A generic roadmap is provided for undertaking an assessment of the accessibility of higher education in a developing country context, generally the first step in planning the design of any development intervention. Following the explanation of the conceptual framework and roadmap for an assessment on the status of students (and faculty and staff) with disabilities in higher education, defined herein as university or technical college education for students who have completed secondary education, potential approaches are examined and these are drawn from developing country contexts.[79]

It is important to point out that development practitioners rely extensively on the review of prior development assessments and programme evaluations in designing new development interventions, including in the education sector. Assessment and evaluation teams will often undertake desk reviews of relevant literature within a country as a component of such efforts. Unfortunately, there is a general dearth of written information on disability in many developing countries and too often donors do not include disability in their assessments or programme evaluations, leaving little in the way of foundational material upon which to draw when planning disability-inclusive development programmes. Moreover, assessments in the education sector undertaken by development donors often exclude analysis of legal and policy barriers or gaps in supporting inclusive education at all levels.

Implementation of Education Projects within a Social Model Framework

Education projects funded by international cooperation must begin with a conceptual design aligned with inclusion. The conceptual starting point

[79] As Gauthier de Beco notes, in many instances students with disabilities are unable to access university education and are often tracked into vocational training or other types of post-secondary education. See Gauthier de Beco, 'Education', in Lisa Waddington and Mark Priestley (eds), *Mainstreaming Disability Rights in the European Pillar of Social Rights: A Compendium* (Academic Network of European Disability Experts, 2018), ch. 2.1, pp. 15–18.

for any disability-inclusive development assessment undertaken to identify barriers and to craft interventions according to the specific needs of persons with disabilities is the social model understanding of disability. An assessment's point of departure, therefore, is that persons with disabilities face barriers in society (attitudinal, legal, physical and communication) and it is those barriers that are disabling.[80] As emphasised throughout this volume, disability is not a purely biomedical phenomenon that is addressable only at the level of the individual with disability through medical or rehabilitative intervention; disability under the social model is addressable through a range of strategies at the societal level. The focus on external barriers is directed at efforts to remediate, accommodate or avoid altogether the environmental factors that limit full participation in society.[81] The field of disability-inclusive development proceeds from this perspective.

An assessment, project design plan, monitoring or evaluation framework undertaken in any aspect of education funded by international development cooperation must be reflective of and responsive to a social model understanding of disability. Its objectives are, put simply, the identification of barriers to inclusive education for persons with disabilities and recommendations for the dismantling or remediation of those barriers.[82] In higher education, inaccessible physical infrastructure, attitudinal barriers among teachers, administrators and students, policies and procedures limiting choice and access to the full curriculum and communication barriers, among others, work as a major disadvantage on students with disabilities.[83]

Gathering Statistics and Data for Development Assessments

Accurate disability data are lacking for most developing countries, although efforts are under way to address existing gaps. Data-gathering requirements are set forth in the CRPD, as well as disability inclusion in the data-gathering framework of the SDGs. This data gap is a major limitation of assessments that seek to gather data in order to make recommendations for the design of inclusive education projects funded by international cooperation. Of note,

80 WHO and World Bank (n. 2).

81 The CRPD aligns with the social model understanding of disability in its reflection of barriers exogenous to the individual in society. See CRPD (n.1) Preamble (e) & art. 1.

82 This framework is reflected in Article 4 of the CRPD which enumerates a series of general obligations to be undertaken by states requiring the identification of barriers and their dismantling through law, policy and other actions.

83 Julie Allan, 'Inclusion and Exclusion in the University', in Tony Booth, Kari Nes and Marit Strømstad (eds), *Developing Inclusive Teacher Education* (Routledge 2003), 130–144.

the Organisation for Economic Co-operation and Development (OECD) reported in 2003 that '[v]ery few institutions keep consistent and reliable data, or profiles on students, special needs and outcomes' and, further, that '[r]esponsibility for data availability is left to institutions in many cases'.[84] Further, developing countries' higher education institutions, where they gather any disability data at all, typically have data only on the students with disabilities who request assistance and these tend to be students with apparent disabilities, such as physical or sensory impairments. Studies from developing countries, including detailed studies from Egypt and South Africa, confirm that data are missing and/or grossly unreliable and that those students who do receive accommodations tend to have visual or physical impairments and that students with cognitive impairments tend not to be served.[85]

While data disaggregated on the basis of disability are spare at all levels of education, this is especially the case in higher education. Students with disabilities who make it into higher education are reluctant to disclose their disability. Universities often operate as fiefdoms with little governmental oversight and have little in the way of disability accommodations. In some instances, a separate ministry exists for higher education, meaning that gains made by a ministry of education in promoting inclusive primary and secondary education will not seamlessly transition over to higher education. Egypt is a case in point. Generally, a 2017 assessment conducted by the US Agency for International Development (USAID) found that 'universities and technical colleges do not capture data on students with disabilities and, where such data are captured, they are not disaggregated as to disability type or gender'.[86] The same study reported that where limited data were available, the universities acknowledged that it was unreliable. An additional factor was the finding that students tended not to disclose their disability, due to stigma, fear of discrimination and restricted choice of studies.[87]

Understanding the numbers of students with disabilities in universities and their circumstances can improve efforts to remove disabling barriers and

[84] Organisation for Economic Co-operation and Development (OECD), *Disability in Higher Education* (Organisation for Economic Co-operation and Development, 2003), 23.

[85] Foundations of Tertiary Institutions in the Northern Metropolis, South Africa, 'Disability in Higher Education', Project Report (New York, NY: Ford Foundation, 2011), 12; Janet E. Lord et al., 'Needs Assessment of Persons with Disabilities in Egyptian Public Universities and Technical Colleges, Final Report and Executive Summary' (USAID/Egypt, 26 December 2017).

[86] Lord et al. (n. 85).

[87] Ibid.

provide appropriate services to students with disabilities at all levels of education. Tracking retention rates of students with disabilities is likewise an important indicator of inclusion.[88] Improving data collection and promoting the disaggregation of data according to disability is an area of major concern, not only for implementing the CRPD but also in order to meet global commitments under the SDGs. Development donors and their implementing partners, when assessing the situation of disability within a country, will more than likely find that it is difficult to obtain or rely on the accuracy of disability data. For example, disability is often not included within the government census and as a result it is often difficult to know the accurate numbers of men and women with disabilities within a country. Due to social stigmatisation, many individuals with disabilities may be reluctant to self-identify as someone with a disability, further skewing statistics within a country. Likewise, many disabilities are 'hidden' (such as developmental disabilities or many psychosocial disabilities) and one cannot ascertain if someone has a disability by simple observation.

Legal Framework for Inclusive Higher Education Supported by Development Programmes

Assessments in support of education projects funded by international cooperation must take due account of the legal framework and assess the extent to which there is an enabling legal environment for inclusive education at all levels. In many developing countries, the disability law and policy environment is wholly underdeveloped and thus provides no foundation at all for the protection of the rights of persons with disabilities.[89] Development programmes that seek to address inclusive education must understand any shortcomings in the legal framework. Any inclusive education programme should, therefore, undertake a baseline assessment that examines the law and policy environment. This can help not only to instantiate non-discrimination and reasonable accommodation into the legal framework where it is missing but also to chart out those elements of the obligation that are progressively achievable. As an example, a baseline assessment should uncover whether and how instruments such as national education strategies, human rights action plans and disability strategies set specific targets and benchmarks for progressively realising inclusive education (e.g. comprehensive barrier

88 Elizabeth E. Getzel, "Addressing the Persistence and Retention of Students with Disabilities in Higher Education" 16 *Exceptionality* 207 (2008).

89 Lord and Stein (n. 51).

removal and retrofitting, budgeting for assistive technology and introducing disability rights law and disability studies into the higher education curriculum).

Beyond assessing the legal framework, surveying the experience of students with disabilities themselves is paramount for understanding barriers that inhibit their full participation in higher education. A study on disability inclusion in higher education in Ghana and Tanzania observed that students with disabilities felt they were regarded as additional and exceptional; they were not anticipated and were therefore not integrated into an inclusive educational environment.[90] Education officials did not grasp the notion of a right to education for these students. In Egypt, while there has been some legal progress to advance inclusive education (e.g. ratification of the CRPD and a decree by the Supreme Council of Universities relaxing restrictions on academic programme selection by persons with disabilities), gaps in law and policy remain, including the non-recognition of reasonable accommodation as an element of non-discrimination and non-ratification of the 2013 Marrakesh Treaty to Facilitate Access to Published Works for Persons Who Are Blind, Visually Impaired, or Otherwise Print Disabled.[91] Further, students with disabilities in Egypt overwhelmingly spoke of the attitudinal environment and lack of understanding, especially among faculty, as to their accommodation needs.[92]

Reform efforts funded by international cooperation too often reinforce discrimination instead of reflecting CRPD rights. Infrastructure projects that include building or refurbishing schools too often neglect accessibility measures in their design. And worse, no efforts are made to fashion locally available solutions, even where they could be cheaply and easily made to facilitate imperfect but achievable access. A large university in Egypt's capital employed a professor who used a wheelchair and had to rely on his driver each morning to get up the staircase into his building. After seeing him struggle for years, his colleagues took matters into their own hands and raised the small sum required to construct a wooden ramp.[93] The university had taken no action. An otherwise well-intentioned effort to build two toilet facilities for

90 Lord et al. (n. 85).

91 As of December 2018, Egypt had not yet ratified the Marrakesh treaty.

92 Lord et al. (n. 85).

93 Author interview with anonymous university faculty member, October 2017, via Skype, Cairo, Egypt.

boys and girls adjacent to a school in Benin was constructed on high platforms with steps.[94]

In other cases, the legal frameworks in developing countries are ill equipped to support the accessibility of higher education for students with disabilities as they are directly or indirectly discriminatory, vague and fail to include disability-specific protections, or are poorly implemented. Insufficient development of regulations also creates barriers to implementation, as governments and ministries of higher education have little awareness of effective implementation strategies to address often complex matters of accessibility. This is so even with the nearly universal ratification of the CRPD. An example from Egypt illustrates the point. Within the Supreme Council of Universities, while there was a good faith to improve accessibility for students with disabilities, there was no in-house expertise on any aspect of accessibility, including in its flagship online learning initiative.[95]

The CRPD provides for non-discrimination and equality for persons with disabilities, full and effective participation and inclusion in society, respect for difference and acceptance of persons with disabilities as part of human diversity and humanity, accessibility, autonomy and gender equality, among others. Accordingly, a component of any legal assessment of Article 24 implementation in higher education must be an analysis of the framework against those principles of the CRPD as a component of identifying discriminatory barriers to higher education for persons with disabilities. Examples of discrimination in higher education that are prohibited under international standards, including the CRPD, include:

- Denying a qualified individual with a disability admission to higher education because of her/his disability;
- Excluding a qualified student with a disability from any course, course of study or other part of its education programme or activity because of her/his disability;
- Counselling a qualified student with a disability towards more restrictive career objectives than other students.

To ensure that their programmes and activities are fully accessible to students with disabilities, universities must provide reasonable accommodations to students with disabilities. Good practice, together with a comprehensive reading of the CRPD, requires higher education institutions to make reasonable

94 Field visit by the author to Cotonou, Benin, 2016. Photograph on file with the author.
95 Lord et al. (n. 85).

modifications in their practices, policies and procedures.[96] Further, they should provide auxiliary aids and services for students with disabilities, unless to do so would fundamentally alter the nature of the goods, services, facilities or other elements provided by the university. This framework divides reasonable accommodations into two discrete categories: (1) reasonable modifications to policies, practices and procedures; and (2) auxiliary aids and services. Reasonable accommodations or modifications can take many forms, depending on the individual student's needs. Examples of modifications that universities could introduce to make their policies, practices and procedures accessible to students with disabilities include:

- Allowing course substitutions for certain required or prerequisite courses;
- Allowing extra time on exams and holding exams in accessible rooms;
- Allowing a reduced course load and extended time within which to complete degree requirements; and
- Providing housing accommodations for a student's personal care assistant.

Auxiliary aids and services can also take many forms, depending on the individual student's needs. Examples of auxiliary aids and services that universities can provide to ensure accessibility for students with disabilities include:

- Qualified interpreters or other effective methods of making aurally delivered materials available to individuals with hearing impairments;
- Note takers;
- Qualified readers, tape-recorded or digitally recorded texts or other effective methods of making visually delivered materials accessible to individuals with visual impairments;
- Class materials, university policies and procedures in alternative formats (e.g. texts in Braille, on audiotape or as digital files);
- Acquisition or modification of equipment or devices.

Studies support the view that the effective inclusion of persons with disabilities in any level of education requires a clear legislative and policy framework underpinned by strong institutional commitment. It is also clear that even where disability laws are in place, stigma and discrimination persist and are reflected in deep cultural and structural bias that impacts the culture of higher education. As in other realms of society, in higher education persons

96 CRPD (n.1) arts.2, 5, 24.

with disabilities are uniformly underestimated and not afforded the same opportunities as their peers. Addressing systemic barriers through a rights-based, whole-institution approach is required.[97] In the light of the foregoing, advancing the right to inclusion in higher education for persons with disabilities in the context of international development is fundamentally important and cannot be addressed in one-off, ad hoc or siloed approaches that only address one or another barriers.

Approaches to disability inclusion in higher education through international development partnerships require an understanding of discrimination that, consistent with the CRPD, proscribes both intentional (direct) and non-intentional (indirect) discrimination and exclusion. Direct discrimination, such as placing restrictions on persons with disabilities to enter university or college, based on type of disability, is grounded on prejudicial assumptions that students with certain disabilities will be unable to complete the course work or persons with certain categories of disability are simply unable to achieve a given area. Indirect or non-intentional discrimination arises from practices that are ostensibly neutral in nature but that generate a discriminatory effect, such as a policy allowing all students to apply to university, including students with disabilities, but in practice, the application process, including forms, are inaccessible. This type of indirect discrimination acknowledges that problems of inequality are both systemic and individual in nature.

When applied in practice to higher education, the duty to provide reasonable accommodation requires the identification and dismantling of barriers in educational institutions arising from physical and communication accessibility challenges, lack of knowledge and understanding by university administration and faculty about specific disability needs and rigid procedures, provisions and practices which are historically embedded in educational exclusion. It requires matching the needs to the appropriate support that brings about equal participation of students with disabilities in learning, participation and development.

Other positive measures are required to achieve full and equal access to higher education. Full implementation of the right to education is subject to progressive realisation and yet states are required to move expeditiously towards full implementation. One measure to demonstrate forward movement is the proactive engagement of development cooperation funding in

97 Mel Ainscow and Anton Florek, 'A Whole School Approach', in Mel Ainscow and Anton Florek (eds), *Special Educational Needs: Towards a Whole School Approach* (David Fulton Publishers, 1989) 1–6.

support of inclusive education. Applying accessibility to higher education thus encompasses access to all aspects of higher education. Students with disabilities should be able to access, on an equal basis with others, the physical environment, transportation, information and communications, including information and communications technologies and systems (ICTs) and other facilities and services, both in urban and in rural areas. The various elements of accessibility and illustrative barriers as they pertain to higher education are discussed in the sections that follow, with a specific focus on integrating these dimensions of accessibility into a comprehensive higher education accessibility assessment framework that could guide baseline assessments of disability inclusion in higher education funded by international development.

Physical Accessibility in Higher Education

Physical accessibility to campus facilities is a precondition for accessing academic programmes and services. Put simply, physical access includes barrier-free entry to a building, a classroom and a physical space or area. Assessment issues should begin with threshold questions like: Can one enter the building? Can one navigate the building? Can one use signs to get where s/he wants to? Can one get around using a wheelchair? Can one get through doors? Even in the absence of local standards on accessibility – the case in many developing countries – assessments of physical access can be benchmarked against standards developed elsewhere and modified.

Physical access to universities and technical colleges poses considerable challenges for students with disabilities. In many developing countries, universities are large, sprawling campuses, and are sometimes spread across a section of a large and crowded city. Cairo University, for instance, is spread out, intersected by multi-lane, traffic-filled streets, and overflows with a student body of 270,000. Even where a campus is self-contained, it may pose major challenges to persons with disabilities due to an overcrowded student population (e.g. at entrances of campus buildings, along pathways) or disrepair (e.g. uneven surfaces, hazards such as uncovered holes in the ground).[98] Utilisation of a comprehensive accessibility audit tool will enable a full range of accessibility considerations to be addressed, and will cover access for wheelchair users and persons with mobility impairments of various kinds as well as hazards posed for blind students and students with low vision.

98 Lord et al. (n. 85).

Such assessments should be part and parcel of any inclusive education development project at any level of education.

Disabled people's organisations (DPOs) and development projects working on physical accessibility in developing countries routinely use standards developed elsewhere and adapt them to suit local contexts. A common approach is to modify the Americans with Disabilities Barrier Removal Checklist, a tool used most recently in assessing the accessibility of public higher education to Egyptians with disabilities enrolled in public universities in Egypt.[99] In another instance in Egypt, the disability organisation HELM also used the Americans with Disabilities Act checklist and piloted it at a large university in Cairo.[100]

Programmatic Accessibility in Higher Education

Accessibility in an inclusive education context should be understood to mean whether a person with a disability can meaningfully receive, participate in and benefit from academic and extra-curricular facilities and services offered by an institution of higher education. This accords with the CRPD in Article 9, which defines 'accessibility' in broad terms and provides important conceptual guidance in addition to setting forth state obligations.

When organisations attempt to make their services accessible to people with disabilities, they may emphasise physical access but fail to take into account the many other barriers to programmes and services in order for persons with disabilities to enjoy equal access. Full access to the academic programme is, of course, an integral aspect of equality of access to higher education. In addition, universities can offer a range of services beyond academic teaching, including job search resources and assistance, field trips and various workshops and training programmes. To create programmatic accessibility, universities must design all of their services and train their faculty and staff so that they can understand and anticipate the needs of a broad diversity of individuals with disabilities.[101] This may include facilitating access to textbooks and other course materials in an accessible format. Where a university does not have staffing resources to accommodate all student needs for accessible formats – whether Braille printers, electronic scanners, audio formats or accessible e-formats – there may be undue delay or failure altogether to

99 Ibid.

100 See www.helmegypt.org.

101 Christie L. Gilson, Stacy K. Dymond, Janis G. Chadsey and Sharon Yu Fang Hsu, 'Gaining Access to Textbooks for Postsecondary Students with Visual Impairments', (2007) 20 *Journal of Postsecondary Education and Disability* 28.

provide appropriate access. Staffing and resources are often cited as obstacles to the provision of sign language interpreters, a problem that is endemic in developing countries. This limitation is likely to fuel further restrictions on deaf students, as in the all too common restriction to all but a handful of academic programmes. Accommodation of persons with learning or other cognitive disabilities is negligible in developing countries, not surprising given that this is an area where higher education continues to struggle in developed countries. The implication for undertaking comprehensive assessments in this context, therefore, is to ensure that programmatic accessibility includes academic programming and all elements required to access programming (e.g. library services) as well as extra-curricular programming.

Access to the Online Environment in Higher Education

An increasingly important element of higher education is accessing and sharing information in the online environment, via university websites and school-related online resources, such as club Facebook pages, online courses and the like. The CRPD Committee has underscored the importance of accessible pedagogic material, inclusive of access to assistive technology and pedagogic materials online.[102] There is no one-size-fits-all assessment tool, but in each case, an assessment must be adapted for the online environment.

A starting point for such an assessment, either on its own or integrated into broader programmes addressing ICT infrastructure, ought to include the following baseline questions in order to align with the requirements for accessibility in the online environment under the CRPD: (1) What, if any, disability-specific services are mentioned on the website? (2) Do students have opportunities to 'enrol' in university services/programmes/activities or to take online courses? (3) Is it easy to find information on the site? Why or why not? (4) Are pictures or graphics (such as logos) included on the website? When a mouse rolls over these, does a text description pop up? (5) Where media content is online, is captioning produced for content and transcripts for audio content? If yes, are alternative presentations (such as text or captioning) provided? (6) Is information available online about programmes or services

[102] See, for example, CRPD Committee, Concluding Observations on the Initial Reports of Azerbaijan, CRPD/C/AZE/CO/1, 12 May 2014, para. 41(a); Concluding Observations on the Initial Reports of El Salvador, CRPD/C/SLV/CO/1, 8 October 2013, para. 50(c); 2013; Concluding Observations on the Initial Report of Korea, CRPD/C/KOR/1, 29 October 2014. The CRPD underscores the need to undertake measures to design accessible pedagogical tools and teaching methods and to ensure that students with disabilities have access to new technologies and the Internet.

for students with disabilities, such as a page for a disability service centre? If yes, is it easy to find and up to date? (7) Does the information provided about disability services (if any) include how to seek accommodations and communication aids and services? The foregoing represents an initial start and should be combined with a technical assessment of compliance with the Web Content Accessibility Guidelines 2.0 which is readily available online as a free service.[103] Such an approach advances CRPD implementation. Moreover, the use of captions and transcripts has added benefits: transcripts facilitate the development of subtitles in a number of languages and improve the indexing of online content. Indexing, in turn, enhances search engine optimisation and the discoverability (and thus accessibility) of a university's online content.

Communication Accessibility

Communication – broadly defined under the CRPD – includes the different modes and formats in which university students, faculty and staff may interact and exchange information and processes inherent to accessing university and technical college services and facilities.[104] Communications accessibility is also relevant when ICTs are used or needed to deliver and enjoy services, including when students with visual impairments use Braille machines to take notes or screen-reading software to access material in digital formats. Relatedly, the CRPD recognises both spoken and signed as well as other forms of non-spoken languages.[105] Likewise, addressing accessibility in inclusive education regarding different modes and formats of learning course material is essential to persons with learning disabilities, who account for the largest percentage of students with disabilities. And yet in developing countries, students with learning disabilities are rarely if ever accommodated as they do not self-disclose, do not have awareness of their disability and need assistance and/or the services that do exist do not have the resources to cater to their needs.[106]

103 Web Content Accessibility Guidelines 2.0, www.w3.org/WAI/intro/wcag.

104 Under the CRPD Article 2, '"Communication" includes languages, display of text, Braille, tactile communication, large print, accessible multimedia as well as written, audio, plain-language, human-reader and augmentative and alternative modes, means and formats of communication, including accessible information and communication technology.' CRPD, art. 2.

105 Under the CRPD Article 2, '"Language" includes spoken and signed languages and other forms of non-spoken languages.'

106 A study of disability inclusion in South Africa underscored that disability services in higher education institutions were under-resourced and focussed overwhelmingly on accommodating

An important element of analysing accessibility in higher education in an assessment concerns information and communication services and devices for students with disabilities. There must be an examination of access to quality sign language interpretation services and the facilitation of other modes and means of communication used by blind, deaf and deaf-blind students. This should include, for example, examining the accessibility of (1) resources for students with disabilities to utilise job/career centres (where available); (2) other career/employment services at universities, whether those are provided for 'self-service' or directly by staff; and (3) information in accessible formats, such as print and electronic resources or alternative formats (e.g. large print formats for persons with low vision) if individuals are unable to access the information and benefit from these services.[107] Obtaining student feedback is critical in order to understand the quality of access. Even where assistive technology is available to make communications accessible, it is important to know whether staff are aware of its presence and how it can be used to facilitate access.

Disability, Gender and Intersectionality

Any assessment of the accessibility of higher education to students with disabilities must address the impact of the social environment on women and girls. Women with disabilities face multiple and intersecting forms of discrimination, and this invariably impacts their experience in higher education. This requires asking the right questions and obtaining the kind of quality data that can guide gender-inclusive recommendations. International standards on disability, including Article 6 of the CRPD, place particular emphasis on gender equality. Further, the SDGs recognise that gender equality is a development goal in its own right and a necessary precondition to sustainable development.[108]

blind and physically disabled students. Foundations of Tertiary Institutions in the Northern Metropolis, South Africa, 'Disability in Higher Education' (2011) 12.

107 Gilson, et al (n. 101).

108 The CRPD in various provisions highlights the multidimensional discrimination faced by women and girls with disabilities, and obligates states, in the implementation of the Convention, to take into account the unique needs of women and girls with disabilities. In Preamble (s), referenced is 'the need to incorporate a gender perspective in all efforts to promote the full enjoyment of human rights and fundamental freedoms by persons with disabilities', and, in Article 6, states 'recognize that women and girls with disabilities are subject to multiple discrimination, and in this regard shall take measures to ensure the full and equal enjoyment by them of all human rights and fundamental freedoms'. CRPD (n.1) Preamble (s) and art. 6.

While gaps in disability data and in disability data disaggregated on the basis of sex may not be readily available, other efforts can be undertaken to be responsive to gender dimensions including, for instance, focus group discussions with students with disabilities, faculty and administrators and online surveys. Mainstream human rights reporting may also yield useful insights as to the particular cultural context and its gender dimension. Particular attention should be given to assessing gender-based dynamics for students with disabilities in higher education regarding admissions, services, accommodations, assistive technologies, facility access and any major inequity challenges and steps that should be taken to reach gender parity.

Effective inclusive education policies have to be supported by financing for schools that will allow for accessible school infrastructure, teacher training and salaries and interventions that support social protection, for example, school feeding schemes. In this context, strategic advocacy in support of inclusive education must be directed towards human rights budget analysis.[109]

The post-2015 agenda presents an excellent platform to address the myriad of inequalities that children with disabilities experience in accessing their right to education. Addressing these inequalities will require the following: (1) collecting and disaggregating data on disability that can be transformed into an internationally agreed framework of categories comprising learners with disabilities and other disadvantages and (2) developing internationally agreed indicators for inclusive education that might include information on the prevalence of different categories of learners by disability, age, gender, place of education (i.e. special school, special class or regular school classes) and teacher–student ratio.

Staffing in Higher Education

Research across the world is conclusive that the attitudinal environment is a fundamental element of student satisfaction for students with disabilities in higher education.[110] Research points to the prevalence of negative attitudes, and low expectations of students with disabilities act as significant barriers to education, leading, for instance, to non-self-disclosure and reluctance to seek

109 See on this point the chapter in this volume on 'Financing Inclusive Education: Lessons from Developing Countries' by János Fiala (Chapter 9).

110 Marie Kraska, 'Postsecondary Students with Disabilities and Perception of Faculty Members', (2003) 25(2) *Journal for Vocational Special Needs Education* 11.

necessary disability accommodations and supports.[111] This, in turn, poses challenges for accurate data collection that can feed into the design and implementation of effective disability supports for students.[112] Likewise, it points to barriers in hiring persons with disabilities in higher education, a crucial element of creating an enabling learning environment for students with disabilities.

Research also underscores the high relevance of faculty attitudes in shaping the experience of students with disabilities in higher education.[113] Attitudinal barriers prompted the drafters of the CRPD to include detailed provisions on disability awareness raising in Article 8. Importantly, the CRPD draws out the connection between inclusive education and the hiring of persons with disabilities as teachers and administrators. Absent implementation of the CRPD holistically in education, taking a 'whole of institution approach', opportunities for persons with disabilities in the education sector will often be limited. First, failures to accommodate students with disabilities at the primary and secondary levels results in poor attendance in higher education, especially in developing countries. Further, universities, much more so than primary or secondary schools, operate more independently, meaning that students with disabilities' experience will vary not only from institution to institution, but within university faculties, and even departments within those faculties.[114]

The CRPD Committee had an occasion to consider a communication submitted under the Optional Protocol to the CRPD by an applicant who

[111] See generally Getzel (n. 88); Sheila Riddell, 'Chipping Away at the Mountain: Disabled Students' Experiences of Higher Education in South Africa', (1999) 8 *International Studies of Sociology and Education* 203.

[112] On the important role that disability inclusion within academic curricula can play in creating awareness of disability, see Chioma Ohajunwa, Judith McKenzie and Theresa Lorenzo, 'Enabling Disability Inclusive Practices within the University of Cape Town Curriculum: A Case Study', (2015) 4(1) *Journal of African Disability Studies* 157 (2015). See, for example, Kraska (n. 110), Shaila Rao, "Faculty Attitudes and Students with Disabilities in Higher Education: A Literature Review," (2004) 38(2) *College Student Journal* 191; Lord et al., (n. 85).

[113] Kraska (n. 110), Rao (n. 112) and Lord et al (n. 85).

[114] Nafisa Mayat and Seyi L. Amosun, 'Perceptions of Academic Staff towards Accommodating Students with Disabilities in a Civil Engineering Undergraduate Program in a University in South Africa', (2010) 24(1) *Journal of Postsecondary Education and Disability* 53.

alleged disability discrimination in hiring at an Italian university.[115] There, the Committee declined to find discrimination under Article 27 in the non-hiring of the applicant on the basis that the Italian university had made a hiring decision based on reasonable and objective grounds, that the applicant had competed in the examination and two other applicants scored higher than he did on the exam. The Committee, however, declined to comment on the implications of the CRPD for advancing person with disabilities into the workforce, as through measures of affirmative action or quota systems. In that case, the Italian system did have quotas for hiring persons with disabilities but chose not to trigger them in the case of the applicant. It is to be hoped that in future communications under the Optional Protocol, the Committee will have the occasion to weigh in more substantively on the role of affirmative action in redressing the gross under-representation of person with disabilities in the workforce and in higher education, and the unworkability of quota systems without monitoring and enforcement.

Admissions and Eligibility

Many of the barriers that children with disabilities experience in primary and secondary school are directly attributable to failures within higher education. As one study on disability access for disabled students in Tanzania and Ghana emphasised, where there is a history of segregated school-based education which is insufficiently rigorous and academic, the participation of students with disabilities is often not predicted and thus not prepared for in higher education.[116]

Restrictive practices on accepting students with disabilities into universities or into certain faculties, including schools of education, seriously impede access to successful role models with disabilities who attained higher education. This vicious cycle of exclusion undermines the CRPD emphasis in Article 24 on having teachers with disabilities in classrooms. Proactive recruitment of persons with disabilities in teaching training programmes is thus worthy of specific attention by donor-funded programmes. Donor-funded programmes in higher education, such as the Erasmus Plus programme of the European Union, could, pursuing an inclusive mandate, open doors for teachers with disabilities from developing countries to attain higher education

115 Committee on the Rights of Persons with Disabilities, Communication No. 9/2012, Views Adopted by the Committee at Its Thirteenth Session (25 March–17 April 2015), CRPD/C/13/D/9/2012.

116 Morley (n. 78) 8–9.

in developed countries with the objective of returning to take on teaching roles in their home countries.[117]

A second element of inclusion impacting access concerns training on accessible ICT. This is vital both to serve students with disabilities who must be able to access ICTs and to ensure that the surge in online teaching, such as e-learning, does not leave students with disabilities behind. Curiously, those faculties best equipped to train university students on accessibility in the ICT context very often do not provide coverage of accessibility in ICTs and often exclude students with disabilities from their courses. Blind students, for instance, are routinely denied entry into faculties of information and communication in developing countries and likewise have trouble accessing faculties of engineering and computer science. This is so notwithstanding the fact that many blind students have an understanding of and interest in the study of accessible ICT on account of their own user experience and expertise. The surge in e-learning opportunities is an avenue for expanding education opportunity in higher education for students with disabilities in developing countries if designed in accordance with web accessibility standards.[118]

Advancing Disability Studies within Higher Education

Integrating a disability perspective into academic disciplines across the academy is essential to promote broad inclusion within society. The same observation holds true for CRPD Committee observations on foreign assistance under Article 32. And yet the entry points for supporting disability inclusion in higher education projects abound. International development initiatives that seek to establish law clinics, to train paralegals, to provide continuing legal education to lawyers and judges or to establish online human rights education are all important platforms for disability rights. Further, providing hands-on experience within schools of engineering and architecture in developing country universities is an obvious but hitherto untapped opportunity within higher education to advance accessibility and universal design for future architects and engineers and experiential learning through barrier removal competitions on inaccessible campuses. University scholarship programmes such as the vast

117 See EU Erasmus Plus Programme: https://ec.europa.eu/programmes/erasmus-plus/node_en.

118 See, for example, Peter Blanck, *eQuality: The Struggle for Web Accessibility by People with Cognitive Disabilities* (Cambridge University Press 2014). See also Michael Stein and Jonathan Lazar, *Global Inclusion: Disability, Human Rights, and Information Technology* (University of Pennsylvania Press 2017).

Erasmus Plus programme supported by the European Union provide opportunities, in theory if not in practice, for students with disabilities from developing countries to study abroad. This may enable them to acquire much-needed skill sets not available in their home institutions and to offer programming for students interested in pursuing career paths that support disability inclusion in society.

Likewise, development programmes that support the education of health professionals offer opportunities to provide education on disability inclusion for future health sector personnel and, likewise, ought to set aside placements for persons with disabilities to be included in health sector education projects. USAID funding has been supporting disability-inclusive approaches to health sector development, with leadership provided by USAID implementer Management Sciences for Health. Failure to do so ultimately undermines health development objectives, as demonstrated by research exposing the neglect of public health development cooperation programmes that fail on disability-inclusion grounds.[119]

Accessing Campus Facilities

Students with disabilities in higher education face numerous obstacles in accessing campus facilities, particularly in developing countries.[120] At first instance, transport to campuses is often an insurmountable challenge where accessible transport – public or private – does not exist. Research in developing countries indicates that barriers in both transport and physical infrastructure are a major problem cited by students with disabilities in higher education.[121] A study of women with disabilities in higher education in Kenya reported major barriers in terms of inaccessible campus buildings and lack of transportation, lack of response by university administration in addressing access concerns and an overall lack of institutional responsibility for improving

119 For how to operationalise disability inclusion in health care programmes funded by international cooperation, see Kate Wilson, *What Does Universal Health Care Coverage Have to Do with Disability Inclusion?* 10 August 2017, https://medium.com/@MSHHealthImpact/what-does-disability-inclusion-have-to-do-with-universal-health-coverage-7959d906a1c4 Leadership, Management and Governance Project Inclusive Health Checklist, https://docs.google.com/document/d/1kfrssDx8NQgM7q6ImjrGlsiT_bAQqLbFvktoPUTvYCg/edit.

120 Lord et al (n. 85).

121 Teresa Tinklin and John Hall, 'Getting Round Obstacles: Disabled Students' Experiences in Higher Education in Scotland', 24 *Studies in Higher Education* 184 (1999). See also Sarah Holloway, 'The Experience of Higher Education from the Perspective of Disabled Students', 18(4) *Disability & Society* 597 (2001).

physical access.[122] Physical barriers impact whether and how students with disabilities are able to access and participate in the array of services offered in higher education, including lectures, library facilities, housing, sport and recreational events and pathways across campus. Accessibility audits point to major challenges in movement around campus, restrictions in campus building entry and egress and lack of signage where there are accessible entrances, among others. Additional barriers include barriers to water and sanitation facilities, hazards on pathways for blind persons and resource limitations especially for retrofitting old buildings.[123]

Extracurricular Activities

Accessibility to the academic programmes (online and in class) provided by universities is but one facet of a student's life in higher education. The accessing of extracurricular activities – in short, access to all aspects of a student's life at an institution of higher education – is a core part of the experience and a major component of assessing the extent to which the institution in question is an enabling environment, socially and otherwise, for students with disabilities.[124] All too often, students with disabilities, whether in higher education or at lower levels, face barriers and outright exclusion from extracurricular programming.[125] Access to extracurricular elements of education may be pegged to Article 24 of the CRPD, which requires equal access by persons with disabilities to all aspects of education at all levels, and to other CRPD provisions, such as Article 30 on participation in cultural life as well as sport, recreation, leisure and play. Article 30 provides detailed obligations as to cultural, recreational and sporting activities, all of which are germane to the life of a university student.

[122] Opini, *Barriers to Participation of Women Students with Disabilities in University Education in Kenya* (2012) 65–71.

[123] Lord et al (n. 85).

[124] Ainscow and Florek (n. 97).

[125] See Janet E. Lord and Michael Ashley Stein, 'Social Rights and the Relational Value of the Rights to Participate in Sport, Recreation and Play', 27 *Boston University International Law Journal* 249 (2009) (arguing that 'even under an energized progression of social rights cases in international and domestic courts, rights relating to sport, recreation, leisure and play remain on the sidelines of human rights practice'). See also Michael Stein and Janet E. Lord, 'Jacobus tenBroek, Participatory Justice, and the UN Convention on the Rights of Persons with Disabilities', (2007) 13 *Texas Journal on Civil Liberties & Civil Rights* 167, 179.

Monitoring CRPD Implementation in Higher Education

The institutional arrangements created by the CRPD, including its annual Conference of States Parties (COSP) and the work of its treaty-monitoring body, the Committee on the Rights of Persons with Disabilities, are important vehicles for advancing inclusive development in the education sector. Both the CRPD Committee and the COSP create global platforms for advancing disability-inclusive development and the rights of persons with disabilities. The effectiveness of these platforms for advancing CRPD implementation in higher education hinges not only on States Parties and the CRPD Committee but also equally on DPOs, NGOs, individual researchers and advocates in harnessing the potential of such venues. To date, very little focus on the accessibility of higher education to persons with disabilities writ large is evident in either the work of the CRPD Committee or of the COSP. The latter performs a function quite different from the more operationally focussed environmental treaty conferences and is all too often utilised as a self-promotional exercise not only for states, but equally if not more for DPOs and NGOs.

The CRPD Committee, in its monitoring of state reports, has consistently underscored the necessity of ensuring that reasonable accommodation is part of the legislative base that protects students with disabilities against discrimination in education.[126] In higher education, reasonable accommodation alleviates the disadvantage that too often persists for students with disabilities as they attempt to navigate conventional requirements for admission and traditional systems rife with barriers to all aspects of the higher educational experience.

While the CRPD Committee has, to some extent, addressed disability inclusion in development cooperation, it could further advance the agenda for disability-inclusive development with the dedication of a General Day of Discussion on the topic and work towards the adoption of a General Comment on Disability Inclusive Development. Further, it could take more detailed account of disability-inclusive development within the framework of its work in other sectors, noting the linkages when reporting on education in a developing country or when reporting on CRPD implementation by donor countries. The effectiveness of such a strategy, however, will largely depend on quality information being provided to the CRPD Committee by DPOs and other stakeholders. Capacity in disability-inclusive development among

[126] See, for example, CRPD Committee, Concluding Observations on the Initial Reports of Azerbaijan, CRPD/C/AZE/CO/1, 12 May 2014, para. 41(a); Concluding Observations on the Initial Reports of El Salvador, CRPD/C/SLV/CO/1, 8 October 2013, para. 50(c).

DPOs is underdeveloped and thus a much-needed area for capacity building by donors. This too is a point that could well be highlighted by the CRPD Committee and ought to be a focus of future COSP meetings.

At the domestic level, the CRPD recognises the essential role of national-level monitoring in advancing the CRPD. In Article 33, it accords monitoring roles to government, requiring a governmental focal point and suggesting a coordination mechanism, necessitating an independent national human rights monitoring mechanism, such as a human rights commission and monitoring by civil society.[127] Here, it is essential that governmental inter-ministerial task forces on disability, or related mechanisms such as coordinating bodies for human rights action plans, include ministries of higher education and any other governmental entity with responsibility for higher education.[128] Further, national human rights institutions should, as part of their role in national-level monitoring of the CRPD, develop linkages to higher education authorities and work to advance inclusive education at all levels of education. There is a clear role for international cooperation programmes to support and provide technical assistance and capacity-building on inclusive education in higher education. Existing programmes – such as scholarship programmes to study abroad, projects to equip universities in developing countries with information and communication technology and support for teacher training colleges – are all opportunities for including persons with disabilities. At the same time, targeted programmes that assess entry points for combatting barriers to higher education for students with disabilities and design programmes accordingly are much needed.

CONCLUSION

The historical and (unfortunately) contemporary approach to disability inclusion in education initiatives funded through development cooperation is limited and could well benefit from more focussed attention by donors.[129] While significant barriers persist in ensuring that children with disabilities have access to primary and secondary education, some attention has been given in recent years to funding inclusive education initiatives in this context. The pipeline into higher education for persons with disabilities is, fortunately,

[127] Gauthier de Beco, 'Article 33(2) of the UN Convention on the Rights of Persons with Disabilities: Another Role for National Human Rights Institutions?' (2011) 29(1) *Netherlands Quarterly of Human Rights* 84.

[128] The provision on coordinating implementation of the CRPD is art. 33(3).

[129] Lord et al (n. 85).

expanding, although much work remains to be done at all levels of education to realise the goals of inclusive education for students with disabilities.[130]

While the work of donors such as UNICEF have helped to advance inclusive education at lower levels of education, it remains the case that too little attention has been given to the barriers evident in higher education. This neglect impacts both the access of persons with disabilities to higher education programmes and, further, affects the capacities of school systems to respond with inclusive practices and qualified teachers, administrators, sign language interpreters and other trained personnel in primary and secondary schools. The persistence of these barriers makes it difficult for students with disabilities to access higher education, especially in developing countries, and those who manage to gain entry face numerous obstacles. Emerging research into the accessibility of higher education to students with disabilities in developing countries suggests that many of the barriers faced are addressable at the level of law, policy and low-cost barrier removal. This will require a more concerted effort by donors to support high-quality assessment work coupled with programming designed to remove barriers experienced by persons with disabilities in higher education.

130 Reiser (n. 76) 31.

13

Harnessing Technology to Realize the Right to Inclusive Education

Deepti S. Raja and G. Anthony Giannoumis

1 INTRODUCTION

"Everyone has the right to education," as stated in the Universal Declaration of Human Rights (UDHR) in 1948.[1] In June 2016, the UN Human Rights Council amended Article 19 of the UDHR to further affirm the importance of access to the Internet to realize human rights.[2] Section 32 on "The promotion, protection and enjoyment of human rights on the Internet" explicitly recognizes the importance of the Internet and information and communication technologies (ICTs) in promoting human rights and socioeconomic development.[3] Literacy and access to information are central to exercising human rights, and hence the ability to access and use the Internet is now a prominent topic in discourses on both human rights and international development.[4] These developments complement the United Nations (UN) Convention on the Rights of Persons with Disabilities (CRPD), which obligates States Parties to ensure access to ICT for persons with disabilities on an equal basis with others.

Over the past two decades, the disability rights community has made significant strides in convincing governments and communities that children with disabilities should have equal opportunities as those without disabilities to receive a quality education.[5] As the attitudinal barriers to inclusive education begin to lower, the conversation and focus turns to "how?" Realizing the right to

[1] Universal Declaration of Human Rights (adopted December 10, 1948, UNGA Res. 217 A(III) (UDHR).

[2] United Nations General Assembly Oral Revisions of June 30 (2017) UN Doc A/HRC/32/L.20.

[3] Ibid.

[4] Paul Jaeger, Brian Wentz, and John Carlo Bertot, "The Intersection of Human Rights, Social Justice, the Internet, and Accessibility in Libraries: Access, Education, and Inclusion," in Jonathan Lazar and Michael Stein (eds.), *Disability, Human Rights, and Information Technology* (University of Pennsylvania Press 2017).

[5] Dorothy Kerzner Lipsky and Alan Gartner, *Inclusion and School Reform: Transforming America's Classrooms* (Paul H. Brookes Publishing Company 1997).

inclusive education is in part dependent on using tools and strategies that can level the playing field for children with and without disabilities.[6] Information and communication technology has emerged as a prominent enabler for access to lifelong education, skills development, and employment.[7]

This chapter focuses on the nexus of the right to education and the right to the Internet and ICT for persons with disabilities. It makes the case that technology must be viewed as a policy strategy to realize the right to inclusive education as well as a tool at the organizational and individual levels to enable individualized learning and successful learning outcomes for students with disabilities. In addition, it discusses different elements of the policy and practice ecosystem that impact and influence how ICT can be harnessed to support quality learning outcomes for persons with disabilities.

2 THE OPPORTUNITY FOR TECHNOLOGY AS AN EQUALIZER IN EDUCATION

The growing evidence of the importance of technology for development has led to the assertion of the right to the Internet and ICT for all,[8] and for equal access to these technologies for persons with disabilities.[9] Information and communication technology can be a catalyst and tool in realizing the right to education for learners with and without disabilities. It can be a disruptive force in the field of inclusive education due to several advantages described later in this chapter.

2.1 *ICT Supports Learning for Students with Disabilities*

2.1.1 Multiple Ways of Communicating and Using Information

Information and communication technology enables the use of multiple means of interaction – voice, text, video, touch, and gestures – to access information, create content, and engage with others, and hence can help to

6 Lee Ann Basser, "Justice for All: The Challenge of Realizing the Right to Education for Children with Disabilities" (2004) 8 *Journal of Gender, Race & Justice* 531.

7 Broadband Commission for Digital Development, G3ict, the International Development Association (IDA), the International Telecommunication Union (ITU), Microsoft, the Telecentre.org Foundation, and the United Nations Educational, Scientific and Cultural Organization (UNESCO), "The ICT Opportunity for a Disability-Inclusive Development Framework" (2013), http://g3ict.org/resource_center/publications_and_reports/p/productCategory_whitepapers/id_297, accessed November 18, 2014.

8 United Nations General Assembly Oral Revisions of June 30.

9 Jonathan Lazar and Michael Stein (eds.), *Disability, Human Rights, and Information Technology* (University of Pennsylvania Press 2017).

address long-standing barriers to communication and interaction. Information and communication technology also allows better customization to individual preferences and functional needs. A range of ICT solutions can be used to enhance classroom and educational participation, including electronic whiteboards, recording and distributing video lectures, task organization and categorization, and memory tools and aids.[10] Figure 13.1 depicts the different ways in which different types of ICT can support the educational participation of students with disabilities.[11]

The practice of using ICTs in inclusive education encompasses three components. First, education service providers can use mainstream computing devices and technologies to deliver accessible content including personal computers, smartphones, tablets, Web browsers, wearables, educational technology such as whiteboards, mobile applications for learning, Web and video conferencing, classroom management and learning portals, cloud-based educational platforms and services, Internet-connected devices, and content-creation and rendering solutions, including word processing, recording, and multimedia creation tools.[12]

Second, education service providers can provide assistive technology that promotes access to mainstream ICT, including screen readers, voice recognition software, captioning, and augmentative and alternative communication (AAC) devices.

Third, education service providers can use digital and multimedia content, including digital textbooks, electronic course materials, audio and video content, online courses and content, massive open online courses (MOOCs), gaming, and virtual and augmented reality for teaching.

2.1.2 Bundled Functionality and Lowered Costs

The advancements and innovations in digital technologies have played a disruptive role in the field of assistive technology by embedding specialized functionalities within general consumer and personal technology. For example, most smartphones and tablets have built-in accessibility features. This is bringing down the cost barrier for families and providers and improving access through off-the-shelf products. While new ICT cannot fully replace or address the needs for specialized assistive technology for some students, it is helping to

[10] Ibid.

[11] Deepti S. Raja, "Bridging the Disability Divide through Digital Technologies," The World Bank Group, http://pubdocs.worldbank.org/en/123481461249337484/WDR16-BP-Bridging-the-Disability-Divide-through-Digital-Technology-RAJA.pdf, accessed October 26, 2016.

[12] Jutta Treviranus (2016). Life-Long Learning on the Inclusive Web. Proceedings of the 13th Web for All Conference, Association for Computing Machinery (ACM).

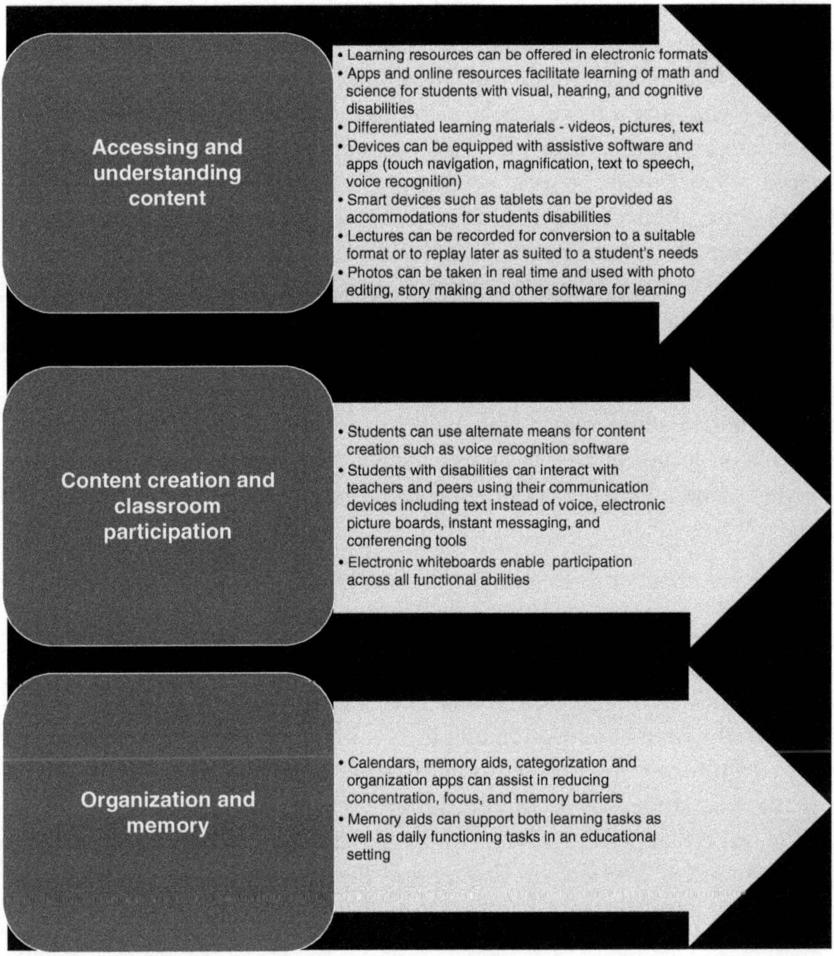

FIGURE 13.1 How ICT addresses barriers to participation in education for persons with disabilities (Source: Raja, 2016)

bring overall costs down. For example, AAC devices can be cost-prohibitive for families in low- and middle-income countries. Today's smart consumer electronic devices can be configured to offer similar functionality with the combination of integrated accessibility features and free or paid mobile applications. Foley and Ferri suggest that even with the use of costly, high-end applications on a smart device, the total cost could come down significantly.[13] This helps to

[13] Alan Foley and Beth A. Ferri, "Technology for People, Not Disabilities: Ensuring Access and Inclusion" (2012) 12(4) *Journal of Research in Special Educational Needs* 192.

open the doors for access to high-end technology solutions for many students with disabilities for the first time.

Many children and youth with disabilities need more than one type of assistive technology solution. In the past, this invariably meant procuring multiple different devices. Many new ICT products bundle multiple accessibility features – for example, personal computer operating systems, smartphones, and tablets come prepackaged with accessibility features such as text-to-speech, voice recognition, preferences for mouse and keyboard navigation, contrast settings, and magnification in one device. This is further enhanced by growing choice in online, Web-enabled and mobile tools and applications. Individuals can find solutions that help with instant captioning, remote sign language interpretation, navigation, memory and organization, assistance with math, composition, reading, note taking, object recognition, and recording personal information to use in case of an emergency. This is promoting affordability, efficiency, and portability of accessible technology solutions for learning.

2.2 *Education Is Embracing Technology as a Mode of Delivery*

There is an opportunistic climate for advocating the use of accessible ICTs in breaking barriers to educational participation and learning for children with disabilities. Figure 13.2 shows how the confluence of several major trends in the field of education and the proliferation of digital technologies offer a significant opportunity to harness the potential of technology as an equalizer for students with disabilities across learning environments.

The first is that pedagogy is moving toward differentiated learning practices recognizing that learners are diverse and that a "one-size-fits-all" approach may fail at appropriately harnessing each student's talent for successful learning.[14] Differentiated learning aims to maximize each student's learning outcomes by engaging students using different approaches, appealing to their varying interests, and providing a range of supports that are responsive to the differing needs of individual students.[15] The underlying assumption is that students' road maps for learning need not be identical to one another.[16] An approach that is built on acknowledging student diversity is intrinsically suited to respecting disability as a part of the human experience.

[14] Gayle H. Gregory and Carolyn Chapman, *Differentiated Instructional Strategies: One Size Doesn't Fit All* (3rd edn.) (Corwin 2013).

[15] Carol Tomlinson, *The Differentiated Classroom: Responding to the Needs of All Learners* (2nd edn.) (Association for Supervision and Curriculum Development [ASCD] 2014).

[16] Ibid.

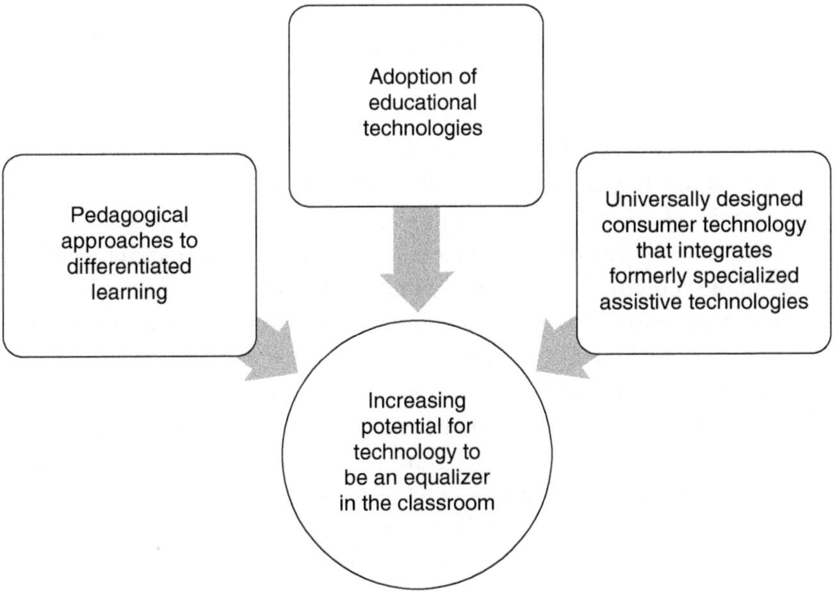

FIGURE 13.2 Major trends impacting the use of technology as an equalizer

Secondly, technology is radically changing and shaping today's formal and informal learning environments.[17] Educational practices are transitioning from learning about technology (e.g., learning basic computer skills) to learning *through* technology. Information and communication technologies are radically and rapidly changing how learning can be differentiated and customized to a student's needs and preferences. Information and communication technologies are being used to offer differentiated instructions and learning by adapting content and process to meet a student's readiness level.[18] Governments are investing resources into modern technologies to promote educational outcomes. Information and communication technologies can help in realizing "effective learning, for all, anywhere, anytime."[19] Web 2.0 tools for learning benefit students with and without disabilities. Technology-

17 Allan Collins and Richard Halverson, "The Second Educational Revolution: Rethinking Education in the Age of Technology" (2010) 26 *Journal of Computer Assisted Learning* 18.

18 William Bender, *Differentiating Instruction for Students with Learning Disabilities: New Best Practices for General and Special Educators* (3rd edn.) (Corwin 2012).

19 Wadi D. Haddad and Alexandra Draxler, "The Dynamics of Technologies for Education," in Wadi D. Haddad and Alexandra Draxler (eds.), *Technologies for Education: Potential, Parameters, and Prospects* (United Nations Educational, Scientific and Cultural Organization and the Academy for Educational Development 2002), www.unescobkk.org/fileadmin/user_upload/ict/e-books/TechEdBook.pdf<u, accessed October 30, 2016.

enabled learning is already a reality and it is important to leverage it for the full inclusion of students with disabilities. In fact, not ensuring that technology-enabled learning is accessible and inclusive will create another phase of disability-based exclusion and marginalization in education.

Finally, several special educators and assistive technology specialists[20] who work with students with disabilities see an overlap between *assistive* solutions and general educational tools and software.[21] This creates new opportunities to regularize the use of assistive and accessible technology solutions for learning, reducing the "othering" of students with disabilities.[22]

It is important to acknowledge that some issues are yet to be fully explored, such as privacy and security in ensuring digital access to education for persons with disabilities.[23] Scholars continue to raise concerns over the erosion of privacy due to monitoring and surveillance conducted by public and private sector organizations.[24] These privacy concerns stem from the mass collection of user data using sensors embedded in mobile technologies and considerations of security.[25] It follows that systems and service providers will have to ensure checks in collecting user data and enhance mechanisms to prevent misuse.

[20] While the authors recognize the formal and informal efforts of stakeholders such as teachers and parents with disabilities in advocating, promoting, and ensuring inclusive education, this chapter focuses on the obligations of educational service providers as a formal organization and as a result does not provide an analysis of the relationship of educational service providers with other external formal and informal organizations.

[21] Trisha O'Connell, Geoff Freed, and Madeleine Rothberg, "Using Apple Technology to Support Learning for Students with Sensory and Learning Disabilities" (Carl and Ruth Shapiro Family National Center for Accessible Media WGBH Educational Foundation 2015), www.apple.com/education/docs/L419373A-US_L419373A_AppleTechDisabilities.pdf, accessed November 2, 2016.

[22] Foley and Ferri (n. 13).

[23] See, for example, Joan M. Mcguire, Sally S. Scott, and Stan F. Shaw, "Universal Design and Its Applications in Educational Environments" (2006) 27(3) *Remedial and Special Education* 166; Foley and Ferri (n. 13). In addition, scholars have examined the right to privacy for persons with disabilities in relation to access to ICT; see Jonathan Lazar, Brian Wentz, and Marco Winckler, "Information Privacy and Security as a Human Right for People with Disabilities," in Jonathan Lazar and Michael Stein (eds.), *Disability, Human Rights, and Information Technology* (University of Pennsylvania Press 2017).

[24] See research by Helen Nissenbaum, "A Contextual Approach to Privacy Online" (2011) 140(4) *Daedalus* 32; Lee Tien, "Privacy, Technology and Data Mining" (2004) 30 *Ohio Northern University Law Review* 389; and Lesa Lorenzen-Huber, Mary Boutain, L. Jean Camp, Kalpana Shankar, and Kay H. Connelly, "Privacy, Technology, and Aging: A Proposed Framework" (2011) 36(2) *Ageing International* 232.

[25] For example, by ensuring privacy policies are accessible for persons with disabilities. For recent analyses of privacy law and policy in the information society, see Kate Crawford and Jason Schultz, "Big Data and Due Process: Toward a Framework to Redress Predictive Privacy Harms" (2014) 55 *Boston College Law Review* 93; Joseph S. Fulda, "Data Mining and Privacy"

3 SHAPING POLICY AND ADVANCING IMPLEMENTATION

Several interconnected, intersecting, and interactive policy spheres and actors are involved in the implementation of ICTs in inclusive education for successful learning outcomes. A wide range of state and non-state actors are involved in the regulation, governing, financing, provision, implementation, and monitoring of ICTs in inclusive education – policy makers at all levels of government, students with disabilities and their families, teachers and educators, school administrators, technology manufacturers and vendors, standards bodies, assistive technology specialists and practitioners, rehabilitation service providers, and civil society. Civil society plays a key role in advocating for technology accessibility in policy and practice. All of these elements and actors are continually influencing and shaping each other. Hence, it is important to take an ecosystem view toward the application of ICTs to promote learning outcomes for learners with disabilities.[26]

Additionally, the policy framework and implementation of accessible ICTs in education must cover all the different levels that impact and shape learner experiences: (i) the learner level, which deals with the direct use and management of technology, the learner's needs and actions, and supportive partnerships with families and caregivers; (ii) the organizational level, which includes educational organizations and institutes as well as all the professionals working within these organizations; and (iii) the systems level, which encompasses the dialogues and consultations between different policy actors, the ICT infrastructure, service delivery, research and development, and monitoring.[27]

3.1 *Theoretical Approaches to Policy Implementation*

Figure 13.3 shows how top-down and bottom-up processes operate to shape the policy and practice of ICTs in inclusive education. Research on policy

(2000) 11 *Albany Law Journal of Science and Technology* 105; Joel R. Reidenberg, N. Cameron Russell, Alexander J. Callen, Sophia Qasir, and Thomas B. Norton, "Privacy Harms and the Effectiveness of the Notice and Choice Framework" (2015) 11 *I/S: A Journal of Law and Policy for the Information Society* 485; Robert H. Sloan and Richard Warner, "Beyond Notice and Choice: Privacy, Norms, and Consent" (2014) 14 *Journal of High Technology Law* 370; Daniel J. Solove, *The Digital Person: Technology and Privacy in the Information Age* (New York University Press 2004); Daniel J. Solove, "I've Got Nothing to Hide and Other Misunderstandings of Privacy" (2007) 44 *San Diego Law Review* 745.

26 Deepti Samant, Rebecca Matter, and Mark Harniss, "Realizing the Potential of Accessible ICTs in Developing Countries" (2013) 8(1) *Disability and Rehabilitation: Assistive Technology* 11.

27 Ibid.

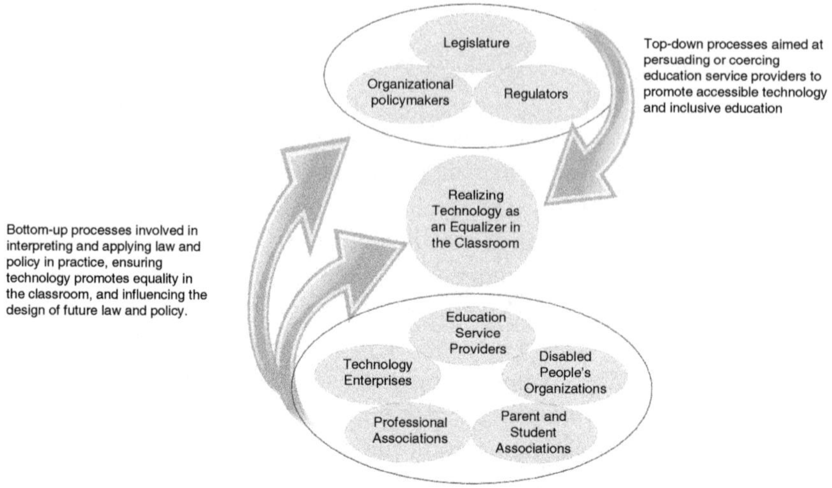

FIGURE 13.3 The role of top-down and bottom-up processes in harnessing ICTs for education

implementation has provided a tripartite distinction between "issues of ends (goals), issues of the relationship between means and ends (whether means chosen are appropriate) and issues of success in adopting means."[28] In this case, the relationship between the means – i.e., accessible ICT accessibility – and ends – i.e., inclusive education – depends on the processes that translate national and international law and policy into action.[29]

Research has examined implementation from top-down and bottom-up perspectives.[30] Top-down processes focus on state-based policy actors involved in designing law and policy, and implementation is based on the sequence of events that follow the enactment of legislation.[31] National education policy frameworks

28 Michael Hill and Peter Hupe, *Implementing Public Policy: An Introduction to the Study of Operational Governance* (Sage 2008).

29 Ibid.

30 Ibid. and Paul A. Sabatier, "Top-Down and Bottom-Up Approaches to Implementation Research: A Critical Analysis and Suggested Synthesis" (1986) 6(1) *Journal of Public Policy* 21.

31 Jeffrey L. Pressman and Aaron B. Wildavsky, *Implementation: How Great Expectations in Washington Are Dashed in Oakland: Or, Why It's Amazing That Federal Programs Work at All, This Being a Saga of the Economic Development Administration as Told by Two Sympathetic Observers Who Seek to Build Morals on a Foundation of Ruined Hopes* (University of California Press 1973).

are influenced by international treaties and resolutions. State-based policy actors provide the means and maintain responsibility for achieving policy goals.[32]

Bottom-up processes emphasize the long-term interactions among policy actors.[33] Policy actors contribute ideas to the design of and compliance with policy objectives.[34] A bottom-up approach focuses on the role of non-state actors and policy networks in implementation processes.[35] Non-state actors contribute to implementation by interpreting and applying policies in practice.[36] A coordinated top-down and bottom-up approach to implementation that combines comprehensive legal and policy approaches with long-term coordination and cooperation with non-state actors can stimulate and accelerate the use of inclusive ICTs in education, while ensuring that technology-enabled learning does not exclude and marginalize students with disabilities.

Implementing inclusive education law and policy, through various forms of social regulation, involves long-term interactions among state and non-state actors in promoting access to education for persons with disabilities. Social regulation does not simply constitute unilateral action by the government.[37] The implementation of social regulations spans the public–private sector divide and includes a multitude of actors engaged in both formal and informal processes.[38]

Thus, the development, implementation, and impacts of policies become a function of the contractual and noncontractual relationships between these various actors,[39] as they are dependent on "each other's resources to achieve their goals."[40]

32 Hill and Hupe (n. 28).

33 Saar Alon-Barkat and Sharon Gilad, "Political Control or Legitimacy Deficit? Bureaucracies' Symbolic Response to Bottom-Up Public Pressures" (2015) 44(1) *Policy & Politics* 41; G. Anthony Giannoumis, "Transnational Convergence of Public Procurement Policy: A 'Bottom-Up' Analysis of Policy Networks and the International Harmonisation of Accessibility Standards for Information and Communication Technology" (2015) *International Review of Law, Computers & Technology* 1.

34 Hill and Hupe (n. 28).

35 Roger Charlton, "NGOs, Politics, Projects and Probity: A Policy Implementation Perspective" (1995) 16(2) *Third World Quarterly* 237.

36 Ibid.

37 David Levi-Faur, "Regulation and Regulatory Governance," in David Levi-Faur (ed.), *Handbook on the Politics of Regulation* (Edward Elgar 2011); David Levi-Faur, "The Odyssey of the Regulatory State: From a 'Thin' Monomorphic Concept to a 'Thick' and Polymorphic Concept" (2013) 35(1–2) *Law and Policy* 29.

38 Ibid.

39 World Bank, *Learning for All: Investing in People's Knowledge and Skills to Promote Development. World Bank Group Education Strategy 2020* (International Bank for Reconstruction and Development/World Bank 2011).

40 Ibid.

3.1.1 Legal and Normative Aspects of Compliance

Research on regulatory compliance provides a basis for investigating the gap between policy objectives and organizational practices.[41] Research illustrates the conflicting interests involved in enforcing regulatory compliance: "the motivation of the firm is to minimize regulatory costs and the motivation of the regulator is to maximize compliance outcomes."[42] Models of regulation have used the strategic choices of policy actors to explain interest conflict.[43] To resolve the conflicting incentives and manage noncompliance, research on responsive regulation suggests using a range of interventions including informing and persuading, publicly discouraging noncompliance, auditing, and financially penalizing noncompliance.[44] By adjusting the regulatory strategy and associated intervention, regulators can enhance incentives for compliance and diminish incentives that obstruct compliance.

Cooperation between state and non-state actors aims to incentivize compliance by encouraging voluntary agreements and compromises.[45] According to some scholars, "[r]egulated firms can cooperate by making good-faith efforts to comply with regulations and voluntarily disclosing their ... violations," and "government regulators can cooperate in regulatory enforcement by forgiving minor regulatory violations and working with firms to solve the root causes of noncompliances."[46] In addition, scholars argue, "firms can establish credible commitments to cooperation by subscribing to a voluntary program" such as "a conduct standard that firms pledge to follow," and "[t]he goal of a voluntary program is to induce participating firms to produce some positive social good beyond what government regulations require."[47]

Scholars have also examined cooperation and compliance in the interpretation of human rights in local settings by community leaders, nongovernmental

41 Russel Hardin, "Compliance, Consent and Legitimacy," in Carles Boix and Susan Carole Stokes (eds.), *The Oxford Handbook of Comparative Politics* (Oxford University Press 2007); Hill and Hupe (n. 28).

42 Ian Ayres and John Braithwaite, *Responsive Regulation Transcending the Deregulation Debate* (Oxford University Press 1992).

43 Ibid.

44 Ibid.

45 Matthew Potoski and Aseem Prakash, "Voluntary Programs, Compliance and the Regulation Dilemma," in David Levi-Faur (ed.), *Handbook on the Politics of Regulation* (Edward Elgar 2011).

46 Ibid.

47 Ibid.

organizations (NGOs), and social movement activists.[48] Some authors have argued that these "intermediaries" "translate the discourses and practices from the arena of international law and legal institutions to specific situations of suffering and violation."[49]

While international legal regimes typically encounter compliance and implementation challenges, self-regulatory approaches can support voluntary compliance by promoting cooperation between state and non-state actors.[50] Scholars argue that "multinational enterprises and global supply chains ... pose major challenges for ... action by the state or ... groups of states, acting ... to control the conduct of economic actors through mandatory legal rules with monitoring and coercive enforcement."[51] Scholars have identified a new approach to international regulation, characterized by "the central role of private actors ... and the correspondingly modest and largely indirect role of 'the state.'"[52] The authors continue, stating that "most of these arrangements are governed by ... firms and industry groups ... [nongovernmental organizations (NGOs)] and other civil society groups."[53] Scholars have additionally characterized this approach as "voluntary rather than state mandated."[54] Research has also establish a typology of international regulatory initiatives, including "joint efforts between NGOs and firms."[55]

Compliance with inclusive education law and policy often involves conflicting incentives. In addition, voluntary approaches to ensuring inclusive education can encourage cooperation among state and non-state actors nationally and internationally. The implementation of inclusive education law and policy involves resolving conflicts between policy goals and practice by translating policy objectives to local organizations and situations. This chapter uses this literature to examine the experiences of non-state actors in supporting the implementation of and compliance with inclusive education and ICT accessibility laws and policies.

48 Sally Engle Merry, "Transnational Human Rights and Local Activism: Mapping the Middle" (2006) 108(1) *American Anthropologist: Journal of the American Anthropological Association* 38.

49 Ibid.

50 Kenneth W. Abbott and Duncan Snidal, "Strengthening International Regulation through Transnational New Governance: Overcoming the Orchestration Deficit" (2009) 42(2) *Vanderbilt Journal of Transnational Law* 501.

51 Ibid.

52 Ibid.

53 Ibid.

54 Ibid.

55 Ibid.

3.2 *The International Policy Mandate for Using ICTs for Inclusive Education*

3.2.1 The Convention on the Rights of Persons with Disabilities

Article 24 of the Convention on the Rights of Persons with Disabilities (CRPD) requires States Parties to ensure that persons with disabilities have access to inclusive education at all levels of education as well as to lifelong learning equal to their peers without disabilities. Recognizing that equal does not mean the same, the CRPD requires States Parties to offer reasonable accommodations and support services to facilitate quality education and learning for students with disabilities. This can include individualized support measures situated in settings that maximize inclusion for academic and social development, and ensuring that they have access to appropriate and alternative means of communication and interaction, including facilitating learning Braille, sign language, and acquisition of orientation and mobility skills.[56]

The CRPD obligates States Parties to ensure access to ICT for persons with disabilities on an equal basis with others. As a general principle of the CRPD, obligations for accessibility cut across all other rights enshrined in the CRPD. The Committee on the Rights of Persons with Disabilities has recognized the relationship between ICT accessibility and the right to education and has argued that accessible ICT and use of assistive technology provide a necessary precondition for persons with disabilities to realize their right to education.[57] The CRPD consistently brings up the role of ICT in promoting the independence and full participation of persons with disabilities across life domains, including education (Article 24), and requires States Parties to make concerted efforts and investments to advance access to ICT.

Enabling an inclusive learning environment can involve the use of alternative and augmentative means of communication, formats for content, and different educational techniques. Information and communication technology is an important enabler of accessibility to systems and services (Article 9), information (Article 21), and meaningful habilitation and rehabilitation (Article 26). The CRPD encourages States Parties to work toward the

[56] Valentina Della Fina, Rachele Cera, and Giuseppe Palmisano (eds.), *The United Nations Convention on the Rights of Persons with Disabilities: A Commentary* (Springer 2017).

[57] See also Mary J. Ziegler and David Sloan, "Accessibility and Online Learning," in Jonathan Lazar and Michael Stein (eds.), *Disability, Human Rights, and Information Technology* (University of Pennsylvania Press 2017); and Charles O'Mahony and Gerard Quinn, *Disability Law and Policy: An Analysis of the UN Convention* (Clarus Press 2017); and Della Fina, Cera, and Palmisano (n. 56), *The United Nations Convention on the Rights of Persons with Disabilities.*

development and distribution of accessible ICTs in collaboration with persons with disabilities. Further, it calls on States Parties to promote digital literacy and access to the Internet for learning.

3.2.2 Sustainable Development Goals

The 2030 Agenda for Global Action (hereafter the 2030 Agenda), with seventeen goals to achieve sustainable development in fifteen years, offers countries and development partners a framework to mobilize resources to address socioeconomic inequities and gaps. Over the period until 2030, countries and development partners will ramp up efforts to achieve these goals by working to meet the related 169 targets. The Sustainable Development Goals, which were announced as part of the 2030 Agenda, are important in the context of the right to inclusive education as they will be pivotal in shaping development investments and resource mobilization undertaken by signatory countries and international development partners.

The 2030 Agenda underlines that all individuals, including those with disabilities, should have access to quality education at the early childhood, primary, secondary, and tertiary levels. Sustainable Development Goal 4, to "Ensure inclusive and equitable quality education and promote lifelong learning opportunities for all," includes *all* men and women as beneficiaries and specifically mentions persons with disabilities. It calls for equal access to all levels of education and vocational training, and inclusive, accessible, and effective learning environments for all students, including those with disabilities. Efforts to achieve SDG 4 will require concrete investments to ensure that learners with disabilities have the supports and accommodations they need. This is complemented by SDG 9c, to "significantly increase access to information and communications technology and strive to provide universal and affordable access to the Internet in [the] least developed countries by 2020."

Countries need to report on their efforts to meet the targets to promote inclusive education on a regular basis. The indicators used to assess progress toward SDG 4 targets are inclusive of students with disabilities. Data used to report on progress have to be disaggregated by disability to the greatest extent possible. Indicators to assess country progress include the proportion of schools with access to the Internet and computers for pedagogical purposes, as well as adapted infrastructure and materials for students with disabilities.

This implies that educational systems need to be reviewed and revised where needed to help countries to meet their obligations under the CRPD as well as the 2030 Agenda.

3.2.3 Relevant Regional Frameworks

In 2010, the European Union (EU) issued the European Disability Strategy 2010–2020 (EDS).[58] As a persuasive policy,[59] the EDS aims to encourage the EU and its Member States to "improve the social and economic situation of people with disabilities."[60] The EDS is part of the EU's overall efforts to eliminate discrimination based on disability and to support the implementation of the CRPD.

The EDS focuses on eliminating barriers in eight areas, including accessibility and education. In terms of accessibility, the EDS aims to "[e]nsure accessibility to goods, services including public services and assistive devices for people with disabilities."[61] The EDS defines accessibility as meaning that "people with disabilities have access, on an equal basis with others, to … information and communications technologies and systems (ICT), and other facilities and services."[62] The EDS goes on to discuss, by way of an example, access to public websites and television broadcasts. The EDS further details the EU's aims to use legislative and administrative measures to "support and supplement national activities for implementing accessibility and removing existing barriers, and improving the availability and choice of assistive technologies."[63] While the EDS recognizes that ICT accessibility is a precondition for participation in society and the economy, the EDS does not provide further detail on the role of accessible ICT in specific areas of social life, including education.

In terms of education, the EDS aims to "[p]romote inclusive education and lifelong learning for pupils and students with disabilities."[64] The EDS recognizes the complexities involved in providing access to mainstream education for children with severe disabilities and urges EU Member States to integrate people with disabilities in the general education system and provide children with disabilities appropriate individual support. Despite the EU's aim to promote inclusive education, the EDS does not detail the relationship

58 European Community, European Disability Strategy 2010–2020: A Renewed Commitment to a Barrier-Free Europe (Commission of the European Communities 2010).

59 Persuasive policies typically attempt to convince non-state actors to voluntarily comply with policy goals by appealing to their sense of morality or social responsibility. In contrast, legislative policies typically require non-state actors to comply with policy goals. See Marie-Louise Bemelmans-Videc, Ray C. Rist, and Evert Oskar Vedung, *Carrots, Sticks and Sermons: Policy Instruments and Their Evaluation* (Transaction Publishers 1998).

60 European Community, European Disability Strategy 2010–2020 (n. 58).

61 Ibid.

62 Ibid.

63 Ibid.

64 Ibid.

between the aims for inclusive education and cross-cutting measures such as ICT accessibility.

The EU, in addition to more than seventy-five countries, has also signed the Marrakesh Treaty to Facilitate Access to Published Works for Persons Who Are Blind, Visually Impaired or Otherwise Print Disabled (MAT).[65] The MAT entered into force in 2016 and aims to, among other things, limit the scope of copyright protections and thereby promote the reproduction and distribution of accessible published works.[66] Copyright typically refers to legal protections that provide content creators with the exclusive right to use, reproduce, and distribute their creative works. The MAT defines a published work as "literary and artistic works . . . in the form of text, notation and/or related illustrations, whether published or otherwise made publicly available in any media."[67]

The MAT recognizes the role that accessible works play in realizing the right to education for persons with disabilities and the role that educational service providers play in creating and providing access to accessible works. It refers to educational institutions as authorized entities that can make accessible copies of copyrighted material to support persons with print disabilities.

3.3 *National- and Local-Level Laws and Policies*

Laws and policies in both the education and technology realms need to facilitate and strategically support access to student-centered and accessible technology for learning. Accessible technology can reform education in terms of inclusion, and educational policy reform will shape the environment and structure in which technology use can thrive.[68] The interplay and extent of cohesion between legislation, policies, and regulation governing education in general, education for students with disabilities (still within the domain of

65 World Intellectual Property Organization (WIPO), *WIPO-Administered Treaties* (World Intellectual Property Organization 2016), www.wipo.int/treaties/en/ShowResults.jsp?lang=en&treaty_id=843, accessed November 9, 2018.

66 For an analysis of the MAT's provisions, see Laurence R. Helfer, Molly K. Land, Ruth Okediji, and Jerome H. Reichman, *The World Blind Union Guide to the Marrakesh Treaty* (Oxford University Press 2017).

67 World Intellectual Property Organization (WIPO), *Marrakesh Treaty to Facilitate Access to Published Works by Visually Impaired Persons and Persons with Print Disabilities* ([S.l.]: Stationery Office Ltd. 2013).

68 Charalambos Vrasidas and Marina S. McIsaac, "Integrating Technology in Teaching and Teacher Education: Implications for Policy and Curriculum Reform" (2001) 38(2–3) *Educational Media International* 127.

"special education" in most countries), and technology ultimately determine the level of access, use, and impact of technology on inclusive education outcomes. In addition, constitutional rights to education and legal instruments pertaining to disability rights will also play a role in shaping how technology is interwoven into inclusive education.[69]

The law and policy structure influencing the use of ICTs in inclusive education must address physical barriers that result when ICTs, learning environments, and content and materials are not designed to be accessible; cognitive barriers when content and teaching methods are not designed with diverse cognitive functional needs in mind; content barriers when students cannot read or understand the material provided, for example, due to linguistic differences; didactical barriers when teachers are not adequately trained to use methods and skills that support inclusive learning; and financial barriers in accessing inclusive ICTs.[70]

Education policy reforms need to address what and how technology is used by instructors and students. Education policies may be slow to evolve and keep pace with rapid innovations in emerging technology solutions to customize and improve learning for all students.[71] Scholars and practitioners are acknowledging that the rapid pace of innovation in technology means that governments and schools are always playing catch-up. For students with disabilities, this can be a twofold issue as separate special education policies often govern access to technology in their schools.

Countries have been focusing on developing strategic and targeted policy approaches to technology in education,[72] most commonly through instruments such as national education technology policies. Such policies mostly address topics of vision and planning, infrastructure, teachers, skills and competencies, learning resources, education management information systems, monitoring and evaluation, research and innovation, and equity, inclu-

69 United Nations Educational, Scientific and Cultural Organization (UNESCO), G3ict, and European Agency for Special Needs and Inclusive Education, "Model Policies for Inclusive ICTs in Education for Persons with Disabilities" (2014) United Nations Educational, Scientific and Cultural Organization (UNESCO), www.unesco.org/new/en/communication-and-information/resources/publications-and-communication-materials/publications/full-list/model-policy-for-inclusive-icts-in-education-for-persons-with-disabilities/, accessed October 26, 2016.

70 Ibid.

71 Ian Quillen, "State, Local Policies Seen to Slow Personalized Learning; Digital Advancements Force Policymakers to Rethink Rules," *Education Week*, March 17, 2011, 42. *Opposing Viewpoints in Context*. July 27, 2016.

72 Michael Trucano, "Analyzing ICT and Education Policies in Developing Countries," https://blogs.worldbank.org/edutech/ict-education-policies, accessed October 31, 2016.

sion, and safety.[73] The inclusion of students with disabilities and the use of accessible technology needs to be considered at the beginning of policy development. This is similar to the argument for promoting universal design – i.e., retrofitting is always more expensive.[74] Education policies and national plans focused on educational technology should consciously include accessibility as well as flexibility on the use of technology for students with disabilities.

This section captures some of the crucial elements that need to be considered in shaping a policy atmosphere that is supportive of the use of ICT in educating students with disabilities.

3.3.1 Incorporating Accessibility in Procurement Processes

In 2009, the US-based National Federation of the Blind (NFB) and the American Council of the Blind (ACB) sued Arizona State University for its decision to use Amazon Kindle e-readers to deliver electronic textbooks to students. Arizona State University (ASU) was among several higher education institutions experimenting with the use of the Kindle e-readers on campus.[75] At the time, the Kindle e-reader did not meet accessibility requirements and was particularly inaccessible to individuals with vision impairments. While the e-readers could convert e-books to audio, their onscreen menus were inaccessible, prohibiting easy navigation and use for students with disabilities. The lawsuit claimed that the deployment of the e-readers violated the Americans with Disabilities Act (ADA) and the Rehabilitation Act of 1973.[76] Section 504 of the Rehabilitation Act and, similarly, Title II of the ADA prohibit public sector organizations or organizations that receive public funding from discriminating against persons with disabilities. In the lawsuit, the NFB and the Association for Computing Machinery claim that ASU, which receives public funding, discriminated against blind students when it distributed inaccessible Kindle e-readers.[77]

73 Ibid.

74 CRPD Committee (2014). General Comment No. 2, Accessibility, Committee on the Rights of Persons with Disabilities, (CRPD/C/GC/2) (2014).

75 Marc Beja, "Advocates for the Blind Sue Arizona State U. Over Kindle Use," *Chronicle of Higher Education* (July 2, 2009), www.chronicle.com/blogs/wiredcampus/advocates-for-the-blind-sue-arizona-state-u-over-kindle-use/7252, accessed October 20, 2016.

76 Jim Fruchterman, "E-Books and Human Rights," in Jonathan Lazar and Michael Stein (eds.), *Disability, Human Rights, and Information Technology* (University of Pennsylvania Press 2017).

77 *National Federation of the Blind* v. *Arizona Board of Regents*, No. CV-09-1359-PHX-GMS (D. Ariz. October 16, 2009).

Following this, the US Department of Justice issued a letter warning institutions of higher education about requiring the use of technology that excluded students with disabilities.[78]

This example highlights one of the main challenges of the increasing use of ICT in education. Technology can remove long-standing barriers to access – as in the case just cited, e-readers can be a good solution to common delays and difficulties in receiving textbooks in Braille or audio – but can inadvertently impose new barriers for students if they are not designed to be accessible. Policies governing the use of technology in schools should incorporate accessibility as a requirement from the beginning. Procurement processes are crucial to ensuring ICT accessibility in education; procurement in publicly funded and private institutes of learning should address accessibility for students with disabilities.

Public procurement is heralded as a means to promote social justice goals through regular market engagement.[79] Evidence also shows that inclusive public procurement policies are a good example of social regulations that encourage non-state actors to actively change their behavior beyond what may be required for compliance. Public procurement policies can have a dual "carrot-and-stick" effect, simultaneously encouraging compliance with accessibility standards and marking accessibility as a competitive edge for vendors, which can further influence their overall approach to designing products and services.[80] A study of ICT accessibility in the United States shows that public procurement policies at the federal and state levels and the Section 508 standards had an impact on the accessibility of products in the consumer market as well, "leading to greater innovation, competition, and choice for accessible technology in the marketplace."[81]

Schools and colleges are sought-after clients for technology companies. Amending procurement policies to ensure accessibility in all ICT devices, software, and services purchased by the educational institution will lead to collaborative processes between technology manufacturers and vendors,

78 Steve Kolowich, "Driving Home the Point on Accessibility," *Inside Higher Ed* (June 30, 2010) www.insidehighered.com/news/2010/06/30/kindle, accessed October 20, 2016

79 Giannoumis (n. 33).

80 Gunela Astbrink and William Tibben, "ICT Accessibility Criteria in Public Procurement in OECD Countries: The Current Situation" (2013) 8009 *Universal Access in Human–Computer Interaction*. Design Methods, Tools, and Interaction Techniques for eInclusion, Lecture Notes in Computer Science 155.

81 The Global Initiative for Inclusive ICTs, "CRPD Implementation: Promoting Global Digital Inclusion through ICT Procurement Policies & Accessibility Standards" (2015), http://g3ict.org/resource_center/publications_and_reports/p/productCategory_whitepapers/subCat_7/id_339/, accessed October 21, 2016.

school or college administrators, IT staff, and students and faculty with disabilities. Public procurement has been seen as an effective mechanism for using the purchasing power of the state to "nudge" the market and promote ICT accessibility.[82] As such, public procurement provides an effective strategy for implementing state obligations under the CRPD as under Article 4, States Parties are required to "adopt all appropriate legislative, administrative and other measures for the implementation of the rights recognized in the [CRPD]."

3.3.2 Adopting ICT Accessibility Standards

Tying accessibility requirements to specific standards and guidelines is important as it sets the stage for the discussion between different stakeholder groups for what practically must be achieved and helps to set the minimum thresholds that educational technology must meet. Standards are also needed for monitoring the accessibility of the technology provided to persons with disabilities.

There is growing transnational convergence on ICT accessibility and standardization globally, largely owing to the growing collaboration, advocacy, and knowledge exchange between policy makers, the technology industry, accessibility advocates and professionals, disabled peoples' organizations, and broader civil society.[83] In other words, as states adopt or amend disability legislation and produce standards and regulations for ICT accessibility, they have sought inspiration from other countries and solicited expert advice and guidance from non-state actors. These transnational relationships and interactions have produced similarities between policy objectives and instruments.[84] Currently, the International Organization for Standardization's ISO/IEC 40500:2012, the World Wide Web Consortium's (W3C) Web Content Accessibility Guidelines (WCAG), the US Section 508 standards, and the EU's EN 301 549 accessibility standard to support public procurement of accessible ICT are predominant.

82 See Gerard Quinn, *Achieving eAccessibility: The Role of Equality Legislation and Other Measures: "The Potential Offered by the Equality Approach"* (National University of Ireland, Galway Faculty of Law 2006); Dónal Rice, "Public Procurement as a Means to Achieving Social Gains: Progress and Challenges in European Legislation and Standards for Accessible ICT" (2015) 29(2–3) *International Review of Law, Computers & Technology* 162; Christopher McCrudden, "Using Public Procurement to Achieve Social Outcomes" (2004) 28(4) *Natural Resources Forum* 257.

83 Giannoumis (n. 33).

84 Björn Hvinden, "The Uncertain Convergence of Disability Policies in Western Europe" (2003) 37(6) *Social Policy & Administration* 609.

The WCAG 2.0 address how to make Web content accessible for users with a wide range of disabilities. The WCAG 2.0 aim to make Web content perceivable, operable, understandable, and robust for users with disabilities. The guidelines have three levels of conformance, with Level A being the minimum level of conformance that must be achieved for accessibility. The W3C claims that WCAG 2.0 covers a wide range of disabilities, including various sensory, physical, and cognitive disabilities, and that following WCAG may enhance usability for all users.[85] As such, WCAG may provide a mechanism for service providers to support States Parties' obligations under Article 4(f) of the CRPD – i.e., to promote universal design in the development of standards and guidelines. According to the CRPD, universal design refers to the design of ICT "to be usable by all people, to the greatest extent possible, without the need for adaptation or specialized design." While the scope of WCAG may extend to all users, this chapter argues that due to the paucity of research on the barriers that people experience at the intersection of disability and other forms of disadvantage,[86] and the lack of practical guidelines on how to meet those barriers, WCAG, only to a limited extent, meets the definition of universal design.

Section 508 of the Rehabilitation Act, which governs the US federal procurement of electronic and information technology, led to the development of the Section 508 accessibility standards. First published in 2000, the standards underwent a refresh process and were updated in 2017.[87] Although Section 508 standards were developed for the federal procurement process, they have had a significant impact on ICT accessibility beyond the federal procurement process, including in other countries.

The EN 301 549 was developed in response to Mandate 376 (M 376) to establish ICT accessibility standards for public procurement. Early drafts of the standard were based on Section 508, and the development process

85 While the authors recognize the impact that the W3C and WCAG have had on ensuring and promoting ICT accessibility worldwide, scholars have noted the limitations of the Guidelines. See, for example, Brian Kelly, David Sloan, Lawrie Phipps, Helen Petrie, and Fraser Hamilton, *Forcing Standardization or Accommodating Diversity? A Framework for Applying the WCAG in the Real World. Proceedings of the 2005 International Cross-Disciplinary Workshop on Web Accessibility (W4A)* (Association for Computing Machinery 2005); and Dagfinn Rømen and Dag Svanæs, "Validating WCAG Versions 1.0 and 2.0 through Usability Testing with Disabled Users" (2012) 11(4) *Universal Access in the Information Society* 375.

86 See Rannveig Skjerve, G. Anthony Giannoumis, and Sumaira Naseem, *An Intersectional Perspective on Web Accessibility: Designing around People* (Springer 2016) 13–22.

87 US Access Board, "About the ICT Refresh" (2018), www.access-board.gov/guidelines-and-standards/communications-and-it/about-the-ict-refresh, accessed November 9, 2018.

occurred in parallel to the Section 508 refresh process. While there are a few differences between the proposed Section 508 revision and the EN 301 549, the standards are very similar and have involved close collaboration and discussion between the actors involved in both processes. The EN 301 549 is a voluntary standard. Both the EN 301 549 and Section 508 standards incorporate the WCAG 2.0 requirements.

Countries that still need to develop their own accessibility standards are looking at incorporating one of the existing ones instead.[88] There are several reasons for this: it can take a long time, and dedicated efforts to develop a local standard could create geographic disharmony in the design of ICT products sold in different countries.[89] In August 2016, the Australian government adopted the EN 301 549 as the technical specifications in the public procurement of Web, software, and digital device services.[90] The Global Initiative for Inclusive ICTs (G3ict) recently released a position paper that made the case for even further transnational convergence on accessibility standards through the development of a global standard for ICT accessibility.[91]

One important consideration is whether compliance with the chosen accessibility guidelines and standards is mandatory or voluntary. As Giannoumis explains, policy actors have to decide between using "mandatory hard" or "voluntary soft" policies to promote ICT accessibility;[92] standards can operate along a spectrum of recommended guidelines to technical requirements for vendors.[93] The resolution at the national or local government level is usually reflective of the country's general approach toward regulations for advancing social equity. With educational technology, school and university administrators will also have to make these decisions. Irrespective of whether standards are mandatory or coordinative, their

88 Several countries, such as Australia, Canada, Germany, Norway, and Japan, have adopted WCAG or used it as a source of inspiration for national or regional ICT accessibility standards after their respective governments ratified the CRPD. This chapter argues that the CRPD, among other mechanisms, has served as an impetus for these countries to adopt WCAG in national law and policy.

89 Ibid.

90 Asha McLean, "Australia to Adopt European Standard to Make Government IT More Accessible," *ZDnet* (August 22, 2016), www.zdnet.com/article/australia-to-adopt-european-standard-to-make-government-it-more-accessible/, accessed October 22, 2016

91 Ibid.

92 G. Anthony Giannoumis, "Self-Regulation and the Legitimacy of Voluntary Procedural Standards" (August 25, 2014) *Administration & Society*, http://aas.sagepub.com/content/early/2014/08/25/0095399714548270.abstract, accessed October 23, 2016.

93 G. Anthony Giannoumis, "Regulating Web Content: The Nexus of Legislation and Performance Standards in the United Kingdom and Norway" (2014) 32(1) *Behavioral Sciences & the Law* 52.

adoption and implementation depends on whether policy actors perceive them to have "democratic legitimacy."[94] [95]

For States Parties that have ratified the CRPD, ensuring the democratic legitimacy of ICT accessibility standards may provide the only means for fulfilling their obligations for ensuring accessible ICT and for taking all appropriate measures to eliminate discrimination against persons with disabilities. This means that the process by which guidelines and standards are created and the nature and diversity of stakeholders involved in both decision-making and monitoring are key factors in their uptake and operationalization.[96] It is important to involve the technology industry as well as users and their advocates in these discussions and negotiations.

Under the CRPD, States Parties have an obligation to substantively involve persons with disabilities and their representative organizations in decision-making processes involving the design and implementation of national ICT accessibility laws and policies. In other words, this chapter argues that States Parties to the CRPD must take into account the substantive involvement of persons with disabilities in efforts to promote universal design in the development of standards and guidelines. In effect, by involving persons with disabilities in the design and implementation of standards for ICT accessibility, States Parties can fulfill their obligations under the CRPD and ultimately promote the democratic legitimacy and adoption of ICT accessibility standards by public and private sector organizations.

3.3.3 Definition and Funding of Individual Assistive Technology

The range of technologies relevant to inclusive education is very diverse and can span from customized and specialized assistive technology hardware or software, to mainstream ICT. Type and allocation of funding are significant factors in determining acquisition and use of inclusive ICTs by individual learners. In most countries, educational resources for students with disabilities are still governed by special education laws, policies, and programs. Funding assistance for assistive and accessible technology for students is usually bound by eligibility criteria, assessment requirements, and limitations on the types of aids and devices to be provided. Laws and policies governing the use of public

94 Raymund Werle and Eric J. Iversen, "Promoting Legitimacy in Technical Standardization" (2006) 2 *Science, Technology & Innovation Studies* 19.

95 Tore Hoel and Paul Hollins, "Learning Technology Standards Adoption: How to Improve Process and Product Legitimacy" (ICALT 2008: The 8th IEEE International Conference on Advanced Learning Technologies, Santander, Cantabria, Spain, July 1–5, 2008).

96 Ibid.

funds for assistive technology usually require that the technology meet a set definition.[97]

The increasing demand for mainstream, multifunctional ICT devices as assistive technology introduces some fuzziness into the common conception of assistive technology and raises the need for policy and funding structures to evolve accordingly. For example, there have been instances in the United States where public and private insurance schemes approve costly, commercial assistive technology but refuse to pay for lower-cost mainstream technologies that offer equivalent functionality based on their interpretation of the definition of eligible technology.[98] Laws, policies, and regulations on the use and acquisition of technology for students with disabilities need to allow flexibility for a range of technology solutions, which may include customized and specialized assistive technology along with mass-market mainstream technologies. The desired productivity outcomes and a good match between a person's needs and the selected technology should guide service delivery and funding decisions.

Financial resources to support the use of ICT in inclusive education must also cover training for the student in the use of the selected ICT and build capacity by improving the knowledge and skills of teachers and support specialists to assist the student in using the device successfully in the classroom.[99] In effect, these resource investments help raise awareness on the rights of persons with disabilities (CRPD Article 8) and ensure that teachers use appropriate pedagogical approaches for students with disabilities (CRPD Article 24(4)).

3.4 *The Role of Non-State Actors in the Realization of Inclusive Education*

The practice of accessible technology for inclusive education is wider than simply the procurement and provision of the technology solution. It is important to consider how the educational, family, and technology ecosystems impact the effectiveness and outcomes of technology use. Policy initiatives and budgetary allocations need to address and invest in building an environment that is conducive to the use of technology for inclusive education.

97 Alber M. Cook and Janice M. Polgar, *Assistive Technologies: Principles and Practice* (4th edn.) (Elsevier 2015).

98 Ibid.

99 UNESCO (n. 69).

Teachers and education service providers play a crucial role in determining the impact of accessible technology on learning outcomes. Accessible ICT for individual learning is most impactful when it is an active part of the student's learning activities rather than "alien to [the] learning environment."[100] Teachers need training and preparation to use inclusive and accessible ICTs to support personalized learning of all students, including students with disabilities.[101] The rate of accessible and assistive technology abandonment and non-use increases if teachers do not include them in learning activities, if they are placed in separate rooms rather than the main classroom, and if they do not receive maintenance or updates in time.[102] Studies on the use of educational technologies show that teachers' attitudes toward and beliefs about technology in the classroom, as well as their experience with using educational technology, are predictors of their use and support of technology for learning.[103] [104] This compounds existing misconceptions, negative attitudes, and perceptions that some teachers may hold about students with disabilities.

It is important for teachers and education service providers to view and value ICTs as a tool to improve the participation and learning of all students, including those with disabilities, rather than an additional administrative burden. Teachers and educational leaders may not understand their role in supporting ICTs for inclusive education, view children with disabilities and classroom diversity as problems and barriers, and often lack guidance, supports, and access to assistive technology specialists to adequately respond to the needs of learners with disabilities.[105]

The United Nations Educational, Scientific and Cultural Organization, G3ict, and the European Agency for Special Needs and Inclusive Education

[100] Helena Hemmingsson, Helene Lidstrom, and Louise Nygard, "Use of Assistive Technology Devices in Mainstream Schools: Students' Perspective" (2009) 63(4) *American Journal of Occupational Therapy*, 463.

[101] UNESCO (n. 69).

[102] Hemmingsson, Lidstrom, and Nygard, "Use of Assistive Technology Devices in Mainstream Schools."

[103] Peggy Ertmer, Anne T. Ottenbreit-Leftwich, Olgun Sadik, Emine Sendurur, and Polat Sendurur, "Teacher Beliefs and Technology Integration Practices: A Critical Relationship" (2012) 59 *Computers & Education* 423.

[104] Courtney K. Blackwell, Alexis R. Lauricella, Ellen Wartella, Michael Robb, and Roberta Schomburg, "Adoption and Use of Technology in Early Education: The Interplay of Extrinsic Barriers and Teacher Attitudes" (2013) 69 *Computer & Education* 310.

[105] UNESCO (n. 69).

propose the following model actions to ensure that teachers are active and engaged actors and partners in using inclusive ICTs for education.

> First, education service providers must provide initial and on-going training on working in inclusive education settings. Second, they must provide training in maximizing the use of accessibility features in mainstream ICTs. Third, education service providers must identify learners' ICT preferences and support learners' self-assessment and self-accommodation of their ICT access preferences. Fourth, they must support teachers' use of personalized learning approaches that are supported by inclusive ICTs.[106]

4 CONCLUDING REMARKS

Accessible ICTs are a strategic tool to advance and realize the right to education for persons with disabilities. Information and communication technologies allow choice and customization in the processes of learning, using content, and interacting with teachers and peers. The trends toward differentiated learning pedagogical approaches, increasing use of educational technology, and accessibility of mainstream ICTs offer an important opportunity to break long-standing barriers to inclusive education. However, the potential of technology to improve educational participation does not automatically translate to changes on the ground. Legislation, policies, and regulation help shape an ecosystem that can harness technology to realize the right to inclusive education for quality learning outcomes.

A bottom-up, process-oriented approach to ensuring compliance can help shape the implementation of the CRPD and inclusive education policies. Policy actors embedded within educational institutions provide a useful mechanism for ensuring compliance with legislative goals and human rights norms. Achieving inclusive education requires a multilevel approach, which involves learners and their families and caregivers, professionals working within educational institutions, and interorganizational relationships between policy actors involved in ICT development and product and service delivery.

Several entry points present themselves in incorporating accessible ICT in the delivery and implementation of inclusive education, including the product development process, content creation, assistive and accessible technology service delivery, teacher training and capacity building, procurement, and monitoring and evaluation. Educational institutions should ensure inclusive education by incorporating accessibility in procurement processes, adopting

[106] Ibid.

international standards and guidelines for accessible ICT, and examining the organizational barriers and opportunities for providing assistive and accessible technology. The results of this chapter provide a useful basis for future research, and this chapter recommends that researchers adopt a multilevel approach to investigating inclusive education by integrating bottom-up perspectives on putting policy into practice with top-down perspectives on regulating the behavior of organizations in the ICT and education industries.

Advancements in educational technology have adopted mobile devices and applications to promote interaction and engagement both in and out of the classroom.[107] Educational technologies have been used to collect data on user interactions in order to provide learning analytics.[108] Educational technologies may include assistive technologies, for example, Braille displays, screen readers, or specialized mobile device applications.[109] This chapter suggests that students with cognitive, learning, and psychosocial disabilities may experience barriers accessing, understanding, or being aware of the privacy and security implications that come with using educational technologies. While research has yet to investigate the privacy and security implications for accessible educational technologies, this chapter argues that educational service providers must consider these issues in the context of ensuring access to ICT and assistive technology for persons with disabilities.

107 See, for example, research by Mohamed Ally, *Mobile Learning: Transforming the Delivery of Education and Training* (Athabasca University Press 2009). Educational technology typically refers to hardware and software systems used for teaching and learning.

108 Ryan Shaun Baker and Paul Salvador Inventado, *Educational Data Mining and Learning Analytics* (Springer 2014). This chapter argues that learning analytics refers to a recursive process of data collection, analysis, learning, and redevelopment of educational processes, strategies, and goals.

109 Assistive technologies often refers to ICT products or services used to "increase, maintain, or improve the functional capabilities of persons with disabilities." See Assistive Technology Industry Association, "What Is Assistive Technology? How Is It Funded?" (2015), www.atia.org/i4a/pages/index.cfm?pageid=3859, accessed November 9, 2018.

14

Indigenous Knowledge–Driven Education Reform as a Means of Achieving Inclusive Education in Indigenous Communities in Canada

Anna Gilmer

INTRODUCTION

The right to education is fundamental to our effective participation in and contribution to society.[1] Aside from being a right in itself, education is an empowerment right: it enables us to benefit from and realise other rights.[2] It is through education that we are able to participate fully in the political process, choose our employment and navigate our own health care.[3] As Nelson Mandela expressed, '[e]ducation is the great engine of personal development'.[4]

However, Indigenous children with disabilities in Canada are inadequately served by – and sometimes excluded from – the education system. The United Nations (UN) and its Member States have worked to protect the right to education and have clarified that under international law all persons have a right to education of the same quality as their peers, without discrimination.[5] Yet, in Canada, as in numerous Member States and other parts of the world, many children face discrimination in education. Indigenous students with disabilities are acutely vulnerable to such discrimination, despite specific international legal instruments that protect their education

1 Klaus Dieter Beiter, *The Protection of the Right to Education by International Law* (vol. 82) (Martinus Nijhoff Publishers 2005) 18.

2 Fons Coomans, 'Clarifying the Core Elements of the Right to Education' in Fons Coomans and Godefridus J. H. van Hoof (eds), *The Right to Complain about Economic, Social and Cultural Rights: Proceedings of the Expert Meeting on the Adoption of an Optional Protocol to the International Covenant on Economic, Social and Cultural Rights, Held from 25–28 January 1995 in Ulrecht* (SIM 1995).

3 Coomans (n. 2).

4 Beiter (n. 1) 1, citing Nelson Mandela.

5 United Nations General Assembly (UNGA), Convention on the Rights of Persons with Disabilities (13 December 2006) A/RES/61/106 (CRPD) Art. 24.

rights as children,[6] as Indigenous people[7] and as persons with disabilities.[8] Domestic Canadian law does not protect those rights on these grounds or permit meaningful enforcement. Reforms are needed in the areas of Indigenous education and education for persons with disabilities, and also at their intersection.

Indigenous knowledge (IK) provides a potential solution. Under international law, Indigenous students have a right to Indigenous-controlled education in their own cultures and languages.[9] In practice, that means a right to education based in IK, or Indigenous worldviews, ideas and ways of knowing. International law also protects the rights of children with disabilities to inclusive education, in which education is structured to provide all students with equitable access to learning.[10] While inclusive education is more economical than segregated education in the long term, the requisite restructuring normally brings additional costs in the short term.[11] The same is true of IK-driven education reform: it requires significant investments.[12] Indigenous knowledge–driven reforms, though, have the potential to achieve real inclusion for Indigenous students with disabilities. By investing in Indigenous-controlled, IK-driven education reform, Canada can make significant strides in fulfilling its multifaceted international obligations to Indigenous children with disabilities in the field of education.

Readers of this chapter should bear in mind that Indigenous communities across Canada vary widely in their cultures, values, laws, experiences, governments and goals. Many Indigenous governments and organisations have already regained control of their education systems and many have implemented IK-based education, and the reforms necessary in those communities will differ from the reforms necessary in a community that currently uses non-Indigenous curricula. Some communities may also prefer to school their children alongside non-Indigenous children, or to partner with other Indigenous communities, and the

6 United Nations General Assembly (UNGA), Convention on the Rights of the Child (adopted 20 November 1989, entered into force 2 September 1990) 1577 UNTS 3 (CRC) Arts. 28 and 29.

7 United Nations General Assembly (UNGA), United Nations Declaration on the Rights of Indigenous Peoples (13 September 2007) A/61/L.67 and Add. 1 (UNDRIP) Arts. 14 and 21.

8 CRPD (n. 5) Art. 24.

9 UNDRIP (n. 7) Art. 14.

10 Committee on the Rights of Persons with Disabilities, General Comment No. 4 (2016) Art. 24: The Right to Inclusive Education (2 September 2016) CRPD/C/GC/4 [11].

11 Gauthier de Beco, 'The Right to Inclusive Education According to Article 24 of the UN Convention on the Rights of Persons with Disabilities: Background Requirements and (Remaining) Questions' (2014) 32 *Netherlands Quarterly of Human Rights* 263, 276.

12 Taiaiake Alfred, *Wasáse: Indigenous Pathways of Action and Freedom* (University of Toronto Press 2009) 199–200.

means of implementing IK in each of those contexts will be different from the means of implementing IK in a community that wants to provide schooling on the reserve. Nothing discussed in this chapter is intended to undermine the political autonomy of Indigenous nations.

Focussed on Indigenous education on reserves in Canada's provinces, this chapter explores the need for reform and the potential for IK to achieve inclusion. First, it describes historical and current inequities in education for Indigenous students and students with disabilities, and the particular marginalisation of Indigenous students with disabilities living on reserves. Second, it clarifies Canada's international obligations towards Indigenous children with disabilities in the field of education. Next, it expands on the ideas of Indigenous-controlled and IK-based education. Finally, it draws parallels between IK-based and inclusive education and proposes IK-driven education reform as a means of achieving inclusive education on reserves.

EDUCATION FOR INDIGENOUS CHILDREN WITH DISABILITIES IN CANADA

Federal Education of Indigenous Children and Resistance to Indigenous Control

In Canada, the federal government is responsible for the education of Indigenous children. The Constitution Act, 1867[13] gives provinces the power to make laws in relation to education,[14] but gives the federal government exclusive jurisdiction over 'Indians',[15] including their

[13] Constitution Act, 1867 (UK) 30 and 31 Victoria c. 3, reprinted in RSC 1985, Appendix II, No. 5 [Constitution Act, 1867].

[14] Ibid. S93.

[15] Three terms appear throughout this chapter that each refer to Canada's original people: *Indian*, *Aboriginal* and *Indigenous*. All three terms encompass First Nations, Inuit and Métis people. *Indian* is the term used in the Constitution Act, 1867 and the Indian Act, RSC 1985, c. I-5, S114(2) [Indian Act], and is also used in this chapter to refer to Indigenous people in interaction with the Canadian state and as perceived by the official mind until 1982. *Aboriginal* is the term used in the Constitution Act, 1982, being Schedule B to the Canada Act 1982 (UK), 1982, c. 11 [Constitution Act, 1982]. It refers in this chapter to the Indigenous people in interaction with the Canadian state and as perceived by the official mind since 1982. It is also the term used in Canadian common law to refer to the group rights of Indigenous people (e.g., Aboriginal rights, Aboriginal title). *Indigenous* is the term used by the international community. It has often been deployed in Canada to refer to original people whether in interaction with the state or not. Recently, though, Canadian ministries have adopted the term (e.g., the recently rebranded Indigenous and Northern Affairs Canada, and Ontario's new Ministry of Indigenous Relations and Reconciliation). In this chapter, it is used as a neutral

education.[16] The federal government has exercised this jurisdiction through the Indian Act, whereby it may 'establish, operate and maintain schools for Indian children'[17] or enter into agreements with provinces or territories for the education of Indian children.[18]

Federal control over Indigenous education has resulted in the non-education of Indigenous children. Statistics on literacy and high school completion show a disparity in education outcomes between Indigenous and non-Indigenous people in Canada.[19] This disparity continues through post-secondary education.[20] Many communities also have 'a history of trauma associated with formal education and relocation'[21] because families were compelled or forced to move to places where the government chose to put schools, not places where families chose to live. Current disparities and distrust are the contemporary manifestations of continued failures by the federal government, which used multiple levers of colonialism to undermine Indigenous interests in providing educational opportunities for children.

The recent Truth and Reconciliation Commission (TRC) report shone a bright light on the Indian Residential School project, whereby Indigenous children were taken away from their homes, sometimes forcefully, and taught in faraway residential schools intended to indoctrinate them into the 'legally dominant, Euro-Christian Canadian society'.[22] In addition to assimilation, coercion, violence and familial disruption caused by the residential school system, 'one of the schools' greatest failings was the very quality of the schooling they provided'.[23] Teachers had low expectations of students, whom they thought 'lack[ed] great mental capacity';[24] students spent considerable time

term for all original peoples in what is now Canada and is not intended to invoke any particular relationship with the state.

16 Constitution Act, 1867 S91(24).

17 Indian Act S114(2).

18 Indian Act S114(1).

19 Statistics Canada, *Aboriginal Statistics at a Glance: 2nd Edition* (Ministry of Industry 2015) 27, www.statcan.gc.ca/pub/89–645-x/89–645-x2015001-eng.pdf, accessed 16 June 2017.

20 Statistics Canada, *The Educational Attainment of Aboriginal Peoples in Canada* (Ministry of Industry, 2013), www12.statcan.gc.ca/nhs-enm/2011/as-sa/99–012-x/99–012-x2011003_3-eng.pdf, accessed 16 June 2017.

21 Ashley Sisco, Margaret Caron-Vuotari, Carole Stonebridge, Greg Sutherland and Gilles Rhéaume, *Lessons Learned: Achieving Positive Educational Outcomes in Northern Communities* (Conference Board of Canada 2012) 25.

22 Truth and Reconciliation Commission, *Honouring the Truth, Reconciling for the Future: Summary of the Final Report of the Truth and Reconciliation Commission of Canada* (Truth and Reconciliation Commission of Canada 2015) v.

23 Truth and Reconciliation Commission, *Canada's Residential Schools: The Legacy*, vol. 5 (Truth and Reconciliation Commission of Canada 2015) 61 [TRC, *Legacy*].

24 TRC, *Legacy* (n. 23) 61, quoting principal R. Baudin in 1883.

working rather than learning;[25] curricula were inadequate, culturally inappropriate and racist;[26] teachers were underqualified;[27] the residential school programme was underfunded;[28] and students left school unequipped for either the traditional or market economy.[29]

In 2008, Canada acknowledged some of these failings through an official apology,[30] but this legacy of racism and assertions of cultural superiority is still felt today. Indigenous students attending off-reserve, provincially run schools continue to experience isolation and racism. Heather Findlay's 2014 thesis on Indigenous students' stories of school at an off-reserve Saskatchewan high school exposed that even where Indigenous ways of knowing are formally included in curricula, Indigenous people are 'essentialized . . . as protectors of nature' in science courses,[31] 'Native studies' is seen as 'an easy credit',[32] and engagement with Indigenous ideas is shallow. Indigenous ways of knowing are certainly not placed on the same footing as European ways of knowing. One participant in Findlay's work illustrated the extent to which her teacher included Indigenous perspectives in chemistry class: 'Just being like, um, First Nations used this as medicine way back when . . . It's not like you have to write a paper on it or anything.'[33] Even today, Indigenous students in Canada rarely see themselves or their ways of knowing in mainstream curricula.

Since the federal government has resisted calls for Indigenous-controlled curricula and has underfunded on-reserve schools, those same curricula are prominent on reserve.[34] Even as Indigenous governments have developed

25 Truth and Reconciliation Commission, *Canada's Residential Schools: The History, Part 1: Origins to 1939*, vol. 1 (Truth and Reconciliation Commission of Canada 2015) 329ff. [TRC, *History 1*].

26 TRC, *History 1*, 300–308; Truth and Reconciliation Commission, *Canada's Residential Schools: The History, Part 2: 1939 to 2000*, vol. 2 (Truth and Reconciliation Commission of Canada 2015) 121–126 [TRC, *History 2*].

27 TRC, *History 2* 113–120.

28 TRC, *History 2* 19.

29 TRC, *History 1* 67.

30 The Right Honourable Stephen Harper, 'Statement of Apology to Former Students of Indian Residential Schools' (Aboriginal Affairs and Northern Development Canada, 11 June 2008), www.aadnc-aandc.gc.ca/eng/1100100015644/1100100015649, accessed 16 June 2017.

31 Heather Findlay, '"Just a Pepper in a Bunch of Salt": Aboriginal Students' Stories of School' (Med. EC&I thesis, University of Regina Faculty of Education 2014) 87.

32 Findlay (n. 31) 80.

33 Findlay (n. 31) 86, quoting participant Wendy (May 2013) 3.

34 Aboriginal Institutes' Consortium, *Aboriginal Institutions of Higher Education: A Struggle for the Education of Aboriginal Students, Control of Indigenous Knowledge, and Recognition of Aboriginal Institutions: An Examination of Government Policy* (Canadian Race Relations Commission 2005).

> the capacity and the institutions needed to control their own education, [federal] government policies and programs have not evolved to recognize the work accomplished and the economic benefit of Aboriginal institutions in Aboriginal communities across Canada.[35]

While the federal government has transferred some control over education to Indigenous governments, such transfers often fail to include control over content. As Marie Battiste explained in 1998, such transfers 'have ushered in yet another era of cognitive imperialism with the requirement in the funding contribution agreements that require First Nations to accept provincial curricula'.[36] In spite of federal resistance, on-reserve schools have attempted to provide culturally appropriate education, but isolation and lack of funding to develop, test and deliver programmes have barred many of these schools from achieving their goals. On-reserve schools 'operate largely independently without a systematic supportive infrastructure to enable parents and educators to address broader issues collectively'.[37] They also receive less funding per student than provincially funded off-reserve schools,[38] and so are not properly funded to effectively deliver the provincial curricula, let alone to develop their own. The current system fails Indigenous students and communities.

Parallels to Education for Children with Disabilities

Persons with disabilities face discrimination in education around the globe. According to the World Health Survey, persons with disabilities 'experience significantly lower rates of primary school completion and fewer mean

35 Aboriginal Institutes' Consortium (n. 34) 8.

36 Marie Battiste, 'Enabling the Autumn Seed: Toward a Decolonized Approach to Aboriginal Knowledge, Language, and Education' (1998) 22 *Canadian Journal of Native Education* 16, 20 (citations omitted).

37 Minister's National Working Group on Education, *Our Children – Keepers of the Sacred Knowledge: Final Report of the Minister's National Working Group on Education* (Department of Indian Affairs and Northern Development Canada 2002) 14, www.afn.ca/uploads/files/education/23._2002_dec_jeffrey_and_jette_final_report_to_min_national_working_group_ourchildrenkeepersofthesacredknowledge.pdf, accessed 16 June 2017.

38 Since the late 1990s, the government has placed a gap on annual increases to core Indigenous education funding, which has remained at 2 per cent: Don Drummond and Ellen Kachuck Rosenbluth, 'The Debate on First Nations Education Funding: Mind the Gap' (2013) Queens University School of Policy Studies Working Paper No. 49, 5. The permitted increases have not kept pace with the rapidly growing Indigenous population, resulting in significant underfunding of on-reserve schools (see further on page 5). A pronounced funding gap has developed between on-reserve schools and provincial public off-reserve schools. Many on-reserve schools lack the funding to maintain their buildings or to provide education even under existing curricula, let alone the resources to provide inclusive and culturally significant education to their students.

years of education' than peers without disabilities.[39] Barriers to equitable access to education include, among others, lack of enforcing legislation, inadequate resources, inappropriately rigid curricula, inadequately supported teachers and violence, bullying and abuse.[40] Canada is not immune. Children with disabilities have experienced exclusion and discrimination in education in a manner that parallels both the experiences of children with disabilities across the world and those of Indigenous children globally and in Canada.

Children with disabilities in Canada – and those incorrectly diagnosed as such – were long subject to institutionalisation, where schooling was either not provided or very poorly implemented. While such institutionalisation did not involve forcefully removing children, against their families' will and contrary to their communities' views and laws, as was characteristic of the Indian Residential School project, the state was very much involved in funnelling children with disabilities into the system. Governments, churches and medical professionals justified the placement of thousands of children into institutions as '[c]hild-saving' or protection, and sought to turn children with disabilities into producers for society.[41] Eventually, these institutions and the systems that created them were exposed as contributing to discrimination, failing to provide real education and permitting the abuse of children. In the province of Ontario, which developed an extensive network of institutions over a period of 140 years, Premier Kathleen Wynne (a former teacher) apologised in 2013 to the former residents of Regional Centres for People with Developmental Disabilities. Her words acknowledged the harm: 'Their humanity was undermined; they were separated from their families and robbed of their potential, their comfort, safety and their dignity.'[42]

As the education system shifted away from institutionalisation, students were often integrated into regular schools but remained segregated in special education classrooms. For instance, in Ontario, the Education Amendment Act, 1980 required for the first time that school boards provide free special

39 World Health Organization (WHO) and World Bank, *World Report on Disability* (World Health Organization 2011) 206.

40 WHO and World Bank (n. 39) 212–216.

41 Margret A. Winzer, 'Confronting Difference: An Excursion through the History of Special Education' in Lani Florian (ed.), *The SAGE Handbook of Special Education* (SAGE 2006) 24–25.

42 Kathleen Wynne, 'Ontario's Apology to Former Residents of Regional Centres for People with Developmental Disabilities' (Ministry of Community and Social Services, 9 December 2013), www.mcss.gov.on.ca/documents/en/mcss/developmental/Apology_December9_2013.pdf, accessed 16 June 2017, 2.

education programmes.[43] But in the decades that followed, students with disabilities often remained segregated from their peers through special education classes and schools, and the education system did not allow them to meet their full potential. In 2001, just less than 60 per cent of students with disabilities were taught in regular classrooms.[44] The majority of those not in regular classrooms were in special education classrooms or schools.[45] Parents of students with disabilities were less likely to feel that their children were being challenged in school to meet their full potential, and there was a significant literacy gap between students with cognitive or emotional disabilities and those without.[46]

Canada has more recently been described as a leader 'in the international community with regards to the right to education of persons with disabilities, specifically concerning inclusive education'.[47] Yet inclusiveness in education varies by province, and 'Canadian courts have stopped short of' demanding inclusion for all children.[48] Educators were apprehensive about the implementation of inclusive education in Canada two decades ago in 1998, and time has confirmed their fears.[49] Research has generally shown a 'gap between policy and practice' in inclusive education, with policy supporting inclusive education reforms, and practice lagging behind, often due to a lack of resources.[50]

Education for Indigenous Children with Disabilities on Reserves: A Particular Failure

Because the vast majority of schools in Canada are under provincial jurisdiction, most changes towards inclusive education in Canada have been done at

43 Ontario Ministry of Education, 'The Education Act' (Ontario Ministry of Education, 5 June 2012), www.edu.gov.on.ca/eng/general/elemsec/speced/edact.html, accessed 16 June 2017.

44 Dafna Kohen, Sharanjit Uppal, Anne Guevremont and Fernando Cartwright, 'Children with Disabilities and the Educational System: A Provincial Perspective' (Statistics Canada, 2003), www.statcan.gc.ca/pub/81–004-x/2007001/9631-eng.htm, accessed 16 June 2017.

45 Kohen (n. 44).

46 Kohen (n. 44).

47 Fatima Ahmad, Suraj Girijashanker and Mariam Kemple, 'The Convention on the Rights of Persons with Disabilities: The Right to Education and the Obligations of States: SOAS International Human Rights Clinic Project' (2011) SOAS School of Law Research Paper No. 06/2011, 53–54.

48 Ahmad, Girijashanker and Kemple (n. 47) 54.

49 Margret A. Winzer, 'The Inclusion Movement and Teacher Change: Where Are the Limits?' (1998) 33 *McGill Journal of Education* 229, 243.

50 See e.g. S. Anthony Thompson, Wanda Lyons and Vianne Timmons, 'Inclusive Education Policy: What the Leadership of Canadian Teacher Associations Has to Say about It' (2015) 19 *International Journal of Inclusive Education* 121, 123, 133–134.

the provincial level.[51] Indigenous students with disabilities, whose education is under federal jurisdiction, have not seen the same developments.[52] This is of particular concern because the rates of disability among Indigenous people are far higher than among the general population and because Indigenous children with disabilities are acutely vulnerable to multiple forms of discrimination associated with exclusion and segregation in the education system.[53]

Exclusion was a reality of the Indian Residential School project, since 'residential schools had no resources to accommodate students with disabilities'.[54] Children did not receive the care they needed and experienced 'bullying and discriminatory treatment from both staff and students'.[55]

Today, Indigenous students with disabilities are often segregated. The lack of special needs services on reserves forces 'families of children with disabilities to choose between keeping their community and cultural connections or accessing disability-related services'.[56] Indigenous students are often forced to leave their communities and to attend provincial schools in order to access special education services.[57] As a result, these children may 'lose contact with their parents, siblings, other community members, their language, and their culture', and families and communities lose a member.[58] Removing students with disabilities from on-reserve schools also has the indirect effect of stagnating those schools' capacity to provide special education.[59]

A matter recently before the Canadian Human Rights Tribunal (CHRT) highlights the discriminatory disparities between services for students with disabilities living on and off reserve. Between 2008 and 2011, the Mississaugas of the New Credit First Nation had an annual special education budget of $160,000–190,000.[60] Two children with Down syndrome, the Miller twins,

[51] Constitution Act, 1867 S93.

[52] Constitution Act, 1867 S91(24).

[53] Disability Rights Promotion International, *Expanding the Circle: Monitoring the Human Rights of Indigenous, First Nations, Aboriginal, Inuit and Métis People with Disabilities in Canada: Systemic Report* (Disability Rights Promotion International 2016) 8–9.

[54] TRC, *History 1* (n. 25) 573.

[55] TRC, *History 1* (n. 25) 573. For further on this point, see Truth and Reconciliation Commission, *The Survivors Speak*, vol. 1 (Truth and Reconciliation Commission of Canada 2015) 183–184.

[56] Deborah Stienstra, 'For Michael Charlie: Including Girls and Boys with Disabilities in the Global South/North' (2015) 2 *Disability and the Global South* 632, 633.

[57] Ron Phillips, 'Special Education in First Nations Schools in Canada: Policies of Cost Containment' (2010) 56 *Alberta Journal of Educational Research* 72, 76.

[58] Phillips, 'Special Education' (n. 57) 76.

[59] Phillips, 'Special Education' (n. 57) 76.

[60] Letter from Kent Elson, Klippensteins Barristers and Solicitors, Counsel for the Mississaugas of the New Credit First Nation to Deirdre Hilary, Investigator, Canadian Human Rights

attended an off-reserve provincial school 'because of their high special needs', and the province billed the First Nation a total of $80,000 per year for the two students, amounting to almost half of the First Nation's annual special education budget.[61] Before the Miller twins reached school age, the First Nation was already using the entire special education budget provided to it by the federal government.[62] Due to inadequate funding from the federal government, not only were the twins unable to attend school in their own community but the community was left unable to effectively support other students with disabilities.

The First Nation brought a claim of discrimination against the government to the Canadian Human Rights Commission (CHRC), citing the lack of clear 'legislative and policy framework for special education on reserve', the inadequacy and impracticability of the federal government's formula-based approach to funding and the imposition of third-party management on bands that run a deficit to pay for special education.[63] The CHRC referred the case to the CHRT in 2012 for further investigation, stating in part that 'the available evidence appears to indicate that children living on reserve are denied special education services and/or differentiated against adversely in the provision of special education services'.[64] The parties were approaching resolution in April 2017.[65]

This case highlights several disparities between special education programmes on and off reserve. One of the most troublesome roadblocks to achieving equality relates to asymmetrical rights to education: while provincial education laws guarantee rights to students with disabilities, there are no

Commission (27 July 2011) by email, Canadian Human Rights Commission File No. 20091016, 8.

61 Letter from Kent Elson (n. 60) 8–9.

62 Letter from Kent Elson (n. 60) 9.

63 Canadian Human Rights Commission, 'Assessment Report' (File No. 20091016), www.firstnationsspecialeducation.ca/wp-content/uploads/2011/11/111228-Commission-Investigators-Assessment-Report.pdf, accessed 16 June 2017 [3].

64 Canadian Human Rights Commission (n. 63) [62].

65 According to Kent Elson of Klippensteins Barristers and Solicitors, counsel for the Mississaugas of the New Credit First Nation (email from Kent Elson to author [3 April 2017] re: Canadian Human Rights Tribunal Case), as of early April 2017, the parties had resolved the portion of the case relating specifically to the Miller twins, and the portion relating to Ontario-wide systemic discrimination was on hold while further study was under way. As part of the settlement and negotiation process, a report was prepared which synthesised information about special education of Indigenous children in Ontario and provided recommendations for moving forward, largely related to control, institutional structures, regulations, funding and resourcing: Peter Garrow, 'Ontario First Nations Special Education Review Report' (May 2017), www.firstnationsspecialeducation.ca/Report.pdf, accessed 10 July 2017.

federal equivalents. Instead, the provision of services to Indigenous students with disabilities on reserve is governed by non-binding 'policies, guidelines, and statements'.[66]

Canadian human rights law does not provide a functional alternative to clear legislation that protects the rights of Indigenous children with disabilities to inclusive education in their own cultures. While the Canadian Human Rights Act may be used to prove discrimination against Indigenous children with disability – as was claimed in the Mississaugas of the New Credit case – enforcement has proven slow, cumbersome and resource-intensive.[67] In a related context, the CHRT declared 'inequitable and insufficient' federal funding of First Nations Child and Family Services Programs discriminatory in 2016, nine years after the First Nations Child and Family Caring Society and the Assembly of First Nations first filed the complaint.[68] Since that decision, the government has failed to remedy the inequities, and in March 2017, arguments were being made about which bodies have the power to enforce orders from the tribunal.[69] It is possible that, even if they were successful at the CHRT, cases like the Mississaugas of the New Credit case would face similar hurdles in implementation.

CANADA'S INTERNATIONAL OBLIGATIONS REGARDING EDUCATION FOR INDIGENOUS CHILDREN WITH DISABILITIES

Canada's Specific Obligations Related to Education for Indigenous Children with Disabilities

Several international legal instruments have been developed to protect the education rights of those vulnerable to discrimination. As a party to those Conventions and Declarations, Canada has clear international obligations relating to education, including specific obligations towards children with disabilities and Indigenous children.

66 Phillips, 'Special Education' (n. 57) 76.

67 Canadian Human Rights Act, RSC 1985, c. H-6.

68 Canadian Human Rights Tribunal, *First Nations Child and Family Caring Society of Canada and others* v. *Attorney General of Canada (Representing the Minister of Indian Affairs and Northern Development Canada)*, 26 January 2016, 2016 CHRT 2 [5]–[6] and [456]ff.

69 Attorney General of Canada, 'Respondent's Factum' (Tribunal File No. T-1340/7008) (FNCaringSociety, 14 March 2017), https://fncaringsociety.com/sites/default/files/AGC%27s%20submissions.pdf, accessed 16 June 2017.

International law has developed to recognise an enforceable right to inclusive education for all children. A general right to education, particularly for children, was protected in the Universal Declaration on Human Rights[70] in 1948, and affirmed in both the International Covenant on Economic, Social and Cultural Rights[71] in 1966 and the Convention on the Rights of the Child[72] (CRC) in 1989.[73] However, the application of this right to children with disabilities remained undeveloped.[74] Non-binding international law that protected the right to education for children with disabilities developed in the 1990s.[75] In 2006, the Convention on the Rights of Persons with Disabilities (CRPD) specifically affirmed a right to inclusive education for persons with disabilities,[76] becoming the first binding international legal instrument to do so.[77] Canada has ratified the CRPD, and has a clear obligation to provide inclusive education across the board.

Inclusion means more than simply placing children with disabilities in the classroom. Instead, it requires 'systemic reform embodying changes and modifications in content, teaching methods, approaches, structures and strategies in education' with a view to providing all students 'with an equitable and participatory learning experience and environment that best corresponds to their requirements and preferences'.[78] The CRPD recognises that disability occurs as an interaction between long-term impairments and various barriers within society.[79] It aims both 'to preserve the dignity of disabled people, by providing them with optimal prospects for autonomy' and 'to abolish the various mechanisms that exclude them'.[80] As such, States Parties, including Canada, have obligations not only to reasonably accommodate individual students with disabilities, but also to create an environment that itself accommodates difference and wherein all students can participate equally and equitably.[81]

70 Universal Declaration of Human Rights (adopted 10 December 1948) UNGA Res. 217A(III) (UDHR) Art. 26.

71 International Covenant on Economic, Social and Cultural Rights (adopted 16 December 1966, entered into force 3 January 1976) 993 UNTS 3 (ICESCR) Art. 13.

72 CRC (n. 6) Arts. 28 and 29.

73 Bronagh Byrne, 'Hidden Contradictions and Conditionality: Conceptualisations of Inclusive Education in International Human Rights Law' (2013) 28 *Disability and Society* 232, 233.

74 Byrne (n. 73) 235.

75 Byrne (n. 73) 235.

76 CRPD (n. 5) Art. 24.

77 Byrne (n. 73) 239.

78 General Comment No. 4 (n. 10) [11].

79 CRPD (n. 5) Art. 1.

80 Gauthier de Beco, 'Protecting the Invisible: An Intersectional Approach to International Human Rights Law' (2017) 17 *Human Rights Law Review* 12.

81 General Comment No. 4 (n. 10) [9].

At the same time, Canada has particular obligations towards Indigenous children. The United Nations Declaration on the Rights of Indigenous Peoples (UNDRIP) protects both the right of Indigenous children to state education without discrimination and the right of Indigenous people 'to establish and control their educational systems and institutions providing education in their own languages, in a manner appropriate to their cultural methods of teaching and learning'.[82] It also requires that states, 'in conjunction with indigenous peoples, take effective measures, in order for indigenous individuals, particularly children … to have access, when possible, to an education in their own culture and provided in their own language'.[83] While Canada voted against the declaration[84] and held objector status for almost a decade, it officially removed its objector status in May 2016 to become a 'full supporter, without qualification'.[85] The federal government has also committed to reconciliation with Indigenous people, including through the implementation of UNDRIP.

Canada's Intersectional Obligations Regarding Education for Indigenous Children with Disabilities

Indigenous children are vulnerable in three respects: as children, as Indigenous persons and as persons with disabilities. These vulnerabilities compound but also intersect to raise a unique risk of marginalisation. The CRC, the CRPD and the UNDRIP, on their own, do not address that intersectionality, since none of these articulate clearly the intersectional education rights of Indigenous children with disabilities. As such, all three instruments have to be applied together, in layers, to allow us to understand the particular education rights of Indigenous children with disabilities.

International law has struggled to address intersectionality. It has developed a focus on historically marginalised groups, identified by a single characteristic or identity, that obscures intra-group differences and even intra-group conflicts.[86] Some UN bodies, including the CRPD committee, have attended to intersectionality.[87] However, no single legal instrument provides a clear view of the education

82 UNDRIP (n. 7) Art. 14 (1).
83 UNDRIP (n. 7) Art. 14(3).
84 Office of the High Commissioner on Human Rights, 'Declaration on the Rights of Indigenous Peoples' (United Nations Human Rights Office of the High Commissioner), www.ohchr.org/EN/Issues/IPeoples/Pages/Declaration.aspx, accessed 16 June 2017.
85 Government of Canada, 'Canada Becomes a Full Supporter of the United Nations Declaration on the Rights of Indigenous Peoples', CNW (New York, 10 May 2016).
86 de Beco (n. 80) 2–3, 8.
87 de Beco (n. 80) 5.

rights of Indigenous children with disabilities. The CRC recognises equal education rights for both children with disabilities and Indigenous children, but does not address their intersection.[88] The CRPD provides clear education rights for children with disabilities, but mentions Indigenous persons with disabilities only in passing.[89] The latest of the three – UNDRIP – names some particular rights of Indigenous children and gives particular attention to Indigenous children and persons with disabilities, but does not provide clear guidance on the unique education rights of Indigenous children with disabilities.[90]

Gauthier de Beco, building on the work of Johanna Bond, explains that international law can take a larger view of rights by adopting a 'qualified universalism' approach.[91] Such an approach involves recognising difference both within and between categories, and 'requires due consideration to those multiple triggers that increase disadvantage'.[92] In this context, qualified universalism would recognise how childhood, disability and Indigenousness combine to create a more severe form of intersectional discrimination,[93] and allow us to understand how those characteristics 'conjointly lead to acute marginalisation'.[94] In order to understand the rights associated with those triggers, we must take a flexible interpretive approach.[95]

One means of doing so is to understand the particular rights recognised by each instrument, and to layer those rights one on top of the other. Like all children, Indigenous children with disabilities have a right to free primary education and accessible secondary education, without discrimination.[96] Like all persons with disabilities, Indigenous children with disabilities have a right to 'inclusive, quality and free primary education and secondary education'.[97] Like all Indigenous persons, Indigenous children with disabilities have a 'right to all levels and forms of education of the State without discrimination', and 'when possible, to an education in their own culture and provided in their own language'.[98] Together, these international instruments oblige states to provide to Indigenous

88 CRC (n. 6) Arts. 2, 21 and 29–30.

89 CRPD (n. 5) Preamble (p) and Art. 24(2)(a).

90 UNDRIP (n. 7) Arts. 14(2), (3) and 21.

91 de Beco (n. 80) 10, citing Johanna Bond, 'International Intersectionality: A Theoretical and Pragmatic Exploration of Women's International Human Rights Violations' (2003) 52 *Emory Law Journal* 71.

92 de Beco (n. 80) 10.

93 de Beco (n. 80) 10.

94 de Beco (n. 80) 10.

95 de Beco (n. 80) 27.

96 CRC (n. 6) Art 28(1)(a) and (b).

97 CRPD Art. 24(2)(b).

98 UNDRIP (n. 7) Art. 14(2) and (3).

children with disabilities state-funded education in their own cultures and languages that is structured to include them on an equal basis with other students.[99]

INDIGENOUS-CONTROLLED, INDIGENOUS KNOWLEDGE–DRIVEN EDUCATION REFORM

The Push for Indigenous-Controlled Education

The federal government's failure to live up to its obligations to Indigenous children with disabilities demands decolonisation of Indigenous education. Decolonisation in this context refers to Indigenous control of Indigenous education systems. Only Indigenous people can create systems based on their own values that truly include Indigenous students. Decades ago, in 1972, the National Indian Brotherhood (now the Assembly of First Nations) released a policy paper on Indigenous education and stated that 'only Indian people can develop a suitable philosophy of education based on Indian values adapted to modern living'.[100] The same remains true today. Indigenous people, communities and organisations have continuously asserted Indigenous jurisdiction over Indigenous education.

Indigenous jurisdiction over education finds its bases in inherent rights, Canadian constitutional law, international law and treaties. Firstly, Indigenous people in Canada have jurisdiction over education as a result of their continued inherent right to self-government, which includes control over Indigenous children's education. The inherent right exists independent of federal or international recognition, and flows instead from the people themselves.[101] Such jurisdiction may also be supported in domestic law: Canada's

99 This was essentially the approach taken by the UN Economic and Social Council in its *Study on the Situation of Indigenous Persons with Disabilities, with a Particular Focus on Challenges Faced with Regard to the Full Enjoyment of Human Rights and Inclusion in Development* (5 February 2013) E/C.19/2013/6 [34]–[36], where it layered the right to an Indigenous education system with the right to inclusion and concluded that '[f]or indigenous children with disabilities who live in their communities, [the right to be part of the general education system] means that the indigenous education system must provide them with the required support'.

100 National Indian Brotherhood [now the Assembly of First Nations], *Indian Control of Indian Education: Policy Paper* (National Indian Brotherhood 1973) 2. This policy paper was renewed in 2010: Assembly of First Nations, *First Nations Control of First Nations Education: It's Our Vision, It's Our Time* (Assembly of First Nations 2010), www.afn.ca/uploads/files/education/3._2010_july_afn_first_nations_control_of_first_nations_education_final_eng.pdf, accessed 16 June 2017.

101 Alex Christmas of the Eskasoni First Nation explains, 'We see our right of self-government as an inherent right which does not come from other governments. It does not originate in our treaties. The right of self-government and self-determination comes from the Mi'kmaq people

Constitution Act 1982 recognises and affirms existing aboriginal rights in Section 35,[102] and the Supreme Court of Canada has not foreclosed the possibility that Section 35 protects an inherent right to self-government.[103] Indigenous jurisdiction over education is explicitly recognised in international law under Article 14 of UNDRIP, which affirms Indigenous people's 'right to establish and control their educational systems and institutions'.[104] Finally, historical treaties between Canada and Indigenous people maintained Indigenous control of education.[105] While several treaties obligated the federal government to provide schools and teachers to Indigenous communities, that educational right was intended to complement Indigenous teachings and ways of knowing, not to supplant them.[106]

Indigenous Knowledge–Driven Education Reform: Furthering Decolonisation

Decolonisation in education would almost certainly involve a shift towards education structured by IK. Indigenous knowledge–driven reform is itself an 'act of intellectual self-determination'.[107] It also helps to remedy the exclusion that Indigenous children experience in Canadian school systems, and achieves cultural inclusion for Indigenous students. Many advocates emphasise the importance of Indigenous students receiving their education in their own cultures and languages, with Indigenous ways of knowing and IK receiving the same weight, attention and respect as Western knowledge systems.[108] In its 1972 policy paper, the National Indian Brotherhood stated, '[w]e want education to provide the setting in which our children can develop the

themselves. It is through their authority that we govern. The treaties reflect the Crown's recognition that we were, and would remain, self-governing, but they did not create our nationhood.' *Report of the Royal Commission on Aboriginal Peoples: Restructuring the Relationship* (Indian and Northern Affairs Canada 1996) vol. 2, 107. While the right is inherent, it finds expression in the Treaties – as Alex Christmas contends – and support in international law: see especially UNDRIP (n. 7) Arts. 3 and 4.

102 Constitution Act, 1982 S35(1) states that 'existing aboriginal and treaty rights . . . are hereby recognized and affirmed'.

103 See especially Supreme Court of Canada, *R* v. *Pamajewon*, 22 August 1996, [1996] 2 SCR 821. The Court in that case completed an analysis assuming without deciding that Section 35 did protect a right of self-government.

104 UNDRIP (n. 7) Art. 14(1).

105 Shelia Carr-Stewart, 'A Treaty Right to Education' (2001) 26 *Canadian Journal of Education* 125, 128. This work is focussed on Treaties 1–7.

106 Carr-Stewart (n. 105) 138.

107 Marie Battiste and James (Sákéj) Youngblood Henderson, 'Naturalizing Indigenous Knowledge in Eurocentric Education' (2009) 32 *Canadian Journal of Native Education* 5.

108 Battiste and Henderson (n. 107) 14.

fundamental attitudes and values which have an honoured place in Indian tradition and culture'.[109] 'Our children' continues to include students with disabilities. What is advocated, in effect, is IK-driven education reform, in which IK informs both the structure and the content of learning.

Indigenous knowledge refers 'to the common-sense ideas and cultural knowledges of local peoples concerning the everyday realities of living'.[110] Indigenous knowledge is a methodology and includes multiple processes or ways of knowing.[111] It is also a completely comprehensive way of knowing that comprises Indigenous epistemology and pedagogies.[112] I do not purport to have drawn out a clear and universal definition of IK. As Battiste and Youngblood Henderson explain, IK as a process defies the 'Eurocentric need for definitions'.[113] Understanding any IK system and its content requires learning through Indigenous processes.[114] And diversity of processes between and within individual nations makes a universal understanding impossible. It is possible, however, to identify common principles, processes and characteristics present in many Indigenous pedagogies that would prescribe aspects of IK-driven education reform.

Four key concepts emerge from the literature on IK and education. First, IK is based in relationships, and so learning involves direct interaction with community members.[115] Second, IK is found in language, and so IK-based education necessarily involves learning in Indigenous languages.[116] Third, IK is dependent on place, and so students learn from place and experience place through visitation.[117] Finally, IK expects difference between individuals, and so teaching is designed to adapt to the needs and abilities of each learner.[118]

109 National Indian Brotherhood (n. 100) 2.

110 George J. Sefa Dei, Irma Marcia James, Leeno Luke Karumanchery, Sonia James Wilson and Jasmin Zine, 'Schooling and Education in North America: Recentering Indigenous Knowledges' in *Removing the Margins: The Challenges and Possibilities of Inclusive Schooling* (Canadian Scholars' Press 2000) 49.

111 Leroy Little Bear, *Naturalizing Indigenous Knowledge: Synthesis Paper* (Canadian Council on Learning and Aboriginal Learning Knowledge Centre 2009) 7.

112 Marie Battiste and James (Sákéj) Youngblood Henderson, *Protecting Indigenous Knowledge and Heritage: A Global Challenge* (Purich Publishing 2000) 39–41; Battiste and Henderson (n. 107) 14.

113 Battiste and Henderson (n. 112) 35–41.

114 Battiste and Henderson (n. 112) 41.

115 Battiste and Henderson (n. 112) 15.

116 TRC, *Legacy* (n. 23) 103, citing Elder Eli Taylor, Sioux Valley First Nation.

117 Little Bear (n. 111) 21; Battiste and Henderson (n. 112) 14; TRC, *Legacy* (n. 23) 98–99.

118 Marie Battiste and Sheelagh McLean, *State of First Nations Learning* (Canadian Council on Learning 2005) 13; Battiste and Henderson (n. 112) 16.

Education based on IK need not exclude Western ways of knowing. Instead, IK fills gaps in Western education.[119] Those advocating for IK-driven education reform have acknowledged the importance of developing both ways of knowing without privileging one over the other. Even during treaty negotiations, Indigenous families and governments have recognised the value of Western education in conjunction with Indigenous education.[120] Battiste explains that parents maintained control of their children's education through the treaties, but acknowledged the value of their children gaining European knowledge.[121]

Several Indigenous communities use IK in curriculum reform, provide education in their own languages or include elders in their education systems. Perhaps the most comprehensive aspirational documents describing an IK-driven education system were developed in Nunavut. In 2007, the Nunavut government released the Inuit Qaujumajatuqangit Education Framework for Nunavut Curriculum, envisioning a new education system built around principles of Inuit Qaujumajatuqangit (IQ) – 'Inuit beliefs, laws, principles and values along with traditional knowledge, skills and attitudes'.[122] The framework highlights the potential of IK-based reform and provides an example of what it could look like. Other communities, including those on reserves, have also made significant reforms.

INDIGENOUS KNOWLEDGE–DRIVEN EDUCATION REFORM AS A MEANS OF ACHIEVING INCLUSIVE EDUCATION

Like inclusive education,[123] IK-driven education reform demands significant short-term investments.[124] As such, two apparently conflicting priorities for Indigenous children with disabilities emerge: providing inclusive education and providing education in the children's own traditions and languages, based in IK. The question then becomes, is the push for inclusive education in conflict with IK-driven education reform, or can one help achieve the other? If

119 Battiste and Henderson (n. 112) 7, 9.

120 For a brief history and different perspectives on treaties in Canada, see Paul W. DePasquale, *Natives and Settlers: Now and Then: Historical Issues and Current Perspectives on Treaties and Land Claims in Canada* (University of Alberta Press 2007).

121 Marie Battiste, 'Constitutional Reconciliation of Education for Aboriginal Peoples' (2009) 5 *Directions* 81.

122 Nunavut Department of Education, *Inuit Qaujumajatuqangit: Education Framework for Nunavut Curriculum* (Nunavut Department of Education 2007) 20.

123 de Beco (n. 11) 276.

124 Alfred (n. 12) 199–200.

IK's goals are aligned with the goals of inclusive education – if investments in IK are actually investments in inclusion – then IK-driven education reform can put Indigenous communities on a path to inclusive education, and can serve as a model for inclusive education in other communities. In sum, they are, and it can.

Indigenous knowledge–driven education reform encompasses four important features of inclusive education: it recognises and values difference, offers individualised support, enables participation in society and demands that education be provided in the community.

Recognising and Valuing Difference: Worldviews on Disability and Exceptionality

Indigenous knowledge and the CRPD understand disability similarly. Inclusion under the CRPD requires not only accepting but also valuing difference. In inclusive education systems, the needs of persons with disabilities 'are understood as integral to the social and economic order and not identified as "special"'.[125] Indigenous knowledge understands them as such.

Indigenous worldviews – more so than Western worldviews – lend themselves to inclusion. The idea that difference is expected and positive is basic to IK. Difference is recognised, but 'is not subjected to relationships of inequality'.[126] Instead, it is described variously as 'unique potential'[127] or as 'gifts'.[128] All students are expected to succeed by using and developing that unique potential or those gifts.[129] This is partly because Indigenous perceptions are free from the European obsession with binaries, including 'the oppressive binaries of able-bodied/disabled, normal/abnormal'.[130] Instead, difference 'is seen as matter of degrees of representation of the sacred forces not of a person's true

125 Office of the High Commissioner on Human Rights, *Monitoring the Convention on the Rights of Persons with Disabilities: Guidance for Human Rights Monitors*, Professional Training Series No. 17 (United Nations 2010), www.ohchr.org/Documents/Publications/Disabilities_training_17EN.pdf, accessed 16 June 2017, 22.

126 Heather Norris, 'Colonialism and the Rupturing of Indigenous Worldviews of Impairment and Relational Interdependence: A Beginning Dialogue towards Reclamation and Social Transformation' (2014) 6 *Critical Disability Discourse/Discours Critiques dans le Champ du Handicap* 53, 70.

127 Nunavut Department of Education, *Inuglugijaittuq: Foundation for Inclusive Education in Nunavut Schools* (Nunavut Department of Education, Curriculum and School Services 2008) 26.

128 Little Bear (n. 111) 19.

129 Nunavut Department for Education (n. 127) 26.

130 Norris (n. 126) 72. Thomas King also discusses the Western obsession with dichotomy in his Massey Lectures: Thomas King, *The Truth about Stories* (House of Anansi Press 2003) 25.

essence', and 'degrees of difference are as sacred as all other formations of sacred forces'.[131]

This is not to say that all IK systems understand disability uniformly, or that all Indigenous communities and people today share the attitudes reflected in IK, or that all Indigenous people with disabilities benefit from these attitudes.[132] Certainly, they do not. There are many reasons why that may be the case, including different personal, cultural or legal understandings of disability, or colonial impacts on worldviews and ways of knowing. It can also be due to the specific impacts of generations of poor schooling and disrupted family lives on parents' abilities to understand disability and exceptionality and to foster positive learning environments.[133] Nonetheless, it is clear that in many Indigenous worldviews, children with disabilities are understood as 'special in a way that they [are] a gift'.[134] Such worldviews – which would inform IK-based education – are compatible with the CRPD and its goals.

Moreover, IK-based education values diversity in all forms, beyond disability. It meaningfully includes Indigenous students in their own learning. The content and structures allow Indigenous students to feel 'valued, respected, included and listened to', consistent with the goals of inclusive education.[135] For IK programmes to succeed in this respect, teachers in IK-driven education systems must understand the context in which their students experience the world, even if barriers to understanding exist. One barrier is that Indigenous communities have been disproportionately affected by transiency in teaching staff – teachers do not have time to learn about the communities in which they teach.[136] In addition, few teachers currently have formal training in Indigenous issues, and even fewer have training in IK content and languages.[137] Supporting IK-based education demands a shift in teacher education, in terms of both what is taught and who is trained. Where possible and hopefully at an increasing rate, the primary educators or teachers in classrooms should be from the community,

[131] Norris (n. 126) 72.
[132] Adele Vukic, David Gregory, Ruth Martin-Misener and Josephine Etowa, 'Aboriginal and Western Conceptions of Mental Health and Illness' (2011) 9 *Pimatisiwin: A Journal of Aboriginal and Indigenous Community Health* 65, 68.
[133] Ron Phillips, '"Try to Understand Us": Aboriginal Elders' Views on Exceptionality' (2010) 20 *Brock Education Journal* 64, 69–71.
[134] Alberta Learning, *A Handbook for Aboriginal Parents of Children with Special Needs* (Alberta Learning 2000) 1, citing an elder from an unnamed community.
[135] General Comment No. 4 (n. 10) [12(e)].
[136] Sisco and others (n. 21) 28.
[137] Terry Wotherspoon, 'Teaching for Equity? What Teachers Say about Their Work in Aboriginal Communities' (2007) 47(4) *Education Canada* 64, 66.

or be otherwise invested in remaining in the community for an extended period, in order to ensure that teachers have or gain an understanding of the context in which they are teaching.[138] Further, teacher education in an IK-based system will address colonialism, racism, Indigenous culture and IK,[139] and teach educators how to deliver IK appropriately.[140] By encouraging development of local teachers and by training all teachers on Indigenous perspectives, IK-based education systems meaningfully include Indigenous students and their diverse perspectives.

Individualised Supports

Indigenous knowledge–driven education reform involves a shift towards the individualised supports required for inclusion. Under the CRPD, States Parties must ensure that '[p]ersons with disabilities receive the support required, within the general education system, to facilitate their effective education',[141] and that '[e]ffective individualized support measures are provided in environments that maximize academic and social development, consistent with the goal of full inclusion'.[142] Valuing difference also means considering multiple identities within 'approaches to teaching, curriculum material, and assessment styles'.[143] At the same time, the CRPD recognises and safeguards the autonomy of persons with disabilities.[144] Indigenous knowledge–driven education reform demands the same individualised educational context.

Individualised support is a key feature of IK-based education. Indigenous knowledge recognises students' individual strengths and gifts and affirms diverse learning strategies.[145] Each child has his or her own 'unique potential'[146] or 'gifts to learn', and teachers are expected to engage in a 'multiplicity' of learning practices.[147] One elder from an unidentified community in Saskatchewan 'stressed the need to "find the key" with students with special

138 Sisco and others (n. 21) 28.
139 Little Bear (n. 111) 16; Battiste and Henderson (n. 112) 14.
140 Dei and others (n. 110) 64.
141 CRPD (n. 5) Art. 24(2)(d).
142 CRPD (n. 5) Art. 24(2)(e).
143 Gillian Parekh and Kathryn Underwood, *Inclusion: Creating School and Classroom Communities Where Everyone Belongs: Research, Tips, and Tools for Educators and Administrators* (Toronto District School Board 2015) 5.
144 See e.g. CRPD (n. 5) preamble (n), Arts. 3(a), 12 and 19(a).
145 Battiste and Henderson (n. 112) 16.
146 Nunavut Department of Education (n. 127) 26.
147 Little Bear (n. 111) 19.

needs and the "gift" that these students give their teachers'.[148] He explained that teachers must support students with disabilities using 'different skills, different ways, different methods. Maybe visual, it may be other ways. But to find that key, that child will learn'.[149] Indigenous knowledge also recognises that we are all in a continuous state of learning – on a learning journey[150] – and so teachers 'meet learners where they are', and continue to build capacity.[151] Another Saskatchewan elder explained 'that "each child is born with the spirit and we have to understand and nurture that spirit"'.[152] Like inclusive education, IK-based education adapts to the child in front of it, and provides individualised support, responsive to his or her changing and different needs.

The Nunavut curriculum documents highlight the potential of IK to ensure support at an individual level. They refer to the principle of *Inuglugijaittuq* (inclusion). Inuit elders described the support necessary for *Inuglugijaittuq* with reference to the *qaggi* (a drum dance), an iconic image in the curriculum documents.[153] In the forefront of the image is *mumiqtuq* (the dancer), who 'represents the child requiring support'.[154] A number of people sit in rows near the dancer.

> The people sitting next to the dancer are *tusariat* (the singers) who support the dancer. They represent supports in the school, community and family that help the child learn. They also represent people, resource equipment, itinerant specialists or Health & Social Services personnel. These supports change, responding to the changing needs of the child. Behind the '*tusariat*' are *qaggipqajut* (the others, usually men, who observe the dancer). They represent other children in the classroom, other teachers, DEA, and community members, older students who all contribute to the caring

148 Phillips, 'Try to Understand Us' (n. 133) 71, citing Elder 2.

149 Phillips, 'Try to Understand Us' (n. 133) 71, citing Elder 2.

150 Gregory Cajete provides an illustration of the journey metaphor among the Pueblo peoples in the southern United States in Gregory Cajete, 'Indigenous Knowledge: The Pueblo Metaphor of Indigenous Education' in Marie Battiste (ed.), *Reclaiming Indigenous Voice and Vision* (University of British Columbia Press 2000) 182:

> Among Pueblo peoples there is a figure called Kokopelli. He is an archetypal figure who symbolically represents the procreative processes and energy in nature. He is said to go from village to village carrying a bag of seeds. In each place that he stops, he plants seeds. He then gathers seeds from that place to plant in the next place he visits. Those seeds are metaphors for thoughts and ideas; they are ways of looking at things. Kokopelli is a metaphor for the kind of understanding each of us must have as we set out on our journey. It is my belief that each and every one of us is Kokopelli. Each of us has a special bag of 'seeds', of special gifts, that we bring and that we plant, and each of us collects seeds to take on the next step of our journey.

151 Battiste and Henderson (n. 112) 16.

152 Phillips, 'Try to Understand Us' (n. 133) 69, citing Elder 1.

153 Nunavut (n. 122) 50.

154 Nunavut (n. 122) 50.

> environment. It is a supportive community – there to support and celebrate the child for what he or she can do, giving voice to his or her song.[155]

The philosophical approach outlined in the curriculum demonstrates how IK accounts for modern resources and structures to support inclusion. It also demonstrates the need for proper resourcing in order to achieve IK-driven education reform in our contemporary setting.

Indigenous knowledge also envisions students as active participants in their learning. As such, 'students must be given the opportunity to make decisions within the classroom and the school regarding their own education'.[156] Individual autonomy is acknowledged and respected, but support is also provided. Education is about helping an individual find out who they are, where they come from, their unique character, their motivation and the role that will help them express it.[157] Indigenous knowledge–based education systems effectively support students on an individual basis, while respecting and enabling their autonomy.

Enabling Participation in Society

Both IK-based and inclusive education expect and ensure that all students are able to contribute to their communities. The right to inclusive education under the CRPD is aimed in part at enabling participation in society.[158] Segregation is a barrier to such participation, and '[c]hildren with disabilities who have been to mainstream schools have greater chances to participate in the open labour market'.[159] Any form of integration, then, better prepares students for participation in society, but inclusive education goes further to ensure active participation. Part of valuing difference is recognising the potential in all students, and 'high expectations [must be] established for all learners'.[160] Indigenous knowledge maintains these expectations and aims to empower all students to participate in their communities.

By providing students with access to IK content, such as Indigenous science, music or poetry, IK-based education more fully prepares students to participate in local and global economies. Indigenous knowledge–based education includes IK in the classroom: the subject matter itself rooted in local

155 Nunavut (n. 122) 50.
156 Battiste and McLean (n. 118) 13.
157 Cajete (n. 150) 183.
158 CRPD (n. 5) Art. 24(1)(c).
159 de Beco (n. 11) 264.
160 General Comment No. 4 (n. 10) [12(c)].

knowledge. The value of IK content is recognised in most or all Indigenous communities, and also in the global community, in an increasing number of fields.[161] Indigenous knowledge–based education that places Indigenous ways of knowing on the same footing as European ways of knowing allows students access to localised knowledge that they would not otherwise learn, thereby allowing them to contribute to their local community and – where permitted by the IK system – to global conversations.

Indigenous knowledge–based education also allows students to participate in their communities by providing them with education in their own language, where key elements of culture are 'accumulated, shared and transmitted'.[162] Indigenous knowledge–driven systems necessarily involve Indigenous language education. Battiste emphasises the importance of language for the 'renewal and respect of Aboriginal knowledge and humanity', noting that 'Indigenous languages offer not just a communication tool for unlocking knowledge; they offer a process of orientation that removes us from rigid noun-centered reality and offers an unfolding paradigmatic process for restoration and healing'.[163] Sioux Elder Eli Taylor explains that '[e]mbodied in Aboriginal languages is our unique relationship to the Creator, our attitudes, beliefs, values and the fundamental notion of what is truth'.[164] Indigenous language education also allows students to participate more meaningfully in their communities and larger society. A study of student experiences in Nunavut garnered positive comments about the usefulness of language learning in primary and junior grades: 'I still use my English and Inuktitut.'[165] Education in their own language allows students to participate more actively in their communities, to communicate more directly about IK and to pass on IK to future generations.

Finally, IK expects something of all students and encourages them to develop their unique skills and to determine a vocation that will allow them to use those skills productively.[166] For instance, for Inuit, there is an 'expectation that the potential of the individual will be developed for the good of the community'.[167] Inuit elders have spoken out against practices such as social

161 See e.g. Kirsten Vinyeta and Kathy Lynn, *Exploring the Role of Traditional Ecological Knowledge in Climate Change Initiatives* (US Department of Agriculture 2013); Mariana G. Hewson, *Embracing Indigenous Knowledge in Science and Medical Teaching* (Springer 2015).
162 TRC, *Legacy* (n. 23) 103, citing Elder Eli Taylor, Sioux Valley First Nation.
163 Battiste (n. 36) 24.
164 TRC, *Legacy* (n. 23) 103, citing Elder Eli Taylor, Sioux Valley First Nation.
165 Matthew Ayres, 'The Impact of Inuit Qaujimajatuqangit on Formal Education in Nunavut' (MA thesis, Royal Roads University Interdisciplinary Studies 2012) 51.
166 Cajete (n. 150) 183.
167 Nunavut (n. 127) 26.

promotion that diminish the 'high expectations that educators should have for students'.[168] Further, '[h]oning skills that demonstrat[e] excellence in one's area of expertise and enabl[e] each person to provide for others' is a fundamental goal, supported by natural law and IQ.[169] Indigenous knowledge–based education ensures that all students graduate able to contribute to society.

Education in the Community and with One's Peers

Indigenous knowledge–based education ensures that Indigenous children with disabilities receive education in their communities, as required by the CRPD. Children with disabilities must have access to inclusive education 'on an equal basis with others in the communities in which they live'.[170] That means that they must receive that education 'within the communities where they live. Students should not be sent away from home'.[171] All persons with disabilities also have a right to 'live in the community' and to 'full inclusion and participation in the community'.[172] Scholars in inclusive education have emphasised the positive benefits of inclusion for children with disabilities and their peers.[173] Indigenous students with disabilities should not be required to leave their communities for education, as they are now. They have a right to education within their communities and among their peers. Indigenous-controlled and IK-driven education reform would effectively safeguard that right.

Indigenous knowledge supports learning in the community and goes further to support learning among community members, in all of their diversity. Indigenous knowledge–based education systems are intended to combat the removal of children, they involve localised and community-based learning, and they require community participation. As such, any IK-based system will necessarily ensure that Indigenous children remain in their communities, in contact with their families, traditions and cultures. That includes children with disabilities too.

Since Indigenous-controlled education is intended in part to combat segregation and to allow communities to recover from generations of removal of

168 Nunavut (n. 127) 23.
169 Nunavut (n. 122) 27.
170 CRPD (n. 5) Art. 24(2)(b).
171 General Comment No. 4 (n. 10) [26].
172 CRPD (n. 5) Art. 19.
173 Sheila Bennett, 'Including Students with Exceptionalities' (2009) 16 *What Works? Research into Practice*, www.edu.gov.on.ca/eng/literacynumeracy/inspire/research/Bennett.pdf, accessed 16 June 2017.

Indigenous children, any effective IK-driven or Indigenous-controlled education system would keep children in their communities. The very goal of decolonisation demands that IK-based education systems serve all children, including children with disabilities, in their own communities.

Indigenous knowledge–driven education reform also demands a shift to place-based learning, which in turn requires that children learn on their own territories. Indigenous knowledge cannot be separated from the land, and is described with reference to it.[174] Indigenous knowledge 'exists in the context of [Indigenous peoples'] learning and knowing from the places where they have lived, hunted, explored, migrated, farmed, raised families, built communities, and survived for centuries'.[175] It can only be transferred in context since it is tied 'to particular landscapes, landforms, and biomes where ceremonies are properly held, stories properly recited, medicines properly gathered, and transfers of knowledge properly authenticated'.[176] Indigenous knowledge–based education would have students experience place through visitation.[177] Place-based learning – which 'anchors the students' lessons in the cultures, the land, the history, and the stories of their communities' – is an essential component of IK-driven education,[178] and such localised learning requires that Indigenous students remain in their communities and learn on their territories.

Indigenous knowledge–driven education can turn schools into hubs of community interactions for students with disabilities, by demanding community participation, and where possible, elder participation. Indigenous knowledge is based in relationships and necessarily involves the community. 'To become human beings, [students] must be continually engaged in all the structures and systems of learning from the parents, the Elders, the leadership, and the community organizations.'[179] Community involvement varies, but may involve parent participation, learning at home or regular class visits by leadership. In communities where elders have retained or gained IK in spite of colonial impacts and are able and willing to participate in educations systems, those elders are indispensable to an IK-based education system. Elders are carriers of knowledge,[180] and Indigenous learning systems involve listening to

174 Battiste and McLean (n. 118) 10.

175 Battiste and Henderson (n. 112) 5.

176 Marie Battiste, *Indigenous Knowledge and Pedagogy in First Nations Education: A Literature Review with Recommendations* (National Working Group on Education 2002) 13.

177 Little Bear (n. 111) 21.

178 TRC, *Legacy* (n. 23) 98–99.

179 Battiste and Henderson (n. 112) 15.

180 Kanatiio (Allen Gabriel), 'A Thanksgiving Address' in Royal Commission on Aboriginal Peoples (ed.), *Report of the Royal Commission on Aboriginal Peoples: Looking Forward, Looking Back* (Canada Communication Group 1996) vol. 1, 4.

their stories.[181] While not all elders are elderly, the very presence of community members of all ages in the classroom carries the additional benefit of demonstrating respect for other kinds of difference and ability.

Indigenous Knowledge's Potential for Evolution

On the face of it, IK-driven education reform achieves most but not all aspects of inclusive education: what is discussed in IK literature does not include everything that the CRPD demands. For instance, the IK literature does not demand that teachers be trained specifically on disability awareness, as required by the CRPD under Article 24(4).[182] As such, it appears at first glance that IK-driven education reform falls short of achieving true inclusion.

However, IK may evolve to include all elements of inclusive education described in the CRPD. Like all ways of knowing, IK is not stagnant, and modern understandings of IK concepts may require all elements of inclusive education described in the CRPD.[183] Take, for example, the IK requirement that teachers accept and support diversity and especially different learning strategies.[184] Such a requirement may, in its modern form, demand the disability awareness training required by Article 24(4) of the CRPD. When IK is deployed in communities, it is allowed to develop and to evolve, and in doing so may come to encompass all of the requirements for inclusion under the CRPD.

Moreover, any shortfalls are unlikely to invite costs beyond what would have been required for inclusive education reform in the same communities. Structural, attitudinal and pedagogical changes will be achieved. What may be missing are technical supports or specific training that can be implemented independently. For instance, the federal government needs to invest in community-based therapeutic services, supports for families of children with disabilities and early diagnosis and assessment.[185] Depending on how IK-based education is implemented, such investments may come as part of the reforms, or they may need to be made separately. In either case, they are needed to ensure that children with disabilities are equally supported in Indigenous

[181] Canadian Council on Learning, 'Nourishing the Learning Spirit: Elders' Dialogue' (4 January 2010), https://youtu.be/GQiDZFiEqp4, accessed 16 June 2017.

[182] CRPD (n. 5) Art. 24(4).

[183] Battiste (n. 176) 12–13.

[184] Little Bear (n. 111) 19.

[185] Alex Wright, Diane Hiebert-Murphy and Gwen Gosek, *Final Report: Supporting Aboriginal Children and Youth with Learning and/or Behavioural Disabilities in the Care of Aboriginal Child Welfare Agencies* (University of Manitoba Faculty of Social Work 2005) 63.

communities and in the provincial system, such that they can participate fully in the classroom.

While IK-driven education reform appears at first glance to fall short of achieving full inclusion, it can evolve to encompass everything required for inclusive education, and can be supplemented with additional supports. As such, it is a strong and appropriate step to achieving inclusive education in Indigenous communities.

DISCUSSION

Within Indigenous communities in Canada, IK supports inclusion of the kind advocated by the CRPD. In other parts of the world, Indigenous peoples may carry similar views, or may provide new insight into disability, education and inclusion. Anyone working on the implementation of inclusive education could benefit from taking IK seriously and from exchanging knowledge with Indigenous communities.

In the Canadian context, IK-driven education reform can help achieve inclusive education in Indigenous communities. There is a pressing need for such reform today, as Indigenous children and especially Indigenous children with disabilities face systemic discrimination in the current education system.

On the international stage, Canada presents as a leader in inclusive education. On the Canadian stage, the federal government emphasises commitment to reconciliation and to its international obligations towards Indigenous people. But on the ground there are large gaps. Federal leadership in both inclusive education and reconciliation means ensuring that Indigenous children with disabilities receive the education they need in order to participate fully in their communities and also on the international stage.

To be a true leader in inclusive education, and to demonstrate a real commitment to reconciliation, the government has to bind itself to deliver to Indigenous students with disabilities living on reserves inclusive education in their own cultures and languages. Federal legislation is needed to ensure that the rights of Indigenous students with disabilities are enforceable in domestic law. In the short term, though, the government needs to move quickly in order to fulfil its own international legal obligations and to work towards reconciliation.

This can start with immediate investments in IK-driven education reform.

B

MECHANISMS

15

Inclusive Education

Perspectives from the UN Committee on the Rights of Persons with Disabilities

María Soledad Cisternas Reyes

1 INTRODUCTION

Contemporary debate on the right to education for persons with disabilities raises the question as to the core elements of the right to education. This chapter examines the core features of the right to education in the light of the United Nations (UN) international legal framework for the promotion and protection of human rights during the twentieth century and the adoption of the UN Convention on the Rights of Persons with Disabilities (CRPD) at the start of the twenty-first century. It does so by incorporating into the substance of the right to education the elements we discuss in what follows. It also provides operational guidelines for the application of the inclusive education model.

Accordingly, at this stage, key questions include: What substantive elements of the right to education of persons with disabilities are emphasised by the CRPD Committee? To what extent has the Committee addressed the right to inclusive quality education? What are the prospects for accomplishing a single education system, eliminating distinctions between mainstream and segregated systems? What guidance is the Committee offering to States Parties?

The chapter that follows reviews the jurisprudence of the CRPD Committee in response to these questions.

2 THEORETICAL ASPECTS OF EDUCATION

2.1 *Conceptualisation*

The right to education is integrally related to the realisation of all human rights and has profound social impact in any community. For the Committee on Economic, Social and Cultural Rights:

> Education has been conceptualized as a human right in itself and an indispensable means of realizing other human rights. As an empowerment right, education is the primary vehicle by which economically and socially marginalized adults and children can lift themselves out of poverty and obtain the means to participate fully in their communities. Education has a vital role in empowering women, safeguarding children from exploitative and hazardous labour and sexual exploitation, promoting human rights and democracy, protecting the environment, and controlling population growth.[1]

Further, the Special Rapporteur on the Right to Education stated that 'education is a fundamental human right. Providing public education is the primary responsibility of governments', and that education is 'a public good'.[2] These understandings form the background to assessing the right to education in human rights law.

2.2 *Education as a Human Right and Its International Legal Framework*

The international human rights conventions adopted in the twentieth and the early twenty-first centuries do not define education.[3] Accordingly, the question arises as to what is the core of the right to education, according to the UN international framework for the promotion and protections of human rights? A review of international human rights instruments provides guidance on the contours of the right to education under human rights law.

The starting point is the Universal Declaration of Human Rights (UDHR), which provides:

> [E]veryone has the right to education. Education shall be free, at least in the elementary and fundamental stages. Elementary education shall be compulsory. Technical and professional education shall be made generally available and higher education shall be equally accessible to all on the basis of merit.[4]

According to the said UDHR:

> [E]ducation shall be directed to the full development of the human personality and to the strengthening of respect for human rights and fundamental

[1] Committee on Economic, Social and Cultural Rights, General Comment No. 13: The Right to Education (Article 13 of the Covenant) (8 December 1999) E/C.12/1999/10 [1].

[2] United Nations General Assembly (UNGA), 'Note by the Secretary-General: Right to Education' (24 September 2014) UN Doc. A/69/402.

[3] María Soledad Cisternas, 'Derecho a la Educación: Marco Jurídico y Justiciabilidad' (2010) 4 *Revista Latinoamericana de Educación Inclusiva* 41.

[4] Universal Declaration of Human Rights (UDHR) Art. 26(1).

freedoms. It shall promote understanding, tolerance and friendship among all nations, racial or religious groups, and shall further the activities of the United Nations for the maintenance of peace.[5]

The International Covenant on Economic, Social and Cultural Rights (ICESCR)[6] recognises the right of every person to education in the same terms as the UDHR, but incorporates two other specific elements: the sense of human dignity as an integral part of education's purpose, and education in all its forms to enable all persons to participate effectively in a free society.[7] The ICESCR emphasises the compulsory nature and free availability of primary education, as well as the progressive introduction of free secondary and higher education. Regarding the latter two elements, the importance of access to the educational process is highlighted.

Additionally, the International Covenant on Civil and Political Rights (CCPR) emphasises the right to a religious and moral education in conformity with a person's convictions, which coincides with the ICESCR in respect of a harmonious coexistence of different sectors, irrespective of their religion.[8]

Notwithstanding this general legal framework, educational exclusion coupled with the marginalisation of certain population groups in education persists. Consequently, a closer examination of other international human rights instruments and the right to education is warranted.

Although the education process develops throughout one's life, it is also true that special attention is given to education in the formative years of childhood and adolescence.[9] The Convention on the Rights of the Child (CRC) reaffirms the purposes of education to encompass:[10]

(a) The development of the child's personality, talents and mental and physical abilities to their fullest potential;

5 UDHR Art. 26(2).

6 International Covenant on Economic, Social and Cultural Rights (adopted 16 December 1966, entered into force January 3, 1976) 993 UNTS 3 (ICESCR).

7 ICESCR Art. 13.

8 International Covenant on Civil and Political Rights (adopted 16 December 1966, entered into force 23 March 1976) 999 UNTS 171 (CCPR) Art. 18(4).

9 United Nations General Assembly (UNGA), 'Implementation of General Assembly Resolution 60/251 of 15 March 2006 entitled "Human Rights Council": The Right to Education of Persons with Disabilities' (19 February 2007) UN Doc. A/HRC/4/29 (Report of the Special Rapporteur on the Right to Education) [15]: 'First, inclusive education should be viewed under an expansive perspective, embracing lifelong learning, stretching from early childcare to vocational training, basic education for adults to life-skills education for older persons.'

10 Convention on the Rights of the Child (adopted 20 November 1989, entered into force 2 September 1990) 1577 UNTS 3 (CRC).

(b) The development of respect for human rights and fundamental freedoms, and for the principles enshrined in the Charter of the United Nations;
(c) The development of respect for the child's parents, his or her own cultural identity, language and values, for the national values of the country in which the child is living, the country from which he or she may originate, and for civilizations different from his or her own;
(d) The preparation of the child for responsible life in a free society, in the spirit of understanding, peace, tolerance, equality of sexes, and friendship among all persons, ethnic, national and religious groups, and persons of indigenous origin;
(e) The development of respect for the natural environment.[11]

The 'best interests of the child' and 'respect for the child's identity' are central principles underpinning the right to education as articulated in the CRC.

The CRC, like earlier human rights instruments, reaffirms access to education, compulsory education and free primary education. It adds to these earlier instruments in its inclusion of additional elements, such as the duties to 'make educational and vocational information and guidance available and accessible to all children';[12] to 'take measures to encourage regular attendance at schools and the reduction of drop-out rates';[13] to 'take measures to ensure that school discipline is administered in a manner consistent with the child's human dignity';[14] and to promote 'international cooperation on these matters'.[15]

From another perspective, the Convention on the Elimination of all Forms of Discrimination against Women (CEDAW)[16] underscores the obligation by States Parties to ensure to women rights equal to men in the field of education. Further, CEDAW mandates the opportunities for access to all education levels, literacy programmes, materials, scholarships, sports, and recreation on the basis of equality. It requires, in this regard, the adoption of measures aimed at reducing any gaps in education existing between men and women, as well as female student drop-out rates, and the organisation of programmes for girls and women who have left school prematurely; and eliminating any

[11] CRC Art. 29.
[12] CRC Art. 28(1)(d).
[13] CRC Art. 28(1)(e).
[14] CRC Art. 28(2).
[15] CRC Art. 28(3).
[16] Convention on the Elimination of All Forms of Discrimination against Women (adopted 18 December 1979, entered into force 3 September 1981) 1249 UNTS 13 (CEDAW).

stereotyped concept of the roles of men and women at all levels and in all forms of education by encouraging coeducation.[17]

The International Convention on the Elimination of All Forms of Racial Discrimination (CERD)[18] establishes that the obligations of States Parties include the duty to enforce the objectives to eradicate discrimination and to guarantee equality before the law in the field of education and vocational training.[19] It also prescribes that states shall 'adopt immediate and effective measures' in this field 'with a view to combating prejudices which lead to racial discrimination and to promoting understanding, tolerance and friendship among nations and racial or ethnical groups, as well as to propagating the purposes and principles' of the United Nations in this field.[20] Like CEDAW, CERD accordingly affirms that measures of equality are central to achieving the right to education and that groups subjected to disadvantage must be affirmatively included in education.

Following this trend, the International Convention on the Protection of the Rights of All Migrant Workers and Members of Their Families (ICRMW) highlights that each child of a migrant worker shall have the basic right of access to education on the basis of equality of treatment with nationals of the state concerned.[21] This includes ensuring that religious and moral education is provided to migrant workers' children in conformity with the convictions of migrant parents.[22] Access to public preschool educational institutions or schools shall not be refused or limited by reason of the irregular situation with respect to stay or employment of either parent or by reason of the 'irregularity of the child's stay in the State of employment'.[23]

Against these developments in the right to education in human rights law, the CRPD is the first legally binding instrument to address with specificity inclusion and diversity in mandating a regulated support system to advance 'inclusive education' at all levels, including in lifelong teaching and learning.

The CRPD recognises two important factors in the education of persons with disabilities: an inclusive education system and the quality of education.

17 CEDAW Art. 10.

18 International Convention on the Elimination of All Forms of Racial Discrimination (adopted 7 March 1966, entered into force 4 January 1969) 660 UNTS 195 (CERD).

19 CERD Art. 5 (e)–(v).

20 CERD Art. 7.

21 International Convention on the Protection of the Rights of All Migrant Workers and Members of their Families (adopted 18 December 1990, entered into force 1 July 2003) 2220 UNTS 3 (ICRMW).

22 ICRMW Art. 12.

23 ICRMW Art. 30.

Under Article 24 of the CRPD, he objectives of an inclusive education system shall be:

(a) The full development of human potential and sense of dignity and self-worth, and the strengthening of respect for human rights, fundamental freedoms and human diversity;
(b) The development by persons with disabilities of their personality, talents and creativity, as well as their mental and physical abilities, to their fullest potential. This must take place in environments that maximize academic and social development of persons with disabilities;
(c) Enabling persons with disabilities to participate effectively in a free society.[24]

Consequently, every person with disabilities shall have the right to a free, accessible, compulsory and quality primary and secondary education. In this way, the CRPD has reinforced the clause of non-exclusion from any educational level on the basis of disabilities.

The CRPD is an important source of guidelines for inclusion in terms of facilitating reasonable accommodations, personalised support and the provision of support within the general education system to facilitate students' effective education.[25] Additionally, it underscores that the teaching and use of Braille and other means, modes and formats of augmentative or alternative communication, guidance and mobility techniques and peer support must be fostered and that the learning of sign languages must be facilitated along with the promotion of the linguistic identity of the deaf community. This entails the presence of professionals and staff trained in these means, modes and formats and the use of material fitted to the needs of students.

The CRPD strengthens the importance of ensuring that persons with disabilities are able to access general tertiary education, vocational training, adult education and lifelong learning without discrimination and on an equal basis with others. To this end, 'States Parties shall ensure that reasonable accommodation is provided to persons with disabilities.'[26]

Especially worthy of mention is that the CRPD lifted the 'respect for the evolving capacities of children with disabilities and respect for the right of children with disabilities to preserve their identities'[27] to the level of a general principle. The inclusion of this principle provides an indispensable guarantee

24 CRPD Art. 24(1).

25 Report of the Special Rapporteur on the Right to Education (n. 9) [81]: 'The existing human rights legal and programmatic frameworks clearly recognize inclusive education as an indispensable element of the right to education for persons with disability.'

26 CRPD Art. 24(5).

27 CRPD Art. 3(h).

for children with disabilities to fully enjoy all human rights and fundamental freedoms, on an equal basis and in accordance with their best interests.[28] This includes the right of children with disabilities 'to express their views freely on all matters affecting them, their views being given due weight in accordance with their age and maturity, … and to be provided with disability and age-appropriate assistance to realize that right'.[29]

Elements of inclusive education set forth in the CRPD represent a qualitative leap in the recognition of human rights for the twenty-first century. The recognition of disability discrimination as meaning 'any distinction, exclusion or restriction on the basis of disability which has the purpose or effect of impairing or nullifying the recognition, enjoyment or exercise, on an equal basis with others, of all human rights and fundamental freedoms in the political, economic, social, cultural, civil or any other field' is a major achievement in disability rights and, moreover, the definition's inclusion of 'all forms of discrimination, including denial of reasonable accommodation' is fundamental to advancing inclusive education.[30]

'Reasonable accommodation', in turn

> means necessary and appropriate modification and adjustments not imposing a disproportionate or undue burden, where needed in a particular case, to ensure to persons with disabilities the enjoyment or exercise on an equal basis with others of all human rights and fundamental freedoms.[31]

Therefore, several infringements of the right to education, either by action or omission, including the refusal to provide reasonable accommodations, can be qualified as discrimination.

Consequently, one can say that the core of the right to education comprises several factors, expressed in different twentieth-century international treaties, and the significant contributions made by the CRPD in the twenty-first century, primarily in terms of inclusion and quality education.

28 CRPD Art. 7(2).

29 CRPD Art. 7(3); Committee on the Rights of the Child, General Comment No. 12: The Right of the Child to Be Heard (1 July 2009) CRC/C/GC/12 [113]: 'The right of the child to be heard has special significance, even more when a decision of exclusion from school is verified, which should be subject to judicial review.'

30 CRPD Art. 2 [3].

31 CRPD Art. 2 [4].

3 THE CRPD COMMITTEE'S JURISPRUDENCE

The work of the CRPD Committee during the first years of its operation demonstrates the commitment of the Committee to advancing the implementation of inclusive education in mainstream education systems. This is reflected in successive Concluding Observations made by the CRPD Committee in its reporting on States Parties.[32]

It is also important to reference the role that the Committee's Recommendations continue to play in advancing the various elements essential to achieving inclusive education. Further, the Committee's practice reveals its understanding of the interrelationship between education for disabled persons with other rights in the CRPD. Its work also demonstrates an interest in the jurisprudence of other treaty bodies and how such bodies can contribute to the progressive development of the right to inclusive education. In examining the jurisprudence of the CRPD Committee in relation to inclusive education, two phases of development may be identified:

During the first period, the Committee concentrated its focus on the advancement of 'inclusive education' for disabled persons. Its practice during this phase tended to urge States Parties to adopt an inclusive educational system that recognised the importance of providing reasonable accommodations and safeguarding and protecting the rights of disabled students at all educational levels (primary, secondary and tertiary).

During the second period, the focus of the CRPD Committee expanded to emphasise 'inclusive quality education' for disabled persons. At this stage, the Committee gave specific expression to elements needed to ensure *quality* of inclusive education. It also directed its attention to the enforceability and justiciability of reasonable accommodations and the recommendation for States Parties to adopt immediate measures towards inclusive education. The sections that follow examine in more detail the work of the Committee in advancing the right to inclusive education and its later focus on quality in the context of inclusive education.

[32] CRPD Arts. 35 and 36. These Concluding Observations consist of a document prepared by the Committee, after finishing the constructive dialogue, approved by its members in a plenary and closed session, which will include – in accordance with its working methods – an introduction, factors and difficulties impeding the implementation of the CRPD, issues of particular concern to the Committee and finally suggestions and recommendations to States Parties. See Committee on the Rights of Persons with Disabilities, Working Methods of the Committee on the Rights of Persons with Disabilities Adopted at Its Fifth Session (11–15 April 2011) (2 September 2011) CRPD/C/5/4.

3.1 *Inclusive Education of Persons with Disabilities*

During the first period of its operation, the CRPD Committee repeatedly recognised inclusive education at all levels within the educational system, and consistently recommended that States Parties take the necessary measures for the full enjoyment of this said right. In this regard, the Committee recognised the importance of access to inclusive education within the general mainstream education system.

In the Concluding Observation for the State Party of China, for instance, the Committee stated that the concept of inclusion is one of the key notions of the CRPD and should be especially adhered to in the field of education.[33] In respect of El Salvador, the Committee recommended the development of an inclusive education model at all levels, in both urban and rural areas. It likewise affirmed the importance of including a gender and cultural perspective, and the provision of reasonable accommodation where needed to ensure that children and adolescents with disabilities can access education.[34] These recommendations understand inclusive education in broad terms and help to eliminate any room for exclusion on the basis of disability in education.

In line with this, and due to the extent that the Committee recognised a sphere of protection to education for persons with disabilities, it recommended to the State Party of Paraguay that education should be inclusive at all levels and throughout the country and should incorporate the gender perspective and be ethnically and linguistically relevant.[35] Similarly, the Committee reiterated the recommendations made to prior States Parties in the Concluding Observations for Mexico. In so doing it affirmed the importance of recognition in law and public policies of an inclusive education system along with the allocation of the necessary budget for reasonable accommodations and adequate training for regular teachers.[36]

The CRPD Committee in its review of Austria urged that greater efforts be made to support students with disabilities in all areas of inclusive education from kindergarten to secondary school.[37] This recommendation expressly

33 Committee on the Rights of Persons with Disabilities, Concluding Observations on the Initial Report of China (15 October 2012) CRPD/C/CHN/CO/1/Corr.1.

34 Committee on the Rights of Persons with Disabilities, Concluding Observations on the Initial Report of El Salvador (8 October 2013) CRPD/C/SLV/CO/1.

35 Committee on the Rights of Persons with Disabilities, Concluding Observations on the Initial Report of Paraguay (15 May 2013) CRPD/C/PRY/CO/1.

36 Committee on the Rights of Persons with Disabilities, Concluding Observations on the Initial Report of Mexico (27 October 2014) CRPD/C/MEX/CO/1.

37 Committee on the Rights of Persons with Disabilities, Concluding Observations on the Initial Report of Austria (13 September 2013) CRPD/C/AUT/CO/1.

recognises inclusive education at a preschool stage. This too gives breadth to the CRPD Committee's interpretation of the right to education under the CRPD.

It the Committee's review of Sweden, it stated that inclusion must be verified in the mainstream education system and, therefore, urged Sweden to guarantee the inclusion of all children with disabilities in the mainstream education system and to ensure that had the required support.[38]

The recommendation for the State Party of Argentina reiterated the importance of developing these inclusive education policies.[39] However, the Committee in its review went deeper by stating that an inclusive education system is a specific right. It also recommended that the State Party develop a comprehensive education policy that guarantees the right to inclusive education and allocates sufficient budgetary resources. Notably, this move signified an express and explicit recognition of the human rights to inclusive education, thus signifying the substantial, indissoluble link between education and inclusion.

Another element considered essential in implementing inclusive education by the Committee concerns the allocation of sufficient resources for the whole inclusive education system. In the case of Hungary, the Committee stressed the importance of allocating sufficient resources for the development of an inclusive education system for children and youth with disabilities.[40] Additionally, paraphrasing the CRPD, it made it explicit that the denial of reasonable accommodation constitutes discrimination, and recommended that the State Party significantly increase its efforts to provide reasonable accommodation to children and youth with disabilities based on students' individual needs.

In its Concluding Observations for Spain, the Committee moved to clarify the nature of the duty to provide reasonable accommodation. In this regard the Committee held that the duty to provide reasonable accommodation is immediately applicable and not subject to progressive realisation.[41]

Aligning with the Committee's view as to the holistic nature of the obligation to provide inclusive education, the Committee made recommendations

38 Committee on the Rights of Persons with Disabilities, Concluding Observations on the Initial Report of Sweden (12 May 2014) CRPD/C/SWE/CO/1.

39 Committee on the Rights of Persons with Disabilities, Concluding Observations on the Initial Report of Argentina (8 October 2012) CRPD/C/ARG/CO/1.

40 Committee on the Rights of Persons with Disabilities, Concluding Observations on the Initial Report of Hungary (22 October 2012) CRPD/C/HUN/CO/1.

41 Committee on the Rights of Persons with Disabilities, Concluding Observations on the Initial Report of Spain (19 October 2011) CRPD/C/ESP/CO/1.

as to implementing inclusive education for adults with disabilities across the whole country, guaranteeing coverage in the most remote areas and incorporating the gender perspective and the cultural and ethnic dimensions.[42]

In another theme emerging from the work on the Committee in the context of education, the Committee has urged States Parties to modify educational terminology drawn from the medical model in its law and policy. Further, the CRPD Committee's practice discloses its clear position on inclusive education in recommending the transition from special and segregated education towards the inclusive model.[43] This move provides clear authority for the proposition that, in the light of the CRPD, the Committee embraces as its governing paradigm inclusive education in achieving the right to education for disabled persons.

The foregoing examination of the practice of the CRPD Committee makes clear that the first period of work is characterised by advancing the implementation of inclusive education in broad terms, at all levels, both in rural and in urban areas. This approach to implementation takes into account the gender perspective and overcomes all cultural, ethnical and linguistic limitations. It underscores that an education system must have: first, inclusion within the general or mainstream system and a clear plan for a transition to an inclusive education system. Further, states must take all measures required to reach such goals regardless of any economic or administrative resource constraints.

3.2 *Quality Education for Persons with Disabilities*

The Committee's development of its jurisprudence suggests the identification of a second period, wherein its practice reveals cross-cutting recommendations for a *quality* inclusive education system. This reflects an important development insofar as the Committee's work seeks to set out a standard of education for persons with disabilities encompassing precise requirements for ensuring quality and inclusive education.

Reference to 'quality' as an element of inclusive education appears for the first time in the Concluding Observations for the State Party of Costa Rica. There, the Committee affirms that disability must be included as a cross-cutting theme to guarantee children with disabilities inclusive education of quality.[44]

42 Ibid.; CRPD/C/ARG/CO/1 (n. 39).

43 CRPD/C/PRY/CO/1 (n. 35).

44 Committee on the Rights of Persons with Disabilities, Concluding Observations on the Initial Report of Costa Rica (12 May 2014) CRPD/C/CRI/CO/1.

Then, with respect to the Czech Republic, the Committee stated that, besides embracing inclusive education as the guiding principle of the education system, to ensure the admission in mainstream school of children with disabilities, the state needs to provide inclusive quality education.[45] Similarly, in the case of the state of Mongolia, the Committee recommended the adoption of specific policies and programmes, with an allocated budget, to implement an inclusive education system in order to ensure quality of education for children with disabilities in their own communities.[46] The Concluding Observations for Turkmenistan,[47] the Cook Islands[48] and Croatia[49] likewise affirm the notion of an inclusive education system that provide quality education.

The Concluding Observation for Germany is worthy of mention in this context.[50] It reaffirms the importance of reasonable accommodation being provided at all levels of education, and being legally enforceable and justiciable before the courts. This too is an essential dimension of providing quality inclusive education. This contrasts with the Concluding Observation for Spain (first period), which stated that reasonable accommodation is immediately applicable and not subject to progressive realisation. The Concluding Observations for Germany also stressed the importance of reasonable accommodation and went even further, noting that if not provided, the duty may be legally enforceable and justiciable before the courts. The Committee's practice reaffirms the inclusion of all persons with disabilities at all education levels by the adoption of immediate measures, stressing that reasonable accommodation must be provided in the general education system.

Also during the second period of the Committee's work, the idea of the transition of students with disabilities from segregated education to inclusive education systems, with responsibility conferred on the Ministry of Education, is given attention.[51]

45 Committee on the Rights of Persons with Disabilities, Concluding Observations on the Initial Report of Czech Republic (15 May 2015) CRPD/C/CZE/CO/1.

46 Committee on the Rights of Persons with Disabilities, Concluding Observations on the Initial Report of Mongolia (13 May 2015) CRPD/C/MNG/CO/1.

47 Committee on the Rights of Persons with Disabilities, Concluding Observations on the Initial Report of Turkmenistan (13 May 2015) CRPD/C/TKM/CO/1.

48 Committee on the Rights of Persons with Disabilities, Concluding Observations on the Initial Report of the Cook Islands (15 May 2015) CRPD/C/COK/CO/1.

49 Committee on the Rights of Persons with Disabilities, Concluding Observations on the Initial Report of Croatia (15 May 2015) CRPD/C/HRV/CO/1.

50 Committee on the Rights of Persons with Disabilities, Concluding Observations on the Initial Report of Germany (13 May 2015) CRPD/C/DEU/CO/1.

51 Committee on the Rights of Persons with Disabilities, Concluding Observations on the Initial Report of the Dominican Republic (8 May 2015) CRPD/C/DOM/CO/1 [45(b)].

The Committee noted, for example, in the case of Croatia, that educational exclusion and segregation are discriminatory.[52]

Another structural measure tied to quality education recommended by the CRPD Committee during its second phase of operation is the need to ensure that inclusive education becomes an integral part of core teacher training in universities.[53]

In line with its progressive development of jurisprudence relating to inclusive quality education during this second period, the Committee held a Day of General Discussion on the right to education for persons with disabilities. There, the Committee drew linkages between the guarantee of lifelong, inclusive, quality education for all persons with disabilities, and at all education levels, and without exclusion.[54]

4 THE CRPD COMMITTEE'S JURISPRUDENCE ON MATTERS LINKED TO THE RIGHT TO EDUCATION FOR PERSONS WITH DISABILITIES

When analysing the Committee's jurisprudence, some matters linked to inclusive education for persons with disabilities can be evidenced. There is an interconnection and complementarities between recommendations on other CRPD articles and education, such as women with disabilities,[55] children with disabilities,[56] accessibility,[57] freedom of expression and opinion and access to information.[58]

(a) Women with Disabilities

The Committee underscores in its practice that women and girls with disabilities must receive appropriate lifelong education according to their choices and needs. This is required regardless of whether they have finished or were excluded from mainstream education.[59]

52 CRPD/C/HRV/CO/1 (n. 49) [36].

53 Committee on the Rights of Persons with Disabilities, Concluding Observations on the Initial Report of Azerbaijan (12 May 2014) CRPD/C/AZE/CO/1.

54 Day of General Discussion (DGD) on the right to education for persons with disabilities, which was held on 15 April 2015, at Palais des Nations, Geneva.

55 CRPD Art. 6.

56 CRPD Art. 7.

57 CRPD Art. 9.

58 CRPD Art. 21.

59 Committee on the Rights of Persons with Disabilities, Concluding Observations on the Initial Report of the Republic of Korea (29 October 2014) CRPD/C/KOR/CO/1.

The Committee's practice also discloses recommendation that States Parties take measures to increase opportunities for adequate education for women and girls with disabilities.[60] Relatedly, the Committee takes the position that consultation with women with disabilities is vitally important. Such consultations should be meaningfully utilised by States Parties as a basis for implementing law reform and policy changes, and for their empowerment, particularly on educational matters.[61]

At the same time, the Committee's recommendations stress the implementation of programmes for women and girls with disabilities, including affirmative action, to eliminate discrimination in all areas of life.[62] Evidently, this recommendation includes the educational sphere of action.

(b) Children with Disabilities

The CRPD Committee in its practice places emphasis on the CRPD provisions concerning inclusive education for children with disabilities. Its Concluding Observations for several States Parties, such as Sweden,[63] Belgium[64] and Denmark, for instance underscores States Parties obligations to provide education for children with disabilities in an inclusive setting.[65]

Likewise, the idea of inclusive education for children with disabilities is reinforced in the practice of the Committee on the Rights of the Child (CRC) in two of its recommendations. In the case of Austria,[66] the CRC Committee recommended that priority be given to ensuring inclusive education for children with disabilities and that the best interests of each child must be the primary consideration in decisions concerning school enrolment.[67] This is fully confirmed in the practice of the CRPD Committee.

Similarly, the CRPD Committee's work reinforces the work of other treaty bodies on inclusive education. The Concluding Observations of States

60 Committee on the Rights of Persons with Disabilities, Concluding Observations on the Initial Report of Denmark (30 October 2014) CRPD/C/DNK/CO/1; Committee on the Rights of Persons with Disabilities, Concluding Observations on the Initial Report of New Zealand (31 October 2014) CRPD/C/NZL/CO/1; CRPD/C/ESP/CO/1 (n. 41).

61 CRPD/C/MNG/CO/1 (n. 46); CRPD/C/HRV/CO/1 (n. 49).

62 CRPD/C/DEU/CO/1 (n. 50).

63 CRPD/C/SWE/CO/1 (n. 38).

64 Committee on the Rights of Persons with Disabilities, Concluding Observations on the Initial Report of Belgium (28 October 2014) CRPD/C/BEL/CO/1.

65 CRPD/C/DNK/CO/1 (n. 61).

66 CRPD/C/AUT/CO/1 (n. 37).

67 Committee on the Right of the Child, Concluding Observations on the Combined Third and Fourth Periodic Report of Austria (3 December 2012) CRC/C/AUT/CO/3–4 [45(e)].

Parties, such as Azerbaijan[68] and Turkmenistan,[69] reflect this emphasis and make cross-references to the Concluding Observations made by the CRC Committee in relation to education. In a similar vein, the Committee in its review of Mongolia issued a recommendation for consultation with disabled people's organisations (DPOs) to ensure early intervention, overall improvement in increasing enrolment of boys and girls with disabilities in primary school education, and the implementation of inclusive early childhood education and opportunities for vocational training for youth with disabilities.[70] Notably, these recommendations are in line with the ones made by the Committee on the Rights of the Child to the State of Mongolia, signalling a cross-referencing practice and highlighting the Committee's approach to implementation of Article 7 of the CRPD on children with disabilities.[71]

Similarly, the Committee shows a tendency to embrace the particular situation of certain sectors of the population in recommending that measures be adopted to ensure that all children with disabilities receive an education, especially those with intellectual and psychosocial disabilities, deaf-blind children and those from indigenous communities.[72] Regarding indigenous communities, the Committee has shown a special concern, and as such has recommended that the appropriate measures be taken to identify and reduce illiteracy among children with disabilities, especially indigenous and Afro-descendant children.[73] The importance of this part of the population being enrolled in the educational system at the compulsory ages according to the laws of the States Parties is stressed.[74] The Committee also noted that it was of essence to provide particular care and assistance to children with disabilities, particularly indigenous children, and to allocate significant resources for their inclusion.[75] In the case of Hungary, the Committee once again reaffirmed the importance of allocating sufficient resources for the development of an

68 CRPD/C/AZE/CO/1 (n. 54) [19]; Committee of the Rights of the Child, Consideration of Reports Submitted by States Parties [of Azerbaijan] Under Article 44 of the Convention (12 March 2012) CRC/C/AZE/CO/3–4 [57(f)].

69 CRPD/C/TKM/CO/1 (n. 47); Committee on the Rights of the Child, Concluding Observations on the Combined Second to Fourth Periodic Reports of Turkmenistan (10 March 2015) CRC/C/TKM/CO/2–4 [43].

70 CRPD/C/MNG/CO/1 (n. 46).

71 CRPD/C/MNG/CO/1 (n. 46) [49].

72 CRPD/C/MEX/CO/1 (n. 36).

73 Committee on the Rights of Persons with Disabilities, Concluding Observations on the Initial Report of Peru (20 April 2012) CRPD/C/PER/CO/1.

74 CRPD/C/ARG/CO/1 (n. 39); CRPD/C/SLV/CO/1 (n. 34).

75 Ibid.

inclusive education system for children and youth with disabilities.[76] This is the same approach the Committee has taken for children in rural areas.[77]

In another line of Committee practice, its recommendations point to the need for an increase of the resources available for school health services to ensure that children have access to and receive appropriate psychosocial and mental health support and psychiatric health care in a timely manner.[78] This recommendation underscores as well the holistic approach the Committee takes in respect of the obligation to provide an inclusive education.

The Committee took a further step by emphasising, in its observations on Article 24 of the CRPD, enforceability on education matters, and recommended that the State Party amend its legislation to ensure that all children with disabilities can submit a complaint to an independent authority if they do not receive adequate educational support.[79]

Recognising the importance of school training for the full enjoyment of rights held by children with disabilities, the Committee recommended raising awareness about the rights of children with disabilities at school, in the family and in the community at large.[80]

(c) *Accessibility*

The CRPD Committee continues to underscore the linkage between the right of education and giving effect to obligations around accessibility. The Committee reflects in its reporting process that education efforts[81] must conform to its General Comment No. 2 on Accessibility.[82] General Comment No. 2 affirms that schools must be accessible, as explicitly stated in Article 9(1)(a) of the CRPD. Further, the Committee makes clear that it is the entire process of inclusive education that must be accessible – not only buildings and physical structures, but all information and communication, including

76 CRPD/C/HUN/CO/1 (n. 40).

77 Ibid.; CRPD/C/ARG/CO/1 (n. 39).

78 CRPD/C/SWE/CO/1 (n. 38).

79 CRPD/C/DNK/CO/1 (n. 61).

80 CRPD/C/COK/CO/1 (n. 48).

81 Mexico CRPD/C/MEX/CO/1 (n. 36); Belgium CRPD/C/BEL/CO/1 (n. 65); Korea CRPD/C/KOR/CO/1 (n. 60); Denmark CRPD/C/DNK/CO/1 (n. 61); and Dominican Republic CRPD/C/DOM/CO/1 (n. 51); Cook Islands CRPD/C/COK/CO/1 (n. 48); Turkmenistan CRPD/C/TKM/CO/1 (n. 47); Mongolia CRPD/C/MNG/CO/1 (n. 46); Croatia CRPD/C/HRV/CO/1 (n. 49).

82 Committee on the Rights of Persons with Disabilities, General Comments No. 2 (2014) Article 9: Accessibility (22 May 2014) CRPD/C/GC/2.

ambient or FM assistive systems, support services and reasonable accommodation in schools.

In order to foster accessibility, education, as well as the content of school curricula, should promote and be conducted in sign language, Braille, alternative script and augmentative and alternative modes, means and formats of communication and orientation, with special attention given to the appropriate languages and modes and means of communication used by blind, deaf and deaf-blind students. Modes and means of teaching should be accessible and should be conducted in accessible environments. The whole environment of students with disabilities must be designed in a way that fosters inclusion and guarantees their equality in the entire process of their education.

Finally, the Committee's General Comment on Accessibility adds that the duty to provide reasonable accommodation is an *ex nunc* duty, which means that it is enforceable from the moment an individual with an impairment needs it in a given situation (e.g. school, in order to enjoy her or his rights on an equal basis in a particular context).

The CRPD Committee underscores the role that communications technology can play in advancing accessibility and implementation of the CRPD. In this regard, the CRPD Committee's practice reveals that the provision of inclusive education and reasonable accommodation in schools and other learning institutions encompasses the provision of, inter alia, assistive technology and support in classrooms, accessible and adapted educational materials and curricula and accessible school environments.[83]

Concerning new technologies, the practice of the CRPD Committee discloses that fostering inclusive education should include the implementation of initiatives and public–private partnerships to design accessible pedagogical tools and teaching methods and to provide students with disabilities with access to new technologies and the Internet.[84]

(d) Freedom of Expression and Opinion, and Access to Information

The CRPD Committee underscores in its practice the importance of sign language recognition as an official language by States Parties. The Committee therefore its reporting practice has recommended giving official recognition to sign languages, including in its review of Paraguay,[85] El Salvador,[86] Republic

83 CRPD/C/KOR/CO/1 (n. 60).
84 CRPD/C/SLV/CO/1 (n. 34).
85 CRPD/C/PRY/CO/1 (n. 35).
86 CRPD/C/SLV/CO/1 (n. 34).

of Korea,[87] Australia,[88] Denmark[89] and Turkmenistan.[90] Moreover, the Committee recommended furthering the teaching of sign language in educational institutions from the primary level.[91] This entails promoting professional training for sign language interpreters and teachers.[92]

In its practice, the CRPD Committee in interpreting Article 24 of the CRPD continues to reiterate that inclusive quality education must be accomplished, with special regard given to the use of sign language, Braille and other forms of accessible formats of augmentative and alternative communication.[93] Finally, the practice of the Committee reflects the importance of making sign language and Braille training available, so sign language and Braille can be used by blind, deaf and deaf-blind students in schools and in public.[94]

5 FINAL REMARKS

Several key elements of the right to education are clearly defined in the practice of the CRPD Committee. Substantive elements of the right include the following:

- The right to education encompasses objectives of personal and social development to their fullest potential, tolerance, pluralism, harmonious coexistence in a free society, understanding, peace, respect for human rights – fundamental freedoms and preservation of the environment;
- Equality before the law, equal opportunities and treatment;
- Non-discrimination, including the elimination of prejudices;
- Respect for beliefs and religions;
- Respect for cultural and linguistic identity;
- Equality between men and women in education;
- Respect for children's identity, their best interest and their right to be informed of matters affecting their education;
- Expression of students' views, which entails the right to be heard, and the assistance required to exercise this faculty;
- Respect for the evolving capacities of children;

87 CRPD/C/KOR/CO/1 (n. 60).
88 Committee on the Rights of Persons with Disabilities, Concluding Observations on the Initial Report of Australia (21 October 2013) CRPD/C/AUS/CO/1.
89 CRPD/C/DNK/CO/1 (n. 61).
90 CRPD/C/TKM/CO/1 (n. 47).
91 CRPD/C/DNK/CO/1 (n. 61).
92 CRPD/C/AZE/CO/1 (n. 54); CRPD/C/NZL/CO/1 (n. 61).
93 CRPD/C/TKM/CO/1 (n. 47).
94 CRPD/C/COK/CO/1 (n. 48); CRPD/C/AZE/CO/1 (n. 54).

- Access, stay and progress in education, at all levels, throughout life;
- Free and compulsory access.

The CRPD Committee in its jurisprudence has substantially contributed to the identification of the two main pillars of education: inclusion and quality. These elements are integral, indissoluble parts of the right to education of all individuals, both being universal in character. Moreover, these two factors are directly proportional, i.e. true inclusion will exist where quality education is available to each and every student. On the other hand, quality education is enhanced and enriched by the inclusion of students in their diversity. Therefore, an inclusive education system lacking quality or existing in a non-inclusive system cannot exist. In other words, should the 'inclusion' and 'quality' elements dissociate, there would be an 'appearance of inclusion' or an 'appearance of quality education', which will undermine the right to education itself.

The CRPD Committee – in the discharge of its monitoring duties and upon consideration of initial reports by the States Parties – is progressively developing the contours of the right to education. Two specific periods are discernible in the jurisprudence development of the Committee. The first period is characterised by the emphasis and consolidation of the inclusive education model for persons with disabilities and by identifying several elements with a view to establishing said paradigm. Then, the Committee progressed towards a second period, which explicitly made quality an essential element of inclusive education.

To the question of whether the CRPD enshrines the right to inclusive education for persons with disabilities, it can be stressed that the Committee has expressly stated so in the Concluding Observation for Argentina.[95]

We can reach the same conclusion when analysing the whole of the Committee's jurisprudence, which has continually emphasised inclusive education as a viable way for persons with disabilities to exercise their right to education. The Committee has even made express reference to the transition from segregated to inclusive education forms.

For these reasons, the right to education of persons with disabilities is necessarily inclusive in nature, as this latter feature is a key aspect of the right's substance.

At the same time, when the Committee emphasises the transition towards an inclusive paradigm, it is setting a goal. Therefore, fulfilment of this goal will entail the existence of only one education system, with no parallelism. In other terms, in the future, the distinction between mainstream and segregated

95 CRPD/C/ARG/CO/1 (n. 39).

education system will disappear. The General Observation to be prepared by the CRPD Committee will provide additional guidelines on the matter.

The Convention also provides guidelines to implement an inclusive quality education. The Committee's jurisprudence adds content to implementation guidelines in defining the tasks to be undertaken by States Parties to achieve an inclusive education of quality, including reasonable accommodations; personalised, effective support; specific learning (e.g. sign language, Braille, inter alia); tutoring and peer support; teacher training and accessibility in several directions, including adapted teaching material. Moreover, the Committee's practice repeatedly stresses that the duty to provide reasonable accommodation is immediately applicable, fully enforceable and justiciable.

The Committee's practice is also reflective of implementation guidance in the form of detailed recommendations to give effect to the right to inclusive education of *quality*. Key features include the Committee's emphasis on sign language, Braille and other means, modes and formats of communication, as well as the relevant training to teaching staff, both with and without disabilities, and full accessibility in all spheres and technological development. Additionally, The Committee's work discloses concern for the situation of women, girls, boys, indigenous persons with disabilities and persons with disabilities in rural areas, and outlined the several forms of disability and their needs.

The Committee has also recognised the right of complaint by students with disabilities who are not afforded appropriate educational services. Related to this is its frequent recommendation to States Parties to undertake legal reform to give effect to the obligation to provide inclusive education. Other lines of recommendation include improving public policies, allocation of resources needed to implement the right to inclusive quality education and ensuring consultations with right holders.

In light of its developing guidance to States Parties on inclusive education, the Committee held a Day of General Discussion on Article 24. This marked the first step in the development of a General Comment on Article 24. In this regard, the adoption of a General Comment on Article 24 may in some sense be seen as a codification o the developed practice of the CRPD Committee during the first phases of its work.

6 CONCLUSION

1. The core of the right to education is found in the numerous UN Conventions on the promotion and protection of human rights, which contain its substantive elements.

2. The UN Convention on the Rights of Persons with Disabilities, in explicitly recognising the right to education of persons with disabilities, also clarifies that inclusion and quality are essential elements of the right.
3. The Committee's jurisprudence on the rights of the persons with disabilities, reflected in its Concluding Observations and Recommendations, reflects two clear phases:
   a. Recognition of inclusive education; and
   b. Recognition of inclusive quality education.
4. The Committee has expressly declared the right to an inclusive education system for persons with disabilities, which means, in essence, the right to inclusive education.
5. From the examination of the jurisprudence it follows that the Committee identifies education quality as a key factor and component of inclusive education. Therefore, inclusive quality education must be provided by States Parties and enforced by persons with disabilities. Inclusion and quality are interrelated, indissoluble components of the right to education.
6. The Committee in its practice sets inclusive quality education as a goal, which, in the future, means that a one and only, wide and universal educational system will exist. Accordingly, the distinction between mainstream and segregated education system is expected to gradually disappear. The right to inclusive quality education – given its universal character – must be applied to persons with disabilities and all sectors of human diversity.
7. To adequately implement the right to inclusive quality education, the Committee has prepared specific recommendations for States Parties, emphasising legal reforms, the adoption of public policies on inclusive education, teacher and administrator training and allocation of sufficient resources to achieve the goal of inclusive quality education.

16

Emerging Trends in the Jurisprudence of the European Court of Human Rights

The Right to Education for Persons with Disabilities

Andrea Broderick

1 INTRODUCTION

The right to education in international human rights law is an end in itself, as well as a means towards attaining all other human rights. Former United Nations (UN) Special Rapporteur on Education Katarina Tomasevski has described education as 'a bridge to all human rights'.[1] Tomasevski observes that 'education is indispensable for effective political participation and for enabling individuals to sustain themselves; . . . it is the foundation for eliminating discrimination. It is the key to unlocking other human rights.'[2] The proper enjoyment of the right to education is of fundamental importance for persons with disabilities as it helps to unlock the systemic disadvantages that disabled persons have experienced for too long. The UN Convention on the Rights of Persons with Disabilities (CRPD) contains a mandate of inclusive education.[3] The CRPD Committee has acknowledged that despite the progress which has

Andrea Broderick, PhD (Maastricht University), LLM (International and Comparative Disability Law and Policy) (National University of Ireland, Galway [NUIG]), Solicitor (Law Society of Ireland), LLB (NUIG), BA International (NUIG and University of Poitiers, France). Part of this chapter draws on aspects of Andrea Broderick, *The Long and Winding Road to Equality and Inclusion for Persons with Disabilities: The United Nations Convention on the Rights of Persons with Disabilities* (Cambridge/Antwerp: Intersentia 2015) and also Andrea Broderick, 'A Reflection on Substantive Equality Jurisprudence: The Standard of Scrutiny at the ECtHR for Differential Treatment of Roma and Persons with Disabilities' (2014) 15(1–2) *International Journal of Discrimination and the Law* 101.

1 Katarina Tomasevski, *Education Denied: Costs and Remedies* (London: Zed Books Ltd 2003) 172.

2 Ibid.

3 See generally Gauthier de Beco, 'Transition to Inclusive Education Systems According to the Convention on the Rights of Persons with Disabilities' (2016) 34 *Nordic Journal of Human Rights*, 40.

been achieved in the realisation of the right to inclusive education, profound challenges remain, including:

> [p]ersistent discrimination against persons with disabilities, compounded by the isolation of those still living in long-term residential institutions, and low expectations about those in mainstream settings, allowing prejudices and fear to escalate and remain unchallenged.[4]

In addition, the Committee has remarked on the 'lack of legal remedies and mechanisms to claim redress for violations'.[5]

In recent years, the European Court of Human Rights (ECtHR) has demonstrated an increasing awareness of the discrimination and disadvantage experienced by certain marginalised groups in society. Furthermore, the Court is displaying a substantive and somewhat transformative approach to equality in respect of marginalised groups, at least in certain respects. The hallmark of substantive equality is its focus on contextual and asymmetrical structures of disadvantage. A contextual approach to equality considers the wider disadvantage faced by marginalised groups, while an asymmetrical approach to equality considers the relevance of the actual group which suffers disadvantage on account of a particular measure. In essence, substantive equality calls for special measures of protection for those with differential characteristics to correct for factual inequalities. Transformative equality goes even further than substantive equality by seeking to address the underlying causes of structural inequalities and disadvantage – the socially constructed barriers, stereotypes, negative customs and practices that hinder the full enjoyment of rights by marginalised groups. Transformative equality requires 'positive measures to bring about change'.[6]

The Strasbourg Court's more recent approach to the interpretation of the non-discrimination norm under Article 14 of the European Convention on Human Rights (ECHR) signals a marked change from its long-standing failure to deal with equality issues under the ECHR in a manner that could address structural inequality. In particular, there have been significant emerging trends in the jurisprudence of the ECtHR related to Roma education and also in the Court's disability discrimination case law. The trends appear to have been influenced, to some extent, by developments in international human rights law (among other

4 Committee on the Rights of Persons with Disabilities, General Comment No. 4 (2016) Article 24: Right to Inclusive Education (2 September 2016) CRPD/C/GC/4 [4(b)].

5 Ibid [4g].

6 Sandra Fredman, 'Beyond the Dichotomy of Formal and Substantive Equality: Towards a New Definition of Equal Rights' in Ineke Boerefijn, Fons Coomans, Jenny Goldschmidt, Rikki Holtmaat and Ria Wolleswinkel (eds), *Temporary Special Measures: Accelerating De Facto Equality of Women under Article 4 (1) UN Convention on the Elimination of All Forms of Discrimination against Women* (Antwerp: Intersentia 2003) 115.

developments).[7] These emerging trends are potentially significant in increasing protection of the rights of persons with disabilities, specifically in the context of ensuring the right to education for disabled individuals. In light of the foregoing, this chapter examines the case law of the ECtHR related to Roma education and disability discrimination. The objective of this analysis is to discern the emerging trends in the jurisprudence of the Strasbourg Court, which can potentially serve as a foundation for advancing disability claims pertaining to the right to education, in particular in light of the mandate of inclusive education contained in Article 24 of the CRPD.

This chapter is broken into five parts as follows: in Part 2, the development of substantive equality jurisprudence in Roma education case law is outlined. In Part 3, the emerging trends in the Strasbourg Court's disability discrimination case law are analysed. In Part 4, the link between disability and Roma rights is outlined in the context of education. Finally, Part 5 contains concluding remarks.

2 THE DEVELOPMENT OF SUBSTANTIVE EQUALITY JURISPRUDENCE IN ROMA CASES: THE GROUP VULNERABILITY APPROACH AND THE SOCIAL-CONTEXTUAL APPROACH

The ECtHR has developed its substantive equality jurisprudence, in particular, by means of the Roma education cases that have come before it. In a string of judgments pertaining to the exclusion of Roma children from mainstream education, the Strasbourg Court has adopted a particular approach in order to justify heightening its standard of scrutiny of Roma rights. The 'vulnerable groups approach' or the 'vulnerability approach' provides a potential means by which to tackle issues of structural inequalities.[8] Lourdes Peroni and Alexandra Timmer are of the opinion that the Court's use of the notion of group vulnerability

> Represents a crucial step towards an enhanced anti-discrimination case law and a more robust idea of equality. The Court's use of the term 'vulnerable

[7] For a detailed elaboration on such developments, see Broderick, 'A Reflection on Substantive Equality Jurisprudence'.

[8] For a detailed examination of group vulnerability in the ECtHR's case law, see the following article: Alexandra Timmer, 'Toward an Anti-Stereotyping Approach for the European Court of Human Rights' (2011) 11 *Human Rights Law Review* 707. See also Maria de Lourdes Peroni Manzoni and Alexandra Timmer, 'Vulnerable Groups: The Promise of an Emergent Concept in European Human Rights Convention Law' (2013) 11 *ICON International Journal of Constitutional Law* 1056. In addition, see Alexandra Timmer, 'A Quiet Revolution: Vulnerability in the European Court of Human Rights' in Martha Albertson Fineman and Anna Grear (eds), *Vulnerability: Reflections on a New Ethical Foundation for Law and Politics* (Farnham: Ashgate 2013) 147–170.

groups' is therefore not mere rhetorical flourish. The term *does* something: it addresses and redresses different aspects of inequality in a more substantive manner.[9]

The vulnerability approach is not a new development within the Strasbourg Court's jurisprudence. In its previous case law, the Court has identified a number of vulnerable groups which suffered differential treatment on account, *inter alia*, of sex,[10] sexual orientation[11] and race or ethnicity.[12] The vulnerability approach has been applied to Roma rights in many cases, including outside the realm of education.[13] Peroni and Timmer highlight the fact that group vulnerability analysis acts as a 'magnifying glass'[14] to the extent that the alleged violation of rights 'looks bigger through the vulnerability lens'.[15] In other words, by virtue of a group vulnerability approach, the Court appears to weigh the special needs of marginalised groups heavily in its analysis of the substantive rights at issue.

In addition to the group vulnerability approach, the ECtHR has also begun to concentrate on the overall social context and disadvantage facing the Roma community as a whole, thereby delving into deeper issues of structural discrimination – that is, discrimination which is systemic to a particular group's disadvantage across numerous spheres of social life. Oddný Mjöll Arnardóttir claims that a social-contextual approach

> [c]an be seen as denoting the general idea that non-discrimination analysis should be conscious of how structural patterns of social disadvantage and exclusion function to keep marginalised groups in the margins. It is, therefore, a perspective on the interpretation and application of Article 14 that keeps in

9 Lourdes Peroni Manzoni and Timmer (n. 8) 1074 (emphasis in original).

10 App. nos 9214/80, 9473/81, 9474/81 (ECtHR, 28 May 1985) [78]. See also *Burghartz* v. *Switzerland*, App. no. 16213/90 (ECtHR, 22 February 1994) [27].

11 See, for example, *Schalk and Kopf* v. *Austria*, App. no. 30141/04 (ECtHR, 22 November 2010) [97]. See *Smith and Grady* v. *The United Kingdom*, App. nos 33985/96 and 33986/96(ECtHR, 27 December 1999) [90].

12 See *DH and Others* v. *Czech Republic*, App. no. 57325/00 (ECtHR, 13 November 2007) [182]. See also *Timishev* v. *Russia*, App. nos 55762/00 and 55974/00 (ECtHR, 13 March 2006) [56].

13 See, for example, *Chapman* v. *United Kingdom*, App. no. 27238/95 (ECtHR, 18 January 2001) [96]; *DH and Others* v. *Czech Republic*, App. no. 57325/00 (ECtHR, 13 November 2007); *Sampanis and Others* v. *Greece*, App. no. 32526/05 (ECtHR, 5 June 2008); *Oršuš and Others* v. *Croatia*, App. no. 15766/03 (ECtHR, 16 March 2010); *Horváth and Kiss* v. *Hungary*, App. no. 11146/11 (ECtHR, 29 January 2013; *MSS* v. *Belgium and Greece*, App. no. 30696/09 (ECtHR, 21 January 2011); and *VC* v. *Slovakia*, App. no. 18968/07 (ECtHR, 8 November 2011).

14 Lourdes Peroni Manzoni and Timmer (n. 8) 1079.

15 Ibid.

mind the object and purpose of eliminating such structures, or at least minimising their effect on individuals.[16]

The increased emphasis on social context has led the ECtHR to elaborate on various positive obligations in the context of the right to education. The aforementioned developments in the Strasbourg Court's case law are discussed in the subsections that follow.

2.1 *Roma Case Law on Segregated Education: The Beginnings of Substantive Equality Jurisprudence*

The case of *DH and Others* v. *Czech Republic* was the first influential authority in the area of segregated education for Roma children.[17] In that case, the Grand Chamber of the ECtHR held that the applicants (a group of Roma children) had been indirectly discriminated against, contrary to Article 14, taken in conjunction with Article 2 of Protocol No. 1 ECHR (on the right to education), by being quasi-automatically segregated from mainstream education on the basis of the results of standardised psychological tests. In essence, the Court held that the state had not taken into account the specific characteristics (cultural and linguistic disadvantages) of Roma children in devising and analysing the relevant tests.

The Court in *DH* acknowledged the fact that 'as a result of their turbulent history and constant uprooting the Roma have become a specific type of disadvantaged and vulnerable minority' who 'therefore require special protection'.[18] In addition to applying the notion of group vulnerability to the rights of the applicants, the Court looked to the overall social context and the disadvantage facing the Roma community in its considerations of the defence advanced by the state for the impugned difference in treatment. The ECtHR ruled that, in light of the fact that the relevant Czech legislation had a disproportionately prejudicial effect on the Roma community as a whole, it followed that the applicants as members of that community necessarily suffered the same discriminatory treatment.[19] This is a significant development since, by focussing on social context rather than solely on the situation of the individual applicants themselves, this enables the Court to address more

16 Oddný Mjöll Arnardóttir, 'The Differences That Make a Difference: Recent Developments on the Discrimination Grounds and the Margin of Appreciation under Article 14 of the European Convention on Human Rights' (2014) 14 *Human Rights Law Review* 647, 664.

17 *DH and Others* v. *Czech Republic*, App. no. 57325/00 (ECtHR, 13 November 2007).

18 Ibid. [182].

19 Ibid. [209].

effectively the underlying disadvantage and factual inequalities faced by Roma in education. Interestingly, the Court in *DH* quoted from international legal instruments in finding that Article 14 ECHR covers indirect discrimination.[20] The Court also cited general recommendations of the UN Committee on the Elimination of Racial Discrimination, which advocate the inclusion in the school system of all children of Roma origin, as well as the consideration of special measures for Roma children in education.[21] This is potentially significant in the disability context, in light of the CRPD's mandate of inclusive education.

2.2 *Increasing Recognition of Positive Obligations in Roma Education Cases*

The findings made by the ECtHR in *DH* have essentially been confirmed in similar cases which relate to the exclusion of Roma children from mainstream education.[22] In the case of *Oršuš and Others* v. *Croatia*, the Court once again took a social-contextual approach to equality.[23] The Court examined the systematic exclusion and structural discrimination facing Roma by taking into account the 'specific position of the Roma population'[24] in its finding that there had been indirect discrimination in violation of Articles 6 and 14 ECHR, taken together with Article 2 of Protocol 1.[25] Owing to the lack of transparency with regard to the transfer of Roma children to mixed classes, the applicants had no choice but to remain in Roma-only classes for substantial periods of time, sometimes during the entirety of their primary schooling.[26] The Grand Chamber's judgment in the *Oršuš* case demonstrates substantive equality analysis. The judgment links the state's margin of appreciation in the education sphere to the types of positive safeguards that the state had put in place in order to ensure that the schooling arrangements for Roma children had sufficient regard for their special needs as members of a disadvantaged group.[27] The ECtHR held that, in light of the

20 Ibid. [95].
21 Ibid. [98].
22 See, for instance, *Sampanis and Others* v. *Greece*, App. no. 32526/05 (ECtHR, 5 June 2008). See also *Sampanis and Others* v. *Greece*, App. no. 59608/09 (ECtHR, 11 December 2012); *Lavida and Others* v. *Greece*, App. no. 7973/10 (ECtHR, 30 May 2013).
23 *Oršuš and Others* v. *Croatia*, App. no. 15766/03 (ECtHR, 16 March 2010).
24 Ibid. [147].
25 Article 6 ECHR was deemed to be breached on account of the excessive length of the proceedings.
26 *Oršuš and Others* v. *Croatia* (n. 23) [182].
27 Ibid. [181]–[182].

high level of Roma children who failed to complete primary education or to attain a sufficient level of language proficiency, the state should have taken positive steps to address the factual inequalities Roma encounter in education. The Court remarked that 'some additional steps were needed in order to address these problems, such as active and structured involvement on the part of the relevant social services'.[28] Specifically, the Court ruled that the state had an 'obligation to take appropriate positive measures to assist the applicants in acquiring the necessary language skills in the shortest time possible, notably by means of special language lessons, so that they could be quickly integrated into mixed classes'.[29]

In a further decision of the Strasbourg Court pertaining to Roma education, *Horváth and Kiss* v. *Hungary*, the Court showed evidence of substantive and transformative approaches to equality.[30] The Court in *Horváth* found that the applicants, two young Roma men, had been indirectly discriminated against on the basis of ethnic origin contrary to Article 14 ECHR, taken in conjunction with Article 2 of Protocol 1, by being placed in segregated education on the foot of a discriminatory testing system. The Court observed that the Roma population suffers from considerable factual inequalities and took note of the fact that the vast majority of Roma children with mild learning disabilities could 'easily be integrated into mainstream schools' and that many were misdiagnosed 'because of socio-economic disadvantage or cultural differences'.[31] By that token, the ECtHR is clearly displaying cognisance of the special needs of Roma, as well as their differential characteristics, in its analysis of the right to education under the ECHR. Furthermore, the Court in *Horváth* noted that a failure to attempt to correct inequality through different treatment may in itself give rise to a breach of Article 14 ECHR[32] (as the Court had recognised in previous case law).[33] This demonstrates an acknowledgement on the Court's part that protection of the rights of disadvantaged groups involves not only scrutiny of differential treatment but also scrutiny of instances in which states fail to take into account differential characteristics. The novel feature of the *Horváth* judgment lies in the Court's call for positive measures to address long-

28 Ibid. [177].
29 Ibid. [165].
30 *Horváth and Kiss* v. *Hungary*, App. no. 11146/11 (ECtHR, 29 January 2013).
31 Ibid. [115].
32 Ibid. [101].
33 See, for instance, *Stec and Others* v. *The United Kingdom*, App. nos 65731/01 and 65900/01 (ECtHR, 12 April 2006) [51].

standing discrimination and 'to assist the applicants with any difficulties they encountered in following the school curriculum'.[34] The Court noted that the Roma children in question had 'received an education which did not offer the necessary guarantees stemming from the *positive obligations* of the State to undo a history of racial segregation in special schools'.[35] In light of the 'recognised bias in past placement procedures',[36] the state had 'specific *positive obligations* to avoid the perpetuation of past discrimination or discriminative practices disguised in allegedly neutral tests'.[37] This is significant as the Court in *Horváth* appears to go further than it did in the previous case of *Oršuš and Others* v. *Croatia*, in which it had ruled that the state had *some* sort of obligation to take steps to remedy factual inequalities in education and to assist the applicants to attain the necessary skills to enable them to enter mainstream education. In *Horváth*, the Court recognised the positive obligations incumbent on the state to remedy structural deficiencies in the applicant's education due to segregation in special schools and, moreover, to actually undo a history of racial segregation.

3 EMERGING TRENDS IN DISABILITY DISCRIMINATION JURISPRUDENCE OF THE ECTHR

In a similar vein to the Court's increasing awareness of the disadvantage faced by Roma in the context of education, the ECtHR appears to be increasingly aware of the historical discrimination to which persons with disabilities have long been subjected, and the need to prevent discrimination against disabled people generally. While the emerging trends in the Court's reasoning in most of its disability equality judgments are not directly related to education (except in one case), it is submitted that the developments witnessed in its disability discrimination line of case law mirror some of the developments highlighted earlier in the context of Roma education.[38] Therefore, the disability equality judgments have the potential to translate to a wider context. It appears that, to some extent, the developments in the Court's line of reasoning in its disability discrimination case law have been influenced by the entry into force of the CRPD. Article 24 of the CRPD provides a clear mandate for inclusive education, through the provision of reasonable accommodations (measures of

[34] *Horváth and Kiss* v. *Hungary* (n. 30) [104] (emphasis added).
[35] Ibid. [127] (emphasis added).
[36] Ibid. [116] (emphasis added).
[37] Ibid. (emphasis added).
[38] *Çam* v. *Turkey*, App. no. 51500/08 (ECtHR, 23 February 2016).

adaptation) and other individualised supports.[39] The provisions of the CRPD, including the right to education, are underpinned by the social model of disability. The CRPD views disability as resulting from 'the interaction between persons with impairments and attitudinal and environmental barriers that hinder their full and effective participation in society on an equal basis with others'.[40] The emerging trends in its case law related to disability discrimination show potential for advancing the rights of persons with disabilities in education, especially when aligned with similar developments outlined previously in the sphere of Roma education. In this section of the chapter, the most significant emerging trends in the Court's disability case law are discussed.[41] In Part 4 of the chapter, the link between disability and Roma rights is elaborated upon in the context of the right to education.

3.1 *The 'Vulnerable Groups' Approach to Disability*

In recent decisions[42] (discussed in the sub-sections that follow),[43] the Court has ruled that persons with disabilities (specifically persons with intellectual and psychosocial disabilities, and persons with HIV) constitute a particularly vulnerable and marginalised group in society on account of past discrimination.[44] Notwithstanding certain drawbacks connected to applying the vulnerability approach to disability, the use of this concept in the Court's legal reasoning appears to be having some positive effects on the Court's judgments related to disability equality, namely a heightened standard of scrutiny and a somewhat more substantive approach to equality.[45] The Court now acknowledges disability as a suspect ground of discrimination and has stated that it will apply a strict standard of scrutiny in respect of alleged violations of the rights of disabled people under the ECHR, in particular instances of discriminatory treatment. This may be significant for the

39 See, in particular, Article 24(2)(c) and Article 24(2)(d) of the CRPD.

40 CRPD Preamble para (e).

41 Section 3 of the chapter draws on Broderick, *The Long and Winding Road to Equality*.

42 See *Alajos Kiss* v. *Hungary*, App. no. 38832/06 (ECtHR, 20 May 2010). See also *Kiyutin* v. *Russia*, App. no. 2700/10 (ECtHR, 10 March 2011).

43 See Subsection 3.3.

44 Categorising HIV as a form of disability might be controversial in some quarters. However, the ECtHR itself has made a link between HIV and disability in certain judgments (see *Kiyutin* v. *Russia; IB* v. *Greece*, App. no. 552/10 [ECtHR, 3 October 2013]). Therefore, in the subsections that follow I discuss HIV as a form of disability in order to maintain consistency with the ECtHR's approach.

45 The concept of vulnerability does not sit particularly well with the disability rights agenda. In particular, there is the fear that it may lead to further stigmatisation of persons with disabilities. See generally Lourdes Peroni Manzoni and Timmer (n. 8).

interpretation of disability rights in the education context, as it provides a potential means by which to tackle the widespread discrimination and exclusion that disabled individuals face throughout Council of Europe Member States. Indeed, cases such as *Horváth and Kiss* v. *Hungary* have illustrated the role that the group vulnerability approach has played in increasing the positive obligations of states related to the provision of education to marginalised groups.

3.2 *Substantive Equality Jurisprudence: First Steps towards Implicit Reasonable Accommodation Duties?*

The case of *Glor* v. *Switzerland* represents a first step forward in the Strasbourg Court's disability equality jurisprudence.[46] The Court in *Glor* found disability discrimination contrary to Article 14, in conjunction with Article 8 ECHR, by virtue of the fact that the state had failed to carve out exemptions to a rule which imposed a penalty tax on persons deemed unfit to perform military service on grounds other than severe disability.[47] The primary relevance of the *Glor* case lies in the fact that the Court adopted a heightened standard of scrutiny, ruling that states have a 'considerably reduced[48] margin of appreciation in establishing different legal treatment for disabled people, on account of the 'need to prevent discrimination against people with disabilities and foster their full participation and integration in society'.[49] The adoption of a stricter standard of scrutiny appears to have been influenced by the entry into force of the CRPD. This assertion is based on the fact that the Court referred to the CRPD as an example of a 'European and worldwide consensus on the need to protect people with disabilities from discriminatory treatment'.[50]

In narrowing the margin of appreciation to the state concerned, the Strasbourg Court commented that it was 'fully aware that where the organisation and operational effectiveness of the armed forces are concerned . . . States enjoy a certain margin of appreciation'.[51] It nevertheless enquired as to what prevented the authorities from 'setting in place special forms of service for people in a situation comparable to that of the applicant'.[52] The foregoing

46 *Glor* v. *Switzerland*, App. no. 13444/04 (ECtHR, 30 April 2009).
47 The applicant in *Glor* had a minor disability and he alleged discrimination on account of the fact that he was subject to the aforementioned penalty tax on the basis of said disability.
48 *Glor* v. *Switzerland* (n. 46) [84].
49 Ibid.
50 Ibid. [53].
51 Ibid. [94].
52 Ibid.

passage can be seen as an implicit recognition of the inclusion of a *de facto* duty to accommodate within Article 14 ECHR. This is similar to the Court's analysis in the *Horváth* case, in which it ruled that a failure to attempt to correct inequality through different treatment may in itself give rise to a breach of Article 14 ECHR. With regard to the right to education for persons with disabilities, recognition of the need for differential treatment, including through reasonable accommodations and other individualised supports, is vital to unlocking long-standing structural inequalities. Therefore, the Court's implicit recognition of reasonable accommodation-type duties in *Glor* may be significant.

3.3 *A Heightened Standard of Scrutiny of Disability Rights, Group Vulnerability and Increased References to the CRPD*

In the case of *Alajos Kiss* v. *Hungary*,[53] the ECtHR adopted an explicit standard of 'strict scrutiny' and, furthermore, applied the vulnerability approach to disability in the context of a man with manic depression who had been placed under partial guardianship and was, consequently, denied the right to vote.[54] The Court categorised persons with intellectual and psychosocial disabilities ('the mentally disabled'[55]) as a 'particularly vulnerable group',[56] basing that categorisation on the 'considerable discrimination'[57] which such individuals have suffered in the past. In that regard, the Court stated that 'the treatment as a single class of those with intellectual or mental disabilities is a questionable classification, and the curtailment of their rights must be subject to strict scrutiny'.[58] The Court grounded its findings partly on the approach adopted in instruments of international law, which it had cited earlier in the judgment (including the CRPD).[59] Referring to the CRPD, and employing the concept of group vulnerability to narrow the margin of appreciation in the case, the ECtHR concluded unanimously that a blanket restriction on the franchise of persons with disabilities, or a category of persons with certain forms of disabilities, was in contravention of Article 3, Protocol 1 ECHR (on the right to free elections), and was therefore not within a state's margin of appreciation.

53 *Alajos Kiss* v. *Hungary*, App. no. 38832/06 (ECtHR, 20 May 2010).
54 Ibid. [44].
55 Ibid. [42].
56 Ibid.
57 Ibid.
58 Ibid. [44].
59 Ibid.

While the outcome of the case is welcome, the *Alajos Kiss* ruling may be criticised on some counts.[60] The nature of the blanket restriction in the case appears to have been a primary factor in the Court's ruling, rather than the wider systemic disadvantage faced by disabled applicants in participating in political processes. The applicant had contended that the restriction imposed on him was incompatible with the CRPD's spirit and text, in particular Articles 12 and 29 thereof.[61] Those articles require support for persons with disabilities in exercising their legal capacity and reasonable accommodations to enable disabled people to participate in political life, respectively. The Court in *Alajos Kiss* blindly accepted the fact that an individualised assessment of a person's fitness to vote could legitimately lead to that person being denied the right to vote.[62] It is of course a legitimate aim to ensure that only persons fit to vote can exercise that right. Nonetheless, while the applicant merely required the same treatment as others – namely, exercise of the right to vote – and while a reasonable accommodation was not actually needed or requested in this case, the Court should have deliberated on the potential measures which could be put in place to assist disabled persons in exercising the right to vote, if so required. The Court's approach is out of step with the social model of disability which underlies the CRPD, since individualised assessments of a person's fitness to vote measure functional deficiencies rather than addressing attitudinal and environmental barriers. It is ironic that the Strasbourg Court actually cited Article 1 of the CRPD (which endorses the social model of disability) in the course of its judgment when referring to relevant provisions of international law.[63] The Court's failure to consider alternative measures for disabled people is also out of line with Article 29 of the CRPD, which calls on states to secure full participation of persons with disabilities in political and public life, if necessary by accommodating their specific needs. This leaves a shadow of uncertainty hanging over the Court's willingness to facilitate the provision of reasonable accommodations and individualised supports in the context of the right to education for persons with disabilities.

In the case of *Kiyutin* v. *Russia*, the Court once again applied the vulnerability approach to marginalised groups, this time in the context of persons with HIV.[64] The applicant in *Kiyutin* had argued that the rejection of his application for a residency permit violated his right to respect for family life, in

60 These criticisms draw specifically on Broderick, *The Long and Winding Road to Equality*.

61 *Alajos Kiss* v. *Hungary* (n. 42) [35].

62 Ibid. [44].

63 Ibid. [14].

64 *Kiyutin* v. *Russia*, App. no. 2700/10 (ECtHR, 10 March 2011).

conjunction with his right to non-discrimination on the basis of his HIV status, contrary to Articles 8 and 14 ECHR. The Court in *Kiyutin* made a link between HIV and disability and, moreover, displayed an increased awareness of the importance of preventing discrimination on the basis of disability (including health-related HIV grounds). The ECtHR's approach appears to have been influenced by the CRPD. In that regard, the Court cited the general prohibition of disability-based discrimination contained in the CRPD in its deliberations.[65] The Court also concluded that a distinction made on account of one's health status, including such conditions as HIV infection, should be covered – either as a form of disability or alongside with it – by the term 'other status' in the text of Article 14 ECHR.[66] In the course of its judgment, the ECtHR cited several articles of the CRPD in the context of relevant international law.[67]

With regard to group vulnerability analysis, the Court noted that:

> If a restriction on fundamental rights applies to a particularly vulnerable group in society that has suffered considerable discrimination in the past, then the State's margin of appreciation is substantially narrower and it must have very weighty reasons for the restrictions in question.[68]
>
> The Court classified HIV-positive individuals as 'a vulnerable group with a history of prejudice and stigmatisation'.[69] This resulted in the ruling by the Court that the state should only be afforded a narrow margin of appreciation in choosing measures that single out that group for differential treatment on the basis of its HIV status.[70] It also led to a finding that the applicant had been a victim of discrimination on account of his health status, in violation of Article 14, taken in conjunction with Article 8 ECHR.[71]

Finally, in the case of *Guberina* v. *Croatia*, the Court held that there had been a violation of Article 14 ECHR, taken in conjunction with Article 1 of Protocol No. 1 (protection of property), on foot of a complaint by the father of a severely disabled child regarding the tax authorities' failure to take account of the needs of his child when determining his eligibility for a tax exemption on the purchase of property adapted to his child's needs.[72] The case is noteworthy by virtue of the fact

65 Ibid. [57].
66 Ibid.
67 CRPD Art. 5 (equality/non-discrimination), Art. 18 (liberty of movement and nationality) and Art. 23 (respect for home and the family).
68 *Kiyutin* v. *Russia* (n. 64) [63].
69 Ibid. [64].
70 Ibid.
71 Ibid. [74].
72 *Guberina* v. *Croatia*, App. no. 23682/13 (ECtHR, 22 March 2016).

that the Court applied strict scrutiny in the area of taxation because the restriction concerned a particularly vulnerable group, namely people with disabilities. The Court also clarified, for the first time in its jurisprudence, that Article 14 covers discrimination by association (because of a relationship with a person with a disability). As Mr Guberina's lawyer (Constantin Cojocariu) points out, this 'may open the door to a more sympathetic understanding of the problems faced by parents/carers, who are frequently left to shoulder the burden of disability in a largely hostile environment'.[73]

In deciding the case, the ECtHR referred to CRPD provisions addressing reasonable accommodation, equality and non-discrimination and accessibility (among others), as well as the CRPD Committee's General Comment No. 2 (2014) on Accessibility.[74] Lisa Waddington asserts that 'this case is unusual for the extensive range of references to the CRPD and related instruments' and for the fact that the Court used the CRPD as more than mere 'relevant legal background material'.[75] *Guberina* appears to indicate a true move towards substantive equality on the Court's part and may be significant in the context of the exercise of the right to education, particularly since the Court placed particular emphasis in its judgment on the key role that accessibility played in the applicant's son's life, by facilitating his personal development and enabling him to participate fully in educative, cultural and social activities.

3.4 *The Social-Contextual Approach: Steps in the Direction of the Social Model of Disability?*

In a similar vein to the approach adopted by the Court in the Roma judgments,[76] the ECtHR has shown itself open to a social-contextual approach to discrimination/disadvantage in *Kiyutin* by examining in great detail the manner in which the stigmatisation and exclusion of HIV-positive persons manifests itself, as well as its consequences for persons with HIV.[77] Alexandra Timmer observes, in that regard, that the Court made 'a real effort

73 Constantin Cojocariu, '*Guberina* and *Gherghina*: The Two Sides of the Court's Disability Jurisprudence' (Strasbourg Observers, 17 May 2016), https://strasbourgobservers.com/2016/05/17/guberina-and-gherghina-the-two-sides-of-the-courts-disability-jurisprudence/#more-3222, accessed 18 August 2016.

74 Committee on the Rights of Persons with Disabilities, General Comment No. 2 (2014) Article 9: Accessibility (22 May 2014) CRPD/C/GC/2.

75 Lisa Waddington, 'Europees Hof voor de Rechten van de Mens, Guberina tegen Kroatie' (2016) 17(6) *Equality and Human Rights Commission* No. 23682/13 (note) [3].

76 See Section 2 of this chapter.

77 *Kiyutin* v. *Russia* (n. 64) [64].

to address the sources of prejudice against people living with HIV'.[78] This 'anti-stereotyping' approach[79] correlates with the approach taken in Article 8 CRPD, which requires states inter alia 'to combat stereotypes, prejudices and harmful practices relating to persons with disabilities, including those based on sex and age, in all areas of life'.[80]

In both the *Alajos Kiss* and *Kiyutin* cases, the Court elaborated on its reasoning for applying a strict standard of scrutiny by acknowledging the extent to which socially constructed stereotypes have in the past perpetuated, and indeed continue to perpetuate, the social exclusion of persons with psychosocial disability and those with HIV, respectively.[81] By showing itself open to the social context of the alleged violation and, therefore, to the social construction of disability/health-related grounds, the Court recognised implicitly that the disabling factors in those cases resulted from attitudinal and legislative barriers to participation.

In the case of *IB* v. *Greece*, the ECtHR once again employed a social constructionist approach to disability (HIV).[82] In finding a violation of both Articles 8 and 14 ECHR (following the applicant's dismissal from his employment on the grounds of his HIV status),[83] the Court spoke extensively about the difficulties faced by persons diagnosed with HIV in terms of stigmatisation and discrimination.[84] The ECtHR repeated its pronouncements from the *Kiyutin* case that, by virtue of the fact that people living with HIV are a 'vulnerable group with a history of prejudice and stigmatisation, States should only be afforded a narrow margin of appreciation in choosing measures that single out that group for differential treatment on the basis of their HIV status'.[85]

While the applicant did not invoke the provisions of the CRPD, the CRPD had obvious relevance to the facts of the case, and it is surprising that

78 Timmer (n. 8) 713.

79 For more information on the ECtHR's anti-stereotyping approach, see generally Timmer (n. 8).

80 CRPD Art. 8(1)(b).

81 *Alajos Kiss* v. *Hungary* (n. 42) [42] and *Kiyutin* v. *Russia* (n. 64) [63].

82 *IB* v. *Greece*, App. no. 552/10 (ECtHR, 3 October 2013).

83 The applicant in *IB* alleged that his dismissal (following complaints by fellow employees that they may be exposed to the HIV virus as a result of the applicant's presence in the workplace) violated his right to a private life under Article 8 ECHR. The applicant also alleged discriminatory treatment, contrary to Article 14 ECHR, on account of the dismissal itself and also in view of the fact that the reason given by the Greek Supreme Court for justifying the dismissal (namely, his HIV status and the necessity to preserve an amicable work environment) constituted unjustified discrimination.

84 See, in particular, paragraphs 72, 80 and 81 of the *IB* judgment.

85 *IB* v. *Greece* (n. 82) [79] and [81].

the ECtHR made no mention of the CRPD in its consideration of the merits of the case, in light of the Court's comparative and evolutive approach to interpretation of ECHR rights.[86] In spite of its failure to mention the CRPD, the social model of disability appears to have infiltrated the Court's legal reasoning in several ways. In the first instance, the ECtHR took the social model of disability into account in its analysis of the scope of application of the right to private life under Article 8 ECHR. The Court stated that there is no question but that situations involving persons with HIV come within the ambit of the right to private life under Article 8, on account of the fact that the HIV epidemic cannot be considered solely as a medical problem. Rather, its consequences reverberate through all spheres of one's private life.[87] The Court noted that the treatment in question, namely the dismissal of the applicant, resulted in his stigmatisation and that this treatment inevitably had serious repercussions on his personality, on the level of respect which others showed him and, eventually, on his private life.[88] Furthermore, in deciding that there was no objective and reasonable justification for the treatment in question, the Strasbourg Court again adopted the social model of disability. The Court acknowledged the fact that

> HIV-positive persons have to face up to a whole host of problems, not only medical, but also professional, social, personal and psychological ones, and above all to sometimes deeply rooted prejudices even among the most highly educated people.[89]

The Court was of the view that the discriminatory treatment in question originated in the attitude of rejection adopted by the applicant's colleagues

86 The evolutive approach to interpretation has featured heavily in the jurisprudence of the Strasbourg Court since its early days. See, for instance, *Tyrer* v. *The United Kingdom*, App. no. 5856/72 (ECtHR, 25 April 1978); *Marckx* v. *Belgium*, App. no. 6833/74 (ECtHR, 13 June 1979); and *Dudgeon* v. *The United Kingdom*, App. no. 7525/76 (ECtHR, 24 February 1983).

87 At paragraph 70 of the *IB* judgment, the Court states as follows: 'It is therefore now established that both employment matters and situations involving HIV-infected persons fall within the scope of private life. The Court cannot but conclude thus, since the HIV epidemic cannot be considered only as a medical problem as its effects are felt in every sphere of private life.'

88 At paragraph 72 of *IB* v. *Greece*, the Court states that: 'It is clear that the applicant's dismissal resulted in the stigmatisation of a person who, even if they were HIV positive, had not shown any symptoms of the disease. That measure was bound to have serious repercussions for his personality rights, the respect owed to him and, ultimately, his private life. To that must be added the uncertainty surrounding his search for a new job, since the possibility of finding one could reasonably have appeared remote having regard to his previous experience. The fact that the applicant did find a new job after being dismissed does not suffice to erase the detrimental effect of his dismissal on his ability to lead a normal personal life.'

89 *IB* v. *Greece* (n. 82) [80].

when faced with his HIV-positive status.[90] On that basis, it concluded that the applicant was a victim of discrimination in breach of Article 8, taken together with Article 14 ECHR.

Of particular importance in the present context is the ECtHR's first disability equality judgment in the field of non-compulsory education, *Çam* v. *Turkey*.[91] The judgment provides strong evidence for the Strasbourg Court's willingness to make use of a social model of disability. The Court in *Çam* held unanimously that there had been a violation of Article 14, in conjunction with Article 2 of Protocol No. 1 ECHR (on the right to education), on account of the refusal of the Turkish National Music Academy to enrol the applicant as a student due to her visual impairment. The case is significant in many respects, not least because the Court focussed on the importance of positive measures to ensure that students with disabilities are provided with education on a non-discriminatory basis. In that context, the Court referred to the CRPD, the importance of inclusive education and, in particular, the definition of reasonable accommodation enshrined in Article 2 CRPD. Significantly, the Court considered that the notion of discrimination on the ground of disability extends to the refusal to provide a reasonable accommodation to facilitate access for a disabled person to education, in line with the CRPD. It is noteworthy that the applicant had not even raised a claim of denial of reasonable accommodation. This leads one to suspect that the Court envisages that discrimination based on disability may extend also to 'lack (and not only denial in the strict sense)' of reasonable accommodation.[92]

The outcome of *Çam* v. *Turkey*, as well as the Court's reasoning in the case, is certainly promising. The other cases outlined in this section also show some interesting trends in the Court's case law. The increased emphasis on the social construction of identity markers has the potential to influence the ECtHR to adopt a mainstreaming approach to disability, which may in turn impact the interpretation of the equality norm and, hence, the right to education.

Mainstreaming disability in the context of ECHR rights would involve the recognition that positive measures (including reasonable accommodations)

90 At paragraph 77 of *IB* v. *Greece*, the Court noted that 'the employer's concern was admittedly to restore peace in the company, but that that concern was rooted in the situation created by the attitude of the applicant's colleagues towards his HIV status'.

91 *Çam* v. *Turkey* (n. 38).

92 See the views of Joseph Damamme, 'Disability Discrimination because of Denial of "Reasonable Accommodations": A Very Positive Connection between the ECHR and the UNCRPD in *Çam v Turkey*' (Strasbourg Observers, 1 April 2016), https://strasbourgobservers.com/category/cases/cam-v-turkey/, accessed 12 October 2016.

are essential to removing the specific disadvantage experienced by disabled people in participating in society.[93]

In the context of the right to education for disabled persons, this might encourage the Strasbourg Court to consider further the positive measures which states can take in order to accommodate the needs, and facilitate the rights, of disabled applicants. This would strengthen the trends emerging from cases such as *Çam*. Notwithstanding this, it is important to note, as Arnardóttir does, that the ECtHR is 'still at an early stage of development' regarding the use of the social-contextual model of disadvantage and that other cases[94] (involving other discrimination grounds) 'continue to be decided without any reference to membership in vulnerable groups, social exclusion, stigma or stereotyping'.[95] Since the Court has not yet had the opportunity to follow up on *Çam*, it is unclear at present how far the Strasbourg Court is willing to go in its disability equality judgments, specifically in the context of the enjoyment of the right to education by disabled applicants.

4 THE LINK BETWEEN ROMA AND DISABILITY RIGHTS

There appears to be clear parallels between the emerging trends highlighted earlier in the Strasbourg Court's Roma education case law and its disability discrimination jurisprudence. The Court has begun to interpret the ECHR's equality norm in a substantive, and somewhat transformative, manner in respect of the rights of Roma and disabled applicants. Through its application of the concept of group vulnerability to the rights of these two marginalised groups, the Court is showing signs of a contextual and asymmetrical approach to equality. The application of the group vulnerability approach to both Roma and disability claims has resulted in a strict standard of scrutiny, which appears to be directly related to the resulting positive obligations incumbent on states, in the context of the right to education of Roma applicants at least. The social-contextual approach to the rights of marginalised groups is also potentially significant in ensuring

93 Broderick, *The Long and Winding Road to Equality* 355. See the comments of Lisa Waddington, 'Unravelling the Knot: Article 8, Private Life, Positive Duties and Disability: Rewriting *Sentges* v. the *Netherlands*' in Eva Brems (ed.), *Diversity and European Human Rights: Rewriting Judgments of the ECHR* (Cambridge: Cambridge University Press 2013) 347.

94 Arnardóttir (n. 16) 654. In that regard, Arnardóttir cites *Kurić and Others* v. *Slovenia*, App. no. 26828/06 (ECtHR, 26 June 2012) (race) and *Vallianatos and Others* v. *Greece*, App. nos 29381/09 and 32684/09 (ECtHR, 7 November 2013) (sexual orientation).

95 Ibid. 654.

that the ECtHR takes into account in its analysis the wider disadvantage disabled applications face. In light of the foregoing, it is apt to examine the Court's stance on segregated education, as well as the link between disability and Roma rights in that regard.

4.1 *The ECtHR's Stance on Segregated Education*

The stance of the Strasbourg Court on segregated education emerges quite clearly from the Roma cases outlined earlier. The Court in *Horváth* accepted the submissions made by the Hungarian government to the effect that the decision to retain the system of special schools/classes had been motivated by the desire to find a 'solution' for children with special educational needs.[96] The Hungarian government had argued that the education programme in its existing form was beneficial to pupils with different abilities.[97] Notwithstanding this, the ECtHR expressed its concern about the existing regime for pupils with special educational needs, stating that it shared the 'disquiet' of the other Council of Europe institutions, which have expressed concerns about the more basic curriculum followed in such schools and, in particular, the segregation which the system causes – even if the applicants in *Horváth* had not been placed in ethnically segregated classes.[98]

The Court in *Horváth* did not condemn segregated educational structures explicitly. However, the ECtHR was not asked to rule on segregated educational structures per se. The Court noted that:

> The identification of the appropriate educational programme for the mentally disabled and students with a learning disability, especially in the case of Roma children, as well as the choice between a single school for everyone, highly specialised structures and unified structures with specialised sections is not an easy one. It entails a difficult balancing exercise between the competing interests.[99]

Moreover, the ECtHR stated that 'as to the setting and planning of the curriculum, this mainly involves questions of expediency', on which it is not for the Court to rule.[100] Therefore, the ECtHR appears to indicate that it will shy away from the issue of segregated education for children with disabilities if

96 *Horváth and Kiss* v. *Hungary* (n. 30) [113].
97 Ibid.
98 Ibid. [73]–[75].
99 Ibid. [125].
100 Ibid.

it is called on to address the issue in future cases. At present, the Court does not appear to consider segregated education as a human rights concern. This is in spite of the fact that, in both *DH* and *Horváth*, the ECtHR acknowledges that children in special schools receive an education which compounds their difficulties and compromises their subsequent personal development, instead of helping them 'to integrate into ordinary schools and develop the skills that would facilitate life among the majority population'.[101] Of course, the very same can be said about children with disabilities in segregated education. As Oliver Lewis points out, 'these statements can be read as the Court (at worst) approving of, or (at best) ignoring the fact that everyone in special schools is denied their right to education'.[102] Lewis maintains that by focussing on the issue of misdiagnosis, the Roma cases 'have had the unintended effect of legitimizing a segregated schooling system as such'.[103] However, he also claims that there are 'some positive elements'[104] stemming from the litigation, 'from which disability activists could build cases'.[105] Notably, the Court in *Horváth* explicitly linked the discriminatory treatment of the Roma applicants in education, and the failure of the state to put in place the guarantees needed to avoid the misdiagnosis and misplacement of Roma, with the vulnerability of persons with psychosocial disabilities, as well as their past history of discrimination and prejudice. In that connection, the Court used the opportunity before it to repeat the sentiments which it had expressed in previous disability cases,[106] namely that due to the special vulnerability of persons with mental disabilities, the limitation of their fundamental rights has to be justified by very weighty reasons, and has to be subject to strict scrutiny.[107] As Alexandra Timmer notes, one 'might say that the Court takes an intersectional approach, combining a Roma-equality perspective with a mental disability perspective'.[108] This would appear to be an encouraging sign from the Strasbourg Court for disability advocates to consider bringing a case related

101 See *DH* v. *Czech Republic* (n. 17) [207]; see also *Horváth and Kiss* v. *Hungary* (n. 30) [125].

102 Oliver Lewis, 'Using Litigation as a Strategy to Challenge Disability and Ethnicity Discrimination in Education' (18 July 2013), http://mdac.info/en/olivertalks/2013/07/18/using-litigation-strategy-challenge-disability-and-ethnicity-discrimination, accessed 13 October 2016.

103 Ibid.

104 Ibid.

105 Ibid.

106 See, for instance, *Alajos Kiss* v. *Hungary*.

107 See *Alajos Kiss* v. *Hungary* [42] and [44]; reaffirmed at *Horváth and Kiss* v. *Hungary* [128].

108 Alexandra Timmer, '*Horváth and Kiss* v. *Hungary*: A Strong New Roma School Segregation Case' (Strasbourg Observers, 6 February 2016), http://strasbourgobservers.com/2013/02/06/horvath-and-kiss-v-hungary-a-strong-new-roma-school-segregation-case, accessed 3 October 2016.

to the segregation of children with learning difficulties throughout certain Member States of the Council of Europe.

In addition, the ECtHR's recent disability equality jurisprudence, particularly *Çam*, illustrates some positive signs that the Court is moving towards a greater understanding of the non-discrimination norm for persons with disabilities, including the requirement for differential treatment and positive measures in the context of education. As highlighted earlier in this chapter, in several recent disability cases the Court has recognised the vulnerable and disadvantaged position of disabled people, in a similar vein to its recognition of the vulnerable and disadvantaged position of Roma.[109] The Court has also advocated a heightened standard of scrutiny and appears to have acknowledged the relevance of social-contextual factors in its analysis of the rights of disabled persons.[110] In its Roma education case law, the ECtHR has recognised that the special needs of disadvantaged groups, as well as their differential characteristics, must be taken into account in the sphere of education. Interestingly the Court in *Horváth* remarked that 'it was not clear whether the applicants had mental (or learning) disabilities that could not have been taken into consideration within the normal education system by providing additional opportunities to catch up with the normal curriculum'.[111] In *Çam*, the Strasbourg Court likewise recognised the special needs of disabled people in education in its analysis of their rights under the ECHR and advocated the adoption of positive measures in that context. The Court should continue to develop this approach, particularly in light of the fact that many Member States of the Council of Europe are also States Parties to the CRPD.

The Court's recognition in *Horváth* of the role of positive obligations in undoing a history of discrimination in the Roma context, and the Court's acknowledgement of the importance of positive measures to ensure that students with disabilities are provided with education on a non-discriminatory basis, lends itself to the tentative conclusion that it might in the future be similarly inclined to consider increased positive measures to undo a history of segregation of disabled children in special schools and, thereby, increase their participation in mainstream education. Although the ECtHR referred quite extensively to reasonable accommodations in the *Çam* case, the Court is at an early stage in its enunciation of these types of measures. Therefore, it is unclear to what extent the Strasbourg Court will interpret the ECHR as requiring the imposition of reasonable accommodations and other

109 See *Alajos Kiss* v. *Hungary*; *Kiyutin* v. *Russia*.

110 See *Glor* v. *Switzerland*, *Alajos Kiss* v. *Hungary* and *Kiyutin* v. *Russia*.

111 *Horváth and Kiss* v. *Hungary* (n. 30) [122].

individualised supports (as mandated by Article 24 of the CRPD) in the context of the right to education in its future case law.[112]

It is also important to note that there are limits to the use of traditional non-discrimination law in the context of education. Therefore, a cautious approach to litigation is mandated, in order to advance disability education claims. As Oliver Lewis points out, 'the lesson surely is that NGOs and lawyers need to be careful in taking future cases, so as to nudge courts into a better space where they use non-discrimination law positively instead of negatively'.[113] Lewis rightly asserts that:

> The challenge for all of us now is to break free from our single-identity boxes, and find an opportunity to mount an assault on segregation, beyond one constituency. Working together in solidarity and in a way which respects and builds on differing positions, the Roma and disability movements can demand a more fulsome sense of inclusion and openness for all children, whatever their labels.

5 CONCLUSION

During the negotiation sessions leading to the adoption of the CRPD, education was described aptly as 'the vector for all human development [a right which is] foundational to society, and . . . a predicate to the full enjoyment of a wide range of civil, political, economic, social and cultural rights, including political participation, freedom of expression, and access to employment'.[114] Let us hope that the ECtHR takes cognisance of these sentiments in its interpretation of the rights of persons with disabilities. The Strasbourg Court is showing promising trends in its disability equality case law, and particularly in the recent *Çam* case. The ECtHR has not been directly confronted with

112 The Strasbourg Court may be reluctant to impose positive duties on states due to the nature of the rights contained in the ECHR (being civil and political rights which are not associated traditionally with a redistribution of resources) and to the self-imposed constraints which the Court has placed on the interpretation of ECHR rights – in other words, the fact that the ECtHR is a quasi-judicial body, which is extremely cautious about the imposition of positive duties on States Parties to the ECHR, particularly under Article 14. For further analysis of this point, see Colm O'Cinneide, 'Extracting Protection for the Rights of Persons with Disabilities from Human Rights Frameworks: Established Limits and New Possibilities' in Oddný Mjöll Arnardóttir and Gerard Quinn (eds), *The UN Convention on the Rights of Persons with Disabilities: European and Scandinavian Perspectives* (Leiden: Martinus Nijhoff 2009).

113 Lewis (n. 102).

114 Judith Heumann, 'Statement by the United States Delegation: At Round Table 2: CRPD Article 24 – Inclusion and the Right to Education Third Conference of States Parties' (United Nations, New York, 2 September 2010).

a case on segregated education for children with disabilities. However, it is hoped that the advent of the CRPD, with its emphasis on inclusive education in Article 24 thereof, and the promising developments highlighted throughout this chapter, may influence the Court to develop its approach to disability equality, specifically related to the right to education. Anna Lawson correctly points out that:

> In the face of the CRPD, coupled with the Council of Europe's own disability policy as expressed in its Action Plan, it would ... appear perverse for [the ECtHR] to continue to insist (as its Second Chamber appears to have done in the *DH* case) that the segregation of disabled people raises no issue of human rights.[115]

[115] Anna Lawson, 'The UN Convention on the Rights of Persons with Disabilities and European Disability Law: A Catalyst for Cohesion?' in Oddný Mjöll Arnardóttir and Gerard Quinn (eds), *The UN Convention on the Rights of Persons with Disabilities: European and Scandinavian Perspectives* (Leiden: Martinus Nijhoff 2009) 93.

17

Emerging Jurisprudence on Inclusive Education under the European Social Charter (Revised)

Shivaun Quinlivan

1 INTRODUCTION

The European Social Charter 1961 (the Charter) and the European Social Charter (Revised) 1996 (ESC(R)) have arguably operated under the radar for decades. It is time for disability rights campaigners and academics to address the hidden existence of the ESC(R) and to bring it into the light. It is evident from the jurisprudence discussed in this chapter that there is ample reason to look to the ESC(R) to assist in promoting inclusive education. This chapter addresses the emerging jurisprudence on inclusive education under the ESC(R). To that end, this chapter introduces the European Social Charters: the 1961 Charter and the Revised Charter of 1996, which have led a somewhat hidden existence. This relative invisibility may be the result of the uneven application of the Charters, the fact that both Charters continue in existence and the overarching complexity of the system in which they operate. The chapter addresses the right to education for children with disabilities and there are two relevant articles: Article 15[1] and Article 17.[2] Because of the dual coverage of the right to education it is necessary to address how the two articles interact. This chapter also addresses the strong presumption in favour of mainstream education, and when segregated or special provision is acceptable under the ESC(R).

In addition to reviewing the articles addressing the right to education, it is important to address the right to non-discrimination. Article E was introduced as an explicit article with the introduction of the ESC(R) and it had no

[1] Article 15 of the European Social Charter (Revised) (ESC(R)) (opened for signature 3 May 1996, entered into force 1 July 1999) CETS No. 163 is titled: 'The right of persons with disabilities to independence, social integration and participation in the life of the community'.

[2] Ibid., Article 17 is titled: 'The right of children and young persons to social, legal and economic protection'. This Article encompasses the right to education.

predecessor in the 1961 Charter. Article E, like Article 14 of the European Convention on Human Rights (ECHR), does not constitute an autonomous right and the wording of both provisions is remarkably similar. The similarities aside, the differences between the provisions are most obviously reflected in their interpretation.[3] Article E has been interpreted broadly and clearly incorporates both direct and indirect discrimination. Finally, the chapter addresses the collective complaints procedure, followed by the enforcement of case law of the European Committee of Social Rights (the Committee) of the ESC(R).

2 THE CHARTERS

The Charter was intended to be the sister of the ECHR; however, it is evident from both the literature and the paucity of cases that the Charter was completely overshadowed by its more famous sibling.[4] Where the ECHR has been 'the jewel in the Council of Europe crown', the Charter, in contrast, has been an instrument with a 'twilight existence'.[5] De Schutter enumerated a number of failings of the Charter, including the failings of the supervisory system, the inability to invoke the Charter before national bodies, limitations within the text itself and the *à la carte* nature of the obligations.[6] An additional criticism levelled against the Charter is that it has not sufficiently stood the test of time and that many of the rights contained in it 'are outdated and lag behind the national laws of states parties'.[7] For example, the Charter contained no right to education, and it referred to the necessity to take measures to place 'disabled persons in employment, such as specialised placing services, facilities for sheltered employment and measures to encourage employers to admit

[3] The European Court of Human Rights (ECtHR) interprets the provisions of the ECHR whereas the European Committee of Social Rights (the Committee) interprets the provisions of both the Charter and the ESC(R).

[4] Olivier De Schutter and Matthias Sant'ana, 'The European Committee of Social Rights' in Gauthier de Beco (ed.), *Human Rights Monitoring Mechanisms of the Council of Europe* (Routledge 2012); Olivier De Schutter (ed.), The European Social Charter: A Social Constitution for Europe (Bruylant 2010); Anne Theodore Briggs, 'Waking "Sleeping Beauty": The Revised European Social Charter' (2000) 7 *Human Rights Brief* 24; Andrzej M. Świątkowski, Charter of Social Rights of the Council of Europe (Kluwer Law International 2008); François Vandamme, 'The Revision of the European Social Charter' (1994) 133 *International Labour Review* 635.

[5] David John Harris, 'A Fresh Impetus for the European Social Charter' (1992) 41 *International & Comparative Law Quarterly* 659, 659.

[6] Olivier De Schutter, 'The Two Lives of the European Social Charter' in Olivier De Schutter (ed.), *The European Social Charter: A Social Constitution for Europe* (Bruylant 2010) 11–12.

[7] Robin Churchill and Urfan Khaliq, 'The Collective Complaints System of the European Social Charter: An Effective Mechanism for Ensuring Compliance with Economic and Social Rights?' (2004) 15 *European Journal of International Law* 417, 453.

disabled persons to employment'.[8] In practice the Charter was 'largely ignored'.[9] Various attempts were made to address some of the deficits of the Charter that culminated in the adoption of the ESC(R).

The ESC(R) has maintained some of the more unusual features that were evident in the Charter, most notably the *à la carte* approach to ratification of the terms of the Convention. Part III of the ESC(R) requires States Parties to be bound by six of the nine core articles (Articles 1, 5, 6, 7, 12, 13, 16, 19 and 20)[10] and by 'not less than sixteen articles or sixty-three numbered paragraphs'.[11] The position with regard to the application of both the Charter and the ESC(R) is somewhat complicated. Where a State Party agrees to ratify the ESC(R), the rights contained in the ESC(R) supersede those contained in the Charter of 1961. However, where a State Party does not accede to a particular right in the ESC(R) and there is an equivalent within the Charter of 1961 that it had ratified, it remains bound by the Charter of 1961. In other words, States Parties cannot use the ratification of the ESC(R) to opt out of particular commitments. Cullen notes that 'the complexity of the structure of obligations undertaken by states'[12] makes it difficult to navigate a State Party's obligations under either the Charter and the ESC(R) or potentially elements of both.[13] This patchwork protection means that the obligations imposed on each State Party may be slightly different depending on which Charter or which articles they have ratified. Thus it becomes important to understand the national position in order to appreciate what form of litigation, if any, can be taken in a particular state.[14]

8 Article 15(2) European Social Charter (opened for signature 18 October 1961, entered into force 26 February 1965) CETS No. 035.

9 Olivier De Schutter, 'The European Social Charter in the Context of Implementation of the EU Charter of Fundamental Rights' (PE 536.488, Directorate-General for Internal Policies 2016) 9.

10 ESC(R) (n. 1) The relevant rights set out in these articles are: the right to work; the right to organise; the right to bargain collectively; the right of children and young persons to protection; the right to social security; the right to social and medical assistance; the right of the family to social, legal and economic protection; the right of migrant workers and their families to protection and assistance; the right to equal opportunities and treatment in matters of employment and occupation without discrimination on the grounds of sex.

11 Ibid. Part III, Article A, Undertakings.

12 Holly Cullen, 'Is the European Social Charter a Charter for Children?' (2005) 40 *Irish Jurist* 60, 61.

13 Only Spain ratified the 1961 Charter in its entirety, and only France and Portugal have ratified the 1996 ESC(R) in its entirety. Additionally the United Kingdom, Iceland and Denmark have only ratified the 1961 Charter. In contrast, countries such as Bosnia and Herzegovina, Serbia and Montenegro have only ratified the 1996 ESC(R).

14 The potential to litigate is also dependent on a State Party acceding to the collective complaints mechanism.

3 RIGHT TO EDUCATION

It is against the backdrop of an ineffective Charter and the necessity to revitalise and update that process that the ESC(R) was introduced.[15] In the context of the right to education, it seems that the old adage *you wait for ages for a bus and then two come along at once* is appropriate. The Charter did not contain a right to education. In contrast, the ESC(R) addresses the educational rights of children with disabilities in two distinct articles. This part of the chapter addresses the impact of the dual coverage of the right to education; the commitment to inclusive education under Articles 15 and 17; finally this section addresses when and if segregated education is permitted under the ESC(R).

3.1 *Dual Coverage*

Article 17 ESC(R) addresses the right of children and young persons to social, legal and economic protection, and provides for an express right to education. Article 15 establishes the right of persons with disabilities to independence, social integration and participation in the life of the community, including 'education and vocational training in the framework of general schemes wherever possible or, where this is not possible, through specialised bodies, public or private'.[16] It is evident that there is an overlap in the material scope of these two articles.

The Committee has established that Article 17 applies to all children, including children with disabilities, but it goes on to provide that in respect of states having accepted Articles 17 and 15, the right to education for children with disabilities is to be primarily examined under Article 15(1).[17] While Article 15(1) covers the right to education of children with disabilities, this does not exclude the relevant issues being examined in the framework of Article 17(2).[18] In practice this means that a failure to ratify Article 15 will not relieve a state from responsibility for the education of children with disabilities where that state has ratified Article 17. In *Mental Disability Advocacy Centre (MDAC)* v. *Bulgaria* the State Party had ratified Article 17 but had not ratified

15 For a detailed discussion of this, see De Schutter, 'The Two Lives of the European Social Charter' (n. 6); De Schutter and Sant'ana (n. 4); Świątkowski (n. 4) chs 1–4; Vandamme (n. 4).
16 Article 15(1) ESC(R) (n. 1).
17 European Committee of Social Rights, Digest of the Case Law of the European Committee of Social Rights (Council of Europe 2008) 121.
18 *Mental Disability Advocacy Centre (MDAC)* v. *Bulgaria* Complaint No. 41/2007 (European Committee of Social Rights, 3 June 2008) [33].

Article 15, resulting in the Committee examining the right to education for children with disabilities under Article 17.[19] In that action it was held that Bulgaria violated the right to education in Article 17(2) and the right to non-discrimination (discussed later in this chapter) of the ESC(R) for depriving children with intellectual disabilities of their right to education. Consequently the interpretations of both Article 17 and Article 15 have an importance when assessing the right to education for children with disabilities.

3.2 *Inclusive Education*

Article 15 explicitly provides that education should take place in 'the framework of general schemes wherever possible'[20] and only if this is not possible should 'specialised bodies'[21] be considered. Article 15 reflects a significant change in disability policy at the Council of Europe level in that there is a clear move 'from welfare and segregation and towards inclusion and choice'.[22] It is evident from the case law and Recommendations of the Committee of Ministers that there has been a profound shift in the values of the Council of Europe as regards people with disabilities.[23] This shift reflects the changes evidenced internationally by the introduction of the United Nations Convention on the Rights of Persons with Disabilities (CRPD).[24]

19 *MDAC* v. *Bulgaria* (n. 18).

20 Article 15(1) European Social Charter (Revised) (n. 1).

21 'Specialised bodies' is the term used in the ESC(R); however, from the case law to date these 'specialised bodies' generally provide education in segregated settings.

22 European Committee of Social Rights, *Digest of the Case Law of the European Committee of Social Rights* (n. 17) 111.

23 Council of Europe Committee of Ministers, 'Recommendation no R(92)6 of the Committee of Ministers to Member States on a Coherent Policy for People with Disabilities' (9 April 1992); Council of Europe Committee of Ministers, 'Recommendation CM/Rec (2009)8 of the Committee of Ministers to Member States on Achieving Full Participation through Universal Design' (21 October 2009); Council of Europe Committee of Ministers, 'Recommendation Rec(2006)5 of the Committee of Ministers to Member States on the Council of Europe Action Plan to Promote the Rights and Full Participation of People with Disabilities in Society: Improving the Quality of Life of People with Disabilities in Europe 2006–2015' (5 April 2006); Council of Europe Committee of Ministers, 'Recommendation CM/Rec(2013)2 of the Committee of Ministers to Member States on Ensuring Full Inclusion of Children and Young Persons with Disabilities into Society' (16 October 2013).

24 See in particular the endorsement of the social model of disability as is evidenced in Article 1 and Paragraph 5 of the Preamble to the United Nations Convention on the Rights of Persons with Disabilities (adopted 13 December 2006, opened for signature 30 March 2007, entered into force 3 May 2008) and see generally Shivaun Quinlivan, 'The United Nations Convention on the Rights of Persons with Disabilities: An Introduction' (2012) 13 *ERA Forum* 71.

This paradigm shift is in essence the move from treating people with disabilities as objects of charity or pity, towards respecting people with disabilities as equal citizens: this is often described as the move from the medical model of disability to the social model of disability.

Article 15 expresses a clear presumption in favour of mainstreaming. Education should be provided 'in the framework of general schemes wherever possible'.[25] This presumption in favour of mainstream educational provision is more than a policy commitment to the inclusion of a child with a disability within the mainstream education system. In order for States Parties to comply with the requirements of Article 15(1) the Committee considers necessary the existence of:

> [N]on-discrimination legislation as an important tool for the advancement of the inclusion of children with disabilities into general or mainstream educational schemes. Such legislation should, as a minimum, require a compelling justification for special or segregated educational systems and confer an effective remedy on those who are found to have been unlawfully excluded or segregated or otherwise denied an effective right to education. Legislation may consist of general anti-discrimination legislation, specific legislation concerning education, or a combination of the two.[26]

This clearly states that the presumption of mainstream education should have a legislative base. Interesting, that legislation could take the form of non-discrimination legislation or a non-discrimination clause within education legislation, thus linking special or segregated education to discrimination on the basis of disability.

Article 17 provides for an express right to education and requires States Parties to take all 'appropriate and necessary measures' to ensure compliance with the provisions of the article. Article 17 addresses the general education system and does not refer expressly to mainstream or special education. The Committee has held that Article 17 does, however, require equal access to education for all and states that:

> Equal access to education must be ensured for all children, in this respect particular attention should be paid to vulnerable groups such as children from minorities ... Children belonging to these groups must be integrated

25 ESC(R) (n. 1) Article 15(1).

26 European Committee of Social Rights, Conclusions 2007: Volume 1 (Albania, Armenia, Belgium, Bulgaria, Cyprus, Estonia, Finland, France) (Council of Europe Publishing 2007) 12; see also European Committee of Social Rights, Conclusions 2007: Volume 2 (Ireland, Italy, Lithuania, Moldova, Norway, Romania, Slovenia, Sweden) (Council of Europe Publishing 2007).

> into mainstream educational facilities and ordinary educational schemes. Where necessary special measures should be taken to ensure equal access to education for these children. However, special measures for Roma children should not involve the establishment of separate schools or classes reserved for this group.[27]

While reference is made to vulnerable groups, no specific reference is made to children with disabilities within the list of groups mentioned. Despite this omission, the list clearly is illustrative and not exhaustive. In addition, the provision makes clear that the default position should be inclusion, not segregation. Reference is made to 'special measures', but those special measures should be taken to ensure equal access to education. Moreover, Article 17 expressly states when referencing Roma children that any special measures should not involve the establishment of separate schools or classes. Arguably the same principles could be assumed with regard to children with disabilities, and where special measures are provided it is contended that they should be provided within the general education system. While this point is not expressly stated in Article 17, its application to the education of children with disabilities is evident from case law.

In *MDAC* v. *Bulgaria*, national legislation introduced in 2002 provided for education for all with a presumption in favour of mainstream education:[28]

> Children shall attend special schools only where all other possibilities of attending mainstream kindergartens and schools have been exhausted, subject to the explicit consent of parents or tutors.[29]

MDAC alleged that the Bulgarian government had failed to implement the legislation effectively. The complaint related to twenty-eight specific institutions where many of the resident children had been either abandoned or orphaned.[30] The complaint alleged that the right to education was being denied to the children as official statistics established that only 6.2 per cent of the children (subject of this action) were enrolled in schools; mainstream schools were not adapted to accommodate the abilities and needs of the children; the education, if provided, was wholly inadequate; and a lack of resources could not in this case serve as a valid defence on the facts.[31]

[27] European Committee of Social Rights, *Digest of the Case Law of the European Committee of Social Rights* (n. 17) (citations omitted) 120.

[28] The situation prior to 2002 denied education to children with severe and profound intellectual disabilities who were classified by law as uneducable.

[29] Order No. 6 (2002) on the Education of Children with Special Educational Needs and/or Chronic Diseases Article 2.

[30] *MDAC* v. *Bulgaria* (n. 18) [20].

[31] Ibid. [18–26].

In response, the Bulgarian government highlighted the passage of the relevant legislation and the practical steps taken to overcome problems of access for this group of children. The government emphasised several action plans as well as a clear political commitment of the Bulgarian government towards integrating children into mainstream schools. The government noted that this was an

> ongoing process, the visible results of which will become evident in the long term and which will require considerable financial input. The Government hopes to achieve the Revised Charter's objectives 'within a reasonable period of time', with measurable progress and with the fullest possible use of available resources.[32]

The Committee stated that Article 17 required States Parties 'to establish and maintain an education system that is both accessible and effective'.[33] The Committee reiterated earlier decisions to the effect that the aim of the ESC(R) is to 'protect rights not merely theoretically, but also in fact'.[34] Accordingly it is not sufficient to enact legislation: implementation is crucial. In assessing whether the system is effective there must be a high quality of teaching and equal access to education for all children, in particular vulnerable groups.[35] In finding against Bulgaria the Committee held that 'teaching in specialised schools must be the exception'.[36] Thus Article 17(2) on its own without reference to Article 15 creates a presumption in favour of mainstreaming.

In *Autism Europe* v. *France* the Committee affirmed that the basic premise 'of Article 15 is one of equal citizenship for persons with disabilities'.[37] Further, the right to education and securing that right for children 'with disabilities plays an obviously important role in advancing these citizenship rights'.[38] Moreover, Article 17 provides for the full development of the child and this is of course as applicable to children with disabilities. The Committee then noted that this approach was arguably more important to children with

32 Ibid. [32], and see more generally paragraphs 27–32.

33 Ibid. [34].

34 Ibid. [38] citing previous jurisprudence of the committee *International Commission of Jurists (ICJ)* v. *Portugal* Complaint No. 1/1998 Decision on the Merits (European Committee of Social Rights, 10 September 1999).

35 *MDAC* v. *Bulgaria* (n. 18) [34]; European Committee of Social Rights, 'Conclusions 2005 – Bulgaria – Article 17-2' (2005/def/BGR/17/2/EN, *HUDOC*, 30 June 2005), http://hudoc.esc.coe.int/eng?i=2005/def/BGR/17/2/EN, accessed 14 July 2017.

36 *MDAC* v. *Bulgaria* (n. 18) [35].

37 *International Association Autism Europe* v. *France* Complaint No. 13/2002 Decision on the Merits (European Committee of Social Rights, 4 November 2003) [48].

38 Ibid.

disabilities 'where the effects of ineffective or untimely intervention are ever likely to be undone'.[39] The impact of the decision in *Autism Europe* v. *France* is that Article 17 as it applies to children with disabilities is guided by the principles contained in Article 15. According to Quinn, this case highlighted a 'natural link' between these two articles, as 'Article 17 was very explicit on the institutions and services required whereas Article 15 was more explicit on the philosophy that should inform these institutions'.[40] This position is reiterated in *AEH* v. *France* when the Committee reaffirmed that Article 15 reflects a shift in values that has occurred in Europe with regard to persons with disabilities. 'Securing a right to education for children and others with disabilities plays a patently important role in advancing these citizenship rights',[41] and such rights should where possible take place in the mainstream system.[42] Consequently, it appears that the right to education in Article 17 as it applies to children with disabilities is to be guided by the principles in Article 15.

All of the decided cases to date reflect a common theme of the exclusion of children with disabilities from the education system; in effect, these cases were about access to education for the children concerned. In contrast, the case of *MDAC* v. *Belgium* currently progressing through the collective complaints procedure is a case of significant interest and importance.[43] This complaint does not focus primarily on access to education for children with disabilities, but instead alleges that the education being received by the children is not in compliance with the ESC(R). The applicants in this action produced statistical evidence that indicates that the percentage of pupils in segregated special education in the Flemish community is the highest in Europe.[44]

39 Ibid. [49].

40 Gerard Quinn, 'The European Social Charter and EU Anti-Discrimination Law in the Field of Disability: Two Gravitational Fields with One Common Purpose' in Gráinne de Búrca and Bruno de Witte (eds), *Social Rights in Europe* (Oxford University Press 2005) 297.

41 *European Action of the Disabled (AEH)* v. *France* Complaint No. 81/2012 Decision on the Merits (European Committee of Social Rights, 11 September 2013) [75].

42 The Committee, in assessing France's ongoing compliance with Article 15(1), found France to be in non-compliance; see European Committee of Social Rights, 'Conclusions 2008 – France – Article 15-1' (2008/def/FRA/15/a/EN, *HUDOC*, 24 October 2008), http://hudoc.esc.coe.int/eng?i=2008/def/FRA/15/1/EN, accessed 14 July 2017; European Committee of Social Rights, 'Conclusions 2012 – France – Article 15-1' (2012/def/FRA/15/1/EN, *HUDOC*, 7 December 2012), http://hudoc.esc.coe.int/eng?i=2012/def/FRA/15/1/EN, accessed 14 July 2017.

43 *MDAC* v. *Belgium* Complaint No. 109/2014 (European Committee of Social Rights, complaint registered 30 April 2014).

44 European Agency for Development in Special Needs Education, Special Needs Education: Country Data 2010 (European Agency for Development in Special Needs Education 2011) 8–9; Serge Ebersold, 'Inclusive Education for Young Disabled People in Europe: Trends, Issues and Challenges: A Synthesis of Evidence from ANED Country Reports and Additional

Consequently, the statistics show that some 6 per cent of pupils require some sort of reasonable educational accommodation and that 85 per cent of those pupils attend segregated education. Of interest here is the fact that the children in question are in receipt of an education albeit in a segregated system and the applicants allege that this is a violation of Articles 15, 17 and Article E in conjunction with Articles 15 and 17 ESC(R). Notwithstanding, the Committee has to date provided an expansive and generous interpretation of the right to education and the right to non-discrimination in the field of education for children with disabilities. Those cases have been about access to the education system for the children concerned. The real potential of the ESC(R) will be put to the test when it addresses the challenges of the very substance of the education provided, or, as with *MDAC* v. *Belgium*, the venue of the education provided for children with disabilities.

3.3 *Provision of Special or Segregated Education*

Evidently, both Article 15 and Article 17 introduce a strong presumption in favour of mainstream education. Further, Article 15 appears to accept that there may be limited occasions when it is not possible to mainstream a child with disabilities and then, in such cases, education should be provided 'through specialised bodies, public or private'.[45] Separate education, where necessary, is narrowly bounded so that any segregated provision must be based on a 'compelling justification', requiring an 'effective remedy' for those 'unlawfully excluded or segregated'.[46]

It is undoubted that the decision in *AEH* v. *France* reaffirmed the strong presumption in favour of mainstream educational provision and from that decision we can extrapolate whether and how segregated educational provision will be acceptable under the ESC(R). The complainant in this action alleged that many children with autism were being deprived of the right to education under the ESC(R). While there were some discrepancies between the parties as to exact figures, it was evident that significant proportions of children with autism were without educational provision.[47] Moreover,

Sources' (Academic Network of European Disability, 24 July 2012), www.disability-europe.net/downloads/72-aned-2010-task-5-education-final-report-final-2–0, accessed 27 June 2017.

45 ESC(R) (n. 1) Article 15(1).

46 European Committee of Social Rights, *Digest of the Case Law of the European Committee of Social Rights* (n. 17) 112.

47 The French government's figures suggested that in 2006, 64 per cent of children with autism received no form of schooling. In contrast to this figure, the associations active in this field estimate that only 20 per cent of children with autism have access to some form of schooling, suggesting that 40,000 autistic children of school-going age have no access to schooling

European Action of the Disabled (AEH) noted that contrary to the requirements of domestic legislation, only a minority of children with autism had access to mainstream schooling. As children moved through the system, the attendance of children with autism in the mainstream decreased significantly.[48] It was further alleged that school integration classes amounted to ghettos within the mainstream.[49] Perhaps of greatest concern was the fact that the

> French state has helped to finance the schooling of children and adolescents with autism in specialised classes run by trained professionals in Belgium.[50]

Thus, France, in effect, exported the 'problem' of educating children with disabilities. Finally concerns were raised in relation to the adequacy of the special education provision, which took place in either medico-educational institutions or day hospital units. These provisions were criticised for failing to ensure that education took place in the mainstream wherever possible.

In response to the arguments raised, the French government pointed out that French positive law was in compliance with the ESC(R). It further argued that France had introduced autism action plans with earmarked funds, and such efforts established 'political goodwill with a view to tackling the problem of autism'.[51] Interestingly, the French government posited that Article 15 does not require education for persons with disabilities to take place exclusively in mainstream schools.[52] The government also challenged the proposition 'that care in a medico-social or health establishment combined with appropriate schooling' does not meet the social integration objective set by Article 15 of the Charter.[53] The government specifically referred to '[s]teering children towards facilities other than mainstream schools'[54] and noted that 'France has established a system allowing for persons with autism's medical, psychological and social treatment while also providing for their schooling'.[55] This is the provision of applied behaviour analysis (ABA), which is regarded as an exemplar among educational interventions for students with autism. Applied behaviour analysis is deemed to be 'primarily developmental and educational in nature

whether in ordinary classes or in other situations. For further, see *AEH* v. *France* (n. 41) [32]–[35].

48 Ibid. [36]–[39].

49 Ibid. [41]–[42].

50 Ibid. [46].

51 Ibid. [49]; this is a direct quote from the respondents reported in the decision.

52 Ibid. [59].

53 Ibid. [60].

54 Ibid. [61].

55 Ibid. [62].

and is aimed at gradually integrating those concerned into a mainstream school environment'.[56] The decision in *AEH* v. *France* is somewhat confused on this point; while the decision is not critical of the actual educational interventions provided, it appears the venue of those interventions was the point of concern.

The Committee in *AEH* v. *France* held that in order for education to happen in a forum other than the mainstream, a variety of factors need to be considered, including 'the type of disability concerned, how serious it is and a variety of individual circumstances to be examined on a case-by-case basis'.[57] It further noted that, in general, states have a wide margin of appreciation in the way in which they implement the ESC(R).[58] That noted, Article 15(1) does not

> leave States Parties a wide margin of appreciation when it comes to choosing the type of school in which they will promote the independence, integration and participation of persons with disabilities, as this must clearly be a mainstream school.[59]

Thus it may be assumed that any automatically exclusionary practices will fall foul of the obligations contained in the ESC(R). What we can take from the decision in *AEH* v. *France* is that segregated education is not in itself inherently in conflict with the requirements of the ESC(R). However, children should not be automatically sent to a segregated provision and any decisions on segregated education should be based on an individual assessment of that child. Any education provided within the mainstream should be suited to the needs of children concerned and the failure to meet the needs of children with disabilities within the mainstream also denies them the right to education.[60] Moreover, States Parties should introduce a legislative presumption in favour of mainstream education, and that presumption should ideally be situated within anti-discrimination legislation.

56 Ibid. [117].
57 Ibid. [78].
58 Ibid. [81] based on *European Council of Police Trade Unions (CESP)* v. *Portugal* Complaint No. 37/2006 Decision on the Merits (European Committee of Social Rights, 3 December 2007) [14].
59 *AEH* v. *France* (n. 41) [78].
60 Ibid. [44].

4 ARTICLE E ESC(R): NON-DISCRIMINATION

The revision of the Charter saw the introduction of a new express article on non-discrimination (Article E). This clearly indicated the desire for a stronger articulation of the principle of non-discrimination. Furthermore, the Committee has expressed the view that the insertion of a separate article in the ESC(R) represents 'the heightened importance the drafters paid to the principle of non-discrimination'.[61] Article E does not constitute an autonomous right which could provide an independent ground for a complaint. It is always necessary to invoke Article E in conjunction with another provision of the Charter. It is submitted that a stand-alone provision would be preferable; however, the fact of this limitation is not fatal to the discussion at hand, namely the right to education for children with disabilities. This part of the chapter addresses the interpretation of the phrase 'other status'; the interpretation by the Committee of the non-discrimination duty; and finally this section addresses the dissenting judgment in *AEH* v. *France*.

4.1 *'Other Status'*

Article E provides that:

> The enjoyment of the rights set forth in this Charter shall be secured without discrimination on any ground such as race, colour, sex, language, religion, political or other opinion, national extraction or social origin, health, association with a national minority, birth or other status.

It is evident from the wording that Article E draws quite heavily from its more famous sibling, Article 14 ECHR. Moreover, the article contains no explicit reference to disability as a protected ground, but the list of protected grounds is non-exhaustive. The Committee in *Autism Europe* v. *France* held that the phrase 'or other status' ensures that people with disabilities are covered by the terms of Article E.[62] Additionally, in this case it stated 'that Article 15 applies to all persons with disabilities regardless of the nature and origin of their disability and irrespective of their age'.[63] It would be incongruous to have an article of the ESC(R) devoted to the rights of persons with disabilities and not have them covered by Article E.

[61] *Autism Europe* v. *France* (n. 37) [51].
[62] *Autism Europe* v. *France* (n. 37) [18]; see also *AEH* v. *France* (n. 41); *MDAC* v. *Bulgaria* (n. 18).
[63] *Autism Europe* v. *France* (n. 37) [48].

4.2 Discrimination

The Committee has from the outset interpreted Article E in a broad and robust manner. *ICJ* v. *Portugal*, the first complaint heard by the Committee, stated that 'the aim and purpose of the Charter, being a human rights protection instrument, is to protect rights not merely theoretically, but also in fact'.[64] As a result of this, the Committee will look beyond the mere introduction of legislation and focus quite clearly on the implementation of that legislation, as is evident from later decisions such as *AEH* v. *France*.[65]

The Committee has expressly accepted 'that Article E not only prohibits direct discrimination but also all forms of indirect discrimination'.[66] The Committee's analysis of Article E provides an intriguing contrast to the interpretation by the ECtHR of Article 14 of the ECHR. The Committee relied on the decisions of the ECtHR, but to a potentially more dramatic effect. *Thlimmenos* v. *Greece*[67] was the first case to suggest that the ECHR may cover indirect discrimination,[68] and the Committee cited the ECtHR, who stated that:

> The right not to be discriminated against in the enjoyment of the rights guaranteed under the Convention is also violated when States without an objective and reasonable justification fail to treat differently persons whose situations are significantly different.[69]

The Committee in *Autism Europe* v. *France* took this statement and stated that:

> In other words, human difference in a democratic society should not only be viewed positively but should be responded to with discernment in order to ensure real and effective equality.[70]

The Committee's interpretation of indirect discrimination is expansive. The Committee requires a State Party to respond positively and with discernment to human difference, thus requiring States Parties to 'take due and positive account' or to 'take adequate steps' to ensure that the rights within

64 *International Commission of Jurists (ICJ)* v. *Portugal* (n. 34) [32].
65 *AEH* v. *France* (n. 41).
66 *Autism Europe* v. *France* (n. 37) [52].
67 *Thlimmenos* v. *Greece* App no. 34369/97 (ECtHR, 6 April 2000).
68 De Schutter in contrast contends that this case represents the first reasonable accommodation case; see Olivier De Schutter, 'Reasonable Accommodations and Positive Obligations in the European Convention on Human Rights' in Anna Lawson and Caroline Gooding (eds), *Disability Rights in Europe: From Theory to Practice* (Hart Publishing 2005).
69 *Autism Europe* v. *France* (n. 37) [52] citing *Thlimmenos* v. *Greece* (n. 67) [44].
70 *Autism Europe* v. *France* (n. 37) [52].

the ESC(R) are really accessible to all. The Committee in this action suggests that states need to have a positive targeted response to human difference that is arguably a stronger requirement than to just prohibit indirect discrimination. In this case, it was not sufficient that the state had legislatively provided for the right to education for children with disabilities – equally it was not sufficient that it had increased the budget spent and its actions in this regard. The Committee held that the French government had not taken 'adequate steps to ensure that the rights and collective advantages that are open to all are genuinely accessible by and to all'.[71] Lord and Brown contend that this case is about the French school system failing to accommodate the individual needs of students,[72] in effect a collective right to reasonable accommodation.[73] Quinn, on the other hand, suggests that it is the very difference in the treaties that gives rise to this different response:

> Unlike the ECHR, [the ESC(R)] is specifically designed to provide for positive rights. So the equality/non-discrimination ideal takes on a different function. It need not be used to generate positive rights – they are already posited under the instrument. Rather, it calls for sensitivity in the delivery of those rights toward difference.[74]

Thus there is a requirement to respond appropriately to human difference and to ensure 'real and effective equality'.[75] Additionally on the issue of indirect discrimination, the Committee has a highly nuanced understanding of the impact of arguably neutral decisions. For example, in response to the decision of *Autism Europe* v. *France*, the French government introduced a number of action plans and policies in respect of the education of children and adults with autism. These actions had been operationalised in the context of significant budget restrictions. The French government highlighted the cuts that were made in the field of education generally, thus arguably affecting all people regardless of whether they are with or without a disability. In *AEH*

[71] Ibid.

[72] Janet E. Lord and Rebecca Brown, 'The Role of Reasonable Accommodation in Securing Substantive Equality for Persons with Disabilities: The UN Convention on the Rights of Persons with Disabilities' in Marcia H. Rioux, Lee Ann Basser and Melinda Jones (eds), *Critical Perspectives on Human Rights and Disability Law* (Martinus Nijhoff 2011).

[73] The duty to provide reasonable accommodation enshrined in the CRPD is an individualised duty; see Shivaun Quinlivan, Chapter 7, this volume. However, due to the collective nature of complaints taken under the ESC(R), such an individualised approach is not possible. As the Committee continues to develop its equality jurisprudence, we may see a further development of this notion of a collective right to reasonable accommodation.

[74] Quinn (n. 40) 298.

[75] European Committee of Social Rights, *Digest of the Case Law of the European Committee of Social Rights* (n. 17) 176.

v. *France* the government contended that the cutting of social protection funding affects everyone covered by that funding and is not in itself discriminatory. The Committee stated that:

> However, in the specific field of disability, the Committee considers that indirect discrimination can be taken to occur where an apparently neutral provision, criterion or practice would put persons having a disability at a particular disadvantage compared with other persons, unless it can be justified . . .
>
> Accordingly, the Committee considers that a person with a disability is more likely to be dependent on community care, funded through the State budget, in order to live independently and in dignity, as compared with other persons in receipt of community care. The Committee takes the view that budget restrictions in social policy matters are likely to place persons with disabilities at a disadvantage and thus result in a difference in treatment indirectly based on disability.[76]

The Committee accepted that cuts might be required in a state's budgetary allocation. However, a State Party must have regard to the impact of such budgetary cuts. This suggests that it may be necessary for a State Party to equality-proof budgetary decisions. This decision underscores the expansive interpretation of the indirect discrimination concept. Moreover, this decision gave rise to a dissent, which is worth assessing as some of the issues raised highlight the novelty and the potential of the collective complaints process.[77]

4.3 *The Dissent in* AEH *v.* France

France, in *AEH* v. *France*, was found to have violated Article E. Addressing the violation of Article E, the Committee reiterated the fact that disability was covered by the term 'or other status', that Article E covered both direct and indirect discrimination, and that positive duties were imposed on States Parties to make sure all rights were genuinely accessible to all.[78] The core of this decision revolved around the cross-border flow of children and adults with autism from France to Belgium. This fact, according to the majority, was illustrative of

> [the French] Government's failure to cater for the specific schooling needs of all these persons within its national territory, thereby imposing on them a way

76 *AEH* v. *France* (n. 41) [143] and [144].

77 Ibid.; the appendix contains the dissenting opinion of Lauri Leppik joined by Monika Schlachter.

78 Ibid. [133].

> of life different from the treatment reserved for persons not suffering from a mental or physical disability and in the same situation as regards their schooling needs.[79]

The cross-border flow of children from France to Belgium was held to be directly discriminatory. No evidence was ascertained during this case to suggest that children without disabilities were travelling to Belgium to receive an education. However, equally there was no evidence to suggest that they were not. It was France's failure to refute this particular element that allowed the majority of the Committee to find a violation of Article E of the ESC(R) taken in conjunction with Article 15(1). The two dissentients, Leppik and Schlachter, questioned the failure to provide substantive reasoning by the Committee in its finding that the flow of people with autism to Belgium was in fact direct discrimination. The dissent stated:

> that an unjustified failure to provide reasonable accommodation for education of children and adolescents with autism would constitute discrimination on grounds of disability, in the instant case the finding of direct discrimination by the majority of the Committee is based on a remarkably relaxed interpretation of less favourable treatment.[80]

Thus the two dissentients appear to accept that were there an 'unjustified' failure to accommodate, that would amount to discrimination. The use of the term 'unjustified' is curious, suggesting that there may be a justified reason not to provide a reasonable accommodation. But the issue in this case was whether the evidential barrier to prove direct discrimination had actually been met. Leppik and Schlachter assessed the necessity for an appropriate comparator and contended that the Committee should be

> able to demonstrate that persons with autism have been exposed to some detriment or disadvantage because of their disability to which persons unaffected by such disability would either not have been exposed or, in the case of indirect discrimination, have been significantly less exposed.[81]

Leppik and Schlachter contended that a cross-border flow of children and adults with autism was not in itself sufficient to find that in fact these people had suffered a detriment. While accepting that the Committee did not follow the strict evidential barriers imposed in individual non-discrimination

79 Ibid. [135].
80 Ibid. appendix.
81 Ibid.

legislation, this is not, in this author's opinion, a failing of the procedure because, as Bell suggests,

> [b]y highlighting the values underpinning the Charter, such as human dignity or social inclusion, [the Committee] has avoided a narrow and restrictive concept of non-discrimination. It takes a purposive approach with considerable stress on ensuring the practical realisation of rights.[82]

It is undoubtedly true that the principle of non-discrimination adopted by the Committee under the ESC(R) lacks the specific procedural and definitional elements found in other legal regimes, clearly the concern of both Leppik and Schlachter.[83] That noted, it is contended that the system of the ESC(R) does not lend itself as readily to the more formulaic system of non-discrimination adopted in individual complaints. It is the very nature of a collective complaints system that the focus is on patterns of behaviour that may disadvantage groups within society that arise from law or practice. Thus the practice of sending people with autism to Belgium to receive their education where there was no corresponding evidence of this happening with any other group was enough to meet the evidential barrier in this instance. Leppik and Schlachter raise an important issue, and that is the lack of clear principles to apply to allegations of discrimination in the context of a collective complaint. It is suggested that, unlike other non-discrimination regimes, the ESC(R) is still relatively new and will in time develop tenets and doctrines appropriate to a collective regime, which it is proposed should be different to the doctrines as they apply to individual litigation.

5 ENFORCEMENT

It seems appropriate at this juncture to give an overview of the collective complaints system and perhaps to raise a cautionary note. There are many positives to the introduction and interpretation of the ESC(R); however, the system has its weaknesses also, most notably the enforcement procedures.

82 Mark Bell, 'Combating Discrimination through Collective Complaints under the European Social Charter' in Olivier De Schutter (ed.), *The European Social Charter: A Social Constitution for Europe* (Bruylant 2010) 47.

83 See for example the requirements of establishing an action for non-discrimination under the European Union. For a more detailed discussion of this point, see Mark Bell, 'Walking in the Same Direction? The Contribution of the European Social Charter and the European Union to Combating Discrimination' in Gráinne de Búrca and Bruno de Witte (eds), *Social Rights in Europe* (Oxford University Press 2005).

The ESC(R) is primarily enforced through the Committee.[84] The Committee has two main functions, first assessing national reports, and second considering collective complaints. The focus of this section is on the enforcement of the collective complaints mechanism.[85] This section sets out in brief the collective complaints mechanism and then addresses the enforcement procedures under the ESC(R).

5.1 *The Collective Complaints Mechanism*

The collective complaints mechanism was introduced in the Additional Protocol to the European Social Charter 1995.[86] This was part 'of the efforts initiated in 1991 to give a new impetus to the Charter'.[87] The procedure is unusual in a number of respects. The procedure allows for three types of organisation to submit complaints;[88] these are international organisations of employers and trade unions,[89] international non-governmental organisations (INGOs) with consultative status at the Council of Europe[90] and

84 Both the Governmental Committee and the Committee of Ministers play a role in the monitoring of the ESC(R).

85 For a detailed analysis of this system, see De Schutter and Sant'ana (n. 4). Briefly, States Parties report annually but not on every right within the ESC(R). The rights have been categorised into four themes: Group 1 addresses employment, training and equal opportunities; Group 2 addresses health, social security and social protection rights; Group 3 addresses labour rights; Group 4 addresses children, families and migrants. What this means in practice is that States Parties report on each right at least once in every four years. Further it is worth commenting on Article 22, which requires States Parties to report periodically on those provisions it has not accepted. It is hoped that the necessity to report on such measures will in time lead States Parties to agree to ratify the relevant provisions.

86 Additional Protocol to the European Social Charter Providing for a System of Collective Complaints (opened for signature 9 November 1995, entered into force 1 July 1998) CETS No. 158; for more information on this system, see Philip Alston, 'Assessing the Strengths and Weaknesses of the European Social Charter's Supervisory System' in Gráinne de Búrca and Bruno de Witte (eds), *Social Rights in Europe* (Oxford University Press 2005); Mark Bell, 'Combating Discrimination through Collective Complaints under the European Social Charter' in The European Network of Legal Experts in the Non-Discrimination Field, European Anti-Discrimination Law Review (European Commission 2006[3]); Régis Brillat, 'A New Protocol to the European Social Charter Providing for Collective Complaints' (1996) *European Human Rights Law Review* 52; Holly Cullen, 'The Collective Complaints System of the European Social Charter: Interpretative Methods of the European Committee of Social Rights' (2009) 9 *Human Rights Law Review* 61; Churchill and Khaliq (n. 7).

87 Brillat (n. 86) 58.

88 For a full list of the organisations entitled to take action, see www.coe.int/en/web/turin-european-social-charter/collective-complaints-procedure1, accessed 13 July 2017.

89 Additional Protocol to the European Social Charter Providing for a System of Collective Complaints (n. 86) Article 1(a).

90 Ibid. Article 1(b).

representative national organisations of employers and trade unions.[91] The Committee must, as part of the complaint procedure, ensure that any complaint by an INGO falls within the field of competence of the relevant body, or where a body is a representative body that it does in fact represent the relevant constituency.[92] The Committee has not adopted an overly onerous test in this regard. Churchill and Khaliq describe the test adopted as 'one of "some competence" with regard to the issue raised by the complaint rather than "particular competence" in the matters governed by the Charter'.[93] Additionally any State Party to the Protocol may also permit national non-governmental organisations (NGOs) within its jurisdiction to lodge complaints against it. In fact, of the thirteen parties to the Protocol, only Finland permits NGOs to take complaints against the state. The failure to allow national NGOs to take a complaint may be one of the reasons why the treaty remains underexploited. De Schutter has contended that the failure to allow NGOs to take cases has not proven a significant barrier as many of the INGOs will allow an action taken in its name.[94] From a disability perspective, there are several important INGOs with consultative status, including European Action of the Disabled (AEH), Mental Disability Advocacy Centre (MDAC),[95] European Disability Forum (EDF), International Association of Autism Europe (IAAE) and Inclusion International – Inclusion Europe.

This procedure is a collective procedure, therefore these complaints must relate to alleged non-compliance of a state's law or practice with the provisions of the ESC(R). Individual actions are not permitted.[96] Unlike most non-discrimination systems, this system assesses a State Party's laws, systems and

91 Ibid. Article 1(c).

92 *Syndicat occitan de l'education* v. *France* Complaint No. 23/2003 Decision on Admissibility (European Committee of Social Rights, 13 February 2004) [4]. The Committee noted 'that for the purpose of the collective complaints procedure, representativity is an autonomous concept, not necessarily identical to the national notion of representativity'.

93 Churchill and Khaliq (n. 7) 428.

94 De Schutter, 'The Two Lives of the European Social Charter' (n. 6) 23. One example of this given by De Schutter is *International Federation of Human Rights (FIDH)* v. *Ireland* Complaint No. 42/2007 Decision on the Merits (European Committee of Social Rights, 3 June 2008). In this case, FIDH endorsed the concerns raised by the Free Legal Advice Centre (a national NGO).

95 Most recently MDAC has lodged a collective complaint against Belgium, *MDAC* v. *Belgium* (n. 43). Lodged in May 2014, this complaint addresses inclusive education for children with intellectual and psychosocial disabilities and alleges a violation of Article E in relation to Articles 15 and 17 of the ESC(R).

96 Churchill and Khaliq contend that there may be a 'grey area ... where complaints may be made that the practical application of legislation or an administrative practice, as shown in its application to particular individuals, is contrary to the Charter. It would seem that as long as there are a reasonably significant number of groups of individuals involved demonstrating

practices. But it may also be possible for an individual who alleges a violation of the Charter or the ESC(R) to contact an NGO or an INGO and request that they take an action on his/her behalf. Such an action would, of necessity, need to be sufficiently general to show 'a general pattern of non-compliance'.[97] Regardless of whether an individual can or cannot litigate, this in itself is not a weakness in the system. Bell highlights that

> [t]he collective dimension to group inequality can be lost within individual litigation. Moreover, individuals from those groups that are most marginalised in society are least likely to be equipped to initiate litigation. In contrast, the collective complaints mechanism does not depend on the identification of an individual victim, but places emphasis on patterns of behaviour and the discriminatory effects arising from law and institutional practice.[98]

The collective complaints procedure is perhaps best described as an attempt to address more systemic breaches of the rights contained in the ESC(R) and the Charter. It is this collective nature of the complaint procedure that has also led to the interpretation that there is no necessity to exhaust domestic remedies, which also means that in contrast to other systems this process is relatively speedy.[99] However, the limitations to this system relate to its enforcement.

5.2 *Enforcement of the Collective Complaint*

The Committee's role is a quasi-judicial role and the Committee will apply the law to the facts presented in order to reach its conclusion. On reaching that conclusion, the Committee then adopts a report which will contain its conclusions in respect of the relevant State Party and whether it is in compliance with the ESC(R). This report is not final as it is necessary to transmit that report to the Committee of Ministers of the Council of Europe, and it is then this body which makes the final decision as to whether the complaint is upheld. Article 9 of the Additional Protocol of 1995 provides that if there has been a finding that either of the Charters has not been satisfactorily applied, then 'the Committee of Ministers shall adopt . . . a recommendation addressed

a generality of practice, complaints of this nature will be admissible.' Churchill and Khaliq (n. 7) 431.

97 Ibid. 432.

98 Bell, 'Combating Discrimination through Collective Complaints under the European Social Charter' (n. 86) 17–18.

99 See www.coe.int/en/web/turin-european-social-charter/collective-complaints-procedure1, last accessed 13 July 2017.

to the Contracting Party concerned'.[100] In practice, the Committee of Ministers more often than not adopts a resolution addressed to the relevant State Party. These resolutions often set out what the state has already done and what steps have been taken, and then specify what measures are still required. This procedure of producing resolutions has been criticised as a 'weak response'[101] and 'highly deferential to states'.[102] This deference is evident when consideration is given to the final outcomes of the decision in *World Organisation against Torture (OMCT)* v. *Ireland*.[103]

OMCT v. *Ireland* is the first case taken against Ireland using the collective complaints system. The case was lodged in 2003 and decided in 2005. Ireland was found to be in violation of Article 17 ESC(R). Briefly, in this case, it was alleged that Irish law failed to protect children from corporal punishment. While statutory prohibitions on corporal punishment were in place, Irish common law permitted the use of moderate or reasonable chastisement of a child.[104] This acted as a defence to a charge of assault against a child. This defence was available to parents and other persons *in loco parentis*.[105] While there were many prohibitions in law and regulations on the use of corporal punishment, the OMCT sought to challenge the 'gaps in legal coverage'.[106] The Irish government defended the action and among its arguments it maintained 'that the law adequately protects children from serious assault in that serious forms of assault/punishment will not attract the defence of reasonable chastisement'.[107] Therefore, where the punishment goes beyond what would be deemed to be the reasonable chastisement of a child, a parent or a person *in loco parentis* could in fact be prosecuted. The Committee found

100 Additional Protocol to the European Social Charter Providing for a System of Collective Complaints (n. 86) Article 9(1).

101 David John Harris and John Darcy, *The European Social Charter* (Procedural Aspects of International Law Series vol. 25, 2nd edn, Transnational Publishers 2001) 367; Bell, 'Combating Discrimination through Collective Complaints under the European Social Charter' (n. 86); Churchill and Khaliq (n. 7); Cullen (2009) (n. 86); De Schutter, *The European Social Charter* (n. 4).

102 Cullen (2005) (n. 12) 77.

103 *World Organisation against Torture (OMCT)* v. *Ireland* Complaint No. 18/2003 Decision on the Merits (European Committee of Social Rights, 7 December 2004).

104 Section 24 of the Non-Fatal Offences Against the Person Act 1997 prohibits teachers from using physical chastisement of pupils; the Child Care (Pre School Services) Regulations 1996 and (Amendment) Regulations 1997 prohibit the use of corporal punishment in preschool; Section 58 of the Child Care Act 1991 prohibits certain categories of child carers from using corporal punishment; Section 201 Children Act 2001 also prohibits corporal punishment.

105 It was alleged that those in *loco parentis* could include foster care, residential homes and in some instances child minders.

106 Cullen (2005) (n. 12) 75.

107 *World Organisation against Torture (OMCT)* v. *Ireland* (n. 103) [40].

that Ireland was in violation of Article 17 of the ESC(R), and in reaching this finding it stated that:

> [T]he prohibition of all the forms of violence must have a legislative basis. The prohibition must cover all forms of violence regardless of where it occurs or the identity of the alleged perpetrator. Furthermore the sanctions available must be adequate, dissuasive and proportionate.[108]

Many elements of this decision are interesting, including the requirement imposed to have a legislative basis for the rights protected within the ESC(R) and the positive obligation imposed on the state to have an appropriate system of sanctions. But what is perhaps of most relevance at this point is to assess the outcome of this decision. The decision was referred to the Committee of Ministers, who failed to adopt a recommendation but instead adopted a resolution.[109] According to this resolution, the Committee of Ministers

> Takes note of the intention of the Department of Health and Children to seek legal advice in relation to amending the regulations to make more explicit the prohibition of corporal punishment of children in care, and on the need for any change required in primary legislation.
>
> Takes note of the intention of the government to keep the introduction of an outright ban on corporal punishment under review.[110]

This resolution hardly equates to the decision of the Committee and is incredibly deferential to the State Party. Moreover, for some time there was little or no response to this decision by the relevant State Party. In its periodic reports Ireland was asked to address the progress in this area and for twelve years Ireland remained in 'non-conformity on the ground that corporal punishment is not explicitly prohibited in the home'.[111] In late 2015, the Irish government finally passed legislation removing the defence of reasonable chastisement.[112] This action was taken twelve years after the complaint was instigated, while disappointing, and indicative of the fact that the enforcement mechanisms are weak, it is equally clear that they are not entirely without teeth.[113]

108 Ibid. [64].

109 'Resolution ResChS(2005)9' (8 June 2005).

110 Ibid.

111 European Committee of Social Rights, 'Conclusions 2011 – Ireland – Article 17-1' (2011/def/IRL/17/1/EN, *HUDOC*, 10 January 2012) 4, http://hudoc.esc.coe.int/eng?i=2011/def/IRL/17/1/EN, accessed 14 July 2017.

112 Children First Act 2015 (Ireland).

113 It was also evident in the decision of *AEH* v. *France* (n. 41) that France had taken significant actions on the basis of the previous decision of *Autism Europe* v. *France* (n. 37).

That concern noted it must be acknowledged that in the majority of cases the Committee of Ministers does not contest the content of the Committee's decisions and equally it is clear that the Committee considers its decision a legally binding interpretation of the Charter. Further, as Bell notes, this is a collective process where 'compliance with the decisions is ultimately an ongoing process'.[114] Equally, Quinn suggests that 'it would be a mistake to telescope the value of the Charter into an analysis of the outcomes it could legally drive'.[115] Rather he suggests that the value of the ESC(R) is 'how effectively it can become an expositor of social values'.[116] It is this author's contention that it would be unfortunate if the case law of the Committee became no more than an 'expositor of social values'. While performing an educative role is important, arguably it is also crucial that these cases drive legal change.

6 CONCLUSION

The review of Articles 15 and 17 of the ESC(R) presents a number of distinct findings. The first significant finding is that there is a significant overlap of the material scope of both articles. Additionally, the failure to ratify Article 15 will ensure that the right to education of a child with a disability will be assessed under Article 17.[117] In the case law to date it has been established that when considering the education rights of children with disabilities, Article 17 is guided by the philosophy of Article 15.

Article 15 is imbued with the concepts of non-discrimination, with references to equal citizenship, 'independence, social integration and participation in the life of the community'.[118] This means in practice there is a strong presumption in favour of mainstream educational provision for children with disabilities; this presumption is evident in the cases decided to date. While there is a presumption in favour of mainstream education, there is an express acceptance that segregated or separate provision may be necessary on occasion. The Committee has held that in order for education to happen in a forum other than the mainstream, a variety of factors need to be considered,

114 Bell, 'Combating Discrimination through Collective Complaints under the European Social Charter' (n. 86) 18.

115 Quinn (n. 40) 283.

116 Quinn (n. 40) 283.

117 European Committee of Social Rights, *Digest of the Case Law of the European Committee of Social Rights* (n. 17) 121; European Committee of Social Rights, 'Conclusions 2005 – Bulgaria – Article 17-2' (n. 35).

118 *Autism Europe* v. *France* (n. 37) [48].

including 'the type of disability concerned, how serious it is and a variety of individual circumstances to be examined on a case-by-case basis'.[119] Thus it may be assumed that any automatically exclusionary practices will fall foul of the obligations contained in the Charter.

Articles 15 and 17 taken together or separately impose explicit and demanding obligations on states to proactively vindicate the right to education protected by these articles. The Committee in its *Digest of Jurisprudence* required States Parties to be able to 'demonstrate that tangible progress is being made in setting up education systems which exclude nobody'.[120] The significance of that onerous obligation was perhaps most evident in the decision in *AEH* v. *France.*[121]

Additionally the Committee in its case law to date has shown a willingness to look beyond enacted positive law that appears on its face to accord with the requirements of the ESC(R) but has assessed the de facto position to determine compliance.[122] Effectively the issue is not about legislating for the rights within the ESC(R) but it is about the effective implementation of those guaranteed rights. All of these cases serve to emphasise the argument that the extent of protection afforded to the right to education for children with disabilities far exceeds that provided for by the more famous sibling (ECHR).

The most problematic element of the ESC(R) must relate to the enforcement procedures. It is contended by many that they lack the necessary teeth to drive legal change, or at least timely change. It is contended here that the case law does result in change – but slow change. This is perhaps best evidenced in the decision of *AEH* v. *France* where France highlighted the extensive actions taken by that state on foot of the earlier case *Autism* v. *France*. So notwithstanding the criticisms of the collective complaint procedure and its apparent lack of teeth, it is undoubted that these decisions do result in change, albeit not at the pace one would hope for. While the enforcement is undoubtedly problematic, other, positive findings point to the potential of the ESC(R) mechanisms to bring about change. Of particular note, the introduction of an explicit article on non-discrimination to the ESC(R) has resulted in a rich vein of equality case law, thus reflecting 'the heightened importance the drafters paid to the principle of non-discrimination'.[123]

Article E very clearly reflects Article 14 ECHR in both wording and applicability. Like Article 14, Article E does not constitute an autonomous right

[119] *AEH* v. *France* (n. 41) [78].

[120] *Digest of the Case Law of the European Committee of Social Rights* (n. 17) 112.

[121] *AEH* v. *France* (n. 41).

[122] *Autism Europe* v. *France* (n. 37); *AEH* v. *France* (n. 41); *MDAC* v. *Bulgaria* (n. 18).

[123] *Autism Europe* v. *France* (n. 37) [51].

which gives rise to an independent ground for a complaint. It is always necessary to invoke Article E in conjunction with another substantive provision of the Charter. As both Articles 15 and 17 are relevant to the right to education for children with disabilities, the parasitic nature of Article E is unproblematic. That noted, this may prove more problematic in the development of a body of equality jurisprudence generally. As with Article 14, Article E has been interpreted to ensure that people with disabilities are covered by the scope of this article by means of the phrase 'or other status'.[124] While there are evident similarities between Article E and Article 14 ECHR, the obvious difference lies in the interpretation of the two provisions.

Article E has benefited from a robust interpretation that from the outset accepted that the provision covered both direct and indirect discrimination.[125] Additionally, the Committee has shown a willingness to impose strong positive obligations on States Parties to respect human difference and to respond to that difference 'to ensure real and effective equality'.[126] It is evident that the level and nature of the duty imposed by the ESC(R) contrasts significantly from those imposed by the ECHR. Additionally while the Committee has yet to expressly base a decision on the failure to provide reasonable accommodation, it is suggested here that the mood music from the Committee suggests that this will be positively received. For example, even the dissentients Leppik and Schlachter accepted the principle that an unjustified failure to provide reasonable accommodation for people with autism in the exercise of their right to education would be discriminatory.[127] The Committee in *AEH* v. *France* ultimately determined that there had been direct discrimination against the applicants. As the Committee grapples with the notion of a collective right to reasonable accommodation, it is hoped that it looks to both the CRPD and the emerging jurisprudence from the CRPD Committee to guide it in its interpretation of the duty to accommodate specifically and more importantly on the right to inclusive education.

124 Ibid.; see also *AEH* v. *France* (n. 41); *MDAC* v. *Bulgaria* (n. 18).
125 *Autism Europe* v. *France* (n. 37) [52].
126 Ibid.
127 *AEH* v. *France* (n. 41) [35].

18

The Scope of Recognition and Protection of the Right to Inclusive Education in the African Human Rights System

Japhet Biegon*

INTRODUCTION

The past ten years (2009–2019) have seen the acceleration of the development of a legal and institutional disability rights framework within the African human rights system. The African Commission on Human and Peoples' Rights (African Commission), the system's principal human rights treaty body, has been instrumental in steering this crucial and exciting development. Inspired by the adoption of the United Nations (UN) Convention on the Rights of Persons with Disabilities (CRPD) in 2006,[1] the African Commission commenced the process of developing an African regional disability rights treaty in 2009.[2] After a protracted process spanning eight solid years, the African Commission adopted the Draft Protocol to the African Charter on Human and Peoples' Rights on the Rights of Persons with Disabilities in Africa (Draft Africa Disability Protocol) in February 2016.[3] In 2017, the Draft Africa Disability Protocol was reviewed by government ministers responsible for matters related to persons with disabilities (PWDs). Its final text was formally

* LLD, LLM (University of Pretoria), LLB (Moi University). Extraordinary Lecturer, Centre for Human Rights, Faculty of Law, University of Pretoria and Africa Regional Advocacy Coordinator, Amnesty International. Email: japhet.biegon@gmail.com. The views expressed in this chapter are solely the author's and do not in any way represent or reflect the views of Amnesty International. This chapter is dedicated to the memory of my eldest brother, Joseph Kibet (1969–1987).

1 GA Res. 61/106, UN Doc. A/RES/61/106 (December 13, 2006).

2 Resolution on the Transformation of the Focal Point on the Rights of Older Persons in Africa into a Working Group on the Rights of Older Persons and People with Disabilities in Africa, ACHPR/Res. 143 (XXXXV) 09 (adopted at the forty-fifth ordinary session of the African Commission on Human and Peoples' Rights, Banjul, The Gambia, May 13–27, 2009).

3 Final communiqué of the nineteenth extraordinary session of the African Commission on Human and Peoples' Rights, Banjul, The Gambia, February 16–25, 2016, para. 11.

adopted as the Protocol to the African Charter on Human and Peoples' Rights on the Rights of Persons with Disabilities in Africa (Africa Disability Protocol) in January 2018.

The development of the Africa Disability Protocol attests to the African Commission's growing focus on the plight of PWDs in Africa. The Africa Disability Protocol sits proudly at the peak of the Commission's work on disability rights. Its other main activity since 2013 has been the adoption of thematic or standard-setting resolutions on various aspects related to the promotion and protection of the rights of PWDs in the continent.[4] These resolutions have animated a system that was hitherto passive and extremely underutilized in terms of securing and safeguarding the rights of PWDs.[5]

An important, yet largely unacknowledged, effect of the African Commission's recent focus on PWDs is the rapidly increasing academic literature on disability rights in Africa. The research door was swung open by Grobbelaar-du Plessis and van Reenen's 2011 *Aspects of Disability Law in Africa*.[6] Then came the launch of the *African Disability Rights Yearbook* in 2013, which, true to its objective, is gradually "bring[ing] into prominence an area traditionally neglected by both governments and academics."[7] Outside these two publications, there is a growing catalogue of peer-reviewed journal articles. Thus far, scholars examining disability rights from a regional angle have focused on two broad issues. First, scholars have debated whether an African regional disability rights treaty is feasible and desirable.[8] With the

4 Resolution on the Attacks on Persons with Albinism in Malawi, ACHPR/Res. 349 (Ext.OS/XX) 2016 (adopted at the twentieth extraordinary session of the African Commission on Human and Peoples' Rights, Banjul, The Gambia, June 9–18, 2016); Resolution on the Prevention of Attacks and Discrimination against Persons with Albinism (adopted at the African Commission on Human and Peoples' Rights, Banjul, The Gambia, October 22–November 5, 2013); Resolution on Accessibility for Persons with Disabilities, ACHPR/Res. 305 (EXT.OS/XVIII) 2015 (adopted at the eighteenth extraordinary session of the African Commission on Human and Peoples' Rights, Nairobi, Kenya, July 29–August 7, 2015); Resolution on the Right to Dignity and Freedom from Torture or Ill-Treatment of Persons with Psychological Disabilities in Africa, ACHPR/Res. 343 (LVIII) 2016 (adopted at the fifty-eighth ordinary session of the African Commission on Human and Peoples' Rights, Banjul, The Gambia, April 6–20, 2016); Resolution on the Regional Action Plan on Albinism in Africa (2017–2012), ACHPR/Res. 373 (LX) 2017 (adopted at the sixtieth ordinary session of the African Commission on Human and Peoples' Rights, Niamey, Niger, May 8–22, 2017).

5 J. Biegon, "The Promotion and Protection of Disability Rights in the African Human Rights System" in I. Grobbelaar-du Plessis and T. van Reenen (eds.), *Aspects of Disability Law in Africa* (Pretoria: Pretoria University Law Press 2011) 53.

6 I. Grobbelaar-du Plessis and T. van Reenen (eds.), Aspects of Disability Law in Africa (2011).

7 F. Viljoen, "Preface" in African Disability Rights Yearbook, vol. 1 (2013) v.

8 F. Viljoen and J. Biegon, "The Feasibility and Desirability of an African Disability Rights Treaty: Further Norm-Elaboration or Firmer Norm-Implementation?" (2014) *South African Journal of Human Rights* 345; Biegon (n. 5); S. Kamga, "A Call for a Protocol to the African

adoption of the Draft Africa Disability Protocol in February 2016, opinions somehow converged.[9] A consensus has been built that indeed an Africa disability rights treaty is necessary. Second, scholars have systematically tracked and documented regional developments relating to disability rights. As expected, their institutional focus is on the African Commission and the African Children's Committee.[10] Other authors have concentrated on developments at the subregional level.[11]

Arguably, the time is now ripe to consider and analyze the emerging scope of recognition and protection of specific rights of PWDs within the African human rights system. In this context, this chapter focuses on the right to inclusive education as read into the existing regional human rights treaties by their respective monitoring bodies and as framed in Article 14 of the Africa Disability Protocol. As part of the burgeoning literature on disability rights in Africa, numerous authors have examined the extent to which the right to inclusive education is guaranteed at the domestic level. The countries covered include Botswana,[12] Cameroon,[13] Kenya,[14] Malawi,[15] Nigeria,[16] and South

Charter on Human and Peoples' Rights on the Rights of Persons with Disabilities in Africa" (2013) 21 *African Journal of International & Comparative Law* 219; L. Oyaro, "Africa at Crossroads: The United Nations Convention on the Rights of Persons with Disabilities" (2015) 30 *American University International Law Review* 347.

9 H. Combrinck, "Disability Rights in the African Regional Human Rights System during 2011 and 2012" (2013) 1 *Africa Disability Rights Yearbook* 361, 367.

10 Ibid. 361; H. Combrinck and L. Mute, "Developments Regarding Disability Rights during 2013: The African Charter and African Commission on Human and Peoples' Rights" (2014) 2 *African Disability Rights Yearbook* 309; L. Wakefield, "Making Progress: The African Committee of Experts on the Rights and Welfare of the Child and the Rights of Children with Disabilities" (2013) 1 *African Disability Rights Yearbook* 369; L. Wakefield, "Baby Steps: Developments at the African Committee on the Rights and Welfare of the Child (2013–2014)" (2014) 2 *African Disability Rights Yearbook* 319, 321–322.

11 L. Murungi, A. Mandlate, and B. Armah, "Disability Rights in the Sub-Regional Economic Communities during 2011 and 2012" (2013) 1 *African Disability Rights Yearbook* 375; L. Murungi, "Disability Rights in the Sub-Regional Economic Communities during 2013" (2014) 2 *African Disability Rights Yearbook* 323.

12 J. Obonye, "The Right to Inclusive Education in Botswana: Present Challenges and Future Prospects" (2014) 2 *African Disability Rights Yearbook* 3.

13 S. Kamga, "Forgotten or Included? Disabled Children's Access to Primary Education in Cameroon" (2013) 1 *African Disability Rights Yearbook* 27.

14 W. Aseka and A. Kanter, "The Basic Education Act of 2013: Why It Is One Step Forward and Two Steps Back for Children with Disabilities in Kenya" (2014) 2 *African Disability Rights Yearbook* 33.

15 E. Chilemba, "The Right to Primary Education of Children with Disabilities in Malawi: A Diagnosis of the Conceptual Approach and Implementation" (2013) 1 *African Disability Rights Yearbook* 3.

16 B. Akinbola, "The Right to Inclusive Education in Nigeria: Meeting the Needs and Challenges of Children with Disabilities" (2010) 10 *African Human Rights Law Journal* 457.

Africa.[17] Understandably, the departure point for such country reviews is Article 24 of the CRPD. This chapter adds to the existing literature by critically looking into the scope of recognition and protection of the right to inclusive education at the regional level.

The chapter is structurally divided into two major parts. The first part examines the existing regional framework relating to the right to education, PWDs, and inclusive education. Both African Union (AU) policy documents and human rights treaties are examined. The practices of the regional human rights treaties are also analyzed. The second part discusses the scope of recognition and protection of the right to inclusive education under the Africa Disability Protocol. It briefly traces the drafting history of the Protocol, provides a quick overview of its contents, and then narrows the analysis down to the provision on inclusive education. Although the right to inclusive education accrues to all PWDs, the focus of this chapter is predominantly on children with disabilities.

EXISTING REGIONAL FRAMEWORK ON THE RIGHT TO INCLUSIVE EDUCATION

The world is home to about 150 million children with disabilities.[18] The majority of these children, 80 per cent to be exact, are in developing countries.[19] In Africa, the prospects for a child with disabilities to receive an education or attend school is acutely slim. According to rough estimates, less than 10 per cent of children with disabilities in Africa receive some form of education.[20] These numbers are staggering and are sustained by the failure of the majority of African states to put in place laws, policies, and structures for ensuring that children with disabilities have an equal access to education. The 2014 *African Report on Children with Disabilities* reveals that children with disabilities are either "absent from, or referred to only marginally in, many public law and policy documents pertaining to education and social development plans."[21] Only a handful of countries, such as Kenya, Sierra

[17] W. Holness, "The Development and Use of Sign Language in South African Schools: The Denial of Inclusive Education" (2016) 4 *African Disability Rights Yearbook* 141.

[18] African Child Policy Forum, Educating Children with Disabilities in Africa: Towards a Policy of Inclusion (2011) 1.

[19] Ibid.

[20] African Child Policy Forum, The African Report on Children with Disabilities: Promising Starts and Persisting Challenges (2014) 67.

[21] African Child Policy Forum (n. 20) 69.

Leone, South Africa, and Uganda, have constitutional provisions or some form of legislation on the right of children with disabilities to education.[22]

The failure of states at the domestic level underscores the relevance of regional or international human rights law, which at its best serves as a "normative beacon, beckoning states to an internationally agreed-upon minimum standard of behaviour, and a 'safety net' for individuals who are denied their rights under the domestic system, or who fall through the cracks of the national legal system."[23] At the African regional level, this "normative beacon" is largely fragmented and incoherent.[24] The normative standards for the promotion and protection of the rights of PWDs in general, and their right to education in particular, are scattered in several human rights treaties. These regional treaties exist within a broader political environment, and in particular, within the auspices of the AU. Ensuring that all children have access to education has been on the agenda of the AU since its inception, and on the agenda of its predecessor, the Organization of African Unity (OAU), as well. In this regard, the OAU/AU has adopted several policy documents that are relevant to the right to inclusive education. In this section, the relevant AU human rights treaties and policy documents are analyzed to ascertain the extent to which they recognize and protect the right to inclusive education.

AFRICAN UNION POLICY DOCUMENTS

In 1979, the OAU adopted the Declaration on the Rights and Welfare of the African Child.[25] The Declaration urged OAU member states to formulate and implement programs in three main fields: health, nutrition, and education. It stated that the purpose of these programs should be to ensure that services in the three fields are "universally accessible to all children within the shortest possible time."[26] The Declaration was specifically relevant to children with disabilities for two reasons. First, it required all domestic-level programs aimed at expanding essential services to pay "particular attention" to children with disabilities.[27] Second, it somehow provided a regional normative basis for the establishment of segregated schools. In specific terms, it suggested that where states find difficulties in providing education within "convention school

22 Ibid.
23 F. Viljoen, International Human Rights Law in Africa (2012) 9.
24 Biegon (n. 5) 67.
25 OAU Doc. AHG/st.4 (XIV) Rev.1(1979).
26 Declaration on the Rights and Welfare of the Child, para. 6(a).
27 Ibid., para. 6(b).

system[s]," they should explore "alternative strategies for establishing educational facilities."[28]

In 1999, the OAU proclaimed the period 1999–2009 the African Decade of Persons with Disabilities.[29] A continental plan of action, outlining twelve broad objectives of the Decade, was subsequently formulated.[30] On education for children with disabilities, the Plan of Action was clearly and openly in favor of integration as opposed to inclusion. It urged states to develop policies aimed at ensuring that children with disabilities have access to "education in integrated settings at all levels."[31] Where it was not possible to provide education in integrated settings, states were encouraged to make provision for special education.[32] The Plan of Action saw inclusive education as an ideal to be promoted rather than a policy issue to be implemented immediately.[33] Essentially, the Plan of Action saw inclusive education as a far-distant goal. It has been suggested that the drafters of the Plan of Action understood inclusive education to mean "integration of learners into the mainstream classroom."[34] However, the Plan of Action itself supports a different conclusion. The Plan of Action proposes two entirely different approaches to integrated and inclusive education. The former should be implemented while the latter should be promoted. Clearly, the drafters knew the distinction between the two forms of education but chose one over the other.

In October 2012, the AU extended the African Decade of Persons with Disabilities to the period 2010–2019.[35] A new continental plan of action is now in place.[36] It fully embraces the concept of inclusive education and drops all references to integrated and/or special education. Persons with disabilities are expected to enjoy "universally inclusive and accessible quality education" during the new Decade.[37] To achieve this goal, AU member states are

28 Ibid., para. 7.

29 OAU Assembly of Heads of State and Government, thirty-sixth ordinary session, Lomé, Togo, July 6–8, 2000, Decision CM/Dec. 535 (LXXII) Rev. 1.

30 African Union, *Continental Plan of Action for the African Decade of Persons with Disabilities* (1999–2009) (2002).

31 Plan of Action (1999–2009), para. 30(a).

32 Ibid., para. 30(b).

33 Ibid., para. 30(h).

34 Unpublished LLD thesis: L. Murungi, The Significance of Article 24(2) of the UN Convention on the Rights of Persons with Disabilities for the Right to Primary Education of Children with Disabilities: A Comparative Study of Kenya and South Africa, University of Western Cape, South Africa (2013) 98.

35 AU Executive Council, Addis Ababa, Ethiopia, January 26–30, 2009, Decision EX.CL/Dec. 473(XIV).

36 African Union, *Continental Plan of Action for the African Decade of Persons with Disabilities*.

37 Ibid., para. 2.7.1.2.

required to implement fifteen priority actions, ranging from ensuring that educational facilities are physically accessible to PWDs to providing "individualized support measures."[38]

At least two other AU policy documents are relevant to any discussion on the evolution of the AU's approach to and activities on the right to education for PWDs in Africa. The first is the Africa Fit for Children Declaration and Plan of Action adopted in May 2001.[39] It called on African states to commit themselves to the provision of "quality, free and compulsory basic education" and to take into account, inter alia, "the special learning needs" of children with disabilities in curriculum development and delivery of education.[40] These calls were renewed in November 2007 during the midterm review of the Declaration and Plan of Action.[41] The second is the Resolution on the Launching of the Decade of Education in Africa (1997–2006).[42] One of the four priority areas during the Decade was access to basic education. A review of the Decade revealed that most of its goals were not achieved.[43] In January 2006, therefore, the AU proclaimed the Second Decade of Education for Africa (2006–2015).[44] The Plan of Action for the Second Decade singled out PWDs for special focus in the provision of basic and secondary education.[45]

It is beyond the scope of this chapter to assess the degree to which AU member states have given effect to these policy commitments. It suffices to say, in the words of the *State of Education in Africa Report 2015*, that "[d]espite tremendous gains in primary school enrolment, no African country has achieved universal primary education."[46] As the statistics previously presented reveal, children with disabilities bear the brunt of this failure.

38 Ibid.

39 African Union, *Africa Fit for Children: The African Common Position as Africa's Contribution to the United Nations General Assembly Special Session on Children, Declaration and Plan of Action*, PANA/FORUM/CHD/DOC.10/Rev.2, Cairo, Egypt, May 28–31, 2001, paras. 29 & (f).

40 Ibid., para. 29(b) & (f).

41 African Union, *Call for Accelerated Action on the Implementation of the Plan of Action towards Africa Fit for Children (2008–2012)*, PANA/FORUM/CHD/MIN/2(II).

42 OAU Assembly of Heads of State and Government, AHG/Res. 251(XXXII) 1996.

43 African Union, *Second Decade of Education for Africa (2006–2015): Plan of Action*, para. 5.

44 AU Assembly, Decision on a Second Decade of Education for Africa (2006–2015) and the Framework of the Plan of Action for the Second Decade, Assembly/AUIU/Dec.92 (VI).

45 African Union, *Second Decade of Education for Africa (2006–2015): Plan of Action*, para. 28(ii).

46 The Africa-America Institute, *State of Education in Africa Report 2015: A Report Card on the Progress, Opportunities and Challenges Confronting the African Education Sector* (2016) 7.

AFRICAN UNION HUMAN RIGHTS TREATIES

Africa has three main regional human rights treaties. These are the African Charter on Human and Peoples' Rights in Africa (African Charter),[47] the Protocol to the African Charter on Human and Peoples' Rights on the Rights of Women in Africa (African Women's Protocol),[48] and the African Charter on the Rights and Welfare of the Child (African Children's Charter).[49] The African Commission is responsible for monitoring the implementation of the African Charter and the African Women's Protocol while the African Committee of Experts on the Rights and Welfare of the Child supervises the implementation of the African Children's Charter.

THE AFRICAN CHARTER AND THE PROTOCOL ON WOMEN'S RIGHTS

The African Charter is the cornerstone of the African human rights system. Both as a group and as individuals, PWDs are entitled to all the rights enshrined in the African Charter. In fact, Article 18 provides that PWDs (and older persons) have the right to "special measures of protection." On the right to education, the Charter provides that "every individual shall have the right to education." Through its complaints or communications procedure, the African Commission has had at least three opportunities to elaborate on the content of the right to education.[50] Unfortunately, it has squandered all these chances. In each of the three cases, the African Commission has found a violation of the right to education but without providing sufficient reasoning for its decision.[51] As such, the African Commission's jurisprudence offers little guidance on the nature and scope of Article 17(1). Such guidance is partly to be found in the 1989 Guidelines for National Periodic Report in which the African Commission require states to

47 OAU Doc. CAB LEG/67/3 rev.3, adopted on June 26, 1981, and entered into force on October 21, 1986.

48 Adopted on July 11, 2003, in Maputo, Mozambique, and entered into force on November 25, 2005.

49 OAU Doc. CAB/LEG/24.9/49, adopted on July 11, 1990, and entered into force on November 29, 1999.

50 *Free Legal Assistance Group* v. *Zaire* (2000) AHRLR 74 (ACHPR 1995); *Union Interafricaine des Droits de l'Homme & Others* v. *Angola* (2000) AHRLR 18 (ACHPR 1997); *The Nubian Community in Kenya* v. *Kenya*, Communication 317/06.

51 C. Mbazira, "Enforcing the Economic, Social and Cultural Rights in the African Charter on Human and Peoples' Rights: Twenty Years of Redundancy and Significant Strides" (2006) 6 *African Human Rights Law Journal* 333, 344–346.

report on the level of access to free and compulsory primary education as well as to secondary and higher education.[52] States are also required to indicate any "special provisions" they have taken in relation to, inter alia, children with disabilities.[53]

In 1981 when the African Charter was adopted, the concept of inclusive education had yet to crystalize into a right recognized in international human rights law. This only happened in 2006 with the adoption of the CRPD. In 2011, the African Commission formally expanded the content of the right to education under Article 17(1) to include inclusive education. In the Nairobi Principles and Guidelines on the Implementation of Economic, Social and Cultural Rights,[54] adopted at its forty-ninth ordinary session (April 28–May 11, 2011), the African Commission stated that Article 17 imposes on states the obligation:

> [t]o ensure that all children with disabilities are provided with inclusive quality and free primary education and access to inclusive quality secondary and tertiary education on an equal basis with other members of their communities.[55]

Essentially, the African Commission read the right to inclusive education into Article 17(1). In 2016, the African Commission provided further guidance on the content of the right to education through Resolution 346 on the Right to Education in Africa.[56] Drawing inspiration from both the CRPD and the Draft Africa Disability Protocol, Resolution 346 clarifies that the "full scope of the right to education" encompasses an obligation to provide "reasonable accommodation measures for children with disabilities and in particular girls with disabilities, [and] to ensure inclusive quality education on an equal basis with other members of their communities consistent with the goal of full inclusion."[57] The Resolution also provides that all children should enjoy "free and compulsory primary education without distinction" and that

52 African Commission on Human and Peoples' Rights, Guidelines for National Periodic Reporting (1989) paras. 41–58.

53 Ibid., para. 47(a).

54 Principles and Guidelines on the Implementation of Economic, Social and Cultural Rights in the African Charter on Human and Peoples' Rights, adopted at the forty-ninth ordinary session of the African Commission on Human and Peoples' Rights, Banjul, The Gambia, April 28–May 11, 2011.

55 Ibid., para. 71(t).

56 Resolution on the Right to Education in Africa, ACHPR/Res. 346 (LVIII) 2016 (adopted at the fifty-eighth ordinary session of the African Commission on Human and Peoples' Rights, Banjul, The Gambia, April 6–20, 2016).

57 Ibid.

educational programs should serve the needs of all sectors of society, including children with disabilities.[58]

The African Commission's Tunis Reporting Guidelines on Economic, Social and Cultural Rights, which were adopted at the same time as the Nairobi Principles, require states to indicate in their periodic reports the measures they have taken to ensure inclusive education for children with disabilities.[59] State compliance with the Tunis Reporting Guidelines is generally low. The majority of states do not delve into the question of inclusive education in their periodic reports. It could be that they are unaware of the Tunis Reporting Guidelines or that they have little to report about. However, South Africa, which has a fairly comprehensive policy on inclusive education, simply mentioned, almost in passing, a case law relating to the right to education of children with severe intellectual disabilities.[60] The country's report provides no further details on the steps taken to implement inclusive education. Nigeria's report exclusively focused on policy measures taken to "integrate" children with albinism (incorrectly referred to as "Albinos") into the "school system."[61] No other information is provided beyond this narrow focus.[62] If Nigeria's report is too narrow, then Ethiopia's is too generic. Examined by the African Commission in April 2015, Ethiopia's fifth and sixth combined periodic report only says that students with disabilities benefit from affirmative action.[63]

Mauritius stands apart from the rest of the countries. In its report examined by the African Commission in October 2016, detailed facts are provided regarding the extent to which inclusive education is guaranteed domestically. The report provides a list of twenty different measures taken by the state

58 Ibid.

59 State Party Reporting Guidelines for Economic, Social and Cultural Rights in the African Charter on Human and Peoples' Rights (Tunis Reporting Guidelines), adopted at the at the forty-ninth ordinary session of the African Commission on Human and Peoples' Rights, Banjul, The Gambia, April 28–May 11, 2011.

60 Republic of South Africa, Combined Second Periodic Report under the African Charter on Human and Peoples' Rights and Initial Report under the Protocol to the African Charter on the Rights of Women in Africa (2015) para. 340.

61 Federal Republic of Nigeria, Nigeria's 5th Periodic Report on the Implementation of the African Charter on Human and Peoples' Rights (2014) 107.

62 It may be speculated that Nigeria's exclusive focus on persons with albinism is related to the African Commission's call in Resolution 263 on the Prevention of Attacks and Discrimination against Persons with Albinism. In this Resolution, the African Commission urged states to "include in their reports . . . information on the situation of persons with albinism including good practices in protecting and promoting the rights of persons with albinism."

63 Federal Republic of Ethiopia, The Fifth and Sixth Periodic Country Report (2009–2013) on the Implementation of the African Charter on Human and Peoples' Rights (2014) 87.

to ensure "no child is deprived of education on account of any form of impairment or disability."[64] The report makes reference to both "inclusion" and "integration," suggesting that though Mauritius remains a top performer on the continent, inclusive education is yet to supplant integrated or segregated education in the country.[65] Another country that stands out is Niger, albeit for a different reason. Unlike other countries, Niger structured its July 2014 report in such a manner that the contents respond to all the requirements set out in the Tunis Reporting Guidelines. On the requirement to report on inclusive education, the state indicates that it has established "inclusive classrooms in primary and secondary education to include children with disabilities."[66] Unfortunately, this is all the information that is volunteered.

The African Commission is also charged with the responsibility of interpreting and monitoring state implementation of the African Women's Protocol.[67] The provisions of the African Women's Protocol on the right to education are pretty extensive. In particular, Article 12 of the Protocol require states to, among other things, guarantee equal opportunity and access to education and training, eliminate stereotypes, protect women and girls from abuse and harassment in schools, and promote literacy. However, the normative contours of the right to education as protected in Article 12 remain unelaborated. Although Resolution 346 of the African Commission relates to Article 17 of the African Charter, it fortunately places particular emphasis on inclusive education for girls with disabilities.

AFRICAN CHILDREN'S CHARTER

Adopted barely a year after the UN Convention on the Rights of the Child (CRC),[68] the African Children's Charter is a product of the actualization of a deep desire among African countries to have "a distinctively African

64 Republic of Mauritius, Sixth to Eighth Combined Periodic Report on the Implementation of the African Charter on Human and Peoples' Rights (May 2009–December 2015) (March 2016) para. 109.

65 See Committee on the Rights of Persons with Disabilities, Concluding Observations on the Initial Report of Mauritius, CRPD/C/MUS/CI/1 (September 30, 2015), para. 33 (noting that the education system in Mauritius remains "mostly segregated" and that many children with disabilities are "completely deprived of any form of education").

66 Republic of Niger, Combined Periodic Report, 2003–2014 (2014) para. 269.

67 African Women's Protocol, Articles 26 and 27.

68 1577 UNTS 3, UN Doc. A/RES/44/25, adopted November 20, 1989, and entered into force September 2, 1990.

framework" for the promotion and protection of children's rights.[69] The Charter has a dedicated provision on children with disabilities. Article 13(1) stipulates that children with disabilities are entitled to "special measures of protection" as a matter of right. Under Article 13(2), children with disabilities and those responsible for them are entitled to assistance at the state's expense, subject to availability of resources. Three areas in which such assistance is due are specifically mentioned: training, preparation for employment, and recreation. Commentators have correctly pointed out that the omission of education (and health care and rehabilitation services) from this list is regrettable.[70]

The right to education is covered under Article 11 of the African Children's Charter. The specific measures stipulated to realize the right include the following: free and compulsory basic education, and secondary education in its different forms and progressively made free and accessible to all.[71] Although the Charter refers to "basic" rather than "primary" education, it is generally understood that the two terms mean one and the same thing.[72] In the case of *IHRDA and Another (on behalf of Children of Nubian descent in Kenya)* v. *Kenya*,[73] the African Children's Committee observed that the provision of free and compulsory basic education "necessitate[s] the provision of schools, qualified teachers, equipment and the well-recognized corollaries of the fulfillment of the right."[74] The Committee is yet to make a definitive pronouncement, say in the form of a general comment, on whether the normative content of Article 11 extends to inclusive education. However, it has indicated on several occasions that inclusive education is an ideal to which all African states should aspire.

In 2012, the African Children's Committee adopted a strategy for promoting and protecting the rights of children with disabilities. The strategy identified seven areas of concern, including and of specific relevance to the present discussion, the general lack of compliance with existing commitments for realization of the right to education for children with disabilities. To improve the situation, the African Children's Committee proposed seven midterm action points for states, four of which focus directly on inclusive education.

69 T. Kaime, *The African Charter on the Rights and Welfare of the Child: A Socio-Legal Perspective* (2009) 3.

70 H. Combrinck, "The Hidden Ones: Children with Disabilities in Africa and the Right to Education" in J. Sloth-Nielsen (ed.), *Children's Rights in Africa: A Legal Perspective* (2008) 299, 311.

71 African Children's Charter, Article 11(3)(a) and (b).

72 Murungi (n. 34) 96.

73 Communication No. Com/002/2009.

74 Decision: No. 002/2009, March 22, 2011, para. 63.

These are transforming mainstream schools to be more inclusive, training teachers on inclusive education, making provision for reasonable accommodation on a case-by-case basis, and promoting inclusive education at the vocational and training level.[75] The Committee also suggested that states should, to begin with, review their legislative and policy frameworks. New laws should, among other things and at a minimum, do the following: (a) guarantee the right to inclusive education in the constitution as well as in children's and education legislation; and (b) provide for the formulation of a policy framework on inclusive education. In May 2014, the AU Conference of Ministers of Social Development considered and endorsed the strategy.[76]

The 2012 strategy placed the African Children's Committee on the right path in connection to matters relating to education for children with disabilities. However, the Committee seemed to have somewhat veered off the road in *Africa's Agenda for Children 2040*,[77] a policy document it adopted in November 2016 setting out a twenty-five-year vision for Africa's children. On education for children with disabilities, the Committee identifies three goals for states to achieve by 2040. First, children with disabilities are included and given necessary support to complete primary and secondary education.[78] Second, "as far as possible, the principle of inclusive education is fully implemented."[79] The third goal is worrying. The Committee proposes that "where appropriate, special-needs schools are opened for children with mild to severe learning, mental and physical impairments."[80] This goal is problematic for at least two reasons.

First, at a time when the emphasis around the world is to establish inclusive schools or transform mainstream schools into inclusive ones, it is disappointing that the African Children's Committee actively encourages states to resort to special or segregated schools. One would have thought that the goal should be to gradually phase out special schools, or as the UN Office of the High Commissioner for Human Rights (OHCHR) suggests, to slowly but surely convert them into "learning resource centers."[81] In essence, rather than

75 African Committee of Experts on the Rights and Welfare of the Child, Strategy for Promoting and Protecting the Rights of Children with Disabilities in Africa (2012) para 6.4.

76 African Union, fourth session of the AU Conference of Ministers of Social Development (CAMSD4), Addis Ababa, May 26–30, 2014, CAMSD/EXP/9(IV).

77 African Committee of Experts on the Rights and Welfare of the Child (ACERWC), Africa's Agenda for Children 2040: Fostering an Africa Fit for Children (2016).

78 ACERWC (n. 77) 19.

79 Ibid.

80 Ibid.

81 UN Office of the High Commissioner for Human Rights, Thematic Study on the Rights of Persons with Disabilities to Education, A/HRC/25/29, December 18, 2013, para. 49.

advocating for the establishment of special schools, the issue that should have concerned the Committee is this: what should happen to the existing special schools? This issue preoccupied the drafters of the CRPD, who were split into two broad groups.[82] The first group thought that special schools should exist side by side with inclusive schools. An earlier version of the CRPD reflected this view. The second group was of the opinion that inclusive schools should be the norm and special schools the exception. This group took the day, but only after accepting some sort of a compromise. The CRPD neither explicitly requires the establishment of special schools nor does it prohibit them completely. As such, it has been suggested that Article 24(3)(c) of the CRPD implicitly permits the establishment of special schools for blind, deaf, or deaf-blind children.[83]

Second, although the African Children's Committee restricts its suggestion for special schools to "appropriate" cases, it appears to define such cases on the basis of the impairments of the PWDs rather than on the barriers to PWDs' participation in society. Perhaps the Committee is of the view that it is utopian to imagine a world in which special schools are completely consigned to the museum. For sure, it may prove practically impossible to offer inclusive education for some children with severe and multiple disabilities. But as de Beco cautions, a very solid treaty-based explanation must be given for placing such children in special schools:

> Providing special education to them [children with disabilities] is however permissible as long as this is not done on the basis of their impairments but on the basis of the barriers to their participation in society. States, thus, have a certain leeway, although they should provide a strong CRPD-based justification if they keep a – partially – segregated education system. Special education may also not be of lesser quality than normal education, because this would again lead to discrimination. The risk is nonetheless that only children with less severe disabilities have the chance to be educated in mainstream schools, whereas the others will remain in special schools.

Still, states have a duty to progressively realize inclusive education. The CRPD is clear that this obligation does not entail actively sustaining special schools alongside inclusive schools.[84]

[82] See G. de Beco, "The Right to Inclusive Education According to Article 24 of the UN Convention on the Rights of Persons with Disabilities: Background, Requirements and (Remaining) Questions" (2014) 32 *Netherlands Quarterly of Human Rights* 263, 285.

[83] Ibid. 286.

[84] General Comment No. 4, para. 40.

TOWARD A CONSOLIDATED REGIONAL FRAMEWORK ON THE RIGHT TO INCLUSIVE EDUCATION

Discussion on the right to inclusive education in Africa will in the future center on the relevant provision of the Africa Disability Protocol. This prediction, of course, is founded on the presumption that the Africa Disability Protocol will eventually enter into force after receiving the requisite number of ratifications. If it does, the Africa Disability Protocol will provide a common reference point for promoting and protecting the rights of PWDs in Africa. As the discussion in the previous section shows, the African human rights system has somehow embraced the idea of inclusive education, but the bodies constituting the system are, understandably, reading from different scripts. As things stand now, a state seeking direction from the system is likely to get lost in the maze that is the African regional normative framework on disability rights in general and inclusive education in particular. The system is sending out mixed signals and its goalposts on inclusive education are constantly changing. The Africa Disability Protocol will usher some sense of a shared position and direction. Or will it? This section takes a critical look at the formulation of the right to inclusive education in the Africa Disability Protocol.

THE AFRICA DISABILITY PROTOCOL: A SNAPSHOT

The African Commission triggered the process of formulating the Africa Disability Protocol in May 2009 when it established the Working Group on the Rights of Older Persons and People with Disabilities. The Working Group was mandated to, inter alia, draft a concept note that will inform the process of formulating a regional treaty on disability.[85] The Working Group quickly, and without preparing the envisaged concept note, proceeded to develop a draft protocol that came to be popularly known as the "Accra Draft." The Accra Draft immediately encountered stiff resistance because it normatively lacked what could be said to be African-specific. It had also been developed without sufficient consultations with PWDs and other relevant stakeholders. The Secretariat of the African Decade of Persons with Disabilities summarized the criticism of the Accra Draft in the following words:

[85] Resolution on Transformation of the Focal Point on the Rights of Older Persons in Africa into a Working Group on the Rights of Older Persons and People with Disabilities in Africa, ACHPR/Res. 143 (XXXXV) 09 (adopted at the forty-fifth ordinary session of the African Commission on Human and Peoples' Rights, Banjul, The Gambia, May 13–27, 2009).

> The Commission had not made any wide consultation with the disability movement in Africa, a phenomena well characterized in the drafting of the UN Convention on the Rights of Persons with Disabilities [UNCRPD]. The circulated draft did not advance any African legal jurisprudence and the document eroded the gains achieved with the enactment of the UNCRPD which currently has 26 ratifications in the continent. Generally, the drafting was poor with contradictions and key concepts left out. The thinking did not unpack the best form of an African treaty body for the proposed mechanism.[86]

In 2011, the African Commission halted any further consideration of the Accra Draft.[87] The Commission subsequently withdrew the Accra Draft altogether and embarked on an entirely new process of formulating a regional disability protocol. This new process began with the Working Group on the Rights of Older Persons and People with Disabilities preparing a concept note making the case for a regional treaty on PWDs and suggesting some of the possible issues to be contained in the treaty.[88] The Working Group then prepared Draft I dated April 2013, the contents of which were motivated by the following four main principles:[89]

(a) The protocol should address African-specific issues;
(b) The drafting should take into account "the way African human rights instruments are crafted";
(c) The protocol should undermine neither the letter nor the spirit of the CRPD; and
(d) The protocol may draw upon existing international and regional human rights treaties.

A series of meetings with relevant stakeholders was subsequently convened to discuss and critique Draft I. In April 2014, stakeholders were invited to comment on a revised version (Draft II) posted on the African Commission's website. Draft III was produced in March 2015 after comments from the public were incorporated. All the members of the African Commission considered this draft and adopted it at the nineteenth extraordinary session held in Banjul, The Gambia, February 16–25, 2016.

86 Secretariat of the African Decade of Persons with Disabilities, *The Architecture for an African Disability Rights Mechanism* (2011) 2.
87 Combrinck (n. 9).
88 L. Mute, "Concept Note on the List of Issues to Guide Preparation of a Protocol on the Rights of Persons with Disabilities in Africa," August 24, 2012 (on file with the author).
89 See "Comments Invited on Draft Protocol on the Rights of Persons with Disabilities in Africa," available at www.achpr.org/news/2014/04/d121 (accessed on June 4, 2017).

The provisions of the Africa Disability Protocol are arranged more or less like those of the CRPD. The substantive articles may be grouped as follows: general provisions and obligations (Articles 1–3); individual rights and duties (Articles 4–24); specific groups (Articles 25–28); specific state obligations (Articles 30–31); and implementation (Articles 32–33). A review of these articles, or their comparison with those of the CRPD, is a task that should be postponed until another day. Still, two general points are worth mentioning.

First, the Africa Disability Protocol places more emphasis on or introduces a few new things not covered or simply glossed over in the CRPD. These include states' obligation to eliminate harmful cultural practices directed at PWDs,[90] stand-alone provisions on older persons and youth with disabilities,[91] duties of PWDs,[92] and state obligation to provide remedies to PWDs whose rights have been violated.[93] Second, the Africa Disability Protocol drops a number of provisions contained in the CRPD or collapses them into single lines or, at best, into just a few sentences. Glaring omissions include the CRPD provisions on privacy, personal mobility, and national implementation.

INCLUSIVE EDUCATION

The right to education is recognized in Article 14 of the Africa Disability Protocol. Article 14(1) provides that "every person with a disability has the right to education." Unlike the CRPD, the Africa Disability Protocol does not explicitly prohibit exclusion of PWDs from the general education system. This is surprising given that, and as mentioned earlier, less than 10 per cent of children with disabilities in Africa receive some form of education. Many factors account for the widespread exclusion of children with disabilities from the education system in Africa. Across the continent, schools with the requisite infrastructure and facilities to cater for the needs of children with disabilities are few and prohibitively expensive. As a consequence, most children with disabilities are unable to attend such schools.

Children with disabilities are also unable to attend relatively affordable schools because they are far from home and physically inaccessible. Other factors that contribute to the exclusion of children with disabilities from the education system include household poverty, stigma and discrimination, and verbal and physical abuse. As the CRPD Committee has observed, the

90 Africa Disability Protocol, Article 9.
91 Ibid., Articles 27 and 28.
92 Ibid., Article 29.
93 Ibid., Articles 8(3) and 9(3).

exclusion of children with disabilities from the school system may also occur in instances when a requirement to pass a common test is imposed as a condition for school entry without reasonable accommodation and support.[94]

Article 12(2) of the Draft Africa Disability Protocol had provided that PWDs "shall on no account be presumed to be uneducable or untrainable."[95] This provision was unfortunately deleted from the final text adopted by heads of state and government in January 2018. In many African countries, certain children with disabilities are not taken to school because their parents or caregivers think that they are uneducable.[96] This practice is rooted in negative cultural beliefs and attitudes about PWDs in general and children with disabilities in particular. In this context, it is not uncommon in many African communities for children with disabilities to be hidden from public view because their birth is considered a curse.[97] The notion that certain children with disabilities are uneducable may actually be the reason behind the failure of many African governments to allocate resources toward the education of such children. For instance, until a court of law intervened, the South African policy on inclusive education did not make a direct provision for the education of children with severe and profound intellectual disabilities.[98] These children could neither be admitted to special schools nor to any other government schools.

Article 14(4) of the Draft Africa Disability Protocol corresponds, more or less, with the objectives of education listed under Article 24(1) of the CRPD. However, one more objective has been added. Article 14(4)(d) provides that the education of PWDs shall be directed to "the preservation and strengthening of positive African values." Borrowed from Article 11 of the African Children's Charter, this provision is included in the Africa Disability Protocol despite the fact that the drafters were initially concerned that it could inadvertently promote those African traditions that undermine the rights of PWDs. At this initial stage (Draft I), the provision on elimination of harmful practices had not been inserted into the Protocol. It would appear that with the incorporation of the provision on harmful practices in Draft II, the drafters felt confident in maintaining the reference to "positive African values."

94 General Comment No. 4, para. 18.
95 Draft Africa Disability Protocol, Article 12(2).
96 African Child Policy Forum (n. 18) 20.
97 Biegon (n. 5) 53–54.
98 See *Western Cape Forum for Intellectual Disability* v. *Government of the Republic of South Africa & Another* [2010] ZAWCHC 544.

Nonetheless, the notion of "African values" is not unproblematic or uncontroversial. Although the term is used frequently in AU circles, it lacks an agreed-upon definition. In the field of human rights, the term is often invoked by African states to push back on what are perceived as "Western values."[99] In June 2015, the AU Executive Council relied on the African values argument in directing the African Commission to withdraw the observer status it had previously granted to the Coalition of African Lesbians (CAL), a South Africa–based NGO working on the rights of lesbians in Africa.[100] The African Commission did not withdraw CAL's observer status. Instead, and in what signifies the lack of consensus on the subject, the African Commission embarked on preparing a "detailed legal analysis" on, inter alia, the notion of African values.[101] This study is yet to be made public. The lack of a common understanding on the notion of African values is part of the broader and largely unresolved debate on who and/or what is "African."[102]

The preamble to the African Women's Protocol comes closer to offering a definition of African values. It indicates that African values are those "based on the principles of equality, peace, freedom, dignity, justice, solidarity and democracy."[103] If defined along these lines, then it may be argued that African values offer an autochthonous foundation for inclusive education in Africa. In particular, the very concept of inclusive education reflects and is embedded in the prominence African societies give to the notions of humanity, diversity, and interdependence. These notions find expression in terms like *ubuntu*, *batho*, and *umoja*, and thrive primarily because of the communal nature of

99 See, e.g., AU Assembly Decision on the Promotion of Cooperation, Dialogue and Respect for Diversity in the Field of Human Rights, AU/Dec.328 (XV). See also a brief comment of this decision in "Editorial" (2010) 10 *African Human Rights Law Journal* v, vi–vii.

100 AU Executive Council Decision on the thirty-eighth Activity Report of the African Commission on Human and Peoples' Rights, EX.CL/Dec.887 (XXVII).

101 African Commission on Human and Peoples' Rights, thirty-ninth Activity Report, para. 50, available at www.achpr.org/files/activity-reports/39/actrep39_2015_eng.pdf (accessed on June 6, 2017).

102 Such a debate took place, more recently, at a roundtable on African approaches to international law, convened by the Centre for Human Rights, University of Pretoria, Pretoria, South Africa, April 3–4, 2017. See "Roundtable at Centre for Human Rights Reflects on African Approaches to International Law," available at www.chr.up.ac.za/index.php/centre-news-a-events-2017/1803-round-table-at-centre-for-human-rights-reflects-on-african-approaches-to-international-law.html (accessed on June 6, 2017). See also African Court on Human and Peoples' Rights, Request for Advisory Opinion by the Socio-Economic Rights and Accountability Project, Advisory Opinion, available at www.up.ac.za/en/news/post_2470942-round-table-at-centre-for-human-rights-reflects-on-african-approaches-to-international-law (accessed on November 27, 2018).

103 African Women's Protocol, Preamble, para. 10.

African societies.[104] Studies have shown that the African traditional way of educating children, like in Latin-America,[105] is not significantly different from what is now referred to as inclusive education.[106] For this reason, Phasha and colleagues recently made a passionate call for a return to such approaches:

> Traditional African communities are about inclusion. If one analyses aspects of African indigenous education, for example, one can infer that we need to create spaces in African schools for parents, elders, families and cultural custodians to come in as teachers to work on a daily basis to complement the work of professionally trained educators. Community teaching emphasizes togetherness, sharing and reciprocity. Inclusion is taken as meaning we all belong and a responsibility of every citizen is to ensure that mutual interdependence is respected as an ideal and a virtue.[107]

This brings the discussion to what the Africa Disability Protocol says about inclusive education. Article 14(3) provides that "state parties shall take reasonable, appropriate and effective measures to ensure that inclusive quality education and skills training for persons with disabilities is realized fully." Pointing to a reluctance to fully embrace inclusive education as a right, earlier drafts spoke of the "goal of inclusive education." References to this language were dropped during the third review, although a single reference to "the goal of full inclusion" remains in the Africa Disability Protocol. The list of measures that states are required to take in order to implement inclusive education is fairly long, and includes the following: provision of access to free, quality, and compulsory basic and secondary education; provision of access to lifelong learning as well as to tertiary, vocational, and adult education; reasonable accommodation; individualized support measures; and schooling choices.[108]

A conspicuous omission in the Africa Disability Protocol is the special attention given in the CRPD to children who are blind, deaf, or deaf-blind, and to the measures required to facilitate their full and equal participation in education and as members of the community.[109] For example, states are not explicitly required in the Africa Disability Protocol to facilitate the learning of

104 See J. Cobbah, "African Values and the Human Rights Debates: An African Perspective" (1987) 9 *Human Rights Quarterly* 309; D. Cornell and K. van Marle, "Exploring *Ubuntu*: Tentative Reflections" (2005)5 *African Human Rights Law Journal* 195.

105 See G. Porter, "Disability and Inclusive Education," paper prepared for the InterAmerican Development Bank, cited in Combrinck (n. 70) 305.

106 See S. Stubbs, *Inclusive Education Where There Are Few Resources* (2004) 84.

107 N. Phasha, "Inclusive Schooling and Education in African Contexts," in N. Phasha et al. (eds.), *Inclusive Education in African Contexts: A Critical Reader* (2017) 1, 5.

108 Africa Disability Protocol, Article 14(3).

109 CRPD, Article 3.

Braille or sign language. Neither are they obligated to employ teachers, including teachers with disabilities, who are qualified in sign language and/or Braille. The only explicit requirement is for states to facilitate the "respect, recognition, promotion, preservation and development of sign languages."[110] The omission of the aforementioned important provisions is regrettable. It deliberately lowers the bar or the standard for African countries. From the outset, the drafters were concerned about "Africa's resource and technical realities" and pondered how to ensure "high-minded/high standard setting phrasing does not undermine immediate possibilities of persons getting an education in 'non-compliant' institutions."[111] This concern led to the active avoidance of language that could imply that the provision of inclusive education is resource-intensive.

One other question that the drafters deliberated on is whether secondary and tertiary education should be free (just like primary education). In Draft I, the relevant provision reads as follows: States Parties shall ensure that PWDs "can access free, quality and compulsory primary and secondary education." The provision remained unchanged throughout the drafting process, though the word "primary" was ultimately replaced with "basic." This may suggest that the drafters' intention is to impose an obligation on States Parties to offer free secondary education. As such, the Africa Disability Protocol offers a higher standard of protection than the CRPD under which the provision of free secondary education is subject to progressive realization.[112] This also means that the Africa Disability Protocol is out of step with other regional and international normative standards. In the Nairobi Principles, the African Commission clearly states that the duty imposed on the state by Article 17 of the African Charter is to make secondary education "generally available and accessible to all by appropriate means, and in particular by the progressive introduction of free education."[113] This wording is borrowed from the International Covenant on Economic, Social and Cultural Rights (ICESCR), which explicitly distinguishes the nature of state obligation insofar as primary versus secondary education is concerned.[114]

The Africa Disability Protocol is unique in one more respect. It requires states to ensure "*appropriate schooling choices* are available to persons with

110 Africa Disability Protocol, Article 14(3)(j).

111 Protocol to the African Charter on Human and Peoples' Rights on the Rights of Persons with Disabilities in Africa, Zero Draft, April 28, 2013 (on file with the author).

112 General Comment No. 4, para. 24.

113 Nairobi Principles, para. 71.

114 ICESCR, Article 13(2)(b).

disabilities who may *prefer to learn in particular environments*."[115] This could mean that even where inclusive schools exist, a person with a disability reserves the right to opt for a special school. On this issue, it is apposite to recall that the possibility of PWDs choosing between inclusive and special schools was discussed and rejected during the CRPD negotiations.[116] However, as de Beco notes, a parent may choose the form of education for her child, but the state has no obligation to offer a choice within public schools.[117]

CONCLUSION

There is little doubt that after many decades of "benign neglect," PWDs are receiving ever-growing attention within the African human rights system.[118] This shift was initially catalyzed by the adoption of the CRPD in 2006. It is now being sustained by the numerous activities on the rights of PWDs within the system, chief among which is the ongoing process of developing a regional disability rights treaty. This process provides a lens through which to examine how the African human rights system is responding to developments at the global level. This chapter focused on one of the innovations of the CRPD – the codification of the right to inclusive education.

Drawing inspiration from the CRPD, the existing regional framework is gradually expanding to embrace the right to inclusive education. However, numerous missteps have been made along the way and a tension still exists between seeing exclusive education as a desirable goal or as a right to which PWDs are entitled. This tension may be addressed if the ongoing drafting process eventually leads to the adoption of an African disability rights protocol. However, as this discussion reveals, it is clear that in certain respects, the right to inclusive education as formulated in Article 14 of the Africa Disability Protocol lowers the bar already set by the CRPD and contradicts previous consensus on important issues.

115 Africa Disability Protocol, Article 14(3)(e) (emphasis mine).

116 De Beco (n. 82) 286.

117 Ibid.

118 T. van Reenen and H. Combrinck "The UN Convention on the Rights of Persons with Disabilities in Africa: Progress after 5 Years" (2011) 8 *Sur: International Journal on Human Rights* 133, 153.

PART IV

PRACTICE

19

Litigating the Right to Inclusive Education under Irish Law

Gerry Whyte

For many children with disabilities and their parents, participation in mainstream education is a significant indicator of their acceptance by society. Where such participation is facilitated, the situation is appropriately analysed in terms of the need for the school to adjust to the needs of the child with disability, to make reasonable accommodation for him or her. However, Irish law provides only limited statutory protection for the right of a person with a disability to participate in mainstream education, and whilst a litigation strategy might be seen as a tempting option for extending the right to inclusive education, it is fraught with risk. In this chapter, I set the context for a consideration of the right to inclusive education in Ireland and then consider whether the provisions of the Constitution offer any protection for this right. I then consider whether the European Convention on Human Rights Act 2003 has any potential application here before, penultimately, briefly testing current provisions in Ireland against the requirements of Article 24 of the Convention on the Rights of Persons with Disabilities. I conclude with some comments about the use of a litigation strategy.

IRISH CONTEXT

First- and second-level education in Ireland is largely state-funded, but in the majority of cases, it is delivered by private parties. Under the 1937 constitution, the state is obliged to ensure that every child has access to free primary education and in the vast majority of cases, the state discharges this duty by funding the educational activities of privately owned schools. This duty does not extend to second-level education, but since 1967, the state has provided free second-level education. Historically the majority of schools in Ireland were owned by religious denominations, and this is still the case (though at the second level, vocational schools are state owned, as are a small number of primary schools). Recent years, however, have seen a growth in multi-denominational and non-denominational schools.

Turning specifically to special educational provision, during the first thirty years of the state's existence, such provision as was made for educating children with special needs came entirely from the private sector.[1] It was only in 1952 that the state became involved and some public funding was allocated to schools for the blind. Another significant advance took place in 1960 when the newly formed Association of Parents and Friends of Mentally Handicapped Children opened a school for children with learning difficulties. The following year, St Patrick's College of Education established a postgraduate diploma in special education and a specialised diploma for teachers of the deaf and blind. According to Griffin and Shevlin, this marked 'the beginnings of official policy in relation to meeting special educational needs provision in Ireland'.[2]

In 1965, a commission established by the minister for health published a report[3] which advocated special school provision for children with mild or moderate learning difficulties, whether through residential special schools, day special schools or special classes in conventional schools.[4] As Griffin and Shevlin note, however, the report considered children with severe or profound learning difficulties uneducable.[5]

By the mid-1970s, more than 100 special schools and a number of special classes in conventional schools catered for the needs of students with learning difficulties though the limited availability of assessment procedures often meant long delays in offering places. Moreover, more than half of all children in need of special education still could not access such education. Such provision as did exist was achieved through voluntary effort until 1977, when a circular from the Department of Education proposed that children with mild learning difficulties should attend special classes in ordinary schools.[6] This was followed in 1980 by a white paper on educational development which called for integration to be considered as the first option for children with disabilities.[7] Then in 1983, an official report, *The Education and Training of*

[1] This account of the development of educational provision in Ireland for children with special educational needs is drawn largely from Sean Griffin and Michael Shevlin, *Responding to Special Educational Needs: An Irish Perspective* (2nd edn) (Gill and Macmillan 2011) chs 3 to 5.

[2] Ibid. 41.

[3] Commission of Inquiry on Mental Handicap, *Report 1965* (Stationery Office 1965).

[4] Ibid. 74.

[5] Griffin and Shevlin (n. 1) 42.

[6] Ibid. 43.

[7] Ireland Department of Education, White Paper on Educational Development (Stationery Office 1980).

Severely and Profoundly Mentally Handicapped Children in Ireland, acknowledged that every child, irrespective of the extent of her learning difficulties, was educable.[8] Ten years later, the *Report of the Special Education Review Committee*[9] 'provided a blueprint for the development of special education that continues to influence policy decisions up to the present day'.[10] Griffin and Shevlin identify two further important factors that emerged during the 1990s which influenced the development of special education.[11] The first was the recourse to litigation by parents of children with learning difficulties to compel the state to improve educational provision for their children, which eventually led to the official recognition of the right of any child with special educational needs to access appropriate education.[12] The second was the enactment of the Education Act 1998, which provided generally for education but which also stated that one of its objectives was 'to give practical effect to the constitutional rights of children, including children who have a disability or who have other special educational needs, as they relate to education',[13] which identified as one of the functions of the minister that 'there is made available to each person resident in the State, including a person with a disability or who has other special educational needs, support services and a level and quality of education appropriate to meeting the needs and abilities of that person',[14] and which obliged every school to ensure that 'the educational needs of all students, including those with a disability or other special educational needs, are identified and provided for'.[15] In the first decade of this century, further acts were passed that had a bearing on special educational provision – these included the Education (Welfare) Act 2000, the Equal Status Act 2000, the Education for Persons with Special Educational Needs Act 2004[16] and the Disability Act 2005.

8 Minister for Education and Minister for Health and Social Welfare, *The Education and Training of Severely and Profoundly Mentally Handicapped Children in Ireland: Report of a Working Party to the Minister for Education and the Minister for Health and Social Welfare* (Stationery Office 1983) [2.4] and [5.9].

9 Department of Education and Science, *Report of the Special Education Review Committee* (Stationery Office 1993).

10 Griffin and Shevlin (n. 1) 45.

11 Ibid.

12 For a detailed examination of this litigation and the government response thereto, see, by the present author, *Social Inclusion and the Legal System: Public Interest Law in Ireland* (2nd edn) (Institute of Public Administration 2015) 305–340.

13 Education Act 1998 S6(a).

14 Education Act 1998 S7(1)(a).

15 Education Act 1998 S9(a).

16 Note, however, that relatively few sections of this act have actually been brought into force.

These factors, together with increasing international recognition of the value of educating children with and without disabilities together, resulted in special educational policy moving towards 'a more inclusive view of special education principally delivered within mainstream settings'.[17]

Having briefly sketched the context for the provision of special education in Ireland, I turn now to consider the protection afforded to the right to inclusive education under Irish law, beginning with an examination of the constitution.

CONSTITUTION

Two provisions of the constitution, Articles 42.4 and 40.1, might be seen to have a prima facie relevance to demands for inclusive education.

By virtue of Article 42.4, the state is obliged to provide free primary education for all children, and in the groundbreaking decision of *O'Donoghue* v. *Minister for Health*, O'Hanlon J held that this duty also applied to children with severe and profound learning difficulties.[18] To date, cases taken under this provision on behalf of children with disabilities have sought to oblige the state to make special educational provision for the children in question, not to place them in mainstream education, but of course it is conceivable that a child with a disability excluded from mainstream primary education could argue that such exclusion infringed his or her right to such education. Two points should be noted about this, however. First, the duty imposed on the state by Article 42.4 is only applicable to primary education, and so this aspect of the constitution could not be relied upon by a student seeking access to mainstream second-level education. Second, where the state has offered some educational provision to a child with a disability, the courts essentially apply a test of reasonableness to determine whether the state is in dereliction of its constitutional or statutory duties to educate. Thus, in *O'Carolan* v. *Minister for Education and Science*, MacMenamin J held, inter alia, that there was a reasonable and rational basis for the proposals advanced by the state in relation to the education of the plaintiff, a child with autism.[19] Peart J adopted a similar approach in *Ó C* v. *Minister for Education and Science*, when he refused to order the state to provide a particular form of education for an autistic child, saying that '[t]here is nothing to suggest that the Minister has acted in some irrational way by

17 Griffin and Shevlin (n. 1) 47.

18 [1996] 2 IR 20.

19 [2005] IEHC 296.

making provision in a way that simply cannot be appropriate to meet the needs of children with autism'.[20] Thus a parent seeking to rely on Article 42.4, in order to have his or her child placed in mainstream education, will have to argue that the provision of special education for the child in a segregated setting would be unreasonable or irrational. In many cases, this may prove very difficult to establish.

While the constitutional principle of equality in Article 40.1 might also appear to have a prima facie relevance to the educational segregation of children with disabilities in special educational facilities, in fact, it may not be of much assistance to such children.[21] There would appear to be a number of difficulties in the way of a student with a disability successfully invoking this principle in support of a claim for inclusive education. First, it is not yet clear whether this principle can apply to decisions of private parties and so, given that most schools in the state are privately owned and controlled, albeit publicly funded, a decision by such a school to refuse to admit a student with a disability may not come within the scope of the constitutional principle of equality.[22] However, this principle would appear to be applicable to state-owned schools.[23] Second, even if it were assumed that the constitutional principle of equality could apply to private parties, Article 40.1 authorises the state in its enactments to have due regard to, inter alia, differences of capacity. Consequently, a decision made pursuant to s 4(4) or s 7(4)(b) of the Equal Status Act 2000 to exclude a student with a disability from mainstream education is likely to be upheld by the courts, provided it is not irrational or unreasonable. Finally, a recent Supreme Court decision would appear to have undermined some positive developments at the High Court level in relation to the application of Article 40.1 to people with disabilities. In two High Court cases, Hogan J held that discrimination on the ground of disability in relation to the administration of justice was contrary to the constitutional guarantee of

20 [2007] IEHC 170.

21 The principal source of constitutional protection of equality is Article 40.1. In *Howard* v. *The Commissioners of Public Works in Ireland* [1994] 1 IR 101, [1993] ILRM 665, Denham J said, at pages 161 and 699 respectively, that Article 40.1 required the organs of government in the execution of their powers to act with due regard to the concept of equality.

22 In *Equality Authority* v. *Portmarnock Golf Club* [2005] IEHC 235, O'Higgins J, in the High Court, stated, obiter, that Article 40.1 did not impose obligations on citizens in their private relations. This point was not addressed by the Supreme Court on appeal – [2010] 1 IR 671.

23 A small number of national schools are owned by the state and it also controls, through the new education and training boards that replaced the vocational educational committees in 2013, a number of second-level schools. In light of the *Howard* decision, constitutional equality claims could arguably be taken against the state in respect of the decisions of such schools, if not by virtue of Article 40.1, then by virtue of Article 5.

equality and, perhaps more significant, that the constitutional guarantee obliged the state, in some situations, to make such 'reasonable accommodation' for people with disabilities as is 'practical and feasible' to ensure that they are held equal before the law – see G v. *District Judge Murphy*[24] and *DX* v. *Judge Buttimer*.[25] However in *Fleming* v. *Ireland*,[26] in which a woman with advanced multiple sclerosis argued that a statutory ban on assisted suicide infringed Article 40.1 because, inter alia, the legislation failed to make reasonable accommodation for persons with disabilities who were unable to commit suicide unaided, the Supreme Court arguably showed a very poor understanding of the concept of reasonable accommodation. Dismissing this argument, the Court said:

> The appellant does complain that s 2(2) affects her by making it difficult or impossible for her to end her own life, because she cannot perform the final suicidal act without assistance. In this she says that she is differently situated from an able-bodied person, a person who does not need assistance. Assuming for present purposes that such a complaint may give rise to a claim under Art. 40.1, this effect does not, of course, result from the provisions of the law, which applies equally to everybody wishing to commit suicide. Since the enactment of s 2(1) of the Act, everyone is free to do so. What prevents the appellant from committing suicide is, on her own evidence, the fact of her disability. The appellant was able to avail of s 2(1) for some time: when she lost that ability it was not through operation of any law before which she is required to be held equal, but the fact of her condition.[27]

It is respectfully submitted, however, that this reasoning fails to understand that a claim for reasonable accommodation is based on the view that society needs to adapt to the particular circumstances of a person with a disability so as to enable that person to overcome whatever limitation in faculty flows from his or her disability. A claim for reasonable accommodation accepts that, as a result of his or her disability, a person is unable to, for example, access a building, participate in a course of education or, in the instant case, commit suicide, and that any such limitation is not directly imposed on the person with a disability by society through for instance a statutory provision as in the instant case. The demand for reasonable accommodation does, however, call on society, rather than the person with the disability, to adapt to the situation so as to overcome the relevant limitation. The Supreme Court decision in

24 [2011] IEHC 445.
25 [2012] IEHC 175.
26 [2013] IESC 19, [2013] 2 IR 417.
27 Ibid .[134].

Fleming, however, does not reflect this understanding of reasonable accommodation.

In light of the foregoing, it seems very unlikely that the guarantee of equality could provide effective protection for a right on the part of a student with a disability to inclusive education.

In contrast to the constitution, which arguably provides no protection for the right to inclusive education, the Equal Status Acts 2000–15 provide some, albeit limited, protection for this right and I turn now to consider this statutory equality code.

EQUAL STATUS ACTS 2000–15

The Equal Status Acts 2000–15 prohibit, subject to certain exceptions, direct and indirect discrimination on grounds of, inter alia, disability in relation to, inter alia, the provision of education. In considering the extent to which these acts protect the right to inclusive education, I first examine those provisions permitting derogation from the principle of equal treatment in relation to educational provision for students with disabilities. Next I consider the extent of the obligation imposed by the acts on educational providers to make reasonable accommodation for students with disabilities.

a) Derogations from the Principle of Equal Treatment in Relation to Education

Section 7(2) of the Equal Status Act 2000 prohibits an educational establishment from discriminating on grounds of, inter alia, disability in relation to the conditions of admission of a student to the establishment, the access of a student to any course, facility or benefit provided by the establishment, any other term or condition of participation in the establishment by a student or the imposition of any sanctions, including expulsion, on a student. However, s 7(4) goes on to provide that the principle of equal treatment in s 7(2) shall not apply:

a) in respect of differences in the treatment of students on the gender, age or disability ground in relation to the provision or organisation of sporting facilities or sporting events, to the extent that the differences are reasonably necessary having regard to the nature of the facilities or events, or
b) to the extent that compliance with any of its provisions in relation to a student with a disability would, by virtue of the disability, make

> impossible, or have a seriously detrimental effect on, the provision by an educational establishment of its services to other students.

Schools (and others) may also justify discrimination on ground of disability by reference to s 4(4) of the act, which provides, in relation to the application of the act generally, that where a person has a disability that, in the circumstances, could cause harm to the person or to others, treating the person differently to the extent reasonably necessary to prevent such harm does not constitute discrimination.

Now, while a presumption in favour of inclusive education for students with disabilities may be inferred from the terms of s 7(4)(b), it is clear that that presumption may be rebutted and so the statutory protection afforded by the 2000 Act to the right to inclusive education is limited. This is borne out by one High Court case and by a number of decisions by equality officers. In *Clare* v. *Minister for Education and Science*, Smyth J held, on the facts of the case, that the expulsion of a pupil with ADHD from a particular school did not constitute discrimination, having regard to s 7(4)(b), and that the making of arrangements for the pupil to be educated in another school was a proper response by the department in light of s 4(4).[28] In DEC-S2009-31, *Mrs A (on behalf of her son B)* v. *A Boys' National School*, an equality officer held that a school did not discriminate when it suspended a student with autism and ADD (who had, on a number of occasions, struck fellow pupils, his special needs assistant and his teacher). The equality officer expressed himself, satisfied that

> the extreme nature of the difficulties presented by the complainant's behaviour, especially in terms of the incidences of striking his teachers/SNA/peers and the disproportionate amount of time that it was necessary for his class teacher to dedicate towards the management of this behaviour, were having a seriously detrimental effect on the capacity of the respondent to provide educational services to both the complainant and the other students in his class.

He was also satisfied that the school had carried out a detailed investigation in relation to the incidents that prompted the suspension of the student. The equality officer further held that the special measures and facilities (including the individual education plan and behaviour management plan) that the school put in place in order to manage the student's behavioural difficulties were reasonable in the circumstances of this case, and that these

[28] [2004] IEHC 350.

measures were sufficient to discharge its obligations under s 4 of the Equal Status Act 2000 to make reasonable accommodation for the student.

In contrast, in DEC-S2009-43, A *Post Leaving Certificate Student* v. *An Educational Establishment*, an equality officer ruled that in order to rely on s 4(4), the onus is on the school to show that i) it had reasonably formed the opinion that the student could cause harm to himself or others; ii) the cause of the prospect of such harm was the student's disability; and iii) the actions the school took to prevent such harm were reasonable and necessary. In the instant case, the only evidence presented was an allegation that the student banged his head against the wall, evidence which was unconvincing. Moreover, the delay between this incident and the removal of the student from the mainstream class would indicate that the school did not consider there to be any significant danger of harm to anyone. Otherwise, any reasonable person would have acted immediately. The equality officer further held that the onus was on the school to show that it had no choice but to rely on the s 7(4)(b) provisions, but also held that the school was unable to provide any convincing evidence that the student's behaviour was having a detrimental impact on the education of other students.

b) Duty to Make Reasonable Accommodation

The Equal Status Act 2000 also provides that discrimination includes a failure to do all that is reasonable to accommodate the needs of a person with a disability by providing special treatment or facilities if, without such treatment or facilities, it would be impossible or unduly difficult for the person to avail himself/herself of a service – s 4(1). This applies to educational establishments as well as to other service providers and is important in the present context as the provision of reasonable accommodation can enable a child with a disability to participate in mainstream education. However, the burden of proof rests on the person with the disability, who must show that without the provision of special treatment or facilities in relation to the operation of the educational establishment, it would be impossible or unduly difficult for that person to avail himself/herself of the educational services in question. Moreover, no definition of 'undue difficulty' appears in the 2000 Act. In addition, s 4(2) absolves the service provider from this obligation where the cost of providing such special treatment is more than nominal. In Decision DEC-S2010-043, *Regan* v. *Old Bawn Community School*, an equality officer held that the cost of providing a sign language interpreter amounted to more than nominal costs for the provider of a part-time adult education programme, providing them with a defence to a complaint of disability discrimination.

Case law has established that an important feature of this requirement to make reasonable accommodation for the needs of a person with disabilities is that there must be a consultation with that person in order to ascertain what his/her disabilities are and how they might be accommodated. In the context of a claim taken under the Employment Equality Acts, the Labour Court said, in *Humphries* v. *Westwood Fitness Centre*, that:

> before coming to [the] view [that the employee was not capable to do the job by reason of her disability], the employer would normally be required to make adequate enquiries so as to establish fully the factual position in relation to the employee's capacity. The nature and extent of the enquiries which an employer should make will depend on the circumstances of each case. At a minimum, however, an employer should ensure that he or she is in full possession of all of the material facts concerning the employee's condition, and that the employee is given fair notice [if extreme measures, such as dismissal for incapacity are under consideration].[29]

On appeal, Dunne J in the Circuit Court upheld the Labour Court's determination.

> I am in no doubt that the employer did in fact have these concerns regarding the plaintiff. However, the way to deal with these concerns was to take medical advice in order to allay those concerns. An employer should take advice from the plaintiff's own doctor or from an independent doctor. The employer had a legal obligation under the Employment Equality Act 1998 to deal with her in that way.[30]

In Decision DEC-S2010-047, *A Student* v. *Galway-Mayo Institute of Technology*, an equality officer indicated that a similar duty to consult existed under the Equal Status Acts. Conversely, it should be pointed out that if a school is unaware of the fact that a student has a disability, it cannot be required to make reasonable accommodation for that student – DEC-S2011-57, *Ryan* v. *DIT*. In DEC-S2012-028, *A Pupil* v. *A School*, an equality officer held that where a complaint of disability discrimination related to an invisible disability – here the student experienced anxiety and depression – a diagnosis of a recognised medical condition, illness or malfunction by a medical professional may be a minimum requirement before the tribunal can entertain the complaint of disability discrimination.

It is important to note that the duty to make reasonable accommodation for a student with disabilities is limited by the concept of reasonableness.

29 [2004] ELR 296, 300.
30 Ibid. 303.

In Decision DEC-S2010-024, *Mr and Mrs X (on behalf of their son, Mr Y)* v. *A Post-Primary School*, the equality officer cited a Circuit Court decision of Hunt J, *Deans* v. *Dublin City Council*, in which the judge stated that:

> reasonableness must be judged according to the context of the individual case ... The City Council is entitled to bear in mind all the extensive and considerable social, legal and policy considerations ... and they are indeed relevant to the decision as to what is reasonable in the particular case ... The Housing Authority is not obliged to submit to every wish expressed by a disabled person in the context of an application for facilities ... All that it is commanded to do by the equality legislation is to devise a 'reasonable' solution to a problem, not to achieve perfection and not to give in to every demand that is made of it.[31]

In the instant case, the equality officer accepted that the school did not have the resources to provide all of the supports that the parents sought for their son, but also that it had put in place a significant range of special measures and facilities to accommodate the boy's special educational requirements.

Deans was also cited in *A Student* v. *A Third Level College*, DEC-S2012-046, in which an equality officer held that the withdrawal by the college of the facility of using a particular computer program in exams amounted to a failure to make reasonable accommodation for a student with dyslexia. In DEC-S2010-009 *Mrs X (on behalf of her son, Mr Y)* v. *A Post-Primary School*, an equality officer held that a school's failure to put in place a coherent individual education plan for the pupil in question in order to address his special educational requirements, its failure to comply with its statutory obligations in terms of the manner in which it dealt with the pupil's absenteeism and its inadequate offer of only five hours of resource teaching per week, without further access to the normal standard of full-time education provided to other students, meant that it had failed to do all that was reasonable to accommodate the needs of the pupil, as a person with a disability, within the meaning of s 4 of the Equal Status Acts. In DEC-S2012-026, *A Parent* v. *Board of Management of a Primary School*, the equality officer held that the school refused a child with a disability a place in the school because he would need special facilities that the school was unwilling to provide and that accordingly the school had unlawfully discriminated against the child on grounds of disability. More recently, in DEC-S2013-017, *A Mother and Father, on behalf of their Son* v. *Respondent National School*, an equality officer held that the failure of a school to transfer a mobile handrail to a classroom, thereby effectively

[31] *Deans* v. *Dublin City Council* (Cir. Ct, 15 April 2008) 34.

denying a student with a physical disability the use of that room, constituted unlawful discrimination contrary to the 2000 Act.

Notwithstanding the limited protection afforded to the right to inclusive education by s 7(4)(b) of the Equal Status Act and the limited nature of the statutory duty imposed on schools to make reasonable accommodation for the needs of students with disabilities, reliance on this legislation has some advantages over other potential legal avenues for asserting a right to inclusive education. First, s 7(4)(b) creates a presumption in favour of mainstreaming and, second, claims taken under the act go, in the first instance, before the Workplace Relations Commission, which is relatively inexpensive.

THE EUROPEAN CONVENTION ON HUMAN RIGHTS ACT 2003

Penultimately, I wish to consider briefly whether a successful case asserting a right to inclusive education could be taken before the Irish courts pursuant to the European Convention on Human Rights Act 2003, s 2 of which directs Irish courts to interpret and to apply any statutory provision or rule of law in a manner compatible with the state's obligations under the European Convention on Human Rights insofar as that is possible and s 4 of which provides that judicial notice shall be taken of, inter alia, any decision of the European Court of Human Rights. In a recent decision, *Çam* v. *Turkey*,[32] a Chamber of the European Court of Human Rights held that the refusal of the Turkish National Music Academy to admit the applicant because she was blind amounted to a violation of Article 14 of the Convention (which prohibits discrimination on the ground, inter alia, of disability) read in conjunction with Article 2 of Protocol No. 1 guaranteeing the right to education. The Chamber held that, as the applicant was qualified for admission to the academy, the decision to refuse to admit her was based solely on the fact that she was blind. Moreover, the refusal of the Academy to make reasonable accommodation for her disability also amounted to discrimination on grounds of disability.

While this is a positive decision for people with disabilities, it does not appear to add anything to the substantive protection already available to students with disabilities under the Equal Status Acts.[33] Moreover, while Irish judges are required by s 4 of the European Convention on Human

[32] App no. 51500/08 (ECHR, 23 February 2016).

[33] From a procedural point of view, the *Çam* case would enable an aggrieved student to initiate a complaint about discrimination in the High Court by relying on the 2003 Act, whereas complaints of discrimination under the Equal Status Act 2000–15 must be initiated before the Workplace Relations Commission, but this is not necessarily a significant benefit.

Rights Act 2003 to have regard to, inter alia, the jurisprudence of the European Court of Human Rights when interpreting Convention provisions, they are not at liberty to anticipate possible decisions of the European Court. As Fennelly J put it in *McD* v. *L*, '[t]he Act of 2003 does not provide an open-ended mechanism for our courts to outpace Strasbourg'.[34] Thus until such time as the European Court goes beyond the *Çam* case in identifying the Convention rights of students with disabilities, the 2003 Act will be of little benefit to such students in the Irish context.

ARTICLE 24 CRPD

Article 24 of the UN Convention on the Rights of Persons with Disabilities (CRPD) provides for a right to inclusive education. However, to date, Ireland has not ratified the CRPD, and it therefore does not bind Ireland in international law. Moreover, even ratification would not be sufficient to enable litigants to rely on the provisions of the CRPD before the domestic courts.[35] For that to happen, the CRPD would also have to be incorporated into domestic law by Parliament.

Nonetheless, it is worth briefly considering how the current Irish position with regard to the right to inclusive education matches up with the requirements of Article 24. Article 24(1) requires contracting states, without discrimination and on the basis of equality opportunity, to

> ensure an inclusive education system at all levels and life-long learning directed to:
>
> The full development of human potential and sense of dignity and self-worth, and the strengthening of respect for human rights, fundamental freedoms and human diversity;
>
> The development by persons with disabilities of their personality, talents and creativity, as well as their mental and physical abilities, to their fullest potential;
>
> Enabling persons with disabilities to participate effectively in a free society.

According to General Comment No. 4 (2016) prepared by the Committee on the Rights of Persons with Disabilities,

34 [2010] 2 IR 199, 317, [2010] 1 ILRM 461, 530.

35 An unincorporated but ratified international convention may, however, have indirect legal effect in the domestic Irish system through the operation of a presumption that domestic legislation is compatible with our international obligations. However, even this is not available in the context of the CRPD given that it is not yet ratified by Ireland.

> *Inclusion* involves a process of systemic reform embodying changes and modifications in content, teaching methods, approaches, structures and strategies in education to overcome barriers with a vision serving to provide all students of the relevant age range with an equitable and participatory learning experience and environment that best corresponds to their requirements and preferences. Placing students with disabilities within mainstream classes without accompanying structural changes to, for example, organisation, curriculum and teaching and learning strategies, does not constitute inclusion.[36]

This is distinguished from integrated education whereby persons with disabilities are placed in mainstream educational institutions but then are required to adjust to the requirements of such institutions. Moreover, the right to inclusive education has to be provided without discrimination, and, according to the General Comment, this includes the right not to be segregated and also to be provided with reasonable accommodation.

> According to de Beco, inclusive education requires a far-reaching adaptation of the general education system. Such adaptation must aim to apply a 'universal design' to education . . . by ensuring that from the very beginning, goods, services, equipment, and facilities can be used by everybody. This involves not only looking at the way in which schools address the individual needs of children who are considered disabled but also designing education systems so as to make room for the variety of children from inception. In order to make schools inclusive, therefore, what is needed is a profound 'change of culture', which can only come through a shift in how education is viewed by society.[37]

Implementing this central obligation of Article 24 will pose a huge challenge to Irish educationalists and to the Irish state if and when it ratifies the CRPD. De Beco argues that the best way to achieve this objective is 'to work incrementally by endeavouring to adapt the general education system' and that this will, in time, lead to less reliance on the segregated system of special education.[38]

Three specific steps that appear to be called for in the Irish context relate to mainstreaming, the provision of reasonable accommodation and the use of individualised education plans. In relation to mainstreaming, while it is true

36 Committee on the Rights of Persons with Disabilities, General Comment No. 4 (2016) on the Right to Inclusive Education (2 September 2016) CRPD/C/GC/4 [11].

37 Gauthier de Beco, 'Transition to Inclusive Education Systems According to the Convention on the Rights of Persons with Disabilities' (2016) 34 *Nordic Journal of Human Rights* 40, 47.

38 Ibid. 54.

that children with disabilities cannot be denied an education in Ireland as a result of the decision of O'Hanlon J in *O'Donoghue* v. *Minister for Health*, in which he held, inter alia, that all children were educable, such children do not enjoy an unqualified right to access mainstream education.[39] As we have noted, both ss 7(4)(b) and 4(4) of the Equal Status Act 2000 permit the exclusion of children with disabilities from mainstream education where this is necessary to avoid rendering impossible, or having a seriously detrimental effect on, the provision of education to other students or to prevent harm to others or to the student with the disability. Section 2 of the Education for Persons with Special Educational Needs Act 2004 similarly permits exceptions to the right of a child with special educational needs to access mainstream education where mainstreaming would be inconsistent with the best interests of the child or with the effective provision of education with whom the child is to be educated. Compliance with the CRPD will, presumably, require the repeal of these provisions.

Turning to the making of reasonable accommodation for people with disabilities, again as noted earlier in this chapter, the duty to make such provision under the Equal Status Acts 2000–15 is heavily qualified by the fact that persons bound by this duty cannot be required to incur more than nominal costs – s 4(2). Again, one imagines that compliance with the CRPD may require a modification of this provision in order to render more effective the duty to make reasonable accommodation for children with disability accessing education.

Finally, by virtue of Article 24(2)(e), the state will be obliged to provide effective individualised support mechanisms in environments that maximise academic and social development. In relation to this obligation, the Committee on the Rights of Persons with Disabilities emphasised the necessity for the provision of individualised education plans.[40] While s 3(5) of the Education for Persons with Special Educational Needs Act 2004 provides for the drawing up of individualised education plans for children who are assessed as having special educational needs, this provision, like most of the 2004 Act, has not yet been brought into effect and clearly will need to be if Ireland is to comply with the CRPD.

39 [1996] 2 IR 20.

40 Committee on the Rights of Persons with Disabilities, General Comment No. 4 (2016) on the Right to Inclusive Education (2 September 2016) CRPD/C/GC/4 [32].

THE PERILS OF LITIGATION STRATEGY

Finally, I wish to comment on the use of litigation strategy to establish a right to an inclusive education. Litigation strategy has been deployed successfully to improve the educational provision for children with learning difficulties. The decisions in *O'Donoghue* v. *Minister for Health*[41] and *Sinnott* v. *Minister for Education*[42] established that children with severe or profound learning difficulties were constitutionally entitled to free education until they reached the age of eighteen and prompted state investment in this area to the point where in June 2011, the state was employing more than 10,800 special needs assistants[43] to work with children with learning difficulties and providing more than 400 special classes for more than 2,500 autistic children.[44] Nonetheless, it is not without its risks.[45] Chief of these is the real risk of losing the case, thereby confirming the current situation (and also exposing the unsuccessful litigant to liability for costs).[46] In addition, litigation in this jurisdiction can be a lengthy process, particularly if the case goes to the Court of Appeal or to the Supreme Court, a process that can take a number of years.

41 [1996] 2 IR 20.

42 [2001] 2 IR 545.

43 Representing a ninefold increase in expenditure since 2001 to a figure of €348m. However in December 2010, a cap of 10,575 special needs assistants was set in response to Ireland's current financial crisis, and in 2013, there was also a significant cut in support hours for children with learning difficulties in response to an increase in the number of children entitled to such support – Genevieve Carbery, 'School Cuts for Special Needs Pupils "Savage"', *Irish Times* (Dublin, 20 June 2013) 5. In June 2016, however, the minister for education announced a 7 per cent increase in the number of special needs assistants followed by an allocation, in October 2016, of an additional 430 resource teachers to support children with special educational needs.

44 In 2006, a report by the Inspectorate of the Department of Education and Science was able to state that '[s]ince the decision in 1998 there has been a significant growth in "autism specific" educational provision, and special education for these children is now provided in mainstream classes, special classes, special schools, and special centres for education'. *An Evaluation of Educational Provision for Children with Autistic Spectrum Disorders* (Stationery Office 2006) 1.

45 For a review of the merits and demerits of litigation strategy based on Irish litigation seeking to promote social inclusion, see, by the present author, *Social Inclusion and the Legal System* (n. 12) ch. 9.

46 Note that in *KRA and another* v. *The Minister for Justice and Equality (no. 1)* [2016] IEHC 289, Humphreys J suggested, obiter, at para 69, that there might be medical conditions such that meaningful or full education is not a practical possibility, or that the cost of providing 'full bespoke education to a particular child in particular circumstances imposes an extraordinary financial or operational burden on the State, well above that involved in the *Sinnott* case'.

Another concern is that, even if successful, litigation establishing a right to an inclusive education might result in the resources necessary to vindicate such a right being taken from the budget of other services or facilities provided to people with disabilities and in the formation of policy on an ad hoc basis. Thus Ware commented, in the aftermath of the High Court decision in *Sinnott*:

> While children with special needs have to have recourse to the courts to ensure that they get appropriate provision, the development of a coherent policy is likely to take a back seat; yet while there is no coherent policy ... recourse to the courts is likely to increase. At best this can only result in improved provision for some at the expense of others, whether at a group or individual level.[47]

Moreover, there is always the risk that gains secured through litigation may be reversed by the enactment of subsequent legislation or frustrated or delayed by bureaucratic delay or inaction. The latter risk is potentially greater where the litigant seeks to compel the state to provide a new scheme or facility, as distinct from extending an existing scheme or claiming damages.[48]

Finally, the dependency of the trial judge on the litigants to determine what issues and evidence should be put before the court may mean that the judge would not be able to take into account all of the interests affected by her judgment.[49]

In light of these concerns, a prudent approach to establishing a right to inclusive education should focus on the political process and seek to persuade politicians and administrators, by force of argument, of the merits of this approach to the education of people with disabilities. If a litigation strategy is to be pursued on this issue, then it should be combined with a political campaign designed to influence the political reaction to any judicial decision.

47 Jean Ware, 'The *Sinnott* Judgement: Have We Grasped the Implications?' (2001) 14 *REACH: Journal of Special Needs Education in Ireland* 75, 82. The subsequent enactment of the Education for Persons with Special Educational Needs Act 2004 means that a coherent educational policy for children with learning difficulties is now in place, but the argument that public interest litigation may benefit one group to the detriment of another remains valid in other contexts.

48 In this context, it note that it is very difficult in this jurisdiction to obtain a mandatory injunction (or affirmative decree) compelling the executive to spend public money in vindicating a constitutional right – see *TD (a minor suing by his mother and next friend MD) and others* v. *The Minister for Education and others* [2001] 4 IR 259.

49 Though the use of *amicus curiae* briefs that facilitate third-party intervention in litigation may alleviate this concern somewhat.

20

Inclusive Education in Flanders, Belgium

A Country with a Long History of Segregation

Elisabeth De Schauwer, Inge Van de Putte and Gauthier de Beco

INTRODUCTION

This chapter examines the situation of inclusive education in Flanders, Belgium. As Belgium is a federal state, education is a domain that falls within the exclusive responsibility of the three communities and, therefore, the federal entity has no say on the matter. Flanders is one of these three communities, the other two being the French-speaking and the German-speaking communities. Given the limited space available, it is impossible to deal with the three communities in this chapter, the educational systems of which are all different and bear no relationship with each other whatsoever.

Flanders has the most segregated education system in Europe according to statistical data. The question is: why is it so hard for Flemish schools to respond to diversity and to develop an inclusive education system? The three authors analyse the current education system, which has in fact a history of two broad, separate and well-equipped systems: regular and special education. In order to achieve the participation of students with special educational needs in the general education system according to Article 24 of the UN Convention on the Rights of Persons with Disabilities (CRPD), a radical transformation is required, one which would take into account Flanders' individual, historical and structural forces.

FOR A LONG TIME: BARRIERS TO INCLUSION IN THE EDUCATIONAL SYSTEM IN FLANDERS

In Flanders, the education for children with special educational needs is mainly dictated by the Law on Special Education of 6 July 1970. Special schools are designed according to the type of impairment. At primary-level special education, there are eight different types of impairment: type 1: mild intellectual disability; type 2: moderate to severe intellectual disability; type 3: children with behavioural and emotional problems; type 4: children with motor problems; type 5: children in a hospital, preventorium or residential setting; type 6: children with visual impairments; type 7: children with auditory impairments; and type 8: children with learning problems.

At the secondary level of special education, there are four levels of education and training. The differentiation between the levels reflects the extent of the individual's participation in mainstream society.[1] Training level 1 involves social functioning and participation in an environment that provides support and that allows for suitable employment participation in an environment with support (to work in a day care centre). Training level 2 concentrates on social functioning and participation in an environment that provides support and employment training in an environment with support (to work in a sheltered workshop). Training level 3 focusses on social functioning and participation and employment participation in a mainstream environment. Training level 4 works on social functioning and participation with or without support, and the receipt of further higher education and employment participation in a mainstream environment with or without support.[2]

Following the Law on Integration in Education (adopted in 1986), special educators were brought into regular education. These special educators are named integration educators (*Geïntegreerd ONderwijs*) (GON) and focus on young people with disabilities and/or learning and parenting difficulties temporarily or permanently, who are partially or fully able to follow the lessons or activities in school with help from a school for special education.[3]

In 1999, Flanders also introduced so-called inclusive educators (*Inclusief ONderwijs*) (ION) who are sent to regular schools from special education type 2 level and above. These special educators provide extra support to children with a moderate or severe intellectual disability. Like GON, they work in regular schools with such children. According to the Flemish Agency for Persons with Disabilities, these children and young people in primary and secondary education are not expected to reach the same learning objectives

[1] Type 8 is not available in secondary-level education. Types 1 and 3 are only offered in training level 3, and type 2 is only available in training levels 1 and 2.

[2] Inge Van de Putte, Elisabeth De Schauwer, Stijn Vandevelde and Leen Poppe, *Onderwijs voor personen met specifieke onderwijsbehoeften: Orthopedagogische werkvelden in beweging: organisatie en tendensen* (Garant, forthcoming) 73–74.

[3] 'Geïntegreerd onderwijs: GON-begeleiding in het onderwijs' (*Vlaanderen*), www.vlaanderen.be/nl/onderwijs-en-wetenschap/op-school/geintegreerd-onderwijs-gon-begeleiding-het-onderwijs, accessed 24 August 2017. Translated by the authors.

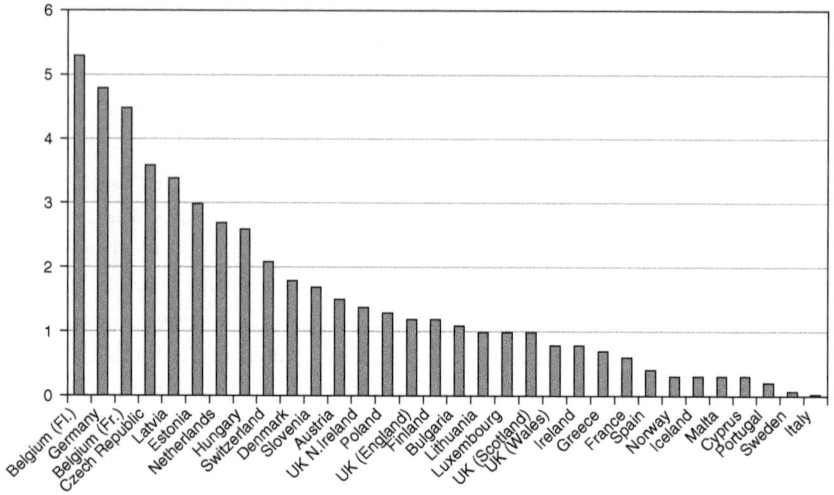

SOURCE FIGURE 1 Pupils in special schools and classes as a percentage of the total school population. Agency for Development in Special Needs Education, Country Data 2010. Retrieved from: www.nesse.fr/nesse/activities/reports/activities/reports/disability-special-needs-1 (p. 19).

and curriculum standards. They can develop their individual learning trajectory. The emphasis is on social integration in the classroom.[4]

Despite the high degree of diversity in society, Flanders has great difficulties in dealing with the variety of pupils. Teachers and schools in Flanders experience a lot of pressure to respond to diverse learning experiences.[5] The number of students in special education in Flanders has been increasing continuously since 2000. Flanders had in 2012 the highest percentage of children (5.2 per cent of the total student population) in special schools all over the EU.[6] The majority are students with

[4] 'Inclusief Onderwijs: (ION-begeleiding)' (*Vlaanderen*), www.vlaanderen.be/nl/onderwijs-en-wetenschap/op-school/inclusief-onderwijs-ion-begeleiding, accessed 24 August 2017. Translated by the authors.

[5] Beno Schraepen, Jo Lebeer and Lies Vanpeperstraete, *Draagkracht ten aanzien van diversiteit & inclusief onderwijs in lagere scholen in de provincie Antwerpen: Projectmatig Wetenschappelijk Onderzoek 2005–2008* (Plantijn Hogeschool 2010) 29–30.

[6] Network of Experts in Social Sciences and Education (NESSE), *Education and Disability/Special Needs: Policies and Practices in Education, Training and Employment for Students with Disabilities and Special Educational Needs in the EU: An Independent Report Prepared for the European Commission by the NESSE Network of Experts* (European Union 2012) 15, 19.

learning problems, mild intellectual disability and behavioural and emotional problems.

Segregation is embedded in the Flemish education system, although there is no empirical evidence of its benefits.[7] Rather, it is a normative choice. Special education is not compulsory for children with special educational needs, but it is provided if it is the choice of their parents. Flanders categorises children according to their ability, and people simply assume that this is the best way to educate children with special educational needs. Moreover, there is a perception that these children act as a barrier for the quality of regular education and that the educational level will necessarily decrease because of diversity.[8] Students with special educational needs who are graduating from special education have their post-school lives marked by unemployment, health problems, loneliness or isolation from community life.[9]

Regarding inclusive education, Flemish teachers state that they are 'scared', 'nervous', 'apprehensive', 'angry' and 'worried'.[10] They find it difficult to tailor their professional selves to the demands of students with special educational needs in regular educational practice.[11] Regular schools spend a lot of time and energy finding out what is 'wrong' with a given child. It appears that 85 per cent of teachers link the particular needs of children to their personal characteristics or to reasons that lie within the private sphere (such as poverty).[12] They moreover blame the child for not meeting the 'norm' and blame the government for a lack of recourses. When the child cannot adjust him/herself, extra support is requested (without which he/she can no longer stay in a regular school). As a result, support by special educators is child-centred, focussed on the adaptation of the child to the school with a view to eliminating difference

[7] Machteld Verbruggen, 'Zijn kinderen met een beperking beter af met het M- decreet?' (2016) 17 *Tijdschrift voor Jeugd-en Kinderrechten* 155, 157.

[8] Raf Feys and Stella Brasseur, 'Dossier M-decreet: Evaluatie 1 jaar M-decreet: een schrijnende balans Crevits durft bevraging leerkrachten nog niet prijsgeven; maar evaluatie & bijsturing zijn dringend! Ook onderwijskoepels, VLOR en onderwijsvakbonden verkiezen stilzwijgen' (2016) 178 *Onderwijskrant* 21, 29–32.

[9] Geert Van Hove, Elisabeth De Schauwer and Inge Van de Putte, 'Looking Back on the Inclusive Education Career of Three Young Adults with Intellectual Disabilities in the Flemish Speaking Part of Belgium: Becoming and Belonging' in Rhonda Craven, Alexandre Morin, Danielle Tracey, Philip Parker and Hua Flora Zhong (eds), *Inclusive Education for Students with Intellectual Disabilities* (Information Age Publisher 2015) 105.

[10] Elisabeth De Schauwer, Inge Van de Putteand Caroline Vandekinderen, *Voorbij de vraagtekens?! Perspectief van leraren op inclusief onderwijs* (Maklu 2011) 12–16.

[11] Inge Van de Putte and Elisabeth De Schauwer, '"Becoming a Different Teacher ... ": Teachers' Perspective on Inclusive Education' (2013) *Erdélyi Pszichológiai Szemle* 245, 245.

[12] Elke Struyf and others, *Zorgbeleid in het gewoon basisonderwijs en secundair onderwijs in Vlaanderen: kenmerken, predictoren en samenhang met taakopvatting en handelingsbekwaamheid van leerkrachten* (OBPWO Project 09.05, UA/KUL/KdG 2012) 79–80.

and reaching the 'norm'. This way of thinking is connected with the deficit framework where the child is perceived as having a problem located in him/herself whereby specialised support is often given as compensation and is focussed on outsourcing, rather than working with teachers to enhance their skills and to develop their teaching methods.[13]

Although Programme for International Student Assessment (PISA) results indicate that Flanders provides high-quality education, they show that the socio-economic achievement gap is among the highest in Western countries.[14] Flanders is not able to combine a good overall performance with equal educational opportunities. This leads to the overrepresentation of students with low socio-economic or ethnic minority backgrounds in special education. In regular primary schools, only 7.66 per cent of students are of ethnic minority background, whereas this rises to 10.82 per cent in special primary schools.[15] Research reveals numerous factors that are not related to any need for transition to special education (such as language problems) to be the cause of this.[16] Another category that is overrepresented in special education are boys, especially in special schools for children with emotional and behavioural problems.[17] Both public opinion and a majority of educational professionals are convinced that segregated settings are the best educational option for students with special educational needs.[18]

CHANGE IS SLOW IN FLANDERS

Over the past twenty-five years, the Flemish government has taken several measures to give a structural framework to inclusive education. It started with steps to ensure the provision of equal educational opportunities through the Equal Opportunities Decree (*Gelijke Onderwijs kansen–decreet*) (GOK

[13] Elisabeth De Schauwer, Inge Van de Putte and Caroline Vandekinderen, 'The Intra-Active Production of Normativity and Difference' (2016) 1 *Gender and Education* 14.

[14] Organisation for Economic Co-operation and Development (OECD), *PISA 2012 Results in Focus: What 15-Year Olds Know and What They Can Do with What They Know* (Organisation for Economic Co-operation and Development 2013) 67, www.oecd.org/pisa/keyfindings/pisa-2012-results-overview.pdf, accessed 22 July 2017.

[15] This statistic has been calculated by the authors using the following website: https://onderwijs.vlaanderen.be/nl/onderwijsstatistieken, accessed 5 October 2017.

[16] Piet Van Avermaet and Kris Van den Branden, *Goed geGOKt? Reflecties op twintig jaar gelijke onderwijskansenbeleid in Vlaanderen* (Maklu 2012) 15–25.

[17] Ides Nicaise and Bram Spruyt, *Het onderwijsdebat: Waarom de hervorming van het secundair broodnodig is* (EPO 2014) 119.

[18] Departement Onderwijs en Vorming, *Meta-evaluatie M-decreet: Synthese van evaluatieve publicaties verschenen sinds de inwerkingtreding van het M-decreet in 2015* (Vlaanderen 2017) 25, https://onderwijs.vlaanderen.be/sites/default/files/atoms/files/Synthese%20tussentijdse%20evaluatie%20M-decreet.pdf, accessed 22 July 2017.

decree). This GOK decree consisted of three phases: 1) adopting measures relating to enrolment (following a 'capacity assessment'); 2) developing an integrated care policy in school with a special attention on students from low socioeconomic backgrounds; and 3) addressing barriers for pupils with special educational needs.[19] In this regard, much attention was paid to the stronger collaboration between regular and special education.[20] During negotiations, the emphasis was mainly on the necessity for special education. The last phase was never implemented.

In November 2008, the preliminary draft of the Educational Care Decree (*Leerzorgdecreet*) was approved. Four key trends can be identified: 1) the international trend towards more participation for people with disabilities; 2) key issues regarding typology and certification; 3) failures in the existing education system; and 4) one common framework with care continuity 'in which the various forms of education (regular education, special education, integrated education ...) get their full potential and through good interaction and collaboration the opportunities for inclusion will maximize'.[21] There was a lot of space for discussion and input from several stakeholders: university colleges, teachers' unions and parents' associations, as well as various actors from regular and special education. There appeared to be no broad societal support for the implementation of the Educational Care Decree. The Flemish government tried to get inclusive education onto the agenda several times, but did not manage to get it through.

With the ratification of the CRPD in 2009, Belgium agreed to create an 'inclusive education system'.[22] This commitment applies to Flanders, which had approved this ratification before the federal entity deposited its ratification instrument. Therefore, the Flemish government is also obliged to achieve inclusive education for all children with special educational needs. The right to inclusive education is subject to progressive realisation, but States Parties must not wait to take measures to reach the objective.[23] Article 24(1) of the CRPD provides that 'States Parties shall ensure an inclusive education system

19 Retrieved from 'Maatwerk in samenspraak: Een vernieuwd beleid voor het onderwijs aan leerlingen met special onderwijsbehoeften' (*Discussietekst voor het parlement*, 8 January 2002), www.coc.be/files/publications/.95/MaatwerkTekst.pdf, accessed 22 July 2017.

20 See for example Frank Vandenbroucke, 'Conceptnota: Leerzorg' (*Eduratio*, 30 March 2007), www.eduratio.be/N_070330_Conceptnota_leerzorg.pdf, accessed 30 July 2017.

21 Ibid. 2, as translated by the authors.

22 United Nations General Assembly, Convention on the Rights of Persons with Disabilities (13 December 2006) A/RES/61/106 [hereinafter CRPD] Article 24(1).

23 Please see the chapter on 'Progressive Realisation' by Gauthier de Beco in the present volume (Chapter 8).

at all levels and life long learning'. The CRPD thus makes inclusive education the primary principle, and special education the exception.[24] Despite Belgium's ratification of the CRPD, Flanders does not seem aware of the implications of this principle for the education of children with special educational needs.[25]

THE M DECREE: THE FIRST STEP TO IMPLEMENT THE RIGHT TO INCLUSIVE EDUCATION

Following the ratification of the CRPD, Flanders adopted a new policy through the Measures for Students with Educational Needs Decree (M Decree). This M Decree was preceded by two other decrees that were proposed following this ratification, and aimed to address the most pressing issues, but neither actually got through.[26] The M Decree was eventually adopted by the Flemish Parliament on 12 March 2014, and its implementation began in 2015–2016. It goes far beyond the inclusion of disabled children and covers all students with special educational needs in regular and special education.

The aim of the M Decree is to achieve inclusive education for children with special educational needs who are able to follow the general curriculum, if necessary, with reasonable accommodation. In the long term, the purpose is to have fewer children with special educational needs referred to segregated settings. Children for whom the general curriculum is not possible are allowed to attend regular schools – provided the school, the guidance centre (*Centrum voor leerlingbegeleiding*) (CLB) and the parents agree on an individual adapted curriculum (*Individueel Aangepast Curriculum*) (IAC) for the pupil in question. The condition requiring a child to be able to follow the general curriculum seems to indicate that making exceptions to the general curriculum is not viewed as reasonable accommodation, and therefore is the reason for the referral of disabled children to special education. Yet this is not in conformity with the CRPD.[27]

[24] Gauthier de Beco, 'The Right to Inclusive Education According to Article 24 of the UN Convention on the Rights of Persons with Disabilities: Background, Requirements and (Remaining) Questions' (2014) 32 *Netherlands Quarterly of Human Rights* 263, 265ff.

[25] Verbruggen (n. 7) 159.

[26] Gauthier de Beco, 'Het recht op onderwijs voor personen met een handicap volgens artikel 24 van het VN-Verdrag inzake de rechten van personen met een handicap: juridische analyse en toepassing in Vlaanderen' (2013) 14 *Tijdschrift voor Jeugd en Kinderrechten* 90, 101–102.

[27] Gauthier de Beco, 'Het decreet betreffende maatregelen voor leerlingen met specifieke onderwijsbehoeften (M-decreet). Een eerste stap in de juiste richting?' (2014) 4(1–2) *Tijdschrift voor Onderwijsrecht en Onderwijsbeleid* 6–7.

The M Decree aims to achieve inclusive education but at the same time further develops special education. The development of the types of special education contradicts the very objectives of the CRPD. The M Decree creates a new type of special education for students with autism who have 'normal' intellectual capacities (type 9). Type 'Basic Entry' (*Type Basisaanbod*) replaces type 1 (children with mild intellectual disability) and type 8 (children with learning difficulties). It is for pupils for whom the general curriculum is not possible with reasonable accommodation. After two years, an evaluation is necessary to determine if special education is still the best option for them. The legislator thereby wants to stimulate a return to regular education.

Main Aspects of the M Decree

1 Regular Education Is the First Option for All Students

A child with special educational needs remains in principle in regular schools. Only when accommodation appears to be disproportionate, or it is unreasonable either to keep this child in a regular school or to provide an individual adapted curriculum does special education come into play. For the first time in Flanders, the applicable legislation therefore guarantees the right to inclusive education to disabled children. The Flemish government does not want a strict interpretation of 'regular education first and then special education'.[28] It wants schools to make more of an effort to allow children with special educational needs to participate in all aspects of daily school life.[29]

The M Decree offers disabled children the opportunity to enrol in a regular school. A school cannot refuse a student because of his/her disability or because he/she demands adjustments to be able to follow the regular curriculum. The M Decree provides for an IAC, but legal access to an IAC is not contained in the law. Children with an IAC get a different kind of enrolment. They have the right to enrol in a regular school but their enrolment is provisional and can be cancelled after a discussion about the reasonableness of the requested accommodations. To link different kinds of enrolment to the curriculum that the pupil follows is not in compliance with the CRPD.[30] The latter requires equal access to inclusive education and full participation in society. Instead, the Flemish government opts for a particular, limited

28 Departement Onderwijs en Vorming (n. 18) 18, as translated by the authors.

29 Ibid. 21.

30 Interfederal Centre for Equal Opportunities (UNIA), *Inclusief onderwijs in Vlaanderen: Een tussentijdse analyse* (Interfederal Centre for Equal Opportunities 2016), http://unia.be/files/Documenten/Tussentijdse_analyse_inclusief_onderwijs-CRPD.pdf, accessed 22 July 2017.

version of diversity and underlines the focus on qualification and cognitive abilities.

Research shows that regular schools report more and more difficulties with students with behavioural problems.[31] Schools have little knowledge and expertise in dealing with students with behavioural and emotional problems. There is a strong assumption that these students do not belong in regular schools.[32]

2 Reasonable Accommodations Are a Right for Children with Special Needs

Every single regular school is required to develop a policy around special educational needs and must explore what reasonable accommodations are available together with the pupil, the parents and the CLB. Reasonable accommodations are individual arrangements that are tailored to the concrete needs of disabled persons.[33] The refusal to enrol them is discriminatory, and parents can complain about it to the Interfederal Centre for Equal Opportunities (UNIA).

Before the M Decree, decisions as to whether a disabled child should have access to a regular school were made after a 'capacity assessment' (*draagkrachtafweging*), a practice that is still in place informally in regular education and that leads to a lot of complaints to the UNIA.[34] This 'capacity assessment' was replaced by reasonable accommodation in line with the CRPD. One year after the M Decree, however, there is still a lot of doubt on what is reasonable accommodation among regular schools.[35] Such accommodation is given on the basis of a diagnosis, especially in secondary education.[36] The problem is

31 Marijke De Smet, Linda Naert and Saar Callens, 'Iedereen mee in de boot van het M-decreet' (*Schoolwijzer Basis*, 23 April 2016) 17, 18, https://cov.acv-online.be/Images/Basis5-SW-iedereenindebootMdecreet-tcm194-387412.pdf, accessed 22 July 2017.

32 Ibid. 19.

33 For a more detailed discussion, see the chapter on reasonable accommodation by Shivaun Quinlivan in the present volume (Chapter 7).

34 Interfederal Centre for Equal Opportunities (UNIA), *Evaluatie: Wet van 10 mei 2007 tot wijziging van de wet van 30 juli 1981 tot bestraffing van bepaalde door racisme of xenofobie ingegeven daden (B.S. 30 mei 2007) (Antiracismewet) Wet van 10 mei 2007 ter bestrijding van bepaalde vormen van discriminatie (B.S. 30 mei 2007) (Antidiscriminatiewet)* (Interfederal Centre for Equal Opportunities 2017) 16, http://unia.be/files/Documenten/Publicaties_docs/Evaluatie_Antidiscriminatie-_en_Antiracismewet_2017.pdf, accessed 22 July 2017.

35 Kinderrechtencommissariaat, *Knelpuntennota M-decreet: Implementatie M-decreet: tussentijdse evaluatie* (Commissie voor Onderwijs 2016), www.kinderrechtencommissariaat.be/sites/default/files/bestanden/2015_2016_11_knelpuntennota_m-decreet_31_mei_2016.pdf, accessed 23 July 2017.

36 Katrien De Munck and Elisabeth De Schauwer, 'De competentiebegeleider doet ertoe! Onderzoek in opdracht van de pedagogische begeleidingsdiensten' (Presentatie gegeven op

not only that focussing too much on reasonable accommodation creates more questions than answers but also that it takes the attention away from changing the whole education system.[37] The obligation to make reasonable accommodation moreover is not accompanied by financial measures and a general strategy to make the Flemish education system inclusive.[38] With few resources to achieve inclusive education, it is doubtful whether Flanders is able to progressively realise the right to inclusive education according to Article 24 of the CRPD. The Belgium Council of State (Raad van State) – which is in charge of assessing the compliance of new legislation with international commitments – considered nonetheless that the M Decree was in compliance with the CRPD.[39]

3 M Decree with the M of Mind Shift

The M Decree requires a shift in mind, asking no longer 'what is wrong with this child?' but 'what is necessary for the school to be able to work with this child?' The premise of the M Decree is that the child with special educational needs is part of the class group and that there should be a focus on the child's participation in the general education system. This is demanding work for the Flemish education system today.

Regular schools must show that they are reflecting upon necessary adaptations and that they try to include children with special educational needs, together with the parents and the CLB. They should no longer ask themselves, 'are we capable of doing this?', which was the underlying idea in the past. In reality, the way in which regular schools handle the inclusion of children with special educational needs is very different: there is a serious discrepancy between theory and practice.[40] Research indicates that regular schools still have difficulties with a transactional framework of collaboration and assign the responsibility of the problems or barriers too easily only to the student.[41] The implementation of the M Decree continues to foster dominant practices of labelling and testing. A diagnosis is often seen as a condition for offering

de studiedag competentiebegeleiders voor alle netten, Ugent Vakgroep Orthopedagogiek, 27 October 2016).

37 Gauthier de Beco, 'Transition to Inclusive Education Systems According to the Convention of the Rights of Persons with Disabilities' (2016) 34 *Nordic Journal of Human Rights* 40, 56.

38 de Beco (n. 27) 7–8.

39 Raad van State 29 October 2013 No. 54.205/1 [3.3].

40 Elke Struyf, *Toeleiding naar het zorgaanbod. Een onderzoek naar bestaande praktijken en verklarende factoren op kind-, gezins- en schoolniveau in het gewoon en buitengewoon onderwijs in Vlaanderen* (Eindrapport OBPWO 13.01, UA en KUL 2016) 76.

41 Ibid. 42.

support and providing reasonable accommodation to children with special educational needs. This creates a danger of creating social inequality, as diagnostic processes are very expensive and are not necessarily a feasible option for all parents.[42]

4 Stronger Regulation on Access to Special Education

The M Decree also describes the new admission criteria for special education. The CLBs play a central role in the referral of children to special schools and will check if regular schools have carefully considered all options. Referrals to a special school solely on the basis of a child's social background are no longer allowed. To ensure that the student's individual needs are met, the CLB is responsible for issuing a certificate for the purpose of special education, which relies on an analysis of these individual needs, the wishes of the parents and the strengths and weaknesses of individual teachers and regular schools. They must also give an overview of the measures taken and possible goals for this student. In many such referrals throughout the first year of the implementation of the M Decree, there was little input on such strengths and weaknesses. The goals for a student's education are often tailored to the place of education where he/she is referred. There has likewise not been much information on effective provision of reasonable accommodation within regular schools.

CHALLENGES WITH THE M DECREE

Enrolment of Disabled Children Is Often Provisional

As mentioned earlier in this chapter, children with an IAC get a different kind of enrolment. They have the right to enrol in a regular school, but their enrolment is provisional. It actually means that they may attend the regular school under certain conditions, but when accommodations are considered disproportionate or when the student makes no progress with an IAC the enrolment can be cancelled. A change in the educational needs and/or in the adjustments demanded during schooling can also lead to such cancellation.[43] This can only happen in collaboration between the school, the CLB and the parents. The school needs to justify and record this decision through official documentation.

42 Wim Van den Broeck, 'Analyse en aanbevelingen n.a.v. de eerste ervaringen met het M-decreet' (Vrije Universiteit Brussel 2016) 6.
43 de Beco (n. 27) 7–8.

Parents of children with special educational needs indicate that enrolment is often problematic. These parents are told that the regular school of their choice does not have the capacity to accommodate such children. They often receive refusals under the table. In a survey among parents, none of them had received a refusal on paper from a school.[44] The procedure of refusal, including the criteria used towards this end, is not transparent.[45] At the same time, this refusal is often backed up by an analysis of support needs by the school without sufficient consultation with the parents, student, previous teachers and support workers. According to the Support Centre for Inclusion, the enrolment for children with special educational needs is a 'waiting station', with unclear information about further steps which can be taken.[46] Parents are insufficiently involved as partners, and no reasonable time frame is set out to concretise enrolment to become permanent. Both the Children's Rights Commission and the UNIA recommend that the difference in enrolment be removed from the M Decree.[47]

There Are Uncertainties about Working with an IAC

The uncertainties about the development of the trajectory and the certification of an IAC are severe obstacles. The quality of an IAC depends greatly on the skills of teachers in regular education to develop and to implement this trajectory. Research shows that the main focus is on actions at the level of the student but rarely on the class or school level.[48] Special educational needs are formulated vaguely and few schools have developed concrete actions to meet the particular needs of the student.[49] Schools also sometimes too easily defer to the option of an IAC in order to get more support in the classroom. There is strong doubt about the legal value of the certificate that is presented at the end of this trajectory.[50]

44 GO! Ouders, *Een jaar M-decreet. Wat denken we daarover? Een bevraging van GO! ouders bij de ouders van het GO! Onderwijs* (GO! Ouders 2016) 13.

45 Steunpunt voor Inclusie, *Drempels en Barrières: Samen met ouders op pad. Ervaringen uit de praktijk in het realiseren van inclusief onderwijs* (Steunpunt voor Inclusie 2016) 25, www.oudersvoorinclusie.be/wp-content/uploads/2016/12/Rapport-Drempels-en-Barri%C3%A8res.pdf, accessed 23 July 2017.

46 Ibid. 19.

47 Kinderrechtencommissariaat (n. 35) 15; UNIA (2017) 29 (n. 34).

48 Struyf (n. 40) 53.

49 Inge Van de Putte and Elisabeth De Schauwer, 'Handelingsgericht werken: Mag het een beetje meer zijn? Onderzoek naar handelingsgericht werken in het Vlaams basisonderwijs' (2015) 34 *Vlaams Tijdschrift voor Orthopedagogiek* 23, 29.

50 Inge Ranschaert, 'Redelijke aanpassingen in het onderwijs: To be or not to be "redelijk"!' (*Studievoormiddag*, 16 June 2017), www.diekeure.be/productblob/docs/212170083(5567).pdf, accessed 23 July 2017.

The Legal Position of Parents Is Insecure

The involvement of families is superficial, as parents are considered to not understand education and should simply be informed by schools.[51] Inclusion is therefore not seen as a matter of choice. The parents are heavily dependent on regular schools with regard to educational choices and are often in a vulnerable position against the school.[52] They do not feel that education professionals listen to them, and have to motivate their choice for inclusive education, not only with regard to teachers but also to support workers (GON/ION), CLBs and other support.

Choosing inclusive education requires substantive effort from parents. This is especially hard for those who have a low economic status. Parents' experience is that it demands a lot of energy to handle the constant danger of being thrown out of school each time difficulties arise, and they express a feeling of loneliness in their responsibility to make sure there is enough support for their children.[53] They also experience a big difference in handling students with special educational needs between teachers themselves.[54] Research also points out the fact that children whose parents have a higher socioeconomic status get faster support, because those parents signal problems to the school on numerous occasions.[55]

Support for Children and Teachers Is Insufficient

The CRPD requires teaching staff to be trained in disability awareness and that support is given to meet the particular needs of children with special educational needs.[56] A number of supported measures were developed to support the implementation of the M Decree. Pedagogical advisors were appointed in order to coach teachers towards more inclusive education. They support teachers to broaden their teaching methods. Several pedagogical advisors testified that they had to provide a lot of information about the M Decree and that they faced heavy resistance by regular schools.[57] This goes in tandem with the experience that too much time and energy go into consultations and reporting, all at the expense of student guidance.[58]

51 Departement Onderwijs en Vorming (n. 18) 55.
52 Nick Hodge and Katherine Runswick-Cole, 'Problematising Parent–Professional Partnerships in Education' (2008) 23 *Disability and Society* 637, 639.
53 Steunpunt voor Inclusie (n. 45) 44.
54 GO! Ouders (n. 44) 3.
55 Struyf and others (n. 12) 83.
56 CRPD (n. 22) Article 24(4).
57 De Munck and De Schauwer (n. 36) 4.
58 Departement Onderwijs en Vorming, *Evaluatie van de pre-waarborgregeling: Basisonderwijs: Procesevaluatie van de implementatie van deze maatregel in schooljaar* 2015–2016 (Vlaanderen

For two school years (2015–2016 and 2016–2017) the Flemish government has focussed on professional development relating to children with special educational needs as well as the M Decree. All regular schools have had the opportunity to follow trajectories on reasonable accommodations, collaborative teaming, handling diversity, working together with parents and implementing the Index for Inclusion.

The budget for special education will gradually become available for the purpose of inclusive education, because more children are making the transition to regular school. The budget that becomes available from special education will be invested in regular education through an 'arrangement of guarantee' (*waarborgregeling*). However, a more constructive and efficient organisation of support at regular schools is necessary and urgent towards this end. The resources for such support should be redistributed. This needs to go further than a guarantee that the budget will no longer be allocated to special education, but rather needs to be a commitment that the budget will be invested in regular education.[59] There should be reform of the support provided to children with special educational needs.

Although there is extra support for disabled children, its extent is rather limited.[60] This extra support does not meet their particular needs and is more available in special than in regular schools. Regular schools continue to consider that support for children with a special educational needs is the responsibility of internal or external experts. They expect guidance to come from outside of the classroom and to be provided on an individual basis. Teachers downplay their own roles in achieving inclusive education and 'are more likely to pass questions [to specialists] because they believe that specialists have' better answers.[61] Indeed, there is more and more outsourcing in regular schools, and research indicates that such outsourcing increases social inequalities.[62] This support moreover is expensive and not accessible to everyone, with the result that inclusive education becomes possible only for a limited group of children.[63]

2016) 62, https://onderwijs.vlaanderen.be/sites/default/files/atoms/files/Evaluatie%20van%20de%20pre-waarborgregeling%20basisonderwijs.pdf, accessed 23 July 2017.

59 Verbruggen (n. 7) 158.

60 Kathleen Mortier, Lore Desimpel, Elisabeth De Schauwer and Geert Van Hove, '"I Want Support, not Comments": Children's Perspectives on Supports in Their Life' (2011) 26 *Disability and Society* 207, 219.

61 Van de Putte and De Schauwer (n. 11) 246.

62 Karine Verschueren, *Buitenschoolse hulpverlening en zorg op school: Samenhang, afstemming en verklarende factoren* (Eindrapport OBPWO 12.01, KU Leuven/UA 2016) 15.

63 Katja Petry, P. Ghesquière, D. Jansen and L. Vanhelmont, *GON en ION anno 2012: OBPWO 10.01* (Katholieke Hogeschool Leuven 2013) 37.

At the moment of writing this chapter, a new support model is being introduced. Special educators (GON/ION teachers) and pedagogical advisors would work together in support teams organised by region. Currently, there is still a lot of vagueness and confusion about this new support model. The distribution of support will stay in the hands of special education.

CONCLUSION

The M Decree is seen by the government as the first step in the implementation of the CRPD. It sits somewhere between 'too little, too late' and 'too fast and too abrupt'. There is currently a lot of pressure to re-evaluate this decree in order to weaken and to revise it. There are even voices in favour of a light version of the CRPD and recognition of the Flemish segregated system.[64]

The Committee on the Rights of Persons with Disabilities (CRPD Committee) expressed its concerns about the limited progress made by Belgium with regard to inclusive education.[65] The coexistence of two separate education systems is not in line with General Comment No. 4 and therefore violates the right to inclusive education.[66] Some students have to travel long distances to attend a special school and this is against the principle of the CRPD that pleads for education in your own community.[67] These worries are still pertinent. There is no coherent strategy to support inclusion in education in Flanders. To break down mind-sets, there should be a profound reform of the general education system.

This led Validity (an international non-governmental organisation previously named the Mental Disability Advocacy Centre) – in collaboration with Equal Rights for Each Person with a Disability (Gelijke Rechten voor Iedere Persoon met een handicap) (GRIP) and one of the present authors[68] – to launch a complaint against Belgium for its lack of inclusive education against the European Committee of Social Rights.[69] Using evidence on the exceptionally segregated education system in Flanders (which is again the most segregated one in the EU), Validity has argued that such practice is in violation of the (Revised) European Social Charter. The decision is still

64 Van den Broeck (n. 42) 3.

65 CRPD Committee, Concluding Observations on the Initial Report of Belgium (28 October 2014) CRPD/C/BEL/CO/1 [36].

66 CRPD Committee, General Comment No 4 (2016) Article 24: Right to Inclusive Education (2 September 2016) CRPD/C/GC/4 [39].

67 Verbruggen (n. 7) 158.

68 Gauthier de Beco in his capacity as GRIP's legal advisor.

69 *Mental Disability Advocacy Center (MDAC) v. Belgium*, Complaint no. 109/2014 (ESCR, complaint registered 30 April 2014).

pending, but should come out in the near future, and it is to be hoped that it will create an impetus towards such a profound reform so as to make the Flemish education system inclusive.

During the transition process, it is, however, important to take the long history of segregation into account. Changes can only take place very gradually. Certain assumptions on deficit thinking, labelling and special education continue to be seen as the best solution for children with special educational needs in Flanders. We addressed in this chapter the difficulties that Flanders shares with other countries, such as adequate support and insecure partnership with parents. A clear vision and strategy by the Flemish government on inclusive education will be important to tackle the numerous ambiguities like provisional enrolment and uncertainties around individual adapted curricula. Further monitoring of the impact of the M Decree will also be necessary to know whether we actually realise qualitative inclusive education for all children.

21

The Implementation of the Right to Inclusive Education in Germany

Thomas Bernhard

I INTRODUCTION

The Convention on the Rights of Persons with Disabilities (CRPD) was ratified by the Federal Republic of Germany on 24 February 2009.[1] Article 24 CRPD, the right to education, is of immense importance in the country. There have not been many articles of public international law which have caused more intensive public,[2] political,[3] judicial[4] and academic[5] debates about which legislative steps the implementation requires, and what

Research assistant at the Chair of Public Law and Public International Law (Professor Markus Krajewski) at the Friedrich-Alexander-University Erlangen-Nuremberg. Some parts of this contribution are drawn from a master's thesis the author submitted to the National University of Ireland in Galway in 2013 for an LLM in international and comparative disability law and policy.

1 United Nations, 'Convention and Optional Protocol Signatures and Ratifications', www.un.org/disabilities/countries.asp?id=166, accessed 1 May 2015.

2 The implementation of an inclusive education system is very often a topic in regional and national newspapers and magazines; see for example Oliver Hollenstein, 'Inklusion – Das soll uns nicht stören' *Die Zeit* (Hamburg, 8 February 2015), www.zeit.de/2015/04/inklusion-schule-behinderung-hamburg-wahlkampf, accessed 1 May 2015. There have also been many documentations and even a film on the subject; see 'Inklusion – Gemeinsam Anders' (*Alpha*), www.br.de/fernsehen/br-alpha/sendungen/inklusion/index.html, accessed 1 May 2015.

3 Almost every federal state (*Land*) has already taken some legislative steps to implement an inclusive education system, accompanied by parliamentary debates, roundtable discussions with disabled people's organisations and expert meetings. See for example, for Bavaria, the Bavarian Parliament document 'Law Draft Printed Matter No. 16/8100 of 28.03.2011' (Lt-Drs) 16/8100 (28 March 2011).

4 So far the courts have regularly denied the applicability of Article 24 CRPD for various reasons, but the legal impact of this article has been discussed in many court decisions already. For an overview of the case law in which courts referred to the CRPD, see Valentin Aichele, 'Die UN-Behindertenrechtskonvention in der Gerichtlichen Praxis' [2011](10) AnwBl 727.

5 See for example Eibe Riedel, *Zur Wirkung der internationalen Konvention über die Rechte von Menschen mit Behinderung und ihres Fakultativprotokolls auf das deutsche Schulsystem* (Landesarbeitsgemeinschaft Gemeinsam Leben, Gemeinsam Lernen Nordrhein-Westfalen 2010); Markus Krajewski and Thomas Bernhard, 'Artikel 24 – Recht auf Bildung' in

immediate legal impact the article has. However, many non-governmental organisations (NGOs) and disabled people's organisations (DPOs) are disappointed about the ongoing debates and the fact that – from their point of view – the right to inclusive education is still not implemented in a manner compliant with international law.[6] In its recently published concluding observations on the initial report of Germany, the Committee on the Rights of Persons with Disabilities has expressed its concerns 'that the State [P]arty has an education system where the majority of students with disabilities attend segregated special-needs schools'.[7]

This contribution examines the implementation of the right to inclusive education in Germany. The first part gives a brief overview of the salient features of the German education system, especially of those that are relevant for the education of people with disabilities. The other parts of this contribution are based on the Concluding Observations on the Initial Report of Germany, which was published in April 2015 by the Committee on the Rights of Persons with Disabilities. In these concluding observations, the Committee commented on the most relevant problems and emerging issues regarding the implementation of an inclusive education system in Germany. This chapter provides further detailed information about the issues mentioned by the Committee, namely the high number of students with disabilities in segregated education (II), the right to access mainstream education (III), the right to reasonable accommodation (IV) and the necessary steps to progressively implement an inclusive education system (V).

II SALIENT FEATURES OF THE GERMAN EDUCATION SYSTEM

Before we can discuss the impact of the CRPD on the German education system, it is necessary to give a brief introduction to this system in order to understand the specific problems the German education system may have in becoming an inclusive system.

Antje Welke (ed.), *UN-Behindertenrechtskonvention mit rechtlichen Erläuterungen* (Deutscher Verein für Öffentliche und Private Fürsorge 2012) 164.

6 Alliance of German Non-Governmental Organizations Regarding the UN Convention on the Rights of Persons with Disabilities, *For Independent Living, Equal Rights, Accessibility and Inclusion! First Civil Society Report on the Implementation of the UN Convention on the Rights of Persons with Disabilities in Germany* (Shadow Report CRPD Alliance, BRK-Allianz 2013) 51ff., http://tbinternet.ohchr.org/_layouts/treatybodyexternal/Download.aspx?symbolno=INT%2fCRPD%2fNGO%2fDEU%2f16323&Lang=en, accessed 1 May 2015 (Shadow Report CRPD Alliance).

7 Committee on the Rights of Persons with Disabilities, Concluding Observations on the Initial Report of Germany (17 April 2015) CRPD/C/DEU/CO/1 [45].

First of all, the German education system is very complicated because the legislative authority for education rests with the sixteen *Länder*, according to Article 30 and Article 70 Grundgesetz (Basic Law, the German constitution), which means that there are different types of schools in these sixteen *Länder*, and also different laws about the education of people with disabilities.

In all of the sixteen *Länder*, pupils go to primary school (*Grundschule*) together for the first four or six (in Berlin and Brandenburg) years. After that, the system divides into different types of schools, as can been seen in Bavaria, for example, with *Mittelschule*, *Realschule* and *Gymnasium*. The *Mittelschule* offers five years of general secondary schooling, the *Realschule* offers six years of intermediate schooling and the *Gymnasium* offers eight or nine years of grammar schooling. Usually the school that pupils attend after primary school depends on the grades that they achieve in the last year of primary school, or on the recommendation of their primary school teacher. Additionally in some *Länder* there exist *Gesamtschulen* (comprehensive schools), which offer nine years of comprehensive schooling (combining the three other school types) and which lead to university-level education as well.[8]

Besides this, there are schools for special education. Special education is classified with regard to pupils' special educational requirements into the following categories: blind, visually impaired, deaf, hearing impaired, mentally disabled, physically disabled, learning difficulties, behavioural problems, impaired speech and pupils with a disease.[9]

These very specialised school types show that Germany has a long and extensive tradition of segregated education for pupils with disabilities. Some decades ago, almost all students with disabilities attended special schools. Since the 1980s, pupils with disabilities have been increasingly included in general schools under school pilot projects.[10] Furthermore, approaches to inclusive teaching have been developed in educational science, and various forms of co-operation between general schools and special schools have

8 See in detail European Agency for Special Needs and Inclusive Education, 'Germany – General Information', www.european-agency.org/country-information/germany/general-information, accessed 1 May 2015; Brigitte Lohmar and Thomas Eckhardt (eds), *The Education System in the Federal Republic of Germany 2011/2012* (Secretariat of the Standing Conference of the Ministers of Education and Cultural Affairs of the Länder in the Federal Republic of Germany 2013), www.kmk.org/fileadmin/doc/Dokumentation/Bildungswesen_en_pdfs/dossier_en_ebook.pdf, accessed 1 May 2015.

9 See further European Agency for Special Needs and Inclusive Education, 'Germany – Special Needs Education within the Education System', www.european-agency.org/country-information/germany/national-overview/special-needs-education-within-the-education-system, accessed 1 May 2015.

10 Ibid.

emerged.[11] Especially in recent years (after the ratification of the CRPD in 2009), all *Länder* have taken steps to implement an inclusive education system.

III HIGH NUMBER OF STUDENTS WITH DISABILITIES IN SEGREGATED EDUCATION

The long tradition of special education is the reason why the number of students with disabilities who attend special schools has always been very high in Germany compared to most other countries. Consequently the Committee on the Rights of Persons with Disabilities has expressed its concerns that Germany 'has an education system where the majority of students with disabilities attend segregated special-needs schools'.[12]

Indeed, it is true that in the school year 2012/13 in total 355,139 pupils with special educational needs attended school, and only 139,605 of them went to regular schools.[13] However it has to be noted that the number of students with special educational needs who attend regular schools has increased constantly since the CRPD has been ratified. In the school year 2008/09 only 88,664 pupils with special educational needs had been enrolled in regular schools.[14] This means that the percentage of students with special educational needs who attend regular schools has risen from 18.4 per cent in the school year 2008/09 to 28.2 per cent in the school year 2012/13.[15] The percentage of students with special educational needs who attend regular schools varies greatly between the different *Länder*, between 14.7 per cent in Lower Saxony and 63.1 per cent in Bremen.[16] The reason for this is that some *Länder* started the development of an inclusive education system earlier. In the school year 2008/09, before the CRPD was ratified, the discrepancies were even more noticeable as the percentage of students with special educational needs who attended regular schools varied between 6.6 per cent in Lower Saxony and 40.9 per cent in

[11] Ibid.

[12] Committee on the Rights of Persons with Disabilities, Concluding Observations on the Initial Report of Germany (17 April 2015) CRPD/C/DEU/CO/1 [45].

[13] Nicole Hollenbach-Biele, *Update Inklusion – Datenreport zu den aktuellen Entwicklungen* (Bertelsmann Stiftung 2014) 11ff.

[14] 'Responses to the Questions from the List of Issues in Connection with the First German Country Review: Volume of Appendices' (Bundesministerium für Arbeit und Soziales 2014), http://tbinternet.ohchr.org/Treaties/CRPD/Shared%20Documents/DEU/INT_CRPD_RLI_DEU_18748_E.pdf, accessed 1 May 2015 (Appendices to Reply to List of Issues), 62.

[15] Ibid. 63.

[16] Hollenbach-Biele (n. 13) 12.

Schleswig-Holstein.[17] However, it is true for all *Länder* that more and more pupils with special educational needs attend regular schools. The most significant increase can be identified in Hamburg (from 14.5 per cent to 54 per cent between 2008 and 2013).[18] Taking the starting point into consideration, it seems possible to identify a progressive realisation of the duty to educate more children with disabilities at mainstream schools in all *Länder*.

However, this result is not as clear as it seems to be at first sight. First of all, the number of students diagnosed with special educational needs has risen from 482,155[19] to 494,744[20] in the same time period. As the total number of students has dropped due to demographic reasons, this means that the percentage of students diagnosed with special educational needs has increased from 6 per cent[21] to 6.6 per cent[22] between the school years 2008/09 and 2012/13. That means that it is possible that the reason for the higher percentage of pupils with special educational needs who attend regular schools could at least partly be the result of changed diagnostics.[23]

It is therefore useful to have a closer look at the share of pupils who attended special schools. In the school year 2008/09, 4.9 per cent of all pupils attended special schools.[24] Until the school year 2012/13, this number has only slightly dropped to 4.8 per cent.[25] This still shows a progressive realisation of the goal to include more children and adolescents in regular schools, but the change is not taking place very quickly.

The official statistics have furthermore been criticised because they do not differentiate between students with special educational needs who are 'really' included in mainstream schools and those who only attend external classes which are classes of special schools that are located in the building of a regular school.[26] The Committee explicitly asked the government to provide data about the students who attend those special classes.[27] That

17 Ibid. 16.
18 Ibid. 16.
19 Klaus Klemm, *Inklusion in Deutschland – Eine bildungsstatistische Analyse* (Bertelsmann Stiftung 2013) 9.
20 Hollenbach-Biele (n. 13) 10.
21 Klemm (n. 19) 9.
22 Hollenbach-Biele (n. 13) 10.
23 Klemm (n. 19) 6.
24 Ibid. 11.
25 Hollenbach-Biele (n. 13) 11.
26 Klemm (n. 19) 9.
27 Committee on the Rights of Persons with Disabilities, List of Issues in Relation to the Initial Report of Germany (12 May 2014) CRPD/C/DEU/Q/1 [18].

was one of the few questions in the list of issues which the government could not answer.[28]

IV THE RIGHT TO ACCESS MAINSTREAM EDUCATION

There has been a debate over the years in Germany about the exact meaning of Article 24 CRPD with regard to the right to access mainstream education. Almost all *Länder* explicitly responded to a corresponding question of the Committee that special education schools will continue to operate in the future[29] and that they 'intend to introduce a system where parents have the right to choose between mainstream general education schools and special education schools'.[30] This has been criticised by the civil society in a shadow report which was submitted to the Committee, because a right to choose would mean that the special needs school system will be maintained.[31] The German monitoring body shares the same opinion that a right to choose would not be compliant with Article 24 CRPD.[32]

On that subject, the Committee on the Rights of Persons with Disabilities seems to agree with the governments of the *Länder*. The Committee does not recommend abolishing all special schools, but it recommends Germany 'scale down segregated schools to facilitate inclusion'.[33] The Committee furthermore recommends 'that the law and policies uphold the duty that mainstream schools enrol children with disabilities with immediate effect if that is their choice'.[34]

On the other hand, this recommendation in the concluding observations makes clear that the Committee is of the view that the right to choose education at a regular school is not sufficiently implemented in Germany so far. This question has to be discussed from a legal point of view with regard to both the relevant legislation (1) and court rulings (2).

28 Committee on the Rights of Persons with Disabilities, 'Replies of Germany to the List of Issues' (15 January 2015) CRPD/C/DEU/Q/1/Add.1 [96].

29 Appendices to Reply to List of Issues (n. 14) 67ff.

30 Committee on the Rights of Persons with Disabilities, 'Replies of Germany to the List of Issues' (15 January 2015) CRPD/C/DEU/Q/1/Add.1 [104].

31 Shadow Report CRPD Alliance (n. 6) 55.

32 Monitoring-Stelle zur UN-Behindertenrechtskonvention, 'Eckpunkte zur Verwirklichung eines inklusiven Bildungssystems' (German Institute for Human Rights, 31 March 2011) 14, www.institut-fuer-menschenrechte.de/uploads/tx_commerce/stellungnahme_der_monitoring_stelle_eckpunkte_z_verwirklichung_eines_inklusiven_bildungssystems_31_03_2011.pdf, accessed 1 May 2015.

33 Committee on the Rights of Persons with Disabilities, Concluding Observations on the Initial Report of Germany (17 April 2015) CRPD/C/DEU/CO/1 [46(b)].

34 Ibid.

1 *Legislation*

The right to inclusive education or to access mainstream education cannot be found in the German Basic Law, because the Basic Law does not include any social, economic and cultural rights. However, Article 3 of the Basic Law deals with equality and non-discrimination. The second sentence of Article 3 paragraph 3 of the Basic Law reads: 'No person shall be disfavoured because of disability.' If the denial to access mainstream education could be qualified as discrimination, the right to access regular schools could be read into that article. This is discussed hereafter in the next section about relevant court rulings.

The specific legislation about education is different in all sixteen *Länder*, because they have autonomy in matters of culture and education, according to Articles 30 and 70 of the Basic Law. It is therefore impossible to discuss all the relevant school regulations in this contribution. However, it is possible to identify some trends that are similar in many *Länder*. To explain the development of the right to access mainstream education, Bavaria as the largest of the sixteen *Länder* is used as an example hereafter.

Of course people with disabilities were never denied access to mainstream education just because of their impairment. However, the thresholds of that right were set very high for a long time in most *Länder*. In Bavaria, it was possible for students with disabilities to be educated at a regular school, but only if they were able to fulfil the demands of that school like all the other students.[35] Of course, reasonable accommodation such as extra time in exams could be provided, but with these accommodations the children with disabilities had to be able to adjust to the norm.

The Bavarian legislator changed this law in 2003. From then on it was possible for students with disabilities to be educated at a regular school if they could 'actively participate' in the classes.[36] This was the case if the students with disabilities could – if necessary with individual support – achieve

[35] Article 21 para. 1 BayEUG a.F. (Bavarian Education Act valid until 2003); for the development of the BayEUG in relation to people with disabilities, see Markus Krajewski and Thomas Bernhard, 'Inklusive Schule im Freistaat Bayern? – Die Änderung des BayEUG vom 13.7.2011 aus Sicht der UN-Behindertenrechtskonvention' (2012) 5 *Bayerische Verwaltungsblätter* 134; Jutta Schöler, Kerstin Merz-Atalik and Carmen Dorrance, *Auf dem Weg zur Schule für alle?* (Friedrich-Ebert-Stiftung 2010), http://library.fes.de/pdf-files/akademie/bayern/07824.pdf, accessed 1 August 2013.

[36] Article 41 para. 1 BayEUG a.F. (Bavarian Education Act valid until 2011).

educational progress and were 'sociable'. This was on the one hand an important step towards inclusive education, because it was not necessary anymore for students with disabilities to be able to fulfil the demands of these schools like all other students. On the other hand, inclusive education was still only possible if the students fulfilled specific criteria such as the ability to actively participate and to be 'sociable'.

In 2011, the Bavarian legislature tried to implement Article 24 CRPD. According to the current Bavarian Education Act, it is not necessary anymore for the students to be 'sociable' or to have the ability to actively participate. Instead, the parents can decide whether they register their children with a regular or special school.[37] There are only three reasons why a school can deny a pupil with disabilities: according to Article 41 paragraph 5 of the Bavarian Education Act, the decision of the parents can be revised by the school authorities if the special educational needs cannot be met at the regular school and the education at the regular school would – having the idea of social participation in mind – jeopardise the development of the pupil with disabilities or the rights of other members of the school community. Furthermore, the cost bearer of the schools has to agree that a child with special educational needs is educated at a specific school.[38] This consent can only be refused if the education at that school would cause 'considerable additional costs'.[39]

A similar development can be seen in many *Länder*. The thresholds of the right to access a specific regular school were lowered in most of the education acts over the past decades. Especially after Germany ratified the CRPD in 2009, many *Länder* have taken legislative steps to implement Article 24 CRPD.[40] However, the three thresholds of the right to access a specific regular school (the available resources, the best interests of the child with disabilities and the rights of others) can be found in many *Länder* in a similar way.

Note that if one of these thresholds applies, this does not inevitably mean that the child with disabilities has to attend a special school. Of course it would be possible to register the child at another regular school where the difficulties do not appear or can be solved.

37 Article 41 para. 1 BayEUG (Bavarian Education Act).

38 *Schulträger*; this can be the community, the district or the *Land*, depending on the school.

39 Article 30a para. 4, Article 30b para. 2 No. 3, Article 30b para. 3 No. 2, Article 41 para. 4 No. 3 BayEUG (Bavarian Education Act).

40 For an overview, see Sven Mißling and Oliver Ückert, *Inklusive Bildung: Schulgesetze auf dem Prüfstand* (German Institute for Human Rights 2014).

2 *Court Rulings*

However, as long as these thresholds exist in the legislation of many *Länder*, there will be cases in which the school authorities deny children with disabilities access to regular schools. In these cases, it is possible to appeal the decision in the administrative courts. It can now be discussed whether the courts apply the CRPD in the right way so far.

It is to be welcomed that the German courts take the CRPD into consideration in many cases.[41] Furthermore, it has already been decided that the CRPD has to be used to interpret domestic legislation and even the Basic Law by the Federal Constitutional Court.[42]

However, the court rulings concerning the right to education have not been convincing so far. First of all, courts still take the view that Article 24 CRPD is not applicable because it did not yet enter into force, because only the *Länder* have the legislative authority to pass legislation in the education sector, but the CRPD was signed and ratified by the federal legislator only.[43] The question when and how an international human rights treaty enters into force when it covers an area in which the *Länder* have the legal competence to act is indeed very complicated.[44] The courts take the view that those elements of the treaties do not enter into force until the *Länder* pass laws to implement the treaty in the domestic legislation.[45] In doing so they mix up the entry into force and the implementation of an international law treaty. In short, it has to be recognised that the federal legislator has the competence to ratify and to put in place international law treaties according to Articles 32 and 59 Basic Law, whereas the competence to implement the treaty for example by passing laws to adopt the domestic legislation to the treaty rests with the *Länder*.[46] As most *Länder* have passed laws to implement the CRPD by now, this dispute is likely to

41 For an overview of the court rulings in the education sector in which Article 24 was mentioned, see Thomas Bernhard, 'Art. 24 UN-BRK: Rezeption in der Rechtsprechung nach fünf Jahren' (2015) 1 *Recht der Jugend und des Bildungswesens* 79.

42 Bundesverfassungsgericht (Federal Constitutional Court), 'Order of the Second Senate' (23 March 2011) 2 BvR 882/09 [52].

43 Inter alia Verwaltungsgerichtshof Baden-Württemberg (Higher Administrative Court Baden-Württemberg), 'Determination of the Special Schooling Obligation against the Will of the Educated Persons' (21 November 2012) 9 S 1833/12 [56]; Hessischer Verwaltungsgerichtshof (Higher Administrative Court Hesse), 'Resolution of 12 November 2009' (12 November 2009) 7 B 2763/09 [5ff.].

44 See in detail recently Dörte Dörschner, *Die Rechtswirkungen der UN-Behindertenrechtskonvention in Deutschland am Beispiel des Rechts auf inklusive Bildung*, vol. 26 (Social Law and Social Policy in Europe Series) (LIT Verlag 2014) 156ff.

45 Hessischer Verwaltungsgerichtshof (Higher Administrative Court Hesse), 'Resolution of 12 November 2009' (12 November 2009) 7 B 2763/09 [18].

46 Bernhard (n. 41) 82.

become less important, because after that the entry into force of Article 24 CRPD cannot be questioned anymore, even by the courts.[47]

The second reason why the courts question the applicability of Article 24 CRPD is that they take the view that social, economic and cultural rights can only be achieved progressively and thus can neither be directly applicable nor establish any individual rights, because they are not sufficiently concrete.[48] This opinion is based on the traditional understanding of social, economic and cultural rights as positive rights which can only be achieved progressively. However, it can be seen in many documents that this opinion is no longer defensible.[49] The Committee on Social, Economic and Cultural Rights has clarified which elements of the right to education have to be understood as being of immediate effect.[50] Recently the General Assembly has adopted a new optional protocol to the International Covenant on Economic, Social and Cultural Rights (ICESCR).[51] This optional protocol now allows an individual to complain to the Committee on Social, Economic and Cultural Rights.[52] Obviously an individual complaint only makes sense when the ICESCR gives rights to the individual person. This modern understanding of social, economic and cultural rights has been given a new impetus with the adoption of the CRPD, namely because it is the first time that states explicitly agreed on this new understanding in a binding treaty of public international law. Article 4 paragraph 2 CRPD reads:

> With regard to economic, social and cultural rights, each State Party undertakes to take measures to the maximum of its available resources and, where needed, within the framework of international cooperation, with a view to achieving progressively the full realization of these rights, without prejudice to those obligations contained in the present Convention that are immediately applicable according to international law.[53]

47 Ibid.

48 Hessischer Verwaltungsgerichtshof (Higher Administrative Court Hesse), 'Resolution of 12 November 2009' (12 November 2009) 7 B 2763/09 [27ff.].

49 See inter alia United Nations Commission on Human Rights, 'Note verbale dated 5/12/05 from the Permanent Mission of the Netherlands to the United Nations Office at Geneva addressed to the Centre for Human Rights ("Limburg Principles")' (8 January 1987) E/CN.4/1987/17 [8]; Committee on Economic, Social and Cultural Rights, General Comment No. 3: The Nature of States Parties' Obligations (Art. 2 Para. 1) (14 December 1990) E/1991/23 [1].

50 Committee on Economic, Social and Cultural Rights, General Comment No. 13: the Right to Education (Article 13 of the Covenant) (8 December 1999) E/C.12/1999/10 [31], [41], [51], [52].

51 United Nations General Assembly, Optional Protocol to the International Covenant on Social, Economic and Cultural Rights (5 March 2009) A/RES/63/117.

52 See further about this optional protocol in Valentin Aichele, 'Ein Meilenstein für die Unteilbarkeit: Das neue Fakultativprotokoll zum UN-Sozialpakt' (2009) 2 *Vereinte Nationen* 72.

53 Emphasis added.

This means that, at least regarding the CRPD, it is quite obvious that all rights can include elements which are immediately applicable and that they can also establish individual rights.

Some courts in more recent decisions again try to question whether the CRPD really gives a right to inclusive education or just to integrative education.[54] This had been discussed in Germany intensively because the official German translation of *inclusive* is *integrativ*, although *inklusiv* is a German word as well and is used in the same way as the English word *inclusive*.[55] Although it has been accepted that the German version is not binding according to Article 50 CRPD, some courts started this discussion again and referenced the French version, which is binding according to Article 50 CRPD and uses not only the word *inclusif* but also *insertion* and *intégration* in Article 24 CRPD.[56] I am of the view that it cannot seriously be questioned whether the CRPD gives a right to inclusive education or not. It is generally acknowledged that if the different translations of a contract in the binding languages contradict themselves, the language of the drafting process is of prime importance.[57] In the concluding observations on the initial report of Austria, where the same official translation as in Germany is used, the Committee on the Rights of Persons with Disabilities clarified that point and noted 'that there is some confusion between "inclusive" education and "integrated" education. However, the Committee commends the establishment of inclusive education models in several Länder'.[58]

To summarise, the courts have to apply Article 24 CRPD because it has already entered into force and the courts have to acknowledge that elements of this article can be immediately applicable and establish individual rights. Furthermore, they should not question that the article really stipulates the goal of an inclusive education system.

[54] Verwaltungsgerichtshof Baden-Württemberg (Higher Administrative Court Baden-Württemberg), 'Determination of the Special Schooling Obligation against the Will of the Educated Persons' (21 November 2012) 9 S 1833/12 [55].

[55] See for example Valentin Aichele, *Die UN-Behindertenrechtskonvention und ihr Fakultativprotokoll: Ein Beitrag zur Ratifikationsdebatte* (German Institute for Human Rights 2008).

[56] Verwaltungsgerichtshof Baden-Württemberg (Higher Administrative Court Baden-Württemberg), 'Determination of the Special Schooling Obligation against the Will of the Educated Persons' (21 November 2012) 9 S 1833/12 [55].

[57] Latham & Watkins LLP, *Völkerrechtliche Fragen des inklusiven Unterrichts in Deutschland im Zusammenhang mit dem Inkrafttreten des Übereinkommens der Vereinten Nationen über die Rechte von Menschen mit Behinderungen* (Bundesarbeitsgemeinschaft Gemeinsam leben – gemeinsam lernen, April 2009) 4.

[58] Committee on the Rights of Persons with Disabilities, Concluding Observations on the Initial Report of Austria (30 September 2013) CRPD/C/AUT/CO/1 [40].

Regarding the right to access mainstream education, the application of Article 24 CRPD would at least have the following consequences: the aforementioned thresholds of the right to access regular schools which can be found in the legislation of many *Länder* have to be interpreted in light of Article 24 CRPD. This means that first of all it has to be acknowledged that generally every child attends a regular school and that education at a special school is the exception to the rule. This is a fundamental paradigm shift for many *Länder*, but most education acts have already been revised to express this new understanding. For the administration and the courts this means that it does not have to be proven by the pupil, the parents or the schools that a child *can* be educated at a regular school, because this is the norm. Instead it has to be proven that this is *not* possible in a particular case if the school authorities want to deny the right to access a specific regular school. This would only be possible if one of the aforementioned thresholds would apply, and the burden of proof for that rests with the school or the school authorities. Furthermore, these thresholds have to be applied in the most restrictive way possible under the wording of the education acts.[59]

If the administration or the courts take the view that it would nevertheless be in compliance with the education act of one of the *Länder* to deny access to a specific school in a particular case, this decision has to be measured against the non-discrimination provision in Article 3 paragraph 3 Basic Law. In having regard to the threshold of the available resources, the decision of the Federal Constitutional Court from the year 1997 has to be overturned. In this case, the court decided that it is not discrimination under Article 3 paragraph 3 Grundgesetz when a school refuses a child with disabilities on the ground that the personnel or material expenses required to support the child are not available at that school.[60] It would only be discrimination under Article 3 paragraph 3 Grundgesetz if the school would refuse the child even though the education at the regular school would be possible, could be shouldered with the available personnel and material expenses, and would not cause any organisational difficulties.[61] This understanding of discrimination is obviously not compliant with the CRPD. This is where the right to reasonable accommodation comes into play: the 'available personnel and material expenses' at a school cannot be decisive. Instead, the school and the school authorities

59 See for example in detail about the interpretation of the Bavarian Education Act (BayEUG) in light of the CRPD in Krajewski and Bernhard (n. 35).

60 Bundesverfassungsgericht (Federal Constitutional Court), 'Order of the First Senate' (8 October 1997) 1 BvR 9/97.

61 Ibid., guiding principle.

have to find solutions for how the child can be accommodated at this school. Of course these reasonable accommodations can include the necessity of additional personnel and material expenses. But according to the definition in Article 2 CRPD, they can only be denied if they would impose a 'disproportionate or undue burden'. Since 'organisational difficulties' can probably be resolved by the provision of reasonable accommodation, they cannot be a threshold of the right to access a regular school.

In relation to the thresholds of the best interests of the child and the rights of others the same problem occurs: it would not be compliant with the CRPD to just examine the conditions at a particular school as they are and then decide whether the education of the child with disabilities at this school would be in the best interests of the child or if it would perhaps interfere with the rights of the other children in the class. As already explained, the schools and the courts have to find solutions to enable the child with disabilities to attend the regular school in a way that is in the best interests of the child and does not interfere with the rights of others. If the schools or the courts take the view that this would be possible but too expensive, neither the threshold of the best interests of the child nor the threshold of the rights of others applies. In this case, the only applicable threshold would be the available resources. This should be expressed properly in the decisions. Consequently, these two thresholds can only apply if the authorities are able to prove that the education at the regular school would jeopardise the development of the child with disabilities or seriously interfere with the rights of other children, although every imaginable individual support would be provided.

This is the way in which Article 3 paragraph 3 Grundgesetz and the thresholds in the education acts of the *Länder* have to be understood and applied by all school authorities and courts now. All decisions which do not take the CRPD into account would be unlawful.

V THE RIGHT TO REASONABLE ACCOMMODATION

The previous sections have shown that the right to reasonable accommodation is one of the core issues regarding the implementation of Article 24 CRPD. The committee is correct to criticise that this right is not yet implemented in the domestic legislation of Germany:

The Committee is concerned that:

(a) Current legislation does not contain a definition of reasonable accommodation and that the denial of such accommodation is not considered a form of discrimination;

(b) The understanding of how reasonable accommodation can be implemented is still largely underdeveloped with respect to administration, jurisdiction and social services provision.[62]

The Committee furthermore makes an explicit statement regarding the right to reasonable accommodation in the education sector and recommends that Germany should 'ensure that reasonable accommodation is provided at all levels of education and [be] legally enforceable and justiciable before the courts'.[63]

Indeed the right to reasonable accommodation is relatively unknown in Germany. In the federal legislation a similar right only exists in employment law.[64] On the *Länder* level, only Saxony-Anhalt has implemented a general right to reasonable accommodation.[65] Nevertheless, there are of course many very specific norms in diverse federal and regional state laws which lay down by law that accommodations have to be provided in specific cases. A study came to the conclusion that these 'regulations may be interpreted to cover the complete provision of reasonable accommodation, subject to judicial interpretation'.[66] All the regulations for examinations, for instance, include provisions about extra time in specific cases and there are also laws which guarantee individual support, including assistive technology.

Nevertheless, the lack of a general norm which requires the provision of reasonable accommodation causes one main problem: without a general norm about reasonable accommodation, schools, education authorities and courts may take the view that they just have to do what is explicitly required by the diverse laws which deal with students with special educational needs. The idea of reasonable accommodation, however, goes far beyond that: the goal is a change of the mind-set of schools and education authorities. When a student with special educational needs wants to attend a regular school, the school cannot just examine whether it would be possible for the child to attend the school in the current situation and decide that it is not possible if there are any barriers. Instead, the school and the authorities have to consider whether it

62 Committee on the Rights of Persons with Disabilities, Concluding Observations on the Initial Report of Germany (17 April 2015) CRPD/C/DEU/CO/1 [13(a)] and [13(b)].

63 Ibid. [46(c)].

64 Section 81 para. 4 Social Code IX.

65 In the new equality act for people with disabilities of 2010 in Saxony-Anhalt (Behindertengleichstellungsgesetz Sachsen-Anhalt), section 4 gives a right to reasonable accommodation, takes the definition of the CRPD and also states that the denial would be a form of discrimination.

66 Lisa Waddington and Anna Lawson, *Disability and Non-Discrimination Law in the European Union: An Analysis of Disability Discrimination Law within and beyond the Employment Field* (European Commission 2009) 77.

would be possible to break down these barriers by any reasonable accommodation. These accommodations may have to be creative and innovative to find a solution for each individual case. It is just impossible to regulate all possible reasonable accommodations in specific regulations.

This is why it is necessary to implement the right to reasonable accommodation at both the federal and the *Länder* level. The general duty to provide reasonable accommodation could for example be implemented in the equality acts for people with disabilities (*Behindertengleichstellungsgesetze*) (BGG) of the Federation and the *Länder*, as it is already the case in Saxony-Anhalt. The non-discrimination provision would fit into the General Law on Equal Treatment (*Allgemeines Gleichbehandlungsgesetz*) (AGG) of 2006. This is the model the CRPD National Monitoring Body argues for.[67]

Furthermore it is important to clarify which body is responsible to provide the accommodation. The Committee mentions the provision of sign language in mainstream schools as a problem.[68] This is one good example in which it was not clear whether the Ministry of Education or the Social Services Ministry are responsible to cover the costs for the sign language interpreter.[69]

As long as the right to reasonable accommodation is not implemented in the domestic legislation, it is at least possible and necessary that the courts interpret the non-discrimination provision in Article 3 paragraph 3 Basic Law in light of the CRPD, which means that the denial of reasonable accommodation can be discriminatory. However, the courts do not do that so far, which shows that the Committee is correct when it indicates that the right to reasonable accommodation is not legally enforceable and justiciable before the courts yet.

VI THE PROGRESSIVE REALISATION OF THE RIGHT TO EDUCATION

Besides these elements that are immediately applicable, the Committee also comments on the progressive realisation of the right to inclusive education in Germany. It recommends that Germany should 'develop a strategy, action

[67] Valentin Aichele, *Barrieren im Einzelfall überwinden: Angemessene Vorkehrungen gesetzlich verankern* (German Institute for Human Rights 2012) 3, www.institut-fuer-menschenrechte.de/uploads/tx_commerce/positionen_5_barrieren_im_einzelfall_ueberwinden_01.pdf, accessed 1 May 2015.

[68] Committee on the Rights of Persons with Disabilities, Concluding Observations on the Initial Report of Germany (17 April 2015) CRPD/C/DEU/CO/1 [46(d)].

[69] See for example Arnold Köpcke-Duttler, 'Eine gehörlose Schülerin in den Mühlen der Bürokratie' (*Legal Tribune Online*, 7 August 2012), www.lto.de/recht/hintergruende/h/kinder-mit-behinderung-muessen-besser-vor-ausgrenzung-geschuetzt-werden/, accessed 1 May 2015.

plan, timeline and targets to provide access to a high-quality, inclusive education system across all Länder, including the required financial resources and personnel at all levels'.[70]

Of course strategies and action plans exist in almost all *Länder*, and most of them have even taken legislative steps to implement Article 24 CRPD in many different areas already.[71] However, it is true that most of them lack clear timelines and targets, which makes it very difficult to monitor whether the steps that were taken are sufficient to be compliant with the duty to progressively realise an inclusive education system. This would be much easier if there were clear timelines and targets, but it would still be difficult. If, for instance, teachers are trained in inclusive education, it may be possible to collect data on how many teachers have been trained, but it is almost impossible to identify the quality of that training.

Despite these difficulties, the Committee was able to identify two main areas in which, in its opinion, the progressive realisation was insufficient so far: 'training of all teachers in inclusive education [and] accessibility of the school environment, materials and curricula'.[72] Although almost all *Länder* have taken steps regarding these two issues, it is true that many *Länder* could intensify their efforts.[73] The training of all teachers in inclusive education is an especially huge endeavour. Due to the aforementioned tradition of segregated education for people with disabilities, for a long time only teachers at special schools have been trained in the special needs of people with disabilities.

VII CONCLUSION

All *Länder* have taken steps to implement an inclusive education system. However, because of the long tradition of segregated education, there is still a long way to go. Many regular schools and the teachers at these schools do not have experience in educating students with disabilities. In my opinion, it is important that the number of students who attend regular schools should be taken as only one of the indicators of the implementation of Article 24 CRPD.

70 Committee on the Rights of Persons with Disabilities, Concluding Observations on the Initial Report of Germany (17 April 2015) CRPD/C/DEU/CO/1 [46(a)].

71 For an overview, see Mißling and Ückert (n. 40).

72 Committee on the Rights of Persons with Disabilities, Concluding Observations on the Initial Report of Germany (17 April 2015) CRPD/C/DEU/CO/1 [46(d)].

73 For a detailed analysis of the legislative steps the *Länder* have taken regarding these two issues, see Mißling and Ückert (n. 40) 33ff. and 38ff.

It is essential to ensure that the education for these students is successful at regular schools. This is why it is necessary to implement the right to reasonable accommodation in Germany and for all teachers at regular schools to be trained in the special needs of people with disabilities.

In its concluding observations on the initial report of Germany, the Committee on the Rights of Persons with Disabilities has exposed these and other weak spots, and identified the core issues. It is thus the turn of the governments and parliaments in the sixteen *Länder* to translate the recommendations of the Committee into practice.

22

The Past, Present and Future of the Right to Inclusive Education in Italy

Delia Ferri*

1 INTRODUCTORY REMARKS

Since the 1970s, Italy has undertaken a process of inclusion of children with disabilities in mainstream schools, has implemented an anti-discriminatory educational policy and has abandoned segregated educational practices.[1] There is a general consensus among legal scholars that, even prior to the ratification of the UN Convention on the Rights of Persons with Disabilities (CRPD) in 2009,[2] the Italian legislative and policy framework was characterised by a relatively high standard of protection of the right to education of disabled pupils.[3] Despite some

* Lecturer in law, Maynooth University Department of Law. This chapter takes into account the legal developments until 10 April 2017.

1 Roberta Caldin, 'Current Pedagogic Issues in Inclusive Education for the Disabled' (2013) 1 *Pedagogia Oggi* 11, 18.

2 Law of 3 March 2009 No. 18 'Ratifica ed esecuzione della Convenzione delle Nazioni Unite sui diritti delle persone con disabilità, con Protocollo opzionale, fatta a New York il 13 dicembre 2006 e istituzione dell'Osservatorio nazionale sulla condizione delle persone con disabilità' in *Gazzetta Ufficiale* (OJ) 14 March 2009 No. 61 Law 18/2009 includes in its Article 1 the authorisation to ratify the CRPD, in compliance with Article 80 of the Italian Constitution (IC), and, in its Article 2, the order of enforcement. The latter allowed the CRPD to have full effect in the Italian legal order. Article 3 of this law, with the aim of implementing Article 33 CRPD, sets up the 'National Observatory on the Situation of Persons with Disabilities'. See Section 3.

3 Paolo Addis, 'Il diritto all'istruzione delle persone con disabilità: profili sostanziali e giurisprudenziali' in Elisabetta Catelani and Rolando Tarchi (eds), *I Diritti Sociali Nella Pluralità Degli Ordinamenti* (Editoriale Scientifica 2015); Silvio Troilo 'Tutti per uno o uno contro tutti? Il diritto all'istruzione e all'integrazione scolastica della persona disabile di fronte alla molteplicità dei soggetti obbligati (ed alla scarsità delle risorse disponibili)' in Giuseppe D'Elia, Giulia Tiberi and Maria Paola Viviani Schlein (eds), *Scritti in Memoria di Alessandra Concaro* (Giuffrè Editore 2012); Silvio Troilo, 'I "nuovi" diritti sociali: la parabola dell'integrazione scolastica dei disabili tra principi e realtà' in Giampietro Ferri (ed.), *La democrazia costituzionale tra nuovi diritti e deriva*

criticism,[4] Italy is often considered a leader in the area of education for students with disabilities.[5] Most recently, this long-standing commitment to implement an inclusive educational system, free of segregation, was commended by the UN Committee on the Rights of Persons with Disabilities (CRPD Committee) in its Concluding Observations (COs) to the Italian initial report on the implementation of the CRPD.[6]

However, notwithstanding a domestic legal framework aimed at ensuring an inclusive education for all children with disabilities, flaws and challenges have emerged in practice and have been highlighted by teachers and pedagogists, by Italian disabled people's organisations (DPOs) and in a series of administrative and civil court decisions.[7] The CRPD Committee itself, in its COs, highlighted some deficiencies in Italian legislation, and identified shortfalls that must be addressed in order to realise a truly inclusive and effective educational system.

In an attempt to solve at least some of the emerging problems, and to fully align the educational system with the wide-ranging obligations enshrined in Article 24 of the CRPD, even before the release of the CRPD Committee's COs, the new Law 107/2015 on the reform of the educational system has commenced a process of altering the existing system.[8] It has also empowered the government to adopt legislative decrees (which have the same status as ordinary laws) inter alia to promote effective and inclusive education for

mediale (Edizioni Scientifiche Italiane 2016); Luca Buscema, 'Il diritto all'istruzione degli studenti disabili' (2015) 4 *Associazione Italiana dei Costituzionalisti* 1; Simone Penasa, 'La persona e la funzione promozionale della scuola: la realizzazione del disegno costituzionale e il necessario ruolo dei poteri pubblici. I casi dell'istruzione delle persone disabili e degli alunni stranieri' in Fulvio Cortese (ed.), *Tra amministrazione e scuola: Snodi e crocevia del diritto scolastico italiano* (Editoriale Scientifica 2014).

4 Simona D'Alessio, 'Inclusive Education in Italy: A Reply to Giangreco, Doyle and Suter (2012)' (2013) 16 *Life Span and Disability* 95, www.lifespan.it/client/abstract/ENG270_6%20D'alessio .pdf, accessed 15 March 2017. See also Simona D'Alessio, *Inclusive Education in Italy: A Critical Analysis of the Policy of Integrazione Scolastica* (Sense Publishers 2011); Simona D'Alessio, '*Integrazione Scolastica* and the Development of Inclusion in Italy: Does Space Matter?' (2012) 16 *International Journal of Inclusive Education* 519.

5 Including by, and among others, Arlene S. Kanter, Michelle L. Damiani and Beth A. Ferri, 'The Right to Inclusive Education under International Law: Following Italy's Lead' (2014) 17 *Journal of International Special Needs Education* 21. See also John C. Begeny and Brian K. Martens, 'Inclusionary Education in Italy: A Literature Review and Call for More Empirical Research' (2007) 28 *Remedial and Special Education* 80.

6 Committee on the Rights of Persons with Disabilities, Consideration of Reports Submitted by States Parties under Article 35 of the Convention: Initial Reports of State Parties Due in 2011: Italy (21 January 2013) CRPD/C/ITA/1.

7 See among others Lucio Cottini, *Fare ricerca nella scuola dell'autonomia* (Mursia 2002) 21ff.

8 Law of 13 July 2015 No. 107 'Riforma del sistema nazionale di istruzione e formazione e delega per il riordino delle disposizioni legislative vigenti' in OJ 15 July 2015 No. 162.

persons with disabilities.[9] The proposal for a legislative decree on inclusive education was released in January 2017 and was finally approved at the beginning of April 2017. At this particular moment in time, therefore, Italy represents a particularly interesting case study to grasp the challenges surrounding the creation of a truly inclusionary educational system that goes beyond a mere integration in mainstream schools, that ensures full and effective participation of all learners and that ultimately meets the standards imposed by Article 24 of the CRPD.

This chapter aims to discuss the Italian legal framework on education of persons with disabilities and its most recent developments. It is divided into six sections. After this introduction, Section 2 discusses the extent to which the right to inclusive education is reflected in the Italian constitution and in national legislation. Section 3 gives a short account of the Italian educational policy for persons with disabilities. Section 4 critically analyses the salient features of the legislative framework and examines its practical implementation in light of domestic case law, domestic monitoring and the CRPD Committee's COs. The section also takes into account the criticism raised by DPOs in their shadow reports. It attempts to identify strengths and shortcomings of Italian legislation in light of Article 24 of the CRPD. Section 5 briefly discusses recent developments: the new Law 107/2015 and the governmental proposal for a legislative decree. Finally, Section 6, by reflecting on the challenges in the implementation of an inclusive and rights-based educational system, discusses the extent to which the Italian legislative framework has achieved the objective of inclusive education prescribed by the CRPD. It ultimately argues that Italy is committed to the full inclusion of students with disabilities, but, so far, the implementation of substantially progressive

[9] Article 76 of the Italian constitution allows the government to exercise legislative functions, only when delegated by Parliament for a limited time and for specified purposes. Parliament delegates to the government the exercise of legislative functions through a delegation law that establishes the principles and criteria that the government must follow and comply with when exercising the legislative function. The delegation law empowers the government to adopt one or more legislative decrees, which are deliberated upon by the Council of Ministers. See Giuseppe Franco Ferrari, *Introduction to Italian Public Law* (1st edn) (Giuffrè Editore 2008) 226ff. The Constitutional Court can declare the legislative decree invalid if it breaches the limits provided by the delegation law. For a broader account, see Enrico Borghetto, Marco Giuliani and Francesco Zucchini, 'Leading Governments and Unwilling Legislators: The European Union and the Italian Law Making (1987–2006)' in Sylvain Brouard, Olivier Costa and Thomas König (eds), *The Europeanization of Domestic Legislatures: The Empirical Implications of the Delors' Myth in Nine Countries* (Springer 2012). For a general overview of the Italian system, see Michael A. Livingston, Pier Giuseppe Monateri and Francesco Parisi, *The Italian Legal System: An Introduction* (2nd edn) (Stanford Law Books 2015).

legislation has fallen short of the objective of inclusive education prescribed by the CRPD.

2 THE RIGHT TO EDUCATION OF PERSONS WITH DISABILITIES IN ITALY: A BRIEF OVERVIEW

2.1 *The Constitutional Framework in a Nutshell*

Article 33 of the Italian constitution (IC) obliges the state to provide a state school system accessible to all children and affirms the freedom for organisations and individuals to set up private schools with no cost for the state. Article 34 of the IC establishes in general terms that '[s]chools are open to everyone' and that primary education, offered for at least eight years, is compulsory and free of tuition fees.[10] Article 38(3) of the IC affirms that 'disabled and handicapped persons are entitled to receive education and vocational training'.[11] However, the general principle of protection and promotion of the rights of persons with disabilities, and in particular of their right to education, is anchored in Article 2 of the IC, which recognises and guarantees 'the inviolable rights of the person, both as an individual and in the social groups where human personality is expressed'.[12] It is also

[10] Compulsory education refers to both enrolment and attendance. It can be undertaken at either a state school or a non-state, publicly subsidised school (*scuola paritaria*) or, subject to certain conditions, through home education or private schools. Law No. 53 of 2003 (in OJ 2 April 2003 No. 77) has ensured the right to education and training for at least twelve years or until the completion of a qualification by the age of eighteen.

[11] The English translation of the Italian constitution is published by the Parliamentary Information, Archives and Publications Office of the Senate Service for Official Reports and Communication and can be found at www.senato.it/documenti/repository/istituzione/costituzione_inglese.pdf, accessed 15 March 2017.

[12] On the interconnections between Articles 34 (right to education) and 38 and the general principle of Article 2, see Silvio Troilo, 'Il diritto allo studio fra Stato e Regioni' (*Federalismi.it*, 2 May 2012), www.federalismi.it/ApplOpenFilePDF.cfm?artid=19978&dpath=document&dfile=28042012102931.pdf&content=Il+diritto+allo+studio+fra+Stato+e+Regioni+-+stato+-+dottrina+-+, accessed 10 April 2017. See also Fabrizio Fracchia, 'Istruzione e differenziazione: la centralità dello studente tra solidarietà intergenerazionale e sviluppo della persona' in Francesco Astone, Mario Caldarera, Francesco Manganaro, Antonio Romano Tassone and Fabio Saitta (eds), *Le disuguaglianze sostenibili nei sistemi autonomistici multilivello* (Giappichelli 2006) 143ff. On the role of Article 3 in the protection of the rights of persons with disabilities in the Italian constitutional framework, see also Carlo Colapietro, 'L'inclusione sociale delle persone con disabilità: un imperativo costituzionale' (2011) 2 *Non Profit* 11, 24. The guidelines of the Ministry of Education on inclusive education also acknowledge the inextricable connection between Articles 34 and 38 in connection with Article 3 (Ministero dell'Istruzione, *Linee guida sull'integrazione scolastica degli alunni con disabilità* (4 August 2009) Prot.n 4724).

underpinned by Article 3(1) of the IC, which provides for the principle of non-discrimination on the grounds of sex, race, language, religion, political opinion and personal and social conditions, and in Article 3(2) of the IC, which establishes the principle of substantive equality. According to the latter, the state is called on to remove the social and economic obstacles that limit the freedom and equality of citizens and prevent the full development of the human being. A wide interpretation of these constitutional principles has led to a paradigm shift, from a paternalistic charitable model of care to a social model based on dignity and equality.[13]

Italy can be described as a regional[14] or even as a 'de facto federal system'.[15] Therefore, besides the aforementioned provisions concerning the right to education, the IC sets forth the division of competence over educational matters between the state and the regions. Article 117(n) of the IC confers on the state the exclusive power to lay down 'general provisions on education'.[16] The Constitutional Court has established that these 'general provisions on education' are concerned with the 'basic characteristics' of the educational system,[17] and comprise: the general organisation of the system, the protection and promotion of the autonomy of each educational institution, the freedom to open private schools and parity between public and private (non-governmental) schools,[18] minimum numbers of school hours per year, the teacher/student ratio, state financial resources, and also the inclusion of people with

13 Carlo Colapietro, *Diritti dei disabili e Costituzione* (Editoriale Scientifica 2011); Federico Furlan, 'La tutela costituzionale del cittadino portatore di handicap' in Carla Cattaneo (ed.), *Terzo settore, nuova statualità e solidarietà sociale* (Giuffrè Editore 2001). See also Chiara Tripodina, 'Article 38' in Roberto Bin and Sergio Bartole (eds), *Commentario breve alla Costituzione* (2nd edn) (CEDAM 2008); Lorenza Violini, 'Commento all'Art. 38' and Emanuele Rossi, 'Commento all'Art. 2', both found in Raffaele Bifulco, Alfonso Celotto and Marco Olvetti (eds), *Commentario alla Costituzione (UTET 2006); Velia Vadalà, La tutela delle disabilità* (Giuffrè Editore 2009) 67ff.

14 Among others Paolo Caretti and Giovanni Tarli Barbieri, *Diritto Regionale* (Giappichelli 2012).

15 Paola Bilancia, Francesco Palermo and Ornella Porchia, 'The European Fitness of Italian Regions' (2010) 2 *Perspectives on Federalism* 123, www.on-federalism.eu/attachments/063_download.pdf, accessed 28 October 2015.

16 This article must be read in conjunction with Article 33(3) of the IC that affirms that '[t]he Republic lays down general rules for education'.

17 Constitutional Court No. 200/2009 [21]. On this decision see Fulvio Cortese, 'L'istruzione tra norme generali e principi fondamentali: ossia, la Corte costituzionale tra contraddizioni formali e conferme sostanziali' (2010) 3 *Le Regioni* 511; Michele Troisi, 'La Corte tra "norme generali sull'istruzione" e "principi fondamentali". Ancora alla ricerca di un difficile equilibrio tra (indispensabili) esigenze di uniformità e (legittime) aspirazioni regionali' (2010) 3 *Le Regioni* 531.

18 Law No. 62 of 10 March 2000 in OJ 21 March 2000 No. 67 Concerning Equality between Public and Private Education.

disabilities.[19] When legislating on the basic characteristics of the school system, the state also addresses (and manages through the Ministry of Education), two core components – teachers' qualifications and recruitment – as well as salaries.[20]

Article 117(2) of the IC goes on to affirm that the state and the regions have concurrent powers over 'education, subject to the autonomy of educational institutions and with the exception of vocational education and training'. The combination of Articles 117(1) and (2) has given rise to interpretative uncertainty to a huge amount of cases on the distribution of powers between the state and the regions referred to the Constitutional Court,[21] and to a wealth of academic commentaries.[22] Within the blurred boundaries traced by Articles 117 of the IC, regions are entitled to legislate on: free supply of textbooks or loan facilities, canteen services, transport services to schools, residential services, scholarships and also specific individualised benefits and services for persons with disabilities (including assistance in schools by communication assistance or socialisation experts and transport to schools), training courses for pupils admitted to hospital and psychological and pedagogical advice to support students in decision-making stages of their studies.[23] Regions also establish the school calendar (which thus may vary across the territory) and the distribution of schools in their own areas. In addition, regions are solely responsible for legislating on, planning and providing vocational education and training, and 'integrated training opportunities' (a combination of education and vocational training).

[19] Troilo (2012) 'Il diritto alle studio fra Stato e Regioni' (n. 12).

[20] In addition, Article 117(m) of the IC empowers the state to determine 'the basic level of benefits relating to civil and social entitlements to be guaranteed throughout the national territory'. The latter competence is aimed at ensuring equality of treatment among users who benefit from the educational services (and more generally social services) across the national territory. Such a cross-cutting national competence implies that whenever a regional law provides for benefits related to social rights (including the right to education), it must be subordinated to the national law that establishes the minimum standards with regard to those rights.

[21] For a general analysis of the Italian Constitutional Court case law on the division of powers between the state and the regions, see Vittoria Barsotti and others, *Italian Constitutional Justice in Global Context* (Oxford University Press 2015) 222ff.

[22] For a general account of this issue, see Annamaria Poggi, 'La legislazione regionale sull'istruzione dopo la revisione del Titolo V' (2005) 5 *Le Regioni* 927; Monica Cocconi, 'Le Regioni nell'istruzione dopo il nuovo Titolo V' (2007) 5 *Le Regioni* 725.

[23] Troilo (2012) 'Il diritto alle studio fra Stato e Regioni' (n. 12).

2.2 *The National Legal Framework*

The conditions and instruments necessary to ensure school integration of pupils with disabilities have been mostly laid down in national laws. The first relevant pieces of legislation date back to the 1970s. Article 28 of Law 118/1971, while not formally abolishing special schools, established that the education of children with disabilities should occur 'in normal classes of public schools, except in cases in which individuals are suffering from serious intellectual or physical impairments of such gravity as to prevent student learning or placement in ordinary classes or make it very difficult'.[24] This law gave families the possibility of placing children with disabilities in mainstream schools, and promoted a cultural shift towards inclusion. It initiated a process to outlaw special schools, and, in order to favour inclusion, provided for free transport to school, elimination of architectural barriers and assistance to students during school hours. Nocera observes that, since 1972 (one year after the entry into force of Law 118/1971), the number of special schools has steadily decreased, and the number of pupils with disabilities attending mainstream schools has increased dramatically.[25] The Italian Constitutional Court, in its landmark decision No. 215/1987, in assessing the constitutionality of Article 28 of Law 118/1971, established that children with disabilities have a right to access mainstream education and, therefore, schools have an obligation to include them.[26] The Court also clarified that the right to education should not be interpreted strictly, but widely as a right to a full social life.[27]

[24] Translated from Article 28 of Law of 30 March 1971 No. 118, 'Conversione in legge del D.L. 30 gennaio 1971 n. 5 e nuove norme in favore dei mutilati ed invalidi civili' in OJ 2 April 1971 No. 82.

[25] Salvatore Nocera, *Il diritto all'integrazione nella scuola dell'autonomia: Gli alunni in situazione di handicap nella normativa italiana* (Erikson 2001) 32.

[26] For commentary, see Carlo Alfredo Moro, 'L'eguaglianza sostanziale e il diritto allo studio: una svolta della giurisprudenza costituzionale' (1987) *Giurisprudenza Costituzionale* 3064, and Raffaello Belli, 'Servizi per le libertà: diritto inviolabile o interesse diffuso?' (1987) *Giurisprudenza Costituzionale* 1629.

[27] Decision No. 215/1987 [6]. This was reiterated by the Italian Constitutional Court in Decision No. 50/1990, and this was reaffirmed in several subsequent decisions. In its Decision No. 52/2000, the Italian Constitutional Court again stated that compulsory education for persons with disabilities should not take place in special classes any longer, but in regular classes of public schools. The Court clarified that special education can be set forth only in residual and exceptional circumstances. In that decision, the Court also stated that participation in the educational process with teachers and non-disabled companions is, in fact, a significant socialisation factor and can make a decisive contribution to stimulating the potential of students with disabilities. See Elena Paparella, 'Il diritto all'integrazione e all'istruzione scolastica dei soggetti diversamente abili: una fondamentale declinazione del diritto allo studio nella prassi amministrativa e nelle recenti politiche governative' in *Studi in onore di Vincenzo Atripaldi* (Jovene 2010) 970ff; Lorenzo Nannipieri, 'Il

Law 517/1977 abolished special schools and differentiated classes for pupils with disabilities,[28] triggering 'an enormous systemic educational change'.[29] This law established the duty for schools to develop specific programmes for children with disabilities and introduced the role of 'support teacher' (special needs teacher), to facilitate learning activities for pupils with disabilities.[30] This law is premised on the understanding that the mere attendance of people with disabilities at mainstream schools does not guarantee in itself the full enjoyment of the right to education on an equal basis with others.[31] However, Anastasiou, Kauffman and Di Nuovo suggest that in the 1980s, while a massive insertion of students with sensory, physical and intellectual disabilities into general education classrooms occurred, appropriate support was not always provided.[32]

Law 104/1992 ('Framework Law for Care, Social Integration and Rights of Persons with Disabilities'),[33] which aims to guarantee the dignity and autonomy of disabled people and to combat social exclusion, is the cornerstone of Italian legislation on disability[34] and reaffirms the right to inclusive education. This law refers to 'scholastic integration' (*integrazione scolastica*), often translated into English as 'inclusion', and states that its objective is the development of the potentialities of the person with disabilities in learning, in communication, in

diritto all'istruzione del disabile nelle fonti nazionali tra problemi definitori, giurisprudenza costituzionale e giudici di merito' (2012) 3 *Rivista AIC*, www.rivistaaic.it/il-diritto-all-istruzione-del-disabile-nelle-fonti-nazionali-tra-problemi-definitori-giurisprudenza-costituzionale-e-giudici-di-merito.html, accessed 13 June 2017.

28 Before 1977, in Italy, there were special schools, mainly aimed at providing education to students with sensory impairments (in particular sight and hearing impairments). Special classes in public schools included children with psychosocial or mild intellectual disabilities that were considered unable to attend the normal classes. Finally, children with intellectual disabilities attended 'medical-pedagogical' institutions. All of these were closed down consequent to the approval of Law 517/1977. Only a few special institutes for pupils who are blind and deaf, as well as schools with specific tasks in the field of education for pupils with particularly severe disabilities, have remained.

29 Dimitris Anastasiou, James M. Kauffman and Santo Di Nuovo, 'Inclusive Education in Italy: Description and Reflections on Full Inclusion' (2015) 30 *European Journal of Special Needs Education* 429, 432.

30 Law of 4 August 1977 No. 517 'Norme sulla valutazione degli alunni e sull'abolizione degli esami di riparazione nonché altre norme di modifica dell'ordinamento scolastico' in OJ 18 August 1977 No. 224.

31 See among others Troilo (2012) 'Tutti per uno o uno contro tutti?' (n. 3).

32 Anastasiou, Kauffman and Di Nuovo (n. 29) 432.

33 Law of 5 February 1992 No. 104, 'Legge-quadro per l'assistenza, l'integrazione sociale e i diritti delle persone handicappate' in OJ 17 February 1992 No. 39. For more on this matter, see Section 3.

34 Domenico Siclari, 'Riflessioni sullo statuto giuridico della disabilità nell'ordinamento italiano' (2015) 28 *Il diritto dell'economia* 553.

relationships and in socialisation (Articles 12 and 13). Law 104/1992 hence embodies a conception of the right to education as both an end in itself and a means towards attaining the enjoyment of all other rights. In terms of educational provision, this piece of legislation requires individualised plans for students with disabilities (Individual Education Plan) (IEP) and the supply of didactic tools and assistive technology to schools, as well as other forms of technical assistance, when needed. A bylaw[35] specifies that the IEP must set forth the learning outcomes objectives, specific 'working itineraries', technology to be used, methodologies and assessment strategies and also specific engagement with the family of the person with disability (which is included in the learning process).[36] Inclusion is in practice ensured by support teachers who develop the IEP in collaboration with the school and provide additional individual instruction and educational support in order to meet the needs of each student with disabilities.[37] Support teachers are qualified teachers who must also obtain further specialised postgraduate training, the requirements of which are established in various bylaws, mainly ministerial decrees. The support teacher's role is complementary to that of the classroom teacher.[38] In its response to a questionnaire issued by the UN Special Rapporteur on the provision of support to persons with disabilities in October 2014, Italy once again clarified that support teachers carry out 'support activities assigned to the classes of the students with disabilities to facilitate their integration process'.[39] Therefore, they are 'not the teacher of the pupil with disabilities, but a professional resource assigned to the class to meet the major educational needs'.[40] In

35 Articles 5 and 6 of Presidential Decree of 24 February 1994, in OJ 6 April 1994 No. 79.

36 A provision was then included in a subsequent bylaw to establish that the IEP must undergo a periodical review (quarterly and any time exceptional circumstances require a verification). Article 3 of Presidential Decree of 23 February 2006 No. 185 in OJ 19 May 2006 No. 115.

37 Law No. 104/1992 also recognises home schooling for those who are temporarily unable to attend school. With regards to tertiary education, Law No. 17/1999 (Law of 28 January 1999 No. 17 'Integrazione e modifica della legge-quadro 5 febbraio 1992, n. 104, per l'assistenza, l'integrazione sociale e i diritti delle persone handicappate' in OJ 2 February 1999 No. 26) modified the Framework Law 104/1992 and introduced a specific provision that guarantees to disabled students attending Italian universities specialised tutoring services and personalised services for exams.

38 Luigino Manca, 'Art. 24 – Educazione' in Sergio Marchisio, Rachele Cera and Valentina Della Fina, *La Convenzione ONU sui Diritti delle persone con disabilità* (Aracne 2010). See also Andrea Canevaro, 'L'integrazione in Italia e i suoi protagonisti' in Salvatore Nocera, *Il diritto all'integrazione nella scuola dell'autonomia: Gli alunni in situazione di handicap nella normativa italiana* (Erikson 2001).

39 'Questionnaire on the Provision of Support to Persons with Disabilities' downloaded from 'Italy' available at, www.ohchr.org/EN/Issues/Disability/SRDisabilities/Pages/Provisionofsupporttopersonswithdisabilities.aspx, accessed 15 March 2017, 4.

40 Ibid.

compliance with the principles laid down in Law 104/1992, a ministerial decree regulates the qualification and specialisation for support teachers, who must undergo (after their undergraduate degree) a two-year postgraduate specialisation course at a university.[41] In 2011, another ministerial decree slightly modified the qualification process for support teachers, and established a requirement for compulsory training on inclusive teaching practices for all teachers.

Since its inception, no major changes to this framework have been introduced. The main previous reform of the education system (Law 53/2003[42]) did not include any specific provisions on the education of people with disabilities, and limited itself to making explicit reference to Law No. 104/1992. In 2008, the Budget Law 2008, as part of general austerity measures and budget cuts, fixed a maximum number of support teachers for children with disabilities who attend classes in public schools, and abolished the possibility of hiring additional support teachers under fixed-term contracts, who would provide specific educational assistance to children with severe disabilities.[43] However, these provisos were referred to the Italian Constitutional Court upon the request of the Sicilian Administrative Council. In its judgment, No. 80/2010, the Italian Constitutional Court declared them unconstitutional and affirmed that they infringed the right of education of children with disabilities, set forth in Article 38(3)(4) of the Italian constitution, and violated the principle of equality. Interestingly, the Constitutional Court in defining the 'content' of the fundamental right to education for persons with disabilities referred to Article 24 of the CRPD, in support of its reasoning.[44] Overall, the Court argued that the core minimum guarantees to make the right to education of students with disabilities effective cannot be subject to financial conditions. The Court pointed out that it is for the legislature to provide appropriate tools to implement the right to education, but underlined that legislative provisions cannot undermine the realisation of a fundamental right by making it conditional on the availability of financial resources. The constitutional judges also pointed out that people with disabilities do not constitute a homogeneous group. There are, in fact, different forms of disabilities, and for each of them there is the need to find the best tools to remove barriers to full participation and inclusion.

41 Ministerial Decree of 10 September 2010 No. 249 in OJ 31 January 2011 No. 24.

42 Law of 28 March 2003 No. 53 'Delega al Governo per la definizione delle norme generali sull'istruzione e dei livelli essenziali delle prestazioni in materia di istruzione e di formazione professionale' in OJ 2 April 2003 No. 77.

43 Namely Article 2 paras 413 and 414 of the Law 24 December 2007 No. 244 in OJ 28 December 2007 No. 285.

44 Paragraph 4 of the 'Conclusions in Point of Law'.

The ratification and entry into force of the CRPD, in 2009, did not bring any substantive change to this legal framework and, until 2015, the most significant innovation was Law 170/2010.[45] This act was passed in order to ensure the right to education for children with 'specific learning difficulties', i.e. children with difficulties in reading (dyslexia), writing (graphic dyslogia and dysorthography) or mathematics (discalculia or numeracy problems). The general objective of this act is to give these children equal educational opportunities to a successful and efficient education in accordance with their needs and abilities in mainstream schools, and to ensure collaboration among teachers, parents and experts of the health services, envisaging targeted flexible educational plans. In addition, this act affirms the need for specialised training for teachers in supporting learners with these disabilities, recognising that it is one of the major challenges to the full and effective inclusion of persons with disabilities in the education system.

3 INCLUSIVE EDUCATION IN ITALY: ORGANISATION AND POLICY

After a short account of the Italian legislative framework, this section aims to give a brief overview of the organisational aspects of the Italian education system in relation to people with disabilities. It also includes some data on current inclusive education practices, in order to frame further critical appraisal and discussions, which are carried out in Section 4.

3.1 *A Decentralised Policy Net: Perfect Shadows on a Sunny Day*

The Italian educational policy system is highly stratified and decentralised,[46] and informed by the principle of subsidiarity and the principle of autonomy of schools and educational institutions.[47]

The Ministry of Education, University and Research (MIUR) is generally responsible for educational policy at the national level. In this capacity, the MIUR has adopted bylaws on the qualification and specialisation of support

45 Law of 8 October 2010 No. 170 'Nuove norme in materia di disturbi specifici di apprendimento in ambito scolastico' in OJ 18 October 2010 No. 244.

46 Since the late 1990s, responsibilities and services have gradually been decentralised, ending up with the granting to regions, provinces and municipalities all the roles and administrative tasks (with the exception of those related to matters expressly assigned to the state).

47 These principles are established in the Italian constitution. The principle of autonomy of schools is implemented by means of the Decree of the President of the Republic No. 275 of 8 March 1999 in OJ 10 August 1999 No. 186 providing schools with didactic, organisational and research autonomy.

teachers.[48] It also has adopted guidelines to facilitate the practical implementation of inclusive education by regional administrative authorities (i.e. regional school offices [RSOs]), local authorities and schools. In particular, in 2009, after the ratification of the CRPD, the MIUR adopted new 'Guidelines on School Inclusion of Pupils with Disabilities',[49] which collate a set of recommendations to improve the inclusion of children with disabilities and to orient the action of the RSOs and the schools. Interestingly, the guidelines refer explicitly to the CRPD alongside constitutional provisions as a standard of protection for the right to education. The guidelines recognise the central role of schools in elaborating the IEP, but require that this IEP is unequivocally aimed towards the personal growth of pupils with disabilities, and towards developing their talents and creativity, enabling them to participate fully in society.[50] It is evident that the guidelines take into account the obligations laid down in Article 24 of the CRPD, and attempt to seek compliance with it. In 2012 and 2013, the MIUR provided guidelines about 'special educational needs' or *BES*.[51] The concept of *BES* is wider than disability and encompasses any form of difficulty experienced in the educational setting, including psychosocial disabilities, learning difficulties and socioeconomic, cultural or linguistic disadvantages. The guidelines have recognised the right to an individualised response and to educational needs, and Ianes affirms that the guidelines respond to the necessity to give adequate support to a diverse student population.[52] They require schools to set out an annual plan for inclusion (affirming that this must emerge from a process of reflection involving all the school staff members) and to have a stable working group on inclusion. Finally, it is worth noting that the MIUR is responsible to pay school staff members, including support teachers, and to annually allocate the total funding resources for the administrative and educational management of schools.

The RSOs oversee the observance of the general provisions for education and compliance with minimum standards. They also distribute the national funding allocated by the MIUR to schools according to their needs. Local

48 See Section 2.

49 Ministero dell'Istruzione, Prot.n 4274 (n. 12).

50 Ibid. Prot.n 4724.

51 Ministerial Directives of 27 December 2011 and 6 March 2013. See also the clarifying directives: Ministero dell'istruzione and Dipartimento per l'istruzione, Strumenti di intervento per alunni con Bisogni Educativi Speciali. A.S. 2013/2014. Chiarimenti (22 November 2013) Prot.n 2563.

52 Dario Ianes, 'Indicazioni operative per promuovere l'inclusione scolastica degli alunni con BES sulla base della DM 27/12/2012 e della CM 6/3/2013' (2013) 12 *L'integrazione scolastica e sociale* 9, 9.

authorities are responsible for providing adequate premises and buildings to host schools, and for the merging and closing down of schools. Local authorities also manage assistance services (including transport to schools and assistance for personal autonomy) which, as mentioned earlier, are regulated by means of regional laws and financed by the regions.[53]

Even though the MIUR is encouraging vertical collaboration among all the authorities involved through regular inter-institutional meetings, and although cooperation between regions and the MIUR is ensured through the Permanent State/Regions Conference, 'the Italian school system can currently be defined as a hyper-loosely coupled organization in which the fragmentation naturally embedded in educational organizations is further intensified by the weakness of intermediate levels of coordination'.[54] The devolution of tasks to different levels has resulted in a patchwork of responsibilities spread across different bodies, and with inconsistencies in how inclusive education is provided across the national territory.

Schools are responsible for the actual provision of inclusive education. They define curricula and educational offerings, organise teaching, assign support teachers, allocate hours of support and lay down the IEP. The school manager, who is the legal representative of the school and is responsible for its overall management, oversees the quality of the educational service provided. Schools are supported by 'Territorial Support Centres', which 'empower schools' stakeholders by developing a peer-to-peer approach, collecting and disseminating best practices, providing advice on managing special needs, and supplying schools with technological devices'.[55] Italy has greatly supported flexibility by giving schools a high level of autonomy to empower them to foster inclusion, taking into account the local context and building on the strengths of school staff members. A study published by the Organisation for Economic Co-operation and Development (OECD) has affirmed that autonomy is likely to improve school outcomes by influencing teacher motivation and capacity, and that schools that make autonomous decisions about curriculum and instruction achieve better Programme for International Student Assessment (PISA) results than schools that do

53 For a more detailed account, see Nocera (n. 25) 107ff.

54 Fabio Dovigo, 'Introduction' in Fabio Dovigo, Clara Favella, Anna Pietrocarlo, Vincenza Rocco and Emanuela Zappella (eds), *None Excluded. Transforming Schools and Learning to Develop Inclusive Education: Conference Proceedings* (University of Bergamo 2016) 17 (references omitted).

55 European Agency for Special Needs and Inclusive Education, *Financing of Inclusive Education: Mapping Country Systems for Inclusive Education* (European Agency for Special Needs and Inclusive Education 2016) 36.

not.[56] However, in respect of inclusive education, empirical research has shown that autonomy has de facto contributed to making inclusive practices extremely heterogeneous across the territory.[57] Despite the guidelines of the MIUR and the attempt to centrally orient the action of schools, Dovigo affirms that inclusion often depends on the school, on 'local custom', and is essentially shaped by school managers and teachers, and the interpretation of what constitutes an inclusive setting 'differs widely among schools, and sometimes even among classes in the same school'.[58]

3.2 *The Role of the 'Permanent Observatory on Integration of Pupils with Disabilities' and of the 'National Observatory on the Condition of People with Disabilities' in Policy Planning*

In an endeavour to promote inclusive practices, in the past few years the MIUR has acted in connection with several bodies and agencies. The two bodies that have contributed to the development of inclusive education are the 'Permanent Observatory on Integration of Pupils with Disabilities' and the 'National Observatory on the Condition of People with Disabilities' (National Observatory).[59]

The Permanent Observatory on Integration of Pupils with Disabilities was established in 1988, in order to translate into actual practice the Constitutional Court decision No. 215/1987, which, as mentioned earlier, established that children with disabilities have a right to access mainstream education.[60] However, it had varying fortunes. Having been scarcely active and basically uninfluential for a number of years, it was closed down in 2009. It was re-established in 2011 for three years, but its activities were still quite limited.[61] As is discussed further in Section 5, in 2015 the new reform reconfirmed this body and gave it a renewed advisory role.

56 The Organisation for Economic Co-operation and Development (OECD), *PISA 2012 Results: What Makes Schools Successful? Resources, Policies and Practices*, vol. 4 (OECD Publishing 2012).

57 Anastasiou, Kauffman and Di Nuovo (n. 29). See also Michael F. Giangreco, Mary Beth Doyle and Jesse C. Suter, 'Italian and American Progress toward Inclusive Education: Common Concerns and Future Directions' (2014) 17 *Life Span and Disability* 119; Michael F. Giangreco, Mary Beth Doyle and Jesse C. Suter, 'Constructively Responding to Requests for Paraprofessionals: We Keep Asking the Wrong Questions' (2012) *Remedial and Special Education* 362.

58 Dovigo (n. 54) 18.

59 See at www.osservatoriodisabilita.it/index.php?lang=it, accessed 15 March 2015.

60 See Section 2.

61 Ministerial Decree of 30 December 2011 available at http://bes.indire.it/wp-content/uploads/2013/11/Decreto-di-costituzione-Osservatorio-disabilità.pdf, accessed 10 April 2017.

The National Observatory was created in order to implement Article 33(2) of the CRPD, by Article 3 of Law 18/2009, which ratified the CRPD.[62] As noted elsewhere, the National Observatory was meant to constitute the independent mechanism, but is organisationally placed within the Ministry of Labour and Social Policies, which finances it, and is chaired by the Ministry.[63] It includes representatives of various ministries, including the MIUR, local authorities, social security institutions, the National Statistics Institute and social partners (trade unions and industry organisations), as well as independent experts and DPOs. While it has monitoring tasks, the National Observatory is also a consultative body in charge of technical support for the elaboration and supervision of national disability policies. It promotes the implementation of the CRPD, and prepares cross-cutting biannual action plans for promoting the rights of persons with disabilities across the whole range of policies, with a view to achieving the objectives established by the CRPD and by the European Disability Strategy.[64] The First Bi-annual Action Plan on Disability was adopted by the National Observatory in 2013.[65] As is further discussed in Section 4, the plan identified critical issues to be addressed by national, regional and local authorities in different fields, including education.[66] It also identified actions to be put in place and strongly encouraged the Ministry and the regional authorities to strengthen regional networks to build structures able to support schools in providing inclusive education.

62 See also the Ministerial Decree of 6 July 2010 No. 167 'Regolamento recante disciplina dell'Osservatorio nazionale sulla condizione delle persone con disabilità ai sensi dell'articolo 3 della legge 3 marzo 2009, n. 18', available at www.lavoro.gov.it/Lavoro/md/AreaSociale/Disabilita/Osservatorio/, accessed 15 March 2017.

63 Delia Ferri, 'Implementation of Art. 33 CRPD in Italy: "Magna Pars est profectus velle proficere"' in Gauthier De Beco (ed.), *Article 33 of the UN Convention on the Rights of Persons with Disabilities: National Structures for the Implementation and Monitoring of the Convention* (Martinus Nijoff 2013).

64 European Commission (EC), 'European Disability Strategy 2010–2020: A Renewed Commitment to a Barrier-Free Europe' COM(2010) 636 Final.

65 This is a bylaw adopted through Decree of the President of the Republic of 4 October 2013 'Programma di azione biennale per la promozione dei diritti e l'integrazione delle persone con disabilita' OJ 28 December 2013 No. 303.

66 The Biannual Plan was prepared by the National Observatory on the Status of Persons with Disabilities. It identifies policies to be implemented, and specifies priorities for action which are streamlined into seven lines of action: (1) revision of the system of access, recognition of certification of disability and intervention model social health; (2) labour and employment; (3) policies, services and organisational models for independent living and inclusion in society; (4) promotion and implementation of the principles of accessibility and mobility; (5) educational processes and school inclusion; (6) health, right to life, habilitation and rehabilitation; (7) international cooperation.

3.3 *Inclusive Education in a Snapshot*

In Italy, public funds to implement inclusive education come for the most part from the state, and only to a limited extent from the regions. The most recent austerity measures had a serious impact on expenditure on education. Public spending on education decreased by 14 per cent between 2008 and 2013. In 2013, total spending on education from primary to tertiary level was equal to 4 per cent of GDP, compared with the OECD average of 5.2 per cent.[67] In addition, according to a report released by the European Agency for Special Needs Education, Italy had a 0.6 per cent decrease in the general expenditure per pupil as a percentage of GDP (2000–2012).[68]

However, despite the overall decrease of national expenditure dedicated to education, funding to support inclusive education has increased. This is mainly due to the rising numbers of learners with disabilities, which increased by 40 per cent between 2004 and 2015.[69] The most recent data released by the National Statistic Office indicate that the figure of disabled pupils in the school year 2015–2016 was around 156,000 (approximately 3.4 per cent of all pupils).[70] As a consequence, the number of support teachers increased by 82 per cent between 2001 and 2014 and, during this period, the spending on support teachers doubled to 6 billion euros. Consequently, there are more than 82,000 support teachers, which translates to approximately one support teacher for every two students with disabilities.[71]

Notwithstanding the actual increase, the number of support teachers is still inadequate to meet the actual needs of students with disabilities. Approximately 68 per cent of support teachers carry out full-time activities in support of different students within the same school. Around 32 per cent of teachers teach a limited amount of hours in several schools. This means that there is not any continuity in the relationship between many support teachers and students with a disability. In addition, more than 15 per cent of disabled pupils in the primary school changed their education teacher during the school year. This percentage rises to almost 19 per cent for disabled pupils in the lower secondary school. The percentage increases dramatically to 41.6 per cent when we consider the support teachers changes from year to year.

67 www.oecd.org/education/skills-beyond-school/EAG2016-Italy.pdf, accessed 10 April 2017

68 European Agency for Special Needs and Inclusive Education (n. 55) 18.

69 Ibid. 20.

70 Istituto nazionale di statistica (ISTAT), *L'integrazione degli alunni con disabilità nelle scuole primarie e secondarie di primo grado: Anno scolastico 2015–2016* (Istituto nazionale di statistica, 21 December 2016), www.istat.it/it/archivio/194622, accessed 10 April 2017.

71 Ibid.

There is also strong evidence to show that roughly 30 per cent of support teachers ask for redeployment as main classroom teachers on average five years after obtaining their qualification.[72] Precariousness is one of the causes. A study authored by De Vecchi and others highlighted that working conditions with children, families, other teachers and other professionals is often extremely draining. Anastasiou, Kauffman and Di Nuovo affirm that support teachers are frequently requested to take responsibility for physical and/or behavioural assistance, due to the lack of support personnel besides teachers (e.g., personal assistants).[73] Ianes and others confirm the problems with the support teachers' role and difficulties with working alongside regular class teachers.[74] As discussed earlier in this chapter, though, Italian law requires the support teacher and the curricular teacher to be collaboratively responsible for the educative process of all the students, which makes everyday interactions more difficult.[75] According to a study published in 2011,[76] the current perception that school managers and curricular teachers have of support teachers is rather critical: they are often considered inadequate to deal with the cases entrusted to them, because they are young, or because they are subject to rapid turnover that prevents the consolidation of skills and experience.[77]

4 A CRITICAL APPRAISAL OF THE ITALIAN LEGAL FRAMEWORK: GOOD IN THEORY, BAD IN PRACTICE?

In spite of a progressive legislative framework, several gaps have emerged in educational provision and in the actual implementation of Law 104/1992. The fragmented educational policy highlighted earlier in this chapter has not

72 Cristina Devecchi, Filippo Dettori, Mary Doveston, Paul Sedgwick and Johnston Jament, 'Inclusive Classrooms in Italy and England: The Role of Support Teachers and Teaching Assistants' (2012) 27 *European Journal of Special Needs Education* 171.

73 Anastasiou, Kauffman and Di Nuovo (n. 29) 435.

74 Dario Ianes, Heidrun Demo and Francesco Zambotti, 'Integration in Italian Schools: Teachers' Perceptions Regarding Day-to-Day Practice and Its Effectiveness' (2014) 18 *International Journal of Inclusive Education* 626.

75 Mirealla Zanobini, 'Some Considerations about Inclusion, Disability, and Special Educational Needs: A Reply to Giangreco, Doyle & Suter (2012)' (2013) 16 *Life Span and Disability* 83.

76 Association TreeLLLe, Caritas Italiana and Fondazione Giovanni Agnelli, *Gli alunni con disabilità nella scuola italiana: bilancio e proposte* (Erickson 2011) 146. See also Fabio Bocci, Anna Maria Favorini, Angela Merola, Daniela Olmetti, Carlotta Ricci and Stefano Zucca, 'L'integrazione degli alunni disabili nella Scuola dell'infanzia. Una indagine esplorativa presso il IX Municipio del Comune di Roma' (2007) 74 *Psichiatria dell'Infanzia e dell'Adolescenza* 785.

77 Dario Ianes, 'Insegnanti di sostegno: un'evoluzione necessaria' (2014) 2 *Italian Journal of Special Education for Inclusion* 35.

facilitated the implementation of an inclusive school system. The data presented in Section 3 also show a 'blurred' situation.

Building on the previous analysis, this section aims to give, from a legal perspective, a critical appraisal of the legislation as it applies to educational provision for children with disabilities in Italy. It compares and contrasts the deficiencies identified at the domestic level with those that emerged in the UN review process. The section first highlights the weaknesses emerging in current educational practice by giving an account of a wide series of domestic court cases. In the second instance, this section discusses the flaws in the Italian education system identified by the National Observatory. In the third and final instance, this section assesses the Italian legislation in light of the CRPD Committee COs, taking into account Italy's initial report, and civil society organisations' and DPOs' shadow reports.

4.1 *Practical Shortcomings Highlighted in Domestic Case Law*

The data presented earlier in this chapter showed gaps in educational provision and a lack of continuity in the support provided by teachers in schools. These gaps, which emerged to a certain extent in the UN review process and in the domestic monitoring, were first highlighted by a series of court cases, mostly initiated by parents of children with learning or intellectual disabilities, in which the parents challenged the appropriateness of existing provision for their children.[78] In general, Italian courts have held that the constitutional and legislative framework in place, read in conjunction with or in light of the CRPD, effectively guarantees disabled students the support measures necessary to substantially enjoy the right to education. However, all these decisions also make evident a failure to properly implement the legislative framework in force.

Most of these cases concern the number of hours the support teacher spends in the class, supporting the student in the learning process. In almost all the cases that end up in Italian administrative courts, the applicants asked for the annulment of the individual educational plan (IEP) adopted by the public educational institution limiting the number of support teacher hours available to the relevant student.[79] Usually, the applicants claimed their right to benefit

[78] According to ISTAT, 8.2 per cent of families of primary school pupils and 5.1 per cent of those in the secondary school level have appealed to the district court or the regional administrative court to obtain an increase in support hours. See ISTAT (n. 70). A review of older cases is provided by Autism Europe, 'Analysis of Italian Case Law' (Autism Europe, 2006), www.autismeurope.org/files/files/caselaw-italy-fulltext.pdf, accessed 10 April 2017.

[79] Among many others see Tribunale Amministrativo Regionale (TAR) del Lazio Sezione 3B No. 2796/2017 (12878/2016); TAR per la Sicilia Sezione Terza No. 557/2017.

from the support teacher either for a greater amount of time or for the entire time of school attendance. In some cases, the applicant alleged inter alia the violation of the CRPD as ratified by Law 18/2009 or only of Law 18/2009.[80] In the majority of cases, administrative courts have annulled the contested measures and held that the '*quantum*' of the teaching support essential to enjoying that right has to be determined exclusively in relation to the need of the student with disabilities, and no other interests can be taken into consideration, not even in cases of understaffed administrations.[81] In many of these cases,[82] the CRPD was cited by the court *motu proprio*, in conjunction with domestic provisions, and often alongside the Constitutional Court decision No. 80/2010,[83] to reaffirm the right to education of students with disabilities. The annulment of measures adopted by the public schools is based not on the mere violation of the CRPD, but rather on the violation of the fundamental right to education which is provided for both in international law (i.e. the CRPD) and in the constitution, as well as ensured by domestic legislation (namely Law 104/1992). However, it appears that the CRPD somewhat encouraged Italian courts to take a definitive stance in annulling decisions that might undermine the effective enjoyment of the right to education. In the same vein, when confronted with some of these cases, under appeal, the Council of State, the higher administrative court, has consistently held that the right to education of the disabled child 'is a fundamental right which must be respected with rigor and effectiveness … in fulfillment of international obligations …, for their own absolute nature of the protection provided by Articles 34 and 38[(3) and (4)] of the Constitution'.[84] In particular, the Council of State acknowledges that

> education is one of the factors that most affect the individual's social relation ships and its possibilities of professional achievement, and its law [i.e. the right to education] takes nature both social and individual, with the consequent need, with reference to the handicapped, to ensure its full implementation through the provision of appropriate integration and support measures[85]

[80] E.g. TAR per la Lombardia Sezione 3 No. 1895/2014.
[81] E.g. TAR per la Calabria Sezione 3 No. 831/2011.
[82] On several other decisions the courts decided only to rely on national law; see e.g. TAR per la Campania Sezione 3 No. 1105/2017; TAR per la Campania Sezione 3 No. 1123/2017.
[83] E.g. TAR del Lazio Sezione 3 No 12914/2014.
[84] Council of State Sezione 6 No. 5428/2015 of 1 December 2015 [5].
[85] Ibid., citing Council of State No. 5317/2014 of 27 October 2014.

Most recently, the Sicilian Administrative Tribunal has clarified that the legislative framework in place prevents the setting of a nominal and insufficient number of support hours and of an inadequate IEP.[86] There is, hence, an evident willingness on the part of these courts to give effect to the right to education of persons with disabilities, which is undermined in practice.

Similarly to the administrative courts (although to a lesser extent), civil courts have also been confronted with different cases concerning the right to education of students with disabilities. In general, the ordinary courts were asked to decide cases in which the applicants had filed a complaint outlining discrimination on the grounds of disability. Primarily, the applicants challenged decisions made by public schools to reduce the employment contract of a support teacher to a limited number of hours due to budgetary concerns, and maintained that these constituted an unlawful discrimination and infringements of the fundamental right to education. In this respect, it is worth citing the judgment of the Court of Cassation of 18 November 2014 No. 25011.[87] In this case, the parents of a child with disabilities had challenged the decision of the public school to reduce the employment of a support teacher for the child from twenty-five hours a week to twelve hours a week. According to the plaintiff, the decision by the school to reduce these hours had been adopted solely on economic grounds. The school attempted to challenge the jurisdiction of the ordinary courts. It argued that the case should have been brought in front of the administrative court, in compliance with the rules governing the jurisdiction of the administrative courts. The Court of Cassation rejected this argument and affirmed that the right to education is one of the fundamental rights of persons with disabilities. The Court referred to the CRPD, alongside the provisions on equality and non-discrimination in the European Union treaties and in the Charter of Fundamental Rights of the European Union. In the Court's estimation, the reduction made by the school of the hours taught by the support teacher can constitute indirect discrimination on the ground of disability, and fall within the remit of its ordinary jurisdiction. Along these lines, the Council of State in its decision No. 3723/2016 affirmed that disputes relating to the implementation phase of the IEP for students with disabilities fall under the jurisdiction of ordinary courts, while the challenge to the IEP itself is under the jurisdiction of the administrative court.[88] This is based on the ground that, after the definition of the individual education plan and the

[86] TAR per la Sicilia Sezione 2 No. 715/2016. See also TAR della Puglia Sezione 2 No. 119/2016.
[87] Cass civ Sez Unite No. 25011 of 18 November 2014.
[88] Council of State Sezione 6 No. 3723/2016 of 26 May 2016.

determination of the number of hours, the school administration is devoid of any power to reduce the number of hours of support laid down therein. It is also based on the ground that any failure in the timely implementation of the plan constitutes an indirect discrimination on the grounds of disability.[89]

A recent decision of the Italian Constitutional Court reaffirmed that the right to education of people with disabilities must be effectively ensured. Broadly speaking, the Court reiterated that a formal recognition is not sufficient, if the right is not guaranteed in practice. The case concerned the transport of students with disabilities to school, and their assistance. In a nutshell, the Abruzzo regional law provided for a grant to be given to local authorities so that they may ensure transport and assistance to students with disabilities only 'subject to the financial resources allocated within annual budgetary laws'.[90] In doing so, the law made the regional contribution aimed at implementing the right of students with disabilities to transport services conditional and subject to budget constraints. The Constitutional court, with a *ratio decidendi* in line with its previous case law and namely decision No. 80/2010, held the regional provision to be unconstitutional. In particular, the Court believed that transportation services for students with disabilities are necessary to guarantee the right to inclusion for persons with disabilities and are an essential element in ensuring the participation of these pupils within the educational process.[91]

All in all, the case law on this issue laid bare the contradictions of a system that ensures the right to education on paper, but easily undermines it in practice. Ordinary and administrative courts have underlined the challenges

89 See also Cass civ Sez Unite Ord No. 5060/2017.

90 Italian Constitutional Court No. 275/2016 [1], citing Article 6(2) – bis of the Abruzzo Regional law of 15 December 1978, No. 78 (*Interventi per l'attuazione del diritto allo studio*), as modified by Article 88(4) of Abruzzo Regional Law of 26 April 2004, No. 15.

91 For a comment on this decision, see Stefano Rossi, 'Limiti di bilancio e diritti fondamentali delle persone con disabilità – Corte cost. n. 275/2016' (*Persona e Danno*, 5 February 2017), www.personaedanno.it/persone-con-disabilita/limiti-di-bilancio-e-diritti-fondamentali-delle-persone-con-disabilita-corte-cost-n-275–2016-stefano-rossi, accessed 15 March 2017; Francesco Pallante, 'Diritti e bilancio: quale equilibrio? Un commento alla sentenza 275/2016 della Corte costituzionale' (*SIDIBlog*, 2 February 2017), www.sidiblog.org/2017/02/02/diritti-e-bilancio-quale-equilibrio-un-commento-alla-sentenza-2752016-della-corte-costituzionale/, accessed 15 March 2017; Adriana Apostoli, 'I diritti fondamentali "visti" da vicino dal giudice amministrativo: Una annotazione a "caldo" della sentenza della Corte costituzionale n.275 del 2016' (Forum di Quaderni Costituzionali Rassegna 11 January 2017), www.forumcostituzionale.it/wordpress/wp-content/uploads/2016/01/nota_275_2016_apostoli.pdf, accessed 15 March 2017; Erik Furno, 'Pareggio di bilancio e diritti sociali: la ridefinizione dei confini nella recente giurisprudenza costituzionale in tema di diritto all'istruzione dei disabili' (2017) 1 *Nomas*, www.nomos-leattualitaneldiritto.it/wp-content/uploads/2017/05/Furno-pareggio-di-bilancio-1.pdf, accessed 15 June 2017.

in the implementation process of the right to education, and (often) the failure of schools and institutions to realise an inclusive educational system.

4.2 *Weaknesses and Shortcomings in the National Monitoring*

Before the ratification of the CRPD, a study to assess the overall compliance of the national legislation with the CRPD was carried out by the Institute of International Legal Studies of the National Council of Research (Istituto di Studi Giuridici Internazionali) (ISGI), upon the request of the Italian Ministry for Labour and Social Policies.[92] This ISGI study, released in December 2008, indicated a general compliance of the Italian legal framework on disability with the objectives of the CRPD. Indeed, the study did suggest some specific revisions to fully align Italian legislation with the CRPD, but no specific amendments were recommended in the area of education.[93] The study posited that a full recognition of the right to education of the disabled is evident in Italian law, which provides 'an adequate protection of the disabled in several respects', in line with Article 24 of the CRPD.[94] The study only affirmed the need 'to pay more attention' to the training of curricular teachers, in order to promote further the inclusion of students with disabilities. Within the educational scholarship, even those who expressed very critical opinions on the Italian legal system, such as Anastasiou, Kauffman and Di Nuovo, affirm that, if Article 24 of the CRPD provides for full inclusion of all students with disabilities in general education, then 'Italy represents the only national example of implementation of a nearly fully inclusive education system'.[95] In fact, the Italian legal framework is premised on the principle enshrined in Law 104/1992 that education must aim to secure the full development of human potential. In that,

[92] Istituto di Studi Giuridici Internazionali (ISGI), *La Convenzione delle Nazioni Unite del 2007 sui diritti delle persone con disabilità: modalità di recepimento, attuazione a livello nazionale e regionale, strumenti di monitoraggio: Rapporto finale* (Istituto di Studi Giuridici Internazionali 2008), www.fiadda.it/upload/uploads/ISGI_Rapporto%20finale_Convenzione%20ONU%20diritti%20persone%20con%20disabilit%C3%A0%20(1).pdf, accessed 15 March 2017.

[93] With regards to the latter, the report affirmed the need to streamline national definitions of disability, which should reflect the role of external barriers in creating disability. The report highlighted the need for definitions of 'reasonable accommodation' and 'discrimination on the ground of disability' in line with the CRPD. It also suggested a number of legislative interventions in the field of accessibility, including the legal recognition of the principle of universal design within Article 5 of Law 104/1992, the recognition of Italian sign language and the development of guidelines for the public administration on accessibility requirements.

[94] ISGI (n. 92) 255 (as translated by author).

[95] Anastasiou, Kauffman and Di Nuovo (n. 29) 429.

this framework clearly aims to realise 'the development by persons with disabilities of their personality, talents and creativity, as well as their mental and physical abilities, to their fullest potential'.[96] Laws 118/71, 517/1977 and 104/1992 ensure that persons with disabilities are not excluded from the mainstream education system on the basis of disability, but integrated into regular schools and provided with support for their inclusion, in compliance with Article 24(2)(a) of the CRPD. Children with disabilities in Italy have the right to access free primary education and secondary education on an equal basis with others in the communities in which they live. In addition, the legislation, as interpreted by the Constitutional Court, provides that persons with disabilities should receive the support required, mainly by means of the support teacher, and aims to ensure that students have access to 'effective individualized support measures ... in environments that maximize academic and social development, consistent with the goal of full inclusion', as prescribed by Article 24(2)(d)(e) of the CRPD.

The National Observatory, in its First Bi-annual Action Plan on Disability in 2013 – which was adopted almost three years before the CRPD Committee's COs – recognised that the legislation in place aims to ensure the full inclusion of all pupils and students with disabilities in mainstream schools.[97] In doing so, and in the same vein as the case law, this plan assumes a general consistency of the Italian system with the principles and the objectives laid down in Article 24 of the CRPD. It does not advocate any general legislative change to the system, but suggests specific and limited improvements to be adopted at the national level.[98] The main legislative innovation that the plan seemed to propose was new legislation, which would make it compulsory for regions to adopt plans on lifelong learning for people with disabilities, and vocational training. In addition, the National Observatory, as did the ISGI, remarked that Italian legislation on education does not include a specific mention of 'reasonable accommodation'. Both of them advocated the introduction of the term *reasonable accommodation* and its definition in the current legislation. In this respect, note that general reasonable accommodation duties are not explicitly included in Italian legislation. Such a duty was explicitly included in the current legislation in 2013,

96 United Nations General Assembly, Convention on the Rights of Persons with Disabilities (24 January 2006) A/RES/61/106 (CRPD) Art. 24.

97 This is a bylaw adopted through the Decree of the President of the Republic of 4 October 2013 'Programma di azione biennale per la promozione dei diritti e l'integrazione delle persone con disabilita' OJ 28 December 2013 No. 303.

98 It also advocates the need for regions and local authorities to play a more active role in the promotion of inclusion.

but it only extends to the employment field.[99] Although the lack of a proviso explicitly mentioning reasonable accommodation is not in line with the CRPD, the 2009 Guidelines of the Ministry of Education refer to this concept and require schools to put in place all the necessary and appropriate arrangements to ensure inclusion. It is also affirmed that the IEP and the support teachers are concerned with the removal of the disadvantage to which a disabled student would otherwise be subjected by standard educational practices or systems. In addition, Italian courts, while not always explicitly, have interpreted current legislation as obliging the schools to ensure accommodations, i.e. to put in place all the adjustments and to take positive steps to ensure that disabled learners can fully participate in education. Other than these, the First Bi-annual Action Plan on Disability underlines the need to improve the operation of the existing system, and to make sure that the right to inclusive education is fully enjoyed by people with disabilities in practice in their everyday life, as the Constitutional Court noted in its decision 80/2010.

The role of the support teacher as a key player to ensure inclusion is not contested by the National Observatory. However, the plan advocates a deeper and more accurate preparation for both support and curricular teachers, in line with what the ISGI had affirmed and in line with the claims of DPOs, supported by data on turnover of teachers.[100] This is intended to ensure that the placement of students with disabilities in regular classes goes hand in hand with the removal of social and environmental barriers to learning processes. The plan proposes the need for better communication between schools and families of people with disabilities, and advocates a more active participation of families in the preparation of the IEP and, though implicitly, in deciding the number of hours of support for the student. It is clear that the National Observatory aimed to put an end to the continuous judicial challenges to the

99 They were included in anti-discrimination legislation only with regards to the employment field in 2013 (Law decree 28 June 2013 No. 76 OJ No. 150 28 June 2013, then converted into Law on 9 August 2013 No. 99 OJ 22 August 2013 No. 196, concerning 'preliminary urgent measures for the promotion of employment, in particular of youngsters, of social cohesion and on and other urgent financial measures'), following the ruling of the Court of Justice of the European Union (CJEU) in *Commission* v. *Italy* C-312/11 (CJEU, 4 July 2013). In this decision, the CJEU found that Italy had failed to fulfil its obligations under the Employment Equality Directive because it had not expressly included a reasonable accommodation duty in its domestic law implementing the Directive. The Italian government argued that, whilst the duty had not been included in Legislative Decree No. 216/2003 implementing the Directive, it was contained in other laws on the rights of disabled people.

100 Dario Ianes and Iacopo Tomasi, *Insegnanti di sostegno: verso la separazione della formazione e dei ruoli?* (Erickson 2015).

IEP by parents of people with disabilities and to the hundreds of lawsuits pending in front of administrative courts.

On a more general note, the plan also suggested changes in the assessment of the quality of inclusive education, and in the collection of data on inclusion. The latter changes are somewhat in line with the recommendations that the CRPD Committee formulated three years later in its COs, and also aims to verify what the real outcomes are of the system in place.

4.3 *Legislative Gaps and Practical Shortcomings in the UN Review Process*

In its initial report, along the lines of the ISGI study and the decisions of domestic courts, the Italian government claimed that the 'conceptual, ethical and normative vision of disability and persons with disabilities' evident in the CRPD 'is reflected in the actions carried out by Italy in the last 20 years'.[101] In respect of the right to education, the legislative framework briefly described is considered largely in compliance with Article 24 of the CRPD. The CRPD Committee itself did not express any specific criticism of Italian legislation as such, and as mentioned earlier, praised Italy for its enduring efforts towards inclusion.[102] The shadow report of the Italian Disability Forum, an umbrella DPO,[103] also acknowledged the advanced legislation and the fact that there has been a financial commitment to ensure all students with disabilities have access to inclusive education.[104] By contrast, a few legislative lacunae were highlighted by the Coordinamento Nazionale Famiglie Disabili (CSS) in its alternative report.[105] The CSS claimed that, at both the educational and

101 Committee on the Rights of Persons with Disabilities, CRPD/C/ITA/1 (n. 6) [1].

102 Committee on the Rights of Persons with Disabilities, Concluding Observations on the Initial Report of Italy (6 October 2016) CRPD/C/ITA/CO/1.

103 The Italian Disability Forum (Forum Italiano sulla Disabilità) (FID) is an Italian not-for-profit organisation of persons with disabilities, and a member of the European Disability Forum. It represents the interests of persons with disabilities in Italy. It is composed of national organisations of persons with disabilities and their families, including the Association of Persons with Visual Disabilities, Italian Association against Epilepsy, Italian Down Syndrome Association, Italian Spina Bifida Association, Disabled People's International Italia and others.

104 Italian Disability Forum (Forum Italiano sulla Disabilità) (FID), First Alternative Report to the UN Committee on the Rights of Persons with Disabilities (FID 18 January 2016) and FID, Italian Disability Forum's Submission for the List of Issues on Italy's State Report to the UN Committee on the Rights of Persons with Disabilities (FID 18 January 2016), both downloaded from www.uiciechi.it/AttivitaInternazionali/fid.asp, accessed 15 June 2017.

105 Coordinamento Nazionale Famiglie di Disabili Gravi e Gravissimi, *Shadow Report on Italy* (2016) downloaded from http://tbinternet.ohchr.org/_layouts/treatybodyexternal/Download.aspx?symbolno=INT%2fCRPD%2fCSS%2fITA%2f25451&Lang=en accessed 7 July 2017.

rehabilitative levels, the legislation does not include specialised approaches focussed on expressing spontaneous communication or implementing other communication strategies. It underlined that alternative communication strategies, such as augmentative and alternative communication, are not legally recognised as forms of communication in exams. Students with severe disabilities are, according to the CSS, 'positioned in a relationship where the aid process prevails' and in which they are 'encouraged to remain in a state of passivity, prisoners of anomalies and behavioural stereotypes'.[106] The CSS also identified in connection with this legislative gap a more practical challenge. A lack of human resources was in fact highlighted, whereby the Italian National Health Service has few professionals specialised in communicative learning for people with cerebral palsy, and/or cognitive delays, or disabilities which fall within the autistic spectrum. The CRPD Committee however, did not follow up on the criticism expressed by the CSS, even though it expressed a general concern about the lack of acknowledgement of Braille and tactile communication as effective tools for the education of blind or deaf-blind persons, when assessing the compliance of Italian law with Article 21 of the CRPD.[107]

The shortcomings identified by DPOs and by the Committee – already evident in the List of Issues preceding the Concluding Observations[108] – all concerned the practical realisation of an inclusive educational system, and the lack of reliable data and indicators capable of monitoring the quality of education and the inclusion of students with disabilities in mainstream schools.[109] The Committee did not engage in any extensive discussion, but recommended that Italy set out 'an action plan – with sufficient resources, timelines and specific goals – aimed at monitoring the implementation of laws, decrees and regulations to improve the quality of inclusive education in classrooms, support provisions and teacher training across all levels'.[110] The Committee somewhat confirmed the analysis of a group of scholars who had claimed that '[t]he Italian system often pays little attention to organisation, which should be not improvised but managed on a scientific basis'.[111] Two particular gaps in the implementation of the right to education were also identified. The first gap highlighted by the

106 Ibid. 5.
107 Committee on the Rights of Persons with Disabilities, CRPD/C/ITA/CO/1 (n. 101).
108 Committee on the Rights of Persons with Disabilities, List of Issues in Relation to the Initial Report of Italy (29 April 2016) CRPD/C/ITA/Q/1.
109 Committee on the Rights of Persons with Disabilities, CRPD/C/ITA/CO/1 (n. 101).
110 Committee on the Rights of Persons with Disabilities, CRPD/C/ITA/CO/1 (n. 101) [56].
111 Anastasiou, Kauffman and Di Nuovo (n. 29) 436.

COs was the lack of availability of accessible learning materials and assistive technology. Secondly, the Committee acknowledged that deaf children are not provided with sign language (LIS) interpreters in school, and recommended that Italy 'desist from recommending general communication assistants as an exclusive alternative'.[112] Statistics from the National Institute of Statistics (ISTAT) annual survey on first degree primary and secondary schools show that for the academic year 2014–2015, around 3,000 deaf students (representing 2 per cent of the total of students with disabilities) have an assistant for communication. However, it is not clear whether the assistant is in fact an LIS interpreter. The Committee therefore embraced the view that sign language interpreters are not de facto guaranteed and their availability depends on the sensitivity of school directors and managers, in spite of the recognition and promotion of sign language in schools being provided for in Law 104/92 and in other regional pieces of legislation.[113] However, Italy is non-compliant with the CRPD due to its lack of formal recognition of LIS. A bill is currently under examination, and following a long stalemate, at the end of January 2017, the text was scheduled for further examination and discussion within the relevant parliamentary commission. However, it is not clear, in the current political turmoil, when it will be approved.[114] In addition, in a time of ongoing and severe economic crisis, the fear of additional financial costs on the public budget might stall the approval of this bill.

Interestingly, the Committee did not engage extensively with the criticism expressed by the Italian Disability Forum (IDF) in its shadow report on support teachers, in particular on their 'excessive turn-over' (which is shown by the data presented in Section 3), and 'their approximate and often inadequate professional profile, as well as by lack of motivation, of specific competences and collaboration of curricular and support teachers'.[115] Once again, however, the IDF's criticism does not concern the role itself of support teachers. The IDF suggests that changes should be made to relevant bylaws to counter the alleged lack of sufficient skills and expertise, and to improve the professionalism of

[112] Committee on the Rights of Persons with Disabilities, CRPD/C/ITA/CO/1 (n. 101) [58].

[113] The latest is the Lombardia Law 20/2016 in BURL of 8 August 2016 No. 32. See also Mark Wheatley and Annika Pabsch, *Sign Language Legislation in the European Union* (2nd edn) (European Union of the Deaf 2012).

[114] In December 2016, Matteo Renzi resigned as Italian prime minister after being defeated in a referendum to change the Constitution, nearly three years after he became Italy's prime minister. Former foreign minister Paolo Gentiloni was then appointed as the prime minister.

[115] FID, First Alternative Report to the UN Committee on the Rights of Persons with Disabilities (n. 104) 64 (citations omitted).

some teachers.[116] Nevertheless, the IDF seems to focus more on the incorrect implementation of the legislation in this respect, than on the legislation itself.

All in all, the review process that occurred at the UN level confirmed that the Italian legal framework is close to meeting the obligations laid down in Article 24 of the CRPD. However, the systemic change in the manner in which education takes place to ensure respect for the needs of all learners, which is required by the CRPD, has not yet been fully realised in practice.

5 THE NEW REFORM OF THE EDUCATIONAL SYSTEM: THE LONG AND WINDING ROAD TOWARDS INCLUSIVE EDUCATION

In September 2014, the government initiated a process of 'modernization' of the whole Italian educational system and put on the table an additional funding of €3 billion to recruit schoolteachers and additional staff, but also to innovate facilities and to introduce high-speed internet and Wi-Fi in all schools. In 2015, Law 107/2015,[117] so-called *LaBuonaScuola* (TheGoodSchool) was approved.[118] This law reforms various aspects of the education provision, and sets forth the criteria and principles that the government must follow when adopting legislative decrees that regulate specific aspects. It engages with many aspects related to the education of students with disabilities, but within the framework laid down by Law 104/1992.

In a nutshell, Law 107/2015 attempts, without questioning the system itself, to improve its functionality and empowers the government to adopt specific provisions that ultimately aim to ensure the full enjoyment of the right to education for people with disabilities. It reiterates the commitment to the realisation of a truly inclusive educational system that must be achieved through a redefinition of the specific training and career path to be undertaken by prospective support teachers, which are to be specifically determined through legislative decrees, together with specific norms aimed at ensuring the continuity in service of support teachers in order to guarantee an effective right to education (Article 1(181)). Law 107/2015 also requires curricular teachers, schools principals and administrative staff to undertake training on inclusion in order to ensure an inclusive environment. This reform law

[116] Moreover, in its shadow report, the FID mentioned several episodes of abuse and ill treatment of students with disabilities, which it attributes to the lack of experience and skills of teachers.
[117] In OJ No. 162 15 July 2015.
[118] Ibid.

intends to promote innovations in terms of how the overall system will function. However, the full inclusion of students with disabilities through the individualised support of support teachers does not change. The law also requires the elaboration of specific indicators for the evaluation of school inclusion. This latter aspect could help overcome the criticism expressed by the CRPD Committee in relation to the lack of reliable data on the quality of education and the inclusion of students with disabilities. Interestingly, Article 1 paragraph 24 also affirms that teaching provided to students with disabilities will be ensured 'through the recognition of different modes of communication' (as translated). This provision could be seen as a gateway to ensure LIS interpreters in schools, though it is arguable that a firmer, clearer, express commitment to interpreters would be preferable. Interestingly, as Carlini affirms,[119] the whole reform law embraces some of the principles laid down in a former legislative proposal to promote school inclusion for persons with disabilities, which had been presented in 2014 by a group of parliamentarians subject to extensive consultation with DPOs.[120]

In October 2016, the Second Biannual Action Plan adopted by the National Observatory also suggested a range of actions to be advanced and to be included in the legislative decree implementing Law 107/2015.[121] Yet, once again, the plan affirms the need to consolidate the system in place and to 'make it more efficient'[122] (as translated), and declares that Italy exhibits clear leadership at the international level, when it comes to inclusive education. Without discussing the action plan in detail, it seems worthwhile to focus on the legislative decree implementing the reform law and laying down rules for the promotion of school inclusion of students with disabilities (Decree No. 66/2017, formerly Draft Decree 378) itself. As established in the reform Law 107/2015, the decree aims to renew the policies already in place for pupils and

119 Antonia Carlini, 'L'inclusione' (2015) 8 *Voci della scuola* 71.

120 Bill 'Norme per migliorare la qualità dell'inclusione scolastica degli alunni con disabilità e con altri bisogni educativi speciali' (Act of the Chamber No. 2444 10 June 2014). On the proposal see the DPOs' comments at http://aipd.it/aipd_scuola/deludenti-i-decreti-sullinclusione-scolastica-del-gennaio-2017-sulla-buona-scuola-atti-governo-n-378/ and www.camera.it/_dati/leg17/lavori/stampati/pdf/17PDL0025500.pdf, accessed 15 March 2017.

121 Ministero del Lavoro e delle Politihe Sociali and Osservatorio nazionale sulla condizione delle persone con disabilità, 'Proposta di ii programma di azione biennale per la promozione dei diritti e l'integrazione delle persone con disabilità in attuazione della legislazione nazionale e internazionale ai sensi dell'art. 5, co. 3, della Legge 3 marzo 2009, n. 18' (July 2016), www.lavoro.gov.it/notizie/Documents/PDA_Disabilita_2016_Agosto2016.pdf, accessed 15 March 2017.

122 Ibid. 9.

students with disabilities, and to define the respective roles of the state, the regions and local authorities in promoting inclusion.

The draft decree was released by the government on 14 January 2017, and submitted to the parliamentary commissions for their examination. After the release draft decree by the government, DPOs criticised several aspects of the decree. First, they claimed a lack of involvement of DPOs in the elaboration of the decree and affirmed that the Government did not ensure a fully participatory process. Secondly, DPOs criticised several substantive aspects, including the lack of obligations on full training on inclusion for curricular teachers, the still insufficient training for support teachers, the increase of total students per class when the class includes a person with a disability and the lack of provisions on specific assessment for people with disabilities in lieu of the general state examinations at the end of each school cycle. They claimed that the increase of total students per class and of the disabled–non disabled student ratio, coupled with the insufficient training for teachers, might undermine the practical realisation of the right to education.

In February 2017, the newly appointed minster for education declared that the text was to be modified in order to take into account the criticisms raised, and claimed that inclusion remains a priority for the government.[123] On 16 March 2017, the parliamentary commissions in charge of the examination of the draft decree[124] released a positive opinion on it,[125] suggesting a few modifications. The final text of the decree was then approved by the government

[123] Ufficio Stampa, 'Miglioreremo decreto su inclusione scolastica. Studentesse e studenti con disabilità devono avere pari opportunità formative' (Ministero dell'Istruzione, dell'Università e della Ricerca, 9 February 2017), http://hubmiur.pubblica.istruzione.it/web/ministero/cs090217quater, accessed 27 March 2017.

[124] The text of the opinion is available at www.camera.it/leg17/824?tipo=A&anno=2017&mese=03&giorno=16&view=filtered_scheda&commissione=0712, accessed 27 March 2017. A few parliamentarians presented dissenting opinions, highlighting gaps and deficiencies. Fossati, for example, affirmed that the decree does not introduce any ameliorative novelty to the system and, by contrast, might hinder inclusion and the right to quality education of students with disabilities, as enshrined in the CRPD. In the same vein, Borghesi criticises the decree. He also points out that the role of families of pupils with disabilities remains too marginal. In addition, Borghesi heavily criticises the obligation of teachers to remain in the role for ten years. Such a predefined period does not guarantee, a priori, inclusion, nor does it ensure quality of education.

[125] The parliamentary commissions, which are competent on the subject matter, must give their opinion on decree schemes within sixty days from their release. The parliamentary commissions in charge of the examination of this decree were the VII (on culture) and the XII (on social affairs). See at www.camera.it/leg17/360?slAnnoMese=201703&slGiorno=16&shadow_organo_parlamentare=2086, accessed 10 April 2017. The text of the opinion is available at www.camera.it/leg17/824?tipo=A&anno=2017&mese=03&giorno=16&view=filtered_scheda&commissione=0712, accessed 10 April 2017.

on 7 April 2017, and was enacted in April 2017.[126] The final text of the legislative decree, now numbered 66/2017, was released and published in the official journal in May 2017.[127] This decree, along the lines traced by the reform law, concerns the performance and quality of school inclusion indicators, certification procedures for school inclusion, school organisation resource allocation, planning and design inclusion and initial training of teachers for educational support. It gives a definition of school inclusion and clearly establishes that it 'concerns all pupils and students, meets the different educational needs and is accomplished through educational and teaching strategies aimed at developing the potential of each individual'.[128] It uses the term 'inclusion' in an attempt to put an end to the incongruence and blurring of the terms 'integration' and 'inclusion' that characterised former legislation. A detailed examination of this decree is outside the scope of this chapter. Some aspects, however, deserve to be mentioned for the purpose of this analysis. First, upon the request of the DPOs, the increase of total students per class and of the disabled–non disabled student ratio, originally provided in the draft decree, was deleted from the final text, and 'inclusive classes' remains limited to a maximum of twenty students (while, otherwise, classes can be of twenty-five to twenty-seven students). Secondly, the decree introduces new rules for access to the teaching career for educational support in kindergarten and primary school, and new requirements for support teachers in secondary schools. In practice, it attempts to counter the harsh criticism raised by DPOs and to strengthen the knowledge necessary to perform the teaching support role. It requires support teachers to acquire a more solid grounding in social inclusion, after the achievement of the qualifying degree in education as a basic requirement for the teaching function. Finally, the decree also attempts to put an end to the turnover of support teachers that endangers the learning experience of students with disabilities and has long been criticised by parents of students with disabilities. The draft text originally included an obligation on support teachers to remain within the role for ten years. The provision raised harsh criticism because, *ex littera lege*, the provision obliged teachers to stay in the support role, but not to remain in the same school or institution. It might be argued that it was unconstitutional to force someone to remain in a role against their will, if other opportunities are available. From a mere speculative point of view, the provision could also be seen as a restriction of free

[126] http://hubmiur.pubblica.istruzione.it/web/ministero/cs070417bis, accessed 10 April 2017

[127] Legislative Decree No. 66 of 13 April 2017 'Norme per la promozione dell'inclusione scolastica degli studenti con disabilita', a norma dell'articolo 1, commi 180 e 181, lettera c), della legge 13 luglio 2015, n. 107. (17G00074), OJ 16 May 2017 No. 112.

[128] Art. 1(1)(a) of Decree 66/2017 (n. 126) (as translated by the author).

movement under European Union law, if the person wanted to take up a job outside Italy. However, the final text removed this provision. It provided a more generic obligation to guarantee continuous and stable support to students with disabilities, to be implemented by more specific bylaws.

At the time of writing this chapter, it remains to be seen whether the decree will actually contribute to realising the right to an inclusive education.

6 CONCLUDING REMARKS

For almost fifty years, Italy has endeavoured to create an inclusive educational system. The Italian legal framework has striven to ensure to persons with disabilities full and non-discriminatory access to mainstream schools. However, there are persistent gaps in actually providing an inclusive education. In this respect, Dovigo affirms that the evolution of the Italian school system shows that the abolition of special schools does not automatically lead to the full, meaningful inclusion of all pupils in mainstream education, and requires constant efforts and the development of educational practices.[129] He also affirms that, when the global scene was still dominated by segregation policies, Italy represented a shining example, but '[n]ow this special status seems to fade away'.[130] Italian schools are facing several problems.

The ratification of the CRPD has contributed to the unveiling of several practical challenges in relation to the implementation of the laws in place with regards to the number of support hours available to students. Caps on the number of hours of support have in most instances been struck down by the courts, or were considered discriminatory, and Italian judges have often attempted to either use the CRPD in support of their reasoning or to interpret Italian law in light of Article 24. The domestic and international monitoring processes have also helped to disclose and to make evident weaknesses in the ways in which legislation has been implemented and practical challenges that the legislation itself has not been capable of avoiding.

The new reform of the educational system and the correlated decrees attempt to meet (some of) the recommendations of the CRPD Committee, and to solve some of the problems that emerged in case law and that were highlighted by DPOs, especially in relation to the practical support ensured to students with disabilities by support teachers. It remains to be seen, following

129 Dovigo (n. 54) 18.
130 Ibid. 22.

the adoption of the legislative decree, how effective these will be. Despite the evident gaps in the implementation, the challenges brought on by the economic crisis and practical shortcomings, Italy continues to demonstrate a strong commitment to the full inclusion of students with disabilities and towards the creation of more equitable and accessible schools.

23

Inclusive Education in China

Zhijun Fu, Bo Chen and Ni Zhen

INTRODUCTION

On 11 January 2017, the Regulations on Education of Persons with Disabilities (Education Regulations 2017) was passed by Premier Li Keqiang.[1] Compared to the obsolete version enacted in 1994, the new regulations clearly maintain the principle of inclusive education for the state educational provision for persons with disabilities and indicates an attempt to incorporate the idea of non-discrimination.[2] However, this new law also encourages the development of special schools and an ableist approach to school enrolment, which undoubtedly compromises the principle of inclusion and the trend towards non-discrimination.[3]

This chapter was collectively contributed by three Chinese scholars. The introduction, Part 1 and the conclusion were contributed by Zhen Ni; Part 2 was contributed by Zhijun Fu; Part 3 was contributed by Bo Chen. Zhijun Fu and Bo Chen edited the whole chapter. Zhijun Fu, PhD candidate of the Law School, Shanghai University of Finance & Economics, adjunct director of the Shanghai Pudong Disabled Persons' Federation (local branch of the China Disabled Persons' Federation [CDPF]).

[1] The draft of the Regulation on Education of Persons with Disabilities (as amended) was passed by Premier Li Keqiang at the executive meeting of the State Council on 11 January 2017. See www.gov.cn/guowuyuan/gwycwhy/20170111c02/index.htm, accessed 30 January 2017. However, at the date of the submission of this chapter, the full text had not been released. The text addressed in this chapter is based on the amended version of the Regulation which was open for public comments and released in 2013. See Legislative Affairs Office of the State Council PR China, 'Notice of the Legislative Affairs Office of the State Council on the Public Opinion on the Education of Persons with Disabilities (Revised Draft)', www.chinalaw.gov.cn/article/cazjgg/201302/20130200384148.shtml, accessed 20 May 2016.

[2] Article 3 of the Draft (n. 2) maintains that 'discrimination on the basis of disability is forbidden in the field of education'.

[3] Article 23 of the Draft (n. 2) stipulates that 'people's governments on different levels should establish special schools to ensure children with disabilities have access to education'; Article 22 maintains that 'children with disabilities who are unable to adapt themselves to the environment of regular schools should have opportunities to attend special education institutions'.

The contradictions in the new regulations reflect long-rooted disagreements about inclusive education in reality. To explore the contradictions and the underlying disagreements, historical, social and political factors must be considered. China has long been active in joining international declarations and human rights conventions, but international standards (the UN Convention on the Rights of Persons with Disabilities [CRPD] in particular) have triggered legislative amendments, including the new regulations.[4] For this reason, attention should be drawn to the interaction between domestic legislation and international standards and conventions. This chapter sets out its analyses by answering two questions. The first question is: how have historical, social and cultural factors influenced today's inclusive education? The second is: what are and will be the roles of laws in improving inclusive education? This chapter sets out three sections. By examining historical, social and cultural events and phenomena, Section 1 firstly explains ideas and theories underpinning China's special education policies. The first section also discusses the origin, problems and influence of the double-track approach to educational provision for disabled children. Then, it examines ongoing educational, legal and social reforms concerning inclusive education in China. Section 2 carries out an in-depth study into Chinese laws on inclusive education and relevant jurisprudence. Section 3 offers a rigorous evidence-based analysis on interactions between the Chinese government, international human rights mechanisms and domestic civil society organisations.

I BACKGROUND AND CONTEXT

In several key government documents on national educational development, the Chinese government persists in developing more special schools.[5] The government (in policies) demands that there must be at least one special school in any prefecture or county with a population of more than 300,000 people.[6] Although there are no comprehensive and detailed statistics about the enrolment rate of children with disabilities, the vague quantitative account provided by the government may still disclose the huge gap in the enrolment

4 Michael Ashley Stein, 'China and Disability Rights' (2010) 33 *Loyola of Los Angeles International and Comparative Law Review* 7.

5 Such documents include the National Long-Term Educational Reform and Development Plan 2010–2020 (see www.moe.edu.cn/publicfiles/business/htmlfiles/moe/moe_838/201008/93704.html, accessed 30 January 2017), the Special Education Improvement Plan 2014–2016 (see www.edu.cn/xin_wen_dong_tai_890/20140121/t20140121_1066692.shtml, accessed 30 January 2017) and the 12th Five Year Educational Improvement Plan (see www.edu.cn/html/e/jygh, accessed 30 January 2017).

6 Ibid.

rate between children with and without disabilities. By the end of 2015, 442,000 children with disabilities had access to schooling, while 1.04 billion children (including children with and without disabilities) in the same age range were receiving school education; in other words, the former amounted to 0.425 per cent of the latter.[7] In 2015, according to China's statistics, China had approximately 85.02 million disabled people, amounting to 6.34 per cent of the whole population.[8] That year, China had 2,053 special schools accommodating approximately 200,000 disabled children, while approximately 239,000 children were studying in either regular schools or special classes attached to regular schools.[9]

Inclusive education in China has a variety of definitions.[10] Some scholars believe that the Learning in Regular Class (LRC) project gives the most practical interpretation of inclusive education.[11] However, other scholars argue that inclusive education in the Chinese context should at least include the deconstruction of special schools on top of placing children with disabilities in regular schools.[12] In addition, these scholars insist that LRC is only similar to the idea of integration in Western countries, which values physical placement of children with disabilities in regular schools but brings about no fundamental change to the educational system and the established special school system.[13] Civil society organisations put forward the argument that reforming the rigid exam-oriented education system should be one of the key elements of inclusive education.[14] No consensus has been achieved

7 Cited from the 2015 National Education Development Bulletin published by the Ministry of Education of China; see www.gov.cn/xinwen/2016–07/06/content_5088866.htm, accessed 30 January 2017.

8 Cited from the Guidelines about Improving the Living Standards for Persons with Disabilities Issued by the State Council; see www.gov.cn/zhengce/content/2015–02/05/content_9461.htm, accessed 31 January 2017.

9 Cited from the 2015 National Education Development Bulletin (n. 8).

10 Meng Deng and Zhiyong Zhu, 'The Chinese "Learning in a Regular Classroom" and Western Inclusive Education: Comparison and Exploration' (2007) 40 *Chinese Education and Society* 21; Meng Deng and Shi Jing, 'From Learning in Regular Classrooms to Equal Regular Education: Reflections on the Localization of Inclusive Education in China' (2013) 8 *Chinese Journal of Special Education* 3.

11 Ibid.

12 Olli-Pekka Malinen, 'Inclusive Education in China' (2013) CEREC Working Paper No. 4, March 2013, www.uta.fi/cerec/publications/workpaper/CEREC%20Working%20Paper%204.pdf, accessed 17 June 2017.

13 Zhicheng Huang, 'Life-Long Education, Education for All and Inclusive Education: A Review of Contemporary Educational Philosophies' (2003) 5(2) *Hebei Normal University Journal* 27–30.

14 Fenming Cui, 'Key Challenges Facing the Reform towards Inclusive Education' (2010) 6 *Educational Development Research* 80–84.

about the definition of inclusive education in the Chinese context, but the ratification of the CRPD and other international documents has established the government's position and has set up boundaries for this discussion.

1 *Special Schools and the Idea of Separation*

The first special school, Mission to Chinese Blind in Peking, was founded in 1874 by William Hill Murray, a British minister.[15,16] Following him, many other Western missionaries set up special schools in China – mainly for blind and deaf children. Nearly half a century later, Chinese entrepreneurs started to invest in building special schools.[17] Before the People's Republic of China was founded in 1949, China had more than forty special schools for blind and deaf students.[18]

In 1951, the State Council of the People's Republic of China (PRC) issued a decision on reforming the entire education system.[19] According to the decision, missionary-founded special schools were taken over by people's governments on different levels. Special schools in the new China were defined as a type of social education rather than as an indispensable part of the public education system.[20] By its very nature, social education was an informal form of education in contrast with formal education provided by public schools. Generally speaking, the informal status of special schools had several negative consequences: education for children with disabilities was considered less important, public schools had no obligation to provide education for children with disabilities and they were obliged to study far away from home, and education quality in special schools was inferior to regular education in public schools. The informal status of special education and its consequence resembles the status of special education in the early days of the former Soviet Union.[21]

15 This section is adapted from Zhen Ni, 'Rethinking Inclusion: Is There a Right to Inclusive Education?' (2016) 11 *Frontiers of Law in China* 486–514.

16 Jianping Lin, 'The Narrow Gate in the Dawn: An Investigation about Protestant Blind Education before New China' (Masters dissertation, Central China Normal University, 2007); Weidong Guo, 'Protestant Ministers and China's Braille System' (2006) 2 *Modern Chinese History Studies* 123–128.

17 Ibid.

18 Ibid.

19 Yongxin Piao, 'The Ten Great Changes of China's Special Education' (2009) 6 *Education Research Monthly* 3–5.

20 Ibid.

21 See Denise Roza, 'Russia' in Mithu Alur and Vianne Timmons (eds), *Inclusive Education across Cultures: Crossing Boundaries, Sharing Ideas* (SAGE Publications, India 2009), 261–273.

Meanwhile, special schools in the new China claimed their mission cohered to contemporary socialist values. In the first place, special schools shoulder the task to transform 'useless disabled people' into a group with basic living skills who no longer burden society.[22] Second, special schools receive a medical mandate to exert on students with disabilities functional compensation and medical correction.[23] The third task of special schools is to separate children with disabilities from the rest of society.[24]

The intentions – to transform, to medically correct and to segregate children with disabilities – are recognised by legislation. Substantive rules and laws on disability and special school education did not exist until the 1990s. The Law on the Protection of Persons with Disabilities was enacted in 1990, defining a person with disabilities as someone who 'suffers from the loss or abnormity of a certain organ or function, psychologically, physiologically or in human structure, and has lost all or in part the ability to normally carry out certain activities'.[25] The Educational Regulations for Disabled Persons was issued four years later.[26] Both the protection law and the regulation reaffirmed measures of physical and psychological compensation and medical interference.[27] At the same time, special schools were confirmed as the main form ('backbone') of educational provision for children with disabilities.[28]

Only in the past decade, several critical events have introduced challenges to the prevailing practice and idea of special education. First, hosting the 2008 Beijing Olympic Games demanded increased transparency of Chinese domestic human rights issues, including disability rights; the domestic disability rights situation since then has had to be measured against international standards. Since then, ideas such as accessibility, reasonable accommodation, inclusion and equal participation have started to receive more attention from the government and the public sectors. Second, China's ratification of the

22 Piao (n. 20) [3].

23 Fei Xiao, Quanli Liu and Zhiliang Qian, 'The Localized Special Education Research: The Thoughts of Professor PIAO Yongxin' (2007) 5 *Journal of National Educational Administration College* 3–10.

24 Xiaguang Peng, 'The Great Changes Facing China's Special Education' (2010) 9 *Chinese Journal of Special Education* 3–8.

25 See Article 2 of the Law of People's Republic of China on the Protection of Persons with Disabilities 1990 (the Protection Law 1990). This definition remains in the revised edition.

26 The Regulations on Education of Persons with Disabilities 1994 (the Education Regulations 1994).

27 Zhen Ni, 'Students' Life in Dongshi School for the Blind: Why Did They Have Uniform Career Plans?' in Wanhong Zhang (ed.), *Disability Rights Studies* (Social Science Academic Press 2014) 1–25.

28 Ibid.

CRPD was eventful for the promotion of disability rights.[29] This led to a wave of legislative amendments after 2008. Third, CRPD shadow reporting by civil society organisations in 2012 raised the issue of the rapid development of special schools to the CRPD Committee; the reporting and the following questions cast on the government by the CRPD Committee compelled the government to think for the first time that developing special schools might have been a misconduct.[30] These emerging dynamics brought about challenges for special schools and opportunities for inclusive education (see detailed discussions in Section 3).

2 *An Inconsistent Approach: The Double-Track System*

In China's double-track educational system, there is little collaboration between special and regular schools; once disabled children are enrolled in special schools, it is almost impossible for them to receive support from any regular school.[31] For children with disabilities in regular schools, however, they receive much less budgetary support. Regular school teachers have limited capacity and motivation to accommodate the needs of children with disabilities. As a result, children with disabilities in regular schools are at risk of being reallocated to special schools. The formation of the double-track system did not take place consequent to careful policy considerations. Rather, the system originated as an expedient measure to raise the level of enrolment of disabled children.[32]

(1) Double-Track Approach: An Expedient Solution to Increasing the Enrolment Rate

The results of China's first disability population census were released in 1987.[33] By then, China had a disabled population of 51,860,000, amounting to 4.9 per cent of the whole population. Taking into account the fact that no scientific record on the size of the disabled population was accessible to the public, these statistics exposed previously invisible persons with disabilities to

29 Article 23 of the Draft (n. 2).
30 Ni (2014) (n. 28).
31 Ni (2016) (n. 16).
32 For in-depth discussions about the nature of the binary regular vs special education system, please see Roger Slee and Julie Allan, 'Excluding the Included: A Reconsideration of Inclusive Education' (2001) 11(2) *International Studies in Sociology of Education* 173–192.
33 See www.cdpf.org.cn/special/dlzt/2005–01/18/content_3234.htm, accessed 11 October 2017.

the whole of society. Also, such conceptualisations began to heighten public consciousness about persons with disabilities and their extreme deprivation.

Part of the deprivation was the extremely low school enrolment of children with disabilities. In 1987, fewer than 40,000 disabled children had access to schooling.[34] This triggered the first serious doubt about the limited capacity of special schools. Since building more special schools to increase the enrolment in a short time was impossible, the government had to explore other solutions to relieve this deprivation. Learning in Regular Class was a pioneering project placing children with disabilities into local regular classrooms. However, thanks to the little support provided, learning in regular class turned out to be 'sitting in class with learning nothing'.

Despite the fact that both special schools and the LRC project failed to solve the problem, the government simply chose to continue with the ineffective solutions. This has gradually developed into a double-track system. On the one hand, the majority of resources continue to be allocated to support the expansion of special school system.[35] On the other hand, the integration approach is intended to place more children with disabilities into regular classes in order to achieve an acceptable enrolment rate.[36] Moreover, the double-track system won legal recognition over time. The Protection Law 1990, the Education Regulations 1994 and even the newly revised Education Regulation 2017 and the Second Special Education Plan (2017–2020) have altogether endorsed the double-track approach; none of them has even challenged the expediency of the approach.[37]

(2) Challenges Facing Inclusive Education in China

Facing increasing pressure from the international community and civil society, the Chinese government has accelerated educational reform by conforming to international standards. However, the reform has yet to achieve fundamental changes. Local conditions are used to explain the unsuccessful implementation of inclusive education – extra-large class sizes, lack of special

34 Zhiliang Qian, 'The Report about the Current Situation of Education for Children with Disabilities' (1999) 1(64) *Journal of Contemporary Special Education* 3–4.

35 Peng (n. 25) [4].

36 Ibid. [4].

37 For the Second Special Education Plan, please see www.cdpf.org.cn/ywzz/jyjyb/jy_254/jywjtz/201707/t20170731_601598.shtml, accessed 22 October 2017. It is the most recent policy document on special education. The plan reaffirms the equally important roles of special and regular schools in achieving higher enrolment rates for children with disabilities in the compulsory education stage – 95% in 2020.

education teachers and limited resources in a developing country.[38] However, the negative consequences of the double-track system draw little scrutiny.

In the double-track system, the long-term absence of some children with severe disabilities and the low performance of those poorly supported entrenched ableism in regular schools. Children with disabilities are regarded as those without appropriate abilities to study in regular schools and thus less valuable. Article 21 of the Protection Law 1990, Article 21 of the Educational Regulations 1994 and Article 22 of the Educational Regulations 2017 all stipulate that ordinary schools should admit school-age children and adolescents with disabilities who are able to adapt themselves to study in ordinary classes. Such requirements downplay schools' obligations to provide reasonable accommodations and other facilities to meet the needs of children. Rather, students are discriminated against on the basis of their physical or mental conditions. This ableist approach is a direct consequence of the double-track system, which takes regular schools as an alternative for children with disabilities and therefore precludes a provision of zero rejection.[39]

Another negative consequence is that the double-track system has given straitjacketed professional roles to teachers working in both regular and special schools.[40] Teachers in regular schools believe that they are not obliged to teach disabled children;[41] instead, they consider themselves teachers of only "normal" children.[42] Teachers in special schools, on the other side, are expected to be experts who could facilitate integration into mainstream schools. This expectation is written into the 1998 Temporary Regulations for Special Schools.[43] However, the fact is that they are neither capable of nor committed to assisting inclusion in mainstream schools. Special school teachers have had a long-term monopoly in educating disabled students, which strengthens their identity as experts within the walls of special schools, but reduces their incentive to promote inclusive education in other settings. The way the government budget is distributed also reinforces the rigid professional identity of special school teachers. By the end of 2015, official statistics revealed that more than 12 billion yuan was allotted to developing special schools.[44] The budget that a special school receives for education is

38 Malinen (n. 13).

39 Cui (n. 15).

40 Zhen Ni, *Untapped Talent: A Systematic Investigation about Barriers to Higher Education for People with Disabilities in China* (2013) NGO Report.

41 Ibid.

42 Ibid.

43 See http://info.jyb.cn/jyfgk/200603/t20060305_12055.html, accessed 20 November 2018.

44 Ministry of Education China, 'The Report on the Special Assessment of Special Education for the Mid-Term Assessment of the National Medium and Long-Term Educational Reform and

determined by the number of disabled students in the school. As a result, all special schools try to recruit as many children with disabilities as possible and try their best to dismiss their role in developing inclusive education.[45]

II DOMESTIC LEGISLATION OF INCLUSIVE EDUCATION IN CHINA

1 *Overview of Inclusive Education in the Context of Chinese Laws*

As explained earlier in this chapter, Chinese legislation adopts the terms 'Learning in Regulatory Class (LRC)' and 'Special Education', which means separated education specially for students with disabilities. The standards and categories of disabilities in China are not the same as in most Western countries. So special education in China does not address all children with disabilities, but only some of them, mostly physically disabled children, intellectually impaired children and some deaf and blind children. Generally speaking, inclusive education legislation is underdeveloped; the technology of legislation needs improvement and it cannot meet the real development of inclusive education in China. This section aims to explore the inclusive education legislation framework in China and then to analyse the relationship between legislation and the real development of inclusive education in China.

China's legal system features written laws which have differing levels of force. Constitutional law has the highest legal force and is named 'mother law' as all other laws are created through it. The second highest level of laws are basic laws made by the National Peoples' Congress and its Standing Committee. The laws at this level include civil law, criminal law, administrative law, the Law of Peoples' Republic of China on the Protection of Persons with Disabilities (LCPD), and several others. At the third level are regulations made by the State Council, and these have less legal power than the first- and second-level laws. One such law on this level is the Regulations of Education for Persons with Disabilities made by the State Council in 1994. The fourth-level laws are made by local provinces' people's representative congresses, which suggest ministry regulations and local governmental regulations. The fifth-level laws include ministries' regulations and local

Development Plan' (Ministry of Education 2015) available from China Education Online, http://xiaoxue.eol.cn/focus/news/201511/t20151130_1343347.shtml, accessed 31 January 2017.

45 Ni (2014) (n. 28).

governments' regulations. In what follows, I expand on the different levels' legislation regarding special education in China.

2 *Inclusive or Special Education Legal Systems in China*

As mentioned earlier, several law levels specifically address special education.

(1) Constitution (the First-Level Law)

In China, there is no mention of the phrase 'inclusive education' under the constitution, but Article 45 of the Chinese constitution stipulates that the state government will arrange employment, lives and education of blind, deaf and mute persons.[46] According to this provision, we can see that the government will develop education for persons with disabilities.

(2) Basic Laws Regarding Inclusive Education (the Second-Level Laws)

A CHINESE LAW ON COMPULSORY EDUCATION (1986) Under Article 9 of this law, local governments should host special schools/classes for blind, deaf and intellectually impaired children.[47] It shows that the objects of special education have been extended to intellectually impaired children, and the places of special education have been extended to special classes in regular schools. It also demonstrates that special education is treated as compulsory education. This provision marked an important beginning for the development of inclusive education in China. Since then, special education has been put in the framework of laws as compulsory education. But it also results in an impact on special education, which is treated as a double-tracked system with regular or mainstream education, which is not good for the development of inclusive education. It may also explain why inclusive education in China is separated from regular education. Most scholars in China have criticised this double-track approach which separates special education from regular education.

B LCPD (PROMULGATED IN 1990 AND REVISED IN 2008) In order to protect the legal rights and privileges of persons with disabilities, the LCPD was enacted in 1990. To make domestic laws compatible with the Convention

46 Constitution of the People's Republic of China Article 45.

47 Chinese Law on Compulsory Education (1986).

on the Rights of Persons with Disabilities (CRPD), the LCPD was amended in 2008 (shortly before the Chinese government ratified the CRPD in 2008).

Under this law, there is one entire chapter (chapter 3) which addresses special education in detailed provisions. Generally, it is clearly stated that receiving education is one of the rights of persons with disabilities under the law. It also provides that education for persons with disabilities should focus on compulsory and vocational education, and it should be a combination of regular and special education.[48] Besides these, there are some detailed provisions on state obligations, development policy, management channels, education funds and special education tools and appliances.

C CHINESE LAW ON EDUCATION (1995) Article 10 of this law explicitly regulates special education, as the state must support and develop special education for persons with disabilities.

(3) Regulations Promulgated by the Chinese State Council (the Third-Level Laws and Regulations)

Among the regulations, the most important is the Regulation of Education on Persons with Disabilities (1994). This is the first administrative regulation relating to the education of persons with disabilities. This regulation sets out the special education organisations' structure, the curriculum arrangement, the teaching modes, the requirement of teachers who perform special education, the rewards and punishments for the development of special education and so on. Due to the amendment of the LCPD in 2008, and in compliance with CRPD, there was a need to amend the Regulation of Education on Persons with Disabilities (1994). After years of amendment, on 11 January 2017, the amended version of the Regulation on Education of Persons with Disabilities (1994) was passed on the executive meeting of the Chinese Government State Council, and came into force on 1 May 2017.

Compared with the Regulation of Education on Persons with Disabilities 1994 version, the amended version has features focussing on equal opportunities for children with disabilities, inclusion education and guaranteeing support and resources. Article 7 of the amended version provides that preschool education organisations and all other category schools must admit disabled students who meet the requirements of laws and regulations. Under the amended version, Articles 17 and 18 stipulate a preference for inclusion

48 The Law of the People's Republic of China on the Protection of Persons with Disabilities Article 23.

education. The amended version encourages children or teens with disabilities to go to regulatory schools or to special classes in regulatory schools for compulsory education. If children with disabilities cannot receive regulatory education, local governments should arrange for them to go to special schools. Article 22 of the amended version requires some accommodations and support to meet the needs of students with disabilities, to guarantee disabled students' equal participation at school. Some other forms of education are provided to guarantee the rights of students with severe disabilities, such as teaching and studying at home and tele-education.

(4) Local Laws Promulgated by Provinces' Peoples' Representative Congresses (the Fourth-Level Laws and Regulations)

These laws are made by local provinces' congresses and implement upper laws within local provinces. An example of such a law is the Shanghai Implementation of the PRC Law on Protection of Persons with Disabilities.

(5) Ministries' and Local Governments' Regulations (the Fifth-Level Laws and Regulations)

One of the regulations on this level is the National Plan to Enhance Special Education (2014). In 2014, the State Council promulgated this regulation which was jointly made by the Ministry of Education, the Ministry of Civil Affairs, the Ministry of Finance, the CDPF, and three other ministries. It put forward the aim of *quanna jiaoyu* (inclusive education).[49] The purpose of the regulation is to promote the development of special education, to improve the special education development level and to safeguard the education right of persons with disabilities. This national plan focusses on the main precautions taken by the state government in relation to the development of special education: to enlarge the number of students receiving special education; to develop non-compulsory special education, including preschool education, high school education, and higher education for persons with disabilities; to promote the development of special education teachers and the reform of special education curriculum and teachings.[50]

49 The notice issued by the department office of the China State Council relating to the Special Education Advancement Plan by the Education Ministry (8 January 2014) can be found at www.mof.gov.cn/zhengwuxinxi/zhengcefabu/201401/t20140121_1037574.htm, accessed 21 May 2016.

50 Ibid.

3 Some Practices in Recent Years

In recent years, special education in China has made some progress and demonstrated some inclusive education practices.

(1) The Resource Centres Play a More Important Role in Some Areas

In some areas of China, local government education sectors have supported and established inclusive education resource centres which give direction to special education in regular schools. The local governments have realised the deficiencies related to the separated two-track system and have piloted some changes. One of the approaches is to make local special education schools into resource centres, and to give guidance to regular schools that have special education. Many local special education schools are used to assist local governments to promote the development of local special education and to fulfil the following functions as entrusted by local governments or the local education administrative departments:

(1) To give guidance to and assess the education of children and juveniles with disabilities in regular classes of the local ordinary schools;
(2) To provide professional guidance and training to teachers who teach children and juveniles with disabilities in regular classes of the local ordinary schools;
(3) To dispatch teachers and other professionals to ordinary schools for guidance and inspection tours of regular classes with children and juveniles with disabilities;
(4) To provide home-based teaching to local children and juveniles with extremely severe disabilities at homes who should be covered by compulsory education so as to ensure their right to compulsory education;
(5) To strengthen cooperation with the local health departments, the civil affairs departments and the local CDPF units and to undertake the tasks assigned by the Steering Committee of the Education for Persons with Disabilities; and
(6) To offer preschool education, ordinary high school education or vocational education to children and juveniles with disabilities.[51]

[51] Committee on the Rights of Persons with Disabilities, Response by the Government of the People's Republic of China to the List of Issues (No. 1 to No. 30) by the Committee on the Rights of Persons with Disabilities (17–28 September 2012) CRPD/C/CHN/Q/1/Add.1 [67].

This is a good practice to promote the integration of special education and regular education (at least in the current Chinese context). Since it is not easy to change the current laws and regulations, some reforms and changes are more important in real practice. In Shanghai and other areas with strong economic situations, such resource centres have the important function of practising inclusive education in China. They act as bridges connecting regular education with special education by providing qualified teachers, accessible teaching facilities and a positive environment. They also help to train regulatory schools' teachers and assist the teaching of students with disabilities.

(2) Some Practices from Civil Society

In June 2014, Li Jinsheng became the first blind person to receive permission to take the national entrance exams to colleges. It was a ground-breaking event in China. Before 2014, blind persons in China could not take national entrance exams to colleges because there is a physical examination regulation excluding them from attending the exam, and there was no accessible exam paper for blind students. In 2015, the Chinese education ministry had to provide an accessible test paper for Li Jinsheng. One of the reasons this blind student could exercise his education right was related to advocacy from civil society and from some disabled people's organisations (DPOs) in China. Due to the endeavours of civil society, a regulation was released by the Ministry of Education and the CDPF in 2015, which provided that exam bodies across the country should offer reasonable accommodations to test takers who have disabilities on the basis of their specific needs.[52] Starting in 2015, test takers with disabilities can enter examination halls ahead of time, and specialised staff members will be there (such as sign language interpreters or guides for blind students) to offer assistance. 'The regulations were released to ensure that people with disabilities can have convenient and equal access to the exams', the ministry said.

Another case is from Guangzhou Province and relates to parents' advocacy of inclusive education. In this province, some parents of students with disabilities were concerned about the special education of their children in

[52] Ministry of Education China and Disabled Persons' Federation, 'Ministry of Education of the People's Republic of China on the Issuance of the "Disabled Persons to Participate in the General Institutions of Higher Education Enrollment National Unified Examination Management Regulations (Provisional)" Notice' (Ministry of Education of the People's Republic of China, 27 April 2015) www.moe.edu.cn/srcsite/zsdwxxgk/201504/t20150427_189466.html, accessed 21 May 2016.

regular school. They understand that the regulatory school cannot provide good inclusive education to their children due to the limited conditions, but they cannot find better inclusive education near where they live. They established a parents-help-themselves organisation and asked the school to provide reasonable accommodation to their children. When the headmaster expressed that there was no policy support from the education authority, the organisation selected two parents' representatives to ask the education authority for policy support. After talking with the school and the authority, the organisation decided to donate money to support the schools and to ask social workers working in that school to provide support for their children in class. Due to support from the social workers, their children attained personal assistance in class, and this assistance has had a good effect on the children's studies. The regulatory schools find it effective to follow the parents' approach in the implementation of inclusive education. So the school committee board introduced some parents into its board meeting and talked about measures of implementation of inclusive education in the school. In the end, the school issued documents to co-implement inclusive education in the school. This positive experience was disseminated and the local education authority adopted the school's method and consequently issued guiding regulations on how to improve inclusive education with the help of parents. This practice of inclusive education has now been expanded countrywide and has been well received.

4 *Challenges of Inclusive Education Legislation in China*

(1) Existing Problems Relating to the Development of Inclusive Education in China

Special education occurred in China in the 1950s when the Chinese State Council issued the legal document 'Regulation on Reform of the Schooling System' in 1951. The inclusive education development process experienced many barriers. These barriers came from Chinese school cultures, economic reasons and citizens' attitudes towards special education, among others.

The first big barrier was the unique Chinese traditional competitive school culture. In ancient China, Keju (the imperial examination system) was the main national examination and method with which people were promoted. From then on, competition and selection have been the main feature of the examination culture in China. Even in current China, Zhongkao (the entrance exam of middle schools) and Gaokao (the entrance exam of colleges and universities) are characterised by selection and competition. So under the influence of the competitive school culture, the selection of excellent students has been the main function of education, and, in some areas, the main evaluation index of teachers' performance. With such a culture existing, the government does not intend to deconstruct the separation of special education and regular education. Instead, the local government intends to encourage the development of mainstream education and to ignore the development of special education. In regular schools, whole-class teaching and performance-based teaching have hindered the development of special education.

Besides the cultural influence, large class size is another challenge of special education in China. The class size varies from area to area, from city to city. In Shanghai, the normal primary school class comprises about forty-five pupils, but in other cities, the class size is bigger. Such big class size has prevented teachers from using individualised curriculums and teaching methods. This means that disabled children cannot be looked after in the class individually. With the exception of physically disabled students, disabled students (such as intellectually impaired students) can only sit in class and cannot participate in the academic activity or class interactions. So inclusive regulatory classes may be not a good place to implement inclusive education in China. Besides the issue of large class sizes, the student–teacher ratio should also be considered a barrier. Because of the large class sizes and the insufficient numbers of teachers, the teacher–student ratio was 1:16.78 in 2014.[53] The large class sizes and the low teacher–student ratio mean that teachers often teach only a few lessons every day. Teachers are busy with class-planning, exercises-rating and off-class activities. They do not have much time to conduct individual tutoring. If the teachers, however, spend large amounts of time tutoring students with disabilities, collaborating with other teachers and taking part in inclusive education development programmes, the inclusive education situation would be improved.

The third barrier relates to economic development levels. In order to develop inclusive education, having sufficient economic investment is crucial, because inclusive facilities are prerequisites to the conduction of inclusive education. For physically disabled students, accessible environments are imperative to facilitate their access to classrooms. For vision- and listening-impaired students, relevant facilitators are also needed in an inclusive environment. Moreover, the qualification of teachers who conduct inclusive

53 Ministry of Education of the People's Republic of China, '2014 National Education Development Statistics Bulletin [1]' (Ministry of Education of the People's Republic of China, 30 July 2015), www.moe.edu.cn/jyb_xwfb/gzdt_gzdt/s5987/201507/t20150730_196698.html, accessed 23 April 2016.

education is incredibly important. Teachers are required not only to have professional inclusive education knowledge but also to have command of inclusive teaching methods. Inclusive education needs more investment, though, to improve basic facilities. For economic reasons, China has a big difference in regional development in terms of inclusive education. Inclusive education practice in south-east China is on average better than that in the western parts of China. It is agreed that economic wellbeing influences the development of inclusive education.

According to national statistics, there are 240,000 children with disabilities who are of an eligible age to go to school, yet stay at home. Eighty per cent of them live in rural areas located in mid-west China.[54] But in south-east China, such as in Shanghai, different inclusive education modes are being conducted. The three main modes are: studying in normal classes, inclusive education resource centres and teaching and studying at home.

Another problem is the lack of inclusive education in senior schools. As mentioned earlier, special education is currently compulsory in China in primary and middle schools. Due to the entrance exam system to senior schools, many children with disabilities cannot enter senior schools as they cannot pass the entrance exams. Very few children with disabilities enter senior schools, so some go to middle-level vocational education schools, some enter community-based care organisations and some drop out and study at home. According to one scholar's statistics, in one of the Chinese provinces, there are only 169 students with disabilities in that province's senior schools, making up a proportion of only 3 per cent.[55]

(2) Possible Suggestions for Future Development

Firstly, inclusive education legislation needs to be strengthened in order to promote inclusive education. It needs to reflect reality and forecast future development. As mentioned earlier, China has disability law and regulations for the education of persons with disabilities, but does not have inclusive education law. Moreover, the scope of students who receive inclusive education needs to be widened in order to keep up with the pace of international development. The recipients of inclusive education should be those who need special education, including not only persons with disabilities, but also genius people with learning

54 Zhu Yongxin, 'The Problems That Special Education Must Face', *Guangming Daily* (21 July 2016), http://news.gmw.cn/2016–07/21/content_21055316.htm, accessed 8 January 2017.

55 Ibid.

difficulties. They are objects of inclusive education, but at the same time they are the subjects of rights. But current Chinese special education only addresses the education of persons with disabilities, especially the education of the blind, deaf and those with intellectual disabilities.

The provisions of Chinese special education legislations are too brief and inapplicable. For example, chapter 3 of the LCPD regulates the principle of special education, development policy, the conduction of special education channels and modes, adult education, teachers/staff members and other elements. But all of these provisions are too general to be applied in reality. The education rights of children have not been exercised or carried out through these overly brief regulations.

Furthermore, the responsibility of special education has not been clearly stated under special education legislation. As per the legislation of Chinese special education, legal liability of performing special education is not clearly provided. According to the Regulation of Education for Persons with Disabilities, schools and individuals bear the responsibility for education, thus ignoring the responsibilities of different levels of government towards inclusive education.

In order to promote Chinese special education development, related stakeholders of special education need to be encouraged to participate in legislation, especially persons with disabilities and their families. According to experiences from developed countries of special education legislation, persons with disabilities and their relatives' involvement have reflected the real needs of even the lowest ranks of society and have promoted the process of legislation. In the history of US special education legislation, parents of children with disabilities expressed their ideas, participated in the discussion of legislation and promoted the development of special education legislation. China needs to learn from these experiences of inclusive education.

Finally, the government needs to repeal laws and regulations that are not in compliance with the CRPD. One such incompliant measure relates to the construction of new special schools. According to Chinese policy, in counties with a population of more than 300,000 people, a special school should exist. This does not comply with the CRPD. It's suggested that the construction of new special schools should be stopped and current special schools should be encouraged to transform into resource centres of regular schools that enrol children with disabilities. Also as suggested by the Committee on the Rights of Persons with Disabilities, resources should be reallocated from the special education system to promote inclusive education in mainstream schools.

By doing so, more children with disabilities can attend mainstream education.[56]

III CHINA'S INTERACTIONS WITH INTERNATIONAL HUMAN RIGHTS LAW ON INCLUSIVE EDUCATION

The previous sections laid out a historical review of inclusive education and an overview of relevant law and policy in China. This section addresses its interactions with international human rights law.

Before looking at the details, it is necessary to explain that international human rights treaties (even though ratified by China) cannot be applied directly by Chinese courts. Neither the constitutional law of the People's Republic of China nor other national law addresses the effectiveness of international treaties in domestic courts in general. In practice (with exceptions in cases involving civil relationships, a contract dispute for example, with foreign individuals or companies[57]), international treaties have to be transformed into domestic law before they become applicable in courts. The Chinese government also upholds this dualist system in its reports to treaty-monitoring bodies.[58] Therefore, the discussion that follows focusses on China's engagement with treaty body mechanisms and the changes in domestic law, rather than the courts' decisions based on international law.

China has ratified several international human rights conventions relevant to inclusive education, including the International Covenant on Economic, Social and Cultural Rights, the Convention on the Rights of the Child, the Convention on the Elimination of All Forms of Discrimination against Women and obviously the CRPD. China has

[56] Committee on the Rights of Persons with Disabilities, Concluding Observations on the Initial Report of China, Adopted by the Committee at Its Eighth Session (17–28 September 2012) (15 October 2012) CRPD/C/CHN/CO/1 [36].

[57] The legal basis of this can be found in the General Principles of Civil Law of the People's Republic of China, which explicitly provides that '[if] any international treaty concluded or acceded to by the People's Republic of China contains provisions differing from those in the civil laws of the People's Republic of China, the provisions of the international treaty shall apply, unless the provisions are ones on which the People's Republic of China has announced reservations'.

[58] For example, see Committee on the Rights of the Child, Response of the Chinese Government to Questions Concerning the Combined 3rd and 4th Periodic Reports on the Implementation of the Convention on the Rights of the Child (23 August 2013) CRC/C/CHN/Q/3–4/Add.1.

also actively participated in the monitoring process of these conventions.[59]

However, it is observed that the reports submitted by Chinese governments to the committees concerning the implementation of inclusive education or education for persons with disabilities primarily focussed on increased financial support and widened access to education (for both mainstream schools and segregating special schools), rather than on education quality or inclusion.[60] Before the entry into force of the CRPD, it seemed that inclusive education was not a key concern of these committees.[61] The game changer was the CRPD and the review of the Chinese initial report particularly, which arguably raised the government's awareness of the substantive element of inclusive education.

1 *The CRPD and the Review Process of China's Initial Report*

China has played a leading role in the drafting process of the CRPD and showed a strong commitment to disability rights on an international level. However, Stein observed a gap between China's commitments internationally and domestically.[62] This comment in general also applies to the issue of inclusive education. As is shown in what follows, China's efforts towards inclusive education draw a mixed picture in light of the CRPD.

(1) China's Initial Report

In 2010, the Chinese government submitted its initial report to the CRPD committee. This initial report adopted a similar approach as in previous review procedures with other human rights committees. Regarding Article 24 on education, it used seven paragraphs to introduce basic tactics, increased access to education for people with disabilities, financial investment in special education schools (including vocational education), teachers' training and

59 For a summary, see Chinese Human Rights, 'China's Reports and Participation to the UN Human Rights Mechanisms' (China Society for Human Rights Studies 13 June 2017), www.humanrights.cn/html/gjrqwj/4, accessed 20 May 2016.

60 For example, see Committee on Economic, Social and Cultural Rights, Implementation of the International Covenant on Economic, Social and Cultural Rights: Initial Reports Submitted by States Parties under Articles 16 and 17 of the Covenant: Addendum: People's Republic of China (4 March 2004) E/1990/5/Add.59.

61 For example, see Committee on Economic, Social and Cultural Rights, Concluding Observations of the Committee on Economic, Social and Cultural Rights: People's Republic of China (including Hong Kong and Macao) (13 May 2005) E/C.12/1/Add.107.

62 Stein (n. 5) [7].

other elements. As discussed earlier, the legitimacy of the double-track system in education is closely related to the principle of non-discrimination. However, the initial report does not address this issue adequately. Instead, these paragraphs emphasise the 'specialised' arrangement, without even mentioning the idea of educational inclusion or accommodation provided by mainstream schools, reflecting a typical double-track system.

Another crucial issue concerning inclusive education is reasonable accommodation and discrimination on the basis of disability. With the definitions given in Article 2, it is clearly provided in Article 5 that the denial of reasonable accommodation constitutes discrimination on the basis of disability.[63] It is also repeated in Article 24 on education that reasonable accommodation is an essential tool to achieve educational inclusion.[64] However, the initial report does not address reasonable accommodation under the section of education. Regarding other parts mentioning reasonable accommodation, it has been argued by a Chinese civil society organisation that the Chinese government misunderstood reasonable accommodation to be a 'convenience' or 'welfare', rather than an obligation without which schools, in the context of education, will breach the non-discrimination provision.[65] For example, paragraph 25 of China's initial report states that '[m]any other laws require that reasonable accommodation be provided to persons with disabilities … The Education Law provides that "the State, society, schools and other educational institutions shall organise education in consideration of the physical and mental characteristics and requirements of people with disabilities and offer them assistance and convenience."' This approach echoes what is discussed earlier in this chapter where the personal or medical model of disability still dominates the sector of education for persons with disabilities. Access to quality and inclusive education seems to be a welfare and convenience – provided one's physical and mental condition is considered fit. Furthermore, as Chinese courts rarely (if at all) apply the non-discrimination clause in cases of education for persons with disabilities, it seems unlikely that the double-track system or the doubtful interpretation of reasonable accommodation will be challenged in domestic courts.

63 United Nations General Assembly, Convention on the Rights of Persons with Disabilities (13 December 2006) A/RES/61/106.

64 Ibid. Article 24.

65 Enable Disability Studies Institute, 'Observation on the Implementation of CRPD in China' (EDSI 2011) [6], www2.ohchr.org/SPdocs/CRPD/6thsession/EDSI_China_ch.doc, accessed 20 May 2016.

(2) The List of Issues, Replies and Concluding Observations

One year after the submission of the report, the CRPD Committee produced a List of Issues to China on 16 May 2012. The Committee unambiguously asked the Chinese government to 'provide the State's educational rationale for "actively develop[ing] special education schools"'.[66] The implementation of reasonable accommodation also clearly drew the Committee's attention. It asked for more information on disability-related discrimination and whether the denial of reasonable accommodation is covered.[67]

In response to the List of Issues, the Chinese government explained its double-track system and introduced its development plan to enhance the quality of education of persons with disabilities in mainstream schools.[68] It also provided that special schools in each area will also serve as resource centres 'for local governments to use and facilitate the education for children and juveniles with disabilities'.[69] In view of this chapter, the reply in this part reflects a promising progress in attitudes towards inclusive education. It at least suggests that the government has become aware that the existing double-track system is not compliant with the CRPD and a gradual reform is required. On the other hand, less progress was observed regarding reasonable accommodation. The reply only added more provisions on reasonable accommodation (as the Chinese government understands it), following the list of provisions prohibiting discrimination on the basis of disability.[70]

The appearance of the exact term 'inclusive education' took place for the first time during the meeting considering China's initial report on 9 October 2012. Mr Lanvad expressed his concern about the high number of special schools and classes for children with disabilities and made clear that '[it] ran counter to the current global trend towards inclusive education'.[71] The differences in the understanding and use of the term 'inclusive' was observable, as at the same meeting the Chinese delegates used the phrase

66 Committee on the Rights of Persons with Disabilities, List of Issues to Be Taken up in Connection with the Consideration of the Initial Report of China (CRPD/C/CHN/1), Hong Kong, China (CRPD/C/CHN-HKG/1) and Macao, China (CRPD/C/CHN-MAC/1) Concerning Articles 1 to 33 of the Convention: China (16 May 2012) CRPD/C/CHN/Q/1 [22] (citations omitted).

67 Ibid. [4].

68 CRPD/C/CHN/Q/1/Add.1 (n. 52).

69 Ibid. [67]. See issue 22 [66]–[67] generally.

70 Ibid. issue 4 [9]–[13].

71 Committee on the Rights of Persons with Disabilities, Consideration of Reports Submitted by States Parties under Article 35 of the Convention (continued): Summary Record of the 78th Meeting (9 October 2012) CRPD/C/SR.78 [30].

'inclusive schools' to refer to mainstream schools that scholars normally call 'integrated education' or LRC in the double-track system.

After this whole process, the Committee on the Rights of Persons with Disabilities provided its concluding observations to China:

> The Committee is concerned about the high number of special schools and the State party's policy of actively developing these schools. The Committee is especially worried that in practice only students with certain kinds of impairments (physical disabilities or mild visual disabilities) are able to attend mainstream education, while all other children with disabilities are forced to either enrol in a special school or drop out altogether.
>
> The Committee wishes to remind the State party that the concept of inclusion is one of the key notions of the Convention and should be especially adhered to in the field of education. In this regard, the Committee recommends that the State party reallocate resources from the special education system to promote the inclusive education in mainstream schools, so as to ensure that more children with disabilities can attend mainstream education.[72]

It also handed down observations relating to reasonable accommodation:

> While commending the legal prohibition of disability-based discrimination in the State party, the Committee is concerned about the lack of a comprehensive definition of discrimination against persons with disabilities. The Committee also worries about the contradictions between many local law regulations and the national law with regard to the prohibition of discrimination. The Committee is concerned that the State party does not consistently apply the concept of reasonable accommodation in relation to the principle of non-discrimination.
>
> The Committee expressly encourages the State party to provide a legal definition of discrimination against persons with disabilities and include in such a definition the prohibition of indirect discrimination. The Committee suggests including a definition of reasonable accommodation in Chinese law which reflects the Convention definition covering necessary and appropriate modification and adjustment applicable in a particular case beyond general accessibility. Furthermore, the State party should ensure that the law explicitly recognizes the refusal of reasonable accommodation constitutes disability-based discrimination.[73]

72 Committee on the Rights of Persons with Disabilities (n. 57) [35]–[36].

73 Ibid. [11]–[12].

2 AFTER THE REVIEW OF CHINA'S INITIAL REPORT

Even though the connection between China's review process with the CRPD and the later attitude changes is difficult to prove, after the initial report, China indeed updated its approach to inclusive education as required by the CRPD through the Revised Regulation on the Education of Persons with Disabilities (Draft).[74]

As discussed previously, the current regulation came into force on 23 August 1994 and its revision began in 2009 – one year after China's ratification of the CRPD. The newest draft was released for public opinions on 25 February 2013. It has seven chapters and fifty articles covering general principles, integrating schools, special schools, special education teachers, monitoring and supervision and legal responsibilities. As it is yet unknown when the draft will be finalised and further become effective, the current draft is our best evidence to assess the extent to which inclusive education in China, if it exists, is compliant with the CRPD.

Although there is huge doubt about the implementation of inclusive education in reality, the progress reflected in the drafts is obvious – especially when compared to the attitudes suggested by reports to various committees.

a. The Draft explicitly acknowledges that educational inclusion is a principle. Article 4 provides that education for persons with disabilities 'shall be open to all persons with disabilities and keep the principle of inclusive education'.[75] Article 10 under the Chapter of Integrated Education also requires local governments to 'progressively enhance the ability of mainstream kindergartens and schools to accept students with disabilities and promote inclusive education'.[76] After all, the explicit embrace of the term 'inclusive education' is still worth applauding, as it at least provides a better baseline for advocacy and reform in the future.
b. The Draft explicitly adopts the term 'reasonable accommodation' and prohibits educational discrimination based on disability. Again, considering that non-discrimination provisions are generally not applicable in Chinese courts, there are huge doubts about whether this provision can be enforced at all. But it is indeed a step forward to connect the principle of reasonable accommodation with non-discrimination, and this will clearly require governments, schools, society and families to

74 Legislative Affairs Office of the State Council (n. 2).
75 Ibid. Article 4.
76 Ibid. Article 10.

provide facilitation and reasonable accommodation in order to achieve educational equality and equal participation between children with and without disabilities.

c. The Draft emphasises the quality of education of children with disabilities in integrating schools,[77] equal participation of activities in all fields[78] and personal education plans.[79]

However, these advances on paper largely diminish if we take their shortcomings into consideration.

The Draft is still built on the double-track system. Although the official explanation of the Draft recognises that integrating students with disabilities into mainstream schools is a better solution to achieve their full development, social inclusion and educational equality, the Draft still accepts the legitimacy of segregating special schools. Some regard it as a 'dangerous inclination towards the argument of separate but equal'.[80] At the same time, it requires students to 'be capable of being educated in mainstream schools' and thus may result in exclusion of students with severe disabilities or those requiring personalised or intensive supports at school. Even for those who can be integrated into mainstream schools, especially high schools, vocational schools and higher education institutions, instead of requiring reasonable accommodations, it requires students to fit in the learning and living environment.[81] Additionally, its encouragement of self-education for persons with disabilities seems open to interpretation as moving against educational inclusion and equality.[82]

IV THE WAY FORWARD

Many social, historical, political and legal factors have resulted in the dilemma of inclusive education in China. A systematic approach has to be taken to address the difficult situation. This approach requires thorough reflections upon the history of special education and struggles for inclusion; also, the important roles of the CRPD and international standards have to be understood as clarifying the idea of inclusive education and increasing the

77 Ibid. Article 15.
78 Ibid. Article 18.
79 Ibid. Article 19.
80 Ni (n. 16) [500].
81 Draft (n. 2) Article 20.
82 Ibid. Article 21.

voice as well as the power of civil society. At the same time, the educational reform has to be deeper and wider in order to engage more stakeholders.

China's ratification of the CRPD and the concluding observations from the CRPD Committee have triggered public discussions around inclusive education. The discussions are critical to the current situation, because the double-track approach and ableist mind-set can only be redressed by public reasoning and consensus coherent to universal values and international human rights law. In doing so, further CRPD shadow reporting and other monitoring processes will play more important roles, since they maintain public space for discussions and actions around inclusive education.

The deeply seated medical model of disability will remain a huge barrier for inclusion, particularly when the medical model is entrenched in laws and government documents. The paradigm shift cannot happen overnight, but urgent actions have to be taken. The Chinese government has been revising policies and laws on inclusive education. Civil society organisations in general and parents, organisations and DPOs in particular play critical roles in raising public awareness and fighting against the medical way of thinking being used for the law-making process. Domestic NGOs and international agencies should collaborate more closely in sharing information and engaging policy and lawmakers.

Furthermore, removal of the double-track approach demands a deeper and wider educational reform. In China, the double-track approach is taken for granted, not only because disabled children are regarded as incapable, but also because education is dominated by examination results. Effective inclusive education needs flexibility in curriculum and assessment, but the examination results–oriented system allows little flexibility. Creating flexibility is relevant not only to disabled children but also to all children; therefore, a systematic educational reform is imperative. Although in-depth discussions about deeper reform are beyond the scope of this chapter, it is fair to say that an important way forward for inclusive education advocates is to initiate a deeper and wider reform, and to engage more stakeholders in the reform process.

In conclusion, scrutinising the historical factors, strengthening domestic and international interactions and reforming the education system are all necessary to further the implementation of inclusive education in China.

24

Legislating Inclusive Education in the Era of the CRPD

The Case of Kenya

Elizabeth Kamundia

1 INTRODUCTION

Education is the key tool for the development of human potential, and is critical for effective participation in society. However, many persons with disabilities in Kenya, and in many other parts of the world, struggle to have access to education.[1] It is approximated that school enrolment rates of children with disabilities in developing countries are as low as 1–3 per cent; therefore, according to some estimates, approximately 98 per cent of children with disabilities in developing countries do not go to school.[2]

The right to education is established in numerous international and regional human rights instruments; in addition, numerous global initiatives touch on the right to education.[3] Human rights instruments that address the right to education include the Universal Declaration of Human Rights,[4] the

By Elizabeth Kamundia, doctoral candidate, University of Pretoria.

[1] See generally, World Health Organization and the World Bank, *World Report on Disability* (World Health Organization 2011).

[2] Andrew Byrnes and others, *From Exclusion to Equality: Realizing the Rights of Persons with Disabilities: Handbook for Parliamentarians on the Convention on the Rights of Persons with Disabilities and Its Optional Protocol* (United Nations 2007); United Nations Department of Economic and Social Affairs, 'Fact Sheet: Youth with Disabilities', http://social.un.org/youth year/docs/Fact%20sheet%20youth%20with%20disabilities.pdf, accessed 18 May 2016. Note that enrolment rates differ according to impairment type. Children with intellectual, sensory, communication, psychosocial and/or multiple impairments generally fare worse than those with physical impairments. For more on this, see World Health Organization and the World Bank (n. 2).

[3] Global initiatives that touch on the right to education include the World Declaration on the Right to Education for all, the Salamanca Statement and Framework for Action on Special Needs Education, the World Education Forum, the Education for All (EFA) Flagship on the Right to Education for Persons with Disabilities and the Sustainable Development Goals.

[4] Article 26.

Convention against Discrimination in Education, the International Covenant on Economic, Social and Cultural Rights,[5] the Convention on the Rights of the Child,[6] the Convention on the Elimination of all Forms of Discrimination against Women,[7] the Convention on the Rights of Persons with Disabilities,[8] the African Charter on Human and Peoples' Rights,[9] the African Charter on the Rights and Welfare of the Child[10] and the Protocol to the African Charter on Human and Peoples' Rights on the Rights of Women in Africa.[11] Currently, African states are developing the Protocol on the Rights of Persons with Disabilities in Africa.[12]

Kenya has ratified or acceded to most human rights instruments that provide for the right to education,[13] including the Convention on Rights of Persons with Disabilities (CRPD). Kenya is a monist state; international instruments ratified by Kenya form part of the law of Kenya by dint of Article 2(6) of the Constitution of Kenya, 2010. The fact that Kenya is a monist state was settled in the 2015 Court of Appeal case *Karen Njeri Kandie* v. *Alssane and another*.[14] In this case, Ouko, Kiage and M'Inoti LJJ interpreted the Constitution as having transformed Kenya into a monist state. The Court of Appeal stated that:

> There can be no doubt therefore that by constitutional fiat, Kenya converted itself from a dualist country to a monist one with the effect that a treaty or

5 Article 13(1).
6 Articles 28 and 29.
7 Article 10.
8 Article 24.
9 Article 17.
10 Articles 11 and 13(2).
11 Articles 12 and 23(a).
12 African Commission on Human and Peoples' Rights, 'Protocol to the African Charter on Human and Peoples' Rights on the Rights of Persons with Disabilities in Africa', www.achpr.org/news/2014/04/d121, accessed 16 May 2016. Article 11 of the Draft Protocol on the Rights of Persons with Disabilities in Africa to a large extent echoes Article 24 of the CRPD. In addition to provisions under Article 24, Article 11(3)(g) of the draft protocol provides that multidisciplinary assessments should be 'undertaken to determine appropriate supports for learners with disabilities'. Under Article 11(4), States Parties are required to ensure 'that persons with disabilities shall on no account be presumed to be uneducable or untrainable, and regular assessments and certification for learners shall be undertaken regardless of their disabilities'.
13 Kenya has acceded to the International Covenant on Economic, Social and Cultural Rights and ratified the Convention on the Rights of the Child, the Convention on the Elimination of all Forms of Discrimination against Women, the African Charter on Human and Peoples' Rights, the African Charter on the Rights and Welfare of the Child and the Protocol to the African Charter on Human and Peoples' Rights on the Rights of Women in Africa.
14 [2015] eKLR Civil Appeal no. 20/2013.

convention once ratified is adopted or automatically incorporated into our laws without the necessity of a domesticating statute.[15]

Despite ratifying the major treaties on the right to education, in practice, Kenya is lagging in ensuring that learners with disabilities access education on an equal basis with other learners at all levels of the education system.[16]

This chapter starts off by establishing the meaning of inclusive education adopted in this chapter in Section 2. Section 3 identifies key issues on inclusive education, with a focus on the African context. These issues are identified through analysing the concluding observations issued by the Committee on the Rights of Persons with Disabilities (CRPD Committee) to the five African states whose state reports have already been considered by the CRPD Committee. These issues include the persistence of segregated education, inadequate law on inclusive education and/or poor implementation of existing law on inclusive education, inadequate training of teachers to facilitate inclusive education, dearth of data on children with disabilities, non-provision of education for children with high support needs and non-provision of reasonable accommodation and accessibility measures to children with disabilities. In Section 4, one of the key issues identified under Section 3 as impeding inclusive education, that is inadequate law, is addressed in detail. In this section, Kenya's Basic Education Act is assessed in order to gauge its adequacy on addressing the issues identified as impeding inclusive education under Section 3. Section 5 concludes and makes recommendations towards ensuring inclusive education for children with disabilities in Kenya.

2 DEFINING INCLUSIVE EDUCATION

The manner in which inclusion is conceptualised has been argued to have 'particular implications for the extent of obligations placed upon States Parties and state actors as duty bearers under international human rights law, and in determining which and what kind of practices might constitute a human rights violation'.[17]

15 *Njeri Kandie* (n. 15) 8.

16 William Aseka and Arlene S. Kanter, 'The Basic Education Act of 2013: Why It Is One Step Forward and Two Steps Back for Children with Disabilities in Kenya' (2014) 2 *African Disability Rights Yearbook* 33, 34; Kenya National Commission on Human Rights, 'The Fourth State of Human Rights Report: Post Promulgation 2010–2014: Human Rights: The Elusive Mirage?', www.knchr.org/Portals/0/StateOfHumanRightsReports/4th%20SHR%20Report.pdf, accessed 19 May 2016.

17 Bronagh Byrne, 'Hidden Contradictions and Conditionality: Conceptualisations of Inclusive Education in International Human Rights Law' (2013) 28 *Disability and Society* 232, 235.

According to the Guidelines of the United Nations Educational, Scientific and Cultural Organization, inclusive education is:

> [A] process of addressing and responding to the diversity of needs of all learners through increasing participation in learning, cultures and communities, and reducing exclusion within and from education. It involves changes and modifications in content, approaches, structures and strategies, with a common vision which covers all children of the appropriate age range and a conviction that it is the responsibility of the regular system to educate all children.[18]

Inclusion 'necessitates the removal of the material, ideological, political and economic barriers that legitimate and reproduce inequality and discrimination in the lives of disabled people'.[19] True inclusion requires that a child with a disability who is attending a mainstream school is guaranteed full access to the curriculum and 'is fully included in all aspects of school life'.[20]

The conceptualisation of inclusive education adopted in this chapter is drawn from Article 24 of the CRPD,[21] the CRPD Committee's interpretation of Article 24 as deciphered from concluding observations issued to States Parties and from General Comment No. 4 on the right to inclusive education.[22] Article 24 of the CRPD establishes the right to education for persons with disabilities and requires the development of 'an inclusive education system at all levels'.[23] According to Article 24, an inclusive education system should be geared towards the development of human personality, potential and sense of dignity. Further, inclusive education is meant to promote respect for human rights and diversity as well as full and effective participation in a free society. To ensure that education is really inclusive (and does not merely amount to integration), Article 24 requires the provision of

18 United Nations Educational, Scientific and Cultural Organization, 'Guidelines for Inclusion: Ensuring Access to Education for All' (United Nations Educational, Scientific and Cultural Organization 2005) 13.

19 Len Barton and Felicity Armstrong, 'Disability, Education and Inclusion: Cross-Cultural Issues and Dilemmas' in Gary L. Albrecht, Katherine D. Seelman and Michael Bury (eds), *Handbook of Disability Studies* (Sage 2001).

20 Byrne (n. 18) 234.

21 It is acknowledged that international human rights instruments prior to the CRPD have addressed the question of education for children with disabilities. However, these instruments and their interpretation by the respective monitoring bodies have been 'constitutive of hidden contradictions and *conditional inclusion*' (Byrne [n. 18] 235). For more on this, see Byrne (n. 18) at 234 and 235.

22 Committee on the Rights of Persons with Disabilities, General Comment No. 4 (2016) Article 24: The Right to Inclusive Education (2 September 2016) CRPD/C/GC/4.

23 Article 24(1).

reasonable accommodation and other individualised support measures to facilitate access to education by learners with disabilities on an equal basis with others.

General Comment No. 4 on the right to inclusive education states that '[i]nclusive education is to be understood as . . . a fundamental human right of all learners' as well as '[a] means of realizing other human rights'.[24] In addition, inclusive education is a principle that 'acknowledges individual requirements' and 'values the well-being of all students'.[25] The General Comment emphasises that inclusive education results from a process of continuously eliminating barriers that impede the right to education as well as changing culture, policy and practice in regular schools in order to accommodate all students.[26]

The CRPD is grounded in the social model of disability, which distinguishes between the impairments that people have and the oppression that they experience.[27] In contrast, the medical model views disability as a 'problem' that belongs to the disabled individual. In the context of education, viewed through the lens of the medical model, the child is faulty and needs to be diagnosed and labelled, and the focus is largely on the impairment.[28] This leads to segregation and the provision of alternative services for the child with disabilities while society remains unchanged.[29] On the other hand, the social model of disability requires the child to be valued and consulted in the identification of his or her needs. Further, barriers to equal access to education are identified and solutions developed, parents and professionals are trained, the child is included and, as a result, society evolves.[30] In essence, inclusive education focusses on changing the system to fit the child rather than changing the child to fit the system.[31]

Inclusive education has not been without its critics,[32] and there has been debate regarding whether Article 24 'bans all special schools for children with

24 General Comment No. 4 (n. 23) [10(a) and (c)].
25 General Comment No. 4 (n. 23) [10(b)].
26 General Comment No. 4 (n. 23) [10(d)].
27 Michael Oliver, *The Politics of Disablement* (Macmillan 1990) 22.
28 Richard Rieser, *Implementing Inclusive Education: A Commonwealth Guide to Implementing Article 24 of the UN Convention on the Rights of Persons with Disabilities* (2nd edn) (Commonwealth Secretariat 2012) 40.
29 Rieser (n. 29) 40.
30 Rieser (n. 29) 27.
31 Enabling Education Network, 'Enabling Inclusive Education: Challenges and Dilemmas', www.eenet.org.uk/resources/docs/bonn_2.php, accessed 19 May 2016.
32 For a detailed analysis of the demerits of inclusive education, see Obonye Jonas, 'The Right to Inclusive Education in Botswana: Present Challenges and Future Prospects' (2014) 2 *African Disability Rights Yearbook* 3, 7–9; for a critique of the CRPD, see Byrne (n. 18) at 240–241.

disabilities'.[33] Studies undertaken in low-resource set-ups have shown that 'overcrowded classrooms, inflexible timetables, unavailability of relevant teaching materials and inadequate specialist support'[34] may render inclusive education meaningless in some contexts. According to the Fourth State of Human Rights Report (published by the Kenya National Commission on Human Rights), public primary schools in Kenya are struggling under the huge number of children enrolled in primary schools following the introduction of free primary education.[35] The report cites important barriers to accessing quality education including low teacher–pupil ratios, 'insufficient learning facilities, and poor learning environment', especially in urban slums.[36] With regard to access to education by children with disabilities in Kenya, the report notes that '[e]ducational facilities do not adequately cater for children with disabilities in terms of teachers trained on special needs education and learning materials used by special children'.[37] The report also highlights that 'accessibility to transport and information and communication by [persons with disabilities] is' also inadequate.[38]

Despite these practical challenges, Kenya has committed itself to ensuring an inclusive education system under various international legal instruments,[39] as well as domestic laws and policies.[40] Implementing 'an inclusive education system in Kenya may not be possible overnight';[41] however, Kenya is obligated to take steps towards progressively establishing an inclusive education system. Article 4(1) of the CRPD highlights various ways through which Kenya can ensure and promote the full realisation of the right to education by children with disabilities. Article 4(1)(a) of the CRPD obligates States Parties 'to adopt

33 Aseka and Kanter (n. 17) 50. Also note that this article clarifies that there is no debate that Article 24 'prohibits a system which assigns children with disabilities to separate, special schools solely on the basis of their label of disability' (50).

34 Jonas (n. 33) 9.

35 Kenya National Commission on Human Rights (n. 17) 58.

36 Kenya National Commission on Human Rights (n. 17) 58.

37 Kenya National Commission on Human Rights (n. 17) 59.

38 Kenya National Commission on Human Rights (n. 17) 85.

39 Kenya has acceded to the International Covenant on Economic, Social and Cultural Rights and has ratified the Convention on the Rights of the Child, the Convention on the Elimination of all Forms of Discrimination against Women, the African Charter on Human and Peoples' Rights, the African Charter on the Rights and Welfare of the Child and the Protocol to the African Charter on Human and Peoples' Rights on the Rights of Women in Africa.

40 The following Kenyan laws provide for the right to education: the Constitution of Kenya, the Basic Education Act, the Persons with Disabilities Act and the Children's Act. Policies that recognise the right to education include: the Kenya Vision 2030 and the Special Needs Education Policy.

41 Aseka and Kanter (n. 17) 50.

all appropriate legislative, administrative and other measures for the implementation of the rights recognized in the present Convention'. This chapter focuses on appropriate legislation for the implementation of the right to education for children with disabilities in Kenya. Specifically, the chapter makes proposals for the amendment of the Basic Education Act as a starting point for Kenya to discharge its obligations under Article 4(1)(a) and Article 24 of the CRPD.

3 ISSUES OF CONCERN ON IMPLEMENTING INCLUSIVE EDUCATION IN SELECT AFRICAN STATES

The Committee on the Rights of Persons with Disabilities has so far issued concluding observations to five African states.[42] Some common issues of concern have arisen in those concluding observations; these issues present a starting point for understanding barriers to inclusive education in the Kenyan context, and therefore introducing key issues for legislative reform.[43]

The first and most prevalent issue of concern relates to the persistence of segregated education in the five African states already examined by the CRPD Committee.[44] In this regard, States Parties have (contrary to Article 24 of the CRPD) promoted segregated education,[45] and/or failed to provide education of children with disabilities in mainstream schools.[46] In one case, early

[42] Kenya: Committee on the Rights of Persons with Disabilities, Concluding Observations on the Initial Report of Kenya (30 September 2015) CRPD/C/KEN/CO/1; Mauritius: Committee on the Rights of Persons with Disabilities, Concluding Observations on the Initial Report of Mauritius (30 September 2015) CRPD/C/MUS/CO/1; Uganda: Committee on the Rights of Persons with Disabilities, Concluding Observations on the Initial Report of Uganda (12 May 2016) CRPD/C/UGA/CO/1; Gabon: Committee on the Rights of Persons with Disabilities, Concluding Observations on the Initial Report of Gabon (2 October 2015) CRPD/C/GAB/CO/1; Tunisia: Committee on the Rights of Persons with Disabilities, Concluding Observations on the Initial Report of Tunisia (13 May 2011) CRPD/C/TUN/CO/1.

[43] While we cannot generalise barriers to fifty-four African states based on the concluding observations issued to only five states, examining the barriers in the five African states whose state reports have already been considered by the CRPD Committee gives us a starting point in identifying issues on inclusive education in the African context. It is also conceded that in fact, the issues of concern identified in the five African states are not peculiar to Africa; concluding observations to non-African states also highlight similar issues in some instances. However, an in-depth consideration of concluding observations by the CRPD Committee to non-African states is beyond the scope of this chapter.

[44] Kenya: CRPD/C/KEN/CO/1 (n. 43) [43(a)]; Mauritius: CRPD/C/MUS/CO/1 (n. 43) [33]; Uganda: CRPD/C/UGA/CO/1 (n. 43) [48(a)]; Gabon: CRPD/C/GAB/CO/1 (n. 43) [52]; Tunisia: CRPD/C/TUN/CO/1 (n. 43) [30].

[45] CRPD/C/UGA/CO/1 (n. 43) [48(a)].

[46] CRPD/C/GAB/CO/1 (n. 43) [52].

education for children with disabilities is carried out by non-governmental organisations, which run special schools, thus preventing inclusion into mainstream schools from the get-go.[47]

A second issue of concern relates to existing laws and policies on inclusive education. In this regard, laws and policies on inclusive education are either being implemented too slowly,[48] not being equally implemented in schools[49] or creating integrated units rather than being geared towards full inclusion.[50] Of particular concern is the breach of 'rules relating to the number of children in mainstream schools',[51] 'and to the management of inclusive classes'.[52]

A third issue of concern relates to the training of teachers in order to enable them to adequately instruct learners with disabilities at all levels of the education system.[53] A key issue of concern on teacher training is the failure to ensure continuous training of teachers on sign language.[54] Additionally, administrators and other staff in schools are often not trained on disability.[55]

A fourth issue of concern relates to the dearth of statistical data on children 'with disabilities disaggregated by age, gender and disability type'.[56] Lack of data is a particular concern with regard to children with high levels of support needs[57] such as deaf-mute children.[58]

A fifth issue of concern relates to non-provision of education for children with high support needs.[59]

A sixth issue of concern relates to the non-provision of reasonable accommodation for children with disabilities[60] as well as the non-provision of accessibility measures.[61] The issue of accessible communication for children with disabilities is of particular concern. In some cases, children who are deaf are taught using verbo-tonal teaching methods, 'instead of providing

47 CRPD/C/MUS/CO/1 (n. 43) [33].
48 CRPD/C/MUS/CO/1 (n. 43) [33].
49 CRPD/C/TUN/CO/1 (n. 43) [30]. An additional issue in the context of Tunisia is that schools are not equitably distributed between regions of the same governorate.
50 CRPD/C/MUS/CO/1 (n. 43) [33].
51 CRPD/C/TUN/CO/1 (n. 43) [30].
52 CRPD/C/TUN/CO/1 (n. 43) [30].
53 CRPD/C/UGA/CO/1 (n. 43) [48(b)].
54 CRPD/C/KEN/CO/1 (n. 43) [43(d)].
55 CRPD/C/TUN/CO/1 (n. 43) [31].
56 CRPD/C/UGA/CO/1 (n. 43) [48(d)].
57 CRPD/C/UGA/CO/1 (n. 43) [48(c)]. In the context of Uganda, the Committee expressed concern about the inability of schools to meet the needs of children with severe disabilities.
58 CRPD/C/KEN/CO/1 (n. 43) [43(b)].
59 CRPD/C/KEN/CO/1 (n. 43) [43(b)]; CRPD/C/UGA/CO/1 (n. 43) [48(c)].
60 CRPD/C/KEN/CO/1 (n. 43) [44(b)]; CRPD/C/GAB/CO/1 (n. 43) [53].
61 CRPD/C/GAB/CO/1 (n. 43) [53]; CRPD/C/MUS/CO/1 (n. 43) [33]; CRPD/C/UGA/CO/1 (n. 43) [48(c)].

education in the language of choice of such children.[62] A final issue of concern relates to the lack of accessible public transport, particularly in rural areas.[63]

4 LEGISLATIVE AND POLICY FRAMEWORK ON INCLUSIVE EDUCATION IN KENYA

The law is an important aspect to consider in discussing inclusive education. It has been argued that '[u]nless disabled children . . . are treated with respect by the legislation governing their educational rights, those involved in their education will not be encouraged to do the same'.[64] The legal framework on the right to education in Kenya can be drawn from various sources: international law, regional law and domestic law. International and regional human rights instruments ratified by Kenya that address the right to education have been discussed earlier in this chapter.[65]

At the domestic level, the Constitution of Kenya 2010 has several provisions that address various elements of the right to education. In the first place, the Constitution guarantees to every person the right to education,[66] and to every child the right to free and compulsory basic education.[67] The Constitution also requires the state to put in place affirmative action measures to ensure that youth,[68] minorities and marginalised groups[69] are provided access to relevant education and training. With regard to persons with disabilities, Article 54(1)(b) of the Constitution provides that a person with any disability is entitled 'to access educational institutions and facilities for persons with disabilities that are integrated into society to the extent compatible with the interests of the person'.

The Constitution also addresses other aspects that are critical to the enjoyment of the right to education by children with disabilities, including accessible communication and information, and accessible public transport. Articles 7(3)(b) and 54(1)(d) of the Constitution address communication and access to information. In terms of these articles, the state is obligated to promote the development and use of Kenyan Sign Language, Braille and

62 CRPD/C/GAB/CO/1 (n. 43) [52].
63 CRPD/C/MUS/CO/1 (n. 43) [33].
64 Jane Fortin, *Children's Rights and the Developing Law* (2nd rev. edn) (Cambridge University Press 2005) 378.
65 See Section 1.
66 Article 43(1)(f).
67 Article 53(1)(b).
68 Article 55(a).
69 Article 56(b).

other communication formats and technologies accessible to persons with disabilities. In addition, the Constitution guarantees to persons with disabilities reasonable access to public transport and to all places.[70]

In addition to the constitution, the Persons with Disabilities Act 2003,[71] the Children's Act[72] and the Special Needs Education Policy also address critical issues of education and training for learners with disabilities. Various committees on education in Kenya have also produced reports on various dimensions of education in Kenya.[73] This section focuses on the Basic Education Act.

4.1 *The Basic Education Act*

The Basic Education Act was enacted in December 2012 and assented to by the president in January 2013.[74] The purpose of the Basic Education Act as expressed in its preamble includes giving effect to Article 53 of the Constitution and promoting and regulating free and compulsory basic education. The Act contains various provisions that specifically address issues of

70 Article 54(1)(c).

71 See Sections 7(1)(b)(i), 18 and 19. Under Section 7(1)(b)(i), one of the functions of the Council is to achieve equal opportunities for persons with disabilities by ensuring to the maximum extent possible that they obtain education. Under Section 18(3) '[s]pecial schools and institutions, especially for the deaf, the blind and the mentally retarded, shall be established to cater for formal education, skills development and self-reliance'. Section 19 provides for special and non-formal education. Note that the Persons with Disabilities Act is currently under review to align it with the Constitution of Kenya 2010 and the CRPD.

72 Section 12 of the Children's Act is to the effect that '[a] disabled child shall have the right to be treated with dignity, and to be accorded appropriate . . . education and training free of charge or at a reduced cost whenever possible'.

73 These include the Ominde Report, the Koech Report, the Task Force on Special Needs Education Report and the Report of the Task Force on the Re-alignment of the Education Sector to the Constitution of Kenya 2010.

74 The Basic Education Act comprises thirteen parts totalling 101 sections. The Act also has six schedules. Part I is a preliminary part and contains the guiding principles to the Act. Part II establishes the National Education Board and lays down the Board's powers and functions. Part III establishes County Education Boards. Part IV addresses free and compulsory education. Part V is on systems and structure of basic education, including promotion of education and the different categories of schools. Part VI is on the promotion of special needs education. Part VII addresses private educational institutions. Part VIII is on governance and management of basic education and training. Part IX is on standards, quality and relevance, and establishes the Education Standards and Quality Assurance Council. Part X is on licensing, registration and accreditation procedures in basic education and training. Part XI is on financial provisions, including financing of basic education, accounts and audit. Part XII comprises general provisions, including general penalties. Part XIII is on repeals, savings and transitional provisions. The schedules to the Act establish certain key bodies in education and lay down the mode of conduct of these bodies.

learners with disabilities. The most comprehensive of these provisions is Part VI (Sections 44 to 48) on the promotion of special needs education.

We can make two important overarching observations on the Act. The first is that the Act does not comprehensively address the range of issues that are necessary in order to guarantee to children with disabilities enjoyment of the right to education on an equal basis with other children. To illustrate, the Basic Education Act does not provide for the reasonable accommodation of individual learners' requirements. In the context of disability, denial of reasonable accommodation amounts to discrimination as established under the CRPD.[75]

The second observation is closely related to the first; the Act is drafted in highly general language and lacks the specificity that is required in order to guarantee true equality in education for children with disabilities. In part, this lack of specificity can be attributed to the fact that the Basic Education Act is a general law on basic education that is meant to address the concerns of all children. To illustrate, Section 5 on the 'functions of the National Education Board' requires the Board to put in place measures to 'ensure all children attend and remain in school to complete basic education requirements'.[76] From a drafting perspective, the words 'all children' would seem sufficient. In practice, children with disabilities in Kenya are barred from equal access to education for a variety of reasons that include lack of accessible transport to schools,[77] inaccessible educational facilities and negative cultural practices.[78] In the absence of further provisions to specifically address these disability-specific barriers to education, the provision under Section 5 to the effect that the Board shall put in place measures to ensure that all children attend school may in reality be merely cosmetic.

Admittedly, it would be impossible to place all the specificities with regard to inclusive education in the Basic Education Act. However, for each especially critical issue from a disability perspective, there should be a general provision allowing for regulations to be developed to provide a greater level of detail. To illustrate this, note that the Act contains minimal provisions on accessibility – in this regard, the Act should be amended to mandate the Cabinet Secretary to develop regulations to give effect to provisions on accessibility to the physical environment in educational facilities, and to information and communications. Such regulations would then be developed in

75 Article 2.
76 Section 5(2)(d).
77 See Kenya National Commission on Human Rights (n. 17) generally.
78 Kenya National Commission on Human Rights (n. 17) 58.

consultation with persons with disabilities and their representative organisations.

The following part of the chapter addresses in detail issues identified under Section 3. These issues are drawn from concluding observations issued by the CRPD Committee to African states whose reports have already been considered by the Committee under Article 36 of the CRPD. In particular, the section examines how the Basic Education Act addresses these issues and proposes necessary amendments to bring the Act into compliance with Article 24 of the CRPD.

4.1.1 Persistence of Segregated Education

In its concluding observations to Kenya, the committee expressed concern about the '[p]ersistence of segregated education institutions in the State party'.[79]

The Basic Education Act entrenches in law special education as the main approach to providing education to children with disabilities in Kenya. Numerous sections of the Basic Education Act provide for a segregated approach to the education of children with disabilities. Section 2 on interpretation defines 'special school' as 'a school established for the benefit of a particular class of children who require some special form of education, treatment or care'. Other words defined under Section 2 that serve to entrench special rather than inclusive education include 'special education needs' and 'special needs education'. Section 25(2) provides that 'the County Education Board shall set up specialized committees on ... special needs education'. Section 28(2)(d) provides for the establishment of special and integrated schools for learners with disabilities. Under Section 39(g), the Cabinet Secretary is charged with providing 'special education and training facilities for talented and gifted pupils and pupils with disabilities'.

Part VI of the Basic Education Act (Sections 44–48) addresses the promotion of special needs education. Section 44 is on the establishment and management of special institutions. Section 45 mandates the Cabinet Secretary to make regulations for special needs education. Section 46 places an obligation on County Education Boards to provide 'for education assessment and research centers including a special needs service'. The functions of the special needs service include the study of children with special education needs within the county,[80] advising parents and teachers as to appropriate

79 CRPD/C/KEN/CO/1 (n. 43) [43].
80 Section 46(2)(a).

methods of education for such children[81] and provision for the special education needs of such children in the identified clinics.[82] Section 47 places a duty on every County Education Board to make a report on the provision that would benefit each child with a disability after he or she completes basic education.

These sections of the Basic Education Act (2, 25(2)(c), 28(2)(d), 39(g), 44, 45, 46 and 47) are crafted in such a manner as to make special schools the first port of call for learners with disabilities. The approach seems to be that all students identified under Section 44(3) ('intellectually, mentally, physically, visually, emotionally challenged or hearing impaired learners; . . . pupils with multiple disabilities; and . . . specially gifted and talented pupils') should obtain education in special schools. This is contrary to the principle of inclusion espoused in the Constitution and in the CRPD.

In the landmark case of *Brown* v. *Board of Education*,[83] the Supreme Court of the United States asserted that '[s]eparate educational facilities are inherently unequal'.[84] Sections 45(2)(a), 47(1) and 47(2)(a) and (e) prove this point poignantly. Section 45(2)(a) provides that the Cabinet Secretary shall make regulations to 'prescribe the duration of primary and secondary education suitable to the needs of a pupil pursuing special needs education'. The education system in Kenya comprises eight years of primary education, four years of secondary education and four years of university education (8–4-4 system of education). Yet the Act makes a clear deviation from the 8–4-4 system of education, and gives the discretion to the Cabinet Secretary to prescribe the duration of education with regard to pupils 'pursuing special needs education'. Arguably, tampering with the duration of education of a certain category of pupils without any well-established safeguards runs the risk of adversely disadvantaging such pupils. In the context of disability, it would be important to proceed very cautiously indeed with regard to the discretion to tamper with the duration of education, given that historically, the capabilities of people with disabilities have been grossly underestimated.[85]

Section 47(1) mandates 'the County Executive Board to consider in relation to each child with special needs belonging to schools in their area, what provision would benefit him or her after he or she completes basic education'

81 Section 46(2)(b).
82 Section 46(2)(c).
83 *Brown* v. *Board of Education of Topeka* 347 US 483 (1954).
84 *Brown* (n. 84) 495.
85 See generally Sophia Isako Wong, 'Duties of Justice to Citizens with Cognitive Disabilities' in Eva Feder Kittay and Licia Carlson (eds), *Cognitive Disability and Its Challenge to Moral Philosophy* (Wiley-Blackwell 2010).

and to make a report to the relevant authority on this issue. According to Section 47(2)(a), County Education Boards' reports shall include 'recommendations as to whether the child would benefit from school education after he or she completes basic education'. Section 47(2)(e) provides that the County Education Board shall 'where appropriate' make a 'proposal of a school of higher learning to be attended by [the learner with a disability]'.

Essentially, Sections 47(1), 47(2)(a) and 47(2)(e) run the risk of denying children with disabilities free choice on what further course to pursue after completing basic education. Non-disabled children are not subjected to this requirement. Ultimately, the choice of whether to continue with formal education beyond basic education should rest with the person involved. Further, the choice of which institution of higher learning to attend should also rest with the student himself or herself. The Act takes a paternalist approach towards children with disabilities; these children are treated as though they lack the capacity to make their own choice of further education. In essence, sections 47(1), 47(2) (a) and 47(2) (e) are discriminatory.

Scholars have argued that it is debateable whether inclusive education can 'be fully realized whilst the option to segregate exists'.[86] Hence, in order to ensure inclusive education for learners with disabilities in Kenya, a key proposal for amending the Act would be to require the provision of inclusive education at all levels of education. It may also be necessary to prescribe a *specific* time frame within which the education system will transition from providing education in special schools to providing education in inclusive settings.[87]

In order to promote inclusive education in Kenya, it is critical that the Act expressly prohibits the general education system from denying admission to children with disabilities.[88] A penalty should also be provided for discriminatory behaviour on the part of learning institutions, including private learning institutions. Increasingly, basic education is provided in private schools; of the approximately 500,000 children in Nairobi, about 60 per cent are enrolled in low-fee private schools.[89] Hence, private schools should also increasingly be

86 John Kenworthy and Joe Whittaker, 'Anything to Declare? The Struggle for Inclusive Education and Children's Rights' (2000) 15 *Disability and Society* 219, 236.

87 CRPD/C/KEN/CO/1 (n. 43) [44(a)].

88 CRPD/C/KEN/CO/1 (n. 43) [44(b)]. Kenya was urged to 'immediately adopt a non-rejection policy for children with disabilities enrolling in regular schools'.

89 Moses Ngware, 'Kenya's Free Education Policy Could Actually Be Deepening Inequality' (*APHRC*, 2 October 2015). http://aphrc.org/kenyas-free-education-policy-could-actually-be-deepening-inequality, accessed 19 May 2016.

required to be accessible to children with disabilities and to provide them with support and reasonable accommodation.[90]

In order to ensure *quality* inclusive education, persons with disabilities and their representative organisations should be involved in initiatives towards inclusion.[91] Article 4(3) of the CRPD provides that persons with disabilities should be closely consulted with and actively involved in decision-making processes concerning issues relating to persons with disabilities. In this regard, it is commendable that many of the bodies established under the Act specifically require within their membership a person with a disability.[92] However, it may still be necessary to amend the Basic Education Act in order to ensure that persons with disabilities are represented in all the relevant boards established under the Act. To illustrate, the Board of Adult and Continuing Education under the 5th Schedule to the Basic Education Act is not expressly required to have a member with a disability. Yet, considering the past discrimination against persons with disabilities in education (and hence high illiteracy rates among adults with disabilities), persons with disabilities should arguably be represented in this board.[93]

4.1.2 Reasonable Accommodation

In its concluding observations to Kenya, the CRPD Committee recommended that Kenya '[i]mmediately adopt a non-rejection policy for children with disabilities enrolling in regular schools, and provide reasonable accommodation'.[94]

Section 4 of the Basic Education Act comprises guiding principles including 'the right of every child to free and compulsory basic education',[95] protection of 'every child against discrimination within or by an education

90 For more on non-discrimination obligations of private entities, see the Convention on the Rights of Persons with Disabilities, Articles 4(1)(e), 9(2)(b) and 21(c).

91 United Nations Educational, Scientific and Cultural Organization, 'The Flagship on Education for All and the Right to Education for Persons with Disabilities: Towards Inclusion', www.unesco.org/education/efa/know_sharing/flagship_initiatives/disability_last_version.shtml, accessed 19 May 2016.

92 Boards that expressly include a person with a disability in their membership under the Basic Education Act include: the National Education Board (Section 10(2)(d)); County Education Boards (Section 20(1)(i)) and the Board of Management for Public Schools (Section 56(1)(f) uses the language 'persons with special needs').

93 In addition, Article 54(2) of the Constitution of Kenya provides for the progressive realisation of the principle that at least 5 per cent of the members of the public in elective and appointive bodies should be persons with disabilities.

94 CRPD/C/KEN/CO/1 (n. 43) [44(b)].

95 Section 4(a).

department or education or institution on any ground whatsoever'[96] and 'non-discrimination, encouragement and protection of the marginalised, persons with disabilities and those with special needs'.[97] However, the Act falls short of recognising denial of reasonable accommodation as amounting to discrimination. The Basic Education Act makes no mention of reasonable accommodation of the individual child's requirement in education. Rather, the approach of the Act is to address 'categories' of learners. To illustrate this point, note that Section 45(2)(e) requires the Cabinet Secretary to make regulations prescribing the 'categories of pupils' requiring special needs education and methods appropriate for the education of such pupils.

The closest the Act comes to individual consideration of each child is Section 46(2). Section 46(1) provides for a 'special needs service' whose functions shall include, according to subsection 2(c), 'the giving of advice to county education boards regarding the assessment of the needs of any child under special needs education for the purposes of any of the provisions of this Act'. In order to ensure that children with disabilities access education on an equal basis with others, the special needs service should be mandated to explicitly recommend appropriate reasonable accommodation measures or individualised support measures that are required with respect to each child.

An important element to provide in legislation with regard to reasonable accommodation and other support measures is that of monitoring, evaluation and quality control. Section 45(2)(h) of the Basic Education Act requires the Cabinet Secretary to make regulations to 'establish a mechanism for monitoring and evaluation to advise the government on the quality of infrastructure and learning facilities in regard to special needs education'. This provision, while commendable, is too narrowly focussed on infrastructure and facilities. The Act does not provide any means for monitoring and evaluating the provision of reasonable accommodation as well as other individualised support measures, which are critical to the implementation of inclusive education. While Section 66 authorises quality assurance and standards officers to facilitate compliance with standards, the Act does not make provision for the officers to monitor the provision of reasonable accommodation measures.

96 Section 4(e).
97 Section 4(s).

4.1.3 Accessibility

General Comment No. 4 on the right to inclusive education distinguishes between reasonable accommodation and accessibility.[98] According to the General Comment, '[a]ccessibility benefits groups of the population and is based on a set of standards that are implemented gradually'[99] while '[r]easonable accommodation relates to an individual and is complementary to the accessibility duty'.[100] Further on accessibility, the General Comment states that:

> The entire education system must be accessible, including buildings, information and communication [tools], comprising ambient or frequency modulation assistive systems, curriculum, educational materials, teaching methods, assessment and language and support services.[101]

In its concluding observations to Kenya, the CRPD Committee recommended that Kenya '[e]nsure that school facilities are accessible for deaf-mute children, and provide materials and curricula adequate to their needs'.[102]

The Basic Education Act does not expressly mention accessibility as it relates to children with disabilities accessing the physical environment or accessing information and communications. The closest the Act comes to providing for accessibility is in Sections 44(4), 45(2)(g) and 59(c). Under Section 44(4), the Cabinet Secretary is required to 'ensure that every special school or educational institution with learners with special needs is provided with … infrastructure, learning materials and equipment suitable for such learners'. Under Section 45(2)(g), the Cabinet Secretary shall make regulations 'to ensure that every special school or educational institution offering special needs education has appropriate … infrastructure, learning materials and equipment'. Under Section 59(c), one of the functions of the Board of Management of a basic education institution is to 'ensure and assure the provision of proper and adequate physical facilities for the institution'.

Sections 44(4), 45(2)(g) and 59(c), while commendable, are narrow, particularly as viewed against Article 9 of the CRPD on accessibility. Sections 44(4) and 45(2)(g) do not include certain elements of accessibility that are critical to ensure inclusive education. These include signage in buildings in Braille and

98 General Comment No. 4 (n. 23) 4.
99 General Comment No. 4 (n. 23) [28].
100 General Comment No. 4 (n. 23) [28].
101 General Comment No. 4 (n. 23) [21].
102 CRPD/C/KEN/CO/1 (n. 43) [44(c)].

in easy to read and understand forms, as well as provision of forms of live assistance including guides, readers and sign language interpreters. Ideally, Section 59(c) should place the obligation to make the physical environment and information and communications accessible on every board of management of a basic education institution. Further, in order to remedy the non-recognition of accessibility in the Act, the Act should be amended to expressly require the accessibility of educational facilities constructed in the future (using the principle of universal design[103]) as well as the ongoing retrofitting of already existing schools.

Section 45(3) provides that '[t]he curriculum used in special needs education shall comply with the requirement of the national curriculum in so far as it is reasonably practicable'. The threshold of 'reasonably practicable' under this section runs the risk of establishing a curriculum that is not equal in quality for children with disabilities. A better way to frame the obligation would have been to require that the curriculum be adapted as necessary to make it accessible to children with disabilities.

An important element to provide in legislation with regard to accessibility is that of monitoring, evaluation and quality control. While Section 66 authorises quality assurance and standards officers to facilitate compliance with standards, the Act does not make provision for the officers to monitor accessibility.

Finally, it is important to link up the provision of reasonable accommodation, support and accessibility with the budgeting process. Section 88 on annual estimates should ideally provide expressly for funding to ensure that these critical elements to inclusion are covered.

4.1.4 Training of Teachers for Inclusive Education

In its concluding observations to Kenya, the CRPD Committee expressed concern about the '[a]bsence of measures to ensure continuous training of teachers on sign language'.[104]

Section 44(4) of the Basic Education Act provides that:

> The Cabinet Secretary shall ensure that every special school or educational institution with learners with special needs is provided with appropriate trained teacher, non teaching staff, infrastructure, learning materials and equipment suitable for such learners.

103 Convention on the Rights of Persons with Disabilities Article 2.

104 CRPD/C/KEN/CO/1 (n. 43) [43(d)].

The first critique of this provision is that it approaches training of teachers for inclusive education from the perspective of 'special schools' rather than 'all schools'. It is difficult to envisage a move to inclusive education in a setup where *all* teachers are not trained on the education of children with disabilities.

Section 95(3)(m) mandates the Cabinet Secretary to make regulations with respect to the conduct and management of schools, including providing for teacher education and development. This is a positive provision; however, once again, it is framed in quite a general manner, as compared with Article 24(4) of the CRPD. Article 24(4) identifies specific skills that should be instilled in all professionals and staff members who work at all levels of education. Such skills include sign language and/or Braille as well as 'the use of appropriate augmentative and alternative modes, means and formats of communication, educational techniques and materials to support persons with disabilities'.[105] The general framing under Section 95(3)(m) may make it difficult in practice to ensure that teachers access the kind of training that they need in order to adequately teach children with disabilities.

In order to progressively ensure the existence of an adequate number of teachers who are trained on inclusive education, the Act should place an obligation on the Cabinet Secretary to ensure that all teachers are continuously trained to meet the education needs of children with disabilities.[106] Over time, such large-scale continuous training would prove a necessary element in the transition to an inclusive system of education. Further on teacher training, it may be necessary to issue a moratorium (to operate after a specified time) against the hiring of teachers who do not have proficiency or competency in one or more of the following: Braille, orientation and mobility, tactile communication, plain language, alternative script, augmentative and alternative mode of communication and sign language or similar proficiencies and competencies.

Teachers who are currently teaching in special schools could play a critical role in the transition from special education to inclusive education. Teachers with qualifications or experience in teaching children with disabilities should ideally provide support to regular classroom teachers on including children with disabilities.[107]

105 Article 24(4).
106 Ingrid Lewis and Sunit Bagree, 'Teachers for All: Inclusive Teaching for Children with Disabilities' (International Disability and Development Consortium 2013), www.eenet.org.uk/resources/docs/IDDC_Paper_Teachers_for_all.pdf, accessed 19 May 2016.
107 Lewis and Bagree (n. 107) 16.

4.1.5 Data on Learners with Disabilities

Kenya's state report on Article 24 provides a glimpse of the condition of inclusive education in Kenya. The state provided statistics on the right to education, reporting that 75 per cent of persons with disabilities had attained at least primary-level education, while only 2 per cent have reached the university level. According to the state report, 39 per cent of the persons with disabilities had attended a mainstream/regular preschool while 37 per cent had attended a mainstream primary school. Only 9 per cent had attended a mainstream secondary school. The state acknowledged difficulties with data, in particular, information on the number of school going children with disabilities both in and out of school.

In its concluding observations on Article 24, the CRPD Committee recommended that Kenya should 'collect disaggregated data on the advancement of the inclusive education system'.[108]

Section 79 of the Basic Education Act requires the County Education Board to maintain a databank of all pupils and students in the county. However, the Act does not require the databank to be disaggregated by features such as gender, age or disability. The 6th Schedule to the Act provides an example of a case where the Act has specifically singled out a certain category of learners and required that data on these learners be provided. Under the 6th Schedule, the National Council for Nomadic Education in Kenya is mandated to 'prepare reliable statistic of nomads and their school-aged children and establish a data bank'.[109] At no point does the Act require the collection of data regarding children with disabilities.

In order to track the implementation of inclusive education in Kenya, it may be necessary to amend the Basic Education Act to require the collecting of data on the following issues: first, information on the number of children with disabilities who are accessing education in inclusive settings, those who are accessing education in special schools, and those not accessing education at all; second, information on the number of learners with disabilities who transition to secondary schools and to third-level education; third, the number of teachers equipped with appropriate skills including in Braille, orientation and mobility, tactile communication, plain language, alternative script, augmentative and alternative mode of communication and sign language to enable them to impart education to children with disabilities; fourth, the number of teacher aides and other support staff members employed by the

108 CRPD/C/KEN/CO/1 (n. 43) [44(a)].

109 Basic Education Act No. 14 of 2013 6th Schedule Clause 1(1)(g).

state to provide support to children with disabilities in inclusive settings; fifth, the number of education assessment and resource centres established in order to advise the regular education system on how best to accommodate children with disabilities.

4.1.6 Access to Education by Children with High Support Needs

In its concluding observations to Kenya, the CRPD Committee expressed concern at the '[l]ack of information on the situation of children with a high level of support needs, such as deaf-mute children'.[110]

The Basic Education Act specifically recognises one category of learners with high support needs – those 'with multiple disabilities'.[111] For these students as well as for other '[c]hildren with special needs',[112] the Act establishes special schools 'suitable to the needs of a pupil requiring special education'.[113] Other students who are identified as having special needs include 'intellectually, mentally, physically, visually, emotionally challenged or hearing impaired learners'.[114] The use of the euphemism 'challenged' is in line neither with the Constitution nor with the CRPD. Ultimately, the Act does not expressly provide any detail on access to education by children with high support needs.

5 CONCLUSION AND RECOMMENDATIONS

Persons with disabilities are now recognised under international law as subjects of rights, with an equal claim to the right to education 'without discrimination and on the basis of equality of opportunity'.[115] In line with this shift in approaches to disability, the push for inclusive education has gained momentum over the past few decades. However, states continue to face challenges in the implementation of inclusive education,[116] and Kenya is no exception.

At the legislative and policy level, Kenya is sending mixed messages regarding its commitment to implementing inclusive education. On the one hand, Kenya has ratified the CRPD, which calls for an inclusive education system at

[110] CRPD/C/KEN/CO/1 (n. 43) [43(b)].
[111] Section 44(3)(b).
[112] Section 44(3).
[113] Section 44(2).
[114] Section 44(3)(a).
[115] General Comment No. 4 (n. 23) [13].
[116] General Comment No. 4 (n. 23) [3].

all levels. The Constitution of Kenya expressly prohibits discrimination on the basis of disability and also comprises enabling provisions guaranteeing persons with disabilities access to the physical environment, to public transportation and to information and communications. On the other hand is the Basic Education Act, which entrenches a segregated approach to the provision of education for students with disabilities.

While commending the Basic Education Act for guaranteeing the right to free and compulsory basic education to all children in Kenya, this chapter has identified key areas where the Act falls short of ensuring equal access to education for children with disabilities. The first key call for the amendment of the Act regards the fact that the Act entrenches special education rather than inclusive education, and in reality makes no mention of 'inclusive education' at all. Secondly, the Basic Education Act does not recognise the denial of reasonable accommodation as amounting to discrimination and therefore entrenches discrimination against children with disabilities in various key areas. The Act also fails to adequately provide for accessibility to the physical environment and to information and communications. Thirdly, the Act does not contain adequate provisions with regard to teacher training for inclusive education. Fourth, the financial provisions under the Act do not sufficiently cover all the aspects that are critical to ensuring inclusive education, including accessibility of the physical environment and of information and communications. Fifth, the Act does not require the collecting of disaggregated data on the advancement of an inclusive education system. Hence, it is important to amend the Basic Education Act in order to ensure the provision of inclusive quality education to children with disabilities in mainstream schools within their communities.

Finally, in line with Article 4(3) of the CRPD, persons with disabilities and their representative organisations should be actively involved in attempts at reforming the Basic Education Act in order to ensure quality inclusive education to children with disabilities in Kenya.

25

Implementation of the Human Right to Inclusive Education in Japan

Yoshihara Ikehara

I INTRODUCTION

Japan ratified the Convention on the Rights of Persons with Disabilities (CRPD) in 2014.[1] It has had a significant impact on disability law and policies in Japan. The conventional separate parallel track system[2] of education, which sorts pupils with impairments[3] into special support schools[4] and other students into regular public schools, has been modified to a certain extent through the influence of the CRPD and other international human rights treaties.

[1] The House of Representatives approved the conclusion of the Convention unanimously on 19 November 2013 and the House of Councillors also approved it on 4 December 2013. The instruments of ratification were deposited on 20 January 2014. The Convention took effect on 19 February 2014.

[2] The concept of the 'separate parallel track' is referred to in an essay by Lisa Waddington and Matthew Diller; 'Under the social welfare model, disability is seen as defect in an individual that renders him or her unable to work or function in society in a conventional way. In this approach, social institutions such as employment and public services are designed to meet the needs of the non-disabled. Rather than adapting these institutions to accommodate disabilities, people with disabilities are directed toward *a separate parallel track* that provides income and services apart from the institutions that serve the non-disabled majority' (emphasis added). Lisa Waddington and Matthew Diller, 'Tensions and Coherence in Disability Policy: The Uneasy Relationship between Social Welfare and the Civil Rights Model of Disabilities in American, European and International Employment Law' in Mary Lou Breslin and Silvia Yee (eds), *Disability Rights Law and Policy: International and National Perspectives* (Transnational Publishers 2002).

[3] I use the term *impairment* in the field of Japanese education law because it is based on the current medical model. As for Japanese legal terminology, the law only provides the term *Shougai*, which can mean both an impairment and a disability, depending on the context. Law does not have any effective terminology to distinguish an impairment from a disability. I use the term *disability* in other fields of law, especially where it is based on the social model.

[4] Education laws and regulations used the term *special education* before 2006, which has since been changed to *special support education*.

However, this system still exists. Although laws and policies have been amended to be more inclusive, they still contain considerable limitations.

This study briefly explores the history of modern education in Japan to demonstrate the conventional intent and philosophy of Japanese modern education. Then, it discusses the improvements in and the limitations of the reform of disability law and policy under the impact of international human rights norms, particularly the CRPD. Finally, it concludes that one reason why full inclusive education is still impeded is due to the deep-rooted conventional intent and philosophy of Japanese modern education.

II BRIEF HISTORY OF MODERN EDUCATION IN JAPAN

i Up to the End of World War II

The modern industrial society in Japan started in 1868 as a result of the Meiji Restoration.[5] The government urged industrial modernisation and a military build-up to catch up with Europe. The government needed to establish compulsory education policies because it was critical to develop people into competent labourers for a modern industrial system and into strong soldiers for modern war. Hence, one purpose of education under the new regime was to nurture children to become these capable labourers and fit soldiers.

The Ordinance on Elementary School of 1880 established compulsory education and provided an exemption for children with impairments. Almost all school-aged children except those with impairments attended elementary school in Japan by 1905. Although the Ordinance of 1880 provided special schools for children with visual or auditory impairments, there were few special public schools for them. Some philanthropists and benevolent people established special private schools for children with other impairments. However, the overwhelming majority of children with impairments were excluded from education.

One aim of the exemption under the Ordinance was to filter out children who could not fulfil the requirements for a competent labourer and a strong soldier. They were sorted out on the basis of medical science.

[5] Ministry of Education, Culture, Sports, Science and Technology – Japan, 'Hundred Years' History of the Educational System', www.mext.go.jp/b_menu/hakusho/html/others/detail/1317552.htm, accessed 17 June 2015.

ii After World War II

a The Separate Parallel Track System during a Period of Economic Growth and Social Welfare

The old regime collapsed as a result of Japan's defeat in the war, and a new constitution, based on democracy and the sovereignty of the people, was established in 1946. This document provides not only civil and political but also social and economic rights. Article 26 provides that '[a]ll people shall have the right to receive an equal education correspondent to their ability, as provided by law. All people shall be obligated to have all boys and girls under their protection receive ordinary education as provided for by law. Such compulsory education shall be free.' The currently standing School Education Law (SEL) of 1947 replaced the conventional exemption system. It provided that the government and municipalities shall establish three kinds of special schools, i.e. special schools for pupils with visual impairments, special schools for pupils with auditory impairments and special schools for pupils with intellectual or physical impairments.[6] Moreover, it stipulated that parents whose children had any of these impairments must enrol their children in a special school. These institutions were named 'special education'. However, the law also provided that the duty of the government and municipalities to establish special schools for pupils with intellectual or physical impairments and the obligation of their parents would be delayed until the Ministry of Education issued a relevant regulation, which was issued in 1979. Thus, children with intellectual or physical impairments were excluded from regular public schools, and the majority of them had no opportunity for education until 1979.

A total of 37,718 children with impairments had been exempted from compulsory education in 1948. However, those numbers decreased to 3,367 in 1979.[7] Thus, the separate parallel track system in education was almost established in that year. Under this segregated structure, children with impairments were separated from other children, and the majority of them went to special schools.

The separate parallel track system was established because of the following factors; first, the new constitution of 1946 provides the right for people to

6 A regular school could create a special class for pupils with impairments based on Article 75 of the SEL of 1947.

7 Ministry of Education, Culture, Sports, Science and Technology – Japan, 'The Situation of Entrance into Special Support Education', www.mext.go.jp/a_menu/shotou/tokubetu/material/013/023.htm#contentsStart, accessed 17 June 2015.

receive equal education correspondent with their ability. However, special education was regarded as 'equal education' because education in a special school was considered to correspond to the ability/disability of a person with disabilities. Separate, parallel educational tracks were considered an equal system corresponding to one's ability. The medical/individual model of disability justified it. Second, the principles of competition and of meritocracy in an industrial society were adopted in education in order to develop competent labourers for economic growth. The Japanese industrial society and the general public believed that the classification of pupils on the basis of individual ability and academic achievement was reasonable. Third, the new constitution of 1946 provides the government with a duty to deliver free compulsory education, but the right to receive education is not construed as a right that an individual citizen can realise through the judicial process based on the judicial self-restraint policy.[8] It is interpreted that the government has the primary authority of deciding how to organise an educational system. The government established the special education system as 'equal education'. It was difficult for a person with disabilities and his/her parents to change it by their right in order to include them in mainstream education. Theoretically they could claim this through political processes; however, their voice was not influential enough within the government because they represent a minority under a majority-dominant democracy.

b The Separate Parallel Track System before the School Education Regulation (SER) of 2006

The separate parallel track system of education has been controversial since its establishment. Its supporters argued that it was the best system for ensuring that a child received an education that corresponded to his/her ability. Its opponents criticised it because its process of categorising children into different tracks was arbitrary. They argued that parents had a right to choose a school and a particular type of education for their children.[9]

Japan ratified the Convention on the Rights of the Child in 1994. At this time, some people also presented the criticism that a child's right to express

8 *Asahi* v. *the Ministry of Health and Welfare* (1967)21(5) Minshu 1043 (Supreme Court of Japan, 24 May 1967) held that the right to maintain the minimum standards of wholesome and cultured living is not a right on which an individual citizen can claim a specific benefit, and that the Ministry of Health has a wide range of discretion on 'the minimum standard'. The right to receive education is categorised into the same class of rights as that mentioned earlier.

9 Kazuyuki Nishinaka, 'Study of Issues on Compulsory Special Education for Children with Intellectual and/or Physical Impairments' (2012) 8 *Core Ethics* 305, 307–310.

his/her own views, as stated in Article 12, was not respected through the categorising procedure. However, attacks on the separate parallel track system were not so much based on inclusion but mainly on the autonomy of the parents/the child or an objection to the arbitrariness of the categorising procedure. However, the Standard Rules on Equalization of Opportunities for Persons with Disabilities, which adopted in 1993, helped create a movement for integration in education. The amended SER of 1993 authorised a special support programme that would be held in a resource room to give special instruction to pupils with slight impairments who were capable of learning in regular public schools. This amendment somewhat opened the door more widely to regular public school for children with impairments who had been sorted into a special schools.

The amended SER of 2002 made minor adjustments to the separate parallel track system. It provided an exception that would permit a child with impairments, who was supposed to be placed in a special school, to enrol in a regular public school if a municipal board of education (MBE) approved that the child could receive appropriate instruction in a regular school. An MBE was required to consider the opinions of experts in pedagogy, medical science, psychology and other relevant fields to provide this approval.[10] The amended SER of 2006 requires an MBE to listen to the parents of a child with impairment as well as experts in deciding whether to issue this approval.[11]

Children with impairments were still principally sent to special schools, although other parts of the SER were amended several times. The SEL of 1947 maintained the separate parallel track system and opened a narrow door to a regular school for a child with impairments, and showed little consideration for the autonomy of the parents/the child.

Adjudication on inclusive education occurred in the early 2000s. In this period, the Tokushima District Court decided as follows:

> The municipality must admit a child into its public kindergarten, unless there is any rational reason not to, in cases where an admission application is submitted by his/her parents. Our whole society must provide human and physical resources for a child with impairments. The municipality that establishes a public kindergarten is expected to fulfil this obligation. When the municipality examines an admission application for a child with impairments, it is not permitted that the municipality denies his/her admission just because he/she has impairments and difficulties in attending a kindergarten

[10] This provision was amended afterwards.
[11] This provision is still effective.

> class. The municipality must search for ways to overcome those difficulties by considering his/her physical and mental condition and the extent of those difficulties. Then, the municipality must flexibly judge whether it is really difficult to admit him/her into its public kindergarten. It is not permitted for the municipality to imprudently not admit a child with impairments into its public kindergarten because of financial difficulty. Because a kindergarten education is important for a child, the municipality is expected to provide resources to the maximum possible extent.[12]

This was a leading decision on inclusive education, particularly preschool education. A child with impairments cannot receive any education if he/she is not admitted to a kindergarten, because there is no special kindergarten for children with disabilities. This situation is different from that of elementary school. The sub-track for an elementary pupil is a special school, but a preschool child with impairments is simply excluded and given no opportunity to receive an education. The court considered inclusive education and reasonable accommodation as critical in the field of preschool education. As can be seen in this decision, the movement for inclusive education has been quietly pushing Japanese society.

III THE IMPACT OF INTERNATIONAL HUMAN RIGHTS NORMS

The Committee on the Rights of the Child (CRC) and the Committee on Economic, Social and Cultural Rights (CESCR) expressed some concerns and provided some recommendations in their concluding observations on Japan.

In the first concluding observation of the CRC,[13]

> the Committee notes with concern the insufficient measures taken by the State party, notwithstanding the principles laid down in the Fundamental Law for People with Disabilities, 1993, to ensure effective access of these children [with disabilities] to education and to facilitate their full inclusion in society.[14]

The Fundamental Law for People with Disabilities (FLPD) of 1993 was enacted just after the United Nations Decade of Disabled Persons

[12] X v. A *Izumi City* [2005] Tokushima District, 'Information of Judgments', www.courts.go.jp/app/hanrei_jp/detail5?id=14834, accessed 17 June 2015.

[13] Committee on the Rights of the Child, Concluding Observations of the Committee on the Rights of the Child: Japan (5 June 1998) CRC/C/15/Add.90.

[14] [20] (brackets added).

(1983–1992). This law provides that all persons with disabilities as a member of society shall be provided opportunities to participate in social, economic, cultural and other all fields of activities. The Ministry of Education, Science and Culture (MESC) amended the SER in 1993, which authorised a special support programme.[15] However, the CRC pointed out its insufficiency, and the MESC made a minor modification to the SER again in 2002, as stated earlier.

The CESCR, in its second concluding observations on Japan, expressed concern

> about the frequently, excessively competitive and stressful nature of all levels of education, which results in school absence, illness, and even suicide by students.
>
> The Committee strongly recommends that the State party undertake a comprehensive review of the educational system taking into consideration general comments Nos. 11 and 13 of the Committee, as well as general comment No. 1 of the Committee on the Rights of the Child. The review should focus in particular on the frequently excessively competitive and stressful nature of all levels of education.[16]

These observations imply that there is little tolerance for differences among students in education and that the nature of education in Japan is excessively competitive, which has been a feature of Japanese education since the country's industrialisation, in the context of the separate parallel track system. It can be said that making the nature of education more tolerant and less competitive would lead to inclusive education and a comfortable atmosphere for all pupils.

The CRC issued its second concluding observation in 2004.[17] It expressed concern about the persistent social discrimination against children with disabilities,[18] the disadvantages that children with mental disabilities face in enjoying their rights as guaranteed by the Convention

15 This is the current name of the ministry. It was until 2001 known as the Ministry of Education.

16 Committee on Economic, Social and Cultural Rights, Concluding Observations of the Committee on Economic, Social and Cultural Rights: Japan (24 September 2001) E/C.12/1/Add.67 [31] and [58]. The second concluding observations of the CRC para. 49(a) expressed the same concern. 'The excessively competitive nature of the education system has a negative effect on the children's physical and mental health and hampers the development of the child to his or her fullest potential' (26 February 2004) CRC/C/15/Add.231.

17 Committee on the Rights of the Child, Concluding Observations of the Committee on the Rights of the Child: Japan (26 February 2004) CRC/C/15/Add.231.

18 Ibid. [24].

and the insufficiency of integration in the education system.[19] The CRC recommended

> the State party undertake all necessary proactive measures to combat societal discrimination and ensure access to basic services for children with disabilities through public education.[20]
>
> Taking into account the Committee's 1997 day of general discussion on the Rights of Children with Disabilities (CRC/C/66, annex V) and the Standard Rules on the Equalization of Opportunities for Persons with Disabilities (General Assembly Resolution 48/96 of December 20, 1993), the Committee recommends that the state party promote the greater integration of children with disabilities into education . . . and increase the human and financial resources allocated to special education and services for children with disabilities.[21]

The Support for Persons with Developmental Disabilities Law was enacted in 2005. In accordance with the law, the SER was amended in 2006 so as to include pupils with developmental impairments, such as autistic disorders, high-functioning autism, learning disabilities and attention deficit/hyperactivity disorder, among pupils with impairments.[22,23] The government explained that the SEL was amended at this time to meet the individual needs of pupils with impairments. It integrated three types of schools formerly classified as special schools, that is, for pupils with visual impairments, with audial impairments and with physical or intellectual impairments, into a unified special support education school. The amended SEL of 2006 named this institution 'special support education'. These reforms seemed partly to comply with the concluding observations of 2004; however, it was not necessarily effective in including children with impairments in a regular public school, because those with developmental impairments who attended a regular public school

[19] Ibid. [43] 'The Committee is concerned that children with disabilities, including mental disabilities, remain disadvantaged in the enjoyment of their rights guaranteed by the Convention, and are not fully integrated into the education system as well as other recreational or cultural activities.'

[20] Ibid. [25]. 'The Committee recommends that the State party undertake all necessary proactive measures to combat societal discrimination and ensure access to basic services, in particular, for girls, children with disabilities, Amerasians, Koreans, Buraka, Ainu and other minorities, children of migrant workers and refugee and asylum-seeking children, through, *inter alia*, public education and awareness campaigns.'

[21] Ibid. [44].

[22] Notification on Amendment of SER, www.mext.go.jp/b_menu/hakusho/nc/06050814/001.pdf, accessed 20 November 2018. See existing Article 140 of SER.

[23] Education law is still based on the medical standard. See footnote 34.

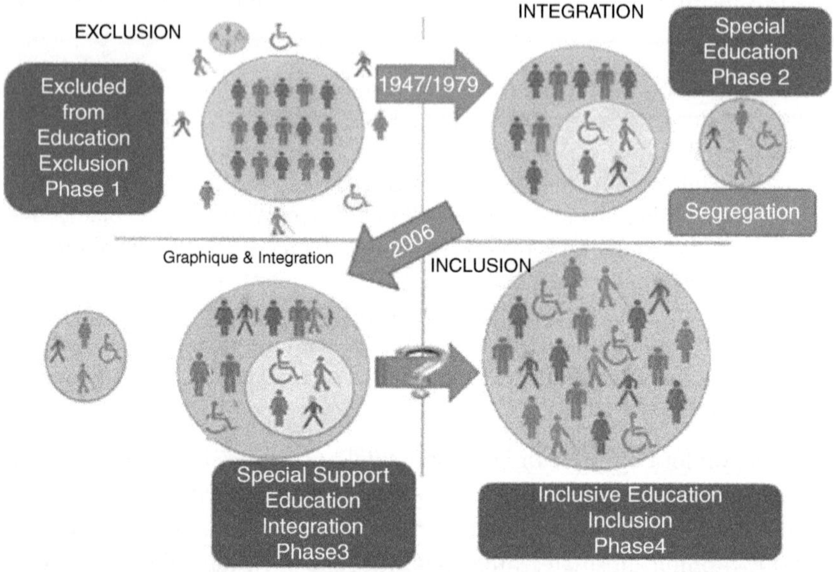

Modified by Reiko lohiki based on LES AVIS DU CONSEIL ÉCONOMIOUE, SOCIAL ET ENVIRONMENTAL
Mieux accomppagner et inclure les personnes en situation de handic.ap:un defiune nécessité (2014.p24)

FIGURE 25.1 Exclusion, segregation, integration and inclusion in education[24]

tended to be sorted into special support education as a result of this amendment.

The total number of pupils with impairments under special support education was 202,000 in 2006, when the SEL and the SER were amended. However, this number increased to 320,000 in 2013 (see Table 25.1).[25] This means that approximately 100,000 pupils who had developmental impairments and had been integrated into regular public school classrooms before 2006 were removed and placed on the sub-track for special support education. Table 25.1 clearly shows that the increase in the total number of pupils with impairments is parallel to that of those who were sorted into special support education classrooms and those who were sorted into special support programmes in resource rooms.

24 Figure 1 from Reiko Ichiki, 'Is Japan Heading for Inclusive Education?' ('Both Men and Women' Center for Labor and Education 2016) 50 (on file with the author). Most children with visual and/or auditory impairment were excluded from education until 1947. Most children with physical and/or intellectual impairment were excluded from education until 1979. Segregated education started in earnest in 1979. It gradually increased integrated settings. After the amendment of the SEL in 2006, a rise in integrated settings has been notable. See Table 25.2.

25 While the population of children who were ready to enter elementary school in 2006 was approximately 1,180,000, that in 2013 was fewer than 1,060,000.

Approximately 100,000 pupils who had been included in regular public school classrooms were excluded from those classrooms. It may be true that pupils with developmental impairments were not sufficiently educated in regular classrooms due to the lack of reasonable accommodation. However, education in a special support education classroom and a special support programme in a resource room is a sub-track that segregates students with impairments from others.

Figure 25.1 shows the difference between 'special education' and 'special support education' in Japan.[26] The main structure of 'special education' was based on special schools in segregated settings. A special class in a regular public school was exceptional. However, Table 25.2 shows that the number of pupils with impairments in a special support education classroom increased the most. This was followed by an increase in the number of pupils with impairments in a special support programme in a resource room. There was almost no change in the number of pupils with impairments in a special support education school.

According to Table 25.2, a special support classroom and special support in a resource room as a kind of integrated setting are distinctive features of 'special support education'. Thus, the trend of Japanese education for persons with disabilities has changed from being a segregated institution to being an integrated institution over the past fifty years, although it still preserves special support schools in segregated settings.

The MESC promotes 'education exchange activities', that is, pupils in regular public school classrooms and those in special support education classrooms and in resource rooms have opportunities to meet, play and participate in a school activity together, although this is based on the separate parallel track system.[27]

The third concluding observations of the CRC recommended in 2010 that

> [the government] equip schools with the necessary facilities for the inclusive education of children with disabilities and ensure that they can choose their preferred school or move between regular schools and special needs schools according to their best interests.[28]

[26] Annual Report on Government Measures for Persons with Disabilities, Initial Report submitted by Japan under Article 35 of the CRPD due in 2016.

[27] Using the Internet for communication without any actual meeting is introduced by the ministry. It deprives pupils of the opportunity to study together in the same classroom.

[28] Committee on the Rights of the Child, Concluding Observations: Japan (20 June 2010) CRC/C/JPN/CO/3 [59 (e)]

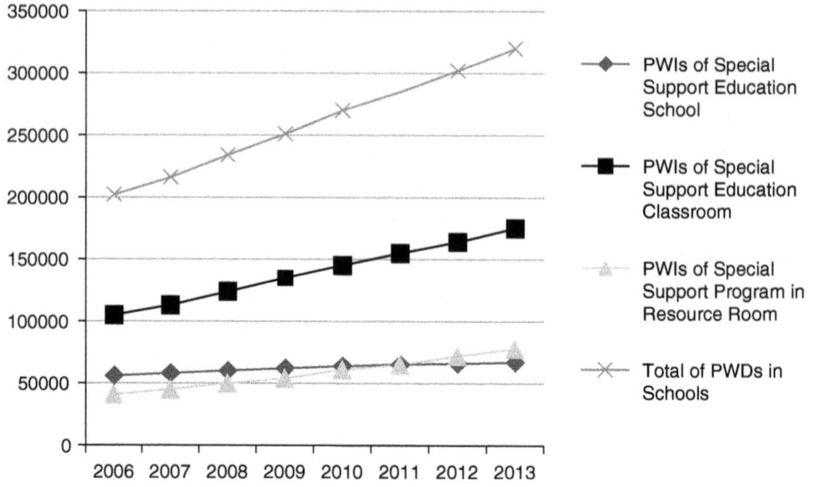

TABLE 25.1 Trends in numbers of pupils in special support education[29]

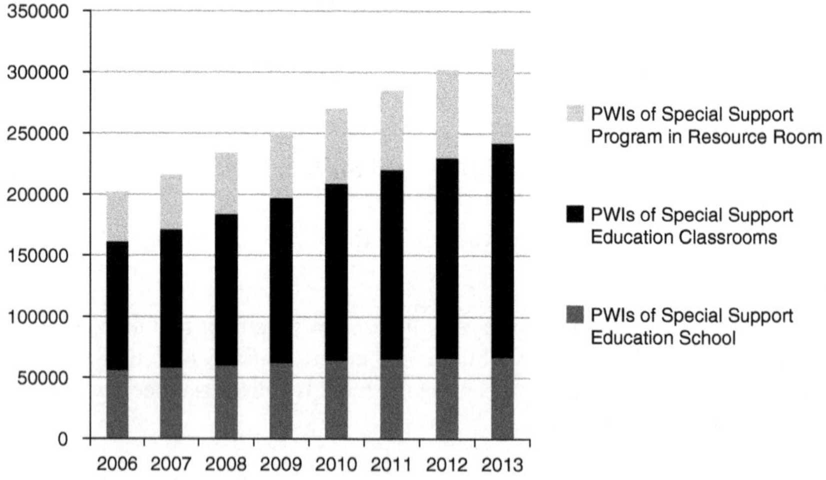

TABLE 25.2 Trends in three pillars of special support education

[29] Table 25.1 and Table 25.2 are tabulated from statistics found on: 'Annual Basic Survey on Schools' (*e-stat*), www.e-stat.go.jp/SG1/estat/NewList.do?tid=000001011528, accessed 17 June 2015.

Furthermore, it recommended that the government consider 'the United Nations Standard Rules on the Equalization of Opportunities for Persons with Disabilities (General Assembly res. 48/96) and the Committee's General Comment No. 9 (2006) on the rights of children with disabilities', which emphasised inclusive education.[30] The CRC distinctively noticed the increasing number of pupils classified as having developmental impairments.[31]

IV THE IMPACT OF THE CRPD

The minister of foreign affairs signed the CRPD on 28 September 2007, and the government planned to ratify it in 2009. However, organisations of persons with disabilities objected that it was hasty to ratify the CRPD without first harmonising the existing law and policies with this framework. Their strategy was to urge the government to reform the existing law and policies in accordance with the CRPD before its ratification, for the government had previously hardly reviewed and reformed the law and policy in line with ratified international human rights treaties. The political party in power changed in September 2009, and the new government tried to reform the prevailing laws and policies in a positive way. It established the Committee for Proactive Reform on Disability Law and Policies in late 2009. The majority of the members appointed to the Committee were people with disabilities, to comply with the slogan 'nothing about us without us'. The Committee outlined a work schedule to complete the reform in four years. The work schedule included three major reforms on laws and policies related to education. The first was an amendment to the FLPD, the second was an amendment

30 Ibid. [59 (h)]. It also recommended ratifying the Convention on the Rights of Persons with Disabilities in para. 59 (i).

31 Ibid. [60]; 'The Committee takes notice of data which indicate that a remarkable number of children have reported low levels of emotional well-being, and that poor relationships with parents and teachers may be determinants. It also notes that the number of consultations on attention-deficit hyperactivity disorder (ADHD) in Support Centres for Development Disabilities is increasing. The Committee welcomes the initiation of research and training of medical professionals on the treatment of ADHD, but is concerned that this phenomenon is regarded mainly as a physiological disorder to be cured by drugs and that social determinants are not given due consideration'; [61]: 'The Committee recommends that the State party take effective steps to address issues of the emotional and psychological well-being of children and adolescents through a multi-disciplinary approach ensuring effective support in all environments. The Committee also recommends that the State party monitor the trends in the numbers of ADHD diagnoses and ensure that research in this area is conducted independently of the pharmaceutical industry.'

to the SER and the Master Plan of Disability Policy and the third was the enactment of an anti-discrimination law for persons with disabilities.

i) The FLPD of 2011

First, the FLPD was amended in 2011. This revision of the law changed the definition of a person with disabilities to one based on the social model. Under this model, 'a person with a disability' is defined as 'a person who has physical, intellectual, psychiatric (including developmental) or any other physical/ mental impairments ("impairments") whose daily or social life is continuously and substantially restricted by his/her impairments and social barriers'.[32] This definition referred to Preamble (e) and Article 4(1)(b) of the CRPD. This revision led to a paradigm shift in disability policies, because the old definition that appeared in relevant laws and policies had been based on the medical model, which is a hotbed of exclusion, and the separate parallel track system. The review and reform of existing laws and policies became inevitable with this amendment. The article on education in the FLPD of 2011 was also amended. It requires the government and municipalities to prepare educational policies to improve and enrich the content and methods of education, accommodating pupils with disabilities to enable them to receive an education with other pupils as much as possible.[33] Article 16–2 of the FLPD of 2011 provides that a pupil with disabilities and his/her parents shall be sufficiently informed and that their will shall be respected as much as possible. Article 16–3 requires the government and municipalities to help achieve mutual understanding between pupils with disabilities and other pupils through the positive promotion of 'exchange and collaborative studies'.[34] Article 16–4 requires the government and municipalities to research and study reasonable accommodation for a pupil with disabilities, to train teachers, to provide appropriate textbooks and to make changes to facilities so that they meet the needs of the pupil.

The FLPD of 2011 also established a new article, Article 4–2, on reasonable accommodation in line with the CRPD.[35] The new article, in relation to

[32] In Article 2–1 of the FLPD of 2011, a 'social barrier' is defined as 'things, systems, customs, perceptions, and all the other matters in a society which become a barrier that hinders a person with impairments in his/her performance of daily or social life' (Article 2–2).

[33] Article 16–1 of the FLPD of 2011.

[34] However, 'exchange and collaborative studies' is based on the separate parallel track system. 'Exchange and collaborative studies' aims to provide opportunities for pupils to get acquainted with each other at school activities, at school festivals and in other classwork.

[35] 'Reasonable accommodation which is necessary to remove social barriers shall be taken so as not to discriminate against a person with disabilities by its negligence, in cases where a person

education, echoes Article 16–4, which provides a general principle on reasonable accommodation.

The FLPD of 2011 made some progress in the area of inclusive education, which is required by the CRPD. However, its approach was eclectic and did not completely generate a paradigm shift in the field of education, although it did represent such a shift in disability policies generally. A separate course of education for pupils with disabilities remains, and the government and municipalities have a duty to enhance inclusion in the field of education, although the FLPD of 2011 qualifies this responsibility with the phrase 'as much as possible'. The government and/or municipalities could potentially use this qualification as a pretext for exclusion.

The MESC officially announced the 'Report on Promotion of Special Support Education to Establish an Inclusive Education System toward an Inclusive Society of 2012'.[36] This report emphasises that it is important to prepare a diverse and flexible system in order to provide each pupil with individual educational needs with instructions that precisely correspond to his or her needs in terms of inclusive education. Furthermore, preparing a series of diverse educational settings, such as a regular class, a special support education in a resource room, a special support education class and a special support education school, is necessary from this point of view. The report adds that the most essential point is whether each pupil can understand school lessons, have a sense of accomplishment, participate in learning activities, spend his/her school days in a fulfilling manner and acquire the strength to live. The report also states that environmental arrangements are necessary from this point of view. However, whether the current education system heads towards the inclusive education that the CRPD requires remains unknown. This is because of the following: first, the 'inclusive education system' is a partly integrated and partly segregated system (Figure 25.1, Phase 3). It is not a fully inclusive system (Figure 25.1, Phase 4). The MESC does not intend to improve the current system and move towards a fully inclusive system. It does not think that the current system is a transitional form of inclusive education but rather that it is an appropriate system that can correspond to the individual and educational needs of each pupil.[37] Second, the 'environmental

with disabilities actually requires removal of those social barriers and unless that reasonable accommodation is an undue burden.'

36 On the MESC website; www.mext.go.jp/b_menu/shingi/chukyo/chukyo3/044/houkoku/1321667.htm, accessed 4 November 2016.

37 Ichiki (n. 23) 52. 'A child with disability and his/her parents are instructed that they should choose a special support education school or a special support education class, because they corresponded to his/her needs. This instruction is the same as before 2006.' Ichiki,

arrangements' that the report points out are different from reasonable accommodation. They do not focus on individual needs but rather on categorised needs. They correspond to the common needs of a certain group of pupils.[38] A pupil's ability to understand school lessons, participate in learning activities, spend his/her school days in fulfilment and acquire the strength to live is mainly assessed from a medical/individual point of view. The MESC and municipalities are reluctant to provide reasonable accommodation for pupils with disabilities and/or to contrive how to teach and run regular classes in order to accommodate pupils with disabilities.

Many pupils with disabilities and their parents realistically prefer a special support education school or a special support education class over a regular public school. This is because special support schools and classes are more prepared to accommodate a pupil with disabilities than a regular public school. Regular public schools scarcely expect to include pupils with disabilities and provide little if any accommodation under the present circumstances.[39] This inclination on the part of pupils and their parents may perpetuate the separate parallel track system because it may allow special support education to more specifically address the needs of pupils with disabilities and regular public schools to be less ready to accommodate them.

ii) Amendment to the SER and the Master Plan of Disability Policy

Second, the SER was amended, and the Master Plan of Disability Policy (MPDP) was prepared in 2013. The SER modified the sorting procedure of the separate parallel track system. The SER of 2002 permitted exceptions, allowing

'Discrepancy between Special Support Education and Inclusive Education', Study on Public Education 2012, Khoki Senda et al., 'Empirical Study on Formation of Curricula for Enrichment of Special Support Education', National Institute of Special Needs Education 2007.

38 A categorised service cannot be customised to each pupil with disabilities, because the right to receive education is not interpreted as a right by which an individual citizen can claim a specific benefit, and the MESC has a wide range of discretion. It is possible for a pupil with disabilities and his/her parents to claim a reasonable accommodation for him/her on the basis of the CRPD and the Elimination of Discrimination against Persons with Disabilities Law of 2013 (detailed later). However, there has been no lawsuit based on those laws, because the law came into effect on 1 April 2015.

39 Examples of accommodations for pupils with disabilities in a special support school or a special support class include providing physical instructions for walking and writing, preparing teaching material correspondent to their particular disabilities, utilising a computer, cooperating with a medical facility for suctioning sputum, providing instructions for basic knowledge of a number and language for daily life and others; from the MESC webpage, www.mext.go.jp/a_menu/shotou/tokubetu/004/003.htm, accessed 15 November 2016.

a child with impairments who was supposed to be placed in a special support school to enrol in a regular public school, if an MBE approved him/her to receive the appropriate education in a regular public school. However, the SER of 2013 permits a child with impairments who is supposed to be placed in a special support school to enter a regular public school, except where an MBE approves that it is appropriate for him/her to enter a special support school.[40] The SER of 2013 seems to replace the principles and the exceptions of the SER of 2002. However, this reversal is not as clear in practice. The MESC issued a public notice on this amendment, which explains as follows: 1) The SER of 2013 makes the sorting procedure a synthetic decision-making process. An MBE shall decide on the basis of the condition of a child's impairments, his/her educational needs, his/her opinion, his/her parents' opinion, the opinions of experts in pedagogy, medical science, psychology and relevant fields and the situation of a school and a community, whether a child with impairments should attend a regular public school or a special support school. 2) An MBE shall provide adequate information to a child with impairments and his/her parents and have maximum respect for their opinions. However, it is appropriate for an MBE to decide ultimately which school the child shall attend, although an MBE, a child with impairments, his/her parents and a school shall build a consensus on the child's educational needs and necessary support in principle. 3) An MBE shall transfer a pupil with impairments between a regular public school and a special support school, depending on the amelioration or deterioration of his/her impairments, whether a change in support is necessary for his/her education, a situation in the educational system arises and other circumstances.

40 Article 22–3 of the SER of both 2002 and 2013 provides a standard for a child with impairments who is supposed to be placed in a special support school: a) a child with a visual impairment, whose visual acuity is below 20/66 or that has other serious visual impairments that preclude or almost preclude him/her from seeing a regular-sized word or a figure with a magnifying glass; b) a child with an auditory impairment, whose auditory capacity is more than 60 db, who cannot or hardly can hear a regular speaking voice with a hearing aid; c) a child with an intellectual impairment, (1) who has difficulty developing mutual understanding and needs frequent help in his/her daily life, (2) who has salient difficulty with social adjustment, while his/her intellectual impairment is less serious than (1); d) a child with a physical impairment, (1) whose impairment makes his/her basic activities of daily life, such as walking or writing, impossible or difficult with a prosthesis, (2) who needs regular medical supervision, while his/her physical impairment is less serious than (1); e) a valetudinarian child, (1) who has a chronic respiratory, kidney, or nervous disease or malignant neoplasm or other disease and needs continuous medical care or has limitations upon his/her daily life activities, (2) whose condition needs continuous limitation of his/her daily life activities. This standard is still based on the medical model.

The SER of 2013 requires maximum respect for the opinions of a child with impairments and his/her parents; however, their right to decide which school the child will attend, that is, a regular public school or a special support school, is not recognised. The synthetic decision-making procedure can easily become one that pressures a child with impairments and his/her parents to enter a special support school, because experts who participate in the procedure form the majority of the decision makers and they believe that a child with impairments should enter a special support school. Although the transfer between a regular public school and a special support school seems to lower the barrier between the schools, it may encourage the teachers at a regular public school to urge a pupil with impairments to transfer to a special support school, and it may discourage them from providing him/her with reasonable accommodation in a regular public school. The fundamental problem is that the SER of 2013 remains based on the separate parallel track system.

The MPDP of 2013 provides the 'establishment of inclusive education' as one of the basic principles of education. It says that

> [w]ith the aim of realizing an inclusive society in which people have respect for each personality and individuality without discrimination against disabilities, the government will build a system that enables a pupil with impairments to receive an adequate education in accordance with his/her age and abilities and on the basis of his/her characteristics together with pupils without impairments to the maximum possible extent, and that accommodates him/her with the necessary support including reasonable accommodation.

The MPDP of 2013 echoes the synthetic decision-making process that is stipulated by the SER of 2013. Thus, the separate parallel track system remains in the MPDP of 2013.

The MPDP of 2013 says that:

> It is desirable that reasonable accommodation is decided and provided in accordance with each condition of one's impairments and educational needs, after a founder, a school, a pupil with impairments, and his/her parents attempt to build a consensus to the maximum possible extent. The government will enrich a 'Multifarious Setting to Study', which is a spectrum of a regular public school, a special support program of a resource room, a special support class in a regular public school and a special support school, to provide a child with individual educational needs with the most suitable instruction for his/her present educational needs from the perspective of his/her independence and participation in society. The government will attempt to provide him/her with the necessary support, including reasonable accommodation and to enable him/her to study together with other pupils in the same setting.

The MPDP of 2013 mentions that a new provision for the educational environment will include the training of teachers and the enhancement of a special support school as a centre for special support education.

The establishment of inclusive education, as declared in the MPDP of 2013, was epoch-making. It was remarkable that the term *reasonable accommodation* was officially adopted in the field of education. However, *inclusive education*, the term used in the MPDP of 2013, was still not fully inclusive. A 'multifarious setting to study', a 'synthetic decision-making procedure' and flexibility to transfer among educational settings did not mean that a pupil without impairments went to a resource room for a special support programme, a special support class and/or a special support school. These concepts represent an inequitable approach. Although the MESC emphasised the significance of 'exchange and collaborative studies', pupils with impairments still seem to be guests in a regular public school.

iii) The Elimination of Discrimination against Persons with Disabilities Law of 2013

Third, the Elimination of Discrimination against Persons with Disabilities Law (EDPDL) was enacted in 2013. This law is a form of anti-discrimination law for persons with disabilities; however, it is not a civil law but an administrative law. The law does not stipulate the rights of a person with disabilities but rather the administrative obligations of public and private entities.

The EDPDL of 2013 requires the government to prepare a Fundamental Plan of Action[41] and ministers to establish a code of conduct for government officials in line with that plan.[42] However, municipalities are only obliged to make an effort to establish a code of conduct for local officials in line with the Fundamental Plan of Action.[43] Governmental and local officials are supervised on the basis of the code of conduct. The ministers are required to develop a guideline for private entities under each of their jurisdictions in line with the Fundamental Plan of Action.[44] A minister can require a private

41 Article 6. The Plan aims for the implementing policies to promote the elimination of discrimination on the basis of disabilities. It shall include a basic orientation to promote the elimination of discrimination on the basis of disabilities, basic matters on measures that the ministries and/or the municipalities shall take to eliminate discrimination on the basis of disabilities, basic matters on measures that private businesses shall take to eliminate discrimination on the basis of disabilities and other important matters concerned with policies to promote the elimination of discrimination on the basis of disabilities.

42 Article 9.

43 Article 10.

44 Article 11.

entity under his/her jurisdiction to report a situation of implementation of the guideline. A minister can also mentor and guide a private entity, or make a recommendation for it based on the guideline.[45] The government and municipalities must provide consultations on discrimination against a person with disabilities, his/her family and/or the persons concerned.[46] Thus, the EDPDL of 2013 does not expect that a person with disabilities will file a lawsuit based on this law. The administrative obligations stipulated by the EDPDL of 2013 are not intended for the use by a person with disabilities but for the authorities. Therefore it is not obvious whether the rights of a person with disabilities can be conversely derived from those administrative obligations and whether he/she can defend his/her rights on the basis of the EDPDL of 2013 in judicial proceedings.

The EDPDL of 2013 basically echoes the anti-discrimination provisions of the FLPD of 2011. However, there are some differences between the two laws. The EDPDL of 2013 provides that:

> [t]he Ministries shall not infringe on the rights/interests of a person with disabilities by unjustly discriminatory treatment in performing his/her duties or conducting their affairs on the basis of disability in comparison with a person without disabilities. The Ministries shall provide reasonable accommodation which is suitable for the gender and age of a person with disabilities and the condition of his/her impairment and which is necessary to remove a social barrier so as not to infringe on his/her rights/interests, where he/she claims that it is actually necessary to remove it, in performing their duties or conducting their affairs, unless it does not impose an undue burden on the Ministries.[47]

Furthermore:

> [a] private entity shall not infringe on the rights/interests of a person with disabilities by unjustly discriminatory treatment in performing its business on the basis of disability in comparison with a person without disabilities. A private entity shall make an effort to provide reasonable accommodation which is suitable for the gender and age of a person with disabilities and the condition of his/her impairment which is necessary to remove a social barrier so as not to infringe on his/her rights/interests, where he/she claims that it is actually necessary to remove it, in performing its business, unless it does not impose an undue burden on a private entity.[48]

[45] Article 12.
[46] Article 14.
[47] Article 7.
[48] Article 8.

The FLPD of 2011 does not require a claim from a person with disabilities for reasonable accommodation; however, the EDPDL of 2013 does require it. The former does not make a difference in terms of a legal obligation to provide reasonable accommodation between public and private entities, although the latter stipulates that the legal obligation of a private entity for reasonable accommodation is just to make effort to provide it.

These discrepancies can be attributed to the change in government. The FLPD was amended in 2011, when the Progressive Democratic Party came to power, but the EDPDL was enacted in 2013, when the conservative Liberal Democratic Party came to power. These discrepancies cause interpretive confusion, as although theoretically the former law is interpreted as providing a general principle, the latter is regarded as detailing a general principle of the former. According to the EDPDL of 2013, a public school must provide reasonable accommodation for a pupil with disabilities, while a private school must merely make an effort to provide it. It appears that, to make this gap narrower, a private school cannot be exempted unless it proves that it has made all possible efforts to provide reasonable accommodation for a pupil with disability.

V CONCLUSION

The CRPD has brought results in the field of education:

i. The FLPD was amended. It requires of the government and municipalities a new educational policy that enables pupils with disabilities to receive an education alongside other pupils to the maximum possible extent.
ii. The SER was amended. A pupil with impairments receives the right to enrol in a regular public school in principle though it is from the wording only.
iii. The MPDP regards inclusive education as the basis for an inclusive society.
iv. The MPDP adopted the concept of reasonable accommodation in the field of education. The EDPDL of 2013 legally requires a school to provide reasonable accommodation for a pupil with disabilities.

However, some critical issues remain:

i. The separate parallel track system is still in place. Therefore, there is concern that the practice of differentiating pupils with disabilities and the exclusion of pupils with disabilities will be reinforced.

ii. There is concern that the synthetic decision-making procedure and respect for the opinion of a pupil with impairments and his/her parents will reinforce the separate parallel track system.
iii. There is concern that the rights of persons with disabilities will not definitely be recognised by judicial procedure and that reasonable accommodation for a pupil with disabilities will not be sufficiently provided for in a private school.

Modern Japanese education has aimed at developing labourers capable of operating in a modern industrial society. The principles of competition and meritocracy, which were the basis of the industrial society, have been incorporated into the education system. Individual ability and effort are respected under this principle and have an affinity with the medical/individual model. The Japanese industrial society and general public have believed that the classification of students on the basis of individual ability and academic achievement is reasonable. An immoderate inclination towards economic prosperity and the development of industry in Japan has resulted in the unification of a sense of value and intolerance for diversity in education. It is conceivable that such unification and intolerance impede full inclusive education, although they are obviously incompatible with respect for difference and diversity. Whether we can surmount these traditional principles and ways of thinking about the CRPD remains to be clarified.

26

Charting a Legal Course towards the Inclusion of Children with Disabilities in Tajikistan

Kate Lapham

This chapter builds on several years of qualitative research in Tajikistan to provide a case study of the interaction between international and domestic legal frameworks and inclusion in education for children assessed with disabilities in Tajikistan. Tajikistan signed the CRPD in February 2018. This will significantly change the international legal framework for inclusive education in Tajikistan, especially in light of the recent General Comment No. 4 released in autumn 2016. Some good reviews of law and policy in the field of disability rights and social service provision have already been published between 2006 and 2012, most notably from Equal before the Law, the Organisation for Economic Co-operation and Development (OECD) and the United Nations International Children's Emergency Fund (UNICEF).[1] These place much of Tajikistan's legal framework in the context of CRPD compliance quite well. Therefore, I focus on the ways that law and policy highlight evolving agreements and disagreements about disability as well as the effects of newer legislation in the widening space for inclusion of children with disabilities in education.

In this regard, the three most important pieces of legislation are the Law on the Protection of Children's Rights passed in 2015, the Law on Education

I would like to acknowledge the support and contributions of Zarina Kurbonbekova.

[1] Eeva Tupi and Pamela West, 'Legislation of Central Asian Countries Regarding Persons with Disabilities and the UN Convention on the Rights of Persons with Disabilities' (Equal before the Law 2012), www.inclusive-education.org/system/files/publications-documents/EBL%20Legistation%20of%20Central%20Asian%20Countries%20Regarding%20Persons ... pdf, accessed 30 March 2017; Mihaylo Milovanovitch and Denise Rosa, 'Tajikistan' in *Kazakhstan, Kyrgyz Republic and Tajikistan 2009: Students with Special Needs and Those with Disabilities* (Organisation for Economic Co-operation and Development 2009); UNICEF Tajikistan, *Child Research Digest No 3: Children with Disabilities in Tajikistan: A Situational Analysis Report* (United Nations International Children's Emergency Fund 2006).

revised in 2013 and the Law on the Social Protection of People with Disabilities passed in 2010.[2] Furthermore, the government is working towards a Codex for Education which would encompass, further clarify and provide regulations for the Law on Education. The timing for these two changes is unpredictable and information about the content of the Codex is limited to copies of public presentations by government officials. This chapter sets the current legal framework in the context of evolving cultural norms surrounding disability and the capacity of the formal school system to provide education to the greatest extent possible with the information available.[3] When possible, I offer commentary on changes envisioned in the Codex and highlight specific challenges that Tajikistan's education system will face following the ratification of the CRPD in 2018.

DISABILITY AND CULTURAL NORMS

Before looking more closely at the legal context, it is important to understand the multiple layers of prejudice that affect children with disabilities in Central Asia.[4] Many of the norms and ideas about disability strongly rooted in Tajikistan's cultural history as part of the historical Persian Empire are also perpetuated by the legacy of defectology, the dominant framework of education for people with disabilities in the Soviet Union. The population of Tajikistan is 90 per cent Muslim, which also influences understanding of disability. In Islam, disabilities have been characterised as deficits that could and should be cured,[5] contributing to stigma associated with disability, which, in the absence of 'rehabilitation', is seen as an immutable incompleteness.[6] As a result, acknowledging a disability within the family can be profoundly shameful. Samadi et al. report on the stigma attached to having a family member with intellectual disabilities in Iran, Tajikistan's cultural

2 Law on the Protection of Children's Rights 2015 (Government of the Republic of Tajikistan).

3 Irina Kholovna Karimova, *National Laws on Inclusive Education: The Current Situation and Paths for Improvement* (Academy of Education of Tajikistan 2016) [in Russian] Ирина Холовна Каримова, *Национальное Законодательство По Инклюзивному Образованию: Нынешнее Положение И Пути Улучшения* (Академии Образования Таджикистана 2016).

4 Hisayo Katsui, *Towards Equality: Creation of the Disability Movement in Central Asia* (Helsinki University Press 2005).

5 Mohammed M. Ghaly, 'Physical and Spiritual Treatment of Disability in Islam: Perspectives of Early and Modern Jurists' (2008) 12 *Journal of Religion, Disability & Health* 105; Mohammed Morad, Yusuf Nasri and Joav Merrick, 'Islam and the Person with Intellectual Disability' (2001) 5 *Journal of Religion, Disability & Health* 65.

6 Fathali M. Moghaddam, Donald M. Taylor and Stephen C. Wright, *Social Psychology in Cross-Cultural Perspective* (WH Freeman and Company 1993).

neighbour.[7] Brown[8] cites the findings of researchers in the Middle East that parents often believe a disability is a punishment from God, a viewpoint that Gatling and Juraeva[9] also found during their work in Tajikistan.

Religious and cultural values of compassion, justice, equality, kindness, generosity and the acceptance of fate as God's will are often prevalent. These can sometimes act as supporting factors for the family. However, they do not completely, or even sufficiently, neutralise the threat to family honour contained in the diagnosis of a disability.[10] The birth of a child with disabilities is considered by many Iranians to be a result of a sin, such that disability becomes a source of shame for the broader family, with negative effects on the marriage prospects of siblings[11] – a view echoed in research specific to Tajikistan.[12]

Gatling and Juraeva further find that in Tajikistan

> Many traditionally minded Tajiks maintain a folk belief that congenital abnormalities are the result of the birth mother engaging in sexual relations outside of marriage or other behavior considered 'antisocial'. Thus the community often sees a child disabled from birth as 'evidence' of such behavior. The community also often concludes that the males in the child's family have lost control of the birth mother[13]

at the expense of their honour.[14] This is a very serious loss of honour for the entire family that is seen as deserved by the community in a context where fidelity in marriage and childbearing are two of the most important fulfilments of social norms for women.[15] Prejudice within the families of children with

7 Sayyed Ali Samadi, Roy McConkey and Greg Kelly, 'Enhancing Parental Well-Being and Coping through a Family-Centred Short Course for Iranian Parents of Children with an Autism Spectrum Disorder' (2013) 17 *Autism* 27.

8 Ronald C. Brown, 'Inclusive Education in Middle Eastern Cultures: The Challenge of Tradition' in David R. Mitchell (ed.), *Contextualizing Inclusive Education: Evaluating Old and New International Perspectives* (Routledge 2005) 274.

9 Benjamin Gatling and Manzura Juraeva, 'Tradition, Stigma, and Inclusion: Overcoming Obstacles to Educational Access in Tajikistan' in Martyn Rouse and Kate Lapham (eds), *Learning to See Invisible Children: Inclusion of Children with Disabilities in Central Asia* (Open Society Foundations 2013).

10 Brown (n. 9) 270.

11 Sayyed Ali Samadi, 'Comparative Policy Brief: Status of Intellectual Disabilities in the Islamic Republic of Iran' (2008) 5 *Journal of Policy and Practice in Intellectual Disabilities* 129.

12 Kate Lapham, 'Redefining the Experience of Raising a Child with Disabilities in Tajikistan' (Doctoral Dissertation, Lehigh University, forthcoming); Colette Harris, *Control and Subversion: Gender Relations in Tajikistan* (Pluto Press 2004); Gatling and Juraeva (n. 10).

13 Gatling and Juraeva (n. 10).

14 Ibid. 24.

15 Harris (n. 13) 86–87.

disability can thus lead to the isolation of the person with a disability, to hiding children with disabilities from the community and to drastic consequences for the mother of a child with disabilities, including abandonment by her husband.[16]

This shame and stigma thus isolates families as well as children, sometimes stopping them from reaching out to others or looking for support, leading to a poor understanding within families of what may be possible for children with disabilities. Enjoyment of life through participation in daily activities, like attending school, is often seen as impossible. The person with a disability is characterised as helpless, having at best a right to food and basic care but not to civic or community participation or education.[17] This is, in turn, further reinforced in the language of modernity and science by defectology's focus on medical assessments and the things that people with disabilities cannot do.[18]

As a result, children in Tajikistan with disabilities often are kept at home or receive education in closed residential institutions or other highly segregated settings. This isolation means that most people in Tajikistan grow up without any experience of peers, classmates or friends with disabilities. In the name of preparing children for re-integration in society through 'rehabilitation', the current system in Tajikistan instead reinforces existing cultural norms and perpetuates fear and stigma associated with disability, which slows down the evolution of cultural norms.[19]

A national coalition of parental organisations opposes these norms. The coalition began with an initiative group set up by the non-governmental organisation (NGO) Zdorovye ('health' in Russian), and the health-focussed NGO Rangikamon in Khujand to help parents of children with disabilities support each other emotionally and practically as they navigate the systems of education, health and social services with their children. The group grew quickly and began supporting like-minded NGOs and initiative groups in other parts of Tajikistan. Mutual support and empowerment of parents was

[16] Katsui (2005) (n. 5).

[17] Hisayo Katsui, 'The Challenges of Operationalizing a Human Rights Approach to Disability in Central Asia' in Michael Rasell and Elena Iarskaia-Smirnova (eds), *Disability in Eastern Europe and the Former Soviet Union: History, Policy and Everyday Life* (Routledge 2013) 204.

[18] Anupam Ahuja and Parvez Pirzado, 'What Is in a Name? Labels and Terminologies Regarding Disability and Special Educational Needs: A Continuing Concern' (2006) 2 *Eenet Asia Newsletter* 6.

[19] Alfredo J. Artiles, Kathleen King Thorius, Aydin Bal, Rebecca Neal, Federico Waitoller and David Hernandez Saca, 'Beyond Culture as Group Traits: Future Learning Disabilities: Ontology, Epistemology, and Inquiry on Research Knowledge Use' (2011) 34 *Learning Disability Quarterly* 167.

one of the foundational goals of this network of parental associations.[20] There are also disabled people's organisations such as Ishtirok (the Union of Disabled Women), which are mostly based in Dushanbe or other cities and focus mostly on physical disabilities. Together, these civil society organisations have leveraged support from international donors (including Caritas, the Open Society Foundations and UNICEF) to advocate for changes in legislation and policies so that people with disabilities can realise their rights as citizens on an equal basis with others.

EDUCATION AND THE LEGAL FRAMEWORK

Tajikistan's monist legal system does not differentiate between national and international law. Once ratified, treaties are fully binding and viewed as part of the same legal system as laws passed by the national parliament and signed by the president.[21] In theory, these treaties and international conventions should form the legal framework for the development of regulations, standards and guidelines for services and thus play a significant role in the design of the Codex on Education.[22] International conventions and treaties ratified by the Republic of Tajikistan include the Convention on the Rights of the Child (CRC), the International Convention on the Elimination of All Forms of Racial Discrimination (CERD), the International Covenant on Economic, Social and Cultural Rights (CESCR), the Convention against Discrimination in Education and the Convention on the Elimination of Discrimination against Women (CEDAW). Tajikistan has also adopted the Salamanca Statement on Principles, Policy and Practice in Special Needs Education. While only the Salamanca Statement specifically references children with disabilities in education, the other conventions provide for inclusion in education on an equal basis for other groups or identities facing discrimination, and the CRC provides guidance in General Comment No. 9 on the inclusion of children with disabilities.

[20] Christopher Michael Whitsel and Shodibek Kodirov, 'Out of the Shadows: The Work of Parents in Inclusive Education in Tajikistan' in Martyn Rouse and Kate Lapham (eds), *Learning to See Invisible Children: Inclusion of Children with Disabilities in Central Asia* (Open Society Foundations 2013).

[21] Milovanovitch and Rosa (n. 2).

[22] Article 4 of the Law on Education also states that 'development in the sphere of education [should take] account of international standards of quality and international education norms', although it does not reference any of these specifically. The concept of a codex is based on the Russian model, which groups legislation, bylaws, regulations and standards into a single legal instrument that would be ratified by the parliament and signed by the president.

There are also several national legislative documents governing access to formal education for children with disabilities. These laws have been developed as the cultural and institutional context described earlier interacts with government reform efforts, international obligations, conditionality tied to international assistance and advocacy from civil society organisations, including parent groups and disabled people's organisations (DPOs). They have been passed and revised at different times and have not necessarily been harmonised with each other.[23] Some parts of these laws reinforce the international frameworks that Tajikistan has adopted. Some even provide specific support for inclusion in education. However, in many cases, they create confusion about how to make education more inclusive, revealing good intentions with a lack of understanding about how inclusion might work or highlighting political and institutional disagreements about the ways in which education should be provided for children with disabilities.

The differing terminology related to disability used in laws passed or revised at different times is one potential source of confusion. While representing a significant improvement over the 1991 law, and in some estimations paving the way for ratification of the CRPD, the Law on the Social Protection of People with Disabilities (LSPPwD) retains significant elements of the defectology/medical approach.[24] Definitions are particularly problematic. For example, the LSPPwD defines a person with a disability (*инвалид*) as someone 'who as a result of unfitness of health due to sickness, injuries, physical or mental defect (*физические или умственные дефекты*) and attendant reduction of the functions of the body, faces barriers to life activities, and needs social protection'. It further defines disability (*инвалидность*) by the level of limitations to life activities resultant of health problems (*нарушения здоровья*) with long-standing consequences for bodily functions. These definitions place the disability squarely with the individual and is a sharp contrast to the preamble of the CRPD, which makes clear that disability stems from the interaction of an individual's characteristics and the social environment.

23 The national laws relevant to education for children with disabilities include the Law on Education (adopted in 1993, revised in 2004 and 2013), the Law on the Defence of the Rights of Children (adopted in 2015), the Law on Higher and Postgraduate Education (2009), the Law on Supplementary Education, the Law on Social Protection of the Disabled in the Republic of Tajikistan (2010), the Law on the Responsibility of Parents for the Education and Upbringing of Children (2011) and the Law on Architecture, Urban Planning and Construction Activities (2008).

24 'Better Services for People with Disabilities in Tajikistan' (Welcome Health Organization, 21 November 2013), www.euro.who.int/en/countries/tajikistan/news/news/2013/11/better-services-for-people-with-disabilities-in-tajikistan, accessed 2 May 2014.

Article 41 of the Constitution and Article 6 of the Law on Education guarantees all citizens of Tajikistan the right to free education through the ninth grade and equal access to education thereafter. The Law on Education is meant to make the realisation of this right explicit. The legal framework for the right to education as it applies to children with disabilities further contributes to confusion. One of the main concerns of the LSPPwD is to provide for the participation of people with disabilities in the social, economic and political life of the country. Article 24 of this law recognises education as an integral part of such participation, guaranteeing people with disabilities 'access and equal rights ... at the level of other citizens to health, education, recreation and tourism'. Some parents of children with disabilities have used this law in court to receive benefits for their children, but in fact there are very few state budget allocations to provide for sustainable, consistent service delivery, often leaving communities to fend for themselves.[25]

The 2013 Law on Education (LE) uses language that is similar in tone, but it does not match the terminology of the 2010 LSPPwD. For example, the definition of special education institutions in Article 1 addresses children with physical and mental delays (*физические или психические отклонения*) and the need for long-term care, but does not use the same terminology of disability or 'defect' used in Article 1 of the Law on Social Protection. The definition of inclusive education in Article 1 of the LE lists several characteristics that could subject children to discrimination. Article 6.1 in the LE provides almost the same list of characteristics, but in a different order, in its guarantee of the right to education. However, neither refers to disability using the terminology of the LSPPwD or other articles in the LE to in any way at all place the burden of clarification on those charged with implementing the law and the court system where experience of disability is likely to be lacking.[26]

Still, Articles 6.3 and 6.7 of the LE leave ajar the door to education in inclusive settings for children with disabilities. Nowhere in the LE does it state that children with disabilities *must* attend special education institutions, only that they *may* if they 'do not have the possibility to study in general education institutions' (Article 22.3) unless a court decides that their behaviour is dangerous to society (Article 22.6).[27] This implies an element of choice in educational placement but at the same time it implies that there is little obligation

[25] Isfara Parent Association, Interview with a father (May 2015).

[26] Interesting, Article 1 does not include political beliefs while Article 6.1 does.

[27] Article 6.3 states that limitations on the right to education based on age, health status (*состояние здоровья*), judicial decision or other factors must be in agreement with the laws of the Republic of Tajikistan. Article 6.8 provides for the continuation of home-based

on the school to provide accommodations. Further space for the development of education in inclusive settings exists in Article 16.5, which lists 'inclusive' as one of the formats that general education institutions may use for the provision of education programmes. Article 6.7 holds the government responsible for provision and financing of education in public education institutions for orphans, children without parental care, children with disabilities (дети с ограниченными возможностями, инвалиды) and others. It makes no mention of special education institutions or any other reference to the type of school or institution where this right must be realised, and this is the only place where the LE uses the same terminology as the LSPPwD in reference to people with disabilities.

Further confusing matters, the 2015 Law on the Social Protection of Children makes regional and local governments responsible for education and gives them the right to develop and implement programmes to fulfil the rights of children with disabilities (Article 8.1, 46.3). The same law also guarantees children with disabilities the right to education and special pedagogical support in accordance with unspecified, other laws (Article 17.2, Article 45.2). The same law also protects children from discrimination based on disability status (состояния здоровья и иных обстоятельств) among other characteristics (Article 11.2, 45.1, 45.4).

The LSPPwD addresses education directly in Article 7, which states that education for children with disabilities must be provided free of charge and that the Ministry of Education and Science is responsible for providing 'pre-service, in-service and professional development training for specialists in the spheres of social service and rehabilitation of people with disabilities, including use of sign language and special writing'. Article 17.2 of the LSP goes further, requiring that the state provide people with disabilities access to preschool, basic and vocational education in general and special education institutions based on his or her individual rehabilitation plan. While this does not mandate education in inclusive settings, it works with Article 16.5 of the LE to create both a space and the outlines of a mechanism for implementation of inclusive education.

Finally, there is some legal recognition of the cultural norms and discrimination attracted by having a disability, although the government addresses this through a charity and rehabilitation lens, and only implicitly with an attempt to control parents' behaviour through legislation and policy. The Law on Parental Responsibility attempts to address some of the consequences of the

formal education, but only for children with an illness (*болезнь*) that keeps them out of school for an undefined long time (*долгое время*).

stigma associated with disability, in particular the tendency of families to hide their children with disabilities. Article 9 of the Law holds parents responsible for providing 'relevant conditions for [the] training and professional orientation of children with physical and mental disabilities'. This reinforces Article 65 of the Family Code, requiring parents not to harm their children's development.[28] In addition, it admonishes parents not to hide their children with disabilities, and 'in the absence of an appropriate environment for the education of these children [they should] apply to the relevant government agencies on education, health and social welfare'. On the other hand, the same law also limits the scope of parents to participate in decisions regarding their children's education by placing expertise and authority solely with education professionals.[29]

In short, the existing legislation is a mixed bag of small and sometimes confusing steps forward but is still heavily skewed to a medical model of disability. It is in need of some revision if it is to comply with the CRPD, and the Codex on Education is likely to continue the confusion surrounding inclusive education with separate chapters addressing general education, inclusive education and special education. Despite these shortcomings and the long shadow cast by the medical model of disability, legislation does not close off the possibility of inclusive education. Negative ideas about disability are reflected in the barriers to mainstream schools, with many claiming that 'they are not ready for inclusion'.[30] A few of these barriers are legal as described earlier. Many are attitudinal, but many also are embedded in the structure of the school day and the physical infrastructure of the education system. In the midst of the confusion about what laws actually mandate and the inertia of school systems, there is space for those who support greater inclusion through advocacy for the regulations and standards, ministerial decrees and other policy documents that fill in the legal framework.

Policy documents can highlight the confusion and disparities in accessing information in different parts of Tajikistan, creating both barriers and opportunities. For example, a working group of government agencies and civil society representatives convened in 2010 and have developed the national Concept on Inclusive Education related to the National Education Development Strategy

28 Tupi and West (n. 2).

29 Christopher Michael Whitsel and Kate Lapham, 'Increasing Programme Effectiveness through Parent Empowerment: The Getting Ready for School Project in Tajikistan' (2014) 22 *International Journal of Early Years Education* 105.

30 Martyn Rouse and Kate Lapham, 'Introduction' in Martyn Rouse and Kate Lapham (eds), *Learning to See Intellectual Children: Inclusion of Children with Disabilities in Central Asia* (Open Society Foundations 2013) 12.

(NEDS), which was agreed between the government of Tajikistan and major donors to education. Although it is a policy statement without the force of law and does not aim for the type of full education inclusion described in Article 24 of the CRPD, it is a positive step that represents hard work and successful advocacy from a variety of civil society actors. Its application also highlights the differences in access to information and legal knowledge in urban and rural areas.

People in remote regions do not know all the laws, they are not familiar with the Concept on Inclusive Education and they do not know the rights of people with disabilities. When we carried out a survey among civil servants, they all said that they needed informational training. Furthermore, they said that they did not need study tours somewhere outside of their jurisdiction – they needed to understand how to do things correctly within the framework of their own laws. There are also differences in people's understanding of the law depending on where they reside; when a person lives in a big city, there are more opportunities for them to discuss and to exchange information. In more remote places, however, information is filtered out by the distance and therefore takes much longer to reach those people. The Concept was approved in 2011, yet some are still learning about it. Thus people's knowledge of the rights of people with disabilities really depends on whether they live far away where there is little information, or in the centre of a city.[31]

Unfortunately, the Concept had parliamentary endorsement by the end of 2014, but it is still not clear whether or how existing legislation might be amended to institutionalise or to sustain progress made within this framework. It could be updated and included in the Codex on Education, and many in the education community would advocate for this. For practical purposes at the present time, this leaves children with special education needs out of policies aimed at integrating people with disabilities into society (as the OECD found in 2009). However, civil society organisations actively refer to the Concept in their advocacy, and there is some evidence that it has been used to pave the way for the inclusion of individual children with disabilities.[32]

Thus, legislation unlocks the door to inclusive education, while leaving the work of opening it to civil society movements and individual schools. Additionally, policies, regulations and especially planning or strategy documents may be significantly more progressive, but may also lack the funds and personnel to move from a mere mandate to implementation, creating a second

31 Mission East, Interview with staff (Dushanbe, July 2016).

32 Findings from interviews conducted with parent groups (Dushanbe, Soghd veloyat and Boktar, in spring 2015).

area of advocacy for civil society as well as a point of collaboration between civil society groups and donors. The section that follows explores the practical and political realities of the education system, in particular the lack of resources available at the school level, and the uncertainty faced by many district officials and administrators, as well as the shape that cooperation and advocacy from civil society groups can take. This provides the context for the conclusions and recommendations that follow.

PRACTICAL REALITIES OF INCLUSIVE EDUCATION

Since the fall of the Soviet Union, Tajikistan has been grappling with education reform amid a series of economic crises starting with the civil war and continuing into the present with the collapse of the ruble in 2015. In most cases, the goal of reform has been sustaining or resurrecting the Soviet system of education, or adopting measures associated with higher achievement in the West. The Soviet legacy of strong education systems with high rates of school enrolment as well as high levels of adult literacy and educational attainment, the strong historical influence of defectology as a defining philosophy for disability and two decades of painful, incomplete and unsuccessful reforms conspire to perpetuate inertia in both the general and special education systems.

Tajikistan's education system is inherited from the Soviet Union and is thus infused with the philosophy of defectology. Originally as an area of developmental psychology seeking to support children with atypical development, defectology evolved throughout the twentieth century as a body of education practices seeking to 'rehabilitate' children with disabilities through specialised education and therapy in special schools or institutions separate from the mainstream, general education system.[33] Defectology in its current form frames disability as a diagnosis for treatment and rehabilitation rather than just one aspect of a whole child requiring adaptations in the learning environment.[34] It has a long history and continues to be influential in the countries of the former Soviet Union.[35] Tajikistan is no exception.

According to UNICEF, a child with a disability living in the Central Eastern Europe and Commonwealth of Independent States (CEECIS) region, which includes Tajikistan, is almost seventeen times as likely to be institutionalised as a typically developing child. Furthermore, the number of

33 Rouse and Lapham (n. 31) 10–11.

34 Harry Daniels, *An Introduction to Vygotsky* (2nd edn) (Routledge 2005).

35 Ibid.

children in institutional care in this region has increased since 2000, with approximately 60 per cent of all institutionalised children registered as children with disabilities. Also, UNICEF further estimates that approximately 1.1 million children with disabilities in this region are not included in nationally collected statistics and thus are likely not to be receiving any formal education or other public services.[36] This phenomenon is likely skewed towards poorer areas within the region, such as rural or remote areas of Tajikistan, where home births[37] that may not be registered until the child reaches school age are common.[38] Research by civil society organisations and DPOs offers some confirmation of this, finding in a shadow report submitted to the Office of the High Commissioner of Human Rights (OHCHR) that as many as 64 per cent of women with disabilities in Tajikistan have never had access to formal education of any kind.[39]

As the poorest republic in the Soviet Union, Tajikistan's education system inherited the defectology approach to programmes for children with disabilities, but does not have as strong a system of special schools as some other countries in the region. Furthermore, the upheaval of civil war, particularly in Khatlon veloyat, and continuing high rates of labour migration mean that those special schools that did exist are often currently providing emergency shelter for children from very poor families or without parental care regardless of their disability status. Combined with poor infrastructure in the public health system to assess children, this blurs the lines between special schools, residential care institutions and orphanages or children's homes, creating layers of confusion and disadvantage exacerbated by the involvement of different ministries and agencies. It is difficult even to get an accurate valuation of the different types of special schools and institutions that exist within Tajikistan's borders.

As a further result of continued political and economic uncertainty, many qualified specialists in the fields of education and health, including

36 Gerison Lawson, 'The Right of Children with Disabilities to Education: A Rights-Based Approach to Inclusive Education: Position Paper' (UNICEF Regional Office for Central and Eastern Europe and the Commonwealth of Independent States 2011).

37 Statistical Agency under the President of the Republic of Tajikistan (SA), Ministry of Health [Tajikistan] and ICF International, *Tajikistan: Demographic and Health Survey: 2012* (DHS Program 2013).

38 The 2012 Demographic and Health Survey estimates that about 25 per cent of births in Tajikistan occur at home, with significantly higher rates (33–35 per cent) in rural and remote areas.

39 Public Organizations of Tajikistan, *The Second Shadow Report on the Realization of the Convention on the Elimination of All Forms of Discrimination against Women* (Office of the High Commissioner of Human Rights 2012).

occupational and physical therapists, psychologists and speech therapists, have emigrated and have not been replaced through pre-service and professional training programmes. There is a shortage of qualified teachers, social workers and school counsellors in the education system more generally. In Dushanbe and large cities, it is still possible to fill specialist positions (albeit mostly with professionals who speak Russian as their first and primary language), but the deficit is particularly acute in smaller towns and rural or remote areas. The specialists who remain also often have substantial private practices, which constrains the reach of their services to only those who can afford to pay for them.[40]

Attending a local school can be very difficult or impossible, depending on the nature of the child's disability and the willingness of the school to accept the child. In some cases, the Psychological Medical Pedagogical Commission (PMPC), which is responsible for the assessment and recommendation of education placement for children with disabilities, recommends that a child receive education at home under the supervision of a teacher from the local school. This recognises the challenges of physical accessibility in school buildings and the lack of available and accessible transportation. However, in practice, this option provides little instructional contact between child and teacher and no social contact with other children outside the family.[41] During fieldwork in Tajikistan in 2015, parents who were interviewed reported teachers who would fill out students' homework themselves, those having poor attitudes towards children with intellectual disabilities especially and those who requested additional informal payments.

The situation in general education schools is hardly encouraging for the prospect of inclusion. As the government of Tajikistan has become increasingly authoritarian, educational policy has become more centralised in terms of the curriculum, assessment and appointment of loyal school principals and district officials.[42] At the same time, fiscal responsibility for education has devolved to the local level in the wake of a near-complete collapse in centralised revenue collection that has not recovered from the civil war.[43] Children are expected to keep up with the

40 Lapham (forthcoming) (n. 13).

41 Ibid.

42 Sarfaroz Niyozov and Stephen Bahry, 'Challenges to Education in Tajikistan: The Need for Research-Based Solutions' in Jaya Earnest and David F. Treagust (eds), *Education Reform in Societies in Transition: International Perspectives* (Sense Publishers 2006).

43 Ibid.; International Crisis Group, *Central Asia: Decay and Decline: Asia Report No 201* (International Crisis Group 2011).

pace of lessons that are often extremely didactic. Teachers in Tajikistan also occupy a difficult position. Low salaries and sharply reduced benefits make the profession unattractive for young people. Graduates of pedagogical universities often work in other fields, even if they are forced to teach for two years after graduation, leaving work in schools to those with vocational pre-service training or no formal teaching qualifications at all.[44] Once part of a respected professional field credited with the huge literacy gains and other accomplishments of the Soviet period, teachers now work in dramatically reduced circumstances with multiple lines of formal and informal accountability.[45] Niyozov likens them to 'meek dictators' controlling their classrooms with little authority and few resources beyond the possibility of giving low marks.[46] Despite the substantial investments of international donors and successful pilots, few teachers have been trained in child-centred pedagogy, activity-based teaching and collaborative learning.[47]

Despite the (problematic) categorisations applied to people with disabilities, there is also a tendency to approach discussions of inclusive education as though children with disabilities and typically developing children were two distinct but internally homogenous groups. Of course, there is great diversity within both groups, and the philosophy of inclusion as well as many of the practices and supports associated with inclusive education would substantially improve the educational experiences of all children in Tajikistan. The understanding of inclusive education has not yet evolved to this point, but the situation is beginning to shift. To be sure, the value and wisdom of including children with disabilities in general education is hotly contested, but there are encouraging signs of progress, such as the fact that schools are testing the waters of working more inclusively despite all of the constraints detailed earlier. Often this progress results from the initiative and quiet advocacy of a small group of individuals interested in inclusion for personal reasons, as the following example of a mother of a child with a disability from Dushanbe illustrates.

44 International Crisis Group (n. 44).

45 Niyozov and Bahry (n. 43).

46 Sarfaroz Niyozov, 'Understanding Teaching beyond Content and Method: Insights from Central Asia' (2008) 40 *European Education* 46.

47 Milovanovitch and Rosa (n. 2).

> *Zamira Nabieva started as a member of the Dushanbe Association of Parents of Disabled Children and came to School #28 eleven years ago with her son. In 2011 she studied inclusive education in India and decided that she wanted to work with the school more closely, setting up a small resource centre called 'Rushdi Inklusiia' (RI) to facilitate the integration of children with disabilities, who had been completely without schooling in some cases, into regular classes. In the first year, the resource centre served ten to twelve students.*
>
> *In its daily work, RI has created a miniature multidisciplinary team that gathers once a month with teachers to discuss students' progress. Children attend regular classes but come to the resource centre for extra support. One of the support teachers at the centre is both the mother of a child with a disability and a member of the PMPC, offering important access to a state structure directly related to education for children with disabilities. Zamira wants to support teachers as well as children, and sees this as an important part of RI's mission. They offer training whenever possible. They also invite teachers to come in for a cup of coffee so that they can ask questions informally. This often ends with teachers asking questions about strategies for working with students in their classes who have not been assessed with special needs but who are struggling nonetheless.*
>
> *Registered as an NGO with an agreement with the school for space, RI can raise funds for materials and, significant, has written permission from the Ministry of Education and Science to implement inclusive education programmes with other schools as well. In this way, RI brings increased access to resources and prestige to School #28 as well as opportunities for professional development for teachers. This centre has become a bridge between parents and teachers, with other NGOs following their lead.*

It is important to note that Zamira had a personal relationship with the school principal that allowed the school staff members to trust her. She was also mindful of the politics involved, calling the attention of colleagues from the Ministry of Education at an opportune moment with an offer to help. The government of Tajikistan has difficulty meeting its budgetary obligations to the education system, and an increasingly authoritarian and fragile ruling coalition keeps close watch on schools as instruments of political control. In this environment, teachers and principals have a rational fear of selective enforcement of regulations and standards that they could not hope to implement with the resources available to them. Thus, fear and uncertainty play a large role in any discussion of including children with disabilities in general education classrooms.[48]

CONCLUSIONS AND RECOMMENDATIONS

This chapter presents the complexity of the interactions between the ratification of international conventions, the development and passage of national laws, the slow and sometimes nearly imperceptible pace of reform and the gaps or spaces for new initiatives based in the attitudes, expertise and funding available in Tajikistan's education system. Legal obligations of the state and other actors are unquestionably important as a basis for analysis and a focus for advocacy. Indeed, civil society organisations, both DPOs and parent groups, through understanding the importance of law and policy have also actively participated in working groups and public commentary on legislative projects as well as alternative reports to international treaty bodies.

Harpur and Bale discuss the importance of national laws for the implementation of the CRPD in both the developed and the developing world.[49] However, in countries like Tajikistan that already have laws with gaps and a history of rigid regulatory frameworks, the most likely place for real change affecting the lives of people with disabilities lies in the standards and regulations that flesh out the intention of the laws. Even in the face of a new law, change can be stalled if the old regulations are simply attached to the new legislative framework. Although it appears that civil society groups and experts are included in consultations organised by the Ministry of Education and Science, no copy of the current text of the Codex is publicly available. This legislative project remains a great opportunity to advance inclusive education for children with disabilities and should be monitored through further research.

However, legal analysis on its own does not capture the complexity of the ways that children's rights are conceptualised, realised and sometimes denied in the public services that follow from existing laws. The political realities of existing systems of segregated education can only be countered through the sustained work of counter-movements by people with disabilities, parents and professionals allied with them by advocating for legal reform, implementation

[48] Lapham (n. 13).

[49] Paul Harpur and Richard Bales, 'The Positive Impact of the Convention on the Rights of Persons with Disabilities: A Case Study on the South Pacific and Lessons from the US Experience' (2010) 37 *Northern Kentucky Law Review* 363.

and rights within a legal system, and their initiatives to fill gaps in service provision. In addition to meeting immediate needs, their services offer models of practice and policy implementation that have the power to open minds and thus to advance the legal basis for inclusion through their subsequent institutionalisation in regulations and standards. This is true in many places, but it is particularly persuasive in Tajikistan where the resources, including teachers and infrastructure, available to the education system as a whole are scarce and shrinking. In many schools, as in the example provided earlier, initiatives led and funded through civil society are the best source of highly qualified and dedicated teachers, as well as prestige and access to external funding.

There is also a great deal to be done outside the education system before education policies and standards can be updated to support inclusion. At the most basic level, standardising the categories and definitions of data collected across ministries and the Agency for National Statistics would make the education sector more transparent for children with disabilities. National data collection through the census and demographic and health survey could be updated to include indicators that are important for the education sector, such as the disability-related questions advocated by the Washington Group. This would also require harmonising terminology across legislation and categories across the health, education and social protection sectors. For example, the current classification system for disabilities does not include autism spectrum disorders (ASD). The reporting form that hospitals use to record a child's birth does not include Down syndrome, and many professionals working with children with disabilities are not aware that Down syndrome exists as an official classification in the register of disabilities.[50]

In both cases, data collection and thus provision of relevant services is made much more difficult. Children are assigned classifications that either partially capture (heart defects in the case of children with Down syndrome, for example) or completely misrepresent the child's needs. Civil society has a role to play here as well. For example, SiDa, a national association of parents of children with Down syndrome and member of Down Syndrome International, has already achieved an informal agreement with maternity hospitals in Dushanbe to refer families whose children are believed to have Down syndrome. However, a change in the reporting form used nationally would allow for official statistics that would further facilitate development and advocacy for services.

[50] Ministry of Health Regulation 9 from 7 January 2013 and Regulation 543 from 2 October 2013 [Russian].

In some cases, this state of affairs is not only a matter of accurate statistics; it is actively harmful to children, as in the case of ASD, which is listed as childhood schizophrenia in the register of mental illnesses and will only be diagnosed after a lengthy assessment stay in a psychological hospital. This is a prospect most families find quite traumatic, which is also completely unnecessary to the assessment of ASD. IRODA, which began as an association of parents of children with autism, is currently working with the Ministry of Health and Social Protection of the Population (MHSPP) to develop a clinical protocol on autism that would allow it to be included in the register of disabilities as a neurological condition. If IRODA is successful in advocating for this clinical protocol, it will mean that children with autism will have the right to a neurological assessment with support from paediatricians and neurologists, and would no longer be subject to the (cruel and counterproductive) treatments for childhood schizophrenia currently included in treatment protocols. In addition, autism would be included in the register of disabilities eligible for a state pension.

These examples illustrate the extent to which the devil can be in the details of regulations and standards that have not been reformed since independence. Even in the presence of adequate legislation, there is a great deal of work left to be done in this sphere. Working groups and policy initiatives like the Concept on Inclusive Education are an important step along this path, but they are not the final destination by any means. Even if the Codex on Education is enacted in its most progressive form, policy makers and advocates must have the time, funds and expertise to continue working through the vast body of regulations and standards that underpin the systems of education, health and social protection as well as the political support to institutionalise their recommendations. They must also have the political will and civic space to continue working together. Ratification of the CRPD would provide some of the necessary political support and an important legal tool for advocacy, but it is also a step along the path rather than a final destination.

27

The Right to Inclusive Education in Argentina

Ana Laura Aiello

1 INTRODUCTION

The aim of this chapter is to explore the right to inclusive education in Argentina, both in theory and in practice, with a particular focus on disabled people. According to different experts, alongside Uruguay and Chile, Argentina presents 'the best educational indicators linked to social aspects'.[1] Also, Argentina (alongside Brazil and Peru) has been deemed a country that has a general law regarding the development of the issue of education for disabled people, as well as an advanced conceptualisation about inclusive education.[2] As evidenced in this research, in Argentina, the right to inclusive education is recognised in various legal instruments, ranging from international to national ones. However, the facts demonstrate that currently there are fundamental problems with the implementation of this right.

The right to inclusive education in Argentina should be read in the country's political and legal context/system. Argentina is a country formed of twenty-three provinces, as well as the City of Buenos Aires. This country has a representative, republican and federal government built upon a separation between legislative, executive and judicial powers.[3] The National Constitution is the norm with the highest status in the Argentinian legal

[1] Paulí Dávila Balsera, Luís Naya Garmendia and Asier Lauzurika Arrondo, 'Las personas con discapacidad, el derecho a la educación y la Convención sobre los Derechos del Niño en América Latina' (2010) 4 *Revista Latinoamericana de Inclusión Educativa* 97, www.rinace.net/rlei/numeros/vol4-num2/art5_eng.html, last accessed 17 May 2017. These authors clarify that such indicators do not reach the poorest population of the country. In addition, note that in this chapter, all translations are mine unless otherwise stated.

[2] Camilla Croso, 'El derecho a la educación de personas con discapacidad: impulsando el concepto de educación inclusiva' (2010) 4 *Revista Latinoamericana de Inclusión Educativa* 79, www.rinace.net/rlei/numeros/vol4-num2/art4.html, last accessed 17 May 2017.

[3] Constitución Nacional de la Nación Argentina, Asamblea General Constituyente, ciudad de Santa Fe, 22 August 1994 (hereafter National Constitution), Article 1.

system.[4] The National Constitution was adopted on 1 May 1853. However, this legal instrument was subject to numerous revisions, with the last taking place in 1994. Departing from this basis, and following Article 31 of the National Constitution, the supreme law in Argentina is formed by the National Constitution, as well as international law and the laws of the nation. Also, it is essential to take into account that, according to Article 75(22) of the National Constitution, international law is above the laws of the nation. Moreover, certain human rights treaties have the same status as the National Constitution (for instance, the United Nations Convention on the Rights of the Child). Therefore, and once again beginning with the National Constitution, the legal system in Argentina is made up of a complex set of international and national laws that differ in status.

This chapter is structured as follows. The next section (2) approaches how the right under analysis is framed in detail in this national case, adopting the definition of inclusive education established in Article 24 of the Convention on the Rights of Persons with Disabilities (CRPD) as the guiding principle. In basic terms, Article 24(1) of the CRPD approaches inclusive education as a 'system at all levels and lifelong learning'. This research will also build upon the interpretation and clarification of Article 24 of the CRPD, as it has been developed in General Comment No. 4, which was issued by the Committee on the Rights of Persons with Disabilities (CRPD Committee).[5] Once the right to inclusive education has been legally framed, Section 3 attempts to analyse the implementation of this right in practice. Finally, Section 4 is dedicated to the overall conclusion for this case study.

2 FRAMING A RIGHT TO INCLUSIVE EDUCATION IN ARGENTINA

As this section demonstrates, in Argentina, there is clearly a right to inclusive education, as recognised by the CRPD – as well as, in a different way, by other relevant human rights treaties. In addition to this international human rights law (which is accepted by Argentina), the national law recognises the right to inclusive education (and/or arguably, to integration in mainstream education) of (among others) disabled people. Subsection 2.1 explores the reception of the right to inclusive education as recognised by different international and

[4] However, as is explained shortly, certain human rights treaties also have constitutional status.

[5] Committee on the Rights of Persons with Disabilities, General Comment No. 4 (2016) Article 24: Right to Inclusive Education (2 September 2016) CRPD/C/GC/4 (General Comment No. 4). The CRPD Committee is the body that monitors the CRPD, www.ohchr.org/en/hrbodies/crpd/pages/crpdindex.aspx, last accessed 23 November 2018].

regional human rights law instruments. In turn, Subsection 2.2 focusses on the way in which the Argentinian domestic law contemplates the right to inclusive education.

2.1 *International and Regional Human Rights Law*

Argentina is part of various fundamental international and/or regional human rights treaties addressing the right to education from a perspective based either on inclusion or on integration. These include the United Nations Convention on the Rights of the Child[6] and the Inter-American Convention on the Elimination of All Forms of Discrimination against Persons with Disabilities.[7] In this research, particular attention is devoted to the CRPD, which, as has already been mentioned, recognises the right to education for disabled people in Article 24.[8] On 30 March 2007, Argentina signed the CRPD and its Optional Protocol. On 21 May 2008, the National Congress adopted Act 26.378, which approved the CRPD and its Optional Protocol. Act 26.378 was promulgated on 6 June 2008. On 2 September 2008, Argentina ratified the CRPD. The CRPD is an international convention, and as such, it has a higher status than the (domestic) laws in accordance with the aforementioned Article 75(22) of the National Constitution. In December 2014, constitutional status was conferred on the CRPD through Act 27.044. In summary, in Argentina, Article 24 of the CRPD is not only regarded as having a higher status than the domestic law, but it has also been incorporated as domestic law through Act 26.378. However, and most important, Article 24 of the CRPD has identical status to the National Constitution.

2.2 *National Law*

Article 14 of the National Constitution establishes the right to teach and to learn, among the rights conferred to all inhabitants of the nation. This Article also specifies that these rights will be regulated by the relevant laws. In addition, Article 75(19) of the National Constitution establishes that the National Congress has the faculty to enact basic laws regarding education. Therefore, various national laws covering the matter of education have been

6 Argentina ratified this convention on 4 December 1990. Also, this convention has constitutional status in Argentina, according to Article 75(22) of the National Constitution.

7 Argentina ratified this convention on 28 September 2000. Argentina also passed Act No. 25.280 in 2000, incorporating the Inter-American Convention on the Elimination of All Forms of Discrimination against Persons with Disabilities to the Argentinian domestic legislation.

8 Section 1 (introduction).

enacted, the most relevant being the National Education Act (No. 26.206). This subsection covers some of the national laws that are most relevant to inclusive education, in chronological order.

The Federal Education Act (No. 24.195) was sanctioned on 14 April 1993 and promulgated on 29 April 1993. Article 6 of this Act contemplates that the educational system has to make it possible for men and women to have an integral and permanent education formation that is in accordance with each person's own capabilities. Article 7 establishes that 'the educational system will guarantee that all persons inhabiting the country can effectively exercise their right to learn, under equality of opportunities and possibilities, without discrimination'. Article 8 recognises as the main characteristic of the educational system that this should be 'flexible, articulated, equitable, open, prospective and oriented to satisfying the national needs as well as the regional diversity'. According to Borsani, the Federal Education Act 'places integrative education, as well as educational special needs, in the category of a matter of state'.[9] In other words, for the first time in Argentina, the issue of integrative education has been recognised as a national/federal law in the form of the Federal Education Act.

In 2002, the Act of Superior Education (No. 25.573) was enacted. This Act modified the previous Act of Superior Education (No. 24.521). For instance, according to the new Act of Superior Education, the state must guarantee accessibility to the environment, interpreters and necessary and sufficient technical support for disabled people.[10] However, Mainardi Remis and Aparicio stress that, 'despite the exquisiteness of certain legislation, it can be evidenced that many persons with a disability are still "invisible" in our universities (as well as in many other environments)'.[11]

The National Fund for the Integration of Persons with Disability was created in 2003 through national decree no. 1.277/2003. Article 4(f) of this decree contemplates that part of this fund will be allocated to the development of programmes to promote integrated education, at all levels. Undoubtedly, the creation of this fund has been a very positive development in regard to the matter under analysis and is another example of the state assuming responsibility in the matter of education.

9 María José Borsani, 'De la integración a la inclusión educativa' (*El Cisne*, 27 July 2016), http://elcisne.org/2016/07/27/de-la-integracion-a-la-inclusion-educativa, last accessed 17 May 2017.

10 No. 25.573.

11 Ana Inés Mainardi Remis and Miriam Aparicio, 'Una universidad posible para personas no invisibles: Eje temático: problemáticas universitarias: Qué universidad para quiénes?' (2012) Simposio: Pensar en la universidad en sus contextos: Perspectivas evaluativas, https://fcecoordinacioneducacion.files.wordpress.com/2012/02/0011.pdf, last accessed 17 May 2017.

In 2006, the Educational Finance Act (No. 26.075) – which had been passed in 2005 – was promulgated. According to Article 1 of this Act, the government (at various levels) would increase investment in education, between 2006 and 2010. The guarantee of 'the inclusion of children and young persons with special educational needs' was made a priority in this Act (Article 2). A leading newspaper stated that, as of December 2010 (the final deadline for the implementation of this law), several of its goals had been achieved (i.e. more extensive coverage offered by the initial and secondary education levels, and an improvement in the salaries of education workers/professionals in the whole country).[12]

Also passed in 2006 was the National Education Act.[13] Article 11(n) establishes as an aim and objective of the national educational policy that disabled people should be provided with 'a pedagogical proposal that allows them to achieve the maximum development of their possibilities, integration as well as a full exercise of their rights'. Article 42 defines special education as a 'modality of the education system'. This Article also establishes that 'special education is governed by the principle of inclusive education, according to subsection n) of Article 11'. However, as just noted, Article 11(n) refers to 'integration'. Article 42 states that, 'special education is focused on all those particular problems that cannot be approached by common education'. Finally, Article 42 determines that the Ministry of Education, Science and Technology, in agreement with the Federal Council of Education, will guarantee the integration of disabled students in education. Articles 43 to 45 are devoted to a range of actions to be performed by the provinces, the Autonomous City of Buenos Aires, jurisdictional authorities and the Ministry of Education, Science and Technology, as well as the Federal Council of Education.

The National Education Act,[14] which replaced the Federal Education Act,[15] received criticism, particularly regarding the matters of integration and inclusion. Hence, for instance, López mentions that 'it would seem necessary to make clearer the ideas of integration and inclusion, in order to advance the discussions and debates around "who" the students are that are included and/or integrated'.[16] More explicitly, the Association for Civil Rights

[12] Stella Maldonado, 'La ley de financiamiento educativo del Bicentenario' (*Página/12*, 2 March 2010), www.pagina12.com.ar/diario/elpais/1–141250-2010–03-02.html, last accessed 17 May 2017.

[13] No. 26.206.

[14] Ibid.

[15] No. 24.195.

[16] Daniel López (coordinator), *Educación Especial, una modalidad del Sistema Educativo en Argentina: Orientaciones 1* (Ministerio de Educación de la Nación, 2009), www.me.gov.ar/curriform/publica/orientaciones_especial09.pdf, last accessed 17 May 2017.

(ADC) affirms that the National Education Act[17] is focused on the integration of disabled people and contravenes Article 24 of the CRPD.[18] According to this association, the National Education Act[19] establishes that 'the educational authorities must guarantee to disabled students living in Argentina that they can attend a common school as long as they can adjust to that school'.[20] If this is not possible, the association states that the National Education Act[21] contemplates that disabled students should attend special schools.[22] Moreover, the ADC offers a number of reasons to support the claim that the National Education Act[23] goes against the CRPD. First, the National Education Act[24] 'establishes a modality of special education'.[25] Second, the National Education Act[26] 'promotes the schooling of disabled people in common schools if their "possibilities" allow them to adjust to those schools'.[27] According to this association:

> Hence, following the approach of integrative education, the student with a disability is 'accepted' in the common school, where children without disability are allowed to learn. However, the organisation of the ordinary school is not revised nor tailored to the needs, interests and proper characteristics of each of the students (included those with disability). On the contrary, the student with a disability has to adjust to [certain] teaching methods and [an] educational organisation that were developed taking into the account the needs and interests of students regarded as 'normal'.[28]

Third, the National Education Act[29] 'promotes the schooling of disabled people in special schools if their "possibilities" or the "complexity of their problem" do not allow them to adjust to common schools'.[30]

17 No. 26.206.
18 Asociación por los Derechos Civiles (ADC), 'Manual para el respeto del derecho a la educación inclusiva en escuelas comunes de los alumnos con discapacidad' (Asociación por los Derechos Civiles, 2014) 22, www.educacion-inclusiva.com.ar/wp-content/uploads/2015/10/ADC-Manual-Educacion-Inclusiva.pdf, last accessed 17 May 2017.
19 No. 26.206.
20 ADC (n. 18) 21.
21 No. 26.206.
22 ADC (n. 18) 21.
23 No. 26.206.
24 Ibid.
25 ADC (n. 18) 22.
26 No. 26.206.
27 ADC (n. 18) 22.
28 Ibid.
29 No. 26.206.
30 ADC (n. 18) 22.

Fourth, the National Education Act[31] 'does not establish a norm that forbids common schools to refuse the enrolment of a disabled student, nor does it reject his/her discrimination on the basis of disability'.[32] Fifth, the National Education Act[33] 'does not promote any process for the transformation of the education system, in terms of achieving a situation in which all schools are prepared to include all students in their rooms'.[34] Despite these criticisms of the National Education Act,[35] the ADC interprets that (in any case) this Act cannot be claimed with the purpose of ignoring or violating Article 24 of the CRPD.[36] This is due to the aforementioned status of the CRPD in the Argentinian legal system (once again, at the least, the CRPD is above the laws of the nation – such as the National Education Act[37]).

3 THE IMPLEMENTATION OF THE RIGHT TO INCLUSIVE EDUCATION IN PRACTICE

This section attempts to show how the right to inclusive education is being implemented and/or exercised in practice in the case of Argentina. In terms of civil society, a fundamental group working on the right to inclusive education in Argentina is the Group Article 24 for Inclusive Education.[38] This is a coalition comprising more than 150 national organisations.[39] Following a Declaration of Principles based on the CRPD, this coalition aims to guarantee the exercise of the right to education for all persons, with an emphasis on disabled people (given the systematic exclusion and segregation suffered by this group).[40] This is just an example (albeit a fundamental one) of the actors involved in making the right to inclusive education a reality in Argentina.

As this section demonstrates, there are various problems in Argentina associated with the effective exercise of the right to inclusive education. For instance, Morales Gorleri (the congresswoman who was chairing the Education Commission in the Buenos Aires legislature) stated during an interview that

31 No. 26.206.
32 ADC (n. 18) 23.
33 No. 26.206.
34 ADC (n. 18) 23.
35 No. 26.206.
36 ADC (n. 18) 23–24.
37 Ibid.
38 See for the website of this group: www.grupoart24.org, last accessed 9 March 2017.
39 Ibid.
40 Ibid.

inclusion 'might be a goal for within 50 years'.[41] Also, she mentioned that the system does not provide answers, due to shortcomings in teacher training, insufficient support resources for the inclusion (of disabled people) in state schools, building problems and discriminatory attitudes (among other issues).[42] Moreover, Gorleri recalled that the education system should not be fragmented.[43]

In order to understand better the rather brief contextual information just provided, the present section attempts to assess the effectiveness of the right to inclusive education in Argentina. To this end, the next subsection (3.1) starts with an analysis of some of the international and regional mechanisms for human rights monitoring and how these mechanisms have approached the matter of inclusive education in Argentina. Subsection 3.2 presents some of the policies that have been elaborated in Argentina with the aim of implementing the right to inclusive education. The final relevant subsection (3.3) explores relevant national case law.

3.1 *International/Regional Mechanisms for Human Rights Monitoring*

This subsection analyses the work developed regarding the right to inclusive education in Argentina through the following mechanisms for human rights monitoring: the CRPD Committee,[44] the Committee on the Rights of the Child[45] and the Inter-American Commission on Human Rights (IACHR).[46]

3.1.1 CRPD Committee

Argentina submitted its initial report to the CRPD Committee in 2011.[47] In this initial document, the country provided information about part of the contents of the National Education Act,[48] the various action lines that the

41 Gabriela Santucchione and Dalile Antúnez, 'La inclusión de personas con discapacidad' (*Página/12*, 4 July 2015), www.pagina12.com.ar/diario/sociedad/3–276370-2015–07-04.html, last accessed 19 May 2017.

42 Ibid.

43 Ibid.

44 See n. 5.

45 This is the body monitoring the United Nations Convention on the Rights of the Child.

46 The IACHR is the body that monitors the American Convention on Human Rights. See Article 33 of this last convention. Argentina ratified the American Convention on Human Rights on 14 August 1984.

47 Committee on the Rights of Persons with Disabilities, Implementation of the Convention on the Rights of Persons with Disabilities: Initial Reports Submitted by States Parties under Article 35 of the Convention; Argentina (28 June 2011) CRPD/C/ARG/1.

48 No. 26.206.

country had implemented in compliance with that Act[49] and information pertaining to the Act of Superior Education,[50] as well as diverse actions revolving around this last law.

In addition, non-governmental organisations (NGOs) – the Network for the Rights of Persons with Disability (REDI), the Center for Legal and Social Studies (CELS), the Argentinian Federation of Institutions for the Blind and Amblyopic Persons (FAICA), the Argentinian Federation of Entities Supporting Persons with an Intellectual Disability (FENDIM) and the Association for Civil Rights (ADC) – presented their shadow report about the situation regarding disability in Argentina (covering the period between 2008 and 2012).[51] This shadow report states that, despite Argentina's domestic legislation as well as its commitment to international treaties, the country does not comply with its obligation to provide disabled people with inclusive education. Quoting the National Institute of Statistics and Censuses (Instituto Nacional de Estadística y Censos) (INDEC), the shadow report highlights that 'only 727.551 (14%) of the 5.061.609 persons older than 3 years, that reside in private homes and present a difficulty or permanent limitation, attend an educational establishment'.[52] The report also states that registration in special schools increased between 2004 and 2010.[53] Overall, this document mentions diverse barriers to access to inclusive education by disabled people (i.e. the lack of resources or qualified professionals[54] or physical barriers that

49 Ibid.

50 No. 25.573.

51 REDI, CELS, FAICA, FENDIM and ADC, 'Comité sobre los Derechos de las Personas con Discapacidad: 8° periodo de sesiones: Evaluación sobre Argentina. Informe alternativo: Situación de la discapacidad en Argentina – 2008/ 2012' [year not available], www.redi.org.ar/Prensa/Comunicados/Informe-alternativo-al-comite-sobre-los-derechos-de-las-personas-con-discapacidad-ONU.pdf, last accessed 17 May 2017.

52 Ibid., quoting www.censo2010.indec.gov.ar/resultadosdefinitivos_totalpais.asp, last accessed 3 August 2012, at pp. 56–57. Note that the most recent statistics about disabled people and the right to inclusive education in Argentina are provided by the document titled 'Censo Nacional de Población, Hogares y Viviendas 2010: Censo del Bicentenario: Serie C: Población con dificultad o limitación permanente' (1st edn) (Instituto Nacional de Estadística y Censos 2014), www.indec.gov.ar/ftp/cuadros/sociedad/PDLP_10_14.pdf, last accessed 17 May 2017.

53 REDI, CELS, FAICA, FENDIM and ADC (n. 51) quoting the Dirección Nacional de Información y Evaluación de la Calidad Educativa (DINIECE) – Ministerio de Educación at page 57.

54 REDI, CELS, FAICA, FENDIM and ADC (n. 51) quoting the Instituto Nacional contra la Discriminación, la Xenofobia y el Racismo (INADI), 'Derecho a la Educación sin Discriminación: 2012', http://inadi.gob.ar/promocion-y-desarrollo/documentos-tematicos/educacion, at page 58.

prevent, and/or cause difficulty in regard to, access to schools for people with physical impairments[55]).

Among the list of issues that the CRPD Committee highlighted in its 2012 document, the Committee asked Argentina to do the following:

> Please indicate what criteria are used in determining whether students should attend a regular or a special school. Please provide data, disaggregated by sex and level of education, on students with disabilities who are enrolled in these two types of schools and show how those figures compare with those for students without any disability.[56]

In its reply, Argentina clarified that work would be done regarding the regulation (among other matters) of the accreditation of disabled students in special or common schools.[57] Regarding statistics, for instance, the following were provided: for the year 2010, a total (nationally) of 127,508 students were enrolled in special education, and a total (nationally) of 10,563,613 students were enrolled in mainstream/common education.[58]

The next step in this reporting procedure was when the Committee issued its concluding observations.[59] At this time, the Committee concluded that it had concerns about the various sorts of barriers, which evidenced a lack of and/or poor implementation of the principle of inclusive education.[60] In particular, the Committee concluded negatively about the situation of disabled children and their right to inclusive education, stating that in Argentina not only are there a 'high number of children with disabilities who attend special schools' but also that there is a 'lack of educational resource

55 REDI, CELS, FAICA, FENDIM and ADC (n. 51) quoting the NGO ACCESO YA [Access Now] from www.accesoya.org.ar/quienes.php?Boton1=Institucional, and www.accesoya.org.ar/camp_escuelas.php, at page 60.

56 Committee on the Rights of Persons with Disabilities, Implementation of the Convention on the Rights of Persons with Disabilities: List of Issues to Be Taken up in Connection with the Consideration of the Initial Report of Argentina (CRPD/C/ARG/1) Concerning Articles 1 to 33 of the Convention: Argentina (16 May 2012) CRPD/C/ARG/Q/1 [22].

57 Comité sobre los Derechos de las Personas con Discapacidad [Committee on the Rights of Persons with Disabilities], Lista de cuestiones que deben abordarse al examinar el informe inicial de Argentina (CRPD/C/ARG/1) en relación con los artículos 1 a 33 de la Convención: Adición: Respuestas del Gobierno de la Argentina a la lista de cuestiones (CRPD/C/ARG/Q/1) que deben abordarse al examinar el informe inicial de la Argentina (CRPD/C/ARG/1) (5 September 2012) CRPD/C/ARG/Q/1/Add.1 [only available in Spanish] [196].

58 Ibid.

59 Committee on the Rights of Persons with Disabilities, Concluding Observations on the Initial Report of Argentina as Approved by the Committee at Its Eighth Session (17–28 September 2012) (8 October 2012) CRPD/C/ARG/CO/1.

60 Ibid. [37].

centres that support the effective inclusion of students with disabilities'.[61] As a result, the following recommendations were made for Argentina:

> The Committee recommends that the State party develop a comprehensive State education policy that guarantees the right to inclusive education and allocates sufficient budgetary resources to ensure progress towards the establishment of an education system that includes students with disabilities. The Committee also urges the State party to intensify its efforts to ensure that all children with disabilities receive a full compulsory education as established by the State party, while devoting particular attention to indigenous peoples and other rural communities. It likewise urges the State party to take the necessary steps to ensure that pupils with disabilities who attend special schools are enrolled in inclusive schools and to offer reasonable adjustments for students with disabilities within the general education system.[62]

Afterwards, the Argentinian government and a group of NGOs issued documents with their replies to the Committee's concluding observations.[63] The government document does not contain any reference to the issue of inclusive education.[64] The document issued by various NGOs only includes a brief reference to inclusive education, namely stressing that the building of the University of Rosario presents architectural barriers and therefore (being an educational institution) violates Article 24 of the CRPD.[65]

On 30 March 2015, the NGOs Association Azul, the Association for Equality and Justice (ACIJ), the ADC and the REDI informed the public that according to information facilitated by the CRPD Committee, the presentation of the next report by Argentina to the CRPD Committee (initially planned for 2014) had been delayed until October 2018.[66] According to this last document, the CRPD

61 Ibid.

62 Ibid. [38].

63 Presidencia de la Nación and Consejo Nacional de Coordinación de Políticas Sociales, 'Comisión nacional asesora para la integración de las Personas con Discapacidad: Informe de seguimiento' [year not available], http://tbinternet.ohchr.org/_layouts/treatybodyexternal/Download.aspx?symbolno=INT%2fCRPD%2fAFR%2fARG%2f16891&Lang=en, last accessed 17 May 2017. Also see the follow-up document elaborated by the NGOs REDI, ADC, FAICA and ACIJ [year not available], http://tbinternet.ohchr.org/_layouts/treatybodyexternal/Download.aspx?symbolno=INT%2fCRPD%2fNGS%2fARG%2f16890&Lang=en, last accessed 17 May 2017.

64 Presidencia de la Nación and Consejo Nacional de Coordinación de Políticas Sociales (n. 63).

65 Follow-up document elaborated by the NGOs REDI, ADC, FAICA and ACIJ (n. 63).

66 REDI, 'La nueva evaluación de Argentina ante el Comité de Discapacidad de la ONU se posterga hasta 2018' (*REDI*, 30 March 2015), www.redi.org.ar/Prensa/Comunicados/La-nueva-evaluacion-de-Argentina-ante-el-comite-de-discapacidad-de-la-ONU-se-posterga-hasta-2018.pdf, last accessed 19 May 2017.

Committee suggested that the civil societies in Argentina should present their alternative reports by April 2017.[67] No further action has been taken to date.[68]

3.1.2 Committee on the Rights of the Child

The Committee on the Rights of the Child issued its last concluding observations about Argentina in 2010.[69] At that time, the committee expressed its concerns about the insufficient efforts in Argentina 'to ensure, through training programmes, that all professionals working with children with disabilities have the necessary knowledge and skills, in particular with regard to inclusive education'.[70] Therefore, among its recommendations, the committee stressed that Argentina should '[e]nsure that children with disabilities are included in the education system', as well as that it should include special education in the school curriculum.[71] Furthermore, when commenting on Argentina's compliance with Articles 28, 29 and 31 of the United Nations Convention on the Rights of the Child, the committee noted 'that the proportion of children with disabilities receiving special education is growing (78 per cent of those between the ages of 3 and 17 years); nevertheless, ... only 53 per cent are integrated into regular educational facilities.'[72] As a result, the committee recommended that Argentina should 'invest additional resources in order to ensure the right of all children to a truly inclusive education'.[73] The Argentinian government has yet to make a public response to these observations.[74]

3.1.3 Inter-American Commission on Human Rights

On 7 July 2016, the IACHR decided on a precautionary measure that required Argentina to guarantee the right to education for a young disabled girl (Irene

67 Ibid.

68 See the UN website: www.ohchr.org/EN/HRBodies/CRPD/Pages/CRPDIndex.aspx, last accessed 15 May 2017.

69 Committee on the Rights of the Child, Consideration of Reports Submitted by States Parties under Article 44 of the Convention: Concluding Observations: Argentina (21 June 2010) CRC/C/ARG/CO/3–4.

70 Ibid. [56].

71 Ibid., at para. 57(a) and (c).

72 Ibid., at para. 67.

73 Ibid., at para. 68(b).

74 As can be seen by the absence on the UN website: http://tbinternet.ohchr.org/_layouts/treatybodyexternal/TBSearch.aspx?Lang=en&TreatyID=5&TreatyID=10&TreatyID=11&DocTypeID=5, last accessed 3 May 2017.

Cuevas). Precautionary measures are established in Article 25 of the Rules of Procedure of the IACHR, for serious and urgent situations presenting a risk of irreparable harm. Two NGOs (the Center for Justice and International Law [CEJIL] and the Network for the Rights of Persons with Disability [REDI]) requested a precautionary measure on behalf of Irene.[75] Irene (who was twelve years old at the time of the NGOs' request) had a neurological impairment and needed various medical treatments as well as therapeutic supports – all of these treatments and supports (which sometimes would have been interrupted) were necessary for her health improvement as well as for facilitating her school attendance.[76] The IACHR considered that the elements of gravity, urgency and irreparability had been fulfilled in this case. The IACHR considered that 'the element of gravity is fulfilled considering the alleged deterioration in the health of Irene (12-year-old), and its possible impact on her rights to life and personal integrity, given the supposed lack of special supports recommended by specialists'.[77] Regarding the element of urgency, the IACHR assessed that this had been fulfilled as 'the continuous suspension of the implementation of the necessary therapeutic care, as well as the over time, could generate an aggravation of Irene's health situation'.[78] Finally, in terms of the element of irreparability, the IACHR evaluated that this element had also been fulfilled because 'the possible violation of the right to life and personal integrity, as a consequence of her [Irene's] actual health situation, constitutes the maximum situation of irreparability'.[79] As its overall conclusion, the IACHR established that Argentina should

> adopt the necessary measures to preserve Irene's life and personal integrity, taking her disability and health situation into consideration, so [she] can have access to the necessary support recommended by the specialists, in the light of the applicable international standards.[80]

In addition, the IACHR requested that the Argentinian government inform the IACHR about the adoption of the requested precautionary measures, as well as regularly updating the information required.[81] According to a newspaper, two months after this decision by the IACHR

75 Inter-American Commission on Human Rights, precautionary measure no. 376–15, Irene regarding Argentina, 7 July 2016, at paragraph 1.
76 Ibid.
77 Ibid. [22].
78 Ibid. [27].
79 Ibid. [29].
80 Ibid. [31(a)].
81 Ibid. [32].

(September 2016), Irene and her parents were still waiting for Argentina's compliance.[82]

3.2 *Policies*

In 1998, a Framework Agreement was issued.[83] The introduction of this agreement defines special education as well as special educational needs.[84] Special education is approached as 'a continuum of education provisions, made by a range of services, techniques, strategies, knowledge and pedagogical resources', whilst special educational needs 'are those experimented by those persons who require help or resources that are not regularly available in their educational context'.[85] This document does not refer to 'inclusion' at any point. Indeed, the approach adopted by this Framework Agreement has been criticised, on the basis that it focusses on the matter of integration, whilst nowadays 'at least at a discursive level, the focus is towards inclusive education'.[86]

The National Plan for Compulsory Education was approved by the Federal Council of Education through Resolution No. 79 (May 2009). This plan identifies the achievement of obligatory education for all people as a political goal:

> To achieve the effective exercise of the right to education of all disabled (and non-disabled) children, teenagers, young persons and adults, through public policies that guarantee the conditions for the universalization of the initial level (for four-years-old) as well as the compliance of obligatory education.[87]

The National Plan for Compulsory Education also recognises that there is a particular problem with inclusive (and compulsory) initial and primary

82 Vanesa Díaz, 'A pesar del fallo de la CIDH, Irene sigue esperando: Los padres volvieron a pedir a la OEA que intervenga' (*Diario Sumario*, 9 September 2016), www.diariosumario.com.ar/sociedad/2016/9/9/pesar-fallo-cidh-irene-sigue-esperando-6448.html, last accessed 6 May 2017.

83 Ministerio de Cultura y Educación: Consejo Federal de Cultura y Educación, *Documentos para la Concertación: Acuerdo Marco para la Educación Especial* (Series A No. 19, December 1998).

84 Ibid., I (Introduction).

85 Ibid., I (Introduction).

86 María Luz Albergucci, 'Educación Especial: Una mirada desde lo conceptual y la información estadística disponible: ¿de la mano o en sendas diferentes?' (Ministerio de Educación, Ciencia y Tecnología, and Dirección Nacional de Gestión Curricular y Formación Docente, 2006), http://repositorio.educacion.gov.ar/dspace/handle/123456789/96160, last accessed 17 May 2017.

87 Plan Nacional de Educación Obligatoria, Subsecretaría de Equidad y Calidad Ministerio de Educación de la Nación, Aprobado por Resolución N° 79/09 del Consejo Federal de Educación (Buenos Aires, 28 May 2009) [9].

education, for disabled (or non-disabled) people.[88] With regard to initial education, paragraph 21 states the need to strengthen teacher training (particularly in urban and rural places), regarding the development of flexible and inclusive institutional models for disabled and non-disabled children.[89] Paragraph 24 recognises that primary education entails the

> challenge of promoting support strategies with regard to the educational pathways of students with or without disability, and with the goal of guaranteeing [their] permanence with quality [standards] as well as the completion of the level – particularly for the most deprived sectors.[90]

Moreover, paragraph 24 stresses that with regard to primary education it is necessary to work on teachers' professional development and (effective) educational teaching policies.[91]

In 2011, the Federal Council of Education issued resolution 155/11 (13 October 2011), which approved the document 'Modality of Special Education'.[92] According to this document:

> The definition of Special Education as a modality implies the offer to disabled students, beyond the type of school that they attend, a clear sense of belonging to the Levels of the System, therefore overcoming previous considerations that made reference to segmented subsystems.[93]

In addition, this resolution acknowledges that the concept of inclusion, included in the National Education Act,[94] is a political concept.[95] In paragraph 18, the resolution states that it is necessary 'that all disabled students are in the school that benefits them mostly, taking the common curricula as the reference'.[96] Moreover, paragraph 19 states that inclusion and integration must be linked and re-evaluated in practice.[97] The resolution clarifies that inclusion is a principle, whilst integration is an educational strategy that looks towards the inclusion of disabled students in common schools (provided that this is possible, and with the necessary

88 Ibid. [21] and [24].
89 Ibid. [21].
90 Ibid. [24].
91 Ibid. [24].
92 Resolution 155/11 (13 October 2011) issued by the Federal Council of Education, Article 1.
93 Ibid. [12].
94 No. 26.206.
95 Resolution CFE 155/11 (n. 92) [15].
96 Ibid. [18].
97 Ibid. [19].

support).[98] Hence, the approach to inclusion and integration provided by the document 'Modality of Special Education' seems to differ from the discussion of inclusion versus integration proposed by General Comment No. 4 (2016) issued by the CRPD Committee.[99] This last general comment differentiates inclusion from integration. Whilst integration is viewed as the 'process of placing persons with disabilities in existing mainstream educational institutions',[100] inclusive education,

> involves a process of systemic reform embodying changes and modifications in content, teaching methods, approaches, structures and strategies in education to overcome barriers with a vision serving to provide all students of the relevant age range with an equitable and participatory learning experience and environment that best corresponds to their requirements and preferences.[101]

The second section of the document is devoted to the numerous policies that are to be put in place with the goal of guaranteeing the comprehensive educational trajectories of disabled students. To this end, the document specifies that the following institutions will be involved in the design and implementation of relevant policies, from 2012 onwards: the Provincial Ministries of Education, the Ministry of Education of the Autonomous City of Buenos Aires, the National Ministry and the National Coordination of Special Education.[102] The third section of this resolution deals with special education in regard to various educational levels. The levels identified are: the initial level (meaning the age range zero to five years), the primary level, education for disabled teenagers and young persons and permanent education for disabled adults.[103]

3.3 *National Case Law*

In terms of the judiciary, Article 108 of the National Constitution establishes that the judicial power is exercisable by the Supreme Court of Justice as well as other courts below it in the hierarchy.[104] Various legal cases have interpreted

98 Ibid.
99 General Comment No. 4 (n. 5).
100 Ibid. [11] quoting A/HRC/25/29 [4] and United Nations International Children's Emergency Fund, 'The Right of Children with Disabilities to Education: A Right-Based Approach to Inclusive Education' (United Nations International Children's Emergency Fund 2012).
101 Ibid. [11].
102 Resolution CFE 155/11 (n. 92) [27].
103 Ibid. [30]–[47].
104 National Constitution (n. 3) Article 108.

the right to inclusive education for disabled people. The following are a few examples regarding the right to inclusive education and physical access to schools, reasonable adjustments required in higher education, the access of a disabled person to a mainstream school and the award of a high school degree.

The judgment in *Asociación Acceso Ya* [*Association Access Now*] *c/ GCBA* (22 December 2009) dealt with issues concerning physical access to the environment, and reasonable adjustments and suppression regarding architectural barriers. The judgment (issued by the Administrative and Tax Court No. 4 of the Autonomous City of Buenos Aires) ordered the GCBA to cease its omission of adopting positives measures to comply with physical access, reasonable adjustments and the suppression of barriers. According to the Association Access Now:

> In 2009 we were notified of the first instance judgement that condemned the GCBA to comply with an accessibility plan in schools. The judgement was appealed, until it was final in 2012. In July of that year, the city's Minister of Education, Lic. [graduate] Esteban Bullrich, signed an agreement with Acceso Ya [Access Now], for [building] works with the purpose of guaranteeing access to schools for people with a physical disability or reduced mobility. The deadline for completion of the works [was] March 2015. However, the agreement foresees an execution plan of works with intermediate deadlines, with the goal of monitoring the effective compliance of the agreement assumed. We already have 500 public schools with basic accessibility (access ramp, adapted bathrooms, accessible rooms and adequate signals) and 215 [schools] with full accessibility (lifts and elevating platforms have been installed), converting this [legal] action in one of our major achievements.[105]

The judgment in *Naranjo, Emiliano Pablo c/ Universidad Nacional de La Matanza s/Amparo* is another relevant illustrative example.[106] The Federal Court No. 2 of San Martín decided on the matter of the reasonable adjustments requested by Mr Naranjo, who had been refused admission to the University Teaching Career in Physical Education (National University of La Matanza – Province of Buenos Aires). As Mr Naranjo was a physically disabled student, he had requested an exemption in regard to complying with the physical performance requirements for his admission to the aforementioned career. In such a way, he had asked to be evaluated after the

105 See 'Acceso Ya, Litigio de Interés Público, Escuelas Accesibles ya, uno de nuestros principales logros', www.accesoya.org.ar/detalle.php?id=12, last accessed 13 March 2017.

106 *Naranjo c/ Universidad Nacional de la Matanza s/ Amparo* (Juzgado Federal No. 2 de San Martín) (25 April 2011).

implementation of reasonable accommodations. The court granted his petition. However, the case was appealed, and in 2015, Procurator General Gils Carbó issued an opinion in favour of confirming the appealed judgment.[107] Afterwards, the Supreme Court of Justice delivered a judgment, confirming the sentence issued by Federal Court No. 2 of San Martín.

The second-instance judgment in *P, AD y Otro c/ Institución Educativa* [*Educational Institution*] *Galileo Galilei s/ Amparo* (case no. 1673644), issued by the Civil, Commercial and Administrative-Contentious Appeals Chamber of Rio Cuarto (Córdoba) on 6 August 2014, interpreted the National Education Act[108] (among other laws). In this case, the petition made by a young disabled person to access a mainstream school came under judicial scrutiny. The first-instance judgment had ordered the Educational Institution Galileo Galilei, a mainstream/common school, that it should admit and register the student GNP in high school. Moreover, the first-instance judgment had ordered that this institution should design and put in place all of the necessary measures needed to overcome the technical and/or physical barriers that could prevent access by GNP to education in the institution that had been containing him since he was four years old. The educational institution in question, with the understanding that GNP could not successfully comply with the requirements of the mainstream high school, appealed the first-instance decision. The Civil, Commercial and Administrative-Contentious Appeals Chamber of Rio Cuarto confirmed the first-instance judgment. The final judgment, which surprisingly does not mention the CRPD, relied on Article 3 of the United Nations Convention on the Rights of the Child to conclude that the superior interest of the (disabled) child should prevail. Regarding domestic laws, and in addition to the aforementioned National Education Act,[109] for instance, the judgment stressed that the province of Córdoba had passed Act 9.870, which recognises that the state is responsible for guaranteeing the exercise of the right to education under equality of opportunities and without any kind of discrimination on the basis of an individual's condition or origin, the social context in which he or she lives, or his or her gender, ethnicity, nationality, cultural or religious orientation or physical, intellectual and linguistic conditions.

[107] See *Procuración General de la Nación, Naranjo Emiliano P c/ Universidad Nacional de la Matanza* (CSJ 94/2014 50-N CS001), www.fiscales.gob.ar/wp-content/uploads/2015/06/CSJ-94–2014-Naranjo.pdf, last accessed 13 March 2017.

[108] No. 26.206.

[109] Ibid.

A different case, decided by the Administrative and Tax Court No. 1 of the Autonomous City of Buenos Aires, involved the right to inclusive education of a young man with Down syndrome. Alan Rodríguez (disabled) had been refused a high school degree. The judgment (dated October 2016) ordered the relevant school, as well as the Ministry of Education of Buenos Aires City, to issue and legalise his degree. This landmark judgment about inclusive education was enthusiastically received by Alan's family.[110] As his mother told the press, Alan had had the chance to work for a company but was told that he could not be hired as he did not have a (high school) degree.[111] After this judgment, this young disabled person began thinking about starting a degree in informatics at the University of Buenos Aires (the institution that had told the newspaper that they would register any student who presented with a high school degree – which would set a precedent, as currently there are no students with Down syndrome who are registered at the University of Buenos Aires).[112] However, according to the press, the government of the Autonomous City of Buenos Aires appealed this first-instance judgment.[113]

4 CONCLUSION

In Argentina's legal system, the CRPD has the highest status (alongside the National Constitution). As such, the scenario for the effective application of Article 24 of this convention is particularly promising. Nevertheless, there are serious concerns about the effective implementation of the right to inclusive education in the country. In terms of domestic law, in Argentina there is still a dichotomy between inclusion and integration. This dichotomy, which is even present in the National Education Act (2006),[114] has been criticised to the extent that Article 42 of this act is considered to breach Article 24 of the CRPD. In terms of population groups in Argentina and the right to inclusive education, the evidence presented in this chapter shows that (despite the serious challenges ahead) major attention has been devoted to the situation of disabled children.

110 Marcelo Maller, 'Ordenan darle el título secundario a un alumno con Síndrome de Down' (*Clarín*, 26 October 2016), www.clarin.com/sociedad/ordenan-secundario-alumno-sindrome-down_0_B1RJX6Rke.html, last accessed 15 March 2017.

111 Ibid.

112 Ibid.

113 'Apelación por un título' (*Página/12*, 29 October 2016), www.pagina12.com.ar/diario/sociedad/3-312954-2016-10-29.html, last accessed 15 March 2017.

114 No. 26.206.

Index

Lightning Source UK Ltd.
Milton Keynes UK
UKHW022239200721
387509UK00006B/439

9 781107 121188